PUNJABI SAGA

Born in 1911, **Prakash Tandon** graduated in science from Government College, Lahore, in 1929. He studied commerce at the University of Manchester and subsequently qualified as a chartered accountant. In 1937, he joined the Unilever subsidiary in India to later become its first Indian chairman. He left the company in 1968 to join the public sector. He served as the chairman of the State Trading Corporation of India for four years and that of the Punjab National Bank for three years. He was Director General and President of the National Council of Applied Economic Research. He has taught at the American universities of Los Angeles, Berkeley and Boston and at the Universities of Punjab (Chandigarh), Delhi, the Indian Institute of Management (Ahmedabad) and the Indian Institute of Technology (Delhi and Kharagpur). Currently, he is the vice-chairman of the Indian Institute of Foreign Trade, Delhi.

Punjabi Century (1857-1974)
'An entirely fascinating picture of India from the inside... Abounding in local colour, the book is full of good stories'

—*The Times, London*

Beyond Punjab (1937-1960)
'Tandon has produced another tremendously readable book'

—*The Hindu*

'Everyone who is interested in factors which have shaped the India of today should read this book'

—*Times Literary Supplement*

Return to Punjab (1961-1987)
'Tandon has a remarkable insight into men...and the situations [in] which they were caught up in their time'

—*Indian Book Chronicle*

PUNJABI SAGA
(1857-2000)

Prakash Tandon

RUPA

Published by
Rupa Publications India Pvt. Ltd 2000
7/16, Ansari Road, Daryaganj
New Delhi 110002

Sales centres:
Allahabad Bengaluru Chennai
Hyderabad Jaipur Kathmandu
Kolkata Mumbai

Punjabi Century first published by Chatto and Windus 1961.
Beyond Punjab first published by University of California Press 1971.
Return to Punjab first published by Vikas Publishing House Pvt. Ltd. 1980.
First published in one volume as *Punjabi Saga (1857-1987)* in hardcover
by Penguin Books 1988.

This edition published by arrangement with the original publishers.

ISBN: 978-81-716-7506-7

Fifth impression 2019

10 9 8 7 6 5

Printed at Yash Printographics, Noida

To
Maya, Manu and Gautam and their generation of Punjabis, wherever they are settled. And to Punjab the eternal.

Contents

ACKNOWLEDGEMENT

Punjabi Century

To Lady Ram Nath Chopra, the lady who was 'asked for' and was promised two years before she was born, for our talks about the charming engagement and wedding customs that have virtually disappeared; for interesting chats on the subject, to Mrs. Som Puri, her daughter, of my generation, who was already driving a car to drop in at her future husband's home; to Har Narain Batra, an excellent check whenever I was in doubt. To S. Natarajan for valuable corrections; to Cynthia Lisely for patient deciphering and flawless typing of the manuscript. Also to a friend of long ago, Donald Forsythe, who introduced me to English Culture.

To Debu and Reba Mukherjee at whose charming bungalow in Mhow I began writing0 and to Col. Sir Ram Nath Chopra at whose hut in the peeaceful pine forest above Gulmarg I finished it.

Beyond Punjab

To many persos this book owes much. Above all to Gärd, to whose support and impeccable sense of the language it owes all.

To Mavis Lely, Phyllis Hoogewerf and Ramakrishnan, who were associated with me at different times as my secretaries, for their many patient hours of deciphering an atrocious handwriting and typing—with always a personal interest; also, to Thiagarajan for retyping many pages; and Jagdish Puri for his help with the proofreading. To those who read the manuscript and made many useful suggestions—Roy Hawkins, Bernard Kaye, Warren and Alice Ilchman, and Fred Weaver. To Maurice Zinkin, as before, my deep gratitude.

Return to Punjab

To Gärd, as before, for her support and impeccable sense of language; to Maya, Manu, and Gautam; to T. Thomas, and Amal Dutt; to John Thompson, Warren and Alice Ilchman, Leo Rose, William Siffin, Leroy Jones, N.C.B. Nath, I.Z. Bhatty, Prem Bhatia, G.D. Khosla, and many others for their advice on the manuscript. To those who deciphered my poor handwriting and helped with the many drafts—G.D. Mathur, Thiagarajan, Padamanabhan, Ram Dhan, D.D. Dhawan, V. Gopinathan, Balkrishna, R.N. Sharma and G.S. Bagga.

To Luci Del Marle for designing the cover pages for all three books.

An amateur author like me always needs the encouragement of a publisher—Peter Calvocoressi of Chatto and Windus, Philip Lilienthal of University of California Press, Aroon Purie of Thompson, Dinanath Malhotra of Hind Pocket Books, Narendra Kumar of Vikas, Gurdial Singh Khosla, who translated the *Punjabi Century* for the Punjabi University, and David Davidar of Penguins. Of their support I am deeply conscious and grateful.

As we enter the new millennium, and the Punjab and India settle down into a new era promising peace with our neighbours, new global linkages and liberal high-technology economy, Rupa & Company has gestured to bring out the *Punjabi Saga* in a new edition. Let our old culture of yesterday flow into our new culture tomorrow.

PROLOGUE

This story deals with a Punjabi family, five generations of which lived through two momentous centuries of change—a family essentially no different from any other family of West Punjab, with a pattern of life that endured through time, change, and strife. The British connection, significant in its own way, was just one of the many conquering waves that came and passed and left its layer of influence on the Punjab like the five rivers that have poured down water and mud interminably and in so doing enriched our soil. Maurice Zinkin who persuaded me to write my first book, *Punjabi Century*, in 1960, summed up that book thus in his foreword:

> Mr Tandon is talking of a past which is over, the flavour of which, had it not been for him, would soon have departed never to be recaptured. His memory, his sense of a scene as a whole, his capacity to recreate the past as it was and not as the present day would have it—these combine to give us the old Punjab as it lived, thought, ate and enjoyed itself. This is how marriages were made, this is how the Indian backbone of the administration got tired of the British, this is what the houses looked like and how one went out for a walk. The society he is describing, the British Punjab as it grew in the years after the Sikh wars and the Mutiny, began to die in the 1930s; it was finally killed in the riots of 1947.

Beyond Punjab, the second book in this trilogy, came out in 1970 after I had left Hindustan Lever. By then, the Punjab I had described had already changed. The book's inscription said:

> To us there was only the Punjab, the land of 'five rivers': beyond it was all Hindustan: and yet beyond, beyond the frozen Himalayas and the warm seas, it was all *Walayat*, the unknown world to where some of our restless men ventured out. And now, suddenly, it was all beyond Punjab.

I described in the book the thirty-one years I spent with Hindustan Lever—1937 to 1968. Lever's experiment in Indianization could perhaps be said to have begun in the 1860's when the Indian Civil Service was first thrown open to Indians; in the British army in the 1920s when a few Indian cadets began to be selected for Sandhurst; and in the 1930s in the last citadel of the British, when their mercantile firms began to admit, selectively, Indian managers. Twenty-three years later, arduous years of mutual dedication to an idea of 'Ization,' as Unilever called it, they made me their first national chairman outside their home companies in England, Holland and America.

Return to Punjab, the third volume of the trilogy, published in 1970 continued to follow my passage through the chairmanships of

Hindustan Lever, the Indian Institute of Management, Ahmedabad, the State Trading Corporation of India and the Punjab National Bank. From a multinational industrial firm to the first business school of India and then through the government's public enterprises I ended in the National Council of Applied Economic Research. These interesting years covered India at the British sunset and its post-Independence dawn. There were two different Indias, but also two different Punjabs.

Today, forty years after partition, our new generation has scattered over India, and the world, in all the professions — the army, medicine, technology, accounting, and management. They are a part of the developing all-India professional-management class, which is a new unifying force in India, of men and women from different parts of the country, working in government, commerce and industry, and developing a new kind of all-Indianness. Qualified from the institutions of excellence and the professions, they are equally at home in India and the outside world and they are the new citizens of both.

From my granduncle who fought the British at Chellianwala, to my grandfather who became a Kanungo in the new administration, to my father in Roorkee College of Engineering in 1898, to my years at University and articled for my chartered accountancy in England of the 1930s, to my sons in the army and a German firm, to my daughter in Washington, and her daughter studying in Boston, the Punjabi saga continues.

The three books were first brought out together by Penguin—in whose early world of classics and contemporary books, one was brought up in England—as *Punjabi Saga.*

Once again a new Punjab seems to be emerging. It is a new Punjab of old vital chaos, through threatening sometimes even to disown its name. But the change in Punjab is no more than the change effervescing in other parts of India, of problems that seem sometimes beyond us to solve; but it is a sign too of a new vitality that, with the healthy instinct of a democracy, externalizes its problems and expresses them to the strong light of debate rather than suppressing them internally.

New Delhi
July, 1987

Prakash Tandon

PUNJABI CENTURY
1857—1947

CHAPTER ONE

Grandparents

Our family were Khatris from the West Punjab countryside. For two centuries we had been moving along the banks of the Jhelum river, sometimes on its eastern and sometimes on its western bank, and for a while in the Himalayan foothills where the river drains into the plain.

We know about our past because in the Punjab it is possible to trace one's family for many generations, owing to the custom of maintaining family records at certain holy places, of which Hardwar on the Ganges is the most important. Whenever there is a death in the family, someone will go to Hardwar to immerse the ashes of the departed. There our family has its own panda, as these priests are called, who at his death is succeeded by his son. He maintains the family records in long, old-fashioned Indian ledgers, covered in red cloth, in which he writes down the length of the page. Every time someone goes he brings these records up to date by entering births, marriages and deaths, migrations and other information about what has been happening in the family. When I first visited Hardwar I had only to say I was a Tandon from Gujrat, and from a crowd of pandas our priest came forward and reeled off our whole family tree for several generations. He had met my father, uncles and elder brother when they had visited Hardwar. He has other Khatri families like ours whom he serves as priest, and whenever we visit we give him some money for assisting us with puja on the bank of the river. That is how he earns his living. The family ledgers are the precious stock-in-trade of these pandas, and they know the genealogies by heart. Having been trained from childhood, like their fathers before them, they develop phenomenal memories.

Other than at Hardwar, our family records are also kept at Kurukshetra, the battlefield of the great epic Mahabharat, and at Matan, in the valley of Kashmir. In the ledger at Matan, I read a message from a great grand-uncle who had walked up the old road from Gujrat over the Pir Panjal passes. The date of the Hindu calendar placed his visit at 1811, just one hundred years before I was born. He wrote in Persian about the arduous journey, the charm of Kashmir, and about our relations. I imagine he conformed to the custom of those days of bringing apples back to the plains, each apple tied in a knot in a turban, and distributed the rare fruit in halves and quarters to friends and relations as a kind of thanksgiving for his safe return. As a child I went to school for a time in Gujrat, where began the old Moghul road to Srinagar through Bhimber and Muzaffarpur. The road was in use until the motor road from Rawalpindi was built. Tongas used to leave Gujrat railway station for Srinagar, a journey that took about a fortnight. I used to love climbing to the top of our house on cold winter mornings to gaze at the snow peaks of Jammu and imagine this uncle winding his way up, walking perhaps ten miles a day and taking twenty days for a journey that is done in a day by motor-car, and today takes less than twenty minutes by air.

During the Sikh period the family farmed and served occasionally with the Sikh armies. Father used to tell us that life was uncertain and sometimes precarious in those days. Although the Sikh empire at one time stretched over the Punjab, Himachal, Jammu, Kashmir and into Afghanistan, only during Ranjit Singh's reign did it wield any kind of central authority. Otherwise, justice was at a discount, for even in my days the word Sikha-Shahi (Sikh rule) still meant high-handedness in the Punjab. But the Sikh regime was never too repressive, and to us Hindus it was perhaps a welcome change from being inferior citizens under the Moslems. After all, we and the Sikhs stemmed from the same stock; most Hindus had Sikh relations, and intermarriage was common. In our own family my elder brother married a girl who was a Sikh on her father's side, but a Hindu on her mother's. Her youngest brother, a soldier in the British and later in the Indian army, married a great grand-daughter of Hari Singh Nalwa, the famous Sikh general who had marched into Kabul. His name had become a legend and we used to hear that even in our days, whenever a Pathan woman wanted to quieten a child she would say, 'Hush, Nalwa is coming.'

We and the Sikhs had the same castes and customs, and they were always members of our brotherhoods—biradaris. In the villages we lived together and celebrated the same festivals. Many Hindus, particularly our women, visited the Sikh gurdwaras to worship. Sometimes a married couple, who had lost hope of getting a son, would take a vow that if they had a boy he would be brought up in the Sikh faith. Although the Hindus got along fairly well under the Sikhs, at least as well as the Sikhs themselves, law and order were poor, and there were no opportunities for development. Local officials were arbitrary and often rapacious, and father told us that people tried to look poorer than they were so as not to attract attention. This had done my family some harm, for when the British began their system of land records we, like many Khatri farmers, refused at first to declare that we owned land. This later debarred us from the special rights which in the Punjab were conferred on the agricultural classes.

Father used to tell us about one of his grand-uncles who had fought the British under the Sikh banner at the battle of Chelianwala in 1849. He was a tall, well-built man in the prime of his life when my father was a boy, and at the festival of Holi he would dress as a lion and carry a whole goat between his teeth. He used to tell the village boys stories of the battle. At Chelianwala the British suffered heavy casualties, and at the cemetry constructed on the field, as late as in my childhood, professional mourners were hired on Saturdays for a few annas to beat their breasts and wail. This uncle used to say that when a British soldier fell down he would put blades of grass in his mouth and say, 'Hamen nahin maro, ham gai hai. Dekho, ham ghas khata hai.' (Don't kill me, I am a cow. Look, I eat grass.) 'How could one kill a cow?' he would ask.

The Punjabis, as old people used to say, were puzzled at the first sight of the Englishmen because they had never seen any people look so implausible. They were used to Pathans, and some of their own people were fair, occasionally with light hair and grey eyes—we had a cousin with ginger hair and a skin that reddened instead of tanning, which he considered a great misfortune, as he was always compared to the posterior of a monkey! But never had they seen people so incredibly red-faced, and dressed in such quaint tight clothes displaying their bottoms so indecently. Never had they seen women who went about barefaced in equally incredible clothes, and spoke to strangers with the confidence of men. Their children they found unbelievably beautiful.

The villagers were, to begin with, frightened of the new conquerors. Women would hide their children. But fear soon gave way to curiosity and then to controversy. What were these Angrez log up to? Their ideas were quite unlike those of rulers in the past. They began by doing the oddest things, like consulting each peasant about the land he possessed and giving him a permanent title to it, with a fixed revenue which was remitted in years when crops were bad. The officers moved about freely, unguarded and without pomp and show. The visiting officials pitched their tents outside the villages, and held their office under a tree where anyone could approach them. Accompanied by just one or two persons they would ride on horseback for hours, inspecting and talking to people. Most of them had learned Punjabi well, some quite fluently. Their women, whom we soon began to call mem sahibs, also moved about freely, asking the village women and children questions. The officers and their wives had insatiable curiosity about our habits and customs and seemed never to tire of getting to know us. Their manners were strange but kindly and considerate, seldom hectoring or bullying. In their dress, manner or speech there was nothing of the rulers, as we were used to, and yet it was soon obvious that there was no authority lacking, and that they had a peppery temper.

I think what impressed our elders most, and what they still spoke about when I was young, was that in the past there had been rulers who were virtuous and mindful of the rayats welfare, but never a whole system of government that was bent to public good, with no apparent personal benefit to its officers. These and many other things at first intrigued the people, and later pleased them.

We Punjabis were fortunate in escaping the rule of the East India Company. For the few years before 1857 Punjab was governed by the Commission under Lawrence and a set of officers whose interest was development rather than trade. We started our British chapter under the new government with no hangover from the Company. In this virgin field, with no regrets from the past, the government settled down to the task in which our family, like many others, was to play a small part, of building an administration; giving the province a new judiciary; for the first time a police; instituting land records and a revenue system; education department; building irrigation canals which changed deserts into granaries; and providing many other services that laid the foundation of a peaceful and prosperous countryside. It was a benevolent bureaucracy which gave much opportunity for building and therefore attracted men who liked pioneering under conditions of scope and power.

When I was at school our textbooks dividing Indian history into three periods, Hindu, Muslim and British, ended with a short chapter, 'Angrezi Raj ki Barkaten'—Blessings of the English Raj. This was always a standard question in our examinations. There was a list of about a dozen blessings like law and order, irrigation canals, roads and bridges, schools, railways, telegraph and public health. In my generation these things were taken for granted, but my father used to explain that while he, too, was born in an era of peace, to his elders the new law and order really meant something. Having lived through the break-up of the Sikh empire, human rights and respect for life and property were an unfamiliar concept to them. They really understood what it meant not to be harassed any more by marauding groups of disbanded soldiers. They had the legends of Jehangir's march to Kashmir in their memory, when his army of two lakh soldiers and camp followers passed through the country like a locust swarm, leaving a line one hundred miles wide that was denuded of all food. The Punjabi language was full of words and proverbs that bore testimony to its tough rulers in the past. 'Never stand behind a horse or in front of an official!' And now, suddenly, the soldiers stopped marauding and foraging. In fact, many soldiers of the Sikh armies, who might otherwise have rampaged around, were engaged in the new armies and given a regular living. The British soldiers were simple, and instead of helping themselves paid fancy prices. If our generation began to be amused at the textbook blessings of the British Raj, my grandfather's generation took them seriously and praised unreservedly. So did my father and his generation, at least to begin with.

I think we must have found something in common between us and the Englishman which made us get on well together from the start. For one thing, there was little or no orthodoxy in us, nor the aloofness and complexity of the southern brahmin. We were willing to accept the foreigners as man to man. Our society was extrovert and adaptable. It had, while retaining its internal structure, adapted itself to each change until, like the exposed cross-section of an archaeological excavation, it showed layers of characteristics piled one upon the other from each external impact. And this, the British impact, was comparatively so gentle and persuasive that the Punjabi for once enjoyed the process of change and adaptation.

Muslim domination of a thousand years, often intolerant and usually zealous, had rubbed off the outward signs of Hinduism, and what was left was driven inward, making it more a belief and a certain way of life than a practice of orthodox rituals. In our names, clothes, food, language, learning, perhaps even in our attitude to women we borrowed freely from the Muslims. Our cooking is mostly Muslim; our names a mixture of Sanskrit, Persian and even Greek; the salwar kameez of our men and women and the semi-purda were also imported. Of my first names, one is Sanskrit and the other, Lal, Persian. Some boys were named Sikandar (Alexander), and some were even called Walayati, a name for foreigners, which became synonymous with the English. This word was later adopted by the English soldiers as 'Blighty' for England. In our language a man who always gets the better of you in an argument is called Aflatoon (Plato); and one who was legalistic in discussions was called a Rattikeen, after the name of a famous English chief judge of the Lahore High Court, called Rattigan. In all this borrowing we may have lost something but we also gained much, at least in directness and adaptability and it was probably that which appealed to the British and made them enjoy their task as builders and teachers, and made us apt and eager learners.

☆

My grandfather, Maya Das, became the first member of the family to join the new government service. The eldest of three brothers, he was born at Kala Serai on the west bank of the Jhelum in about the year 1840, before the British took over the Punjab. He went to a small school in the village Sikh dharamsala, where they taught children how to read and write Persian, and simple arithmetic. Persian was still the written language of the Punjab. After leaving school he was taken on as a kanungo, a minor official, in the Revenue Department at a small salary, I imagine about twenty rupees per month. As his work dealt with the farmers, it meant gifts of vegetables, ghee and other produce, for it was considered a normal thing to offer such gifts; in fact, the farmers regarded it as no imposition if it was left at only that.

The early years, when the new services were being organised, were, according to our father, full of problems, some human and amusing. One aspect of the British which was not understood, was their sense of discipline—something quite new and alien to the people. Our grandfather related the story of one of his colleagues who was appointed a patwari. It was a simple enough job and required the barest of training in maintaining a register of land records and transfers. But like all jobs in the new regime, it imposed a type of discipline which this man found hard to grasp. He was asked to maintain a diary in which entries were made of his daily work, but he was told that every Sunday was a holiday, when he need not work. There were, of course, the festival days which were also holidays, but the idea of not working on Sunday, which up to now had been a day like any other, was new and one which this man never quite understood. Some time later, the British revenue officer paid an inspection visit and looked into his diary, and found that very little work had been done, and that ineptly. What, however, disgusted the officer most was a frequent entry: 'Today a Sunday was celebrated.' The officer decided that the wrong man had been recruited and discharged him. This man did not mind very much losing his job, as in those days of simple wants and plentiful food, living in a village without a job was no particular hardship, but what really upset him was the Sahib's lack of appreciation of his gesture in celebrating this Christian holiday with such flattering frequency.

The dismissal of this colleague of my grandfather was something odd to everyone at the time. Surely one has to consider things in their proper perspective. A funeral, an illness, a wedding, a call for help from a neighbour or relation are all things which must receive preference over work in hand. It may require several days' absence from one's work, but these are duties which must be performed unquestioningly. You just down tools or tether the bullock, strap your horse and go. This poor man was merely following the custom of his society, of course taking advantage of the new rule which allowed holidays. Dismissal was, therefore, a punishment wholly undeserved. What would the widowed aunt say if he did not turn up for at least two days to attend the head-shaving ceremony of her son; more so now that he was a government official and a man of some importance. His presence was necessary, and he went, but he took the wise or, as it turned out to be, unwise precaution of treating the absence under the new rules as a Sunday and entering it meticulously in the diary.

Looking back, I suppose that for discipline to grow gradually in a society as the result of changing economic and occupational conditions is one thing; for it to be imposed suddenly must have been totally incomprehensible to our people, and could only be regarded as an idiosyncrasy of the rulers. It did not begin to be really understood until my father's generation.

My grandfather died young. Having started modestly in a profession he had keenly felt his lack of education and realised that going to a dharamsala school was not enough. People were now talking of the new high schools where they taught the English language, the key to new skills and professions. He decided to send the brightest of his younger brothers to Gujrat, forty miles away, which had the nearest high school. This was the school to which my father and uncles and we brothers and cousins all went later in continuation of the new process of professionalisation that had begun in a small way with grandfather.

☆

My grand-uncle, Thakur Das, was born in 1850, the year after the British fought their last battle in the Punjab at Gujrat. According to custom we never take the names of our ancestors, as far as we know, but this grand-uncle was named after an ancestor six generations ago. The reason for defying this ban was strange. Our great-grandmother had a dream while she was pregnant, in which this distant ancestor Thakur Das appeared and told her that he was going to be reincarnated in her womb. When she bore a son, he was named Thakur Das in deference to the wishes of this ancestor. In the family records at Hardwar I could only see this one instance of a name repeated.

Thakur Das grasped the opportunity for education that grandfather gave him, and studied with avidity like most Khatri boys of his time who for generations had been deprived of their right to opportunities in service. He was the first in the family to pass matriculation, and we were told that there was great jubilation in the village. He was immediately given the title of Babu. This title had been brought by Bengali and U.P. clerks who came with the British to man their services, but so far there had been few Punjabis to acquire enough education to earn it. He was a bright pupil and was noticed by the English headmaster who after school took him on as a teacher.

At this time, in about 1870, government was encouraging the practice of law in the newly formed courts. Through the influence of his headmaster, grand-uncle was offered a year's legal training in Lahore. To our village this was indeed the wonder of all wonders of the new times. He was probably the first from the village to travel as far as Lahore, but to study in that town, in one of the new colleges, to learn to argue, defend and cross-question before an English judge, was indeed something to talk about. What was more, he was supposed also to have acquired a knowledge of the English language. He could 'git-mit git-mit', as they said when they first heard English spoken. A year later, my grand-uncle finished law and with great pride and ostentation displayed a painted metal board with a wooden frame, declaring his name and profession in an arc in English letters and a straight line in Urdu underneath. Fifty years later, we used to decipher the faded English lettering. It said, 'Lala Thakur Das Tandon, Pleader, Gujrat.'

The process of professionalisation was now proceeding rapidly. Next door another pleader soon set up his board, a Kochhar Khatri, who later caused much admiration in the town by giving college education to three of his sons, the eldest of whom became one of the first Indian judges in the Punjab, the second a pleader, and the third a doctor who joined the army. The small town would indeed have marvelled had it known that his grand-daughter would marry an army officer from far away Maharashtra who was to become Chief of Staff of the Indian Army.

Innovation was also fast catching up. As his practice prospered, grand-uncle left the city and built a house just outside the city wall, facing one of the gates. It was built in a new style, which bore the first traces of influence of the British bungalow. Houses had so far been built inside the city wall, usually two or three storeys high. With pressure on the limited space, they seldom had only a single storey, and rarely more than three, with an open room or two on top to catch the breeze or escape from the rain when people slept out on the terrace on summer nights. With peace and safety people began to leave the city, though no one as yet dared to go as far as the civil station where the English officers lived in large bungalows. They could not have gone to live so far away from their people, virtually into the jungle, nor would they have had the courage, even had they been allowed to do so by the sahibs. The first move was to go just outside the city wall.

Our grand-uncle's house had a high wall around it which was blank on three sides, while on the fourth side, facing the road, it had open arches and a high old-fashioned studded gate, barred at night from inside. These arches were rented, partly as a source of income, but also for protection since the house was outside the city wall. As the house faced the main city gate, its front soon became a tonga stand from where these two-wheeled horse carts went to the railway station of Gujrat, to some neighbouring small towns and villages, and to Kashmir. Inside the main gate of the house, as you entered, there was a rectangular courtyard with rooms on two sides, a shed for grand-uncle's tonga, and a stable on the right, and a blank wall opposite the entrance. The rooms were occupied by grand-uncle's clerk, servants, some nondescript distant relatives, people from our village, and his clients. It was customary for clients from villages to sleep at the pleader's house, though they boarded outside. A courtyard full of resting and sleeping clients was a visible sign of a pleader's success.

In the left corner of the courtyard, through the blank wall, there was another gate that led to the inside of the house where the family lived. Just within this gate was a dark vestibule called a deohri, which was as far as the tradesmen could go uninvited. In it there was also a deep well, known as a baoli, from which the family drew water. Through another door at the top end of the deohri you entered the house, which was also built around a square courtyard. On the opposite side of the entrance was a wing with kitchen and store rooms; facing it was a wing with living rooms; on the right a blank wall, and on the left a room which occupied the full length of the wing and was used as grand-uncle's sitting-room and office. This room had a door opening to a passage by which the visitors and clients came in from the outer courtyard without going through the family quarters. The passage ended in a small square sunken garden behind the house, which had a grove of fruit trees and some jasmine and rose bushes to provide grand-aunt with flowers for her morning puja. The garden with its oranges and mangoes was a great temptation to us, but we never dared to go beyond picking fallen fruit. The luxury of a private garden, adjacent to the house, was a novelty. Some city people had fruit orchards, but these were outside the city and more like farms.

The house was built of the old, thin, hard Punjabi brick, more like a small tile compared to the later thick English brick. Afterwards they stopped building houses like grand-uncle's. As the pressure of population grew inside the city suburbs began to spring up. When they saw the first Indian officers living in government bungalows in the civil station, some people took courage and moved out to their vicinity, into bungalows of English style. Others went to the suburbs and built houses rather like those in the city but with ugly modern touches. The style of grand-uncle's house somehow went out of favour.

Inside, the house was spacious, with high ceilings, cool in the summer but so very cold in the winter that you tried to keep close to the kitchen fire or a charcoal brazier. It was sparsely furnished, with string charpoys or niwar, cotton tape, beds and low string and niwar stools, called pirhis. They all had gaily lacquered legs. In the main bedroom, faded with age, was a rather elaborately worked pirhi with a high back. It had a coloured string seat and ornately turned sides and back studded with mirrors and ivory pieces. It was the pirhi which grand-aunt, like all Punjabi brides, brought in her dowry. Near it was an old bed of elaborate design which had been her bridal bed. This furniture was very like the style still seen in Gujerat and Saurashtra. In our own house we had a very old bed on which our father's grandmother had lain on her wedding night. The rest of the furniture consisted of many steel and wooden trunks; there was the very large steel trunk in which grand-aunt brought her dowry. They contained clothes, linen, blankets, shawls, quilts, utensils of copper and silver, jewellery and ornaments, and tapestries called phulkaries.

The sitting-room called baithak, literally meaning where you sat, was an impressive long room furnished in the old style. It served as a study, office and reception room. The entire floor was covered with a cotton carpet, durrie, with a white sheet, known as chandni, meaning moonlight. On it were placed flat white cushions to sit on, and tubular cushions, known as gao-dum (cow-tailed) takias, to lean against. Near the cushions were low octagonal, ivory inlaid mango-wood tables and brass spitoons. At the head of the carpet was a large divan-like cushion where grand-uncle used to sit. Near this was a low ornamented hooka with a long stem. The whole effect of the room was one of extreme neatness, cleanliness and chasteness. Before entering you left your shoes outside. In the walls there were small modelled and arched recess with shelves, some of which had shutters of carved rose-wood, while others were open. The walls were lime-washed in white, and the inside of the open cupboards was washed in green.

At the north end of the baithak there was an alcove with a low thara, a brick platform, also covered with durries, chandnis, and gao-dum takias. This part of the room was used for an office and had modern revolving wooden shelves containing uncle's law books. It also had some low desks with sloping sides for writing. On the desks were ceramic ink-pots containing rags soaked in Indian ink. The pens were cut from hard reeds and sharpened to a point at one end. There were also modern English pen holders of porcupine quills with metal nibs. For blotting the ink there were brass cups with perforated lids to sprinkle sand.

The alcove had a number of pictures hung in a line, all tilting forward from the wall. The pictures were quite a fascination to us children. They were prints of Ravi Varma, of the royal family of Travancore, who painted a large number of Indian mythological subjects, depicting practically the whole story of the Hindu faith. The settings were the lush jungles, hills and waterways of Travancore which in dry dusty Punjab looked unfamiliar but very beautiful. The women in the pictures, the Shakuntalas and Damyantis, the Sitas, Lakshmis, and Saraswatis, were large, handsomely proportioned fair women looking more like women of the north, but presumably modelled on the lovely grey-eyed Tia women of the Cannanore coast.

Interestingly enough, the place of honour in the drawing-room was given to an English coloured print, which was as popular as the Ravi Varma pictures for nearly fifty years. This was a picture of life in steps of ten years till they reached the prime and then descended. It began with birth and ended with death, both events being blessed by angels. On the first step there was a baby in a cradle, and on the next a flaxen-haired girl playing badminton. She was soon a young woman in the arms of a smooth-faced young man, saying a shy yes to him. On the next step stood a bearded man and this ripening woman, both looking fondly at their baby in a cot. Then came the top step with a greying man and woman as proud parents of a family. After that the steps went down, through grandparenthood to decrepitude, till a very old woman was sinking into the arms of an angel. This was life, though depicted in symbols foreign, some to us seemingly immodest, like the young couple in each other's arms. Mercifully they were not kissing, as then the picture could not have been displayed at all. It was much appreciated and always caused wise comment by my grand-uncle and his visitors.

Our grand-uncle, with white hair and a square cut white beard, was a distinguished looking man in my childhood memory. He always wore loose white pyjamas, a white shirt, a cream cotton or grey woollen long coat, a starched loosely-tied white turban, and strong Punjabi shoes. He had a very courteous manner and spoke to us children with old-fashioned politeness, which was very flattering but made us giggle. It was the custom in those days for elders to receive and talk to visiting children as if they were grown-ups. But grand-uncle always amused us because in his polite speech he always addressed us as langoors, long-tailed monkeys, an affectionate reference to Hanuman's monkeys who in the Ramayan followed Ram and Lakshman in their battle with Ravan. We were pleased at this reference too because in the local annual depiction of the Ramayan we boys tried hard for parts in Hanuman's monkey army.

Grand-uncle's day began early. He would sit in his office, and the munshi, his clerk, would bring in the clients whose cases were coming up for hearing in court that day. A client, usually a simple villager, would at once begin a long account of the wrong done to him, his complete innocence and the equally complete perfidy of the opponent, his full faith in grand-uncle, who next to God must know the whole truth, and his confidence that justice was going to prevail—in his favour. And so these clients would declare at length as grand-uncle went through his preparatory notes on the case, asking some questions and instructing the munshi to impress upon the clients not to say more than what had been agreed upon.

After working till about nine o'clock in the winter months, grand-uncle would go in for his meal, a breakfast and lunch together. During the winter he ate in the inner courtyard in the sun. His food was always cooked by grand-aunt and served by one of the children if they were about. The custom of servants cooking and serving came later. Usually, grand-aunt cooked outside and my uncle sat near her. After the meal he had a quiet pull at his hooka in the courtyard, or in his office if he had some last-minute work at the cases. At about ten o'clock he would tie his turban, put on his coat and shoes and leave for the courts. His tonga was waiting outside and solemnly he and his munshi would get in with the law books and files. Making much unnecessary but quite musical noise with the foot-bell, fixed in the dashboard, the syce would drive away very importantly, for there were few private tongas in Gujrat in those days.

We never quite knew what happened in the courts; how the cases were argued; what the judges did. But in the afternoon grand-uncle would return at four o'clock, and after some sweets or fruit and milk, or in the summer almond or some fruit juice—tea was unknown in those days except as a remedy for chest troubles—he began his work again, usually receiving new cases. At night he worked again after dinner in his office, consulting the law books and preparing the cases. In the summer months the courts began at seven in the morning and sat till midday. He then did his preparatory work very early in the morning and in the cool of the night.

Every evening water was sprinkled on the dusty brick-paved floor of the outer courtyard, and grand-uncle would sit there in a reed chair which later gave place to an English deck-chair, smoke his hooka and receive visitors. His friends, relations and clients would drop in for news, to chat, or to seek advice. The relatives would also drop in on the family in the inner courtyard. He was over seventy when I first remember him. He spoke in clear Punjabi laced with chaste Urdu and Persian and an occasional English word, punctuated with much conscious wisdom and many Punjabi, Persian and Urdu proverbs. At that age, everyone expected him to speak with the dignity and wisdom of age, education and experience. He was one of the first to receive higher education, to travel outside the Punjab, and to speak with the English in their own tongue. These things, combined with age, gave him a natural position of leadership in the town and community.

He was a man of considerable interests. He collected old coins and was reputed to have a rare collection at a time when few Indians went in for such hobbies. On special occasions, when he came across anyone who showed an interest in the subject, he would take out his collection from a locked cupboard in the drawing-room. My uncle, who had once been present, said that it was quite a ritual. Grand-uncle kept the coins in cloth bags tied with strings, and would take out one coin at a time. Uncle said he did not trust the visitor with his collection; but then this uncle did not like him, and was the first in our family to rebel against the authority of an elder. He was later to break away from grand-uncle altogether, something then akin to apostasy. Another interest of grand-uncle's was to trace the family history. For this he did a considerable amount of research in the villages along the Jhelum and often spent his holidays at Hardwar with the pandas, delving into family records. When I first went there in 1950, the panda had heard from his grandfather of old Lala Thakur Das and his researches. I do not know what happened to his records over which he spent much time and care.

Grand-uncle was over eighty when he died in 1931. Till the end he regularly took his walks in early morning and in the evening, along the Bhimbar road. On cold winter mornings, muffled in his grey coat and a thick shawl, he used to walk through the avenue of leafless shisham trees. Above the trees, catching the early rays of the sun, were the peaks of the first line of the Himalayas, a rose pink against the deep blue of the foothills. In the evening he gazed at them again as he set out, but then they looked a light mauve above the very deep mauve, sometimes purple, of the North Indian winter line. In summer the hills were hidden by the dust except after rain when the air was washed clean. He loved his walk, which was often punctuated by people joining him, if they wanted some private advice or to get their side of the story in a family quarrel first, which they found difficult to do at the evening gatherings in his house.

He loved his life, which was something new and exciting. His generation was the first span of the bridge that began in 1850. With my father began the second span and with me the third. Grand-uncle was born seven years before the Raj began, and father died seven years after it ended.

CHAPTER TWO

Parents

My father, Ram Das, was born in 1876 in Kala Serai, three miles from the town of Jhelum. He was only about twelve when our grandfather died, leaving him the eldest of four brothers and two sisters. Normally, as an orphan, he would have hung around the village, but the custom of familial responsibility came to his rescue. In this case there was also an old debt. My grand-uncle had been educated under similar circumstances by my grandfather; it was now his turn to educate my father. This debt my father repaid, when his turn came, by educating his three younger brothers.

Father moved to Gujrat to live with his uncle who put him into his old school. In district towns government had opened high schools, and in smaller towns middle or primary schools. About the same time the English Protestant missions were also starting schools in the Punjab, and some of them built a great reputation for themselves. The high schools in my father's time still had English headmasters, who in their own way did much pioneering work in evolving curricula, translating textbooks and writing new ones. My father used to speak highly of his headmaster, who must have worked hard for a small pay, so far away from home. This admiration he was often to express for many of the Englishmen he came across at school, college and in service. Most of them had no doubt been put there by circumstance, having been born in India, and had they even wished they had nowhere else to go. But he looked at it in another way. They could have behaved like unhappy exiles and done just enough to keep their heads above water; but he admired those, and there were many of them, who seemed to love India and threw their roots deeply into its soil and from whose suckers grew many trees in my father's generation.

Some of them could have left India but stayed on through choice, sometimes in obscure corners of the country. A fine example was Dr. Taylor who, after resigning from a successful career in the medical service, settled in a small village, Jallalpur Jattan, about ten miles from Gujrat, where he began to practise eye surgery. He rejected the idea of working in the comparative comfort of even a district town like Gujrat where he would have had the company of his compatriots because, he argued, Gujrat already had a hospital and he could do more good in the country. He made a great name for his charity and his skill, and patients came to him not only from Gujrat but sometimes from several hundred miles away. His name became a legend. He specialised in the cataract operation where through simple surgery he restored sight to many. He was not the only one; there were many like him. There was Miss Brown who started a women's hospital in Ludhiana which was later to become, I think, the first women's medical school in India.

Father's life in his uncle's home must have been quite hard. While, thanks to the system of family responsibility, poor relations, particularly young ones, were taken care of, they were actually barely tolerated and their dependence was often made clear to them every day of their life. Women were perhaps the ones to blame. Men were indifferent, and they might not give the same affection to the dependant child as to their own children, but the women were adepts at making the dependant's life miserable. While grand-uncle treated father with kindly indifference, so long as he filled his hooka properly—a chore which must have put him off smoking for the rest of his life—grand-aunt monopolised all his spare time outside school hours for running errands and doing shopping. She made sure at the same time that he was kept constantly reminded of his position.

Years later, when our father was well settled, we children used to call on grand-aunt and listen deeply impressed to how she had looked after our father, how she had swathed the poor boy with affection and care so that her own children sometimes felt envious. She would express lachrymose doubts whether our mother felt for us the way she did or our father. We used to be touched by this eloquent expression of an affection of so long ago and envied our father as a little boy. We thought of the many good things we missed in life for, according to our aunt, while she firmly believed in not spoiling her own children, she made sure that the poor orphan never went without anything he ever wished for. She conjured visions to us of our austere, stern father spoiled and doted on. It was only when we grew up that we began to discover the humour of the situation, but one who knew it all the time but never saw the joke of it was our mother who, being in the position of a daughter-in-law, dared not retort. Back home she used to be very upset. Our father never said anything.

At school father did well. Despite the many chores his aunt gave him, he worked hard at studies when he could. This was the age for hard work. Boys were avidly soaking up the learning that was being imparted in the new schools. There were stories of boys who literally mortified themselves to learn. To prevent sleep, they would tie their top knot with a string to the ceiling so that each time they nodded with sleep they woke up in pain when the hair was pulled up with a jerk. To prevent their eyelids from closing with the heavy sleep of youth they would put drops of acrid rapeseed oil, which smarted and burnt their eyes but kept them awake. In the cold freezing winter nights they woke up at three o'clock in the morning, went out of the warmth of the quilts and the closed rooms and bathed in icy water to wake themselves up thoroughly and then settle down to long hours of study until daybreak. They would do hard physical jerks and exercises to keep awake. The privilege of education came virtually free, and the results it was leading to in the shape of new careers were so glittering that they studied with a dedicated obsession.

The English headmaster of the Gujrat government school may have thought that this was perhaps going too far, but he must have been secretly satisfied, I imagine gratified and touched, by this naive and hungry desire to learn. The boys had coined a Punjabi expression, remembered even in our days, wishing that they could grind the books into a pulp and extract the knowledge out of them and drink it. They could learn so much more that way, for it would become a part of their system. If it is wondered what kept men like this headmaster going, one only has to think how moved they must have been at the response they evoked. People wanted more and more of them; their needs and demands were limitless. In India, service, genuine and freely given, soon becomes elevated to saintliness. Saintliness is never conferred; no formal declaration makes saints; they are made by popular opinion. Some of the early pioneers of education and social service in the Punjab acquired such haloes.

My father held his generation of schoolboys as an example to us. This was not just a case of the nostalgia of each generation for its past, for his generation did work hard all through life. Education and opportunities were new and they fell on virgin soil, which blossomed soon into a meadow of a very industrious, able and conscientious professional class. The Punjabi Khatris had for generations been deprived of their right to administration; and now suddenly opportunities were thrown before them; anyone's to pick up. The Khatris, and soon the other castes, ran forward to grasp them. The Khannas, Kapurs, Chopras, Malhotras, Sahnis, Dhawans, Talwars, Puris, to mention only some among the Khatris; Batras, and Kumars notably among the Aroras; were soon to spread all over the Punjab government civil list, the medical service of the army, the first commissioned service open to Indians, and the professions of lawyers, barristers, doctors, scientists and professors. Many rose from the lowest ranks through sheer integrity, hard work and self-teaching. One of the earlier Indian deputy commissioners, nearly fifty years ago, had joined revenue service forty years earlier as a satchel bearer. Many of them even left India and went across the forbidden black waters to the Mauritius Islands, Fiji, Malaya, Burma and East Africa, in search of greater responsibility and better opportunities. Many young munshis, as they taught English probationers Urdu and Punjabi and explained Punjabi life and customs to help them pass service examinations, were also teaching themselves, quickly and assiduously, till the pupils discovered the talent of their teachers and assisted them, sometimes to reach high posts.

After passing matriculation from Gujrat, father went to Lahore to join the Dayanand Anglo-Vedic College. Before finishing college he decided to compete for the entrance examination to the Roorkee Engineering College. This college had been started in 1844 for training of the Royal Engineers and was run by that corps. After the consolidation of the Punjab, government began to take on a few British and Indian civilians for manning the newly created department of public works, with its branches of irrigation, and building and roads. This department expanded so rapidly with the growing network of irrigation canals and roads in the Punjab and western United Provinces that the demand for engineers soon necessitated reserving the whole college for training civil engineers.

The Thomason Engineering College at Roorkee had a succession of able teachers, and a stiff competitive examination for admission. The number of entrants was limited, and each one who passed was assured service. This made entrance to Roorkee a coveted prize. Father travelled to Roorkee without mentioning it to grand-uncle. He was anxious to make his way quickly, but he missed admission by one place. Putting aside his disappointment, he went up to the principal and asked if he could not squeeze in another student. The Englishman was somewhat taken aback by this simple country boy suggesting such an innovation, but to father's surprise he was at least not visibly annoyed, and asked him to come back the following day. Fortune favoured father, for the next day one of the boys decided against joining the college, and so there was a vacancy which fell to him. His uncle was very pleased and agreed to pay for the two years' course. It was a very expensive education for those days; it cost thirty rupees a month.

He sometimes spoke to us of his stay at Roorkee as a dream. The thought that in two years he might become an engineer—he had never in his life met one—in one of the coveted government services, with a fixed salary of an amount he would hardly know what to do with, spurred him to work as he had never worked before. The end of studies seemed near and the reward of a post within his grasp. It would also mean the end of his dependance. He would go back to Gujrat and to his village with an air of importance, the first engineer from his village and the second from Gujrat. It is difficult to imagine his elation, and I find it hard to compare with anything in my life. Perhaps my joining a British commercial firm marked among us something just as new and daring, though without the aura of government service.

In 1898 father qualified as a civil engineer and joined the irrigation department of the Punjab government. His uncle's pride was justifiably great. He had repaid the debt to his elder brother. His aunt felt that her anxious care was the factor most responsible for his success.

At the time my father began his career, the service rules, like the Indian caste system, were clearly defined, well understood and fully accepted. You accepted them as the natural order of things. There were three grades in service, virtually like the Hindu castes, because entry was preordained and determined by birth. There was a grade for the British-born, which was the seniormost; followed by a middle grade for the locally born British, pure or mixed; and a junior grade for Indians, irrespective of their caste. Between the English-born and the Indian-born British we were unable to make a distinction. They all looked the same, spoke the same language and seemed to live alike. The difference was too subtle for us to appreciate. It could only be inferred that those who were born in England belonged to superior families and received better education than their local kinsmen and therefore were better qualified for superior posts; but strangely enough, the locally born talked of 'home' with the same nostalgia.

My father's generation for two reasons accepted the position without any resentment. First, the initiative lay with the British officers, who were developing the country and the services, and it therefore seemed only right that as teachers and leaders they should enjoy a superior position and the privileges of gurus and mentors. We are used to giving our gurus and seniors respect. In the primary school my father went to, the boys swept the teacher's house, did the shopping, tended the cow, chopped wood and brought daily offerings of milk, curds, vegetables, grain and fruit. In fact, this is how in kind and service the teachers used to be paid, but even later, when school fees were given in cash, the custom of service and gifts continued for a long time. Even I took milk and curds to the master besides the English newspaper to which my father was one of the few in the town to subscribe. Thus, the British were not begrudged this privilege which they were entitled to by their special position. It was when the position gradually changed and they no longer were the teachers—when many of them were being trained by Indians—that their privileges began to be questioned. But that was to come later. When my father joined service the order was unquestioningly accepted. I wonder sometimes if the British during those first fifty years were so busy teaching and building that they did not look ahead to the time when their pupils would be mature enough to demand equality; or were they convinced that that stage was never going to be reached and the teaching would somehow continue for ever; a trust in perpetuity, where the ward would never become his own trustee. Actually the process took its natural course, jerkily but always upward. At each stage of transition there was a jerk, a delay and some frustration, but soon someone would jump the cataract and begin to swim steadily upstream towards the higher reaches of responsibility and power. My father having started low struggled hard till he reached the nirvana of his service, the cadre of the Imperial Service of Engineers.

All that he had endured in his early years—the dependant life of an orphan, the concentrated effort to equip himself for a profession, and the strain of reaching the upper rungs of his career—made father into a quiet, determined and taciturn man. He was conscientious and meticulous at work to the point of being a perfectionist. From the first month at Roorkee College when he sat at the drawing boards he maintained a spirit of never being satisfied with whatever he did, drawings, calculations or discharging obligations. He always felt that he could do still better. His only enjoyment in life was work, and I do not even know whether he really enjoyed working. Perhaps it was the only thing he knew how to do, and he did it well. But most of his colleagues that I knew were also like that; they lived and talked only about their work, though they envied the ability of their English colleagues to combine it with rest and play. Father, who never relaxed from work, explained it to us by saying that the Englishmen could afford to relax because if things went wrong they managed to explain it to each other, and took the attitude that things do sometimes go wrong. But when an Indian made a mistake the reaction, if an understanding one, was that the job perhaps was too difficult for him; 'after all they did not have the skill or the experience; one must be careful with giving responsibility too soon, perhaps one should have kept a closer eye'. Such quite well meaning remarks hurt, even when there was no imputation of negligence. Being always on test like this made him, if possible, even more conscientious and punctilious. He thus worked and worked, and took his first holiday twenty-eight years after joining service. He had taken odd short spells of leave to attend funerals and weddings, but leaving work to rest and relax he did only once in the thirty-five years of his service. By then his career was assured and he was senior enough not to worry about others. So he took six months' leave, and he and I went trekking in Kashmir. We walked, waded and climbed, and he never spoke about work. We followed our great grand-uncle's footsteps and brought the family ledger at Matan up to date.

For years father was so busy at work that he never gave any thought to religion. Our home was not irreligious; we feared God and invoked His name, but there was no daily worship or ritual, or much visible influence of religion on our daily life. We were only conscious of our religion at festivals and fasts, weddings, namings or death; and then only in a mechanical sort of way. Sometimes my mother performed a kind of ceremony, as for instance on my recovery from chicken-pox, when some simple offerings were made to Durga, the goddess of small-pox. For big functions, requiring more complicated ceremonies, a brahmin was called in, who usually appeared to us almost as ignorant as ourselves.

There had never been much formal religion in our homes and villages anyway; invasions and the bigotry of the invader had erased much of it from the surface. Furthermore, my father and most others of his generation had been too absorbed in learning their professions. From a simple boy in a village he had become an engineer doing complicated trigonometric calculations—a transformation where religion had played no part. Through his school and college days and his early working life in the jungles he remained disinterested, but when he was first posted in a town both he and my mother came under the influence of the Arya Samaj. This reformist movement, started by Swami Dayanand Saraswati, had found a more receptive soil in the Punjab than in the home of the founder in Kathiawar, or even in progressive Bombay and Poona. To our new professional class it provided a western social reorientation combined with simple Vedic belief and ritual. Its opposition to orthodoxy and idol worship, and its revival of

Vedic ritual in modern form, without temple and priest, made a direct appeal to the Punjabi intelligentsia. Actually two schools of thought had developed within the Arya Samaj; those who harked back to a purely Vedic education, known as the Gurukul party, and the others who wanted to combine the Vedic with the modern, and became known as the College party. The former founded an old monastic type of teaching institution in the Kangra hills, called Gurukul Kangri, with an emphasis on Sanskritic education. The Anglo-Vedic school made a wider appeal, and its focal points, the Dayanand Anglo-Vedic High School and the College by the same name in Lahore, commonly known as the D.A.V. School and the D.A.V. College, became the backbone of the progressive section of the Punjabi Hindu community. Its emphasis on modern education, its opposition to child marriage and sponsoring of widow remarriage were in line with the modern concepts in which my father had been trained. We began to profess this new creed and attend the mandir, which did not look like a temple, but more like a lecture hall with a pleasant open courtyard and a garden. Worship took place in the courtyard or in the open hall. There were no priests except visiting swamis who were modern, educated men. The prayer, sandhya, was Vedic, as also the hymns; and in the centre of the congregation a votive fire was lit with incense and sandalwood. The whole ceremony was simple and beautiful. Men, women and children prayed together, and afterwards there was an informal sermon from a swami or a member of the congregation. We also did the sandhya twice a day at home, in the morning and evening. But this zeal did not last very long, and after some time my father began to lose interest even in the mild discipline of the Arya Samaj and did his sandhya irregularly, nor did he often go to the mandir, though in the house we continued to follow the Arya Samajist rites.

The Arya Samaj had a certain polarising effect on my father's already somewhat unconventional thinking. Even in his class he was ahead of his time. He set his face against many old customs, important and unimportant, and it was characteristic of our society that he was seldom censured for it; in fact, there was even some grudging admiration. When, for instance, he arranged the marriage of our cousin, his dead sister's daughter, with a boy from Bahawalpur, whose language and custom were as far removed from ours as to be almost non-Punjabi, it caused at first considerable consternation in the family, but at the wedding many realised that it was a very good match, and that was what really mattered. He had even allowed the boy to visit our home and meet the girl before the marriage. He was opposed to ostentation, to gold and jewellery, lavish spending on weddings and ceremonies; in fact, to all the non-productive expenditure in which our Hindu society commonly indulged. He was willing to be considered mean rather than to accept such, in his opinion, senseless obligations. In all this he was helped by our mother, though perhaps somewhat hesitatingly since she felt that on occasions he was callous in his beliefs. She thought it selfish of him to believe that everybody should move at his pace; others without the advantages of his education and position in the community could not, in fairness, be expected to ignore custom as he did.

A characteristic which also led him into difficulties was his flat refusal to secure jobs and favours for relations, who considered it quite natural to turn to him for help, and equally unnatural that he should withhold it. If he turned away his relations they could not very well turn to others who, after all, had their own obligations and demands to fulfil. This was a dilemma in which many of his generation were placed, the difficulty of fitting a new definition of integrity into the traditional pattern of duties towards the family and caste. Father used to envy his English colleagues who, being far away from home, had no relations demanding favours. He also attached much importance to the honesty of his service. The new administration in the Punjab had acquired a reputation for incorruptibility, at least at the level of its officers. At the lower levels the traditional graft continued, though in a subdued way, but in the higher ranks there was hardly anyone who was corrupt. But, as he explained, desisting from corruption was easy enough. You were under no obligation to a stranger to do him a favour and accept his money. It was the importunities of the relations that were difficult to refuse, as when your widowed aunt came and sat at your doorstep and left her young son in your care to provide for. Once we had a cousin living with us for nearly two years, till even he got tired of the free support and went away in disgust.

As children we did not understand our father's problems, and we saw him as an austere, colourless person, without any relaxations or enjoyments that we could share, interested only in his work and our future. He continually exhorted us to work and looked upon play as an exercise which you needed at regular intervals in order to work even harder. He continually advocated simplicity in clothes, food and thought. Explaining to me the proverbs in Nesfield's English Grammar, he paraphrased the whole list in his own way of thinking. The one I remember particularly as being at variance with what our teacher had explained was 'wine in, wit out', which he carefully explained meant losing your wits as soon as a drop of wine went in. I protested that that is not what Nesfield could have meant because the English were known to us for their fondness of liquor. That nettled him, for although he held them in high regard for their many virtues, their conscientiousness, sense of responsibility, industry and integrity, he was inwardly sorry that they drank. He almost felt they let him down. He must have tackled one of them on the subject, and I think he must have been told that they did it only for the sake of their health, because soon afterwards a half-bottle of Hennessy brandy appeared in our house which he began to take in medicinal doses with hot water on winter evenings. It never became a habit, and after a while he gave it up, finding the taste too unpleasant and also, I suspect, because we began to ask questions.

There was no contradiction or ambivalence in his make-up; he was all of a piece and lived up to what he preached. His generation founded the new Punjabi middle class and added some modern values to the old Punjabi character, but what they lost in the process was the colour of my grand-uncle and his age.

☆

My mother was a Vinayak Khatri, whose family came from a small town, Hadiabad, in Kapurthala State in East Punjab. It was rare in those days for someone to marry so far away, nearly two hundred miles, from home. When we asked mother about this unusual thing, she would only shrug her shoulders and quote the Punjabi saying, 'You go wherever your grain and water takes you.' She did not belong to the plains, for she was born and brought up in the mountains and lived there till she left to marry father. Her own father was a postmaster who spent most of his working life in the hills of Kangra and Chamba. It was a delightful source of wonder to us that she had been familiar with mountains, forests and snow, things we had never seen. She would describe to us how snow fell, but we could not quite picture it. She must have found the early years of her life in the plains somewhat trying, but the canal post near Madhopur headworks, on the river Ravi, where she first joined father, was near the foothills and from there she could see snow peaks. Although it never snowed the water in the canal was always ice-cold.

She had the build and complexion of the hills; she was small, wiry and pale-skinned, and for years she spoke with the accent and diction of the hill Punjabi which, free from the influence of Urdu and Persian, was nearer to Sanskrit. She was brought up simply, but was given education in Hindi, which for those days was unusual for women. Her father had belonged to the orthodox Gurukul wing of the Arya Samaj and had sent her only brother to the Gurukul seminary in the Kangra hills. The education they gave was amazingly out of tune with the changing times, and he always remained very unworldly. Our mother was more practical; she was remarkably firm and determined, and could take care of herself in most circumstances.

Father must have tried in the early years of married life to expose mother to English influence. For a while he must even have persuaded her to wear English clothes, because in an old photograph of theirs we saw her incredibly dressed in a European blouse, long skirt and shoes, and with her head uncovered. Father's experiment could not have lasted long, or perhaps it went only as far as this photograph, because we could not remember seeing her in anything but Punjabi clothes. His attempts at modernising her eating habits made no headway at all. She belonged to the very strict school of vegetarians that would not even tolerate onions in cooking. Her food was consequently cooked separately from ours, and while she did not mind onions entering the kitchen, meat and fish had to be kept and prepared outside. On nights when we children wanted to snuggle into her bed and be kissed by her, we would share her food. She did not say no, but we knew she did not like us smelling of meat. I could tell the way she kissed that she found it distasteful.

She quite enjoyed meeting the wives of father's English colleagues, but often twitted him that they were not as rational as he made them out to be. They were as full of contradictions and conservative as we were. She admired them tremendously for their ability to bear separation from their children for the sake of their husbands. To put children to school in England, and be separated from them for three or four years at a time in order to be near their husbands struck her as a great sense of duty towards both children and husbands. When my brother, and later I, left for England for our higher studies, her eyes did not even look misty. I learned afterwards that when she returned from the station she went and lay in bed and sank into deep coma for many hours. This was a strange habit with her: she seldom complained or lost her temper, but when she could stand things no longer, she would quietly go to bed without anyone knowing it, and lie there in a faint, sometimes for several hours. We would go about the house in a normal way, and hours later she would slowly open her eyes, get up and go about her work as if nothing had happened. She did not like to be asked how she felt.

Mother had an uncanny sense of premonition of danger. This was something that never failed to intrigue us, for she was unerringly right about future events, especially deaths in the family. There were occasions when she told father that she must leave at once because someone was about to die. Father scoffed but she went, and she was right. Usually she did not share her premonitions with us, though sometimes we could tell from her restlessness that some bad news was on the way. She woke up one morning and said she knew that our youngest uncle, still in his thirties, recently married, and perfectly healthy as far as we knew, was going. We received news of his sudden death the same day.

After the short experiment at westernising her father must have left mother alone, but she kept pace with his development, though at her own distance and without letting go anything she cherished. Generally speaking, throughout the process of change, our women showed enough attachment to tradition to prevent the change from swamping old values. Our fathers changed rapidly, our mothers slowly, and between them my generation managed to learn the new without entirely forgetting the old.

CHAPTER THREE

Life in Canal Colonies

After joining service my father moved about the Punjab from one canal post to another. We lived in small canal colonies—at some headworks, a new construction project, or at operating posts along a canal. I was born in one of these colonies, at Bullokee, where a headworks was under construction to take a new canal out of the river Ravi. It was for those days a large project, designed and patiently built in brick and mortar without the aid of any plant and machinery. The whole barrage was made by hand, brick by brick, joined with hand-crushed brick mortar and lime. There were no trucks, earth movers or Euclid dumpers; only men and beasts. The animals used were always donkeys, who were more manoeuvrable on the rough sites than bullock carts. The donkeys threaded their way through dumps of materials and construction work carrying their loads in two bags slung astride. Dams then were small but took many years to build. Bullokee was one of those small dams on which my father, as a young man of thirty-two, was posted. My recollection of Bullokee was solely a beautiful solid gold watch which he received as a gift commemorating the construction of the dam and the part he played. Father told us that on the day they opened the sluice gates to let the first water into the new canal, everyone from the chief engineer in charge of the project to the workmen received a gift. The watch had a white enamel dial with Roman figures in blue and finely shaped gold hands. On the inside of the gold cover at the back was an inscription which I still remember: 'Presented to Ram Das, Sub-Divisional Officer, by the King Emperor of India, for service on the construction of Bullokee Headworks.' It was considered too precious for everyday use, and for years it remained locked till some burglars stole it. Of all the things we lost in the burglary father tried hardest to trace this watch, but the police only discovered that the thieves had sold it for seven rupees. We offered to buy it back for much more, but it could not be traced, although ironically we got back some old clothes.

When the project was finished father was transferred down the new canal to a small colony near a village called Mangtanwala. Our nearest railway station was the famous Sikh Gurdwara of Nankana Sahib. We lived here till I was seven, and its memories have stayed with me for ever, so clearly etched that time has neither diminished nor effaced much. It was a lonely, flat, unbroken and dusty country, but as my childhood in these surroundings was happy and contented I have continued to love this kind of vast and open countryside. Dust and flatness have never depressed me. I love the treeless west Punjab country, with its far horizons, as much as the mountains, in whose distant acquaintance I later lived in Gujrat. Small towns like Gujrat I do not mind, but life in big cities I have never cared for. And yet, with this aversion I have had to live the last many years in Bombay, and before that in Manchester. I suppose with no choice in the matter, I became attached to them both, but my heart is still in places like Mangtanwala.

Our colony was half a mile away from the canal bank. A road led from a point where a fall had been built in the canal to allow for the gradient in the land. Its rushing noise could be heard on still evenings from quite far. It was a big canal, some two hundred and fifty feet wide, and we were not allowed to go into the water, but our uncle, whenever he came home on holidays from his college in Lahore, used to organise swimming parties, and he and his friends sometimes gave us a dip in the grey swirling waters under the fall. Occasionally the man who lived in a brick cabin at the fall and took readings of the canal caught a fish and sent it to our house. This was a rare treat which somehow always coincided with the visits of our young uncle, who would himself clean and fry the fish for our evening meal. On those days we were not allowed to drink milk or eat any milk preparation, for it was believed that mixing milk and fish caused leprosy.

The colony was built in a square. On the front, where the road from the canal joined it, there were three bungalows, the first a rest house for visiting officers, the second the residence of the executive engineer under whom my father worked, and the third our home, which stood in complete contrast to the other two houses. The first two were built in the style of dak bungalows of the late nineteenth century, red baked-brick structures with wide verandahs and flat roofs in which old steel rails were used as rafters, with brick paved ceilings in arches. Our bungalow, the oldest of the three, was unusual as it belonged to the earliest style of British bungalows in the north. Its high walls were made of sun-baked mud and straw bricks, and lime-washed. It had gables and a sloping roof covered with a very thick straw thatch. The single-storied thatched cottages I occasionally saw in England always reminded me of our old bungalow.

Behind the row of bungalows were the office buildings, a dispensary, staff quarters, workshop and telegraph office on one side, and fruit and vegetable gardens on the other. The colony was well planted with a variety of trees and flowering shrubs, both local and exotic. There were mangoes, rosewood, flame of the forest, coral, Indian laburnum, pipal and avenues of eucalyptus. Pleasant and shady, trimly maintained, like all other canal colonies and bungalows it bore the stamp of successive English officers. Having its own water channel from the canal it was well watered and green, and during the hot months an oasis in the dry parched country around. The drinking water we drew from our own wells. There were no shops, and one had to go to the village of Mangtanwala a mile away for simple necessities, while for other shopping our nearest place was Nankana Sahib, and the nearest big town Lahore.

As the canal system was first started and for many years run by officers of the Corps of Indian Engineers, its organisation was based on military lines. Our colony was the headquarters of a division which extended about fifty miles on either side along the main canal and included its lateral distribution channels which carried the water to the fields. The whole division was connected by its own telegraph, and later by a telephone system as well, which also connected us with our neighbouring divisions. In our own division there were two more subdivisional officers like father, but they were posted away and lived in their own colonies, smaller but set up like ours.

Father was responsible for operating and maintaining his part of the canal. After a certain amount of water had been received, he had to ensure its flow with the minimum of losses. From the main canal smaller channels, and from them still smaller channels took the water into the fields. At the distribution points men were posted to let out water at fixed intervals. The farmer waited at the appointed hour, day or night, to receive the water in his field, and for the whole of his turn he stood guard to make sure that his neighbours did not divert the water to his own land too soon. He stood there with the spade over his shoulder ready to strike. Water was his life blood and quarrels over it often led to murder, almost as commonly as quarrels over women. A Punjabi proverb attributed all troubles in life feuds and murder, to zamin, zan, zewar—land, women, gold.

All along the canal men were also posted at such key points as falls in the canals and at the junctions when the smaller channels left the main line. They were on round-the-clock duty to take readings every few hours which they telegraphed to father's office. All day long and till late in the evening, and sometimes even in the middle of the night, these telegrams would keep coming in, but the calm way in which father read them and put them aside intrigued us. But sometimes he would leave his meal to point to his office room and send for a clerk or an overseer to telegraph a message to some operating point. In an emergency he would go away himself. Run on a strict regimen of constant communication and speedy action, our colony was on duty the whole time and always in a state of alert.

Occasionally there was an alarm, as when there was a breach in the canal bank, and then it was truly like a battle. A canal would break its bank and water rush into the fields, flood the country and keep on advancing. The farmers around the breach were in a panic and would run with their cattle to dry ground. Their standing crops may be ruined; land waiting for the next crop or land just sown may be flooded; mud huts may collapse and altogether much loss may result. If the flood was serious, in this flat country it might cause waterlogging for a whole season. The farmers at a distance on the other hand might benefit by the unexpected supply of water, provided it was timely, and breaches in the canals were therefore sometimes suspect.

S.O.S. messages were telegraphed to the divisional headquarters and to the circle superintending engineer. Aid was rushed from all directions; farmers from the neighbourhood were pressed into emergency service; and large numbers of men fought ceaselessly to fill the breach. Thousands of sandbags, brushwood and earth were dumped into the breach to stem the rushing water. It sometimes took days to patch a breach. In the meantime the flow of water in the canal would have been closed, but if the breach was at a long distance from the head it would take some days before the flow was exhausted.

A canal breach was something to talk about for a long time in a colony, but while the fight was on there was hectic activity at the base. Men and material were rushing out, and the base was denuded of all staff except the telegraphist and an odd clerk. All operating staff, the overseers, sub-overseers, mates, workshop men, labourers, in fact all able-bodied men would be rushed to the spot. Couriers dashed backward and forward from the temporary base at the breach to the headquarters carrying messages for the telegraphist to relay upward, and to carry instructions received from the circle officers to the breach base.

Slowly the news would begin to arrive that the men were getting the upper hand and the gap was closing. Until then the men at the breach had been too busy to think of sleep or food—just eating scratch meals of dal and chappaties from the field kitchen. Now the families would despatch some food from home, and the men had their first decent meal. When the breach was filled our father would arrive back slumped half-asleep in the saddle, worn out, unshaven and caked with mud. His return was the sign that the crisis was over, but there was still plenty of work ahead. Reports had to be made and arrangements put in hand for the permanent work to restore the water flow.

Father was a big-set man of strong constitution that took seemingly unlimited strain. Over forty years later, when he was an old man of eighty, paralysed by a stroke, I watched him once shuffling from his bedroom to the bathroom, holding the wall as he moved across a distance of ten feet in almost as many minutes. We never helped him till the end, because independent movement, however slow, kept him going and retained his pride. On this occasion my mind flashed back to seeing him in a state of virile fatigue, and I reminded him of it. I said, 'It took you ten minutes to walk ten feet; what was the longest you ever rode?' The courageous man that he was, he brightened at the question and said he was once in the saddle for twenty-four hours and must have ridden well over a hundred miles. And instead of rueing his fate, he avidly began to describe the occasion.

Maintenance work on the canal went on the whole time. There were bridges, falls, breakwaters and masonry work to be looked after, banks to be trimmed and their berms repaired, roads on the sides to be kept serviceable, and many other jobs for the proper care of the canals. There was always some new construction work and remodelling, surveying and designing; and whenever the canals were dry the work that could not be done otherwise had to be quickly finished before the flow began again.

The colony was self-contained and provided all its own services. We had our own doctor, and father had also engaged a schoolmaster. On festival days there was much excitement, especially at Diwali when everyone lit lamps at night, and at Besakhi, the end of harvest festival when we all put on new bright clothes and went to the canal bank. Sometimes there was a wedding in the colony, and then there was great festivity. The girl's father would ask permission to hold the wedding there because it was cheaper than going home. Everyone helped by lending utensils, cots, bedding and by serving the guests. The wedding party would arrive from Nankana Sahib railway station in tongas and on horses, with its own brass band. A gas-lamp at night created a brightness we had never seen before. At births, illness, occasionally deaths, the colony doctor came into prominence. He was usually a simple man who continued to apply with diminishing skill whatever he had learned many years ago. Some doctors were bold enough to experiment, but most of them relied on an array of ten bottles, numbered serially, which were dispensed according to the diagnosis, and sometimes tried in turn.

For us the most exciting place in the colony was the telegraph office with its gadgets and instruments. We were mystified by the morse code which conveyed messages many miles away and brought the reply back instantaneously. The decoding of the tickticking by the 'tar babu', the telegraph clerk, never failed to thrill us. Some years later when the telephone arrived and we could hear a squeaky voice from points many miles away, our excitement knew no bounds. Another place of interest was the guardhouse where an iron chest, called the treasury, was kept. The guards were under the command of a barquandaz, 'the one who wields lightning', as the artillery men were then called. Our guards carried swords which had never been used to anyone's knowledge. The barquandaz was a very distinguished looking old man with a beard dyed red and a well tied turban from which hung a gold embroidered flat tassel. He spoke to us with clipped dignity, and his flattering address of huzoor and janab always made us giggle.

In front of the guard-house was a wooden tripod with a flat gong on which the guard on duty beat the hour melodiously. At night it gave a feeling of security to the whole camp to know that the guard was on watch. There were also two chowkidars who did the rounds. To announce their presence, both to those sleeping in the camp and to possible intruders, they used to utter some blood curdling yells. A really good night watchman had to have a powerful voice that could strike terror in a thief. He always developed his own style of announcing his presence every quarter hour or so. One of our best chowkidars, a one-eyed puny bhayya from the U.P., though known for his unprepossessing physique and presence, was yet a man transformed at night. Few intruders, even if they knew him well in the day, would dare to cross his path at night for fear that the magic of his nocturnal voice might have given him some demonaic strength unsuspected by day. Every quarter hour he would begin by clearing his throat in a stentorian manner, then hold the phlegm, of which he could produce prodigious quantities, for several minutes and finally spit it out with an ear-splitting noise. This was enough to scare most strangers. He would then proclaim loudly in a voice that could be heard in the village a mile away, that those who were sleeping should continue to sleep; others beware!—'sone walo sote raho, baqi khabardar'. It was a testimony to the day's toil that everyone did continue to sleep. His imprecations were also a clear warning to the intruder that he was directly taken note of as not being asleep. After that Lachhman would make a suitable pause to let his warning sink in, and then suddenly hell was let loose. He yelled a long blood-chilling ha, ha, ha, like a pack of howling hyenas. This set all the pariah dogs as far away as Mangtanwala barking and sent the neighbouring jackals in full retreat. But the colony continued to sleep. Once we had a burglary, and in the morning we found Lachhman gagged and tied. He never lived down the indignity and eventually resigned.

There was much bustle when the superintending engineer arrived in camp with his staff of clerks, orderlies, guards, horses and camels. For days ahead the colony was tidied up and made spick and span. While he stayed in the rest house, tents would be put up for his large staff. His orderlies and guards looked resplendent. To add to all the excitement, the superintending engineers in those days were always British, and in an out of the way place like ours theirs were the only English faces we ever saw. Looking back, it is interesting to think that here in a large government colony of a technical nature, in a country ruled by the British, as far back as before the First World War, one seldom saw any Englishmen. The executive engineer in charge of our division, his three sub-divisional officers and the entire technical staff were already Indian.

We children led a happy existence. There was no school, and we had only a private teacher who taught us under a tree or in the sun, according to the weather, with none of the irksome discipline of a regular school. There was plenty of time to play and a lot of space to play in. Our games had always something to do with the work of our fathers. One of us would be the horse, with a string round the shoulders and under the arms, the others would be the officers and overseers, and we would go on inspection tours. An English officer had to speak with accented Hindustani, with the tongue rolled in the mouth, and the others had to call him sahib the whole time.

We also greatly looked forward to the visits from relatives, especially our young uncles, who being brought up by our father used to spend their school and college holidays with us. Life would then be very exciting. They would organise sports and games and in the evenings tell us tales of Lahore, a strange and fabulous city where there were motor-cars, shops, many-storied buildings and rare fruits and sweets.

A few times in a year we accompanied father on tour. This was the greatest event of all. The night before, a string of camels would arrive at the bungalow to load the baggage, which meant practically half the household. First the office desk would be dismantled, and in the drawers of the two cupboards of the desk were carefully packed files, stationery, red and black inkpots, drawing instruments, pens, pencils, diaries and paper-weights. The cupboards would be slung over a camel and the desk-board tied on top. On the other camels were loaded the trunks, bed rolls, crates containing cooking utensils, crockery and glass, foodstuff and luggage of the staff. There was much commotion in loading the camels as each animal was made to sit down to strap the baggage. Willing and patient as camels are, they grumble a great deal when they are made to sit or get up, and keep up a constant barrage of protesting noises. When the caravan was ready, the barquandaz with his sword in scabbard would stand in front of the first camel, which had a bell and a lantern hanging from its neck, and at a signal from him the train started, accompanied by the guards and followed by the servants and father's riding horse. The first camel as the flagship carried the khazana, the chest with money, which was to be disbursed in payments and salaries. With the solitary swaying light and the tinkling of the bell, the camelcade travelled through the silent night and arrived at destination in the early hours of the morning. Some sleepy dak bungalow would suddenly come to life as the camp was set up.

We would wake very early the next morning to savour the excitement of our departure to the full, and hope that no last-minute telegram would delay the start. We would run to the stables and watch the horse harnessed and hitched to the tonga, a two-wheeled trap with a seat in front and a seat at the back on which people sat with their backs to each other. Our father, the syce, a servant, we brothers and father's black-japanned despatch-case would set off after breakfast to the first dak bungalow ten or twelve miles away. We drove along the canal, on the road built on one of its banks. On the canal side there was a protective berm while on the other side the bank sloped steeply outwards and was flanked by a regular row of shisam trees. The surface of the road was kutcha but well dried and smooth and the tonga sped along, but never for very long. There were always interruptions on the way. There would be work going on which father had to inspect; the overseers met him on the way to discuss their work; the records of the check posts had to be examined. These to us were dull delays; but more interesting were the supplicants on the way. Farmers would hear that the engineer was passing their way, and individuals, groups, sometimes large parties of them, would wait for him. Their requests were usually of two kinds, either to increase the size of the water outlet, or a remission of irrigation revenue because the crop had been poor. Sometimes they would come with personal complaints and grievances, which they felt any government officer ought to be able to redress.

The interesting thing about these delegations was their style. A group of stalwart Muslim or Sikh farmers, bearded, with large loosely tied turbans, long home-spun shirts and brightly coloured tahmads wrapped round their legs, and sturdy Punjabi shoes with turned-up leather spurs, would move forward, bow and stand with old-fashioned courtesy of hands folded over their stomachs. Slowly their spokesman would begin reciting the grievance or the request in old-fashioned Punjabi, embroidering it with some very flattering remarks mixed with great hopes and choice blessings. 'Janab,' he always began, 'huzoor, we are in great distress. Only you, the generous supporter of the poor can help us.' And so he would continue, considering it unmannerly to come to the point too soon. At suitable moments an elder in the group would prompt him, sometimes by underlining a point, at other times by politely disagreeing with him. The latter was a practical gambit. 'No,' the elder might say, 'not at all, huzoor will understand the thing himself; he is so wise and perspicacious that now that he knows our predicament he will insist in his wisdom in giving us a water outlet twice the present size and not one and half times that we ignorant jats are asking for.'

These peasants were men of dignity and charm, shrewdness and much cunning, but centuries of oppression had taught them to be self-effacing. That is why they always began with professions of great distress which made the task of an officer somewhat difficult. He never knew how much to discount, and some discounting was essential if one were to be fair to others. A curious weakness with them was their pride, usually tinged with boastfulness. A cousin told me a story which is an amusing illustration of this pride. As a young magistrate visiting a village he was approached by two men with a dispute about a buffalo. One of them claimed that he had left the buffalo with the other when he had gone away, but now that he had returned and demanded it back the other man refused to give it. My cousin tried in such cases to bring about a settlement instead of taking official cognisance which would lead to a long-drawn suit. He asked if they were interested in a peaceful settlement, or preferred to fight it out, in which case he had to demand their presence at his court in town which they would have to attend several times.

The prospect of travelling to town for several hearings and engaging pleaders had a chastening effect upon both; but, said the defendant, while he admitted that the buffalo had been left behind with him—in fact he had never denied it—the animal had been in a wretched condition at the time; and yet look at it now! He had fed it and looked after it like his own beasts so that today it was one of the best buffalos in the village. Had the original owner continued to keep it, the buffalo would have died long ago. He rightly refused to return the beast, at least not until he had been paid for all he had spent on it, both in care and money. He would be reasonable and buy the buffalo at the price the animal was worth at the time he took it over. The argument now resolved into deciding a suitable price.

The original owner naturally started with a price which the present custodian thought outrageous, and one he could never pay. He simply did not have the two hundred rupees that the owner asked, and the buffalo was not even worth half that sum anyway. The owner was adamant about the price and refused to believe that the other could not afford to pay two hundred rupees. He informed my cousin that the other man had just taken his groundnut harvest to the market and sold it for three hundred rupees. How could he then deny that he had not enough money? This apparently went straight home. This farmer was one of the first in his village to grow groundnut, and he was very proud of his yield, which was well above what the agriculture department people had told him to expect. That he should be told before the magistrate, and in full hearing of the village, that he had only been able to get three hundred rupees, when in fact he had got nearly twice as much, was an insult he could not bear. 'Huzoor,' he shouted, 'this man is a liar. Mine was no mean little crop like his; I grow groundnuts, not grams. I harvested twice as much from my land as this liar, and I cashed not three hundred rupees but six hundred. Huzoor, here is this liar's full price for the buffalo; here is two hundred rupees. I will not have my groundnut crop run down by anyone.' And the slighted groundnut grower insisted on paying the full amount because his farming pride was deeply hurt.

These West Punjab farmers could also be very violent, and the canal officers had to handle them carefully. Water to them was life. In a dry country with scanty rainfall, irrigation canals had created some of the best farming land out of desert and scrub. Rain came from above as God willed it, in plenty or otherwise, and nobody could stand face to face with God and demand adequate rain, but one could go up to a canal officer and demand water; all he had to do was to enlarge the outlet. And so the eternal demand for more water went on.

In three or four hours we would reach the bungalow, having covered only ten miles. In the bungalow, which had lain deserted since the last visit, there was much activity. Our camel caravan had arrived several hours earlier and camp life had begun its routine. The house was open and ready to receive us. Father's office looked exactly like at home; the bedrooms were ready; in the dining-room the next meal was waiting to be served; the bathrooms had jugs and tubs of cool water drawn from the well; there were flowers in all rooms and a large basket of fruits and vegetables from the garden to show the skill of the mali. Outside, staff, clerks, peons and guards were installed in their quarters, and life in the camp hummed with activity. To us it added to the excitement that everything revolved round the centre of authority that was our father.

If it was summer, we would feel drowsy and after lunch go to sleep. Somehow the lunch, cooked by the same man who cooked everyday at home, and perhaps not so well in camp, tasted so much better. In the afternoon, while father worked in his office and saw an interminable string of people, we nosed about the camp or went swimming in the channels, which were just deep enough for us. We would dive and play in the muddy water, while the village children watched us with curiosity. Soon they would throw off their clothes and take running dives in the Punjabi fashion, folding their knees in the air. They were born swimmers and divers.

Father's day began early next morning. In camp in the summer he was up before five and out on inspection before six. He would go in the tonga or ride his horse, visiting the spots where farmers had complained and petitioned. He returned at eight or nine and did office work till one o'clock. After a meal and rest he worked again in his office from four till seven. He would then go for a walk or visit another site. After dinner he worked again for an hour or two. When the gong struck ten and the chowkidar began his rounds the camp turned off the lights and went to sleep. On summer nights we slept on the high terrace where lying in bed you had everything below you and only the sky above. You did not see the trees or buildings but looked up into the vast dome of the sky, velvety black on moonless nights, studded with uncountable bright points of scintillating light. The whole country stretched around like a flat black saucer, featureless and immense. Its silence was broken in the early night by distant voices from the neighbouring village, an occasional barking of a dog. The continuous sound of the crickets, of the water in the canal rushing down the fall, hastening to its destination of thirsty fields, all merged into the silence of the night. The sound of cascading water in this flat dry country was a music born with the canals.

CHAPTER FOUR

Childhood Years

The farmer boys among whom I grew up were a remarkable lot, well made, self-confident and fearless. They would jump from trees, dive into the canal from high overhanging branches, ride horses bare-back, drive a herd of buffaloes cursing and swearing like grown-ups, and try to tie their turbans like their fathers. They grew on a simple diet of milk, curds and ghee; wheat and maize chappatis; cooked and raw simple vegetables; gur and fresh cane. It was healthy though un-varied. During the dry season, when there were no vegetables, the farmers would have just curd, butter, salt and bread for lunch, bread and dal for dinner; and last night's bread with butter and churned curds for breakfast.

When the boys grew up some of them went into the army, others stayed on the land, while very few went to towns. Their childhood was short as they were put to work at the age of three or four, even if it was only taking a horse to water or grazing the cattle. In the evenings they played gulli danda with a stick and a bail sharpened at the ends, or kaodi. In this game two teams were ranged against each other across a line. A boy from one side would run into the other side calling kaodi, kaodi in one breath. The opponents would try to tackle the runner as he pranced about trying to touch someone. If he managed to return to his own side of the line without losing breath, any that he had touched were out, but if the other side made a successful tackle he would be pinned down till he lost his breath, and then he was out. Among other exercises a favourable pastime was massaging and wrestling.

As small boys they sometimes played with girls, mostly hopping and running, but soon they became self-conscious and stopped mix-ing, and if a soft boy wanted to continue to play, the girls would peck him away with their sharp tongues and with slaps. While the boys were confidently growing into men, the girls were cockily developing into self-assured Punjabi women. There was no purda and growing girls went about freely, but as past playmates met at the well they would be seized by shyness, conscious of the change in each other. The girl he had fought and whose pigtail he had pulled had acquired new contours of rounded softness. She had lost her level, cheeky gaze and now looked on the ground or aside at her girl friends, upon which they would all burst into a titter. The boy whose face she had scratched and clawed now looked hard and angular, his voice had become husky. He seemed anxious to help her draw water when she could pull the bucket as well as he. At other times there would be bantering between boys and girls, and as long as the whole crowd joined no notice was taken, but as soon as a boy and a girl exchanged glances which showed the slightest signs of individual interest, someone would immediately warn the parents, who took it as a sign that it was time to think of arranging her marriage. 'Youth has come to your girl,' some neighbour would tell a mother; 'it is time you "had her asked" by a good family.' Engagement is charmingly known as 'being asked', mangna. Marriage would follow within a year, usually after the next winter harvest when the wheat was in.

As soon as the girl had been asked boys stopped looking at her. She acquired a new status in her family and especially among her girl friends who would talk to her about the future when out fetching water. She would listen but never join in the conversation, for that would be immodest. If the boy was from the same village she would know him; if he was from another village she might not even know what he looked like. Her friends would tantalise her by sometimes painting the picture of an ogre and sometimes of a prince. She was innocent enough to accept both and be frightened by one and thrilled by the other. At times she would cry at the uncertain prospect before her and the parting from her family and friends when she would have to go and live in another village. The girls would try and console her. 'Don't worry, he is tall, taut and handsome; he will come riding on a horse, with a high plume in his turban. He will seat you behind him, and as soon as you have put your arms around him he will spur his horse and gallop away. We know you will be crying, but you will soon forget your tears and all of us. A few days later he will bring you back but you will not be the same; he will not bring back the girl he took. And you will no longer play with us or tell us what happened to you. And then you will return only occasionally, till one day you will come big and heavy, waiting to fill the apron of your shirt.' 'Stop it, you immodest girls, have you no shame?' would protest the betrothed girl, hot with embarrassment but yet excited. She would say protestingly, 'How do you know all this; you should not be thinking of these things; you are telling lies.'

In this bantering talk were woven their own day-dreams, longings and fears. Their playmate has been asked for; their turn cannot be far behind. Deeply attached to their mothers, the girls have been taught from a very young age that parting is inevitable. The mothers have referred to it in anger, admonition and gentleness. Each time the girl made a mistake, burnt the food or dropped a stitch, the mother would say, 'What are they going to say—is this how I taught you.' From mother and father it is always 'they'. They, who will come to take you away one day. They, to whom you belong. They, to whom we must turn you over, well endowed and well trained. And now, with the betrothal, 'They' have asked for her and she has been promised. From now on she is 'Theirs'. She is already part of another family. If anyone insults her, 'they' will avenge it, arriving with sticks and spears. And there may even be murder if the insult is great and the family proud. Her own people would join in the revenge, if they had not already taken it themselves. If the boy's family came to suspect that the girl's parents had not taken enough care to guard her modesty, or if there was the smallest suspicion that the girl was immodest herself, the betrothal would immediately be broken off. Such girls brought shame upon their families. It was best to return the shagan, the gifts received at the engagement ceremony.

Illicit love between the unmarried was rare, and if it happened the only recourse for the boy and girl was to elope. This was a risky business for they would soon be missed and chased on horses. It was difficult for this flat, featureless country to hide a runaway couple. The girl would be dragged back home 'by the hair' which, to teach her a lesson, in the old days was cut off and her face blackened. Irate father and brothers might even kill her. Chances of pre-marital love were also made small by the early marriages. Virginity was sacred, and girls were married before there was much chance of their losing it. Illicit love was more common between married men and women or married women and unmarried young men, and the rendezvous usually the tall millet or sugar cane fields. Such affairs were few but not so rare, and a fruitful cause of crime. The husband would go into a towering rage, pick up his axe or spade and rush out to seek the man and cut him down on the spot. He might also kill his wife if she confessed the affair and seemed brazen about it.

There were sometimes rapes and abductions, but mostly with the woman's consent or connivance. It usually became known as rape if they were caught, and abduction if she changed her mind after eloping. When in love, it was not uncommon for a woman to poison her husband. The country abounded in poison-lore, and with the help of some old woman, a married girl would poison her husband to be free to marry her lover. At other times the lover might murder the husband. In this fertile, otherwise peaceful canal country the passionate nature of a virile farming stock led to love intrigues and murders, poisoning and witchcraft.

☆

The country like its people had its varying moods. It quivered under the blazing heat of summer, when temperature in the day could hit one hundred and twenty-five in the sun, and in the winter at nights a white blanket of hoar frost covered the ground and temperature dropped sometimes to the twenties. A change in temperature over a range of a hundred degrees made both farming and farmers hard. After the bitter cold of winter nights and the many wet days, when a piercing wind blew from the Himalayas, spring came gentle and balmy, with the first touch of warmth, which gradually rose to the crescendo of dry searing summer when man and beast panted breathlessly for the relief that the rainy season would bring. After the rains came the freshness of autumn containing the first touch of winter, crisp in the morning and chill in the evenings. Our Punjab country had five seasons: winter, spring, summer, rains and autumn.

Spring harvest was the climax to the farmers' toil and hopes. For days whole families worked out in the fields harvesting, threshing, winnowing and bringing in the corn. Women, tall and slim, would stand on low wooden stools, erect like taut bows with their breasts pointing upward, their arms stretched high above their heads holding flat reed trays. Like the opening movement of a dance, when from stationary feet a movement would shiver upward and end in the finger-tips, these women would gently tilt the trays with a quivering movement into the wind and shake them like bells. The wind would sweep the chaff while the grain fell into a heap below. The wind outlined their supple bodies as it swept their clothes back. Few sights are more graceful than women winnowing, except perhaps women walking from the wells with pitchers of water on their head. They walked along narrow banks of twisting and turning ditches and channels, talking, laughing, gesticulating and occasionally stopping to pick out a thorn from the foot. Their bodies swayed in a rhythm, arms swung freely, but the pitches filled to the brim never lost a drop. Another typical sight, one of greater interest to the menfolk, was the women walking at noon to the fields carrying victuals. They carried flat reed baskets on their heads with thick oven-baked unleavened bread wrapped in a napkin and some cooked vegetables. On the basket rested a small pitcher full of lassi, buttermilk. Tired and hungry, the man kept looking towards the village till he caught sight of his wife. From afar he would recognise her and keep turning his head to look at her. He stopped work when she came near and walked to his well under a tree, leading the bullocks in front. He watered them and spread some straw before them and after a wash himself sat down to eat his meal. She sat in front of her man and helped him to the food, but never ate herself; she always ate alone when she returned home. He ate silently while she talked about the morning's happenings, the children, the neighbours, in restful, small talk. After she had seen him eat his fill she collected the food left over and started to walk back. There was no farewell but a simple, 'Achha main chalni han—right, I am going.' The farmer eating under a tree, his wife sitting beside him and a baby lying on the ground was one of the first stories we read in our Urdu textbook.

When the harvest was over and the grain was in, there was leisure. In the canal lands the crop was usually good, because the canal water, unlike rain, seldom failed. And now it was time to think of chores, digging ditches and repairing bunds, a well or the house, buying new bullocks or a horse, marrying a daughter.

Besakhi was a secular festival, the only one of its kind in which Hindus, Muslims and Sikhs all participated alike. Though celebrated both by town and country, it was essentially a farmers' festival, a kind of thanksgiving, but of a bacchanalian kind; an orgiastic feast to relax the tensions of months of hard work at the rabi, the main crop of the year. It was held on a river bank to which families trekked on foot, on horse, in bullock carts and in tongas. The men were dressed in new clothes and brightly dyed turbans; the women in new salwar kameezes, and dupattas as brightly dyed as the men's turbans; the boys dressed like their fathers and the girls like their mothers, but the very little boys had special clothes. I can remember exactly how I was dressed one Besakhi. A pill-box red velvet cap with gold embroidery, a brightly striped shirt, new white pyjamas, cut out at the bottom and in front to save my mother the trouble of carrying spares, and embroidered red leather Punjabi shoes, which being new hurt the whole time. I do not know how proud my mother felt but I certainly was really happy.

The farmers went about in groups. Some of them were drunk, others pretended to be, or, as they said in Punjabi, had just wetted their whiskers with it. They danced the bhangra to the rhythm of a double flute, and a wooden rat fixed to a stick which went up and down the stick as it was pulled by a cord, making a clacking sound. The rat and the double flute were the only instruments beside a drum, but the jats made up for that with a great deal of vigour and vitality as they danced in a circle. The tune was a long simple descending recitative melody which was picked up at the end by a shout and then went on again. Their movements were curiously feminine, in fact, hermaphrodite. They would start by holding both arms stretched high above their head, not unlike the graceful movement of women winnowing, and dance backward and forward. The left hand then held the loosely tied tehmad round their legs, while the right arm was held above with the hand drooping down gracefully, and first one foot was put forward and then the other. They danced like that to a low melody on the flute, almost softly, with a lithe and sinuous grace; but suddenly the flute lifted up to a high note and with a yell their bodies burst into a masculine, powerful whirling dance. Danced by strong bearded men, Sikhs or Muslims, it was a curious sight, at first ludicrous but soon beautiful. The ludicrous touch was deliberate, and the name bhangra has come to mean merriment with a lot of noise and chaos.

Many years later bhangra was adopted as one of the folk dances at the Republic Day celebrations in New Delhi, and a team of Patiala Sikhs toured the country. Although many other dances had far greater artistic value, it proved the most popular item. I saw them in a Bombay drawing-room, a tall, handsome lot, their beards tightly tied and their clothes colourful. The sight of these men starting with the feminine opening movements of bhangra was curious. I was looking at the faces of the people to see their reactions, and noticed with interest that while the women soon came under the spell of the dance the men were less impressed. The gentle opening followed by the triumphant, powerfully suggestive yells, seemed to fascinate the women. That these tall sinuous men could be as soft one minute and as strong the next seemed to stimulate them, as indeed is the whole purpose of the dance.

The sandy bank of the river was used as fair ground. Hundreds of shops made of bamboo and gunny bags were erected. The shops sold a variety of goods but commonest were the booths with highly coloured sweetmeats and drinks. After a ceremonial dip in the river we had a picnic meal and then set out to enjoy the fair and spend our money. The village women could not be torn away from the general merchandise shops which attracted them with an assortment of colourful glass bangles, bead necklaces, mirrors and combs, kohl, highly perfumed hair oils, and such other luxuries that they could not buy in the village shops. The children were thrilled by the wooden hand-painted toy birds, animals and carts. The mechanical Japanese toys had not yet arrived. The villagers wandered about, gaping at the sophistication of the town shops, while the shopkeepers leered at them and tried to pull them in.

There were numerous other attractions, wooden giant wheels, merry-go-rounds, acrobats, conjurors, animal tamers with bears, monkeys, snakes and mongoose, and medicine men. The latter applied their skill with amazing boldness. A dentist would virtuall y hypnotise a group and then proceed to pull out perfectly healthy teeth, quite painlessly, of one person after another. The proof of his skill was the painless extraction, whether needed or not; no one questioned the necessity but everyone admired the way he did it. An optician would fit old men with second-hand glasses, testing their sight by the simple process of trying two or three pairs and then asking with which of them they saw best. An occulist cured all eye troubles with some drops whose great merit was their fierce stinging action. For minutes the victim would contort his face in pain and press his eyes, while all the by-standers watched the effect of the drops. When the pain gradually disappeared and the man at last opened his eyes he was so happy to see daylight again, having fully expected the painful darkness to stay for ever, that he shouted happily that he had never seen so well before. There were a variety of one-pill-or-powder healers who convinced everyone who stopped to listen that he was positively ill. One farmer will admit to backache and dizziness when he stands up after digging a ditch; another is caught with the disease of urinating whenever he excretes. At this revelation the doctor will challenge them all to deny that they suffer from the same complaint, for he can tell from their faces; and they all nod assent. Another quack who specialises in women's diseases will not be perturbed by the fact that he has only men in his audience. It is easy enough to convince them that their women suffer silently.

Astrologers and amulet sellers also had their market, but the weirdest of all these benefactors displayed a revolting array of dead iguanas, small lizards, baby crocodiles, snakes, animal skulls, all pickled in a trayful of oil, out of which he dispensed in small bottles for rubbing on rheumatic joints, for general massage, or as aphrodisiac.

The favourable spot for men at the fair was the wrestling pit, where anyone could compete, though the greatest interest was aroused by the professional bouts. There were games, kaodi and gripping the wrist; gatka, where one man would fight several opponents with short sticks; and then there were horse races where simple jats raced on a variety of horses and ponies, yelling and shouting and waving their arms, with more enthusiasm than speed.

Troubadours and bards sang and recited ballads and legends; professional entertainers specialised in parody, mimicry and farce. On the singing and nautch girls men showered coins whenever they rendered a particularly touching verse or a suggestive dance movement in a confusion of tinkling ankle bells. When the girls cast longing glances or flicked them with their long silk handkerchiefs, the farmers wished that they had not brought their wives, who were busy shopping somewhere but would soon come to drag them away.

As the spring afternoon paled, tired, hot and dusty families began trekking back to their villages. The bullocks groaned and snorted as they pulled the heavy creaking carts over the sandy river bed. While the crops were ripening, and during harvest, the bullocks had little work to do, except to pull the persian wheel for an hour or two a day, to water the vegetable patch and to fill the bathing and washing tanks. The threshing of corn was easy work, for they had just to walk round and round unhurried on a bed of harvested stalks. Now that the men had leisure the bullocks were going to be busy. Grain and enormous piles of straw had to be pulled to the market; the wedding season was coming, and after that they would start the next ploughing.

☆

The time had come for weddings, and the country echoed to the beating of drums. Gaily dressed women and children, packed in bullock carts, with the men riding or walking in procession, happy, shouting, bantering and raising much dust on the village roads was a common sight everywhere. The guests arrived at the wedding house with voracious appetites. If they gorged themselves they would be twitted for not having enough to eat at home, but a barat, wedding party, that did not eat well was criticised for being finnicky. So they usually put up with it good-humouredly and vied with each other in stuffing themselves. In between meals the men played games and took exercise in order to do justice to the next meal. The young and strong among the visitors would challenge their hosts to wrestling and games, and the two sides competed earnestly to uphold the honour of their village. In the evenings there was drinking and dancing girls, story-telling and boasting about houses, fields and cattle. The hosts could not retaliate easily; in fact, they had to restrain themselves. But their case was taken up by their village mirasis, the professional clowns and entertainers, who had the traditional liberty to exercise their sharp tongues upon the guests.

On the third day they packed the dowry, and with the bride in a palanquin the procession of bullock carts and horses started back for home. Swathed in red, the bride, a mere girl of fourteen or so, sobbed and cried as she left for a strange home. Consoling words from friends and parents were forgotten in the loneliness that gripped her as she sat huddled in the rocking palanquin which passed fields and villages she did not recognise. When the party reached the village a procession of women would come out to receive the bride and bless her. They would raise the curtain of the palanquin and lift the veil to see her face. If she was beautiful there would be unreserved admiration, she would be compared to the moon; but if she was plain there would be a chill praise which made their opinion equally clear. The groom strained his ears to discover what his bride looked like, while she tried to look from the corner of her eye through the uplifted veil to get a glimpse of her man.

When the excitement died down and the over-fed guests went to catch up with lost sleep the little palpitating red bundle was led to the innermost room in the house where the groom was nervously waiting. Before closing the door his mother would say, 'Son, take care of her.'

☆

When the weddings were over, there were trips to the market to sell the grain. In fact, a few trips had already been made to settle with the money-lender and to raise cash for the weddings. There was an air of fursat, leisure, of the year's job done. Spring was losing its balminess, the sun was rising earlier and setting later every day. The days were becoming warm, but the nights were still pleasant. At first people moved out of the rooms at night to sleep in the verandahs, then into the courtyard, but with the first signs of real summer they moved their cots on to the roof terrace at night. On moonlit nights the country became ethereal and unreal. Sometimes you would wake with a large, bright white moon staring down in your face. The full moon would stare at couples sleeping on roof terraces. It would make the shy bride feel guilty in her husband's embrace as this intruder looked shamelessly on her body which she was just discovering for herself. In all poetry around the moon, masculine in our lore, legend has him condemned to eternal sleeplessness because he once pried on his mother bathing. His brother the sun, more modest, his mother said, will rest peacefully every night. But the moon was nevertheless, perhaps just because of his boldness, the favourite. With the face of a moon, is how the mothers like their babies to be described. The moon's face framed in black clouds, is how the poet describes his beloved lying on a pillow with her black hair loose.

When nights became hot and still and the summer gathered full strength, the dust storms arrived, sometimes followed by a cooling shower. Everyone would wake up with a start, and then there was commotion on all the roof terraces in the village. Drunk with sleep people staggered down with their beddings and cots to the verandahs below.

During the day, under a hazy sky the country burned and languished. High whirlwinds raced across the land picking up dust and dry leaves along their path. The cattle herded together in the shade, and the farmers sought the pipal trees near the wells. These were most trying days for both man and beast. Healthy and strong men suddenly crumpled up from heat stroke. Cattle died of no seeming illness. The days got hotter and hotter until men felt they could stand it no longer. Dust storms of various colours would blow out of nowhere. They were usually brown, but sometimes yellow, red and even black. The black sand-storms were frightening, for the hard white daylight of an afternoon would suddenly become almost pitch black so that you could not see a few feet ahead. The red storms were the colour of blood and awesome; in the yellow storms there was an eerie amber light.

When the earth could stand no more and the parched soil cracked; when the air was so dry that one could drink a large pitcher of water in a day without a drop of sweat but only some grains of salt on the brow, the horizon would darken one afternoon, and instead of the hot dusty breeze there came a cool fresh wind with the smell of moist dust. The sky became covered with seething billowing, white-edged clouds, which approached like an angry army. Peals of thunder and long forks of lightning rent the sky, and large rain drops began to fall, at first slowly and deliberately but soon racing madly down to earth till they were like long needles of glass bursting as they hit the ground. They beat a terrible tattoo on the dry caked earth, and the noise swelled to a deafening roar. The rainstorm lashed the hungry earth which seemed to delight in its violence. Big trees which had stood for years fell like toys, sometimes over men and beasts cowering under them.

Little rivulets ran gurgling with red brown liquid everywhere. Slowly the fury of the storm began to abate, and the rain settled down to a more gentle persistence. The farmers praised God and gave Him several grateful names as the peals and flashes became more and more distant and receded into the western horizon. By the evening the frogs croaked, the sloping banks of ditches were touched with tender green, and there blew a cool and fresh breeze. 'Zameen noo vatar aa giya,' the farmers said. The soil has received the proper moisture, and with a little sun would be right for the plough. The wet spell would last for three or four days and then one morning when the sun shone bright out of a blue sky, flecked with white fleecy clouds, the farmers lifted their ploughs and led their bullocks to the fields singing their simple yodelling songs. The earth yielded softly to the plough and the clods broke easily. The new cycle of growth had begun.

Savan was the poetic month of rains. It was the month for picnics by canal and river banks, when large parties went swimming for the day and cooked their food outdoors. It brought friendly clouds and nourishing moisture, but also floods from swollen rivers which, while doing damage to standing crops and villages, added another layer of alluvial topsoil. About drought, floods or locusts the Punjabi farmers complain mildly. If God gives He is kind; if He does not give He has merely withheld. They were not an especially religious lot, Hindus or Muslims, but they were godfearing. Canals gave greater certainty to their lives and a plentitude they had never known before, yet they thanked God for timely rains. They were a contented lot.

When the rains stopped the sun shone every day again but now it had lost its fierceness. It rose lower in the sky and the days got shorter. Mornings, had a pleasant touch of cool turning into cold. People who had left the terraces at the beginning of the rains now found it cool even in the verandahs. First the blankets and then the quilts came out of the big trunks. It was also a season of illness. The stagnant water bred mosquitoes which brought malaria. People shivered with cold and ached, then became hot and broke into perspiration. Sometimes the fever came every day, at other times every other day, and it took its regular yearly toll of life, young and old.

The autumn became chillier but there was no leaf fall, for the leaves had fallen at the end of winter. Autumn was only a season of change between summer and winter, and one day the wind would blow cold from the north. It came from the fresh snows of the Himalayas. Winter was the pleasantest time of the year in the Punjab. The invigorating air brought life and vitality back to bodies drained by the desiccating summer. The mornings were cold and misty; often there was frost, and sometimes the water in the ditches had a thin film of ice. The sun would rise like a big orange in the mist, and as it rose higher and gathered strength the mist would slowly dissolve. Days were crystal clear, and everyone warmed himself in the benign rays of the golden sun. There was much work in the fields, and many crops grew in these winter months. Sugar-cane was ready in early November, but wheat, barley, grams, peas and mustard ripened through the winter. Near the towns there was much market gardening as well. It is the season when the flat Punjab country looks at its best with the rich lush green of the growing crops. In a single well-watered field there may be as many as four different things growing together.

While the men worked in the fields in the wine-like air, the women sat in the afternoon sun spinning and embroidering while they sang together, before starting to cook for their men. They embroidered phulkaris, literally meaning flower work. They were tapestries of red handloom cotton cloth embroidered with silk thread of gold, blue and green. The designs were traditional and geometric, in long diagonal stitches. The really beautiful ones, called bagh, garden, were a closely embroidered field of gold with a small red border left at the ends. They took many months to finish. Phulkaris were never sold but handed down from mother to daughter, and were worn wrapped like shawls on auspicious occasions beginning with the wedding day.

It was the season of healthy appetite and rich food. The Punjabi love of food, of curds, buttermilk, thick chappatis and sarson sag, the cooked mustard leaves, knew no bounds. Women put extra lumps of ghee into the sag and big chunks of freshly churned butter on the yellow maize chappatis. It was the season to feed the men. Fresh cane juice boiled off into gur, plain or spiced, was eaten in large quantities. Special sweets, pinnis, made of equal quantities of sugar, ghee and roasted gram flour were considered essential to resist the cold. 'Feed him and give him strength in this season,' was the older women's advice to the young women, and as the young ones snuggled with their men under thick quilts at night they felt that food had given them a new vigour. It was also the season of mating horses and cattle.

In the middle of winter arrived the Arabian monsoon, short, useful but bitterly cold. For days the sky was leaden and low, the air damp and chilling to the bones, but the farmers were happy; it provided moisture to the crops. And when the sun shone again the wheat and mustard were standing high and waving joyously in the breeze. The green rippling waves of wheat contrasted with the pure gold yellow of the mustard flowers—a sight I have felt the need to see every year, even if for a day. Like people returning to their mountains, valleys or seashore, I long to return to the Punjab to see its flat land clothed in its exuberant colours of growth; its many greens, the green of the chilli fields, the green of the wheat, of the gram and rice; and its yellows of mustard, cotton and snogra, the Punjabi flax.

As the wheat yellowed and the mustard flowers bleached and formed into seed, the winter's pace began to slacken. The sun became warmer and rose higher each day. Spring was heralded by the festival of Basant. Men and women dyed their turbans and mantles yellow in honour of the ripening corn, the mustard flowers, the yellowing pods of peas and grams, the yellow flowers of cotton, and all the bounties of nature associated with yellow. Yellow halva and yellow sweets were eaten in large quantities. Winter was over and with it the worst the weather could do to the crops, which would now ripen safely. And when the harvesting is over and grains are taken in will come again the boisterous festival of Besakhi.

The flowering trees added their own contribution of colour in spring. They shed their leaves, and against the bare tracery of branches the corals burst into their blood-red spiky bunches of flowers; the dhak, known as the flame of the forest, with its long flowering branches packed with velvety pink petals; amaltas, the Indian laburnum, with its drooping cascades of incandescent yellow flowers; the big siris, the rain tree, with its small, delicately formed brush-like pink flowers. They all dabbed their patches of colour on the country in one last heroic effect before summer spread its withering fingers.

☆

Our language, Punjabi, has no script and hardly, until lately, any except religious literature. For centuries the Muslims had used Persian which the Sikhs continued as their court language. The Sikhs had evolved the Gurmuhi script for writing Punjabi by modifying the Sanskrit alphabet, but this they did to avoid the sacrilege of recording their holy book, the Granth Sahib, in Persian script, the script of the Muslims against whom they had revolted. Persian however continued to flourish as the language of culture and communication. Educated Punjabis were therefore bilingual, speaking Punjabi and reading and writing Persian.

The British brought Urdu with them from the United Provinces and Delhi, and supplanted Persian. At the same time they brought English, and from then on education was imparted both in Urdu and in English. Persian, along with Sanskrit and Arabic, became a classical language, and we had the choice of one of them. By the age of ten I was learning English and Persian, my curriculum was in Urdu and I spoke Punjabi at home and outside. Official business was transacted in both languages, at the higher levels in English and at the lower levels in Urdu. The district level was the dividing line. My father, when he was in the districts, had a stenographer for English and a munshi for Urdu.

Hindi, in the Devanagri script, arrived later and was confined at the beginning to the Brahmins and to our women, the latter through the influence of Arya Samaj. Literacy among our Hindu women thus began with Hindi, and this created some amusing situations, because in my mother's generation there were many women who could not communicate with their husbands when they were away from each other, as they could only write in Hindi and their husbands only in Urdu or English. In our generation the same problem was solved by the middle class girls learning English. At home, like their parents, they spoke Punjabi with their husbands but their correspondence was in English. The girls were in fact trilingual as they spoke Punjabi, wrote in Hindi to their mothers, and in English to their fathers and husbands.

In the early years the Englishmen were also trilingual. They spoke in English to the westernised Punjabis, in Urdu to the Punjabi with ordinary education, and in Punjabi to the rayat. In fact, the English official then had a rather better knowledge of Urdu, and usually also of Punjabi, than the average educated Punjabi had of English. This helped both sides, but particularly the Punjabis. Speaking in Urdu or Punjabi gave them a poise and a dignity which later suffered badly during the early period of anglicisation; a pose which only those recovered who achieved mastery of the English language and familiarity with its culture.

A snob value began to be attached to knowing first Urdu and later English, and Punjabi was relegated to the home, the women and the illiterates. The language consequently began to lose its purity, and by my days it was so mixed with Urdu that except for the verb endings and prepositions it was almost Urdu. The well educated went further by adding English, and their speech became a mixture of a little Punjabi, some English and much Urdu. I have often wondered what effect it has had upon Punjabi character to have no language of our own, only an unwritten dialect and that also heavily mixed. I imagine it has helped to make the Punjabis what they are, practical, not over-cultured, at ease when transplanting themselves.

Punjabi is a quaint language, slow, indelicate and lusty. When the U.P. babus came with their refined speech and manners, we became acutely aware of our crude ways and indulged in self-depreciation, which however in Punjabi make-up goes hand in hand with boasting. A Punjabi will often refer to himself as a yokel, a jat, and an ox, but somehow manage to make it sound like a boast. He will firmly run himself down, but always in a frank, open manner, without any trace of selfconsciousness. Equally, he will boast with the casualness of making a self-evident statement. The language lends itself to both.

Punjabi excels in love and in abuse. Its abuse is of the genealogical kind which can trace one's family history in the most revealing and incestuous terms. Father used to relate the story of an English colleague who appeared for his departmental examination in Punjabi. The examiner asked him whether he subscribed to the popular view that the Punjabis were a rude and rough people. In reply the young probationer burst into such choice Punjabi, tracing both the legitimate and illegitimate ancestry of those who held such a view, that the examiner interrupted him to say that quite obviously the candidate's knowledge of the language was both classical and sufficient for the department's normal requirements.

Our language is worth listening to when a villager prods a particularly stubborn bullock under a plough, or when he chastises an unwilling buffalo out of the pond. The animal will listen contentedly as the man improvises particularly lurid situations out of its ancestral past, and offer just enough resistance to keep the flow of words from changing to serious use of the stick.

A classical use of the language was made by women quarreling with a neighbour. Such quarrels were an institution that provided a relief to the dull routine of their daily life. A quarrel would always begin in the afternoon, when morning chores were finished, but before the evening's work began. One of the parties, the aggrieved or the offending one, would come to the platform in front of her house and begin to mutter vaguely as a warm-up till the opponent felt it was time to take notice and come out to her platform to take up the challenge. The neighbouring women would hastily put away their work and appear on their thresholds. And now the quarrel began in right earnest. The preliminary sparring was over, the audience had settled down to an afternoon's fun, and there was no retreat. Minutest details from the past were brought out and painted in word pictures of the most damaging colours, with ogress, eater of her dead children, eater of husbands, immodest, burnt, drowned, all generously used as adjectives. A great accusation was meanness, which in the Punjab is a cardinal sin. Stories, true or imagined, were remembered and embellished of meanness to guests, meanness at births, weddings, and funerals, meanness to relations and neighbours' children; in fact, meanness of all kinds was treasured like scandal to be used on some such occasion.

As the afternoon wore off, the quarrel ran its course like a mountain stream, angry and rushing, as it swept past each obstacle. The neighbours listened approvingly or disapprovingly as the contestants cleared a hurdle or baulked at it. The liveliest to watch were the quarrels between two equally matched opponents, but of rare interest were those between an older woman and a young one, where experience clashed with inexperience and astute thrusts were met with headlong impetuosity. Each stroke of the experienced woman was known to the neighbours, but there was excitement in the possible contribution of the beginner. Occasionally, when cornered, youth would fall back on the weakness of age and having found the delicate spot turn the weapons mercilessly. Such weakness might be the lost looks of a wife and the roving eye of the husband.

Like the stream, the quarrel went on. The Punjabi language and its idiom would rise to heights to be remembered for many a day, perhaps made use of in a future bout. Sometimes in the heat of the fray, a casual thrust might draw blood from a spot unknown and unsuspected by the person dealing the innocuous blow. The victim would burst into a long wail and sob bitterly. An old hurt or a healed wound would suddenly gush, and the quarrel was at once over. The neighbours would rush to the side of the defeated in genuine solace, while the victor was left shamefaced with a hollow victory, protesting that she did not realise. Such dramatic endings were rare though.

As the afternoon lengthened and the time approached for the return of the menfolk, the quarrel would begin to flag. In South Punjab one of the parties might dash in and bring out a reed stool and lean it upside down against the front door. This meant that the quarrel would be renewed the following afternoon. There was no retreat now unless the other party felt she had had enough, in which case she disappeared, and no upturned stool picked up the gauntlet. Back in the house, the woman decided whether the husband was going to be drawn in or not. Usually they did not involve their husbands.

If a woman decided to bring her man into it, she would with great adeptness create an atmosphere of complete gloom to meet him when he came home. She would sit in a corner and sulk, the light would not be lit, and hearth left cold, there would be no cooking, the children left unfed, so that the man came home to an air of desolation which immediately made him sense that something was wrong. And slowly, never all at once, the story would come out. Usually the man would shrug his shoulders and consider it wise to ignore the affair; sometimes he would talk to the other party's husband, and both of them would make some wise or cynical comment about the ways of women and leave it at that.

Vivid in quarrel, Punjabi can equally convey its vigour in love. In Heer Ranjah, in Sohni Mahinwal, in Sassi Punna, in its ballads and folk songs, it has been enshrined in all its simple, but vigorous poetry. But whether in the ballads, the improvisation of the peasant in the field, or the women quarrelling in the mohallas, its purple passages are those tinged with the facts of life. They are earthy and direct. Love and death to the Punjabi go together. 'May you die' is what the peasant says to his valuable ox, the mother endearingly to a naughty child, and the lover to his beloved. 'May I die,' is her ecstatic reply to each caress. The Freudian death wish is common in Punjabi; in love, in disappointment, in culmination, in frustration, in triumph and in defeat.

Although not written down until Urdu came in the last century, Punjabi has through the ages accumulated a great fund of folk tales, folk poems, fairy tales, heroic legends and old stories, tales which were passed down through the professionals when they were in verse and through the families when in prose. There was a great variety of bards who sang the balads to their own tune on a simple string instrument. Stories were told us at nights by parents and elders, at home and in the squares, till we knew them by heart. On winter nights we would sit huddled in our thick quilts, with only our faces peeping out, and in the summer we sat on our cots on the terraces listening to these stories, embellished and animated by the skill of the story teller. It was customary to sit in a ring in front of the teller, who before starting would appoint someone in the audience an 'anghara bharne wala', whose duty it was to keep the story teller company by making suitable interjections like, 'yes; and then what happened; and so the prince said.' As children we always competed for this task.

These stories fell into different categories. There were fairy tales of enchantment, with a princess as the reward of adventure, usually living under a spell in an underwater palace guarded by a snake or ogre. A variation on this theme was the famous Gul Bakavli, where the quest was for a flower with magic properties of cure. There were heroic tales of adventure and drama, and humorous tales. They told of princes, princesses, ailing mothers and fathers who could only be cured by a certain remedy; stepmothers, either revengeful, if they were old, or in love with a younger member of the family, if they were young themselves but were married to older men; ogres, ogresses, jinns and giants; birds and animals as companions to the prince. An unusual character in some stories was a half brother who always insisted on accompanying his elder brothers on their adventures. He was not half in the sense of relationship but literally half. He had only one eye, one ear, one arm, one leg, and so on, but that did not deter him from setting out with his brothers. He made up for his deficiencies by distinguishing himself in an emergency in an amusing manner.

Stories were always told at night because there was a belief that if you told stories during the day travellers would lose their way. We always said that this was a ruse to put us off from bothering the grown-ups in the day time, but our elders genuinely believed in this superstition and would only relate stories at night, when everybody was safely home after the day's toil and travel.

Another interesting pastime was conundrums, mostly in quite beautiful couplets. Some were meant to teach us the complex system of relationships by asking us to guess the relationship that was involved in a complicated chain. In Punjabi each relationship, even the wife's father's sister's husband has a specific name, and we have to learn them all. To our great amusement the answers to the conundrums were sometimes something as simple as father or mother, but you arrived at this solution by a tortuous route.

CHAPTER FIVE

Khatri Background

We Tandons are a sub-caste of the Kshatriya caste, or the Khatris as they are called in the north. We belong to the first group of twelve Khatri houses, known as the Bahris; these are followed by another fifty-two houses, thus called the Bunjahis; and then the Sarin Khatris. Originally these sub-castes must have been the equivalent of tribes or clans, and they continued to maintain a kind of tribal cohesion. We usually married among the Bahris, and the other groups among themselves, but while you could accept a daughter-in-law from a sub-caste lower than yours, you never gave a daughter to an inferior sub-caste. Sons could marry 'beneath' them but never daughters. As all marriages were arranged these rules were seldom broken.

There were other restraints on marriage. We could never marry into another Tandon family, even if there was no known relationship. Consanguinity was also strictly barred, and we could not marry the most distant cousin. All cousins, however remote, were your brothers or sisters. These were eugenic precautions which worked well to maintain the stock free from the usual signs of interbreeding. But I suppose such strictness will only work as long as marriages are arranged.

Caste pride among us did not lie in arrogating privileges or exercising authority; it took mainly the form of a code of conduct in regard to marriages and hospitality. To a Khatri a daughter was a debt which must be discharged honourably. She must be married into a caste of equal or higher status; a dowry must be raised; and having got her married, one must never accept anything from her or her in-laws. Parents, and even brothers, sisters or relations, unless they were younger than her, would never stay at her house. When they visited her they would not accept any food or drink, but if under any circumstances food had to be accepted, it was scrupulously paid for, and at a generous rate. An elderly aunt made such a fuss that she was a joke in the family. At the end of a half-day visit to her married daughter she would count up a long list of items that she would insist on paying for; one anna for a glass of water, another two annas for using the mat to sit on, and so on. We always reminded her that she had not paid for visiting the closet.

The marrying of a daughter was called kanya dan, literally, the gift of a daughter. It was a sacred duty, and having performed it one never took anything back that might savour of repayment. In its own practical way it was a precaution against the wife's relations, particularly the mother, imposing upon her, but like the eugenic precautions it was carried to a meaningless extreme just to rule out all chances of its ever happening. Having too many daughters was clearly a misfortune among us, for even after they had been married and provided with dowries, usually beyond one's means, gifts in cash and kind had to be provided by the parents and brothers on all possible occasions. And if the daughter or her in-laws were calculating enough, this could become an intolerable burden.

Hospitality with us was equally a matter of pride and social obligation, and its rules were inculcated from a young age. If a person from your village or a relation was visiting your town, but was staying with someone else, you went formally to invite him and his family. Etiquette made them protest by saying that wherever they were they were eating your food, so why should you trouble. You insisted and they protested, but after the procedure had taken its conventional course they very modestly agreed. There was a fresh protest when you asked them to both meals of the day. That really was too much trouble, they would say, but you always retorted that you were Khatris, not Sonars, that you should ask them to one meal only. The Sonars were the goldsmiths, who as a caste had been dubbed mean.

Formalities of the invitation settled, someone of the family, usually one of us children, had to go to fetch them even if they knew their way. Unless they were close relations, they came only just before the meal, which always began with a sweet, never with a salt dish. You always 'sweetened the mouth' at the start. The meal was literally a battle between the host and the guests, in which the latter must, after much seemly protesting, eventually lose. Men and women ate separately, our mother eating alone, last of all. After lunch one of us would walk back with them, and again fetch them in the evening for the second meal.

When we boys were sometimes staying with relations, other people in the town used to invite us. When we returned home mother would ask searching questions about where we had been invited, and make sure that all those who ought to have invited us had in fact done so. From the full account we gave she also made certain that we had gone through all formalities properly. Did we protest the right number of times; did we suggest that one meal would be enough, and did we accept only after the Khatri-Sonar analogy had been given; did we pretend at the meal that we were not hungry; did we begin the meal by eating the sweet; did we put forward our hands with fingers outspread over the plate when the hostess wanted to help us to more? These and many other questions were asked to make sure that we did not behave as we would have liked to by accepting the invitation with alacrity and falling upon the food like young wolves.

Next to our Khatri caste were the Aroras who were usually merchants and traders. They had their own sub-castes, but among them there were not the same strict gradations. They could marry in any sub-caste they liked, but of course the strict rules of consanguinity, common to Hindus, applied. Their rules about marrying daughters were the same as ours, but with an interesting exception. They could sometimes 'exchange' daughters, that is, marry a brother and sister to another sister and brother. Such a custom the Khatris frowned upon for two reasons. It introduced an element of bargaining in your daughter's dowry, because at the same time you were receiving a dowry from the other house for your daughter-in-law. While this went against our Khatri pride, there was a shrewd and practical reason as well. The invariable misunderstandings between the bride and the mother-in-law in one household could have repercussions on the other.

Khatris and Aroras were the two props of our Hindu society, and around them was built the structure of the service castes, both Hindu and Muslim. All the service castes were hereditary. Some of them worked on the jajmani system whereby each family was hereditarily attached to a group of jajmans—families to whom they ministered. We had a family barber, whose father before him had been our family's barber, and so the barber's family and ours were indissolubly bound. Good or bad we could not get rid of him, nor could he refuse to serve us, unless we went to live in another place and adopted a local barber family. But whenever we returned to our home town the old barber was there, and there was no changing him.

The first and most important in the jajmani system were the Brahmins. That they could be the leaders of society, in a position of privilege, I only discovered when I went to live outside the Punjab. With us the Brahmins were an unprivileged class and exercised little or no influence on the community. Perhaps the Muslims had so discouraged temples and external worship that the Brahmins had no place left from where to exercise their authority. In towns like Gujrat, and more so as you went further west of the Jhelum river, there were very few temples of any size. Only in Lahore, and that in the deep heart of the city in Hindu mohallas, did one come across any big temples; mostly our temples were holes in the walls or little shrines under pipal or banyan trees, easily demolished and just as quickly set up again. The importance of the Brahmins was therefore limited.

Our Brahmins did not as a rule even have the role of teachers, because until the British opened regular schools teaching was done by Muslim mullahs in the mosques or by Sikh granthis, scripture readers, in the gurdwaras. Our Brahmins were rarely erudite; in fact many of them were barely literate, possessing only a perfunctory knowledge of ritual and knowing just the necessary mantras by heart. As the occasions requiring their aid and knowledge were few, to earn their living they had developed a system of charity. Every morning members of a Brahmin family would visit the homes of their jajmans to collect cooked food—a chappati, some cooked vegetable or lentils, and buttermilk. The food would last the Brahmin family for both meals of the day; sometimes there were chappatis left over which they would dry and eat later soaked in hot milk. Handa, as such gift of food was called, was always in cooked food. It could never be claimed in its equivalent of raw food, for that our women would have considered an imposition. While mother could always manage the handa out of whatever was cooked for the family, to give it raw would have meant dipping into her stores. While the handa took care of the family food, gifts in money and clothes on ceremonial occasions helped the Brahmins to eke out a thin living. It was a frugal life, and there were rarely any affluent Brahmins.

Without erudition and because of their daily dependence on the other castes, there was a touch of mild derision towards the Brahmins. The very address 'oh Pandita' or 'oh Brahmina' had gentle sarcasm about it. They were never elders of the community, nor was their advice sought on mundane matters. On the other hand some respect was shown to the astrologer pandits, who were the élite of our Brahmins, or the learned pandits who gave religious discourses, but astrologers and learned pandits were few. To the astrologers we went for establishing auspicious moments for betrothal, marriage, a business venture or a journey. They interpreted the almanacs, called jantris, and advised on the influence of the heavenly bodies upon individuals. These jantris, produced by the great pandits of Banaras and Hardwar, were essential for Hindu homes, sometimes the only book a family might possess. They were calendars with information about stars, planets, moon and the sun, whose interpretation was the specialised task of astrology. The basis of each individual's life, as it was governed and influenced by the heavens, was his horoscope which the astrologer cast at birth and consulted before all important moves and occasions in life. Astrology was the preserve of Brahmins.

The other Hindu service castes were the artisan castes of Sonars, the goldsmiths; Tarkhans, the woodworkers; Jhewars or Mehras, the cooks, chars and water carriers; and Kalals, who sold liquor and were on the fringe of the social scale. Of these only the Jhewars were included in the jajmani system, and were in daily contact with us. A woman or girl from our Jhewar family would come every morning to clean and wash the utensils, while a man would bring water from the nearest well, and later from the hand pump on the ground floor. At weddings, or when we had a lot of guests, their men came to do the cooking.

The goldsmiths and carpenters were independent and dealt with whoever needed their services. The Kalals, before the British introduced liquor, sold opium, hemp and other narcotics. Liquor among us was practically unknown and addiction was mainly to eating opium, although even that was an uncommon habit.

There were no Hindu untouchables in the West Punjab, and such work as that of sweepers, skin-flayers and leather workers was done by Muslims. They were presumably untouchable Hindus who had at one time become Muslims to escape their lot, which they apparently did not manage to do even though they acquired some kind of theoretical equality with their Muslim brethren. They had the right to worship in mosques and to mix at an uneasy distance with poor Muslims, but they were compelled to retain their unwelcome professions.

As a boy I would feel quite ashamed when my mother, asking for a glass of water at some Muslim house, would be told with ingratiating courtesy that both the glass and the water had come from a neighbouring Hindu family. But slowly I saw the change come in. Our father made no bones about eating with Muslims and bringing them home. Interestingly, this problem was solved in our home, as in many other homes where a similar change was at work, by the introduction of chinaware. Our women, who objected to Muslims eating off our metal utensils, willingly shared china plates, cups and saucers. These were somehow considered uncontaminable. Their gleaming white, smooth surface, from which grease slipped off so easily, somehow immunised them from contamination. My mother would not at first use the chinaware herself and reserved it for the menfolk and for Muslim, Christian and English guests, but she soon began to weaken.

This led to the next stage, that of accepting unpeeled fruit in non-Hindu homes.

Then followed the acceptance of tea and manufactured biscuits and the English bottled lime cordial, but mother never reached the stage of eating cooked food with Muslims or even with my father's English colleagues. This also used to puzzle me, because I could understand the traditional taboo on Muslim food, but how did this taboo attach itself to the English? I think it came from the discovery that like Muslims they ate beef, and that only Muslim cooks would serve them. As a child I could never understand how the Muslims and the English swallowed such insults from us and did not retaliate. It took the ideal of Pakistan and a separate Muslim nation in the 1940's to create an occasional feeling in Punjabi Muslim minds that they should also not accept food or water from the Hindus. The English, I suppose, just left it as one of our idiosyncracies and bothered no more about it.

There were a number of other Muslim service castes who plied hereditary professions. Two of them were in the jajmani system. I have already mentioned the barbers. In addition to his professional chores of haircutting, shaving and some surgery, the barber enjoyed the important function of go-between for arranging betrothals. At the weddings the barber, Raja, as he was always courteously called, had a place of honour second only to the Brahmin. As a barber we children of course never took to him because he always knew better than we how our hair should be cut. Just at that time the English style of hair-cut, known to us as the 'Bengali fashion', was becoming popular, but our Raja insisted on giving us a close crop. To add insult to injury, he said it was good for us because it did away with the need for dressing the hair and thus losing valuable time every morning which might otherwise be spent on studies. We despised him, but dared not say so, and in any case his argument about work appealed to our father. But whatever his skill as a barber, the Raja enjoyed much prestige among his jajmans for arranging betrothals, when he literally held the honour of a family in his hand.

Another Muslim caste in the jajmani system was that of Mirasis. The Mirasis beat drums and played the shehnai, a flute with a trumpet end, at weddings and other auspicious occasions, but their speciality was wit and repartee which they could exercise with traditional immunity on the highest and the lowest in the society. The victim could not take umbrage at the Mirasis' wit. They would come to weddings and other gatherings, invited or uninvited, and begin to poke fun at guests and hosts alike. Their wit was inherited down the generations and practised from childhood; it was sharp and very quick, and at times brilliant. Woe betide a man who tried to retaliate and get the better of them, for they could reduce him to rags before a company. A problem with the Mirasis was how to send them away satisfied; anything short of that would lead to a special session against the poor host; and it was the respected custom to let the Mirasi say whatever he liked without showing anger and rancour. In any case, retaliation could only lead to an admission of lack of humour; the Mirasi had nothing to lose. The Mirasi women also worked, playing small drums and singing, but they never excelled in wit, only in vulgarity. Men and women sang praises of the family and recited its genealogy at weddings. They were also the vehicle of old ballads and songs. The word Mirasi in the Punjabi language has come to mean witty and funny in an overdone, vulgar manner. They lived as a close community in their own mohallas. Although Muslims, other Muslims never intermarried with them. Their women were slim and attractive in a brazen way, and of easy virtue.

The Mirasis moved with the times and took to brass bands, an influence from the army, which gradually replaced the shehnai and the drum at weddings. Dressed in the quaintest uniforms which were a mixture of those of the regimental bands and of the court dress of the King Emperor as shown in pictures, the Mirasis led the wedding processions and gave their customers the maximum value out of their new instruments, drowning the din of the party and even challenging the fireworks.

Not far removed from the Mirasis were the Kanjars, the community that bred prostitutes and singing and nautch girls. They were of course not in the jajmani system. Their men lived like drones, condemned to this because illegitimate birth of such low origin prevented them from going into any occupation. They were also Muslim, although the ranks of prostitutes drew castaways and fallen women from all communities. As with the Mirasis there was no intermarriage between them and other Muslims. The professions of singing, nautch and plain prostitution were graded in that order in their community, on account of the requisite skill and talent required. It took only good looks to make a prostitute, while dancing, despite the low level to which it had dropped, still required some years' training and a lithe figure; but singing needed both talent and intensive training of many years. The singing girls were the élite of their community. They were no common prostitutes, and gave their favours only when they wished. The Mirasis provided them with musical accompaniment.

Other professional castes of interest were the Bhands, Bazigars, Saperas, Madaris and Behroopis. Bhands and Rasdharis were a community of clowns and jokers whose specialities were farce and impersonation. At weddings and parties they gave traditional performances or improvised skits on the company present. They were ingenious in both humour and farce, and never performed anything serious or classical. The word Bhand in Punjabi is synonymous with clown.

Bazigars (acrobats) and Madaris (jugglers) were also hereditary professions. They moved from place to place, the Bazigars as a troupe but the Madaris always single. Sapera, the snake charmer, must also have formed his own caste, but somehow one never knew where he came from.

A Behroopia's speciality was to disguise himself and act a role in such a realistic manner that people did not suspect it to be play-acting. He might arrive at a party as an old toothless hag, and no one would know until the end, when he suddenly threw away his garb and declared that he was a Behroopi. People used to be so taken in that they would gasp with wonder and reward him suitably. They were consummate artistes. The word Behroopi in Punjabi has come to mean someone with a deceptive appearance. Rasdharis on the other hand went about in groups and put up plays and dramas. Dressed in colourful costumes they would arrive in a town and give short performances of old legends, stories or plays at street corners and at weddings.

The trades of weavers, tailors, washermen, blacksmiths, potters, oil pressers and vegetable growers were also practised only by Muslims. In some cases there was probably no question of caste involved, for when the British brought Hindu regimental tailors and barbers, some Punjabi Hindus also took to this work. To some trades like blacksmiths and weavers, resistance was broken by the arrival of machines; but to others like oil pressing, pottery and vegetable growing the Hindus never took. Even the agricultural Hindus never practised market gardening. For this there was a special Muslim caste of Arains who only grew vegetables. An ordinary farmer might grow some vegetables for himself but never a surplus for sale.

All these castes did not make ours a multi-layered society; it would be more apt to describe it as a multi-unit society, in which each caste had its functional place without oppression by a higher caste. The different castes were united into biradaris, literally meaning brotherhoods. There was an overall Hindu biradari; there was a Khatri biradari, an Arora biradari, and biradaris of sub-castes and of each service caste, Hindu or Muslim. These biradaris were loose and undefined, but in time of need they formed themselves into close-knit groups. They gave you certain rights and expected some duties. They were led by elders of the group, not formally elected but just the senior and most respected men. Your rights were your duties. At weddings and funerals everybody helped the family ungrudgingly. At a daughter's wedding the biradari members served the guests and helped with many chores; at death, when the immediate members of the family were too stunned to be of much use, the whole biradari was a source of strength.

The biradari also had a useful legislative function, that of altering customs which with changing times had begun to be onerous. At one time our Khatri wedding parties used to stay for a whole week at the girl's house. With rising costs and urbanisation this became an imposition, but no one dared to 'lose his nose' by asking the guests to stay for less than seven nights. Ultimately the Khatri biradaris reduced the number to three, and once this was sanctioned we could all follow suit. Later the three nights were reduced to two and then to one. The biradari also served as a forum for disputes between its members. If a difference could not be settled between two parties someone would suggest that they might put it before the biradari. The biradari would either hear the complaint in public or appoint an arbitrator. The rulings of the biradaris, whether on disputes or on obsolete customs, usually relied upon persuasion for their implementation. Occasionally they might pass a stricture or utter a caution. Only rarely, when either wilful defiance or serious immorality was involved, did they resort to the extreme penalty of excommunication, which consisted in stopping hooka pani. No one would then offer or accept a smoke or a drink, enter into a marriage alliance, or have any social intercourse with a person thrown out of the biradari, but fortunately such complete ostracism was rare. If your own biradari threw you out, no other biradari, even of a caste lower than yours, would accept you. How could you belong to a biradari which was not yours by natural right? The worst effect of such excommunication was that it made also your children unacceptable, both socially and in marriage. The sons might yet move to another town to settle and marry there, but the problems of marriageable daughters brought most recalcitrants to heel.

Stopping hooka pani was such complete punishment that it usually did not last long, provided you made amends for your misbehaviour. You went to some elders and begged their pardon, suggesting that the biradari might gather to reconsider their decision. Gatherings, of the biradari were interesting affairs and provided lively entertainment to the community. The meetings took place in the evening after dinner in the open square of a mohalla, and all members could attend. The accused and the complainant, if there was one, were called to appear before the biradari panchayat, the five elders, which sat in a group at the head of the congregation. The meeting might last one or more evenings until a decision was reached. There was much lobbying and many private discussions in between. Witnesses were called; anyone could charge, accuse or defend, the whole procedure an open forum with the community sitting in judgement, guided and tempered by the elders. Often the mere public ventilation of a grievance, the sympathy it evoked and the condemnation aroused, was sufficient to satisfy the complainant or the biradari, and mild regret closed the matter. On more serious occasions, such as the awarding or a revision of the hooka pani punishment, the guilty person would take off his turban, the repository of his honour, and place it at the feet of the panchayat. This was an expression of the deepest regret and humility, before which the biradari must by convention relent. Although women did not usually attend the biradari meetings and were not members of the panchayats, they exercised great influence from behind the scenes.

I remember a particular case of stopping of hooka pani soon after the first world war. There was a Khatri who had made a very large fortune during the war, and in the first flush of his new wealth he decided to remarry, even though his first wife was still alive, in sound health, and had borne him sons. Members of his own biradari, and even of the lower castes, refused to consider such an alliance, but he found an old man in poor circumstances who agreed to give his very attractive daughter, much younger in years than the wealthy suitor. The old man felt that this was an excellent match for his daughter, far beyond his best expectations. From poverty she would rise to living like a rani, in luxuries undreamt, with untold silver, gold and servants. Besides the suitor was a high class Khatri and a very generous man, who offered to see that the old man and his sons would want no more.

When people heard of the proposal they were outraged. It was an injustice to the first wife, also a woman from our town. Had she not borne him sons and was she not, besides, still young and fertile? She was good enough for him, in fact originally better than his station; she came from a better family, and was married to him when he was still struggling in life; what if he had amassed a fortune since? Had she died or become mad, or had she been barren, or had she produced only daughters, remarriage would have been understandable, but here there was no justification at all. Self-respecting families had rejected his offers and now he had obviously lured this wretched old man into giving his daughter. It was clearly a case of selling a daughter, a black mark which no forehead of a Khatri in living memory had worn. Elders of the biradari tried to dissuade the old man from this transaction, but the betrothal went through and a date was fixed for the wedding. There was nothing the biradari could do to the rich man as he came from another town, and in his own town he was too big to care. But on the wedding day, when the bridegroom's party arrived at the railway station, it was met by a jeering crowd which drowned the half-hearted music of the brass band. The old man was ostracised; no one came to the wedding; no one helped to receive and serve the guests; and all the way back to the station the next morning the party were jeered again. In fact, the barat only stayed for one night. Knowing the reception they were going to get from the town they 'stole in like thieves at night and crept away before dawn'—a metaphor which was reserved for morganatic and ostracised weddings where a small barat would come late in the evening and leave by daybreak because it dared not show its face to the town.

The rich man never came again to our town; he died a few years later. The old father lived a despised unhappy life despite his new affluence which turned bitter in his mouth. Occasionally his daughter visited him, but no one went near her and her wealth and pomp were scorned. The first wife was treated with added respect and sympathy. The incident was never forgotten, and the lesson was not lost on the town.

There was another interesting case of biradari punishment where a member of the panchayat decided to break the rule that he himself had agreed to introduce. The Hindu biradari of his town had decided to ban fireworks at weddings on the ground that they were a wasteful expense. This wealthy man, a pancha himself, decided to hold a most lavish wedding for his daughter, for which he ordered fireworks specially from another town. The biradari reminded him that it looked ill for a pancha to break a rule, but he proudly ignored their advice. When the barat arrived there was consternation, for not a soul turned up to receive and to serve, except a few immediate relatives. It taught the man a lesson. All the elaborate arrangements he had made, the pomp and show which should have drawn great applause turned to dust. Worse still, he was reduced to insignificance in the eyes of the visitors who naturally wondered what sort of a family their boy was marrying into. But if it taught him a lesson, the biradari learned ds to the pigeons in long whistles, and they would wheel round and round in wider or narrower circles according to the varying tone and length of the whistle, till they were told to settle back on the loft. This daily routine combined traits lesson too, for soon afterwards the ban on fireworks was relaxed. It was a harmless, though wasteful, custom, and people liked their fun at weddings, which it was unwise for the biradari to interfere with.

Even when the biradaris were powerful, they were seldom harsh or vindictive, nor were they easily influenced by the well-to-do and powerful members. Through centuries people had learned to rely upon them. The panchayat elders would forfeit respect and confidence if they transgressed the limits of natural justice. A strong man could defy the biradari for a while, but ultimately he had to get his sons and daughters married, and sometimes he had to take out a funeral. He could not therefore afford to stand apart for too long.

Our lawyer uncle used to explain that the weakening of the biradari system began when the British brought codified laws, impersonal courts, professional advocates and judges, high stamp duties, rules of evidence and procedure. Though the new justice was impartial, it was cumbersome and costly. The judges at first were unfamiliar with the ways of people, but as they began to understand them people also learned that this new impersonal justice could be deceived by casuistry and false evidence. It was difficult to sustain a lie before a biradari—if you were not found out then, you were bound to be caught later—but before a judge, to whom you were merely a plaintiff or a defendant, perjury was only actionable if it was found out at the trial. Time came after the First World War, when the farmers made so much money from a good crop that a man might publicly declare that he was going to put aside so many thousand rupees to settle a score by murdering someone, and later fight it out with the help of a leading criminal lawyer. And get away they often did.

If the introduction of law courts deprived the biradari panchayats of their function to adjudicate and arbitrate, the growth of western education and the movement away from home weakened their social importance. People developed personal standards which made them decide social issues in an individual light rather than according to custom. Our father lived most of his life away from our Khatri biradari in Gujrat, and altered custom as he saw best in the light of his newly acquired western education, which naturally challenged many of the old beliefs that had so far been taken for granted. He began to apply, in fact, the same procedure which the biradari has applied collectively and over a period, the changing of outworn customs; but in his case it was he who decided when the custom was outworn. The weakening of the biradari system meant in time a weakening of the caste system, as obligations to your caste were enforced by the biradari through the restraints that they exercised by day to day contact, backed ultimately by the threat of sanctions. But once you moved away from your town the biradari ceased to have a hold on you. In the new place you formed new friends, and sometimes new relationship, and although you tried to keep contact with your original biradari the ties soon began to weaken. You might join a local biradari, but somehow its ties were never quite so strong.

CHAPTER SIX

Life in Medieval Towns

Gujrat is the place I came to regard as my home. I have no recollection of Kala Sarai where the family originally came from. The canal colonies we lived in had a transitoriness about them, but Gujrat with our own house, our biradari and relations, was a home to us. In the Punjab your home, whether referred to in the simple Punjabi word, ghar, or in the more poetic Persian word, vatan, meant a lot. It was the first question you asked a stranger even before you asked him his name or caste; and if you both came from the same place or nearabouts a relationship was immediately formed. In a strange town you made a biradari of your two families with all its obligations and rights, and exchange of gifts of fruits and sweets on ceremonies, festivals and weddings. If his wife came from your town she became your sister, if he came from there, he was your brother, and if the wives came from the same town, they became sisters. The children referred to them according to the acquired relationship.

Travelling in a train you might suddenly discover that a man in the compartment hailed from the same village or town. There would be an immediate shout of 'Lao, tusan te sade vatni hoay, sade apne ghar de, sade bhara, wah, wah!' 'Take it, you are our countryman, from our home, our brother, well, well!' A feeling of warmth welled up, especially if you were a long way from home. Everyone in the compartment felicitated you on this coincidence. In a strange part of the Punjab you both regarded yourselves, as exiles, and commented on the air, water, milk, vegetables, the size and sweetness of cabbages and cauliflowers, dialect and everything else as being not quite what you were used to. You were abroad and such differences were to be expected, but it was good to have someone from your home. The locals would accept it all in good part, and remark that it was but natural that things away from home are never the same. Gujrat provided the anchor in our itinerant life.

Gujrat was founded, probably in the twelfth century, by a dynasty of cattle-rearing tribes, known as Gujars, who also founded the state of Gujerat. Its population in 1917 of under twenty thousand was probably less than it had been in its days of glory. It lay on the Grand Trunk Road of Sher Shah, between Peshawar and Lahore and between the rivers of Jhelum and Chenab. To the north, about thirty miles away, began the foothills of the Himalayas, to the west, at the same distance, the low hills of Pabbi, where the plateau of Puthowar began to rise towards Rawalpindi. Gujrat was thus situated in a triangle of flat land with hills at the apex and rivers on two sides, while at its open base the flat plain of the Punjab stretched endlessly to the south. Its strategic position can be easily realised. After the invaders from the north-western passes crossed the Jhelum and descended down the Pabbi they came upon Gujrat, a walled fortified town built on the only hill for miles. It was the only well fortified town up to Lahore.

The city was built on a kind of right-angled hill, one side of which rose steeply. The town sloped from the small crown of the hill down to the plain below. There was a city wall all round with five gates, in addition to the main gate on top of the hill. Being contained by the wall it remained for centuries very congested, and it was not until the end of last century that the first houses, among them grand-uncle's, were built outside the wall. Thirty years of uninterrupted peace, which looked good for a long time to come, tempted people for the first time to venture out. Inside, the city had remained unchanged for eight hundred years, perhaps longer, since its strategic importance was such that there must have been some habitation even before the Gujars founded it; they perhaps only renamed and rebuilt it into a strongly defended town. Apart from its age we knew nothing of its history.

The city had a kind of defensible planning. It was divided by three main streets in the shape of a bow with an arrow. One of these streets ran roughly north south connecting two gates, like the string of a bow; another ran from the eastern gate to the citadel on the crown of the hill, like the arrow in the bow; the third street went in an arc from the vicinity of the northern gate to the southern gate like the bow itself. These main streets were quite narrow and contained the shops, which were ranged in groups of the same kind. There was one bazaar of gold and silversmiths, another of confectioners and cook shops; then there were groups of dry grocers, dyers, metal workers, cloth merchants, general merchants, book shops and stationers, shoe shops, and so on. In the side streets were groups of potters, weavers, and odd professions like brass bands. In one area lived the prostitutes and nautch and singing girls, and in another the Mirasis.

Inside the sections made by the three main streets were mohallas, small blocks of houses opening on to a square. The mohallas had usually two openings, a lane leading in at one end and leading out at the other, though some mohallas ended blindly. The lanes, called gallis, were quite narrow and had houses on both sides. One called the bheeri galli, the narrow lane, was indeed so narrow that if you saw someone coming from the other side you waited to let him come out first. Two grown-ups could not pass each other even sideways. It was just about two feet in width, and on both sides it had high blank walls. The walls must have been several hundred years old, and the old thin brick had been rubbed through the centuries up to a man's height into a smooth lacquer-like surface that shone black. There were other lanes not quite so narrow where two persons could just pass each other. Many of these lanes went through two or three small mohallas, eventually ending in a cul-de-sac. The mohallas were purely residential and had no shops. They were originally occupied by people of the same caste, but this tended to disappear in our time, though most Hindus and Muslims still generally lived in separate mohallas. Our small mohalla was a mixed Hindu and Muslim locality. The service castes had their own mohallas.

Because of the limited space within the city the houses were high, nearly all of three stories, more than which it was difficult to build with bricks and timber. Each house had a platform in front with two or three steps leading up on either side. The main door was in the centre of this platform, which was called thara and served several purposes. Women sat there in the afternoons spinning, sewing, embroidering and gossiping or quarrelling. From their respective tharas they could talk to each other without leaving their own domain. Upon the thara the itinerant merchants spread their wares while the women looked at them from their windows above, coming down only if they became interested.

You arrived in Gujrat by railway train. The station was about one mile from the city, and outside it was a large cluster of tongas. Red-shirted coolies took your luggage to the tonga shed where you were at once surrounded by all the tonga-wallas and dragged in all directions. You could either take the whole tonga or share it with others. After piling up the luggage you had the inevitable argument with the coolies, the usual rule being to offer a low amount and gradually raise it. Four people with some children in their laps settled in the tonga, and it started towards the town. Half way, the Grand Trunk Road from Peshawar crossed the city road, and there you were stopped at the octroi post to pay toll on anything unused that you brought in. Passing through the eastern gate the tonga would go by one of the main streets and stop at a small well, called Khari Khui, because its water was brackish, an uncommon phenomenon in this part of the country. Here we alighted from the tonga and found someone to carry the luggage. The lane twisted and turned past tall houses, at places barely five feet wide between the projecting platforms, till we reached Kuanungo Mohalla, a small mohalla with two tiny squares. The narrow lane connecting these squares was about thirty feet long and went between the blank walls of two houses like a tunnel. These two houses joined on top forming a roof over the lane, which then led to the next square and stopped there.

Our three-storied house in the second mohalla was typical of other middle class houses, but perhaps more ornate than most, both inside and outside. It had a large wooden door, fretted and chiselled, with carved wooden knobs with iron studs in them. At night a stout rectangular wooden bar let into a recess in one wall was pulled behind the door and slid into a recess into the opposite wall. This old safety device, known as erl, was common in our homes. Each storey had windows and fanlights with small panes of coloured patterned glass. The windows were painted a light blue, and the facade of the house was plastered in mat pink. The whole facade was symmetrical, ornate, and quite attractive. It was a square house with an open well in the middle, and the rooms on each floor opened into a verandah, running all round the well. On the first floor the well was covered with a wooden frame with iron bars; on the other floors it has a wooden railing fence around it. As the house had blank walls on all sides, except the front, where the entrance was and some windows, the purpose of the well was to provide light and ventilation and to keep it cool in the summer. In winter, to prevent the cold wind from outside from blowing through the house, we had to keep all windows closed. During the rains the water poured into the well and flushed out through the drains into the street, and in early spring when it hailed it made a carpet of white on the ground floor. Thus in the congested heart of the city, the house was open to the elements.

The entrance door opened into a vestibule known as deohri, which was a sort of reception room for strangers and hawkers. Nobody could proceed beyond this room unless invited. On the left of the deohri a door opened to a narrow staircase leading upstairs. Small at the base compared to the height, the old Punjabi houses had to have steep stairways with very high steps, and a rope to hold on to as you climbed up On the right-hand side of the deohri another door led to the ground floor rooms, and if the two doors were closed the deohri itself could be left open. The groundfloor rooms around the well received little direct light, and the blank walls at the back made them totally dark. We used them only as store rooms. On the ground floor there was a tube well with a hand pump. A pipe went up to the floor above so that water could be pumped up.

When visitors and traders knocked at the door with the padlock chain, if the men were out mother would look out of a window from upstairs to see who it was. If the visitor was a relation she would come down, but traders were never allowed upstairs, nor would they have found it easy to carry their loads up the narrow steep steps, so mother would either go down herself or would lower a basket by a rope, or ask the man to leave the stuff. If the men were at home during the day the deohri door was left open, and it was customary for visitors to call from downstairs and be told either to come up or to wait outside or, if the weather was inclement, inside the deohri. Women visitors just called and climbed upstairs, as also relations or close friends of the family.

The deohri had another and tragic use. On a death the men coming to condole waited out in the street or sat on the platform, but the women came into the deohri. Relations and close friends of course went upstairs. When the body was brought down it was placed in the deohri for arranging the bier. On the days following the women called every morning and sat in the deohri to mourn.

At weddings the deohri also had its use. The bride, as she left home, tarried there awhile to take a last farewell from her parents before she stepped into the palanquin. When she reached her new home the deohri was her reception chamber. After the first few days when the initial shyness had grown into intimacy the young bride would run downstairs to open the door, in the hope of a quick embrace from her husband in the dark deohri. An understanding mother-in-law would tell her to go down and open it. Girls in young unrecognised love would sometimes stand in the deohri behind the entrance, and make some sound to attract the boy inside, only to meet in the confusion of a clumsy kiss.

From the deohri we climbed up the dark steps to the first floor. At the landing there was a niche in the wall in which in the old days, before the pump was fitted, the water-carrier poured water from his goatskin into a duct that led into the kitchen. From the landing the door opened into the verandah round the well. On the right there was a long room, our sitting-room, the baithak; opposite there were two rooms, one we used as a bedroom and one for storing blankets, quilts and other things that might be needed more often than the goods stored in the locked rooms on the ground floor. On the third side was another bedroom opposite the baithak and of the same size; the fourth side was the kitchen. The bedroom doors were blank wooden shutters but the baithak doors were panelled with coloured glass. The kitchen had no doors; it was an open alcove.

The second floor was similar to the first except that on the side facing the kitchen there were no rooms but an open space. This floor had more light, and with the small open terrace it looked more spacious. The terrace had an open air oven which was used on summer evenings for baking bread and keeping the food warm.

On the third floor were terraces with high wooden walls to give privacy. The stairs led into a closed landing beside which were the dry closets. Steps led from outside the landing room to the open roof above it from where we had a fine view of the city standing in a hump on the side of the citadel and sloping down to the green fertile country around. In the distance the first peaks of the Himalayas rose above the ground haze. In winter, after a rain, the mountains rose majestically above the green belt of the surrounding country, their peaks covered with snow, touched by pink in the mornings and mauve in the evenings. After sunset, before the cold early night descended, the mountains were a sombre dark blue, while the snow peaks still reflected light from the sun which had disappeared.

The walls in the verandah around the well on the first and second floors were ornately decorated with paintings in Persian style. The main motif was slender vases with large spreading branches and flowers painted in a formal style. The flowers were roses, pomegranate, narcissi and irises. I do not know when these walls were plastered and painted, but both plaster and paint had endured well. The plaster was nearly all intact, and the paintings had only slightly faded. The lines were exquisitely drawn in long, fine brush strokes.

We lived in a very informal style. There was little privacy, and we ate on the floor in the kitchen. If there were guests the servant brought the food into the baithak. If relations visited we received them in the lower baithak, but if strangers and formal visitors came the men were taken to the upstairs baithak while the women stayed below. The mode of living changed from one season to another. During the winter we spent the days in the sun on the open terrace of the second floor or on the roof, and in the evenings we moved downstairs to the snugness of the first floor rooms. During summer we spent the days in the dark cool rooms of the first floor, and in the evening we moved up to the second floor terrace and, as the weather became warmer, to the roof terrace.

There was still a great deal of self-containedness in our homes; we bought household commodities in bulk and stored wheat, rice and pulses from one crop to another, and till quite late times mother ground the wheat and maize herself on a stone mill. She bought raw cotton, ginned it on a small wooden gin in the house and had it carded by an itinerant carder, who came with his long bow which he suspended with a stout string from the ceiling. She spun the yarn on a wooden spinning wheel and gave it to the Julaha for weaving. She bought coconut oil and soda which she gave to the soap boiler for making washing soap; she made her own preserves, pickles and jams, while she gave the ingredients to the pansari for extracting essences and preparing sherbets. She embroidered, stitched and sewed, and had we had sisters she would have been steadily preparing and storing away their dowry. She minded or supervised the feed of the cow and the buffalo that we always kept by mixing oilcake, cottonseed, bran, salt, unrefined sugar and dried left-over wheat chappatis. She bought metal utensils by weight and had them tinned, and if they broke she sold the metal by weight. We even bought logs and had them chopped on the front thara by Kashmiri labourers who wandered about the Punjab during winter when their own land was frozen and unproductive. We also maintained a ritual contact with land by growing symbolically in a small pot a few plants of the grain in season.

Our mohalla was mixed, and in both its squares there were Hindu and Muslim homes. Except for the burqa, with which the Muslim women veiled themselves when they went outside the mohalla, there was very little difference in the dress. The Hindu ghagra, the voluminous ankle-length skirt, had practically gone out by my time and only a few old women wore it. The women always wore salwar kameeze. There was no social stratification in our mohallas, and amongst our neighbours there was a Muslim lawyer, a Hindu confectioner, a Muslim clerk in the municipality, and a Brahmin family. Boys and girls played together, and in the afternoon the women would take out their low stools and embroidery and sit on their tharas, talking and gossiping.

People rose early in the morning. Many men had the village habit of going into the country for their morning ablutions. Some took a walk in the fields or on one of the roads leading out of town. On the way they cut a green neem or wattle twig and chewed one end which was made into a kind of brush to clean their teeth and thrown away after using it. They stopped at a well with a Persian wheel and had a bath. In winter well water is warm and in summer cool. There they met other men and exchanged news. Newspapers had barely reached Gujrat. On the way back through the town they passed through the open market square to buy fresh vegetables which had been plucked early the same morning and brought in from the market gardens surrounding Gujrat. After an early morning cooked meal men left for work by ten o'clock. Those who worked in offices returned home by five, but the shopkeepers, who began the day early, returned home at midday and then worked till late in the evening. Working hours varied from summer to winter. During the hot weather schools and offices opened at six in the morning and closed at midday; in the winter one worked from ten o'clock till four. In summer everyone slept in the afternoon, and in the evening the men went out for a walk or visiting friends. Sometimes after dinner husbands and wives went out together to visit relatives or friends, but without a specific purpose this was rare. Usually people retired early to sleep. Life thus ran on an even, slow tempo quickened occasionally by festivals, weddings and visits of relations from other towns. All such events were looked forward to long in advance.

The Hindu festivals were many, but those celebrated with enthusiasm were Lohri, Basant, Holi, Besakhi, Rakhri, Dusserah and Diwali. At Lohri, which came in January, large bonfires were lit in pits dug in the ground. There were special sweets of nougat covered with sesame seed and parched rice to eat, and there was always a special celebration for a baby who was having his first Lohri. We also exploded fire crackers. Little boys gathered firewood for days ahead. In the evening men, women and children gathered around the fires, which in the cold of a January night were most welcome. Late at night we went home to bed, tired and sleepy, with the sound of crackers still in our ears.

Basant came with spring and was the festival of the yellow colour of ripening crops, celebrated in the same way in towns as in villages. It marked the beginning of the kite flying season. Then came Holi, a festival of sheer rowdiness which every year seemed to grow worse. It was a day of complete licence when one splashed coloured water or threw powdered colours on each other and smeared colour on people's faces. Everybody put on old discarded clothes, for at the end of the day they would be a mess. The clothes were put aside for the next Holi, but it took a lot of scrubbing and washing to get the colours off faces, heads and hands. Some streets were notorious because the inhabitants would stand on their roofs and throw ashes, dust and contents of dustbins, even night soil on passers-by in the street below. But no matter what one did nobody could complain or take it ill. Everything had to be treated in good humour. Even staying indoors was no protection, as friends came to your house and dragged you out into the street, and once you were drenched in colour you might as well go with them and take your revenge. Women played Holi in the mohalla while men ran berserk in the streets. Holi, it is said, shares its origin with April Fool's Day.

After Holi came Besakhi in April. We used to celebrate it on the banks of the Chenab six miles away. It was, though in a quite different way, also full of noise and rough merriment; a pleasant combination of river picnic and festival.

Then came a long break in the hot summer months till the next festival in August, Rakhri or Raksha Bandhan, meaning the protection tie. Sisters tied rakhri, a coloured silk bracelet, round the wrist of their brothers and cousins. If a girl had no brother she would adopt one. The rakhris gradually became very ornate with little silk pompoms and glass pearls which we greatly admired round our wrists. To absent brothers the rakhris were sent by post in advance. Originally the custom meant a pledge of protection by brothers and male cousins, but now this meaning was more or less lost, and brothers had to pay some money to the sisters in return for the rakhri, something which we as young boys quite resented. We would be given silver rupees to pass on to our local adopted sisters, since we had no sisters of our own, and we used to protest that surely we boys could make a better use of the money than the girls who would only put it in their money boxes.

After Rakhri came the best festival season of all—Dusserah and Diwali. Both originated from the Ramayana; Dusserah enacting the battle between Ram and Ravan, at which the demon king of Ceylon was defeated, and Diwali in celebration of Ram's return home after fourteen years of exile. Well ahead of Dusserah a town committee was formed to collect money for a performance of the entire Ramayan. Local dramatic talent was selected for acting and production, and a stage was erected in the market square. The whole story of Ramayan was acted progressively each night for about a month. It was an entirely amateurish effort, all the actors were boys and men, and the performance was free to all. Some of the improvisations could be amusing and ingenious, and each year people wondered how the director would tackle a particular stage problem. Amongst the ticklish problems were the scene of Ram, Lakshman, Hanuman and their army crossing the water between India and Ceylon; Hanuman's flying to the Himalayas; and Lakshman ungallantly cutting Saroop Nakha's nose when he could stand her overtures no longer. Sometimes a difficult scene would be missed out and at other times they would use symbols, substituting words for action, or a combination of words and action. One director hinted the day before, that he was really going to make Ram and his army cross the sea, and we were all very curious about it, for no one had tackled this problem before. How could you run water on the small rickety stage? At the appropriate moment, anxiously awaited by all, two men appeared on the stage with a long half dry white dhoti, each holding two ends. They were swaying the dhoti as if to dry it, so that it billowed from side to side and heaved like a sea. Then Ram and his companions appeared on the stage and after some suitable words jumped over it to the other side to Ceylon. The whole thing was simply but effectively done and drew much applause. Living nearly a thousand miles from the sea it did not occur to us that the dhoti might have been blue.

We little boys used to hang around the Ram Leela hoping to be given a small part, usually that of a monkey in Hanuman's army. With a red mask of a monkey's face, red shirt and short pants and a tail sticking out at the back, holding gaily decorated red bows and arrows we pranced about and got in everybody's way. Hanuman would cuff us now and again and send a young monkey howling, while others jeered at the victim for being a fake warrior. Every evening after dinner we carried our own chairs to the Ram Leela if we did not want to sit on the ground. The performance went on till late at night, and next day people would minutely criticise the previous night's performance and compare it with the years before.

The performance varied in quality from day to day and from one year to another, but people were surprisingly charitable, not for want of local rivalries and jealousies but, I think, because the sight of a colourful stage with Ram, Sita and other characters of their Ramayan, whom people worshipped every day, alive and talking, moved them deeply. Dasarath's grief when Kaikeyi demanded her step-son Ram's exile so that her own son Bharat should ascend the throne; Bharat's loyal insistence on following Ram into exile; Sita's cries as Ravan carried her from her forest cottage; Lakshman's fainting after the wound in battle and Ram counting the night's hours waiting for Hanuman, who had flown to bring the sanjivani herb to save Lakshman's life from the Himalayas two thousand miles away, were some of the many poignant moments that brought tears to the eyes of the audience. These simple men and women, moved by the realism of the acting, wanted to go forward to worship the heroes of their life and thought. But there was much conscious and unconscious humour too, as when the Lakshman who was known to dislike the fellow playing Saroop Nakha acted with such realism that he nearly took his nose off. The very genuine howls of Saroop Nakha brought the house down. The little boys who stuck pins in their arrows to give painful jabs to the boys in Ravan's army also provided a realistic touch, much appreciated by the audience.

Night after night the Ram Leela continued to unfold the great epic till we reached the last scene of the defeat of Ravan. This was acted on an open field on the afternoon of the Dusserah day. An enormous, hideous effigy of Ravan surrounded by smaller effigies of his brother Kumbh Karan and his son Indrajit, made of paper and bamboo and stuffed with fire crackers, were erected. In bright new clothes we collected at the fair and spent recklessly the four or eight anna piece given to us, till the Ram Leela's moment of climax arrived. At dusk Ram, Lakshman and Sita drove up in an open horse carriage and amidst great applause Ram dramatically shot an arrow at Ravan, his coup de grace. Immediately Ravan and his companions burst into flames. Crackers exploded and rockets shot out of the effigies. There was great commotion and din when after a whole month's narration of our beloved epic, virtue at last triumphed over evil, and the wicked demon, Ravan, collapsed, his body racked and tortured by crackers and flames. We returned home with full stomachs, sad that the season of Ram Leela was over, but we would soon brighten up at the thought that the best of all festivals was yet to come, and so soon. In twenty-one days there will be Diwali.

Diwali has a touch of Christmas about it, particularly, as I was to discover later, the Scandinavian Christmas. It is a festival of the home when families unite. It was auspicious to be home on Diwali day to receive the blessings of the goddess Lakshmi. The preparations began many days ahead, and everyone in the home was given something to do. The women prepared sweets and made hattis on the wall. A portion of the wall was plastered with cowdung and painted white with red swastikas. Little projections, called hattis, of mud and straw, were fixed on the wall for placing the lamps. Earthenware cup-shaped lamps called diwas, which give Diwali its name, were first soaked in water. Little girls would roll wicks out of cottonwool and put them into the lamps which they filled with mustard oil. Latterly coloured wax candles appeared on the scene. Father would have to have the house painted, bring some new silver rupee coins, and buy sweets from the bazaar. There were so many things to make and to buy—special sugar sweets in white, pink and yellow, moulded in the shape of horses; gaily painted clay figures of people and horses; coloured prints of Ram, Sita, Lakshman, Hanuman, Lakshmi and other gods, goddesses and scenes from mythology; paper and bamboo lanterns; candles and fireworks.

On Diwali day there was hectic activity, hanging the lanterns, placing the diwas and candles in rows, beginning with the steps before the house and going up all the way, on windows, wall parapets, inside the house and on the hattis. In the evening when everything was ready we would bathe again and put on new clothes. From then on we became impatient and urged the parents to begin the Diwali, only to be repeatedly told that we had to wait till it was dark; you cannot light lamps in daylight.

In November night falls early, and with our excitement pitched to frenzy we would rush to light the lamps. This was quite a task if it was breezy, for the flame on the wicks in the open earthenware diwas would flicker and go out and leave dark gaps in the lighted rows. Usually the evening was still, and row after row of little trembling flames would outline our house and the neighbouring houses until the whole mohalla was a mass of lights. We shouted to the children in the neighbouring houses, vying with each other who put up the better show. But we still could not eat the sweets until the family puja had been done. Our mother collected us all and we sat in front of the hattis for puja. On the floor, in front of the lighted lamps she placed a tray with silver rupees spread on it. The coins were smeared with saffron and covered with grains of rice as an offering to Lakshmi; it was called Lakshmi puja. There were trays of sweets lying on the floor, and when the puja finished we were given some prashad, an offering of sweets. As soon as the puja was over we rushed out to light the fire crackers. Our narrow mohalla became a fairyland with sparklers, rockets, coloured candles, and fireworks that delighted our simple tastes and were known by such beautiful names as moonlight, flower shedders and pomegranates, which threw cascades of sparkles like a fountain of fire.

A treat we always looked forward to was a visit to the bazaar to 'see the Diwali'. We were taken to the bazaar by the elders, holding their hands so as not to get lost in the crowd. It was a wonderful sight; rows of houses outlined with flickering lamps and candles, lanterns in different colours hanging from the balconies, and the confectioners' shops brilliantly lit with gas-lamps and with tiers of sweets sloping up to the ceiling. The sweets were made in all colours and arranged in decorative pyramids on shining trays. They were wrapped in very fine gold and silver foil. In the midst of this colourful mountain of temptation the halwai sat, fat and paunchy, weighing out sweets to his customers standing in the street, and giving an even shorter measure than usual. We returned home to find all the doors open, every room lit and the tray of saffron-covered silver rupees still at the puja altar. The rows of lamps and candles were still flickering but many of them had gone out. Tonight Lakshmi, the goddess of prosperity, visits every home, so all the doors must be left open and the lights burning to give her an open welcome. A curious custom had grown of propitiating Lakshmi by gambling. For days ahead people played games and gambled, and on the night of Diwali our parents let us also play, but with cowrie shells which were then still the lowest denomination of money.

Next morning we awoke with a feeling of anti-climax. Diwali was gone, and there would be no more festivals for over three months, till Lohri came again. We felt sad but tried to brighten the gloom with the thought that it was still a holiday. We busied ourselves with collecting wax from the bottom of the burned out candles. Then we melted the wax and made some half-hearted attempts at shaping candles, but real Diwali was over.

Festivals that we celebrated with great enthusiasm and eclat were in later years spoilt by the growing bitterness between Hindus and Muslims. The Hindus resented the Muslims slaughtering cows on their Bakri-Id, and the Muslims objected to the noise and music of our festivals, and would not let Dusserah, Diwali and Holi pass without trouble, sometimes leading to bloodshed. It reached such a pitch that for some years we did not celebrate our festivals for fear of provoking bloody riots. Even Ram Leela was dropped. On the other hand we began to add more festivals to our already sizeable list. Christmas is today celebrated in more clubs, restaurants, army messes and even homes in big towns than it was during the British days. Clubs hold children's Christmas parties and New Year dances. Republic Day and Independence Day are also acquiring the air of festivals; so while we acquire new festivals many of the old ones are losing their significance.

CHAPTER SEVEN

Life in Medieval Towns

We stayed in Gujrat for about a year to complete our schooling, and seven years later I returned there to join college. As child and adolescent I got into tune with the spirit of the town, and a spirit it certainly had. It possessed a self-contained medieval unity of life in which people worked at their hereditary crafts and professions, and lived in their biradaris, friendly and tolerant of each other. In such a congested town, where everyone knew everyone else and his affairs, I suppose tolerance was essential. Yet underneath it there flowed currents, sometimes in complicated convolutions which caused embarrassment to the society, but usually without any tumult on the surface. The town had through the ages acquired a character and a reputation, unsavoury in parts, but of which its inhabitants were quite proud. Like its famous industry of forging weapons, swords and guns, it had a stored-up vitality which went ahead in a surge when opportunity came at the end of last century. There will be few successful professional families in the West Punjab who do not stem from this town and its district. Later, as the development spread, other districts like Sargodha, Shahpur, Sialkot and Gujranwala also made their contribution, when castes like the Puris of Ghartal, Sahnis of Bhera, and the Batras of Girot, all three from small places, unknown in the past, spread through the services and professions.

Though newcomers to Gujrat, through our grand-uncle we joined the local biradari and soon got to know most of the families. As a child I would sometimes accompany my mother when she went out visiting and shopping. Our progress was slow as she often stopped to talk. We would walk through the covered lane in front of our house into the second small square of our mohalla. She would be called by one of the Muslim women from her balcony. 'Bibi-ji, where are you going? You are taking your boy with you. By the grace of Allah, he has grown. I suppose he will be a big engineer like his father one day.' My mother would reply, invoking Parmatma, the Hindu name for God, in response to the neighbour's Allah. The neighbour's little girl, Fatima, would look at me curiously and ask if I would like to play hide and seek. The mother slapped her on her head and told her not to be so bold. Years later, when I came back to live in the same house, Fatima had grown into a lovely girl. She wore a burqa when she went out of the mohalla, but underneath the conventional demureness she was as bold as ever with a roving eye. On the other side of the square lived a Hindu confectioner whose wife used to come down and join my mother with a 'Behnji, how are you keeping?' And her little girl, Rupa, stood by her looking at me as if I was too good a boy to want to play with little girls. She also grew to be a beauty with flashing eyes. Both Rupa and Fatima were lively girls and there was talk that they were both in love with a Muslim boy of a wicked reputation. When Rupa's parents heard about it they immediately betrothed her and married her off inside a few months. The poor thing got married tc a widower twice her age. When her doli left she cried bitterly, but in her case, as we in the mohalla knew, it was not for parting with her parents, who had dealt her hard, but for exchanging her flowering love against a dull old husband.

It was strange that in the narrow lanes of the confined city, under the strict watch of parents and neighbours, such affairs could develop at all, but secretly they did occur. Someone or the other always knew, because they had seen the girl disappearing into a dark deohri, or making signs from a balcony to someone passing below, or perhaps throwing a small tightly screwed-up ball of paper; a really daring one had climbed over a wall separating the terraces of two houses; another had thrown back the hood of her burqa in a lane far from home, where she thought no one would recognise her. Although such affairs sooner or later became known, people never talked too loudly. Somehow the city felt that everything must be contained within its walls, and it was practical to be discreet. It could always happen in your own family. Occasionally an affair would burst the bounds of propriety, but in such cases too it was somehow hushed and settled, though any time it might be raked up in a quarrel and thrown in someone's face.

My mother and I would walk on into the next lane which had only Hindu houses, and she would talk to some women sitting on a platform, gossiping, spinning but, like good Punjabis, always eating something, horse radishes with salt and pepper, sugar cane, parched gram and corn or whatever else the street vendors had to offer. The talk was usually about sickness in the house, especially of children; death, births and marriages; what they were cooking for the night. The profoundest discussion would be about some remedy which was known to have cured someone. And so we walked on, and though these conversations were dull to me there was always a chance of someone offering me a sweet or fruit. The next lane was a wholly Muslim one, known as Sheikhans' Gally. Sheikhs were Muslims who had been converted from Hinduism and given this high title as an immediate reward. Here also my mother knew many women but we felt strange because of a heavy garlic smell that emanated from their houses and the uneasy consciousness of their eating cow's meat. There was also a sense of strangeness in their invoking Allah and Khuda instead of Ishwar or Parmatma.

From here the lane opened into one of the main streets, and as soon as we entered it mother pulled her mantle over her face and held my hand. She crossed over into another lane to avoid walking in the street. This lane was inhabited by courtesans. It was like any other lane, but to me it had a mystery about it. I could not understand what these women were and why they seemed to have no menfolk and children. They looked like other Muslim women, for they were usually Muslims, and the odd Hindu girl strayed into their fold adopted their customs and manners; yet they had tired faces and bold, almost brazen, manners. They left their heads uncovered, for instance. In the mornings when other women looked fresh and clean after the bath these women looked haggard; and in the evenings when other women were tired and work-worn, they were all dressed and made up. Most of them were old, but some were young, mysteriously attractive, made up and decorated in a way that even our new brides did not dare; beautiful in a quite different way to our young women. These young ones did not seem to have the customary respect for the older women. Were they even related to them? They did not look like their daughters or nieces. And what were those curious strains of music that came from some room upstairs—a sitar, a tabla, the jingling ankle bells and a girlish voice endlessly repeating a refrain. I dared not ask my mother questions because I somehow felt that she would evade the explanation. I once saw some red colour coming out of a drain and trembled to think that they were doing some sacrifices inside the house.

An old courtesan sitting on a platform would talk to my mother who stopped to answer. She would make simple enquiries about our family. There was never any hesitation on my mother's part to talk to them, though I noticed that my young aunt or the men never did. But no one avoided that lane. These women were not pariahs or outcasts, they lived among us, and Gujrat contained them as a part of its life. Like other castes they served a purpose and were not scorned because they served it. They were not accepted or respected, but neither were they treated with contempt or prudery.

From the lane of the courtesans we would go through the Sonar Mohalla where all the gold and silversmiths lived together in a tight community. The Sonars were supposed never to give you full measure of gold and silver in ornaments. It was said that a Sonar who once made an ornament for his mother without keeping back part of the gold could not go to sleep for worrying over this deviation from a principle. He woke his mother in the middle of night and asked for the piece back, saying he had made a mistake and could not sleep till he had put it right. The Sonars married in their own biradari but without observing our rigid codes. We would usually stop at the house of the Sonar who made jewellery for us and talk to his wife. As usual, my mother treated her as an equal even though her husband would be very deferential in my father's presence. Somehow caste inequality in terms of social behaviour expressed itself more prominently in the case of men than women. It is interesting to think that while Khatris and Sonars had lived amicably in adjacent mohallas for generations there had never been any inter-marriage, inter-dining, or much social intercourse.

From the Sonar Mohalla we went through the Bheeri Gali, the narrowest lane in the city. We children loved sliding our shoulders against its lacquer-smooth walls. At the other end we entered a Khatri mohalla, and after exchanging some small talk with the women we met we passed on.

This mohalla had recently had a scandal. There was a head clerk in a government office and his wife, an elderly couple, living in this street. They had a daughter who at the age of nearly twenty was still unmarried. Many friends and people in their biradari had spoken to them about the inadvisability of leaving a daughter unmarried till such an age; it was risky and marred the chances of a good marriage because people became suspicious; and where would you find an eligible young man of twenty-five or more who was still unmarried? You would have to look for a widower. Yet the old man did not heed their advice. The girl was quite attractive and healthy, and everyone felt it would be understandable if she went wrong. One night there was great commotion, and the whole mohalla was awakened by the cries of 'Chor! chor!' It appeared that the old babu had got up in the night and found his daughter in the arms of a man. The moment she saw her father she cried out 'Thief! thief!' and pushed the man away as if in a struggle. The 'thief' disappeared quickly, but as he ran down the street he was recognised as the son of a prominent family with a mysterious reputation. He had already been suspected of various affairs, but burglary was something new. His family was affluent enough, and nobody really believed that he had tried to steal the girl's bangles; he was sure to be visiting the old babu's daughter with her consent. The scandal died down gradually, and the elders spoke to the old man seriously. The young man accepted the charge of attempted burglary and squared it up as best he could with the police.

It was the unwritten rule in such affairs that if the pair were caught the girl would immediately disclaim all acquaintance and accuse the man of assault, burglary or anything she could hastily think of. There was no question of sticking by her man, for such affairs were not supposed to lead anywhere, and the girl surrendered herself to the man on the traditional, tacit understanding that he took the entire risk. Somehow the society also helped the girl, presumably because it would be a very unpleasant task to take action against her. Instead, she was left to the mercy of parents or husband. Her partner could always fend for himself, so it did not matter too much if the blame were foisted on him. Actually, such affairs were not too many, and the society was almost puritanical in its morals and conventions, but it was pragmatic in its approach to the old lapse and infraction. Gujrat probably had more such affairs than other towns and its boys and girls had a reputation for liveliness. The erring girl, married or unmarried, brought enough shame on her family to be sufficient punishment in itself. She put a black mark on their brow which was not easily washed off. People knew, even though they pretended not to notice. In new alliances and the biradari dealings it was visible for a long time.

Virginity was sacred. An unmarried girl was called a virgin. Premarital affairs were an exception, but not so rare were happenings within the family which never came to light. They were usually affairs between brother and sister-in-law, between a young aunt and nephew, and occasionally between a young stepmother and a stepson. There were many causes. One was the joint family system where people lived not in a single unit of husband, wife and children, but in a big crowd of relations all together in one house. Another cause was the arranged marriages which, though mostly happy, did occasionally bring together totally antipathetic personalities who, had the choice been theirs, would never have selected each other; for instance, a frigid husband and a passionate wife. Were it the other way round, the man could discreetly resort to the courtesans, but an unsatisfied woman had no such outlet and might therefore resort to liaison within or without the family. Yet another cause was occasional disparity in age, again due to parents' choice. A mere girl would be married to a man as old as her father. A younger brother, son or nephew of the husband might attract her, where the husband repelled. Between a wife's younger sisters and the groom there is a tradition of bantering which begins at the wedding when they ask him tough and embarrassing questions, hide his shoes and play tricks. Such bantering sometimes led to a casual affair. Lastly, a young widow condemned to lifelong loneliness might have an affair with the late husband's brother, sometimes even his father. Being voiceless in the family, widows were easy victims.

Young widows were, in fact, a great problem, for while people would not accept remarriage at any cost, they did not know what to do with them. Whether a widow stayed with her own or her husband's parents or brothers she was a burden. Her misfortune was considered to be her fault; at least it was her fate. While her parents and brothers had sympathy, other relations showed none, particularly her mother-in-law who felt that she had brought evil luck and 'eaten up' her son. She was forbidden to dress and eat well, to share the family's festivities and joys, and often she was just an unpaid servant in the house, without the freedom to leave. The lot of the widows improved somewhat with the spread of the Arya Samaj which advocated remarriage, or education to befit them for a teaching job, but people were slow to react and continued to hold the old belief that God had so willed it. In our family, under the influence of father, two widows in fact managed to arrange their own marriages, but that came many years later.

☆

From the Khatri mohalla we turned into the Mandi, Gujrat's marketplace, which was a large square with wholesale and retail grocers and grain merchants' shops. The square was paved, and there were heaps of grain, pulses, gur, rice and other foodstuffs from which both retailers and consumers bought. In the centre of the square was a large banyan tree under which women sat on the ground selling vegetables which were grown outside the city wall and brought in fresh twice a day. The fresh and colourful vegetables were a very pleasant sight, arranged neatly in reed baskets. The vegetable sellers were always women and girls from the special Muslim caste of Arains. Unlike the ordinary Muslim farmers, they specialised in market gardening and never went in for cultivation of crops. The Arain men and boys worked at growing the vegetables and the women did the selling. My mother would stop and look at some vegetables, and the buying was always done after the same formula. 'How much are the brinjals, sister?' my mother would ask. 'Sister, what am I going to ask you, give whatever you like. They are half anna per seer,' was the vegetable woman's answer. There was a little bargaining, but as the low price left little scope for reducing it, the woman would weigh the quantity and give one or two brinjals extra as jhoonga. Jhoonga was a great institution: you were entitled by custom to receive a small quantity of what you bought in addition to the proper number or weight. As children we would always press the shopkeeper for more jhoonga, and the success of our buying was judged not so much by the bargain we drove but by the jhoonga we received.

I saw a fire for the first time in this market. It was a big fire, and next to the shop where it broke out was a kerosene store. Gujrat had never heard of a fire engine, so the whole town turned out to help. A long chain of buckets conveyed water from the nearest well, and for hours people fought a desperate battle. In a congested city like this, built of brick and timber, fires could be murderous, as a fire at one end of a narrow lane could seal off a large mohalla. Surprisingly, fires were a rare occurrence, and I do not recall another.

After buying our vegetables and exchanging enquiries about children my mother took her change, and we walked into the main street which led up the slope to the top of the city. This was a street of much interest to me. It began with a soda water shop with row upon row of coloured aerated drinks, of which there was a prodigious variety of synthetic flavours and colours. This shopkeeper boasted over fifty; and for one of his special customers, a local barrister who had been to England, he compounded an aerated mixture of beer and pink rose sherbet. After the drinks shop came a number of fruit shops, then cook shops which made Punjabi delicacies like potatoes and grams, nan, the Persian ovenbaked bread, liver, kidneys and kababs and potato chops. As these delicacies sizzled on the coals, on a plate or a spit, their aroma rose tantalisingly to my nostrils. Next were the confectioners whose coloured sweets were an equal attraction to me and the flies. Then came the general merchants selling manufactured household articles, which in those days were mostly imported. The goods were usually British or German, and many of the brands had become household names. Japan had not quite entered the market. One could buy knives, scissors, buttons, cotton and silk thread, mirrors, soaps, bottled hair oils, razors, socks, woollen and cotton knitwear, etc. These imported things always held more glamour for us than the local ones. We preferred the imported combs to the hand-made wooden ones, the electroplated Sheffield and Solingen knives and scissors to the solid steel ones made by our local smiths, Pears and Vinolia soap to the home-boilded desi soap, and the shining coloured buttons to the simple cloth ones.

The street then began to rise towards the Chowk where the four main streets met. On the left was the Sonar bazaar, with the shops of gold and silversmiths; on the right the Pansaris, who sold herbal medicines, spices, rose petal jams used as a laxative, preserves, essences, rose and kewra waters, almonds, pistachio, assofoetida and many other interesting and exotic things. Nearby were shops where they made gold and silver leaf for spreading on sweets. Tiny particles of silver and gold were put between brown paper sheets about eight inches in length and five inches in width. A sheaf of such papers interleaved with the gold or silver particles was placed on a flat stone and beaten with a stone pestle until the gold and silver particles were beaten into the flimsiest leaves about four inches square. To spread these leaves on a sweet you pick it up still attached to the paper sheet and delicately let the leaf waft down. It looks decorative and is supposed to have tonic value. The sound from these shops as the leaves were beaten was like the tonk-tonk of the coppersmith bird.

Once passing this street I saw a strange and frightening sight that I could not understand. In a shop, completely empty of goods, there sat a man in a rigid pose of silent meditation in front of a tall brass lamp with a single wick in a bowl of oil. The man was dressed in plain white clothes and the lamp cast his shadow on the bare wall behind. As people passed in the street they stopped to look but no one talked to him, and he would not raise his eyes to look back at them. It was early in the morning and I could not understand why this man had to sit in broad daylight in front of a lamp and talk to no one. There was no wailing or crying in the house above and no sign of death. I did not dare to ask anyone till I reached school, and there I learned that this shopkeeper was declaring himself bankrupt. The word for one who goes into bankruptcy is diwalia, meaning one who lights a lamp, the diwa. The act is called 'diwala nikalna', to take out the lamp. In due course the creditors will open discussions with the bankrupt, and his biradari or its panchayat may have to be called in, but this morning people merely watched the sad sight. This public confession, and the ritual of penance would not be forgotten for generations. 'Was not his father a diwalia; or was it his grandfather who took out the lamp?' someone will ask. And debts had to be honoured by sons and even grandsons.

The street continued to rise steeply from the square to the citadel, with narrow lanes on either side leading to other lanes and mohallas. Here the entrance to each mohalla was barred by a strong wooden gate with many stout erls at the back. It was the oldest part of the city and totally medieval. It had an old well, baoli, which was reached by a steep flight of steps and was supposed to be very deep, and so it must have been, as the citadel was high above the ground level. There was an old hamam, a steam bath, dating back into the Moghul or perhaps pre-Moghul times. We climbed up the main street till we turned into a lane to go into the house of some relations. In the citadel the houses were narrower than below, as the pressure on land must have been greater in the old days in this most secure part of the city. Some of these lanes and houses saw the sun for less than an hour in a day and were therefore dark and chilly in the winter, though cool in summer. We made some more calls, and while my mother talked to the women I watched other boys play in the lane. In this congested area there were hardly any open squares; only narrow twisting lanes, flanked by tall houses. One shuddered to think what happened here during invasions in the past. When the city was lost people retired into the citadel, barred the mohallas and houses and waited on housetops with cauldrons of boiling water and oil, while the invading soldiery ran about, mad with lust for loot and rape. When we read in our history books of Nadar Shah's qatil-e-am in Delhi, the order for three days' general massacre which he gave his soldiers, it meant something to us living in a town like Gujrat.

Equal devastation was caused whenever plague broke out. In the dark lanes and houses, plague spread with the speed of duststorms. It blew through every gali, mohalla and house picking victims at random. As it swept through a lane it would rush up the narrow steep stairs of a house and touch an inmate with its hot fingers, then jump over the terrace wall into the next house and through it down into the street below. Its victims would burn and writhe in pain for a day or two. The family and neighbours were scared when they helped, but help they did, although they knew that apart from the little comfort it gave, help was quite useless. The delirious victims hardly knew. Sometimes there were so many dead in a street that they had to wait for their turn to be taken out of town to the cremation grounds. When the mourners came back from the cremation, those next in order had been brought down, and as their funeral procession passed through the hushed streets people would ask who was it now. Sometimes it wiped out a whole family. Once when there was a mild outbreak of plague I myself lay in bed feeling hot and giddy. In my groins was a swollen gland which the old family doctor said was the dreaded sign. Everybody agreed except my uncle's wise munshi who said that though there was plague in one part of the town and the gland was good evidence, he somehow did not believe that I had it. He looked carefully down my leg till he saw a tiny, almost healed, cut under the ankle. This, he suggested, was the cause. And so it was.

From the citadel we returned to our house by a short-cut through the mohalla known as the Small Well with the Pipal Tree. I used to like returning this way because in the whole city, apart from the market, it had the only tree. It was a large, spreading pipal with a well underneath, always the coolest spot in the summer. Pipal is a lovely tree and rightly declared sacred by our ancestors. Its beautiful, bright green, perfectly formed and delicately-veined leaves are so fine and light that they tremble melodiously in the merest breath of wind, and each one of them acts like a fan. There is always a cool breeze under a pipal, and as it often has a well underneath, the spilled water adds to the coolness. The banyan tree has a severe majesty, while the pipal has a gentle friendliness about it. It is at its best when it has new leaves, smooth, pink and unbelivably soft and delicate, like the palms of a baby's hands. Under its maternal spread people sleep, worship and take vows, but we never went under it in dark because we were warned that it sheltered dains. We were told how to distinguish a dain. She is a beautiful woman, but her feet are turned backwards. And if you do not look out and get close to her she will take you away to eat you, for human flesh is her only food.

On the way we called at a Jhewar house, where my mother asked the wife to help with cooking and cleaning the utensils next week because we were expecting some guests.

By the First World War a ring of buildings had sprung up along the road which skirted the city wall. Among them were a number of institutions, a jail, a mission hospital and school. One or two enterprising shopkeepers had also ventured out. But there had long been a Civil Station, a kind of suburb of Government offices and bungalows. The early British officials built their bungalows in spacious surroundings outside the towns. In time these colonies grew into small self-contained townships of a standard pattern that was rather pleasant. In the residential part of the civil station there were large bungalows, each with its own fruit, vegetable and flower garden, cookhouse, servants quarters, stables and dhobi ghat. A long tree-lined drive led from the gate to the bungalow. They had rooms with high walls of sixteen feet or more, and deep verandahs all round, usually with well proportioned round columns. In the gardens they grew flowers, vegetables and trees imported from England, and that is how many of the flowers, and vegetables so familiar to us today were introduced to us. Many of these flowers which we looked upon as English, grew in their wild state in the Himalayas, but to our gardens they came via England.

In the non-residential area of the Civil Station there was a post office, a branch of the Imperial Bank which worked for the Government, a hospital, school, sometimes a college, Government offices, law courts, police headquarters and barracks, a parade ground, and the Company garden. These gardens were started in the days of the East India Company, and although most of them after 1857 were renamed Victoria Gardens, they continued nevertheless to be known as Company Gardens. There were usually in the larger towns a general store, run by a Parsi, selling European tinned and bottled provisions, liquors and general merchandise. In a part of the Company Gardens there was a club for the British residents. Later, as the number of Indians in the professions and services grew, they formed their own clubs. Ironically, the club named after the town was always exclusively British, presumably because it started as the first one. Each Civil Station, to round off its British origin, had a small Protestant church and a few local Christians with biblical names like Daniel and Samuel. Roman Catholicism never made much headway in the Punjab. They were a small, sad community living around the church, in a no-man's casteland between the English and us; lost to us and never accepted by them.

☆

My school, the Government High School of Gujrat, which my father, uncles, and before them my grand-uncle, had attended, was situated in the Civil Station, and it was typical of Government schools from the last century. It was a single storey brick building in the shape of an H. In front, facing the road, was a garden, at the back playgrounds, and on one side a hostel and some staff quarters. The English headmasters of my father's days had gone and were replaced by Indians. The school had ten grades and was divided into three sections: the first five years were known as the primary, the second three years were called the middle, and the last two years the high school. Teaching was in Urdu in the primary and the middle schools, and in

English in the high school. We began by learning calliagraphy and numerals on wooden boards, which we smeared with yellow clay every day. We wrote with reed pens which were sharpened every morning, and in small earthenware inkpots we soaked a rag in ink crystals made from lamp black. With this we learned to write on the clay surface Urdu lettering in the beautiful Persian script. At the end of school we washed off the clay and the writing and smeared on some fresh clay to prepare the surface for the following day.

Our curriculum was perhaps better than the one I came across in the more advanced schools in Bombay thirty years later. For example, we learned our geography in three stages; in the primary school we were taught the geography of our district and then of our province; in the middle school the geography of India and Asia, and in the high school the geography of the world. Similarly, our history teachings were divided into four sections: the Hindu, Muslim and British periods of Indian history and, as an optional subject in the high school, the history of England. I was therefore astounded to find that my daughter's first introduction to history and geography in a Bombay convent school was through the British Isles. She knew King Alfred and the towns and ports of England before she had heard of Ashoka and Calcutta. Despite the naive dose of the blessings of the Angrezi Raj, the English Directors of Public Instruction in the Punjab had designed our studies well. The medium of instruction was first Urdu, but during the last five years of school we had to learn English and one of the classical languages, Sanskrit, Persian or Arabic. The whole curriculum was well balanced.

Events of interest at school were the annual cricket tournament, the visits of the school Inspector and the Governor of the Punjab, and fine days in the summer. Fine days were an institution that could only have been developed in the dry country of West Punjab. After a long succession of hot summer days, the monotony would one day be broken by a cloudy sky or, better still, a wet day when it rained heavily. Word would go round in the classrooms that it was a shame to be indoors working when it would be so much nicer to be out playing and getting wet. The luxurious feeling of running out into the rain and getting soaked is something only those who have lived in our dry climate can understand. Some bold ones among us would get together and write out an application to the headmaster. It ran something like this:

To: The Headmaster, Gujrat,
Government High School, Punjab.
Gujrat, Punjab.

Honoured Sir,

Today, by the grace of God, is a fine day. Therefore, we the students of the Government High School, Gujrat, Punjab, request that a holiday should be declared. For this act of kindness we shall for ever pray for your long life, happiness and prosperity.

Yours most obediently,
The Students
of the Government High School,
Gujrat, Punjab.

To make the best impression the application had to be written in English; it also had to invoke the grace of God, just in case God changed His mind and the sun came out. We would watch anxiously for the clouds to stay, and for some word from the headmaster. Suddenly, out of its hour, the school bell rang chaotically to say that the school was closed, and three hundred boys ran out with yells and whoops of joy. God and headmaster had both been kind, though now it did not matter even if God changed His mind.

Cricket was a popular game in the West Punjab, and Gujrat had a very fine team. The annual tournament was therefore a great event and cause a display of much enthusiasm. The days of the match were holidays, and we would relax in the winter sun, cheering and praying for our team, hoping the match would last its allotted span of four days. In the mornings and evenings we would hang round the hostel where the visiting team was accommodated. Whether we won or lost it was sad to see them depart, and to return to our classes. We also played the Indian games of gulli danda and kabodi, and football, volley ball, basket ball and hockey, but cricket interested us most.

The Schools Inspector came once in a year, and how we looked forward to it, for it was known that he came not to examine us but to inspect the work of the teachers, especially the headmaster. For days we would discuss with much bravado how we held the future of our masters in our hands; we could ruin them if we wished. By innocently giving ignorant answers we could make the Inspector think that the cause of our ignorance was bad teaching, and should the teacher try to explain that we were feigning ignorance, it would not look well for his discipline. If we wanted to we could convey in a few moments that we did not like our master. The masters knew all this and for days ahead were sweet and anxious. We enjoyed care and kindness unknown since the last visit of the Inspector. The brighter among us were carefully primed; the dull ones told to keep quiet, and if they were asked a question, the bright ones were to cut in enthusiastically so as not to give the dull ones a chance. But we knew too and the masters gently hinted at it, that scores could always be settled after the Inspector's visit; there was a limit to how far we could go. I can still remember the smile of blissful satisfaction on the master's face as I once stood in class reciting with great feeling and grand gesticulation:

Twinkle, twinkle, little star,
How I wonder what you are,
Up above the world so high,
Like a diamond in the sky.

The Inspector was so touched by my recitation that he gave me a two-anna piece as a prize. I could do no wrong for days afterwards in class. Throughout my school and college career that was not only the highest but the only distinction I ever achieved.

The visit of a Governor was a great event. It combined everything good in life—a holiday, sweets, fireworks and days of preparations when classes became a pleasure. We made streamers and buntings; mottoes of welcome and felicitation in letters of golden paper on red cloth; decorations of banana stems, mango leaves and marigolds; paper and cloth Union Jacks, and decorated pictures of the King Emperor and the Empress with loyal messages underneath. We learned to sing 'God Save the King' in both Urdu and English to different tunes. The day before the visit, dyers from town came to the school to dye our turbans at school expense, each class in a different colour, pink, saffron, blue, green and others.

The next morning, hours ahead of the time, we lined up in front of school on either side of the road, well scrubbed and washed clean, both the road and the boys. The two rows of brightly coloured turbans gave the effect of a rainbow in the decorated settings of foliage, flowers and coloured paper. In our hands we held the Union Jacks. The air was pleasantly scented by flowers, but our sensitive nostrils took in more keenly the odour of sweetmeats, usually yellow laddus, being prepared in the booths that the halwais had set up in the school. There was going to be a free distribution of sweetmeats, but we had to wait till the Governor had passed.

At last the procession came, led by the police band and marching policemen—we had no army in Gujrat. They were followed by a row of phaetons and victorias, belonging to the local gentry and specially painted and groomed for the occasion. There were then no motor-cars in Gujrat. In the phaeton in front sat the Governor and his Lady Sahiba, both dressed in quaint clothes, though even quainter was the A.D.C. who sat there in a high red plumed helmet. The Governor kept doffing his grey top hat and his wife waved to us and smiled, somewhat immodestly we thought, as we waved our flags and shouted lusty hurras for the Governor, hurras for the King and Queen, hurras for the Empire, hurras for Great Britain. In the phaetons behind came the other Government servants, the local titled gentry of Rai Bahadurs and Khan Bahadurs, members of the Municipal Committee, and some leading zamindars of the district. As soon as the procession had passed, we broke ranks and ran to the school to claim our paper bags with five laddus each. In the evening there would be fireworks in the Company Gardens, and a visit to the railway station to look from a distance at the Governor's special train, painted in a beautiful ivory colour, guarded by soldiers.

There were other great events of this nature, the Victory Day in 1918, and the visit of the King's uncle, the Duke of Connaught. On Victory Day we were marched up to the parade ground where we were given special bronze medals, heard speeches and sang songs about the invincibility of Great Britain, the greatness of our King Emperor, the perfidy and never-in-doubt defeat of Germany. For the Duke of Connaught also medals were struck, sweets distributed and parades organised. We certainly enjoyed these events although they were not really meant for our enjoyment but, I suppose, to inculcate in us a sense of loyalty and attachment. We certainly learned to associate high British dignitaries with a holiday, bright turbans and sweetmeats, but the pomp and importance was of an impersonal kind. With their strange appearance and their distance, they meant very little to us except that they were great people for whom everybody was told to turn out. For the grown-ups it certainly meant more. To be invited to the parties in their honour was a mark of distinction that the important and the aspiring did not want to miss. It was an honour to be invited and proof of your insignificance if you were not. The crested ivory invitation cards to the Governor's party were treasured by some people and kept carefully wrapped in cloth to be displayed to some British official as a mark of acceptance. I wonder if the British felt it to be more than just a formality; they cannot have imagined that the loyal songs we sang and the naive expressions of loyalty from our elders meant much in spite of the elation of the moment.

Later, in England, when I saw an English crowd cheering the King and Queen I sensed at once the differece. A simple remark by someone, such as, 'He is looking well', conveyed a pride and affection that sprung from deeper sources. The Governor's face of purple-veined red hue, or his lady's powdered countenance, gave in any case no indication to us of their real feelings. Our earlier generations looked upon them with gratitude as symbols of justice and peace, but we were born to the 'blessings, of the British Raj' and accepted them as the natural order of life. But even this order was soon to be disturbed, without much warning or build-up, and in the small town of Gujrat life was never to be quite the same until it ended in the cataclysm of 1947 which completely changed the pattern of centuries. For the second time a new idea reached the Punjab through a man from Kathiawar. First came Swami Dayanand's ideal of Arya Samaj, an now Gandhiji's new nationalism.

In Gujrat we felt the tremor only very slightly. Lately, some outsiders had given lectures on a subject that at first we found difficult to understand. The only public lectures we were used to hearing were the Kathas, religious discourses, and in more recent years, the Arya Samaj sermons, but political lectures were something quite new. These visitors spoke about the freedom of India, and this intrigued us; but when they talked in familiar analogies and idiom about the Kal Yug, we saw what they meant. Had it not been prophesied that there were seven eras in India's life and history: there had been a Sat Yug, the era of truth, justice and prosperity; and then there was to be a Kal Yug, an era of falsehood, of demoralisation, of slavery and poverty. This was Kal Yug, when man's word meant nothing, when he could swear falsely in these new courts of law and retain the fruits of falsehood. Man had lost respect for custom, for the guru, for the elders; he could defy his biradari and indulge in practices which yesterday would have forfeited caste and honour. 'An' (a great word meaning much more than just food) and milk and ghee were becoming scarce, where yesterday they flowed through Hindustan in rivers. This wealthy land was now a golden sparrow inside a cage, its feathers plucked one by one. These homely analogies, illustrated by legend and history, registered easily, but not so easily the conclusion to which they were linked, that it was all the fault of the Angrezi Sarkar. We could not readily see how the British were to blame for Kal Yug, which had been foretold so long ago.

Word reached us about the simple, small man from Kathiawar who spoke in the new idiom. Gandhi rechristened India Bharat Mata, a name that evoked nostalgic memories, and associated with Gao Mata, the mother cow. If this struck a chord in the Hindu mind, the Muslims soon responded to the Khilafat call, in support of the deposed Khalifa of Turkey and the name of Madar-i-Hind, mother India. He preached the new language of national pride and spoke about the peace of the British as the peace of slavery. Gradually a new picture began to build in our minds, of India coming out of the Kal Yug into a new era of freedom and plenty, Ram Rajya.

When the news of Gandhi's arrest came there was trouble also in our Gujrat. A young handsome cousin of ours, grandson of granduncle Thakur Das, led some young men to cut telegraph wires and march about the city, until they were picked up and put into the local jail. But in Lahore we heard that martial law was declared. Our mother happened to be in Lahore just at the time on a long-deferred visit to a cousin of our father, and suddenly she found herself cut off from home. She was not to be daunted and made several attempts at getting out but each time the soldiers sent her back to the city. I suppose she looked too simple and innocent a young woman to be suspected of breaking the martial law with any political intentions. Although no trains were running, she argued with the British soldiers that she must get to the station and sit there and wait. Knowing her, I think if she had got past them she would have walked home to Gujrat, eighty miles away.

All kinds of rumours floated out of Lahore of beatings and mass arrests, of people being made to crawl on thier bellies on the roads, of students made to walk every day to Lahore Cantonment six miles away in the hot sun just to salute the flag. And then came the news of the Jallianwala Bagh at Amritsar. We heard that General Dyer took a position with his machine-guns at the only entrance of this densely packed sunken garden surrounded by tall old mansions, and fired and fired till his ammunition was exhausted. The crowd heaved in a blind mass, it climbed up the trees and over the shortrun of a low wall, but the guns kept gathering it back into a heap. At last, it was said, when there were no more bullets left to feed the over-heated guns, Dyer and his soldiers, tired, picked up their tools and went away, leaving the garden to wailing widows and orphans searching the heaps. Triumphantly Dyer declared that he had the whole rebellious city at his mercy and felt like reducing it to ashes, but then took pity on it and refrained. Truth and rumour spread like lightening.

People in Gujrat were stunned and fumbled back in their memory to Nadirshah. But Nadirshah was just an adventurer, a bandit who claimed he had an excuse: some of his soldiers had been murdered after Delhi had capitulated, and the order of general massacre was the punishment he prescribed for Delhi breaking its word. But this Sarkar was different; it had been kind and benign, it had ruled for sixty years without the traditional marks of power. Why this sudden change? After sixty years we in Gujrat had almost forgotten that we were ruled by the British. In the city you never saw an Englishman except some rare salesman throwing free cigarettes out of a tonga to promote the habit of smoking. You had to go out of the city gates into the Civil Station to see one of the three or four Englishmen posted in Gujrat, the Deputy Commissioner, the Superintendent of Police, sometimes the Executive Engineer, possibly the Sessions Judge, and perhaps the Padre Sahib. Indians were already becoming senior officials. In this atmosphere of calm acceptance the banging of the mailed fist seemed strange. Nobody had taken much notice of what the politicians had said, it was the sort of platitudes we were used to from our elders. They had always said: 'India was once the land of milk and ghee, look at this Kal Yug now.' And if some spoke about freedom and equality, was not that what our English books also taught?

There was now growing up a third generation of Punjabis, educated in English thought, who were beginning to think accordingly for themselves. My father's generation of professional men read the news and editorials in the Tribune and though they spoke discreetly, they began to think about politics for the first time. Everybody discussed; even we boys in school learned new names like Gandhi, Tilak, Lajpat Rai, Ali Brothers, Mother India and Azadi. Was a change under way? In their inevitable succession dynasties and kingdoms rose and fell like tides in a sea. The wise began to wag their heads again and utter old wisdom. When a Hakam, a ruler, is harsh out of proportion to the occasion, it can only be that he is afraid and unsure. If this does not work he will have to be harsher still the next time until he exhausts himself to no avail. Somehow these new Hakams did not look the kind who would relish harshness for very long. To the Punjab change was nothing new; it had been a recurring phenomenon for so long that the Punjabis had learnt to smell it like the distant rain on their parched and dusty soil.

In such simple terms we discussed and reasoned as the new movement spread in the Punjab, though the non-co-operation and satyagraha of the next few years somehow did not affect us much in Gujrat. There were occasional political meetings and hartals, some picketing of the one foreign liquor shop and the many cloth stores, but generally Gujrat took little interest in politics and continued its medieval tempo.

CHAPTER EIGHT

Engagement, Wedding

While we were living in Gujrat mother and father arranged the marriage of my uncle, who had now settled in a law practice.

Having taken his time over passing his degree he was now nearly twenty-four, an unusual age among us to remain unmarried. A lot of people were asking questions about the delay, and my mother felt that his marriage could not be postponed any longer. If the elders had had their way he would have been married long ago, while he was still studying, but times were changing and it was in accordance with father's own ideas that uncle preferred to wait for his marriage till he was settled in life. To the old way of thinking this was irrelevant. You married when you came of age and not when you began to earn. Marriage and earning were two separate things. Marriage was a social, familial and religious obligation, while earning was a matter of circumstance. To allow my uncle to remain unmarried till he was twenty-four was something that had never happened in our biradari. But now that uncle was earning, father agreed with mother that marriage was opportune, and this was made known.

In an arranged marriage there are many cosiderations which thoughtful parents take into account. The girl should of course be a Khatri, and a Bahri, and she should possess some education which in those days only meant that she should not be illiterate. As my uncle was well-built and tall, the girl should also be of good physique, but as he was of a pukka colour, a euphemism for being dark, the girl ought to be fair. Temperamentally she should be sober and serious, because my uncle had been wild in his college days. In short, what the parents were looking for was a girl who possessed his good points and compensated for his weaknesses. A new consideration that had developed in our class was that she should belong to a family that had taken to professions.

We began to receive many feelers from in and around Gujrat. Many of the girls my mother had seen herself or heard about from others, but as the boy was in her opinion accomplished, and as she was not worried about any other boys or girls of even near-marriageable age in our family, she could afford to be discriminating and finicky. Why should she not be, everyone agreed. The boy was good-looking, he was earning and had a well placed brother and uncle, even if he had no parents. If he had been wayward at college, a reputation that had reached Gujrat, it only meant he was experienced and knew the world. Nevertheless mother was advised not to wait too long, because too many refusals would make people talk. Just as my mother was beginning to relent, an offer came that interested her.

In Peroshah, a small town not far from Gujrat, in the direction of Bhimber and Kashmir, there was a Bahi Khatri family of the caste of Vohra. The father had recently retired from Government service as a revenue officer. From a small beginning he had risen high and had been awarded the title of Rai Bahadur. He was a personal friend and protege of the Governor of Punjab, O'Dwyer, whose munshi and companion he had been in his youth. Both had served and risen together. One of his sons had been to America for education. The girl was excellent in every way and the match most flattering to us. My mother spoke to father about it and suggested that we should call in the family barber, a Muslim, respectfully referred to by the title of Raja to open negotiations.

Raja heard the details carefully and offered to travel to Peroshah. When he reached there, he first approached some other family barbers, and then spent some time in the bazaar putting tactful questions about his mission. Having satisfied himself he repaired to Rai Bahadur's house, where he was received with courtesy when he declared that he was Raja to some of the respected families of Gujrat. His mission was obvious, though he was in no hurry to come to the subject. He fully savoured the importance attached to his errand and the consequent hospitality. He was treated with great respect because of his ability to make or mar the reputation of two families. As he smoked his hooka, he wisely discoursed on the subject of worldliness, bringing out carefully the satisfaction to parents of possessing good children. Such satisfaction of course was only really fulfilled when the children were suitably and happily married. Rai Bahadur and his visitors listened with suitable appreciative exclamations of agreement.

When the other visitors had left, Rai Bahadur asked Raja in confidence where he had come from. Raja gave only enough information to satisfy Rai Bahadur; he was not going to rush in with all details, for there was still the morning's hospitality to think of. In any case, both sides had to proceed delicately in such matters, with proper decorum and lack of curiosity. There must be no hasty or premature enquiries that might be taken for anxiety or eagerness. After that Rai Bahadur left him with instructions to his servants to make him comfortable for the night. Inside, he spoke to his wife who agreed that the proposal should be pursued.

In the morning when Raja had amply breakfasted on hot milk, parathas and sweets he belched appreciatively and pulled thoughtfully at his hooka. Instead of coming to the subject he launched on a well worded eulogy of Rai Bahadur, his name, his fame and his family. Having put his host at ease he began to talk about our own family, and eventually he landed on the exact spot, that is uncle. I think my uncle would have enjoyed listening; it would have appealed to his sense of humour. All his weaknesses were delicately turned into an individual kind of strength. He had spent many years at college, not just failing his examinations, but because the professors were so fond of him that they did not want him to go. He was an ornament of the college they could ill afford to lose. He had the skin of Lord Krishna, the blue of dusk. God had taken away his parents but amply compensated him with a brother and sister-in-law who had brought him up as their first child. His brother was a great engineer who had built the Bullokee Dam single-handed, and to the farmers in the new canal areas he was God.

In the afternoon, after further consultations inside, Rai Bahadur told Raja in simple words with emotion behind them, that they were very flattered at the proposition, and he was willing to give his youngest child, his favourite in old age, to us. He was sure she would be happy in her future home. He thanked Raja and praised him much, genuinely and feelingly.

Raja returned to Gujrat in a tonga the same evening, a journey that he would ordinarily have done on foot. He was much satisfied with himself and his delicate handling of the mission, and sent word to us that he had much to tell and would present himself in the morning. Again, Raja was not the indelicate man to hurry; but the message said enough to satisfy us. In the morning he came to see father and gave a detailed account of his mission. Suitably rewarded, he went away blessing both families and setting great expectations on such a union, and no doubt including the hope of richer rewards for himself at the time of the wedding.

After sounding uncle, who agreed with due modesty and said that he would be guided by their wishes, our mother decided to visit Peroshah herself. Accompanied by an elderly aunt she travelled up a few days later and arrived at the house of Rai Bahadur where they were already expected. My mother slowly came to the subject.

Young and inexperienced she proceeded without the sureness of Raja, but being in loco parentis gave her the natural dignity of her role. Mother praised uncle and Rai Bahadur's wife likewise praised her daughter. In fact, the very sweets my mother had eaten were prepared by the girl, and the cushion on which she was sitting had been embroidered by her. She was a talented, educated girl. Nowadays boys demanded education, and so girls had to be given some schooling; not too much, for that made them too forward and interfered with their domesticity. On the cushion not only had the girl embroidered the word welcome in Hindi but, it might be noticed, in English as well. They believed in bringing up their children well. It was so necessary nowadays. And so the girl's mother went on, not knowing how to stop, till my mother delicately suggested a desire to see the girl. This was the crucial moment.

All mothers have their natural pride, however anxious they may be to find a suitable boy for their daughter, to discharge their debt in life, to send her to a good home where one day she will be Grihalakshmi, goddess of the house. Though mothers like to think their daughters perfect, there is always the lurking fear that the stranger, a mother herself, may be so proud of her son, that her own jewel of a girl may not appear good enough. There will be other offers, if God wishes, just as good and possibly even better, but each refusal hurts the mother's pride.

The daughter had been sent away the moment these strangers entered the house. She had guessed the purpose of their call and was nervously trying to do some work in another room while her future was being decided. A hundred questions darted anxiously through her innocent mind, and as she was agitatedly trying to piece together her thoughts, her mother called. 'Prepare some sherbet and bring it out here for the guests, my son.' Fond parents in affectionate moments referred to their daughters as son, putra. Shyly, with the mantle half hiding her childish face, the girl walked up to my mother with a shining bronze jug full of sugared water. My mother had been carefully watching her as she walked across the courtyard to see if she limped or had any other physical defect. And now she scrutinised her from her feet upward to make sure that she was sound of limb. The girl bowed before my mother. She was simply dressed, without any jewellery, as became a virgin. She wore a plain white salwar, a red kameez of a subdued pattern, a home-dyed green dupatta. On her slender wrists she had coloured glass bangles and in her ears thin gold rings, more to keep the pierced lobes open than as ornament. Her black hair was parted in the middle and tied into a single plait woven with a black cord. Her figure was childish, her breasts immature, and although she was seventeen mother thought she looked less. She had the demure simplicity of a well-bred girl. Her face, my mother thought, was beautiful, and flushed in shyness.

'What is her name?' asked mother.

'We call her Savitri,' her mother answered.

My mother deliberated for a moment and then said, 'It is a beautiful name and suits her well. We haven't got a Savitri in our home.' That settled the matter.

☆

In due course the horoscopes of uncle and Savitri were shown to the pandits to make sure of their compatibility. We were assured that the gods agreed to the match. Here was a youth whom the sun had blessed with power, and Venus, with us a male, with manliness and vigour; a girl who would run her home wisely, blessed by Jupiter. On an appointed day Rai Bahadur's family came to Gujrat to offer shagan, the ceremonial earnest of betrothal. From the girl's side only the male relations came. They brought with them a procession of men carrying large trays containing sweets, fresh and dried fruits, which must include coconuts, almonds and dried dates. They also gave one hundred and one silver rupees in cash. One gave cash according to one's capacity, but the amount given on all auspicious occasions was in odd sums of eleven, twenty-one, thirty-one, fifty-one or one hundred and one rupees, the only exception to this rule being twenty-five rupees. If the engagement was broken the cash was returned to the girl's parents. We received the guests with grave courtesy, and my uncle bowed and touched the feet of Rai Bahadur who put a saffron tilak mark on his future son-in-law's forehead. Other relations from both sides exchanged tilak, and Rai Bahadur gave token amounts of a few rupees to each of our relations present. With further exchange of courtesies the guests departed. The sweets were later distributed by us among our relations and biradari in proportion to closeness of relationship, and to the biradari according to the adopted practice. The horoscopes were again consulted to fix an auspicious date for the wedding.

In the old days girls were betrothed at an early age, though the wedding took place when they reached puberty. In fact girls were sometimes promised by their parents as babies in arms to a family with whom they were on close terms. An elderly lady once told me that she was engaged even before she was born, and the reason was quite accidental. Her mother had once gone to some good family friends with her baby girl of two. She was a pretty child, and as she played with the four-year old boy of the other family, both mothers looked at them proudly. The boy's mother said that she must have this little girl as her future daughter-in-law. The girl's mother agreed to the proposal in principle, but as she felt that a difference of only two years in age was too small she promised that she would give them her next daughter instead. A couple of years later she produced another daughter, the said lady. The difference of four years between her and the boy was considered suitable, and so they were engaged.

Like all mothers, almost from the day Savitri was born her mother had begun to collect her dowry, but about a month before the wedding preparations started in real earnest. Tailors, embroiderers, furniture makers, coppersmiths and goldsmiths arrived. The confectioners came with their enormous vessels and lit big fires to make maunds of sweets for the wedding feast and for distributing. Arrangements had to be made for receiving the wedding party, putting them up for three nights and feeding and entertaining them. Rai Bahadur was the leading man of Peroshah, and as this was the last wedding in the family everything had to be done in great style. Weddings were exhausting affairs for the girl's family in more ways than one.

The first ceremony after the shagan was to send bhocha to our mother. They sent her some money, and a set of clothes, some ornaments, copra, dried dates, rice, sugar and money. Some days later they sent another set of gifts known as gad, consisting of a heavy mantle with gold border, some lighter clothes and dried fruits, rice and sugar. In fact, from the day of shagan this interminable traffic of gifts in cash and kind from the girl's people had begun. All through her married life a girl will receive gifts from her parents, brothers and uncles—when her children are born, at the various ceremonies for the children, and when they get married.

As the day of the wedding drew near relations began to arrive. First came the women and children, later the men. The local invitations were sent through their Raja who called on each home and left two tablets of soap. This was an old custom to enable people to wash their clothes for coming to the wedding. The whole house was full of guests, and there was much confusion. The elderly women used to relish the opportunity to ventilate old grievances, real or imagined. All relations were assembled and it was a chance too good to be missed.

A grand family row sent away everybody pleased and satisfied.

☆

At nights, women and girls used to gather in the large courtyard and sing to the accompaniment of a small, oblong, two-sided drum, called dholki. The songs were traditional, handed down the generations, and were known as suhag de geet, to wish the girl a happy married life. They were in dialogue form.

Father : *My daughter, why are you standing behind the sandalwood tree?*

Daughter : *I am standing here, father, because I want a good marriage.*

Father : *My daughter, what kind of husband do you want?*

Daughter : *Father, among the stars as the moon stands bright;*
Beside the moon as Krishna stands bright;
I want a match like him.

The girl then turns to her brothers, and to her uncles in similar refrain.

Till late in the night the beat of the dholki and the singing continued while the girl sat quietly in one corner in a reverie. She had not seen her betrothed, but these songs seemed to reassure her.

There was a series of ceremonies to perform during the last two days: the gana, mayan, shanti path, choora and the wedding proper. Savitri was dressed in simple old clothes, wrapped in an old blanket and made to sit in a back room while excitement and confusion mounted in the house. Raw sugar and salted cakes were placed in her lap. Mouli, the auspicious thread, was tied round her wrist and she was told by her girl friends, who were now in constant attendance, to tie the so called gana really tight because it would have to be opened by her husband when he took her home. The girls smeared her hands and feet with henna, and put the paste on their own hands and feet too. They also made tears in Savitri's old clothes. These two last days were called mayan, and special songs were sung:

Blessed be the mother who bore such a daughter,
'In old and soiled' clothes in mayan she put her.

Early on the wedding morning, before the stars had faded in the sky, men came into the ladies' courtyard to make the vedi, a pavilion of leaves and flowers, in which the wedding ceremony would take place that night. They brought four big banana plants and a lot of foliage. The banana plants were put as pillars, and a top covering was made of twigs and mango foliage. Inside the pavilion were placed two new square reed baskets, of the kind that vegetable-sellers used, upside down to serve as stools. The vedi had to be completed before sunrise. During the day women and children continued to decorate it with flowers and garlands, sprinkle it with red powder and hang coconuts on it.

After sunrise there was the ceremony of shanti path, the way of peace, at which prayers were said so that all might go well at the wedding. Savitri came out of the house and sat in the vedi, still in her old clothes. Garlands of cowrie shells and copra were tied to her wrists. Her mother's brother and his wife brought the choora, a set of red ivory bangles reaching from wrist to elbow. They were to remain on her arms as a sign of her newly-wed status for a whole year, so that wherever she went people would know she was a new bride. After a year the choora would be taken off ceremoniously, but should the husband die before the year was out she would break the bangles herself on her arms. She was anointed with oil, and a dried date was put into her mouth. After this ceremony Savitri got up and returned to her room. Since the previous night everyone in the house had been fasting. Now the fast was broken by all except by Savitri and her parents who would continue to abstain from food until the wedding ceremony was over.

Savitri never took off her choora!

The evening came, the time to prepare her for marriage. Savitri had not bathed or changed clothes for two days. A young married couple were chosen to go to a well with the pandit. There they did puja and drew a pitcher of water. In this blessed water Savitri was bathed. After that the women busied themselves with the pleasant task of making-up and dressing the bride. She was anointed with sandalwood oil, and her hair was dressed into long plaits; her hands and feet had already been dyed red with henna; her lips were stained with red juice of wattle bark; her eye lashes darkened with kohl. She was now dressed in red clothes, rich and beautiful, for red is a bride's colour in the Punjab. She was bedecked with gold jewellery from head to foot, one special piece for each part of the body. On her head was a round cup-shaped ornament, chownk, which lifted her dupatta gracefully. There were two smaller pieces, called phool, flowers, on either side. All three were delicately worked and each had a blue stone studded on top. On each side of the hair parting were flat, broad pieces, twitarian, with rows of little pendants, joined over the parting with a fine gold chain. Suspended from the hair with another gold chain was shingar patti that rested on her forehead like an inverted new moon. In her ears were heavy rings in the shape of inverted cups with pendants, called jhumke, and in one of the nostrils a clove-shaped pin, called by that name, laong. Around her neck was a flat ornament, known as gulu band, and a long garland of old English sovereigns alternating with small round buds of gold. She had five rings, one on each finger, each ring connected with delicate gold chains converging to bracelets round the wrists. On her arms was the new bright red chọora, and round the wrists she had gold bangles and bracelets. Above the elbow she wore a single heavy bangle with the ends in the shape of a tiger's head. She also wore flat anklets called paonchies, which rested gracefully over her feet; on her toes she wore little bells which tinkled as she walked. She wore a red velvet salwar and kameez with heavy gold embroidery round the collar and the cuffs, the hem of the shirt and on the edges of the salwar. Her dupatta, the mantle, was also red with a gold border. She was wrapped in a red phulkari of the bagh design. Tall though Savitri was, she was weighed down by the heavy clothes and jewellery. Tired by the strain of the last two mayan days and the fasting, nervous at the ordeal of the long wedding ceremony and of the departure and all that lay in store for her, unknown and unfamiliar, her knees turned to water as she tried to rise on her feet. She was supported and led into her room. Women looked at her in admiration; her girl friends in envy. After the two days in old clothes, without a bath, she now blossomed out like a flower. The old women said that mayan was a good custom; it helped to produce a contrast and it also rested the girl.

Back in her room, Savitri waited through the long tedious hours till midnight, which the pandit had declared as the auspicious moment for the wedding ceremony.

☆

While all this was going on in Peroshah, we were also busy in Gujrat. A month before father had sent out invitations. The English custom of printed invitation cards had already reached our town, and we asked the small local press to print the cards. The text was in Urdu and invited you to collect at our house on the afternoon of the wedding day and proceed with the party to Peroshah where there would be sehra bandi in the evening; milni later at the bride's house, followed by dinner; and the wedding ceremony at midnight. The barat would stay in Peroshah for three nights and return on the morning of the fourth day. In the bottom left-hand corner was a pompous though cryptic R.S.V.P. which was the latest superfluous imported refinement. It was superfluous for no one ever refused a wedding invitation. Each card was sprinkled with saffron and stained red to mark the auspiciousness of the occasion. Lists were carefully made of all those attending and the total number was discussed, almost negotiated, with the Rai Bahadur's family. We had over two hundred persons to invite. Raja went to see Rai Bahadur who, though welcoming such a large number, protested that Peroshah was after all a small place and it would be difficult to put up so many guests for three nights and to do their very best. Eventually, a number was agreed upon. The girl's side nevertheless allowed for more, knowing full well that there would be last-minute invitations, and people would bring along their own guests.

Guests from outside Gujrat had to be put up at our house and the houses of our relations and friends. The near-relations arrived with their families days ahead, and our house was as full as the bride's. On the bride's side they prepared a dowry, daj; on our side we were busy preparing clothes and jewellery for the bride, called vari. In addition, sets of clothes had to be made for presenting to the bridegroom's sisters. We also performed ceremonies of shant, gana and mayan; and of course we had gifts to send to Peroshah needed for the ceremonies in the bride's house.

On the wedding day all the men assembled, dressed in new clothes, happy and eager, at the tonga stand by my grand-uncle's house outside the town, to set out for Peroshah. All the tongas in town and from the neighbouring places had been hired to take the barat. This was before the convenient motor-buses had arrived. The barat was accompanied by a brass band, the fireworks people carrying their stock of crackers and contraptions of bamboos with spiral fireworks, and people carrying gas-lamps. But the most colourful sight of all was the horse on which my uncle was to ride that night to his bride's house. They had decorated the horse in advance, always a mare for this purpose. She had been specially washed and groomed till her skin shone when her owner brought her to our house. She was caparisoned and saddled magnificently, and auspicious coloured threads were tied to her mane and to the reins. When the mare stood in front of our house, she was fussed and decorated, and our aunts, the bridegroom's sisters, brought a large tray full of grams covered with silver leaf and fed her. The horse was having its day too, for it was carrying a bridegroom, who has the status of a king, and a king's mount has its own importance. Before leaving the house, the last ceremony was the bag pharai, when our uncle was handed the reins of the horse by his sisters. He had to give them some money for that and they sang the song of bag pharai:

Brother, what will you give for holding your reins
What are you going to give your sisters.

And with blades of grass dipped in saffron the sisters sprinkled him before he left the house.

The barat arrived in Peroshah in the afternoon and was met by relations and friends of Savitri's family and escorted to the dharamshala, the temple inn. Here they rested and were given sweet drinks and light refreshments. Many of them were going to stay at the dharamshala, others were taken to the janj ghar, a hall built by the community for the reception of barats. Important guests like my uncle and our family were put up at one of Rai Bahadur's own houses. The whole village had turned up to see the barat and to make critical comments on the groom and his party. After all, the Rai Bahadur was somebody in Peroshah and they wanted to satisfy themselves that his Savitri was going to a house of equivalent status. They took the customary privilege of making caustic comments just sufficiently loud for us to hear. Some wags in the barat matched their wit with the locals, and there was much amusement all round. 'If you have any other girls bring them out; it is not often that you in Peroshah have the honour of getting grooms from Gujrat,' shouted one of the baratis. To this one of the locals retorted, 'Go away, we have heard the reputation of Gujrati goondas; what surprises us is that Rai Bahadur agreed. This boy looks all right, but as for the rest of them, they look as if there is going to be a famine in Peroshah after they leave.' And so the bantering went on.

Tall, trim and upstanding, uncle Dwarka Prashad looked a striking figure dressed in the classical robes of a khatri warrior king. The old custom is that if a king meets a wedding party on its way, it is he who dismounts as a mark of deference. On his head he wore a silver crown over his turban, on which was tied gold braid and then another garland of roses, jasmines and marigolds that fell over his face in a cascade of gold threads and flowers. It was called sehra. It was blessed first by the pandit and then by grand-uncle, followed by all the baratis as they came forward to touch it and wish him well. He wore a long red, buttonless cloak, tied with tabs and trimmed on the edges with gold; on his legs a pair of tight trousers; on his feet gold-embroidered Punjabi Pothowari shoes with turned up spurs in front; and around his waist a sword in a red velvet scabbard with silver mountings. Behind him in the saddle sat my elder brother, for according to custom the groom rode to the bride's house accompanied by his best man, always a young brother, cousin or nephew.

Through the streets of Peroshah, headed by the brass band and men holding gas-lamps over their heads, while fire crackers were exploding, the colourful procession with our uncle sitting on his horse wended its way by a circuitous route to cover the main streets. Some people carrying silver carafes were sprinkling rose water. On the way we stopped by a jandi tree, where uncle alighted from his horse and with his sword made a ceremonial cut in the gnarled hard wood, a custom meant to test the khatri groom's prowess and the sharpness of his sword. In the old days he was supposed to slice the stem or a thick branch of the tree with one blow. However great our hero-worship for our athletic uncle, his khatri skill with the sword was small, and he made the merest scratch. The procession continued midst much noise and music. As we reached the Rai Bahadur's house the procession solemnly came to a halt. Awaiting us, under an archway of leaves and flowers, stood the male members of Rai Bahadur's family, headed by the old man himself, a handsome figure dressed in the pink turban customary for the bride's father, a white cloak-like double-breasted long coat, which bore an influence of the English frock-coat, white salwar and Punjabi shoes. Deferentially behind him stood his brothers, brothers-in-law, sons and other relations in that order. We also formed in similar order. In the absence of a grandfather, we had grand-uncle at our head. There was a short ceremony of anointing the groom with oil, as the two processions stood facing each other in silence, and then followed milni, the ceremony of a formal introduction of the two families.

Rai Bahadur moved forward from the bride's side; from ours our grand-uncle stepped forward. They embraced each other, and Rai Bahadur put a garland round grand-uncle's neck, and then took out a saffron-stained envelope containing some money, which after passing twice round grand-uncle's head he presented to him. They were followed by Rai Bahadur's brothers, in order of seniority, meeting our father and his brothers. According to prior agreement a selected list of relations did milni with each other, and in proportion to their importance our side received money from their opposite numbers. At this stage, while the two groups stood facing each other and uncle still sat on the horse, a sehra was recited. A friend of the family with poetic pretensions had composed a poem, also known as the sehra, in which he eulogised uncle, felicitated the company, and wished him on everybody's behalf a long and happy married life. The poem, written in illuminated letters and framed in a colourful Persian border, was presented to uncle.

After milni the groom alighted from his horse, which in all its splendour was taken away. Led by womenfolk Savitri, with her head bent and veiled, came forward to receive the groom and put a garland round his neck. She was then led back. The groom was taken inside the house and surrounded by the women and girls who put him through a quiz-ceremony of teasing him and testing his wit. The mother-in-law, sisters-in-law and others put him questions which he had to answer in verse. Usually the grooms were coached by the womenfolk at home. Some were very bold and improvised answers which made the girls giggle and then go into peals of laughter. Such grooms were very popular. News would soon reach the bride how the groom was faring: girls would run in and give exaggerated accounts of what he looked like, his wit and intelligence. The women pressed money into his hand, and the ordeal over, he was allowed to leave.

In the courtyard the barat was being fed, and how the wedding guests used to eat! They would sit in long rows on the ground and in front of them metal trays and cups were placed. The food was cooked by professional cooks of Jhewar caste, but never served by them, for in those days it would have been a mark of disrespect to have the guests served by hired men. Members of the family and biradari would personally wait upon them. Nor did the girl's side sit down with the guests; they always had their meal afterwards. It was also a custom to serve sweets on the first or the second afternoon, sometimes in a khurli, which literally meant a manger. White sheets would be spread in front of the guests, and the sweets piled from one end to the other, like filling a manger. There was naturally many times more than they could consume, and the guests were therefore given coloured silk handkerchiefs in which they could take away what they could not finish. The Khurli was very expensive and few could afford it. It therefore created a sensation which was remembered for years.

After dinner most of the guests left, and preparations began for the wedding ceremony which was due to start after midnight. The pandit came with trays of incense rubbed in ghee, holy water from the Ganges, puffed rice, wheat flour, honey and sacred thread. He sat in front of the hawab kund, an iron receptacle in which the sacrificial fire was burning. In the four corners around the fire he arranged piles of fruit and burning incense. The time was now drawing near, and close relations sat down on the carpets spread on the floor. The pandit was seated in front of the fire, and on the other side the bride and groom were led up. Swathed in the red phulkari, with her red mantle drawn low over the face, Savitri was barely visible. Demureness combined with nerves and fatigue made her look like the victim of a sacrifice as she was escorted to the fire, affectionately supported, according to custom, by her maternal uncle. Our uncle walked up with not a great deal more confidence. They both sat down on the upturned reed baskets facing east, she on his left, with the side of her phulkari tied to his sword, a symbolic tying together of their fates, her honour represented by her head covering and his protection by the sword.

Savitri had still not seen her bridegroom and was anxious to know what he looked like, yet she dared not raise her mantle or look up. She could only see his knees and calves covered in tight trousers. They looked sturdy. She could tell that he was tall, but was he good-looking? Was he going to make a good husband like her father, who still affectionately called her mother rani? She was already tied to him and his for ever. Many years lay ahead, happy years probably, as most marriages were happy. Her mind became bolder as her thoughts ran on. Would she bear him many children? At this she felt shy and guilty and was awakened from her reverie by the fire which rose into a flame as the pandit finished the first mantra with a long intoned 'om swaha', and we all picked up a handful of incense and threw it into the fire.

The pandit went on chanting the mantras, and the fire would flare up each time he finished one. The ceremony, which lasted for many hours, seemed to consist of three parts: the worship of the fire by the bride and the groom, the vows, and ritual symbolising the union. The vows ran like this:

Savitri's father to the bridegroom:
I give you my daughter, whom I have brought up with great love and affection, as a gift to you. Look after her; that is your duty.

Uncle:
I accept her. She is half of my body. I will look after her.

Savitri to her bridegroom:
I offer you my body, my mind and my possessions. I will serve you; you are my master; you are everything to me, after God. I will never look at another man. Apart from you, all other men will be like father, brother or son to me.

After the vows they both go up, stiff and tired, having sat rigidly and self-consciously for long hours. Tied to each other, now man and wife, they walked twice round the fire, he in front and she behind him in an anti clock-wise direction. They then walked twice round the fire again, now she in front and he following. This ceremony seemed to establish their equality, each leading the other twice round the sacred fire. They then embarked on the symbolic journey of life, the yatra of seven steps; one step for health, another for prosperity; a third for children and so on.

Dawn was breaking as the long vedic marriage came to an end. By now a number of baratis had joined, having rested a few hours after the sumptuous meal. As the ceremony finished, Savitri's brother gave her parched rice; she gave it to her husband, who threw it into the fire. It now remained for the two family priests verbally to witness the marriage. Each purohit on behalf of his family recited its lineage: Dwarka Prasad, son of Maya Das, son of Suhawa Mal....

Savitri and Dwarka Prasad, total strangers still, were now man and wife, married in ancient vedic rites, without any written word. They sat again on the reed stools while people showered rose petals on them. Everybody got up and one by one walked up to them to give them blessings, ashirvad. They both thanked with joined hands. As they got up rose petals scattered on the floor. Savitri was led away into the house, and my uncle walked back to where we were staying. They were man and wife, but they would not be together till she reached our home in Gujrat. The ordeal of ceremonies was not over yet; her worst trial, leaving her ancestral home, was yet to come.

When the guests left Savitri's father and mother, who had not eaten for over a day, broke their fast. Having completed the kanya dan, the gifts of his daughter, the father was now given some milk. The others complimented the father on having performed his duty well, and the daughter thanked him for what he had done for her.

Others : *The father drinks milk out of a bowl, and the brother bathes in Ganga.*

Daughter : *Bless, you, father, for spending your earnings on me.*
Bless you, mother, who give birth to me.

In this refrain the songs continued.

On the last day, Savitri's dowry was displayed. In the courtyard charpoys were covered with durries and on these were arrayed the clothes, jewellery, linen, household utensils and cash. There was furniture, a big bed, a low chair and some modern pieces for her new home. The dowry also contained phulkaris which went down from mother to daughter, and some inherited clothes, but these had become merely symbolic because no one wore them any longer. The bride's friends and relations and nearly half Peroshah came to look at the daj. The elder women examined it with critical eyes and stored every article in their memories: the number of suits of clothes for Savitri and her husband, their quality and value; the workmanship and the weight and value of the gold in the jewellery; the number of utensils, their metal and weight. Later they would discuss it and compare it with other dowries. The most important points to note were the gold and the cash.

As people walked around and praised the dowry, Savitri's mother and father accepted the compliments with the simple and modest answer: 'This is nothing'. Our grand-uncle on our behalf thanked the Rai Bahadur in well-chosen words and said, 'How can we take all this; you have given us so much'. Savitri's mother gave him some money as daj dekhai, dowry showing. The women sang a song to express the thanks of the groom's father:

You have filled our house inside, outside, in front and behind;
And the beautiful daughter you have given us will be its ornament.

Later in the day a procession came from our side carrying vari, gifts of clothes and jewellery for the bride and the groom. It was taken indoors and examined carefully by the womenfolk who selected one suit of clothes and jewellery for the bride to wear at the time of her departure. After that one of our uncles took charge of both the vari and the daj, made a list of all the articles in the daj and had them packed, ready for leaving the next day. The departure was set for ten o'clock in the morning.

The packing and carting away of Savitri's daj was a sign to her parents and family that the time for parting had come at last. For days her father and mother had been too busy to think of anything but the needs of the moment. Now the wedding was over, the daj on which they had worked for months was packed and gone. Tomorrow Savitri would also leave, and with her all the guests. The house that had been full of people, noise, music and happiness would suddenly be quiet. Rai Bahadur had not kept good health of late, but the hustle and bustle had kept him active and busy. With this sudden sense of anti-climax he felt old and tired; life would be empty without any children in the house, and Savitri who had come much later than the others was his favourite.

That night the barat had an early dinner, without the usual liveliness. Back in their room for their first early night's rest, Savitri's mother and father tried to console each other with the satisfaction of a job done, of a debt discharged. The thought of the parting in the morning left them both with a hollow feeling. Savitri's mother pulled herself up and with a mother's fortitude began to talk of the future. Savitri is lucky, Dwarka Prashad is a fine young man, handsome, healthy; a man who will take good care of our girl. She will have children, and living so close she will come and visit us often. The house will have children's laughter again and they themselves will go to Gujrat frequently to see her. And with these thoughts, combining sadness with courage, they went into a fitful sleep.

Savitri lay huddled in her bed, with many other women in the room. They were all tired and slept soundly, but her confused thoughts kept her awake. A girl of barely eighteen, brought up in simple surroundings, she knew no more about life than a child. She had always been close to her mother, as the only child in the home for many years. She had played with other girls and had hardly been conscious of growing, till the other day when two women arrived from Gujrat and she was told in advance by her mother that they were coming to look at her. Her mother had explained that she was now a grown-up girl and could not expect to stay with her parents much longer, however hard it would be for them to lose her. And now she was the wife of this stranger whose face she still had not seen. Tomorrow she would leave her home for good, to return to it only occasionally as a visitor. She lay wide awake, half afraid and half curious, with sadness sweeping her as the night grew shorter and the hour of parting came nearer. She tried to console herself with the thought of returning home next week with her husband; the joy of meeting again her parents and friends; the importance of coming home as a married woman, an object of curiosity and admiration. But fear and sadness soon returned.

The household was up very early. Last evening's sadness had given way to the excitement of the biggest moment of the wedding, the departure of the doli, the bride's palanquin. Friends and neighbours were collecting to see the bride leaving. The village dai, the midwife who had brought her into the world, was present to accompany her, as the custom was, on her first venture into a new world. Savitri felt consoled by this thoughtful custom. Till she returned home next week the dai would be close to her. 'My child, do not be afraid, I will be with you the whole time; you will talk to me about everything; I will be your mother.' With these words the dai encouraged Savitri. 'I brought you into the world and I will now launch you on your new life.'

The palanquin bearers arrived with the doli. Covered with a red cloth with white trimmings, it was placed near the front door. Inside Savitri surrounded by her parents and relations was waiting for the final moment. They all blessed her, and her father and mother gave her their last words of advice. 'Beta, you have to go now. You are going to your new home, and though you will not forget us, you must think of your husband and your new home first. You should make a dutiful wife.' These were Rai Bahadur's last words. Her mother held her close to her breast, loath to leave. She put some money into her lap, and one by one her sisters and aunts came up and hugged her and gave money. At last her maternal uncle gathered her in his arms and with faltering steps Savitri walked up to the doli. Her mother and other women moved forward to take a last look, before the flap of the doli was lowered. Savitri cried as if her heart would break. Her mother could not contain herself any longer, and sobbed. The women chanted the farewell song of the doli:

Father you have put your daughter in the doli;
People shower blessings on you.
Bless you father for all you have showered on me;
Bless you mother who bore me.
They are taking me away, father, in the doli.

We on our side stood silently gazing at Savitri's parents. All eyes were wet, even ours. Grand-uncle, erect and venerable with his white beard, stepped forward and made a short valediction. 'Rai Bahadur, you must not be sad; this is not the moment for sadness. You have discharged your duty well; you should be proud. We are happy to take your daughter away; she will be the light of our home. Your loss is our gain.' Rai Bahadur bowed his head in gratitude at these words. They embraced each other.

'Let us go, it is getting late,' said grand-uncle, and at that the bearers lifted the doli by its poles and the procession moved on. Savitri's people walked behind the doli, the women singing, the men silent, till they came to the end of the street. We moved on towards Gujrat.

We reached Gujrat by midday, but the doli could not be taken into the house until it was dark and the bride had been shown the evening star. In the evening the doli was taken through the streets and lanes of Gujrat to our house and placed on the platform in front. Our lane was full of our biradari and neighbours waiting to receive the doli. Our grand-aunt, in the position of mother-in-law, received Savitri, passed a bowl of water round her head and drank it. The bride was then taken into the deohri where the ceremony of showing the bride's face took place. The women came up and lifted Savitri's veil, blessed her and gave her money. Savitri bowed deeply and touched our grand-uncle's feet. She was then taken upstairs into her new home and given some food, which she barely touched. It was now late in the night and she was led to her bridal chamber. The last one to leave her, with affectionate words of encouragement, was the dai.

Today, Punjabi weddings are different. Gone are the horoscopes, the barbers, the songs, many of the symbol-rich ceremonies; the noisy pleasures which for simple people were the only entertainment in life; gone are the phulkaris and the heavy classical jewellery. Gone too is the bride's fear of an unknown future; gone the sadness of the parting.

CHAPTER NINE

Child birth, Death, Funeral

Childbirth was held in terror in those days, especially the first one, when a girl was said to come back to her husband's house for the second time as a gift from God, provided things went well; and so often they did not. Childbirth always took place at home and was entrusted to the care of the family dai. Dais were usually old Muslim women who had earned a reputation for midwifery. Like the family barber, there were family dais who over years delivered succeeding generations. Savitri was therefore greatly encouraged when after the first confused realisation that she was going to have a baby my mother told her that they would send for her old dai. Raja was once again called in and told to go to Peroshah to break the good news. To our relations in Gujrat the news was delivered through the family priest, the Purohit, but to the biradaris and friends through Raja. In a few days Savitri's people sent some gifts and a new set of clothes in honour of the coming event, and her mother came over herself, proud and happy, and asked us if she could take Savitri to Peroshah for a few days to show off her expectant daughter. This was a custom largely meant to reassure the young bride, because back in familiar surroundings and among her friends and relatives who fussed and congratulated her, she lost the initial fear and began to feel important.

Back in Gujrat, Savitri led a relaxed life and filled her leisure with dreams. With her red ivory choora still on her arms, wearing her bridal clothes of velvet and brocade, she would go out visiting with my mother in the afternoons, on display as a happy bride whose fulfilment was coming in such auspicious time, in less than a year of her wedding. She was congratulated and blessed wherever she went, and given much advice. A bride so young and pretty, fruitful already, with the double bloom on her face of bridal happiness and the coming motherhood, must indeed have been blessed by the gods. And whom the gods blessed, everyone else also was eager to bless. 'May you have a son like four moons.' Passing through the street of the courtesans, mother would stop to talk to the women as they looked enviously at Savitri. With their own bodies overfulfilled, yet never loved, with occasional maternity whose only purpose was to bring forth a nameless daughter to provide for their old age, they looked at Savitri, demure and happy, with a far-away look of sadness. Her joy was never to be theirs. They blessed her too. Mother took Savitri to the Arya Samaj, and had the havan done at home, for the sacred fire to purify it. For luck she took her to the temple too to be blessed by the immortal pair, Shiva and Parvati.

Some time before Savitri was due, the dai arrived. She took charge of everything and bustled about. She checked what preparations had been made. She hoped that her husband as a good Khatri had done his duty and told her the appropriate heroic tales to make the boy brave. She must not go near maimed or ugly beggars. Mother dutifully accepted the role of taking instructions from the dai and did as she was told. She remembered her own dai.

When the time came, we children were sent away to a neighbouring mohalla to father's maternal uncle's house, but we kept dropping in to find out what was happening. One morning we were awakened early to be told that Savitri had given birth to a son at night. We rushed to our house, but as we climbed upstairs we felt there was something wrong. There was hushed silence, not the happy chaos usually prevailing at the birth of a son. Mother took us aside and told us that the baby was not well and Savitri had fever. After that we were ignored and nobody seemed to mind if we hung around.

Later in the day Savitri's mother and father arrived because Raja had been sent immediately to Peroshah to give the news cautiously. The dai had recognised the danger, and her inability to meet it, and had suggested that the big doctor from the hospital should be sent for. Uncle Dwarka Prashad rushed out, and as he went through the mohalla the anxious neighbours guessed. Some hours later when the doctor came out of our house and walked back through the mohalla, alone, followed only by the peon carrying his bag, they all knew.

☆

When the doctor realised that further effort was no use, he whispered to my mother the dreaded Hindu formula, 'I think the girl should now be lowered on to the floor.' Helped by others, she lifted Savitri from the bed and put her on the floor, which had been hastily plastered with water and some cowdung. She was laid with her head to the north and feet pointing south, as countless generations of Aryans had been laid over the axis of mother earth. From the top of the head the soul was supposed to leave the body towards the ancient home of the Aryan ancestors near the North Pole. A few drops of water from the sacred Mother Ganga were put into her mouth, and the aromatic leaf of the holy Tulsi plant, which is grown in a pot in every Hindu home, was placed between her lips. Slowly life was leaving Savitri's body, burning with the heat of the fever, her baby lying already lifeless near her. A small lamp made out of dough, with melted ghee and a cotton wick, was put near her. As life would stop flickering in one body it would symbolically rise in a tiny flame in another. The soul would soar up and perhaps somewhere enter another body, till purified of all sin it would rise and merge into Nirvan, to be reborn no more. Who knows, my mother thought, where Savitri's soul was first born, and whether she was its last home. Had it finished its eternal quest, or would it continue the search for peace? Whatever its past or future, whether it stopped here or continued, in its sojourn, through Savitri's body, innocent and sinless, it could only have gone upward to a higher existence. It could only have gained a step nearer to Nirvan. Under the first impact of the shock her thoughts raced on, but she awakened herself from her reverie as she heard the sobs of Savitri's mother and father. She rushed out of the room to busy herself with all that had to be done. Outside she told uncle Dwarka Prashad to go in. She whispered into his ear, 'The boy looked just like you.' She then went down to the deohri, where Raja was waiting. She told him to go immediately to the family Brahmin and on the way to warn the acharyas to be ready.

The pandit came and performed the shanti path, bidding peace to the soul on its onward journey, like shanti path had been performed on the morning of Savitri's wedding to bid her well on her journey into her new life. The pandit suggested that some wheat and rice should be given in charity. Some wheat and rice were symbolically brought on a plate and the pandit made Savitri touch the grains. He coaxed her to utter the Gaytri Mantra as her last invocation. She whispered OM, and as she could whisper no more, her eyes were closed, her mouth gently shut and her arms folded across the breast. The pandit announced that the soul had departed. His task over, he left the room and sent for the acharyas, the Brahmins who take over when death sets in.

As the acharya came into the room he offered condolences and said a few formal words in praise of the departed. As Savitri had no sons, my elder brother was chosen to perform certain ceremonies. He was bathed, Raja shaved his head, and he was put into a new, unwashed raw silk dhoti and had to sit by the oil lamp, in a corner of the room. The lamp had to be kept filled with mustard oil to keep it burning for ten days until all the ceremonies were over. Food would be served to him first and brought to him to eat near the lamp. As a mere boy, my brother was somewhat frightened by the role he was called upon to play. He must have thought of the happier role he had played as uncle's sarbhala when he rode behind him on the horse on our way to Savitri's house for the wedding.

An elder in the family was given the duty of writing post-cards to relatives and friends announcing the death. Each card bore a simple message that at this time, on this day of the month and year, Savitri had gone heavenward and taken the new-born child with her. The card was torn at one edge to indicate, even before it was read, that it brought a message of death. Telegrams were sent to those relatives who were near enough to reach in time for the funeral.

As the news spread members of our biradari began to drop in. As they passed through the street our neighbours joined them. Durries and mats were spread on the thara in front of our house and in the mohalla square for the callers to sit on. Our elders stood at the door, and as visitors came with folded hands and said, 'Very much grieved, how much we cannot say', they replied with their hands stretched out in a gesture of infinity. 'God's will.' The elderly callers touched Dwarka Prashad on the shoulder and said, 'Son, have patience, there is no alternative but to accept God's will with fortitude. Bear the loss like a man, it will give courage to everyone else, especially to her mother and father.'

One member of the biradari always came forward on these occasions and offered to make all the arrangements for the funeral rites. Others, who were good at helping at weddings and funerals, came up behind him and asked to be told whatever task they were considered fit to undertake. These were the moments when the biradari came into its own. Everything would be taken off the hands of the bereaved family, and without fuss, very quietly, everything would be taken care of. It was a great feeling for the family, a feeling of importance, of belonging and affection, to be waited upon in their grief. With smooth and experienced efficiency the men and women divided up their tasks, and some one took overall direction. One person ran to the post office to send the letters and telegrams; another went to buy materials for the ceremonies—incense, ghee, mouli and rice; another went to buy new unstitched cloth for the shroud, and handwoven red, purple or magenta cotton or silk for covering; another to buy flowers; another to buy bamboo sticks, some fagots of sandalwood, a mat woven from date-palm fronds, some string, an earthenware pitcher and bowl. A large variety of materials was needed for the coffin and the cremation. In villages a handcart would go round and the biradari members would each give an unsplit log of wood as their contribution for the funeral pyre.

Inside, four women washed Savitri. Her body was first smeared from head to foot with milk curds and then washed with water. Her mother wished her to be dressed in her wedding clothes, her hair oiled and dressed and a red mark placed on her forehead and in the parting of her hair. The choora was taken off because it was inauspicious to burn it. She was then wrapped in a scarlet silk shawl and garlanded round her neck, and flowers were heaped on her breast. So dressed, she looked the bride she was not so long ago. And like the bride she was taken down to the deohri, where she was placed on the bamboo and mat stretcher and tied to it. Now that she was ready to leave, just as when she had arrived, the women came forward to lift the covering and look at her face. While the men stood at the back sobbing silently, the women gave unrestrained vent to their grief, and suddenly one coalesced wail rose through the well of the house. Grand-uncle stepped forward and gently pushed the women, who were smothering Savitri's face with kisses. 'It is getting late,' he said. 'It is time to start.' He had said just those words standing by Savitri's palanquin.

Men came forward and lifted the bier and moved on. While passing through our mohalla they held it low so that the neighbours and others waiting in the street could take a last look. At the end of the street they covered her face and lifted the bier on their shoulders and started at a brisk pace. Every few steps another mourner would join the carriers out of duty and piety. It was considered a blessing to carry it. To the monotonous chant of 'Ram Nam Sat hai', God's name is truth, sprinkling water with a tuft of kusha grass, throwing coins in the air over the body for the poor to pick up, the procession moved on through the streets till it reached the cremation grounds. They lowered the bier to the ground at the entrance, and the acharya performed the symbolic ceremony of braking the earthenware pitcher full of water. The pitcher had to be dropped in such a way that its neck also broke, to prevent death visiting the family again too soon. The women were persuaded to return, and reluctantly they started back, stopping on the way to bathe at a well.

The acharya performed the last rites, the ceremony of prayer for eternal peace to the departed soul and for the welfare of the family. Some people had arrived earlier to arrange the funeral pyre. The big and heavy logs were placed at the bottom, then the smaller ones; the still smaller logs formed rests for head and feet. Three iron bars were stuck in the ground on each side to prevent the logs from rolling off the pyre. The body was placed on the logs and covered with a few pieces of sandalwood and then smaller logs with some big ones on top again. A bundle of dried twigs and reeds was made into a small pillow and pushed between the logs under her head. Incense and ghee were then poured all over the pyre.

When everything was ready, some elders led Dwarka Prashad to the final and the most painful act. Everyone fell back and left him and the acharya sitting near the pyre. The acharya recited some last mantras and lit a torch of dried reeds which he handed over to Dwarka Prashad, and then walked away.

Dwarka Prashad stood alone, staring vacantly at the pyre. Between the logs he could see the still form of Savitri which he had learned to know so well. He saw the shape of her head, the curve of her breasts and her thighs, and her feet pointing up. In deep youthful sleep he had sometimes seen her lying on her back covered under a bedsheet, as still as she was now. As intimacy grew he had seen her whole body lying expectantly vibrant, but now she looked so relaxed. He felt the growing heat of the torch but he stood still. His feet would not move. As the torch burst into a fierce flame and he still would not move, grand-uncle came forward and put his hand under his elbow and led him close to the pyre. 'Dwarka Prashad,' he whispered hoarsely, 'this is something which only you must do.'

There was a little smoke from the pillow of dry grass, crackle and then a small tongue of flame leapt and licked the red silk shawl. It grew into a fire which spread to the dry logs. Fed by incense and ghee, as it rushed through the pyre, the fire raged and flames leaped high. The mourners fell back as the intense flames consumed everything in their way. 'Let us now go,' said grand-uncle.

Some other mourners had taken the baby to the river Chenab, a few miles away. There they made a small stretcher from bamboos and reeds, and covered it with soft rushes and leaves. On it they laid the baby wrapped in a piece of red silk and covered with marigolds. The little bier then floated gently downstream. Babies and children were floated on the rivers, or if the river was far away, buried, but they were never cremated.

On their way home the mourners stopped at a well to bathe. The acharya again performed the prayer of peace. As the last prayer was said, the mourners, sitting behind the acharya, all facing in the direction of the town, picked up a straw which each person threw behind over his shoulder. They all got up and walked back to Gujrat.

Back in our mohalla, people sat on the mats in front of the house and planned the future ceremonies, the one for the fourth day, the Choutha; the Daswan of the tenth day; and the Kirya on the thirteenth day. These decided men of our family stood up and with folded hands said, 'Please come.' So soon after the going away of a dear one, it is not appropriate to say 'Please go.' The mourners folded their hands, bowed and departed.

No fire was lit in the house but the neighbours and the biradari had thoughtfully prepared a simple meal and sent it to our house in the evening. They coaxed us to eat at least a few morsels with the formal words, 'By giving up food you cannot bring back the dead. Your loss is irreparable, your grief so deep, but you must keep body and soul together because in this world life and death go side by side.' Such words of condolence and encouragement were traditionally uttered.

On the fourth day the biradari gathered at our house in the morning to go and collect 'the flowers', as the bones were called because of the way they burst at the ends. A bone from each limb of the body was placed on a tray and washed with milk. They were then put into a new earthenware pitcher which was tied in a red cloth and marked with Savitri's name. The jar was handed over to the sadhu who lived at the cremation ghat. The ashes were collected in a bag to be immersed in the nearest stream of flowing water.

The Daswan and the Kirya ceremonies over, the acharyas were sent away with a complete set of new clothes, bed linen and utensils, for it was believed that the gifts reached the dead. At the last ceremony Savitri's parents sent Dwarka Prashad a turban to signify their continued relationship. The acharya blessed the family and prayed for peace to all. This marked the end of mourning. Next morning everything in the house was washed or put in the sun, and after this we began usual social life again. On the seventeenth day some Brahmins were called in and fed and given a dakshina of cash, fruit and food, which is also believed to reach the dead. Members of the family will not partake of this food.

The very last rites for Savitri took place at Hardwar where uncle went later. He took the 'flowers', and on the steps of the ghat on the Ganga, where the river leaves the Himalayas and enters the plains, he sat with the family panda and performed the last rites. The 'flowers' were then taken in a boat into the midstream and scattered on the fast-flowing river. This broke his last link with Savitri, and from then on she was only a memory. In the evening, as dusk fell over the hills and the river, he went to the ghat again. In a cup-shaped boat made from the thick, waxy leaf of the dhak tree, the flame of the forest, he filled roses and jasmines and placed on them a little earthenware lamp. His little boat, with many others like it, with their lamps lit, floated gently downstream. On still nights hundreds of these boats with their flickering lights floating on the silvery breast of Mother Ganga is a sight so delicately symbolical of life itself.

After making a sad entry of his visit in the family book, uncle left Hardwar to return home.

☆

We had finished our school examinations and had been staying on in Gujrat, waiting for aunt Savitri's baby. But now there was nothing to do, and mother was glad that uncle Dwarka Prashad declined her offer to stay on for a while to look after him. He said he preferred to be alone, and my mother felt that he did not want us around. She was relieved to leave the house where she could still hear Savitri's ebbing moans. Father had put his foot down that there was to be no mourning in the traditional style. He felt that it insulted the grief of the bereaved. Rai Bahadur and his wife were completely broken and did not care. They withdrew to Peroshah and we never saw them again. First the Rai Bahadur, and then Savitri's mother died within the year.

If engagements and weddings were complex and prolonged, so were funerals and mourning. If we enjoyed long and heartily at weddings we paid back dearly at mourning. The Punjabis never did anything in half measures, especially our women, with whom mourning had become an art and a test of both skill and stamina. Often the grief was borne with great courage, but the spirit and flesh broke down under the strain of mourning. The original, symbol-rich ritual had become mixed with some very ugly mourning customs. Curiously, while the prolonged mourning, with its ugly passages, was entirely on the women's side, when men congregated to condole there was calm, dignified silence, broken by words of philosophical wisdom. 'What God gives He takes back; who are we to protest', was the general theme. They sat silently, with covered heads, and with occasional sighs praised God and the departed.

The women seemed to find in death some physical and mental catharsis. They cried, they wailed, they beat their breasts, in rhythm and in rhyme. They did it to traditional pattern, with improvisations. They would sit in a group, with their faces covered with their mantles, holding one end of it, the pala, which gave this form of mourning its name. With the pala they dabbed their eyes and blew their noses as they cried in a song. The leader improvised the dirge as she went along, and the others followed. To express their sympathy, each would in turn come up to the bereaved, put her hands on her shoulder and cry in an intimate language and tone, occasionally hugging her. As further evidence of her grief she would blow her nose often and profusely into the pala of her mantle. They never gave relief to the poor woman, already in deep distress.

The most gruesome spectacle of all was the siyapa, which used to scare us children. The women would form a mourning squad in the deohri and one of them, the most experienced of them all, who had perhaps led at a number of deaths, would lead the siyapa. She would select the squad and then stand in the middle with the rest. Twenty-five or more, in several rings around her. They would all bare their breasts and gird up their garments to bare their thighs, and at a word from her begin to beat their breasts, their cheeks, their foreheads and thighs rhythmically in that order, keeping time with the mourning song, sung in a quick tempo. The leader usually sang the song she had improvised at the death of her son or husband; others followed her. While directing the siyapa she kept a stern eye on the performers and sent away anyone who could not keep pace or made an awkward movement. The women turned out would sit crestfallen with the others on the floor and join the pala. The noise of the beaten flesh and the quick song, with an occasional fainting, made the whole thing so horrible that in our days the biradaris finally said no and the custom died rapidly.

CHAPTER TEN

A Medieval Nawabi State

Sargodha, where we joined father at his new posting, was a town barely twenty years old and part of the new phenomenon of development in the old Punjab. The land between the rivers had been covered by the new canal system, whose special contribution was the irrigation of the desert area in the west and south-west Punjab. Till the end of the last century this was just scrub and waste, inhabited very sparsely by some wandering herdsmen, who were called junglis. They kept sheep, goat and buffalo, and raised a little grain.

The new canals brought water to the land which had always lain fallow because of a scant and uncertain rainfall. But it was fertile because since time these rivers had broken their banks in flood, continuously altering their course and adding fresh layers of rich alluvial top soil. And now these canals brought a perennial supply of water, and in their wake communications, roads and railways. Having dug the canals, the task before the Government was to people this land. They raised a cadre of energetic men called Land Settlement Officers, who set about attracting people from the populated Punjab to this land of opportunity. People were at first hesitant to go into the jungle, whose main inhabitants were jackals, hyenas, foxes and deer. But those who did sent back enthusiastic reports. The virgin soil, with its energy stored for millenia, seemed to hunger for the thrust of man's plough, and the seed he scattered brought forth crops that astounded him. And a man could ask for as much land as he wanted; the more he asked the better it pleased the sahibs, who happily filled in the squares on their maps. One enterprising man, the story went, got on his horse and rode beside the sahib, first in one direction and then in another. They rode all day till they arrived back in the evening to where they had started, and that, said this young stalwart, was all his land, if the sahib agreed. The sahib was only too happy to agree; he would work all night to fill so many more squares in his settlement plans. This was the first of the famous Tiwanas of Shahpur, near Sargodha. The man in charge of the colonisation of the Sargodha area, to whose energy and drive the scheme owed much, was Malcolm Hailey, later governor of the Punjab. It was ironical that having done so much for the province, when he came to govern it the rise of political consciousness made him quite unpopular.

Wherever a few families settled together they made a village, but Government were anxious to found new towns to provide outlets for the produce from the villages and serve as centres of administration and education. Sargodha was such a town. There were others, Lyallpur and Montgomery, entirely new, while many small hamlets soon became tehsils and district towns. The untiring Settlement Officers literally dragged people to these new towns. 'Take some land in this town,' they would press a farmer while he was receiving his arable squares. 'All right, Sahib, give me a "peg of land" enough to tether a horse. It may be useful when I come into the new town to pay my revenue dues.' 'No, no,' the sahib would urge, 'take an acre, two acres, more if you like.'

Starting from scratch, these towns were made in the image of the Settlement Officers, practical, orderly and colourless. Methodically planned, Sargodha was so different from the medieval Gujrat. It was built in a square, bounded by the new canal on one side and by the new railway line that went across the canal at a right angle on another; on the third side it had a belt of gardens, fruit orchards and vegetable patches through which ran a water distributory; and on the fourth, set apart from the city, there was a mandi, the wholesale produce market next to the railway station. The town was divided into two parts, the city and the mandi on one side of the railway line, and the civil station on the other. On the outskirts there were three more innovations, the waterworks, a seed farm, and an area set apart for factories, mainly cotton gins, flour and oil mills and a new luxury, an ice factory.

The mandi was a big square with ground floor shops on all sides. Here the produce of the surrounding country, wheat, cotton, millets and oilseeds, came in. The farmers brought the commodities in large carts drawn by pairs of bullocks or male buffaloes, or on camel back, and unloaded them in the square in mounds. Most picturesque were the heaps of cotton, pure white and fluffy, like fresh piles of snowdrift. The farmers, the wholesale buyers and commission agents, among them the representatives of the large European produce firms of Ralli Brothers, Louis Drayfus, Volkart Brothers, and their Japanese counterparts, Toyo Menka Kaisha, Mitsu Bishi and others, and the professional auctioneers would move from one pile to another. Men would pick up a handful of wheat, look at it casually and let it drop through their fingers, as the auctioneer sang the bids in a soft voice. No one spoke, but at a nod from someone the auctioneer varied the pitch of his monotonous, sing-song four rupees two annas, four rupees two annas, four rupees two annas, to four rupees three annas. At another nod he changed from the three annas to four annas, and suddenly without a word he stopped and moved away to another heap followed by the silent crowd, while a munshi entered the completed transaction in a notebook. In another system of auctioning, the broker and the bidder stretched their hands under a towel and the bidder made his offer by holding the auctioneer's fingers. This was a cumbersome method and gave way to the open bidding. Month's toil, hopes and fears were settled in a few minutes. The farmer would walk back to the shop of his arhti, the man who advanced him money and sold him his seed, to settle his account before harnessing his bullocks. From the railway station next door the produce packed in gunny bags would be sent to destinations all over the Punjab, India, and it was said, even across the sea.

The Civil Station was built in a large rectangle along the railway lines. The bungalows varied in size with the importance of the official, and there were also some private bungalows belonging to some big zamindars. British social life centred round the church, the club and the polo ground. In Sargodha their wine and provision store rejoiced in the name of London House. In 1918 the senior district officers were mostly British, but Indians had already begun to arrive on the scene, and the first problem of social adjustment had begun. When the deputy commissioner was an Indian, as the head of the district he could not be kept out of the club, unless he solved the problem by being of the older type, and therefore glad to be spared the onerous honour of mixing with the Sahibs. But if he belonged to the I.C.S., educated at Oxford or Cambridge, there was a problem; at least the Service had to be honoured. Within the British membership there were also problems. The I.C.S. deputy commissioner, his assistant commissioner and the sessions judge formed one natural group in which the police superintendent fitted in if he was an ex-army man, and for reasons of practical courtesy the civil surgeon also, because it was always well to make the doctor feel your equal, and in any case he was usually also from the army and had university education. The status of the engineers depended upon their background. If they came of the right background, they were accepted, otherwise, like the bank manager and the police officer they were just tolerated. It helped too if you were a Scot and had retained the accent, because then like the parson and the doctor you acquired a certain social neutralness and a fairly high minimum level of acceptance. This concession did not however automatically apply to the Irishman, who along with the

Scot was the backbone of the earlier services. And a complicating factor in the Sargodha British community was the neighbouring army remount depot, where the service corps had a stud farm for raising horses and mules. It had a number of British officers of an inferior social grade. Fortunately the depot was a few miles away, and as motorcars had not yet arrived in Sargodha the remount officers could not come to the club every evening, but at week-ends they came in strength. At Christmas, New Year, and when the Governor visited Sargodha, the club was one well-knit community; at other times, while it offered a solid facade to us it had its own layers inside.

On the other side of the railway lines were the Company gardens and the hospital. After that began the city, which extended up to the fruit and vegetable gardens. The city was planned in square blocks, of which by our time there were sixteen. It could only expand in one direction and there already a seventeenth block was going up. There were two main roads with shops running laterally, and two vertically with the residential areas behind them. A residential block had two entrances from opposite sides and enclosed a spacious square, with a wide lane running behind containing another two rows of houses. Provision had been made for a high school, a market place, an orthodox Hindu temple, an Arya Samaj, a Muslim Mosque and a Sikh Gurdwara. There was a waterworks and piped water supply system. The blocks were numberd, and while some were exclusively Hindu, Sikh or Muslim, others were mixed. An area had been set apart for the prostitutes, singing and dancing girls.

Sargodha, as can be imagined, was a much cleaner and healthier city than Gujrat. It was planned, well laid out and had plenty of light and air. Its streets and lanes were wide and straight. Somehow the clean, hygenic, impersonal layout seemed to mould the population into the pattern that the settlement officer of the late Victorian period must have had in mind. There was more social and political awakening in Sargodha; its municipal affairs were better run; its communities had started new schools. The singing and dancing girls were moved out of the city, first near the canal bank, and then still further away. It was typical of the new spirit of Sargodha that its biradaris tried to stop wasteful expenditure at weddings by banning fireworks, and had they got away with this they would probably have stopped music and entertainment as well. But with all this Sargodha was drab and had none of the colour of Gujrat, neither the city nor its people.

To Sargodha people came to settle from all over the West Punjab, professionals, traders and businessmen, artisans of all castes. Old ties were severed, and new ones were formed. The block we lived in contained mostly professional families, both Khatris and Aroras, and a new affinity sprang up between them. It began with the men, thrown together in work, and spread to the women. In Sargodha our mother hardly visited any but professional homes, Khatri or Arora. In fact the bonds of education and work supplanted the old caste bonds, and a new society emerged with four castes whose membership was cutting across the traditional pattern. They were the professionals drawn from all castes; the traders, who were Aroras, but with an odd Khatri amongst them; the artisans; and in the surrounding villages, the samindars, often very wealthy. This re-grouping had not yet started to affect the marriage customs. Khatris still married only Khatris, and Aroras other Aroras, but they were not any longer so strict about the right sub-castes. Instead, professional families married into families of the same social standing and education, and traders among traders, zamindars into other farming families. The old, tightly knit biradari system was going, and there was a new more broad based sense of relationship. Among us the Arya Samaj took the place of the old biradari.

While we were in Sargodha the influenza hit the Punjab. Postcards with edges torn began to arrive almost every week. Father went down also and lay hovering between life and death for days. Perhaps his iron constitution, the result of years of hard outdoor life, saved him. Two of his nephews and both his sisters died within a week. We wondered what this plague was, though we had heard that it came from Europe, from its battlefields. Slowly he recovered from his illness, and when he was able to move about the house mother arranged a havan ceremony to cleanse the home of the illness. She distributed sweets and hoped that this strange foreign affliction would not come our way again. Yam-doot, the messenger of the god of death, had visited our family too often in the past year.

Perhaps in celebration of father's recovery, or because time was ripe otherwise, the first mechanical contraption arrived in our house. It was a Singer sewing machine, shining black and chromium-plated, with a highly polished case in wood. Few homes as yet possessed one. With it came a colourful calendar showing Singer's popularity in different countries of the world. This was my first introduction to people of other races, if only in pictures. Father now regaining strength and interest in life, at once converted to advantage the slogan on this calendar, 'Singer preferred in every country.' He exhorted us to learn singing in addition to studies. Even if we had no special talent for it, we must work hard because singing was a great accomplishment. He was convinced in his humourless way that the Singer people were using to good advantage the international love of singing.

☆

After two years at Sargodha father was transferred to Muzaffargarh, the last town in the south-west corner of the Punjab, near the river Indus. There was still another town, Dera Ghazi Khan, further west, but that was on the other side of the Indus and was considered out of the Punjab. All these towns on the Indus, like Dera Ghazi Khan, Dera Ismail Khan, Issa Khail, Moosa Khail, Miram Shah, Shalozan, Parachinar, with their sonorous names, were considered Pathan and not Punjabi. Though the Hindus there were Punjabis, mostly merchants, and spoke Punjabi and frequently married in the Punjab proper, somehow because of their Pathan looks, often with fair skins and grey eyes, their clothes and manners, we never regarded them as quite our kind. But marriages into these frontier families were popular, I think because of an atavistic preference for the race and colour type derived from our Aryan ancestors.

The admiration of a fair colour probably stemmed from the time of the Aryans. It was almost an obsession with our society in a way that I never came across even among the British whom we believed to be very colour and race conscious, judging by their racial aloofness in India. From the time a baby is born its complexion is all important. The second question asked about the newborn is always, 'Is it fair or dark?' Mothers put a black mark every morning on a fair-skinned child's forehead, and a black cord round its waist to ward off the evil eye. A little girl with dark complexion is a mild source of worry to the parents from the beginning: 'How shall we find a suitable match; who will have her? We shall not be able to find a handsome fair boy; we shall have to raise a big dowry.' When it came to marriage, the first question is, 'Is he fair; is she fair.' Fairness could cover many defects and sins. Whether the proposed match was tall or short, plain or handsome, clever or dull, fairness offset everything. The face of a moon, the skin of jasmine, the complexion of rose; who cared if she could not cook and sew. Later, in the Tribune, the paper of educated middle class Punjabis, matrimonial advertisements would always begin by asking for a fair bride. But dark boys and girls also had to be married, and if the fair only married the fair, we would in time have had two unrelated colour castes. To avoid this the society instinctively developed an excuse. It appears to have been discovered that Lord Krishna was dark, the colour of dusk.

The Muslim invaders of Turkish and Moghul blood must have strengthened our colour consciousness. With their poetry of 'saman araz' and 'gul araz', the jasmine and rose hues, they re-emphasised our traditional preferences. There was however a limit to fairness. When the British came, their very fair hair and pink skins fell outside our acceptable scale. They were too fair. With us the hair must always be dark, the skin pale but not white, and the cheeks have only a touch of rose in the cold winter. European fairness was too extreme for us to appreciate and, besides, it reddened in our sun. Similarly, the eyes were best dark, though a wine colour could be attractive; but light coloured eyes, grey or blue, were signs of faithlessness and untrustworthiness as also light colour of hair. The ideal of beauty was summed up in these similes: hair dark and thick as billowing rain clouds, eyes soft and black as a gazelle's, and skin the colour of wheat.

Muzaffargarh was barely Punjab as we knew it. Far from the mountains, it had a landscape of date groves and soil covered with patches of saltpetre, looking like a fresh fall of snow; the houses were built of mud and straw instead of baked brick, the people were smaller and sharp featured, seldom Khatri and mostly Aroras, usually poor and humble before the Muslims, calling themselves in self-disparagement poor Kirars. Even the animals were different, for here donkeys were used instead of horses and the camel instead of the bullock. We found the people and the land very strange at first. We had already felt some change in the Sargodha people, in their accent and slightly un-Punjabi ways, but these people were almost incomprehensible. But soon we began to recognise the Punjabi Hindu society in its familiar framework, the castes and sub-castes, the customs, rituals, fasts, fairs and festivals; and the newly-started Arya Samaj immediately offered us a kind of biradari.

The land was in part sour with the saltpetre, kullar, which seemed to rise out of the ground in patches of soft, powdery white. It would rise on walls of buildings and eat up the plaster and then the bricks. Nothing seemed to stop it. The more you removed it out of the ground the more it came up. It sometimes covered a whole field or it came up in small patches. Nothing would grow in it and nothing seemed to kill it. People accepted it as a white scourge. They made no use of it. There were some nonperennial canals which brought water during the summer months. Rainfall was scanty. The summer monsoon barely reached here, but there were some showers from the winter monsoon off the Arabian sea. Whatever water the canals brought was therefore most welcome. In this dry rainless climate the only thing that grew in abundance was the date palm. It was almost a date economy. The flesh of the dates was eaten fresh or dried; the stones were ground into a flour; the fronds were used for thatch, while the young shoots were dyed into bright colours for basket weaving; the stalks which bore fruit were used as brooms; its bark made fuel; and when the tree died the long stem was made into a channel for use on a persian wheel, while out of the root came a succulent, white porous vegetable matter which was a delicacy eaten raw or pickled. Date was their wealth and the kullar seemed not to bother it. But we boys bore a grudge against the date palm, for our school masters loved to whittle the stems of its fronds to make steeped and supple canes which cut viciously into the palms of our hands, where the Punjabi boys traditionally received their punishment. On cold frosty mornings, when our fingers refused to move in the open draughty classrooms, a sadistic teacher would use such a stick to 'thaw' our hands.

Muzaffargarh as a town was already unlike other Punjabi towns, for it had a touch of the trans-Indus Baluch country and the Persia beyond. Its square mud brick houses were in the Muslim style of a high blank wall with inner and outer courtyards. We did not live in the canal colony as there was no accommodation, and we took a house on the outskirts. It had high blank walls on four sides, with a shuttered gate in the front wall. The outer courtyard, as you entered, was shaped like a reversed L. On the left there was the reception room used for my father's office and two living-rooms for men visitors. At the top of the right-hand side of this courtyard were servants quarters, stables and tonga and cattle sheds. Through a door protected by a purda wall you entered the inner courtyard, with the residential quarters built on the left, and a wing facing the entrance containing the kitchen and pantries. Through one of the living-rooms you entered father's office and came out into the outer courtyard. As we did not observe purda we did not use the two courtyards for their different purposes, but among Muslims life flowed in two separate streams, in the outer courtyard of the men and in the inner courtyard of the women. Only members of the family, close relations, women, and maid-servants entered inside. In this town we had our first experience of strict purda. Among us, in the upper Punjab, women pulled the dupatta over their faces, but being usually diaphanous it made only a formal kind of veil, while Muslim women wore burqa, which covered them from head to foot, with a piece of net or lace sewn in the portion over the eyes. But in Muzaffargarh the purda was more strict, and while the Hindu women did not actually wear burqa they often wrapped a sheet round themselves and had a thick veil over the face. Across the Indus even the Hindu women wore burqa.

Muzaffargarh was on the edge of a desert which began only a mile away on its western side. It was a desert of sandhills and valleys. Some hills were more than fifty feet high, and changed their shape whenever the wind blew hard. The sand shifted from day to day and gave them ever-changing contours. The landscape had a strange beauty of voluptuously curved hills, bare and soft, with the sand on the surface furrowed by the wind. In the summer it burnt during the day; at night it was cool and fresh, lapped by a caressing desert breeze. In the winter it was cool by the day and freezing by night. The landscape had a great variety of moods, expressed in colours, changing during the day and from one season to another. It was remarkable how the one single tone of grey could change into so many colours and tints with the sun and the moon. It was at its most spectacular in the hour before the sun rose and after it set, the hour between the day and the night. On the nights of the full moon the landscapes almost ceased to be earthly.

It became our favourite touring country. We insisted on accompanying father as often as we could. It lacked the lushness of growing crops on the rich, fat lands of the perennial canals, but it offered something new, the sand desert and the Indus country.

We never forgot our first introduction to the desert. My brother and I strayed from our dak bungalow one evening and roamed into the dunes. We walked up the hills enjoying the feeling of treading on soft sand which gave way underfoot and left a large trail behind; we rolled down the slopes like logs, and we ran after the camels that had brought the camp baggage and were now turned loose to graze. We chased them through the valleys and up the hills, laughing at their ungainly long-legged trot. As the sun went lower in the sky we were amused at our long shadows, which looked as if we were walking on stilts and made us appear as long as the camels. Occasionally we stopped to pick the small pink and yellow succulent peeloo fruit from the gnarled, thinleafed bushes, the only thing that bore fruit around here. When we were tired and felt we had enough of the camels and the sand, we decided to return home, but now all the dunes looked alike. A brisk wind had sprung up as the sun went down and it had covered our tracks with new waves of sand. We became frightened because we knew we were lost and we had walked a long way from home. We wandered about, and luckily in the end we were picked up by the camel-drivers, who had strayed in our direction looking for their beasts which we had driven away. They delivered us back at the bungalow from where rescue parties were setting out with hurricane lanterns. Our worst punishment was however to come the next day when our ears full of sand began to ache with excruciating pain.

Further west of this strip of desert the country dipped gently to the Indus. The road and the railway line stopped at a small terminal station at the village of Ghazi Ghat. From here the Indus began, and in the summer it stretched sometimes for nearly twenty miles in width and at places was over fifty feet deep. It was like a brown, muddy sea as far as the eye could see, across which an old paddle steamer used to ferry passengers. In the winter the river shrank to a few shallow streams over which a pontoon bridge of boats was fixed. Elsewhere on the Indus people crossed the river on goat skins. These were sewn up skins, inflated and tied at the neck. On one of them the 'passenger' and on the other the ferryman would lie on their stomachs and paddle their way across. The ferryman used his feet as rudder while he paddled. The passenger was sort of towed along. Occasionally one could see crocodiles basking on sandbanks in the morning sun. The country along the river banks was thickly overgrown with reed and abounded in game, deer, hare, pig, fox, jackal and porcupine, whose quills we greatly prized for making pen-holders.

A great sport in Muzaffargarh, and a quite unusual one, was camel fighting. The animals were specially bred for it, and the fights took place in a sand valley with a ring of high dunes forming a vast natural amphitheatre. They were held on Sunday afternoons and were free to the spectators, who settled down on the slopes of the hills, safely out of the camel's way. Two fighters would be led into the arena and let loose. Their docile and placid look was misleading, for the fighter camels were a vicious lot and fought with tremendous anger. They growled and made the most weird noises, they kicked and bit each other savagely, but mostly they fought with their long necks, and blood streamed down their heads till one of them had had enough and ran away from the arena into the desert, followed by his angry owner. The victorious camel ran around, now growling happily as he was dragged away by his master to make room for the the next fight. People bet on their favourite camels and jeered as the vanquished one ran away. There were many other side-shows, cock fighting, quail fighting, partridge fighting and wrestling. The bird fights were clean sport, unlike the gruesome ones I saw in Manila years later, where they put long, razor-sharp spurs on the cocks so that the fight ends in a kill in a matter of moments. Our birds fought with their bare claws and the fight would last a long time, till one of them ran away. There was rarely a kill.

Life in Muzaffargarh did not always run evenly. There was great commotion when one of our classmates was murdered. He was the son of the municipal dai, a widowed woman with only this child. She had delivered a young woman who died in childbirth. The girl's father, who also had only this one child, began to brood over his loss and imagined that it was the fault of the dai. People tried to dissuade him, but in vain, and his belief gradually took on a hideous shape. One afteroon, as school was closing, he met this boy and told him that he had been asked by his mother to fetch him. The boy happily went along and lured by sweets accompanied him to the dunes outside the town. There he was murdered near a water hole. The demented man choked him to death as with a pencil he stuffed his nose and mouth with mud. Such a tragic and cold-blooded murder the town had never known before. We all flocked to the sessions court on the day the judgement was to be delivered. The judge, one of the first Punjabis to hold the post, was a very impressive looking man in a black closed collar coat and a white turban. He spread a black handkerchief over the turban when he came to delivering the sentence. 'Bhai Amir Chand....' In chaste, well chosen Urdu, beginning with the common appelation of brother, he went on impassively to analyse the evidence, deliver the judgement and to sentence him to death. Amir Chand showed no signs of shock, or a trace of emotion; he had probably totally forgotton the young boy and was only thinking of his daughter; he perhaps even welcomed the sentence. The judge must have been moved by this because he ended softly by asking Amir Chand to forgive him.

In Muzaffargarh I saw the British for the first time in numbers. So far one occasionally saw an Englishman, seldom many together except when the governor visited, but now a British regiment had camped outside the town. On the first evening when the British soldiers came to town in twos and threes, in their immaculate white walking-out uniforms, with well pressed forage caps at jaunty angles at the parting of their fair hair, with swagger canes under their arms and in shining black boots, we just stared. We sat on the school compound wall, discreetly out of the way. Their faces and bare knees, the red colour of newly burnt brick, were strange, but the strangest thing of all was that they all looked alike. We could not understand how their officers distinguished one from the other. Someone suggested that they were numbered for that purpose. Gradually we became bolder and tried out small English, but neither side could make out much. Their accent we found totally unlike the English we were used to learning. We wondered where they came from. Someone suggested that they were specially bred for the army, which needed so many of them every year, in the poor parts of London; and the theory was put forward that they were all illegitimate and were collected for the army. As we became familiar we began to exchange hockey and football matches. At hockey we managed well, but playing football with bare feet was hopeless against their heavy boots. Gradually there was much fraternising and friendliness as both sides began to make something of each other's English, but it came to an end abruptly. They were fond of visiting the prostitutes' bazaar, and one day one of them stabbed a reluctant girl and the city was put out of bounds. We never saw them again.

☆

Father's usual spell of three years posting was over and we were expecting a transfer any day. There was always a pleasant anticipation about the next post. Would it be back in the jungles or would we get a town? As we were growing up the place we might go to was of great importance for our schooling. Father had been recently selected for what was then called the Imperial Service of Engineers, which was looked after by the Secretary of State for India in London. He was therefore looking forward to his first new posting in this cadre with the important ring, but we were not a little surprised when he received orders to go to Bahawalpur State, where he was appointed as personal assistant to the State Engineer, a Scotsman under whom he had worked before and who had in fact asked for him. If Muzaffargarh was not quite Punjab, Bahawalpur was almost foreign. As a border state between the Punjab, Sind and Baluchistan, its customs, language and way of life was more akin to Sind and Baluchistan, and it had little in common with the Punjab. We were therefore thrilled with the prospect of 'leaving' the Punjab. The anticipation was further enhanced by the first news from father, who had, as was usual on a transfer, preceded us, that our new house had electricity. So far we had only seen it in railway trains and on odd visits to Lahore. In 1921 very few towns in the Punjab could boast of such modernity. Bahawalpur had besides a college, a club, gardens and palaces. Its proudest boast was a Mall Road, which only the big cities like Lahore, Amritsar and Rawalpindi possessed. Based on some legendary origin in England, the name Mall Road spelled urban luxury to us.

Bahawalpur was interesting because it contained in it a world of the past which had died in the British Punjab years ago. It was an unprogressive world, with intrigues and cruelties which had elsewhere given way to reform and justice, but it possessed also colour and pageantry. To us it had the excitement of a real ruler, a king, his durbar and palaces. Its ruling family of Abassis came from further west some centuries ago. With a young Nawab at the centre, the court and family formed a large circle, none of whom did any work. His father had had many wives and each one's family had given up work from the day of the marriage. Royal dignity demanded that they quit work and live on patronage. Then there were the surviving relatives of his grandfather's numerous wives. He himself was a young man, but before he was eighteen he had also been married more than once. His first marriage was with his maternal cousin as was customary among Muslims.

One of the young members of a closely related family was at our school and a person of considerable interest and curiosity to us. It was an unusual decision to send him to school, and he was flatteringly ignored by the teachers and given immunity from studies and examinations. He had a princely disdain for work but realised its onerous nature sufficiently to express his sympathy for us who had to pass examinations. He was preparing to become an aide one day. In the meantime, he was working hard learning car driving, shooting and acquiring the capacity to do nothing for long periods. He was already learning the mysteries of sex and its infinite variations, which knowledge, apart from personal pleasure, he seemed to regard as a qualification. Some senior boys would hear lively descriptions of his affairs with the bandis in the palace.

The bandis, literally meaning 'the tied', were maids in the harem, usually daughters of female servants. As young women they were often a prey to their masters; to the young in pursuit of their initial adventures, and to the old as 'tender morsels' for a change. They would beget children from the family and were usually married off to manservants, often the sons of bandis. The senior ladies of the family tolerated the institution, partly because it was the traditional way of providing cheap household labour, tied to the home because it belonged nowhere else; but they must have seen in it also the additional advantage of keeping the young men from experimental liaisons with growing cousins or from straying out to the courtesans and bringing disease to the cousins whom they would marry in due course. Mixed with members of the family, and with their blood continually freshened from outside, the bandis were usually good looking and robust. Curiously, they seldom formed any long liaisons or exercised any influence upon the men in the family. There were cases of women, even courtesans, rising to positions of great influence upon rulers, but one rarely heard of a bandi rising to a position of eminence.

A matron with the help of a wise old bandi might arrange to place a young woman in the way of an exploring adolescent. Our unsuspecting schoolmate prince talked of his first affair in terms of a great exploit with this 'relucant' innocent bandi. Later as the emboldened youth really began to exploit, when he visited his estates, the village girls would be kept in purda for fear of his depredations. If one of them took his fancy he might marry her and put her behind the high walls of one of his many palaces and mansions; or having had his fill of her he might return her to the family with some money. The family could gnash their teeth if they liked, but they could do no more. Being poor and simple, they accepted their fate and were happy if the girl was kept in the harem. Occasionally the patrician would cast his discretion to the wind and show illicit interest in a woman in one of the other households. Such an insult would be avenged by intrigue, not openly, but usually by poisoning. The little wheels of intrigues would move fast but quietly on such occasions, for if the slightest scent of the plot reached the threatened party, wheels on his side would move faster still. The story went of a patrician of long ago who saw one of his young companions coming surreptitiously from the harem. He declared that very day that while in the past he had hunted wild animals with his dogs, on the following day he was going to try the variation of hunting a man. The whole retinue was commanded to witness the spectacle which, everyone knew, would consist of burying the man up to his waist and setting the dogs on him. The young aide immediately scented the danger, and as it was now his life against the master he moved with a speed born of despair. With threat and bribery he and his friends reached a point where hatred and frustration had simmered for many years. Although this deep wound had healed on the surface and was forgotten by others, now given the chance to open, with just the right pressure from someone who had remembered its existence, it gushed and took its long-stored poison in one dart to the masterful victim. The story went that before the night watch went on duty, within barely six hours of the uttering of the threat, the great man lay gasping for life, begging for water, but help had already been ruthlessly barred. The heir was not altogether sorry to succeed the next day to the riches of the estate, innocent though he was of the misdeed. The windfall of power banished any thought of investigation and revenge. Prudence also demanded a discreet acceptance, for a re-opening might lead to another desperate throw of the dice, and this time perhaps also a bid for power. Securely guarded in high-walled harems, the women on these occasions worked side by side with men with even greater boldness and cunning.

The women of the harem were well guarded from public gaze. Soon after our arrival we heard that the ladies of the palace were going to move from Bahawalpur to the old family seat. Years of drill had trained the police in a smooth operation of this exercise. The town criers went about with their drums, and wherever they stood and beat them a crowd collected to hear that on the afternoon of the appointed day no one should be on the road which led from the palace to the railway station, not even on the connecting roads. As far as the eye could see on this route no human being should be visible, not even a woman, in case that was a ruse. People whose houses even distantly overlooked the road were told to stay inside the rooms on the ground floors. All these precautions were taken notwithstanding the fact that the ladies were in any case going to travel in purda cars, completely screened from outside.

Two hours before the appointed hour the police began to clear the roads and order people to shut all doors and windows which could be seen from the roadside. They blew whistles and shouted at anyone they saw from the road. Soon a deserted silence descended, of a kind that was unimaginable. It was eerie because it was in broad daylight and carried with it a threat of the dungeon and even death. We two brothers could not restrain our curiosity to see what exactly was going to happen. We went on the terrace and crouched behind the brick grill of the parapet wall. Mother called us down when she discovered this, but did not dare to go up the open stairs nor shout for fear of the police hearing as it was now close to the hour.

Suddenly the police whistles began to blow, and as each man sounded the signal he about-turned and stood motionless with his back to the road and his head bowed. A cavalcade of cars rushed down the road with their special dark glass windows up and thick cotton sheets tied around them, exposing only the windscreens for the drivers to see through. The partitions between the driver and the rear compartment in which the ladies sat was of course also screened by a blind, and so was the rear view window by the sheet outside. As the procession went out of view the policemen blew their whistles again and life began to creep back to the roads. At the railways station the cars drove up to a separate purda siding which had been built for the purpose with high walls on both sides. The cars went up the platform to the waiting private saloons with closed venetian shutters. Out of the front cars rushed some old bandis to hold sheets and form a purda lane between each car and the railway coach. In the meantime the motor drivers had walked away out of sight. When the ladies were safely in the compartments, the doors were closed and police guards stood watch outside with their backs turned and heads down. Shortly a railway engine came and took the coaches away. At the other end the same exercise was performed to take the laides from the station to the palace, and once they were inside their one annual excursion was over. It was the only 'outing' they ever enjoyed.

The sisters of a Nawab, according to custom, were not permitted to marry. In the north the word for wife's brother, sala, has somehow become a term of abuse. The Nawabs therefore considered it an unbearable insult to become a sala to someone; they would rather not marry their sisters. But it was a risk to keep them in the palaces for fear of some scandal arising, and they were therefore banished to an old inaccessible fort in the desert. There, under a heavy guard, they lived their long lonely lives like prisoners, lost to the world and looking back to their childhood, the only short spell of happiness they had ever tasted. Relations rarely came to see them, and thus condemned they could only have received scant attention from the fort authorities. But stories went about of strange happenings in this fort of the living dead.

The fort of Drawar must have been built centuries ago. It was twenty-six miles from the nearest town and was surrounded by a featureless desert which had no roads and little life except herds of deer and some wandering camel tribes. We once visited it by car, an old 'T' model Ford, which with its high chassis and light weight was then the only thing on wheels that could have done the journey. Every now and again its wheels would get stuck in sand and we had to get out and push, sometimes literally lift it out. Deer stood observing us innocently and at some movement on our part would bound away, carrying their fat sleek bodies gracefully over mounds and bushes on their ludicrously thin legs. In this barren country of camels and lean men they locked oddly fat and well fed. Drawar rose suddenly out of the desert as we reached the brow of a hill; a magnificent fort built of mud and yellow stone. Its walls rose sheer out of the sand. From the main wooden gate you entered into a scene of centuries ago. With small mud houses, narrow winding lanes, and people walking behind their donkeys or leading camels, the scene looked older than anything one saw in the Punjab. They were tall, proud men with sharp features, thickly bearded and dressed in loose baggy trousers and long kurtas, usually dark blue or black, their loosely tied turbans of a dark red colour. The women, thin and tall, dressed similar to the men, were equally striking. Some men carried swords, others old matchlocks. We passed by a group of rare interest, a very tall, handsome man of erect and proud bearing and his family group of a small son, wife and camel. He was wearing a turban printed with a hand-block design of red with small white squares, a long white shirt to his knees, with silver chains and tassels to the buttons, a red velvet waistcoat whose edges and pockets were trimmed with gold, a blue salwar and black gold-embroidered shoes. A sword hung from his waist in a red velvet scabbard. In his arms he was carrying his young son, gorgeously attired, his eyes thickly dabbed with kohl. The boy had long black hair, like his father whose long hair curled at the ends into ringlets and fell over his shoulders. They were combed back over the ears and came out as a full plume from behind his turban. His wife had an arched red mouth, deep kohled eyes and hair intricately woven in long plaits falling over her ears. She walked proudly behind him, holding the reins of their dromedary equally well decorated with red tassels and a handsome saddle. They must have been going to a wedding.

The population of Drawar was small because water was a great problem. They collected it in underground holes from the odd showers they had during the year. In the fortress apart from the royal virgins there lived also some forgotten men locked up at the ruling family's pleasure. Some had been sent up years ago because they had incurred the momentary wrath of a Nawab. And today no one remembered them. The Governor of the prison fort himself must have felt condemned and no better than the inmates. It was not exactly a prize post and could only have been earned as the result of some lapse or by the successful intrigue of some opponent. This is what Drawar was, one of many picturesque forts in the desert east of Bahawalpur and in west Rajasthan.

The young Nawab, Sadiq Mohammed Khan, was a very handsome youth of finely chiselled sad features. He dressed like the people and wore his curly hair long. They flowed out of his turban in a well-oiled pack of ringlets. He was intelligent and had considerable charm and must have had to fight against the family tradition. With not enough to do and with no scope for his energies, he was restless and sometimes petulant, as when he would stop his car to berate someone who had not alighted from a tonga as he passed by. He had a special type of horn fitted to all his cars. It consisted of a rubber bulb with a long chromium-plated tube on the outside of the car ending in a horn in the shape of a crocodile's head fixed on the fender. It uttered a deep melodious sound, and as his car passed you were expected to get out of your vehicle and stand respectfully by the road. Sometimes one barely recognised the car as it majestically swept past in a cloud of dust, but you nevertheless got out in case he noticed you through the rear view mirror. On a rare occasion he even whipped people for their disregard of this elementary courtesy. Being a charming and courteous young man himself, he could not stand discourtesy in others. Once we had literally to drag our mother out of the tonga, but we managed it just in time. He possessed a magnificent variety of cars, Armstrong Siddeleys, Daimlers and Rolls Royces, all custom-built jobs, but unfortunately for the people, they were swift and silent, and as he was frequently on the road travelling between his country palace and Bahawalpur, at all hours of the day and night, one had always to be alert. But he soon began to lose interest in the manners of his people and did not care whether they stood to attention or not.

When he reached the age of eighteen the Government of India agreed to instal him on the gadi, and Lord Reading, the Viceroy of India, came to perform the installation ceremony. There were great preparations. The railways station, where the Viceroy was to arrive in his special train, and the entire route of the drive were scrubbed clean and decorated with arches, plants, flags, festoons and mottoes of welcome. The guest palace was re-furnished. Plans were made for a great durbar at which the ceremony of investing the Nawab with the full powers of a ruler was to be held. Arrangements were made for a banquet that night, and for the sake of His Excellency and the British officers and their wives, who were going to be present, Goan cooks and waiters, complete with the ingredients of the meal, were specially brought from Lahore, two hundred and fifty miles away. It had to be an English meal consisting of soup, tinned paté, salmon also out of a tin, with white sauce, a variety of roast birds, caramel custard pudding, Kemp's bottled coffee and a savoury on toast. The Indian guests were greatly disappointed at the Goan cooking which they considered tasteless. Boiled fish and white sauce with boiled eggs chopped in, unsalted and unseasoned roast meats and baked pudding served with an array of unfamiliar instruments was quite an ordeal.

They longed for the spicy, saffron-tinted cuisine of the famous palace cooks.

The durbar was an occasion for felicitation and expressions of loyalty. Honours were conferred, and the young Nawab became His Highness, Nawab Sir Sadiq Mohammed Khan, K.C.I.E., etc., ruler of Bahawalpur State and entitled to a salute of fifteen guns. His privy purse was raised to Rs. 3 lakhs out of the state's total revenues of Rs. 40 lakhs. In addition he would, of course, enjoy many amenities, and everything was tax-free. The Viceroy particularly commented on the young Nawab's progressive outlook. The day before he had lain the foundation stone of a public library, an institution whose fulfilment though was postponed for a number of years.

On the following day there was a duck shoot. Detailed arrangements had been made well in advance. A list of the bags was drawn up; the Viceroy would have the biggest bag of several hundred ducks; the Nawab would follow with a slightly smaller bag, decorously conceding the lord's greater prowess at shooting. The protocol continued down the line, zigzagging between Indians and Englishmen. But to make sure of such a vast number of duck special arrangements had to be made. Large nets were spread over the jheels and hundreds of birds were snared. Their wings were gently clipped, so that for some days they would be unable to fly strongly when disturbed. The arrangements worked well, and on the day of the shoot there was great carnage. Thousands of birds were shot, and with great mounds of dead birds in front of them the Viceroy, the Nawab and their party, dressed in khaki shooting clothes and leaning on their guns, were photographed and filmed. A special film unit had been brought from Bombay to prepare a record of the installation ceremonies.

This was the world of the ruling family, a world of the past in which the only new touches were the Rolls Royces, occasional trips to Europe, some new gee gaws for the palaces. Favourites came and favourites went; they came into power overnight and they left just as quickly. Once a venerable, white-bearded old chief minister, illiterate but astute, rose to great power. There was no question with him of any delegation of authority or sharing of responsibility; everything went through the one man. Even the lowliest jobs were filled at his recommendation. His word decided everything, and nobody acted until he had spoken. But one afternoon, at the height of his power, he was told to quit the State within the next few hours. By midnight he was in Multan, impoverished, finished, and soon to be forgotten.

The wheel of fortune never stopped turning. One day a man was right on top and the next day he might touch the hard floor. Those who got on it knew what they were in for and accepted it philosophically. Those who fell off it tried desperately to scramble on it again, and those who reached the top tried vainly to stop the wheel. The game of intrigues was played not only for the results, but also for its own enjoyment. There was the case of an Accountant General of the State whom a contender challenged for the job. That the new man had no qualifications was beside the point. The incumbent was a man of great integrity, but word was gently passed around that he was getting too old. One day, at the end of busy day's work, when he was anxious to leave office, a sheaf of cheques was brought for his counter initials. The clerk on duty, with a blotting-pad in one hand, very cleverly made him initial them without much scrutiny. Among them was one cheque deliberately filled in for an astronomical amount which would have emptied the State treasury for many year to come. The treasury immediately returned the cheque, and word was taken to the ruler at once that the finances of the State were in the greatest of danger. This was proof that the old man was indeed becoming senile and unfit for such a responsible task. He was promptly retired.

Another man, a minister, again totally illiterate, had the habit of denying instructions whenever anything went wrong. On one such occasion the written order was produced with his signature underneath. He had learned just enough writing to doodle his signature. He cunningly asked for the paper to be shown, held it in front of his face and quickly licked off the signature with his tongue. He then berated the subordinate for falsely issuing the orders, when he had not signed anything of the kind. There was an Inspector of Schools who had also learned to sign his name at the time he was appointed to this job. An Inspector General of hospitals had before been in charge of a jail. Qualifications for a job were trifles that never stood in the way of selection; what mattered was boldness and influence and a courageous assurance that they could do anything.

Administration in the State was based on the most advanced lines, years ahead of the Punjab, at least on paper. There was a cabinet of ministers, if such a mixed set could be called a cabinet. Each pulled the ruler his own way, and everybody interfered and intrigued against the others. The portfolios were Home, Finance, Law, Public Works and others, but the formalities of either the division or the sharing of responsibility were barely observed. Then there were the secretaries, including one for Foreign Affairs, who was supposed to deal with outside affairs of the State, though in fact that was the close preserve of the British Resident, and one on which even the Nawab dared not trespass. The Resident was a jovial and well-fed Irishman who had earned an odious name as a Deputy Commissioner during the martial law days. His visible interests in life were eating roasted quails whole, drinking whisky and nursing his gout; and his work was mainly keeping an eye on the ruler. The Residents were usually men of great administrative ability, and with one or two advisers they could have exercised much constructive influence. Their colleagues in the Punjab with much less powers were rebuilding the country. These Residents seemed only to aim at maintaining a medieval museum, making sure that nothing was disturbed, like in Bahawalpur's Noor Mahal palace where illuminated calligraphed Qorans, Persian rugs, swords and armour of ancestors buried centuries ago, heirlooms for which bloody battles had been fought, were on display alongside the oleoprints of their Britannic majesties and pictures of race horses and champion dogs cut out of the Sketch and the Tatler and framed in gold.

When time came we children were sad at leaving Bahawalpur. The Nawab Sahib, his ever-changing motor-cars, palaces, durbars and processions, elephants and dromedaries, polo and tent-pegging, the stories of court intrigues; all this we were going to miss at father's next posting in some staid British-organised district. But times were moving; we had sold our tonga and the mare, Bijli, lightning, who could march to music, salute by lifting her right leg and put all her four feet on a low stool a foot square; and we had placed an order for a new Chevrolet car for our next station. We might now have electricity wherever we went.

From Bahawalpur I went back to Gujrat to join the newly-opened Intermediate college, and after two years I went to Lahore, where I stayed another two years to finish my degree.

CHAPTER ELEVEN

Lahore, Old and New

Legend has it that Lahore was founded by Lav, son of Rama whose other son Kush founded Kasur, a small town about thirty miles away. Whatever the truth, it must be a very old town. In our days there were actually two Lahores, the Lahore of the Lahorias, people who lived inside the old walled city; and the Lahore of the ring of suburbs that grew after the city began to respond to the new peace and order. This new Lahore belonged to the Punjab and was the centre of the life of the new province. The two Lahores were quite different in appearances and character.

The old Lahore was like Gujrat on a bigger scale, except that it was quite flat. It had a city wall with several gates and a fort inside. Its narrow streets and lanes, its fortified mohallas, whose large wooden or iron gates were stoutly barred every night, its many bazaars, each specialising in a different ware, its busy and crowded markets for cloth, jewellery, embroidery, metal work, household ware, fish, vegetables, dry groceries, all seethed with vitality and colour. On the high road to Delhi and at the ford of the Ravi, Lahore must have felt the shock of untold waves of invaders as they advanced and retreated, but it had learned not to be overwhelmed. Its people likewise learned to combine a mixture of meekness and bluster. They were meek before a powerful invader but full of bluster to the one licking his wounds as he retreated.

They were resilient like all Punjabis, but whereas in the countryside people could scatter Lahore was a concentrated target which had learned to suffer and to rise again. Self-commiseration was no part of the Punjabi character; much less of the Lahoria. To watch him in a fight was really to know him. While the going was in his favour, he was bold and on the offensive, but the moment he felt the ground slipping he became the personification of tact and reasonableness. 'Oh kings, why do you not listen, why are you getting upset? I am only doing the talk of your benefit.' And if the tide turned slightly in his favour he was up again. 'Look, everybody, look, darkness has descended; I was doing the talk of his benefit and he comes riding on my head. Hold me back, people, anger is coming over me.' He lay low to let the invader continue to Sirhind, and to strike the best bargain he could with him, but if the stranger was staggering home, reeling under the blow of the defender, I am sure he pinched his pocket.

Circumscribed by the city wall the people of Lahore led a self-contained life. They were born, bred and married in their mohallas, and upon death they were taken outside to Ramu Gardens on the banks of the Ravi for cremation. They had so lost touch with the country, that the Lahoria children proverbially asked how high was a wheat tree. In times of trouble the city closed within its shell. Every house had its store of wheat, pulses, ghee and sugar; every mohalla its own well; the mohalla gates were barred, and the stout erls were pulled behind the studded door of each house; the mohalla defence squads kept vigil; and every home kept its pots full of boiling water and oil. Trouble had always been part of Lahore's life, but for a period of sixty years, from the time the British took it from the Sikhs till they put it under martial law in 1919, it enjoyed uninterrupted peace. Then its life of trouble began again, first the martial law and them the communal riots, ending with the conflagration of 1947, and the Lahore we had known and loved was gone.

Although they belonged to our casts and sub-castes, the Lahorias were different. They seldom married outside, and their customs bore the stamp of city. In Lahore they never entertained at weddings. When the barat arrived at the girl's house, they would do the milni and then bow to the guests and say, 'Achha Maharaj.' This was a signal for the barat to turn back from the door, and only the groom and members of his immediate family were admitted in. Lahore had certainly learned not to waste its food in communal feasting. Their living was frugal, and to us they appeared self-centred and mean. Some of the richest men of Lahore were famous misers. One philanthropist was commonly reputed to collect rental in annas and pies from beggars and lepers who sought shelter at night in a serai he had built. Could you marry among people like that? Your daughter would starve among them, was the attitude of the outsiders. But there were also families in Lahore who had settled from the districts, in some cases for several generations, and they still continued to practise their original customs. These outsiders either looked for a match in another outside family or in the town they had come from. Intermarriages between Lahorias and non-Lahorias began only in recent times.

Like Gujrat Lahore could not have changed much in a thousand years. If one overlooked the signs of electric supply the city must have been just as Bentinck saw it when he called on Ranjit Singh, or even

Babar when he hurried past it to meet Ibrahim Lodi. Apart from fires and house collapses, destruction by invaders, and a slow and imperceptible change in the style of houses, the city must always have looked the same. Though built in the style of Gujrat, it was even more congested. With not enough light and air the Lahorias had a distinctive pallor, unusual in the Punjabi. The only 'open spaces' inside the city were the markets, the most spacious and colourful being Hira Mandi, the area of the courtesans, euphemistically called the gem market. It was an institution to which there was nothing similar elsewhere.

Whereas in Gujrat the courtesans lived in a small lane, here it was a whole district, with bazaars, gallis and squares. Hira Mandi by day was quiet and deserted, but after the sun went down it came into a dazzling and brilliant life. It was typical of the old Punjabi way of containing different aspects of life that even in Hira Mandi there were middle class residential areas in which people of all communities lived in streets adjacent to those of the courtesans.

Late in the afternoon the girls would wake up from their slumber and loll about the house comparing notes, sometimes cursing the race of man, sometimes praising a kind exception, or looking at their wardrobes and cosmetics. Some strayed down to the bazaar and walked about desultorily in their slept-in clothes, untidy in appearance, or stood in front of a pan-biri shop chewing pan and smoking. The mirasi musicians and the kanjar drones, also loafing about and taking the air, might make some rude cracks, which the girls were well able to answer, for after all they were the breadwinners. Slowly they would drift back to start the evening toilet, which was a long and careful process. A scrub and bath, frequently a shaving of the whole body hair, enjoined by Muslim custom, powdering, rougeing, perfuming, hennaing, combing and plaiting, and a careful choice of clothes would finally be set off by passing the silver stick dipped in kohl powder between the eyelids. All ready, they waited for instructions from the mother or the mistress, hoping against hope for that rare treat of an evening's assignment away from the house, at some men's quarters, or more exciting still, a secret rendezvous, when a girl might be taken in purda to remain unseen. But the best treat of all was a journey away to somewhere in Kashmir or some other distant holiday place as an ostensible wife trying to look homely and domestic. However hard their life they were naîve and simple at heart, and while there was hope they prayed for a love affair, one that might even lead to marriage, which might be rare but was not unknown. When that happened they could make truly great wives.

The principal of a college, whose son was at school with us, had made such a marriage. He was an aristocratic man with the great Muslim charm of the culture of old Delhi. He had fallen in love with her while he was still at college and she was just starting. She must have been deeply devoted to him because even now, over twenty years later, you could still see a worshipping look in her eyes, which seemed never to have quite lost a touch of some inner anxiety. She was a woman of extraordinary grace and beauty, and dressed in dupatta, kameez, chooridar pyjamas and embroidered shoes she looked like a late eighteenth century Moghul princes. Her daughter, an image of herself, and her son, who was tall and lanky like his father, were brought up in the old Delhi tradition. It was altogether a charming family and, in spite of its antecedents being common knowledge, cultivated by all. Our mother had no hesitation in getting to know them, and their son was our playmate. I think she also felt that playing in their house would have a good influence on us because they were so cultured, in a way that we Punjabis never were.

As the evening darkened lights began to go up in the houses and balconies and the girls took their appointed places. There were four classes of houses, the very select ones of the well-known singing girls, those of the nautch girls, of the special courtesans, and of the common prostitutes. There were of course different grades within each category. The leading singing girls lived in luxurious homes and enjoyed a measure of respectability. Their names usually carried the courteous suffixes of begum or banu, and if they were Hindus, as they sometimes were, bai. They were frequently invited out to weddings and other functions; they sang for the recording companies, and later for the Lahore Radio, and still later as playback singers in films. To visit their houses was quite respectable. They received in the hall, a long, well proportioned room with an ornate ceiling and painted walls. The floor was covered with thick quilted mattresses, spread with spotlessly white sheets. Against the walls there were white or coloured velvet cushions, with low carved tables and polished brass spittoons. You sat relaxed along the walls and were served pan supari. The singing girl would prepare the pan herself from her fretted silver box, and a maid would pass it round with scented betel nut and little wads of cottonwool dabbed in attar on a silver tray.

The formalities of reception and the pleasantries over, she would sit surrounded by her musicians, usually three men, one playing the harmonium, another the sarangi, and the third the tabla. She led. After a lot of tuning of the sarangi and the tabla, the musicians would slowly begin. They carefully watched her right hand and its outstretched little finger, as she slowly conducted them in a song-symphony. Years of meticulous training had given her a flawless diction, and each word was uttered with beautiful precision. The opening movement, the alap, might take ten minutes or more, going slowly and repetitively over the scale and gradually culling out the theme in a very relaxed way, till she and the musicians all floated in unison on the wave of melody. As she sustained a long note, the harmonium merely followed in a single low resonant note, the tabla whispered in little taps, but the sarangi sometimes followed and sometimes led her through alternating variations and quick glissandos through the second movement, the vilambit, till both of them, she and the sarangi player, gazing at each other in ecstasy, slowly lost themselves. The tablawala then came in to gently waken them by a slight but compelling change in rhythm, and slowly he took her over, while the sarangi hovered in the background. He would fix his eyes on her, beseeching, cajoling, waking her from the deep reverie of her song which was called khayal, 'thought'. A great khayal was a great thought on the part of the singer, something personal, something uncharted; it was a dream thought which the accompanying musician sometimes found difficult to follow. Lost in her reverie, they did not know where she would come up again; so they retired muted into the background, not daring to disturb her, but on hand for her return. And slowly a smile flickered on the tablawala's face; he shook his head with the quickening rhythm as each beat, louder than the one before, brought her back to their midst. The sarangi now sang joyously because it had recovered the leader again. It talked tremulously and petulantly to her, dancing around her in sheer happiness; but melting into pure adoration as the khayal built to its cadenza, the tans in drut, the musicians appeared not quite certain of themselves till the finish. They beamed with relief as she gave them a tired smile that conveyed her appreciation.

The audience woke from their own dreams as she gently lowered them to earth. They uttered decorous wah wahs and offered silver coins and notes, which they would pass round the head of the girl before offering them. And then began a chaste appreciation of the song in Urdu laced with pure Persian, carefully savouring the melody, the words and the subtle thoughts behind them. They would go over a single line or a phrase, analysing its construction and poetry, and congratulate her on her delicate interpretation. The servants broughts drinks, sherbets and whisky, and perhaps the amber-coloured Rajput-Moghul liqueur, when the weather was cold. It was made from saffron, pigeon and partridge blood, and a variety of spices. It was served only in thimble glasses, and a few drops of it were enough to produce a wonderful feeling of warmth which spred through the body and made one fell hot on the coldest night. Conversation went on in polite tones, and requests were discussed for the next song; was it to be a thumri, a dadra, a kajri or perhaps another khayal in the rag? There were ragas for the sunrise, for the lighting time, for the rains, for all times of the day and for all seasons. And on their merits the discussion continued till the tablawala started his taps again and her right hand began to sway tentatively.

In their humbler homes the courtesan girls, many beautiful even in their prematurely tired youth, would sit on the balconies under a strong light and look smilingly down at the men walking in the lane below. There were jasmine-tinted Kashmirans, wheat-skinned Punjabans, grey-eyed Paharans, delicately modelled Delhiwallis, taut and proud-looking Rajasthanis, an occasional hawk-faced Baluch or a rosy, blue-eyed Pathani. They came from all over the north, from the mountain passes of Karakorum to the hills of Kumaon, from the Nagin of Srinagar to the lakes of Udaipur, dressed in their different clothes and hair-styles. Men from below would look up, vacillating in their choice, till someone, would separate from the crowd and dive into the dark staircase, lit by a solitary earthenware lamp. As he entered into the glare of the reception room the girl left the balcony. She would come and sit near the man and they exchanged formal pleasantries, while the maid sat in a corner watching them ingratiatingly and shrewdly. The girl would size up what kind of a man he was and what to ask. Mostly it was a dull routine with a succession of bullying and blustering men, weak and old men, young and fumbling men, mean and demanding men, prudish and hypocritical men, an endless monotony of types that she knew by sight, but occasionally there came a simple man, undemanding, generous, with deep emotions, reaching uncertainly for a fulfilment somewhere but not daring to ask for it, not willing to talk about it. Instinctively she would rise and tell the maid to close the shutters of the balcony, bolt the street door and go away. The understanding mother or mistress encouraged such occasional lapses into humanness because it freshened her up and kept her going. In the seclusion of the reception room, she would talk freely, trying to know him. She would bring him something to eat and drink, and indulge in the beautiful picture that her man had returned home after the day and needed her relaxing care. Almost shyly she would hold his fingers and lead him to her room, both trying to forget themselves and who the other was. Perhaps she even wondered if the time had not come to think of her baby, a thought which had to be faced some day, because if she did not marry, for which the chances were small, she would need the support of a daughter one day.

These girls were superstitious and insisted on some kind of religious sanction. Most of them became Shia by faith so that by a simple invocation they could marry each man as they took him, and dissolve the marriage afterwards. The law of the Shia sect of Muslims permitted marriages of such temporariness.

In the houses of the nautch girls there was much gaiety, music and drinking. But for these girls North Indian dancing might have perished as an art. They were a merry, wily lot who loved dancing and enjoyed their life; they danced and made love because the rhythm in their limbs and their quivering bodies needed a relaxing fulfilment. There were some among them who became famous and kept exclusive establishments like the well-known singing girls, but somehow they never quite achieved their status.

The houses of the common prostitutes were gay and busy, men coming and going all the time, and the girls exchanging ribald repartee with them. They were popularly known as the four anna and eight anna walis. Their bodies exhausted, their looks faded prematurely, they provided just satisfaction. When they failed to do even that they joined the ranks of maids, except the few who were shrewd enough to become independent.

This was Hira Mandi, also known as Tibbi, as much an institution of Lahore as Lahore was an institution of the Punjab. Glittering and gay, it had an honest immorality about it. No high principled finger was pointed, nor had any reformers suggested closing it down. It was there for those who needed it, and such needy ones came from all classes.

☆

Though cooped up in a congested city people had a number of places they could go to on holidays, festivals and fairs in the environs of Lahore. Near the northern gate was Maharaja Ranjit Singh's marble samadhi, where the great Sikh king's ashes were buried. It had become a shrine for both Hindus and Sikhs. Next to it was the Juma Masjid, with its graceful minarets and the open courtyard where the special Id prayers were said. Across the river on the west there was

Jehangir's tomb with its spacious park and gardens that offered a pleasant picnic spot; and across the road from his magnificent inlaid-marble tomb is a small ruin of the mausoleum of his queen, Noor Jehan, and her only child, a little daughter. The tragic prophecy of this great Moghul lady, expressed in her own couplet, was more than fulfilled.

On the grave of us poor, neither a lamp nor flowers;
Neither the scorching of the moth's wing, nor the sound of a nightingale.

On the eastern side of the city there was Shalimar Garden, also made by Jehangir, and patterned on the famous Nishat and Shalimar Gardens of Kashmir; the samadhi of Haqiqat Rai, a young martyr who was buried alive in a brick wall by a fanatic qazi; Shahu di Garhi, the shrine of a Muslim saint; and the more recent British addition of the Company Gardens, named after Lawrence, containing parks, zoo and an ornamented hill.

Lahore, despite its frugal habits, knew how to enjoy itself. Added to our many Punjabi festivals it had a number of local fairs, the big fair at the samadhi of Haqiqat Rai, and a particularly beautiful one called the Mela Chiraghan, the fair of lights, which dated back to Jehangir's days. It was held at the Shalimar Gardens, on whose walls, pavilions and canals thousands of earthenware oil lamps were lit, to make the whole garden look like a fairy land. People of all communities came to this fair, and an interesting feature was the Mina Bazaar, held on the third, the last day of the fair, which was attended exclusively by women. Visitors and stall holders were all women. No man was allowed inside, but every year some daring young men would enter, dressed in burqas. Some would invariably get caught and be given the traditional shoe beating by the women. The wretched youths were turned out of the garden to a jeering crowd of men waiting outside the gate for their womenfolk.

The favourite sports of the Lahorias were exercises at the wrestling pits, the akharas, and flying kites and pigeons. Every evening young men, amateurs and professionals, would go to the akharas of well-known old wrestlers, to do hard massage and exercises and practise wrestling. Occasionally great champion wrestlers came for tournaments. Each wrestler was taken in a procession through the city by his special followers. With the garlanded hero walking in front, followed by a drummer, the procession would go through the bazaars introducing the wrestler to the city. There was great enthusiasm on the day of the matches, and thousands would collect at a large akhara outside the city to witness the giants battle. These wrestlers were man mountains of tremendous strength, and they followed a complicated etiquette and ritual in both their daily life and their fights.

The kite flying season commenced on the day of the spring festival, Basant, when the sky would be covered with thousands of yellow kites of all shapes and sizes. One usually flew kites from a roof terrace, and in the excitement of the fights the sport always took its annual toll. The cord used with the kites was prepared by dipping it in a solution of powdered glass and glue which made it stiff and sharp. A kite flyer would get his kite high up in the air and then challenge another kite. After considerable manoeuvering you got your kite to do a roll under the other kite, and as it came up you pulled it jerkily so as to cut the other kite's thread. There would be an uproar from the neighbouring roof tops, as the beaten kite floated helplessly downward, and people tried to snatch it with long poles.

Flying pigeons was another old aristocratic and expensive roof top sport. It required a lot of patience to rear and train the birds. The pigeon loft was made from a long bamboo pole with a split-bamboo square platform on top of it, and was fixed on a roof terrace where the pigeons alighted to rest at night, safe from the cats. In the late afternoon the pigeon fanciers would get their flock up into the air and fly them as a team in a circle. The owner gave commands to the pigeons in long whistles, and they would wheel round and round in wider or narrower circles according to the varying tone and length of the whistle, till they were told to settle back on the loft. This daily routine combined training and exercise for the birds. Sometimes there were competitions with other owners, when you made your flock gang up with another flock, or a part of it, and entice it back to its own loft. The decoyed pigeons stayed as part of the winning flock until their owner could decoy them back.

Outside the wall Lahore had developed very pleasantly into spacious parks, gardens and suburbs. Two famous features were the shopping centres of Mall Road and the legendary Anarkali, and the numerous schools and colleges.

Lahore was the first town to start schools and colleges, and although educational facilities eventually spread all over the Punjab, higher education in arts, science, medicine, law, engineering, teaching and veterinary science was concentrated in Lahore. Each generation, my grand-uncle, father, uncle and we ourselves, studied at Lahore. When you settled in a profession or service, most of your colleagues were old friends from Lahore; you married into some family whose sons and daughters had been to Lahore. Gradually people also began to retire to Lahore. Thus Lahore came to acquire a very special position in our society. There was an overall class of Punjabi professionals who had been educated at Lahore, and this was not a caste of birth and inheritance, for in many colleges, especially those started by charitable trusts, there was a large number of students from humble homes in towns and villages. Punjabi parental ambition to give their sons, and soon their daughters, higher education was indeed great, and often touching. It made Lahore such a large centre of university education with about twenty-five colleges and well over ten thousand students, both boys and girls, more than thirty years ago.

The shopping centre of Lahore was another institution that made it the centre of Punjabi life. There was a range of shopping facilities which no other town provided. Inside the city there were bazaars that specialised each in a different kind of merchandise. In Dabbi Bazaar you could go from one shop to another, all selling only textiles, cotton, silks and woollen, from all parts of the world; you compared, bargained and chose from a competitive variety offered by a hundred shops. If you wanted a bamboo you could go to a bazaar where shop after shop sold nothing but bamboos of all sizes and lengths. But quite different was Anarkali, the street of pomegranate blossom, named after the tragic courtesan girl who was Jehangir's calf-love. Legend has it that Akbar had her murdered to make the young prince Selim forget. The bazaar was built close to her small tomb, and it was not just a bazaar of Lahore, it was a bazaar of the whole Punjab. Sitting in Malerkotla, Muzaffargarh or Mianwali, you talked of having bought this or that in Anarkali in a manner that seemed to convey that Anarkali was a bazaar in your own town. Generations of college students had gone to Anarkali, and they continued the habit throughout their life. At shopping week-ends in Lahore you met old friends and their families in Anarkali. The wives became acquainted and called each other behnji, and sometimes it resulted in future relationships. The shopkeepers remembered you from college days, and you lightly taxed them for charging you just as high prices even though there was no longer the same fear of defaulted bills. And then like good Punjabis you all adjourned to the latest popular restaurant. The old Kesari's, once the pioneering catering establishment which always served the latest in coloured fizz, was still going strong. You stood in the gutter and tried Kesari's latest concoctions in gas and liquid. Then came Stiffles, Kailash's and Standard's, leading in a wide range of eating places, down to the snack shops outside the Shalimi Gate, to satisfy the Punjabi's insatiable love of eating. You took your choice, and while the women talked about the homes they came from and about their children and compared notes about marriageable brothers and sisters the men went back to their college days and exchanged sly references to the places they used to visit in seach of varied fare.

It is a charming trick of fate that poor Anarkali, who was poisoned lest she became Jehangir's spouse, is commemorated by a bright and gay street, while Noor Jehan, who ruled both Jehangir and Hindustan, lies in a silent, lonely ruin hidden in the reed thickets on the bank of the Ravi, with only jackals and bats to keep her company.

Next in popularity as a shopping centre was the Mall. In a magnificent curved sweep it began at the foot of the Government College hill, wended its way through the Gol Bagh, and at the Bhangi Gun developed into a wide street flanked by the Arts College, the Science Laboratories, the Senate Hall and the Museum. After that it became a shopping centre. For two miles it proceeded as a wide boulevard with handsome shops of western type, where the British from all over the Punjab came to do their purchases. At its western end were a number of motor-car showrooms, hotels and restaurants, and thereafter the Mall merged into the Lawrence Gardens and some very charming, leafy suburbs.

☆

I came to Lahore in 1927 and managed to enter the coveted Lahore Government College, the first stage of the Punjabi middle class ambition in those days. The second stage was entry into the Indian Civil Service.

Entry into Government College had become a masterpiece of complicated official planning. A few boys were taken in because they had topped the lists in the examinations; thus high merit was unquestioningly rewarded. Some were admitted because they were outstanding in sports and athletics. If they were good enough to get into a college team, no further questions were asked. After having assured the academic elite and the leading athletes the complicated ritual of selection began. There were many areas for reward: families from the states, titled families with record of loyal service to the British Government, sons of high officials and zamindars, nominees of the Political Department, a few Christians and Anglo-Indians and an odd Parsi. The English principal carefully went through the applications, also considering any secret reports that might have come in from the police about a boy's or his family's political leanings. In fact, we all had to sign an undertaking that we did not possess nor would acquire any interest whatsoever in politics. Lastly, a few boys, I among them, were admitted who possessed none of the above qualifications but somehow appealed to the principal because their sheer mediocrity might hold some unsuspected promise. Patterned on Oxford and Cambridge, with a number of British and British-educated Indian professors and lecturers, Government College aimed at giving an all-round education. Its academic standards were naturally high because of its well qualified and hand picked staff which belonged to the well paid senior cadres of government educational service.

Despite Government's attempts to keep politics out of student's way, our interest in it was daily growing. Some of the attempts were pathetic. After one summer vacation two boys were called up by the principal who thrust some papers before them. These were the statements they had signed when they joined college, agreeing not to take part in any political activity. The principal reminded them that on a certain date they had attended a political meeting. With difficulty the boys recalled that out for a walk one day they had seen a crowd collected in a street and had stopped to look. It was a small labour meeting protesting about something or the other, and they moved on. Such strict surveillance however missed the point. It overlooked the fact that what was making real headway was the simple moral of Gandhiji's teachings that we should be independent and free, which one did not have to learn by participation in politics, and which was amply demonstrated by all that we read in English political and literary thoughts; and those few who were attracted by active politics were not to be defeated by threats of expulsion anyway. Politics was permeating our daily discussions at home and outside, which mattered more than what appeared to bother the government—the terrorist movement among young students. The Punjabis, with one exception, made poor terrorists anyway.

CHAPTER TWELVE

Voyage to England

One day in 1928 my father asked me if I had decided what I was going to do after finishing college next year. To three generations of young Punjabis the unquestioned choice had been the Indian Civil Service, and I assumed that this was what my father would expect of me. I was therefore taken aback by his next question. Did I see any future in the I.C.S. or, for that matter, in Government service? I took in his point, but I was surprised that political doubt had crept in even in my father's mind. I had not expected this of his generation. In someone as disinterested in politics as my father any question about the future of government service was indeed a sign of change. I had till now thought that he would see it in the elementary terms that the British had brought peace and development, and while some administrative concessions and improvements were necessary here and there, the question of independence and freedom had no meaning. And yet what he said was that though the present agitation would no doubt die down, how long would the British be able to carry on. Although he would not admit it, I feel that these thoughts came to him as a result of growing personal frustrations. This I could only guess.

I think these doubts in father's mind began not from any growing political conviction, because apart from what he read in the daily bible of the educated homes, the Tribune, he seldom read about politics or discussed it, but from a change that was taking place in the relationship between his generation and the new generation of Englishmen coming into the department.

I think father's contemporaries had learned and worked unquestioningly for long enough. At first they were grateful for the opportunity, but as time went on they became proficient at their jobs. They had grasped the opportunity well and made a success of the chance afforded them, but naturally time came when the sense of gratitude wore off and they judged themselves on their own merit. Also, by now, young Englishmen were being put under them, and they in turn became teachers. And there was much to be taught, because the specialised nature of the type of work that was peculiar to the Punjab meant imparting training which these young men had not received at their engineering colleges in England. Besides, they were not the pick of the British universities, whereas the young Punjabis from Roorkee were better than ever since the competition for entrance had become so stiff that only the province's ablest youth gained admission.

Furthermore, the English newcomers were not the pioneering type of fifty years ago. As our knowledge of English grew, their facility in Hindustani and Punjabi began to diminish; the ease of travelling and the spread of amenities helped to weaken their interest in the land. Twenty years earlier, when they came on tour they travelled for several days by horse and tonga, spent much time with each assistant and in his area, and stayed a day or two at each dak bungalow, which gave the neighbouring farmers a leisurely chance to meet them. When the motor-car arrived, the superintending engineer could tour through his whole circle of a radius of a hundred miles or more in two days. The amenities of the headquarters towns, the club, electricity, ice and fans, made them reluctant to travel. The new generation were also beginning to send their wives home to look after the children's education, which naturally made them lose interest in the country.

Three or four of father's earlier chief engineers had settled in Mussoorie, where they had bought houses while still at work. There they sent their wives every summer except in the years of furlough, of which there were only four or five in over thirty years of service. They were born here, had studied at Roorkee, married and worked, and here they died and were buried under the thick spreading branches of the rhododendron trees in Mussoorie facing the perennial snows of the Himalayas, which fed the canals they had built and run. Their children mostly returned to India and also married and worked here. Father had enjoyed working under these men, sharing language, food and hardships. Mother knew their wives well too, for usually also born in the country they spoke excellent Hindustani, and often Punjabi as well. When they came on tour she would specially cook and send them their favourite Punjabi dishes; they would teach her knitting, crochet, embroidery and making curtains and cushion covers, or cutting khaki shorts for us. She felt at home with them, and the men felt at ease in one another's company.

The new generation came from the British universities, men coming out to India for the first time. Mostly prospects had brought them out: good salaries, quick promotion, liberal leave, concession passages and an early superannuation offered an easier career than at home, at least to the mediocre. While the I.C.S. may still have attracted a type that was interested in India, I doubt if that could be said of the engineers any longer. And they were formal men, with different values, ambitious to get on and perhaps not specially interested in the Punjab. In father's kind these new men found little in common or of interest. They found them industrious but dull, interested only in their work, and I think father was quick to sense the change. He was an old-fashioned Punjabi whose only modern sophistication lay in his skill and social thought. He did not belong to the newly westernised class of Punjabis, nor did he have any problems on that score. He was not eager to be cultivated socially by the British colleagues or to become a member of their club. He was quite satisfied with his own ways and equally with the changes that the British contact had made in him. He wore his turban, but accepted English trousers and coat for working convenience and lived at home in simple Punjabi style. But while between the older generation of the English and his kind there had been a kind of bridge; with the new generation there was no link outside the work. I think the attitude of the new lot hurt him. They stuck to their own ways and made little attempt at understanding his. He had a feeling that they did not think of him as an individual beyond his industry and integrity. They probably found him even a trifle ludicrous, and what the older generation had considered attractive old-fashionedness struck them as backwardness. He never gave expression to his feelings, but I know that he felt it. He also began to resent their assured and privileged position. For an ordinary engineering graduate, with no training in irrigation engineering or building work, to start ahead of the highly trained talent of Roorkee in the name of a 'ratio' seemed indefensible. To spend some years in training such raw youths and then to watch them maintain a lead all their life seemed all wrong. He felt the unfairness of it and equated it with the injustices that the political leaders were speaking about. This wrong belonged to the bigger wrong, the exploitation of the country. And as time went on many wrongs began to appear in his department. Indian engineers, even the ablest in the department, never got beyond a point. Somehow when they came near to the top post of the chief engineer something was found wanting in them. In this race for the top only the English seemed to win, not through declared policy but by the frustrating process of knocking out each Indian contestant individually. Father, of course, was not in the running, or anywhere near it. At the beginning it was accepted that Indians could only go so far; later frustration was avoided by the barriers being successively lowered; but now with plenty of able Indians crowding in at the penultimate post there was growing bitterness at being deprived of the goal.

By the late twenties social tensions also began to appear. In Sargodha, where father was reposted while I was studying at Lahore, there were two clubs in the Civil Station. The Sargodha Club's exclusive Europeanness had been slightly modified by admitting a few senior Indian officers and some big zemindars like the Tiwanas, but not their wives, on the ground that most Indian women were either in purda or socially too backward to be admitted. As a result a separate club had been started by Indian officers and city professionals. The interaction of the two clubs on the Civil Station was interesting.

The Sargodha Club had at that time two Indian officers, the deputy commissioner, an Indian Christian, and the sessions judge. The deputy commissioner accepted the honour but seldom visited the club, but the sessions judge was unsure of himself and felt that he must go there regularly to keep the privilege alive. He played tennis there every evening but felt diffident to join in the purely social activities, so he always turned up afterwards at the Indian Club for a game of bridge and a chat. We had in the station a young Kashmiri, the first Indian accountant of the local Imperial Bank, who was very westernised, extremely lively and sporting. His English manager had invited him to join the Sargodha Club but the young Kashmiri bluntly refused because his wife would not be admitted, and in any case, he considered the honour dubious. He joined the Indian Club, and with his youthful exhuberance gave the poor old sessions judge a bad time. Every evening as he turned up after tennis the Kashmiri twitted him about deserting his English friends. He would hold forth about the whole Anglo-Indian social problem amusingly, but with much thrust and truth. From there he would stray to politics, and simple old-fashioned people like my father listened with much interest because it added a new dimension to the editorials in the Tribune, a dimension of personal feelings vividly expressed. He was much travelled and well connected, distantly, we believed, to the Kashmiri family leading in politics. He spoke about injustices all round, touching familiar chords and providing blunt answers. This handsome Kashmiri soon became the favourite of the club, the political mentor of father and his contemporaries. He gave shape to thoughts that had hitherto vaguely arisen in their minds, thoughts they had had no one to discuss with.

He was incidentally also responsible for the choice of my career. He suggested that I might think of a new profession of Chartered Accountancy, of which there were so far only a handful in India. Father was willing to consider any suggestion from him. Thus it came about that I set out a few months later for England to serve articles and qualify as a Chartered Accountant. My professors and colleagues were astonished at the choice, and I felt important at almost blazing a trail in career. The first Punjabi Chartered Accountant had just returned from England, but as he had not begun to work no one was any the wiser about this new profession.

At the age of eighteen I began the long journey from Sargodha to London. I was an immature eighteen, having never been further than two hundred miles from Lahore. Leaving home at two o'clock at night did not make the start any easier. A waning moon cast a gloomy light as the car went down the drive, while I felt waves of sadness, thrill and plain fright. I thought of the unknown prospects and the pledge father had asked me to sign before leaving. It was typical of him to make me promise that I would not drink, smoke, consort with women and thus lose sight of the main object of my journey.

☆

At Karachi I had my first sight of the sea. To a Punjabi who has never seen a stretch of water wider than a river in spate, the sea is beyond imagination; but on the overcast August afternoon it looked not so unfamiliar. It was a vast heaving sheet of brown, not unlike the desert; only it broke against the Keamari wall with a deafening roar, instead of the silence of sand. It was as if the petrified desert had suddenly begun to heave into life and sound, with its hillocks and dunes swaying in rhythmic movement.

The coastal mail boat from Karachi to Bombay rolled and lurched in the monsoon and filled me with a misery I have never tasted before. Home-sickness merged into sea-sickness. I understood how the brides must feel as the doli lurches on the shoulders of the bearers. My little wooden cabin, with the curtains drawn to hide the swinging horizon, was as lonely as the swaying doli. I also longed for the solid home, parents and friends, and wished the journey would turn back instead of leading on. What would England be like and its people? Would they be the forbidding, unfamiliar kind we usually saw in the Punjab? We had heard that even the coolies in England were Englishmen, dressed in coat, trousers and hat. Would I be able to ask one of them to carry my baggage? I had heard from one recently returned that in a public convenience you paid two annas to an English sweeper, dressed in a collar and tie, smoking a pipe and reading an English newspaper; what was more, he called you sir and thanked you if you gave him another two annas. There were girls in restaurants who brought you food, and you did not call them madam, they called you sir instead. You lived in strangers' homes and paid them money, and the lady cooked and washed for you and made your fire. The streets were crowded with men and women rushing all the time, walking very fast or riding on railway trains that sometimes disappeared under the ground. As I lay in the heaving bunk, whose spring mattress added acutely to my discomfort, I tried to piece together a picture of the future life from what I had heard, but it was a flat, unreal picture without any familiar dimensions.

The change from the small coastal boat to the large eight-thousand-ton mail steamer at Bombay made me forget all my misery in a wave of wonderment. The new boat was enormous and luxurious, a maze of passages, stairs and decks. I was a bit cowed by the number of English people about, especially the officers and stewards in starched whites, and it added to my nervousness when I discovered that I was going to share the cabin with an Englishman. Excitement rose as in a confusion of new discoveries and crowded decks the siren blew and Ballard Pier slowly receded from the ship. A number of us young Indians stood together in a frightened herd, taking courage from each other's ignorance. A steward came and announced lunch, my first lunch, for meals had always been meals without names. Hungry and curious, I sat subdued at a table laid with a bewildering array of dishes, glass and silver. The menu card conveyed nothing, and I readily accepted the steward's suggestion to have some cold roast mutton. There could have been no worse introduction to English cooking. Boiled, floury potatoes, raw leaves of lettuce and tomatoes, cold grey and pink, spongy slices of mutton and thick boiled wads of watery cabbage, all unsalted, unflavoured, with doughy white bread and artificial looking yellow butter were as unfamiliar as the thick white soup and the boiled cake pudding. By now the ship had turned round Colaba lighthouse and met the big monsoon waves in the open sea. It began to do all the familiar motions of the Karachi boat, and via the lavatories I hastily made my way to the cabin below.

The next five days were pure misery. With the portholes closed the cabin was hot, damp and smelly. I picked up a pillow and a sheet and went upstairs to lie on a wooden bench in a passage where it was a little fresh and cool. Some other Indian students had also discovered this place and were lying in half-dead heaps, past the stage of feeling sick, past all sense of feeling, while the ship reeled on its course ploughing through mountainous waves. Four of us were Punjabis; as it turned out, three from Government College in Lahore, where we had seen each other. We talked about home, the firm flat land, which however hot or cold at least was always stable under your feet. We longed for the sharp, static horizon instead of this uneven line of grey waves which went up and down like a mad swing in all directions. We went back to our school physics and agreed that the fact that this ship did not sink could only be due to Archimedes being right. Gloomy, wet days merged into night, as the ship shuddered, reeled, and dived we lay inert, not caring if the storm got the better of the ship.

One afternoon the ship suddenly steadied itself and began to move with just a pulsating sound instead of the creaking and groaning of ploughing through big waves. We got up to look at this miracle, and saw the barren hills of the Red Sea and calm blue water with a white wake, as the ship gracefully cut its way forward. It was a wonderful feeling which dissolved all the gloom of the past week. We rushed down, shaved, bathed, changed and rushed up again to discover the thrills of the voyage. The decks were again full of life and laughter; the passengers bent upon making up for the lost days, and the stewards rushing round happily busy.

I discovered my cabin mate, an English customs officer from Bombay who drank from breakfast till after midnight. He seemed to drink and smoke all the time, except for the few hours he spent sprawled on the bed where the steward dumped him every night. This was the first time I saw anyone drunk; in fact, but for the time when we had that half bottle of brandy in the house I had never seen anyone drink. His only attempt at conversation ended abortively. He asked me whether I was going home, but I could not follow his accented speech nor the reference to home and said the Punjabi 'hain'? He told me to say 'pardon', not that 'hain'. I felt hot with shame, and I think he sensed it, because he never spoke to me again. Such problems were cropping up everywhere on the boat. The older experienced Indians, who were familiar with the English ways, knew how to go about; but we were simple and natural and ran into plenty of minor trouble. Some of the hardy passengers who came up on deck during the storm had objected to us lying in heaps on the benches. Eventually the Captain came, but he must have understood our misery, for he let us lie there till we were a little better. We spoke loudly and sometimes called to each other across the deck; we stared at the makeup and the strange clothes of the women, especially when they put their arms round men and without any trace of shame slid to music across a chalked floor. One of the boys disturbed them during after-lunch coffee by trying to strum an Indian tune out of the piano, and they again complained to the Captain. A Tamil brahmin boy who was going to Cambridge for I.C.S. boldly decided to retaliate by sitting cross-legged on the deck next morning with all the marks and stripes on his arms, forehead and chest, chanting mantras interminably till he cleared the whole deck. He knew that religious practice gave the immunity that he did not enjoy in the state room at the piano.

We were told by experienced Indian passengers that these were the usual tiffs between Indians and British on English boats. It always began from Bombay and lasted till Port Said, but once the boat entered the Mediterranean the atmosphere would change. On the opposite way, a pleasant atmosphere existed until Port Said, and then it would suddenly become stiff and unpleasant as the boat went east of Suez. Although in the second class the English themselves were mostly the lower middle class and even the working type, from the customs, port trusts, telephones and railway workshops, we did not even conform to their standard of social sophistication and behaviour; and being simple themselves they were quick to show it. So we went about in two groups, the English and the Indians, never speaking to each other and with unconcealed mutual dislike. A young Bengali, an art student who claimed to be an ex-terrorist, enjoyed the opportunity of giving us education in politics. He told us that he had been picked up as an experiment by an English police officer, who had recommended him for painting murals in India House in London, in the hope that a stay in England would wean him from politics.

We Punjabis were more than anything else worried by the problem of food. We yearned for our thick chappatis, chalk-white butter and curd, till we decided to go to the crew's quarters and appeal to the Pathan and West Punjabi engine-room men. They understood our difficulty, and in spite of the chief officer's protests we became their regular guests. We were also bothered by the English omnivorousness. They seemed to relish all kinds of animals and all parts of them. We were revolted by ham and bacon, roast pork and beef, steaks and ribs, and we were told they even ate the head, feet and tripe of the unfortunate animal. Surely, we argued, they must draw the line somewhere. One morning as some of us were going up to breakfast, a Muslim boy came running down and shouted excitedly that they even ate that part of the animal, its most private part. He could barely explain with excitement, but as he calmed down a little he informed us that he had just been to the dining-room, and the steward had brought him some liver, kidneys and this extraordinary part of the animal's anatomy. He had not even waited to ask. He swore he was telling the truth, and he was, because as we hesitatingly sat at the table, we saw a plateful of sausages. After that we were prepared to expect anything.

At Port Said we made a bee line for the cook shops, and to the disgust of the Bengali, Gujrati, Tamil and Parsi boys our Punjabi group preferred a solid evening of nan-gosht to the sights of the first non-Indian city. With vast quantities of unleavened chappati like bread, and meat that tasted like camel we arrived back fortified for the rest of the voyage. But from the next day, exactly as our experienced Indians had forecast, the atmosphere on the boat thawed. The first whiff of cold European air seemed to change our co-passengers from Anglo-Indians to English, friendly and attractive. The strain of several years' heat and work seemed to slide off their shoulders. They asked us about our home, where we were going, what we were going to learn, and gave us advice. We began to feel at home with them. They smiled encouragingly at our attempts at picking up their ways. Being imitative by nature I began to learn rapidly their language and mannerisms, their politeness and quiet-spokenness, and to acquire taste for their food and familiarity with the confusing variety of table instruments; so that by the time we reached Marseilles, I was feeling confident already at steering my way through the new life.

As the boat train reached London each one became absorbed in thoughts about the future. There would be many years in a strange land, away from home and parents; there would be successes and failures, disappointments and crises, all to be faced and settled alone. We would spread all over England, Scotland and Wales in universities, workshops, hospitals and offices, reading a variety of subjects and learning many trades and skills. Some would keep a straight course towards their goals, some through either misfortune or fault of their own would stop half way, some would begin to drift, pleasantly at first, and then get caught in a whirlpool and be cast aside, ending their days in mean jobs, usually as waiters in Indian restaurants, never daring to go back home or even contact other Indians in England. And what would be awaiting us on our return home? That was to be the gnawing fear right through the stay. Jobs were scarce in India. As the boat train rushed through miles and miles of backs of houses with their little yards, all looking alike, we sat awed by the present and the future, till we were spewed forth into the immensity of London.

Everyone had someone to meet him at the Victoria Station, a relation, friends or introduction. I had my elder brother, Manohar, waiting for me, meeting every train from Paris since the morning. In reply to his cable on the ship I had told him the day of my expected arrival, little realising that there were many trains to London in a day. He looked so different from when I had last seen him four and a half years ago that I barely recognised him. I felt a little self-conscious at the difference between us. He looked so un-Punjabi, so English; even his skin had paled several shades; his clothes were differently cut, his soft hat and shoes were unlike what I had specially bought in Lahore; even his Punjabi sounded unfamiliar, its construction distinctly English. We spoke awkwardly about home and the journey. In the taxi I told him about the little problems on the voyage, and he explained to me that I would find the English quite different here, and I must forget what I had thought of them in India.

England was to be my home for the next eight years. I was to discover at the end that I did not care whether I returned; that the people known for their strangeness and formality were sentimental at heart and held back nothing, provided you became one of them, and I did.

CHAPTER THIRTEEN

Studying at Manchester

London was just too big for me and the two days I spent there so overwhelming that I was glad to leave for Manchester. My brother had arranged some digs in advance so that I settled in straight away. On the following day I went to meet my new principal to whom I was going to be articled, and then to the University. Life opened at a chapter in which almost everything was new. Whether in the digs, at college or in town, impressions came big and fast. The independence I enjoyed in my affairs, the academic and social freedom of University life, the stimulating lectures and the Union activities gave me a most exhilarating feeling; so much so that I began to have a peculiar nightmare. I would dream that I was suddenly recalled home and had to leave this wonderful new life; I would awake with a sense of great relief that it was in fact only just beginning.

Life had a fullness I had never known before. At college in Lahore, extra-curricular activities had been limited to an occasional debate, with a professor in the chair, and an odd lecture by a visitor, again with a professor presiding. You merely listened because questions were not encouraged. The debates were on strictly non-political subjects and the talks on topics as harmless as possible. And now suddenly I was thrown into an atmosphere of freedom undreamt of and so stimulating that I had to remind myself that it was real. I went around in a maze, attending lectures, debates, meetings of innumerable societies, talks, seminars, symposia, concert and socials. The days were so packed with interest that the nightmare often returned. But before I could really be part of this life I had a problem to solve.

The habit of sticking together had begun on the boat and continued in England. In class and in spare time Indian boys formed into groups. Whenever you came to the college Union after a lecture you gravitated to a corner where there was a small group of Indians, simply because it needed no introduction to talk to Indians you did not know, nor had you to look for a subject of conversation; an enquiry about home was enough. On the other hand, you could not very well walk up to an English group and introduce yourself; for one thing their conversation was on unfamiliar lines, and their idiom was not always easy to follow. Very soon all Indians knew each other, and some made friends and explored together their new environments. One mutual interest was Indian food, because then there were no Indian restaurants in Manchester. Some practised landladies could produce a recognisable curry but we mostly learned to rely on our own skill, which with some, especially the Punjabis, was soon quite considerable. But the major link was getting our bearings and testing conclusions on each other, especially on those who had arrived earlier. You could put your problems to them without self-consciousness. But this habit of sticking together had its obvious disadvantages; it closed all windows, except the one to studies. Outside lectures you led a life very little different from that at home. There were few points of contact with your environments other than the simple ones of receiving service. Your observations were dulled by being impersonal, tested only by a point of view that was close to your own. It soon began to pall and made me restless.

Participation in the life of a foreign country is not easy. We blamed the English in India for being exclusive, but, except for the fact that they were the rulers, and therefore created problems by their exclusiveness, there was little difference in our difficulties in England and theirs in India. The question is where to begin and what you consider the trouble worth. Most difficult is leaving your own group, which usually regards such an attempt as unncessary defection, convinced that it can provide you with a self-contained social life. If you want company to go to the pictures you do not have to look for an English student, there will be plenty of Indians whom you can ask. If you sat with some English boys in the refectory or went out to lunch with them, you were told that you were going over to the other side. Attempts at fraternisation dubbed you as one of them and ashamed of your own people. Many undoubtedly found it flattering to be able to mix freely with Englishmen because of the hidden inferiority complex produced by the English attitude in India which made some exaggeratedly friendly, and others unnecessarily suspicious. Few had a natural poise. The group's general attitude was that as they ignored us in India, why should we cultivate them here.

It was altogether a complex situation which some well-meaning Englishmen and women, sympathetically interested in India, tried to improve by inviting us to their homes and social gatherings. I genuinely admired these people because it was not an easily rewarding task. Many of us responded with a sneering attitude, others with long harangues on British injustices. Occasionally, then someone mildly defended or suggested another angle, we considered that the very proof of an imperialist outlook which never saw the Indian point of view. Usually we had a sympathetic hearing, which made us alternately lachrymose and arrogant. Poverty, illiteracy, child marriage, and a host of other Indian problems were placed at the British doorstep; we were the blameless victims of it all. They were to be blamed moreover because they did not put things right by brushing aside our own opposition.

One day I attended a lecture by Lord Meston of Agra, an ex-governor of the U.P. He was a mild old man, and I was struck by his unassuming and modest manner. I met him on the road and he asked me the way to the building where he was to give his talk. To see an English lord and ex-governor walking on a wet pavement in a mackintosh, carrying his own bag, was a sight I could never have imagined. We climbed the stairs together, and when we entered the room he looked hesitatingly about till he was recognised by the secretary of the society. In his talk, which was otherwise balanced and informative, he irritated me by his bland assumption, reiterated more than once, that the British record in India was nothing but good, of which he would like young Englishmen to be entirely proud. Had he been addressing the Primrose League this might have gone down well, but here there were a number of sprouting socialists, I among them, and he got a rough handling during question-time. As he left he whispered to me that perhaps I should not have left India. I never quite made out what he meant.

Soon afterwards I got up to speak at a debate on the British Empire. My heart thumped as I fidgeted in my seat, trying to sum up enough courage, and when I did begin, all the lights in the hall went out. They told me to carry on, and undaunted I continued while the lights came and went. I do not remember what I said but I think I demolished the case for the Empire with a barb or two and much eighteen-year-old earnestness, though with a sense of appreciation of what they had done in the Punjab. I discovered that while these young people could be very patient with undiluted criticism, they much preferred it when it was mixed with some humour and fairness; but this does not come easily to us when we criticise or oppose. We usually like to state our wrongs clearly and unequivocally, without relief of any kind.

After this debate I devoted myself to every phase of university life except earnest work. I marvelled at this freedom where boys and girls could organise any activity they liked, and no one in the University seemed to mind. No professors ever entered the Union uninvited, much less directed its activities; and conservatism, communism, nihilism, Marie Stopes, or anything we wished could be discussed. The culmination was the most hectic and the bitterest of all debates, the one on the King and country motion: 'This house will not fight for its King and Country under any circumstances.' To my joy and horror the motion was carried. It was soon followed by a lecture by Saklatvala, a member of the Parsi house of Tatas who had settled in England and was the first communist member of Parliament. He was brilliant and bold, and there was a near riot in the debating hall. It had been bad enough to hear Englishmen talk heresy about the King, but to hear an Indian, a communist, voted to Parliament by Englishmen and women and, to wit, so amusing, was more than the young conservatives could stomach. 'Never, sir, in the history of this beautiful hall has so much filth been poured on its walls; it will take years and generations to wash it off,' said one young Tory in a voice charged with suspiring emotion.

Both at the King and country debate and at the Saklatvala talk I was too astonished to get up. Moreover, it seemed their own fight. My emotions were mixed. I was happy at the thought of so much freedom; sad that in India we should probably never be allowed to enjoy it. But the Indian problem was fast receding from any mind. I felt a sense of elation I had never experienced before. I was drawn into the vortex of a new life, and I cared less and less for the life I had left behind.

Some Indian boys reacted badly and attributed the change in me to the traditional 'Punjabi loyalty to the crown', which ironically enough was a British expression that we could not live down. Some Bengali boys warned others that I was a spy and came from a family of police service. For a time it became quite unpleasant as I argued back extolling British qualities and deprecating Indian shortcomings. Before we condemned the English so wholeheartedly we must take a critical look at ourselves. I argued. A much older student, a lecturer from Roorkee College, who had recently arrived, agreed with my enthusiasm but warned me that on my return I would find the British there a disappointment.

Time passed very pleasantly now, going from one interesting activity to another, welcomed for an exoticness that had taken roots so naturally and easily. I revelled in adopting their ways. After a particularly thick evening I even relished a plate of tripe and onions. My brother had gone to the heart of his English friends by his genuine liking for Bury black-puddings, something for which I was never able to raise great enthusiasm; otherwise I dropped all my inhibitions. I developed a liking for beer, fish and chips, hot-pot and parkin, smutty stories, soft aitches and broad a's and generally got as close to the heart of Lancashire as one could. But one day I found myself sitting between a Lancashire and a Yorkshire couple at Old Trafford at the annual cricket event. Then I was really lost and walked away disgusted with myself, for I could not raise any enthusiasm for the proper rose in this time-honourd vendetta. But I found I had enough natural affiliation left to give a whole half-crown extra to an old cartman who moved some stuff from one place to another, when he said, 'Give us another half crown, Sir; there is many a time I have sat and watched your great Ranji at Old Trafford. He was a cricketer ba goom!'

Lancashire speech and accent was something I took to, and in those days no one regarded it as a sign of inferior education. At college, lecturers and students all had the soft north country speech with it melodious intonation. The class was full of such names as Walker, Winder, Entwistle, Laithwaite, boys and girls from the valleys of Lancashire and the mines of Wigan, with an unassuming, coarse-spun and direct manner that I found very close to our own. Many of them were practically bilingual, for they spoke an archaic kind of language at home and modern English with a Lancashire accent at college. It was not always easy to get to know them because they were inclined to leave you alone, but once they took to you they gave much genuine warmth.

An embarrassing occasion, whose humour completely escaped me at the time, was when I nearly became a Christian. A family invited me to Sunday tea, and I cheerfully accepted because they had an attractive daughter. After tea, over which the usual polite enquiries were made about India, with assurances that at the proper time, no doubt, India, would be an equal member of the Empire, especially when she had more people of my kind, I was asked if I would like to go to church. Of course, I did not have to, but if I liked to accompany them it might be nice. I had little choice if they were all going, including the daughter.

The church turned out to be a tabernacle of some strange order, presided over by a fiery Scotsman. It was a plain hall with a platform on which sat two women, one who played a harmonium and another the violin. I had never before been to a church service, but this was different to what I had imagined. After some lusty songs, rendered with great fervour, the shock-haired priest in a lounge suit came on the stage. He began slowly, discursively as he looked at the congregation, fixing each person with a keen gaze. When his eye alighted on me I tried to look intelligently interested in the proceedings and smiled approvingly. That, I was to discover, was my undoing.

The preacher slowly warmed up, and in rapt silence men, women and children listened to him as if they had never heard him before. Soon his voice was thundering across the hall, hurling bolts at his congregation. His hands in the air, his body quivering with pious rage, his dark hair flying like a sombre cloud, he stood firmly on his feet and threatened his followers, inexorably, mercilessly, without offering any hope. Fear began to permeate them, and as he thundered at them, 'Will ye burn alive in hell', they replied sotto voce, 'No, save us.' In a soft voice, suddenly gentle and reassuring, he whispered, 'Yes, I will save ye.' But the next moment he was back with the whiplash. 'If ye are fit to be saved; if ye want to be saved.' 'Save us,' they pleaded in unison. 'Save us, we want to be saved.'

I was getting lost. I could not understand what had possessed them. What had they done wrong, these simple people, to be afraid of chastisement? And why was he threatening them; and what would he do to save them? He scanned the hall and shouted again, 'I will save ye, be ye white or brown; be ye English or furrin; be ye Christian or heathen.' Now everybody knew, and they craned their necks to see the object of this special reference. Some of them had seen me come in, others guessed. My hosts proudly looked back, and I began to shrink in my seat.

The chase was now joined in earnest. This was going to be a glorious Sunday, with a young brown heathen on the platter. Such a saving had not taken place before. He bullied and cajoled, rasped and whispered as he tried to persuade me to be saved. The whole congregation was with him. Some young men and women got up and offered to be saved, largely, I think, to encourage me. But I had a problem which no one understood. I had a vague idea that a Christian saving meant a batpism and that meant a public bath. For one thing it was freezing cold, and for another, I did not like the idea of undressing in public to be diped under the gaze of all, so I did not take the risk and held fast.

As I thanked my hosts after the service, they wanly asked me to come again, but it was clear that it has been a great disappointment to everybody. I was miserable too, for I would have liked to make everyone happy.

☆

It was interesting to be in England at a time of great changes. As I got to know the country, its institutions and its people, I could even participate in a way in the intellectual process that lay beneath the change. I got the opportunity of joining a committee on University life, I was elected to the Union executive, led an Indian debating team to the English Universities, and was invited to participate in many interesting activities. This was also the time of the great depression, the hunger marches and 'Love on the Dole'. Living with a family where the man was thrown out of work brought home to me what unemployment could mean. For a time, while the family pride resisted the dole, I was their only employment.

In this family both husband and wife were staunch conservatives while I was becoming ardently labour. I could follow the process that influenced my own thinking, but I found it hard to understand in the beginning what they had in common with conservative politics. Gradually it became clear to me. It was of great fascination to watch their near working-class way of living and the intense struggle she put up to climb clear of the dividing line; and I think it was that which had decided her to take in a boarder. We at first lived in a street of an unbroken row of houses with backyards and front steps, which she felt as a hateful symbol of working-class living that she must get away from. With a slight improvement in the husband's commission and the apparently quite reasonable amount that I contributed, she felt she could afford to get away to something of her choice. 'The idea of bringing up children in houses with backyards and no front gardens—well, it may not have been posh where I came from, but we at least had a little lawn and a couple of trees at the back. And I am going back to where I belong.' I loved the defiant toss of her head, as she shook her bell-shaped hair, and the sound of her soft Lancashire speech, as she waxed eloquent about each class living the way it was ordained.

After a lot of cogitation my landlady came to the point and asked me one day if I was happy staying with her, because if I was, and as I was paying her well—not that, mind you, she did not give me full value—she would like to flit. She would like to leave this neighbourhood. She had nothing against her neighbours, but she would like to move into a council estate house, with a front and a back garden; a semi-detached house which was 'fit and proper for them and the kids'. I was touched because she had begun to regard me as one of the family, and by the simple though practical manner in which she asked me I felt that I had become a part of the family's progress and ambition. I assured her that as long as I was here I reckoned I would continue to stay with her; but I had already acquired enough northern hard-headedness to add that so long as she looked after me well she had not to worry.

So we moved into a council house with its own gate and a wire fence. It had a little lawn in front, a small garden at the back that would keep her man respectably busy mowing and digging his own place instead of going to the allotments like a working man. The house had a proper bathroom with a tub and a separate water closet upstairs instead of a privy in the backyard. It had two bedrooms and a small one for the children, a front room which was allotted to me as my study, a dining-room and a kitchen. There was also a tiny hall and a cupboard under the stairs. The family were in raptures over the house, the locality, the proper road that ran in front of it instead of a street, and the fact that the estate had a name. There was a shopping parade with a Co-op, a public house with a car park and all other signs of class. And if they had a lodger it was a proper Indian gentleman who went both to the city and the college, not just a working man. She would now order her shopping to be delivered and would occasionally include some special things like grape fruit for the gentleman staying with them. The children went to a better school where they wore a uniform. We now regularly had a roast on Sundays and high tea, with canned fruit instead of the cheap fresh fruit in season.

I watched with interest the difference between a thrifty Punjabi woman and my landlady. Where the Punjabi woman would have tucked away small amounts in gold ornaments and clothes, this Englishwoman bought bits of furniture—a half-moon rug, and easy chair, a cupboard. Instead of changing her gold bangles into heavier ones, she traded her dining-room suite for something in better wood. Watching her at work and leisure I learned a new definition of house pride. She worked far harder at polishing and scrubbing than our women ever did. I learned, too, that where our women took pride in discharging obligations and duties to the family and the biradari, this woman lived entirely in the world of her own home. I was surprised at the little contact she maintained with her husband's or even her own relations. She seldom visited relations and they rarely came, except at Christmas and christenings. A question they frequently put to me was whether we attached the same importance to home life as they did, but I realised that home to us meant something different. On special occasions we combined as a family of parents, brothers, and sisters, uncles, aunts and cousins even thrice removed, whereas with them years might pass without even brothers meeting. I sometimes wondered whose was the better system; perhaps theirs because instead of dispersing energies and resources widely it concentrated them for the benefit of the immediate family. Their attitude certainly had its advantages when things were going well, but when trouble came, as with the depression, I saw its harsher side. There was a time when I was closer to them than their own relations, to whom it was a matter of hard luck that they had fallen by the wayside. To me it was a misfortune to be shared. While we could rely upon relations, they might turn to a friend, but there was never any question of predetermined obligations.

The depression began as one of those things that start in the States, but Lancashire soon began to feel it. For a while the blame could be put on the ineptness and inexperience of the Labour Government, and Harry would hold forth at length on what you could expect of ex-engine drivers and miners running a government. You must leave it to the Tories, for they were born gentlemen and knew the job since generations. We would have long arguments about socialism, League of Nations and free trade, all of which he considered unsuitable for the Englishman, though he would not grudge them to foreigners. I was acquiring it all as part of my education. It did not take a young Indian in England long to discover socialism as his political creed. We were vexed by the imperialist attitude of the conservatives, their easy assumption that they were in India and elsewhere for the good of those countries, on a sacred mission, even though the misguided inhabitants did not always see it that way. The socialists on the other hand considered the conservatives as much a problem and a menace as we did. The socialist sympathy for the underdog anywhere naturally appealed to us. They spoke about free trade, equality of races, ridding the world of poverty; and they included everybody in the future hope of the world. At the Conservative Association meetings at the Union the talk was instead about preserving the glory of the Empire and taking a firm line everywhere. India should gratefully wait for a long time to be free, if she did not want to sink into complete anarchy. Conservatism of those days did not seem to be interested in us as a people and had nothing to offer for our problems.

The extent to which Indian political and economic thinking has always veered left must be largely due to generations of young Indians having been influenced by fabian and socialist thought during their student years in England. They sensed in it a genuine sympathy for Indian aspiration and saw in the doctrine a solution to the problems of India. When Independence came it was but natural to turn to a socialist pattern.

As the depression deepened a sense of fear began to spread. Now my landlady would tell me over my meal about Mrs. So and So's husband who had been laid off, and the latest plant to go on short time. Harry's firm was not doing too well, and unfortunately the creeping fear was pushing him to drink. He began to arrive home late even on evenings other than Friday, the pay day. This worried her because drink had run in his family, and she was afraid that if he went too far it might be taken as an excuse by his employers to lay him off. Just that happened. He began to drink during lunch hour and was ultimately dismissed. There followed a grim struggle. Pieces of furniture began to go as they had come; things on hire purchase were returned; and she would spend long hours mending and darning things beyond repair. Pride had ultimately to be swallowed and the dole accepted; but only once during those dismal times did she weaken. She said to me one day, 'Prakash, if only I can count on you to stay with us I am sure we will get by.' The years of depression showed me enough to learn a deep respect for the courage of these people, courage amply displayed a decade later.

CHAPTER FOURTEEN

Punjabi – Viking Linkage

I took my degree and tried unsuccessfully to do some economics research, but soon strayed into the pursuit of delving deeper into English life. In effect it meant doing nothing at all, and for more than a year I led a pleasantly aimless existence. I went to Hallé concerts, to the new Reference Library, I read the *New Statesman,* worked on the Union affairs, heard Oswald Mosley, Winston Churchill and Harry Pollit, played games, walked extensively in the north country, and sported a snuff-colored shirt and green and orange ties. Among my friends were at least three who had been doing medicine for ten years and more. It was an amiable life whose only flaw was the weekly letter home, but the chore done with a routine skill I felt good for another week. My allowance of fifteen pounds per month with a small extra amount once a year was ample for my needs. And so life would have carried on in a lazy current that would inevitably have landed me on the mud flats, if she had not arrived on the scene. She appeared providentially at just the right time. I met her at a student congress at Oxford in early spring. Two days before the end there was a choice of visits to Whipsnade Zoo and Stratford-on-Avon, but as the former was half a crown cheaper I took it. Since almost everybody preferred Stratford, Whipsnade had to be cancelled and I was left with no choice in the matter but to improve my mind. She in any case was full of a Nordic earnestness to follow up her history of literature studies at Uppsala. She was chubby and greeneyed with a flat pale face and sturdy ankles, but what took my fancy was her nose. Its Scandinavian arch ending in an up-tilting tip was something I had never seen before, because our Punjabi noses are often straight, with sometimes a middle-eastern curve, but they never point upward. The following evening, our last in Oxford, I realised that life was beginning to do some complicated zigzags, which I did not seem to mind.

Back in Manchester I tried to sort things out. Sweden was where matches in India came from, and that was about as much as I knew about the country. I went to the library to consult the *Encyclopaedia Britannica,* but it could only coldly inform me that Sweden had the highest rate of illegitimate births in the world; otherwise it had timber, iron ore and a long dented coastline. Looking at some typical pictures of lakes and forests it seemed about as different from the Punjab countryside as it was far from it on the map. And she came from a small island in the Baltic, which looked even farther. As usual, I decided to accept life as it came, with her as a part of it. It seemed so much nicer that way The few doubts I had her viking romanticism and islander's practicalness soon brushed aside. She seemed atavistically willing to burn her boats behind her, once she decided that she liked where she had landed. She cancelled her plans for the rest of her educational tour to the Continent and wrote home to her mother about it. Drawn from a long line of windjammer skippers from the Baltic, going back, may be, to the adventurers with the long boats, she never suffered from doubt; in fact, her determination and the way she ignored the problems I thought the future would hold somewhat frightened me. Her mother sent back a simple invitation to bring me back for summer vacation.

Before going to Sweden I took her to a favourite spot of mine where I turned up for a week-end whenever I could manage it. It was a Quaker guest house in the Ribble valley, on the border of Lancashire and Yorkshire, an old converted farm-house with a magnificent view. Living in Manchester always made me long for a distant horizon, and whenever I could not stand any more the interminable rows of houses, wet pavements and the glistening tramlines, I would pack a small bag and take a bus to this place. The greyness of Manchester continued in another thirty-odd miles of Bury, Bolton and a string of other towns, until the road came out of this industrial tunnel into the open air of the valley of the river Ribble. Now it was a clear sky, green grass, the light and the smells of the country. From the sleepy cobbled little town of Clitheroe, where the bus dropped me, I would walk along a lane that climbed past fields and farms, inhaling deeply the English country smells with their infinite variety of shades.

Hay's Farm was situated well above the valley and commanded an extensive view of the land as it dipped into the wooded hollow that was the river valley, and rose again on the other side through woods and farms to the noble form of Pendle Hill. At the back of the house there was a beautiful old English garden which in early summer was alone worth coming all the way from Manchester to see. The friendly Quaker who was in charge of this guest house told me that during his visit to Lancashire at the time of the Round Table Conference Gandhiji had stayed a night here. He arrived in the evening in his chappals, dhoti and white wollen shawl and took a walk in this garden which just then was in the blaze of its full glory. It had astonished him that Gandhiji did not even seem to notice the flowers. I consoled him that it was quite characteristic of Gandhiji, that though he passionately advocated a return to nature he completely lacked interest in its beauty.

A sense of peace used to fill me as I walked through the garden and stood on the terrace looking at the valley and Pendle beyond. I had got to know every fold and contour of this hill, its every shade of colour through the four seasons, and the changing lights of day and night. I believe I loved it in a peculiarly personal sort of way so that I felt I should do some detransference, and thus it was that I brought Gärd here. Before she introduced me to her country there was a small part of England that I wanted to show her first. We walked through the woods and ravines formed by the streams and brooks that drained the hills into the Ribble. From the valley we climbed the Pendle and roamed for hours over the sombre moors where the wind always blew hard. We sat on an old stone wall and watched the seagulls poised on the currents in the air, occasionally uttering their primitive cries. I had often slipped away from the guest house and climbed the Pendle alone; today I felt a different kind of exhilaration, for the mountain seemed to matter less.

☆

I gazed through the window of the train from Gothenburg to Stockholm at the long succession of outcrops of granite, still blue lakes and silent pine forests. Every now and again you saw a factory in a forest clearing, usually on the edge of a lake, but the train never ran through miles and miles of smoke-stacks with the houses of workers clustered around them. I looked at her face in the opposite seat, and at the faces of other passengers, pale and impassive, with calm blue eyes. They looked so placid and yet you felt underneath there was a strength of passion that I had already recognised in her. It looked all so far from the Punjab, so different, and yet I sensed a commonness and felt at home. As I got to know them well I realised that we were both products of essentially rural societies. Like us, they were a rural people, to whom land and family ties still meant much.

We spent a few days in Stockholm, a city of elegance that blended its architecture, both old and new, so naturally with its fresh and clear waterways and surrounding forests. She happily showed me around its palaces, galleries, parks and linden avenues, the old city and the new town hall, its statues and, what to the Punjabi in me made a great appeal, its variety of restaurants and food. Hand in hand we roamed about from early morning till late at night, and she felt a new thrill of seeing it through my eager eyes. The evenings were long and the nights short, when the sun left a velvety purple dusk behind and soon returned to a rosy dawn which turned into a silvery day. To us even the long day were too short.

In the mornings, we met outside the Concert Hall to watch the fountains play on the glistening wet bodies of the indescribably beautiful group of Milles' 'Orpheus Waking up the Dead'. We would wander among the flower-sellers with their gay tulips, narcissi and hyacinths, and decide that what we needed more immediately was breakfast. We would sit in a 'Norma' with a variety of breads, cheeses, butter and milk between us. We then walked along the river where on a little island stands the Singer to the Sun, lifting his arms to the sky in the gay ecstasy of a Swedish summer.

On the last evening we sat on the slopes of Skansen watching a deepening blue mantle gently descend over the city. The brick walls of the Town Hall changed from red to purple, the surrounding waters became a blue black, and the three golden crowns on its main tower stood burnished by the last rays of the sun. Stockholm spread below in a blue shadow. We looked back on the last fortnight and were reluctant to leave. Later in the evening we caught the boat train for the night steamer to Visby on the island of Gotland.

In Stockholm we could get lost, but now it was going to be different. Gotland is a small island and Visby a very small town. On her mother's side her family had lived there for centuries. Her father had migrated from the mainland and had taught generations of schoolboys at the Cathedral school. Her mother's father had been captain on the Gotland-mainland boats and his father before him had perished in a sailing ship. Girls from the island had often married men from faraway countries, but this was the first time that one of them was bringing an Indian home. News had already spread of this unprecedented happening. The moment we stepped on board the mate saluted smartly, an old schoolmate of hers, and disappeared to tell the Captain who graciously waddled down to welcome little Ingegärd and her Indian boy on his ship. Almost everybody, except the mainland tourists knew her on the boat as a schoolmate, or as the daughter of the old teacher, Dr. Skoglar, and Tante Hedvig, and I was lost in endless handshakes, bows from the waist and välkommens to Gotland.

At midnight the boat left Nyanäshamn and on a mirror calm sea set course for Visby. We sat on the top deck watching the beautiful phenomenon that is a northern summer night. To me, coming from the lower latitudes, it had a strange beauty about it. The long twilight reluctantly dissolved into a soft darkness which the sun seemed to insist on keeping in a loose embrace. A pale orange light travelled from the point where it had set and edged along the horizon, never letting the darkness assert itself. I thought of the contrast of our Indian-ink nights where, its job done, the sun was so firmly excluded and pure darkness prevailed. Here sun and darkness mated in half-somnolence, till he gently pushed her aside and began to rise out of the sea. The darkness slowly melted away, lingering for a while in a colourful dawn. By two o'clock he possessed the earth in broad daylight. The sea and the sky were now tinted a china blue, and another Nordic summer day had begun in its resplendent glory. I shivered in the early morning cold and moved closer to her. I wondered why they had shed their worship of the sun when we still held it a god.

The chalk cliffs of Gotland with Visby clinging to their slopes now rose out of the sea. The city wall, the black spires of Santa Maria, the Hanseatic ruins, and the red and green sloping rooftops drew nearer as the steamer swung in its course towards the narrow harbour entrance. I waited to see the vista life held around the next bend. She pressed my hand to reassure me but it somehow felt a little unsure.

Many years later Gärd was to tell me, when she first visited the small town near Lahore where my parents had settled after retirement, how much she felt at home, adding that I must have found the same familiar touch on my first arrival in Visby. In a small town in Sweden, as in a small town in the Punjab, such arrivals were everybody's business. I realised that I had become English enough to find it tiresome at first, but I soon got used to being on display and bore it patiently. From the moment of my arrival Mamma's coffee-pot did not stop boiling for days. She and the maid must have spent days baking cakes to serve all the callers. Mostly women, they came singly or in small groups, and each time, to the delight of everybody and Mamma's special pride, I faultlessly went through the Swedish formula for introduction and farewell. My fixed smile had to make up for my lack of speech. They commented, according to Gärd, on my regular white teeth and my thick unruly black hair, and asked innumerable questions about home which she blithely answered in Swedish without referring to me, though now and then she paused to tell me what the question had been.

I had had advance tuition on the Swedish Lloyd steamer, and had learned the drill well. Each time a guest came I stood stiffly to attention, with the heels together, to shake hands, and bowed from the waist, bending my head so that the hair fell into my eyes. I remembered this vividly when years afterwards, back in Sweden, I saw her giving a gentle push to the heads of our little boys to make them give a correct performance. Most charming was the way girls and young women curtsied to their seniors by bending at both knees, and how the little boys clicked their heels and jerked their heads in a bow. I had also learned that with coffee you had to take one cake of each kind of a whole array, and if you helped yourself to another the hostess took it as a compliment. But you needed some practice to consume so much confectionary. We then had to return the calls, which meant more coffee ceremonies.

In Sweden, besides the many holidays and festivals of religious origin, though more observed for their special fare, there are also those of purely gastronomical significance. Such is the first of August, the feast of the crayfish, when the night is already dark, and in gardens, week-end cottages and outdoor restaurants Chinese lanterns are strung in their honour. Crayfish parties go on through the whole month of August, while it is permitted to catch them in the brooks. I had my proper initiation in Swedish eating and drinking when we were invited to the crayfish party of the local Yacht Club.

The Visby Yacht Club was a truly democratic institution. Anybody who owned a boat, whatever its size, or regularly sailed with friends, could become a member. The president was the jovial Herr Vice-Consul for Latvia, who besides a yacht also owned what must have been the last commercial sailing ships of Gotland. He was there with all his family. The owner of a big store brought also his assistants who used to take turns as crew; a bookseller who employed only girls brought them all along. It was quite a cross-section of small town society, for when it came to boats all were brothers.

The party lasted all night. Swedes have retained the sensible habit of eating and drinking together, but how much they could eat and drink was another matter, and it was hard for a foreigner to keep pace. Before the scarlet guests of honour, the crayfish, arrived on the table there was a prodigious smörgosbord accompanied by the fiery brännvin. You lifted a glass of this unmatured spirit, faintly flavoured with aniseed, and tilted it with a smart jerk so that the entire contents went searing down your throat to explode in a muffled wallop at the pit of your stomach. With the crayfish the time-honoured rule is 'one for every claw'. Through the night drink followed drink and everyone wanted to say skol to the foreign guest. When so addressed, you look straight into the other person's eyes, raise your glass, drink, hold it in front of you again and look again into his eyes before putting it down. With so many drinks everybody started remembering snatches of school-book English and happily engaged in conversation with me. In between bouts of food and drink we went out to dance in the open air, and Swedish dancing was full of vigorous abandon.

I somehow lasted the pace, and the next morning, which was Sunday, agreed to go sailing to the club meet down the coast. There was a high wind, and few set sail, but Gard and her brother, Sune, put their yawl to sea. Had I remembered my lesson from the Arabian Sea I might have treated the Baltic more respectfully. Last night's crayfish and raw spirit, the kerosene and linseed smell of the boat, the high seas and the cold wind soon showed the whole family that there was a long distance between a sea-faring Gotlander and a land-locked Punjabi. I hardly heeded Sune's assurance that the yacht was specially constructed to ride storms and had seen much worse. Only three boats arrived at the meeting place, and an enormous lunch remained uneaten. I said I would rather walk the eighteen miles back to Visby. Mamma decided to keep me company, but luckily we caught a bus.

Gärd and I went on a bicycle tour of the island starting out on the road that follows the coast to the north of the city. It was a rugged country of pine forests, spruce and juniper, and chalk cliffs. The sparse soil on the stony shore had a violet shine of the thyme that filled the sun-drenched air with its scent. The wind-bent fur trees turned all their branches towards the land, while the low stunted spruce spread like a carpet in the shelter of the rock. Below the cliffs the tideless Baltic lay calm and inert after its last summer storm. When evening came we had to look for somewhere to sleep, so like all wandering youth we walked into a lonely farmhouse and asked the farmer's wife if she could put us up for the night. It turned out that the farmer could speak English as he had been to America in his youth. Most Swedes had kinsfolk in the States, but this man was one of the few who had turned back from there. While Gärd and the farmer's wife busied themselves upstairs fixing the beds he told me about the girls he had known over there.

Our hostess treated us to the best supper she could produce at such short notice, and coffee in the morning, and when we left she would not hear of payment. She asked us to call on her sister a few miles up the road, which we did and were asked to stay to coffee and cakes. And so it was always; whether it was a small farm like this one, or one of the stately stone houses in the rich farmland further south in the island, you were offered free hospitality wherever you went. I was also struck by the way you could trust everybody. One of our bicycles broke down and we just left it on the roadside, without there being any doubt about picking it up the next day. Anything you left by the road was safe. The farmers built little wooden platforms where their approach roads joined the main road. On it postmen and delivery truck drivers left parcels. Crime was virtually unknown, and the samll jail in Visby was rarely inhabited.

We had another home in Sweden, the farm her father came from which is still in the family, in the county Dal, near Sweden's biggest lake, Vänern. A road leading to the lake divides the estate; on one side is the garden where four century-old linden trees flank the gate. The path leads to a white and yellow wooden house with grey slate roof; on the other side are stables and barns. The fields are a clearing in the pine forest, the main source of the farm's income.

I first saw Hultet in darkest winter, a darkness yet unrelieved by the snow. She had met me in Gothenburg and we were on our way to Visby for Christmas. I had not realised before what winter darkness meant. Apart from a few hours of grey twilight, impenetrable blackness ruled over the country. In the house the lights burned all day. In the early morning of Saint Lucia's day, which heralds the long Swedish Christmas, her youngest cousin in a long white nightgown with a crown of lighted candles on her yellow head went round the bedrooms. She carried the coffee tray, with saffron bread in the shape of the swastika, the ancient symbol of sun worship the Scandinavians shared with us.

I saw Hultet again in early summer when the scent of the linden blossom floated in the air, weighed with the heavy perfume of the honeysuckle that swarmed all over the veranda. The garden contained many trees not usually found in that latitude, yew, copper beech, walnut that did not fruit. They had been planted by her father who loved the soil he had left. In late summer the forest was full of red and black berries, and all hands not needed for farm work were sent out with baskets to gather enough for jams and juices for the long winter. This was also the time when the local school children arrived to help with the replanting of saplings to replace the trees felled during the winter.

I began to understand the progress of Sweden as I sensed its sturdy society, firmly rooted in the soil and untouched by feudalism, free from inhibitions, and with sex morals that must date back to pre-Christian times. The Swedish tolerance of pre-marital relationship was often mistaken by foreigners for laxity. Here in a corner of Swedish countryside, which was at the time deeply religious in an old-fashioned Lutheran way, it was considered the natural thing for a young couple occasionally to spend a night together at her parents' farm, provided their relationship was accepted by the neighbourhood as one meant to end in matrimony. Any suspicion of wantonness was frowned upon. Sometimes for obvious reasons marriage came sooner than intended. When for practical reasons, such as the youth waiting till he could own his own farm, the engagement had to last long, it could be borne without frustrations. The boy and the girl worked contentedly through the week, and without a sense of guilt they could meet on Saturday night. A sane and practical outlook seemed to be common among the Swedes.

☆

After the long summer in Sweden and a return at Christmas, Gärd, who had left Uppsala the year before, decided to return to her studies. This seemed a signal for me also. For over a year I had done no work, and unless I returned to my articles now it might become too late. It was a stiff enough course if you stuck to the rigorous discipline of work and study, but the way I was going, my Yorkshire principal with a tongue like a cat-o'-nine-tails told me, I had no chance at all. In any case, he wondered if I would ever die a qualified accountant, even if I lived to be a hundred. Stung by this, next week, dressed in my striped trousers and black coat, and for a while, as an earnest of my intentions, with a bowler hat as well, I returned to the office and somehow stuck it for three years. It was difficult to get away from the college Union altogether because these were the exciting days of Mussolini, Hitler, the wars in Spain and Abyssinia, but generally I immersed myself in unexciting things like executorship law and consolidation of balance sheets. Occasional visits to the Hallé, the bawdy Hume Hippodrome, the last musical hall left in Manchester, and the Rusholme Repertory theatre helped relieve the monotonous attempt at belying my principal's gloomy prognostication. Once in a while I managed to escape to the Ribble Valley.

As five, six, seven years passed since I had left India, I began to feel not so much the absence of home as the strain of living in a large town, with a damp and chilly climate. In spite of its smoke and grime I loved Manchester, but the absence of sun and a yearning for the open sky over a flat country began to tell. During the wet, foggy winter months I used to look every morning at a rowan tree outside my window. If the berries were profuse and bright red it was said to mean a severe winter. They seemed to last a long time, till the back of the winter was broken and the bushes on the small road island in front of the house showed small swellings on their bare twigs. My spirit would begin to rise at this first sign of the coming spring, but the liftman at the office damped my enthusiasm. 'You don't know our weather; you don't know our March and our April; we won't be through till May is out, and then tha can cast tha clout.' He was a lugubrious looking man, completely hairless and wore a red toupee, and he was usually right. I laughed hopefully at his gloomy prediction as, during my last winter, one mild February day followed another, and the little rowan, despite the warning of its own red berries, started sprouting little silky green leaves. I looked at its progress every day and thought that perhaps in this unpredictable climate spring might have come early for once. But the liftman was right, and both the rowan and I were proved hopelessly wrong. Winter came back, the greyest, chilliest winter I could remember. The leaves of the brave little rowan shrivelled with the frost, and I sat down to the hard grind, determined to make this my last winter.

The examinations over in a November week of dense fog and marrow-chilling cold I left Manchester to await the result in Visby. Such a luxurious sense of the job-done descended over me that I stayed on in Sweden through spring and summer. Gärd was now teaching at her father's and her own old school, and I spent the months contentedly going through his sizeable library. Hitler was becoming menacing, and I had left behind the first air raid protection posters in England. Even in this peaceful island war seemed inevitable, and I wondered sometimes whether Gärd would ever be able to follow me to India. I let the months lazily go by till time came that I must return.

CHAPTER FIFTEEN

Journey to India

The future was already casting a shadow, the big question of finding a job on my return home. So far, Government had been the only employer of managerial talent in the Punjab, where there was no industry or commerce, but Government service was getting riddled with caste and community considerations. There were ratios for Hindus, Muslims, Sikhs and others; there were weightages for all but the Hindus; preference was given to agriculturists; and on top of all that there was pull and favour. And it did not stop there, because all through the service promotions, and even postings, were beginning to be made a communal consideration. Government service was thus ceasing to be the attraction it used to be. I decided to look for a job in the commercial and industrial Bombay or Calcutta.

Before leaving England, I had applied through the University Appointments Board to a number of British concerns operating in India. One or two suggested I contact their local management in India, but an oil company asked me to come for an interview. My hopes ran high, as this company was reputed for having taken a few Indians at salaries equalling those of the I.C.S. But the interview intrigued me. The man seemed totally uninterested in my qualifications and enquired only about my family connections and background. He asked me if I thought I would fit in well. I said I imagined so, though I did not know the work involved and their accounting methods. He looked bored and said he meant, was I able to fit in with their people and senior government servants in the station. This alarmed me. I did not care for this criterion of ability; and I also expected social problems, especially with the general English prejudice against intermarriage. The inaffable interview came to an end, and a few days later I received a short note to say that they had nothing to offer, though I might call at their local office and pursue the matter. It was quite plain that they had no interest in me.

Something that followed came as a shock. As I happened to be in London I called at the Indian High Commissioner's office for advice about jobs in India. In those days this office was Indian only in name; except for the High Commissioner it was run mostly by British officials who seemed generally uninterested in the needs and aspirations of Indian students. At my arrival, eight years earlier, I had gone there only to get my Punjab University provisional certificate endorsed. Since then I had had nothing to do with them, and I was therefore astonished to find that the man who received me had in front of him a thick file of papers with my name prominently on its cover. He had nothing to offer by way of help or advice, but I left his room puzzled. We knew that Indian students in England were kept under careful watch, but I could not understand what valuable information could have made such a thick dossier on me. Apparently my every movement had been recorded. Next day I left for home.

The journey back by P. & O. was uneventful. Although it was a one-class boat, the English tried to segregate themselves into two classes, according to the cost of the fare. The fact that everybody was doing it cheaply did not prevent those who paid fifty pounds from feeling superior to those who paid only thirty-two, but between the English and Indians the atmosphere seemed generally a lot easier than eight years ago.

The Indian passengers were returning students, and a few not so prosperous businessmen. They mixed more freely and easily. I discovered that after years' lack of practice I felt awkward at speaking Hindi and Punjabi, and I had to try quickly to improve at least my Punjabi before meeting my parents. We mostly discussed politics and the prospect of self-government and Dominion Status; total freedom was still so distant a dream that we did not think of it seriously.

My cabin mate was a mild-mannered Bombay businessman who had gone to Europe to pick up new ideas. He discussed at length a particularly lurid one. He had his eyes on the Juhu beach of Bombay where thousands came for fresh air in the evenings. He wanted to fill its entire length with hoardings to convey the latest marketing messages to the backward masses. He used to wax eloquent on the moving signs and neon lights of Piccadilly Circus and the lovely posters along the British roads. I ventured a suggestion that Juhu was probably a pleasant palm-fringed beach that might look well as it was. This made him sad. The whole trouble with India, he said, was that things had been left alone for too long. I had the chagrin of meeting him again on the same subject.

Back in India I called on a European working in a Bombay firm with a letter of introduction from a mutual friend. He was very frank and painted a discouraging picture. His own firm like others, he thought was not yet ready to take Indians in management. An odd young Indian had been engaged, but only because of influence or because he was an Oxford or Cambridge blue. There was the further complication of my proposed marriage. European firms might not like it. In their own firm they had taken on a highly connected Indian married to an English girl, and this had created complications and much unhappiness to the couple. Among his colleagues there was an unspoken disapproval, expressed in a social taboo which the girl felt keenly.

So things stood, and I felt it might be best to join an Indian firm, where such problems would not exist; and somehow the prospect of working for the good of India had its attraction. I heard from a friend of my father that a big Indian company, interested among other things in shipping, were looking for an accountant. There was no question, however, of just walking up to their door and asking for a job. One had to know the manager, preferably belong to his community, or at least know someone to whom he was under some obligation. Why should he throw a good job away on a perfect stranger, when he might oblige a friend or relation by employing somebody equally well qualified.

Armed with an introduction, I went to see the general manager. A shock of a different kind awaited me. This man only wanted to know the minimum salary I was willing to accept. I said rather naîvely that I was keen to join an Indian firm, but had no great interest in the starting salary, so long as there was scope. If, after a time, they found that I possessed ability, they would no doubt offer me a decent pay, but until then the salary did not matter much. This seemed to annoy him, for he delivered a long harangue on the exaggerated notions of people with foreign qualifications. Did I think that this was the I.C.S. where I could expect a big salary? I tried to protest that I had not even named a figure yet, but he had me out of the room soon with sound advice to be modest in my demands and drop swollen ideas. As to my desire to serve in an Indian firm I must not exploit such a sentiment. So the interview ended, and I left him more confused than ever.

It was no use trying to obtain an interview with the only other large, Indian firm, because I had exhausted my only contact. Furthermore, they were said to favour their own community. So I decided to call on some European firms. Here I found I could walk in and send my card to the general manager and be called in. Most of them said that their head offices were in Calcutta and I would have to go there; others had no interest, but all received me encouragingly and seemed to imply that they were perhaps not ready to start Indians in management, although Indianisation was not far off. One manager showed some interest and asked me to see their chief accountant. This highly competent looking person, with a broad north country accent that made me nostalgic, also gave me short shrift, for he had no use for qualified accountants in industry. With tactless innocence I asked how else they managed to run their accounts. Once again there was an abrupt end to the interview, and I was told that they built up their accountants the hard way and did not believe in high-fallutin degrees and qualifications. He reminded me so much of my Yorkshire principal whose exterior belied his heart. I reported laconically to the manager that they apparently had no need of an accountant. I think something must have touched a sympathetic chord, because he said it would seem a pity to let me go; could I return the following day? He would like to think it over.

He was a sensitive looking man, with a surprising decisiveness in his speech and manner. He outlined a proposition to me with just the right touch of knowing his mind, but with a fine sensibility to my interest. They were going to open a new department in marketing research, which someone from their head office was coming to start, and they needed a young Indian to receive training under him. The prospects would be just as good whether I began in advertising or in accounts, but I would be making no use of a specialised training of many years. The chances of going into their accounts department were obviously small, he added, with a frank grin. He suggested that I think it over and meanwhile go to Calcutta to try to find something in my own line. I travelled across to Calcutta and began the search again, but I wandered through Clive Street and Dalhousie Square with some experience and confidence gained from Ballard Estate of Bombay. There were few Indian firms of sufficient size or inclination to offer employment. The British business houses were polite but reluctant to try out Indians as managers. An influential youth had been taken on here and there, but Indianisation as a policy had not begun yet. A rubber company chief accountant told me that they had recently employed an Indian chartered accountant at two hundred and fifty rupees per month. 'You may have noticed him sitting outside my office, as you came in. We will see how it works.' The practising firms were cold and aloof, and their partnerships were sacred. The managing agencies sent for young commercial officers from home!

I summoned enough courage to call on the oil company again, and the chief passed me on to their accountant, an Australian who had served his articles in England. This time I got on well. He asked me for several interviews, mainly discussing where we thought the profession would lead to in the future. I became greatly enthused over this subject; and he seemed to enjoy listening to a newcomer in the profession. We hoped for the time when accountants would leave their ledgers and take their share in operating management. Finally he told me that if I could wait for two or three months they might have a position to offer, but would I let him know if I accepted the Bombay post in the meantime. I asked him whether I would be required to fit into the firm and its environments socially. He said we would have to see that, but added slyly that as an Australian he saw my point.

I decided to join the firm in Bombay. The people I interviewed were likeable; they manufactured in the country; and they seemed earnest in their desire to experiment with Indianisation. What attracted me no less was the accent and manner of the north country origin of the firm reflected in many of them. Work seemed their principal concern in life, and that was the criterion I had inherited from my father. There would be a long process of adjustment and many problems and pains, but being the first in their experiment was in itself stimulating, and leaving my training behind me gave an edge to the challenge.

This great problem out of the way, I went to Lahore to meet the family.

CHAPTER SIXTEEN

Sunset over Lahore

For the first generation of professional men in the Punjab it had been the natural thing after retirement to go back to the place they came from, and spend their last years as respected elders in village or small town society. But father's generation had grown away from their background, for them it was a question to find a congenial place to settle down. While I was still in England my father retired from service, and built himself a house in Model Town, a suburb six miles out of Lahore.

Model Town was a place, the like of which had never been and will never be seen again. It was almost entirely populated by retired government officials, who all addressed each other as Rai Sahib, Rai Bahadur, Khan Sahib or Khan Bahadur, Sardar Sahib or Sardar Bahadur.

Somebody had conceived the idea in 1925 of acquiring a big tract of jungle wasteland, a few miles out of Lahore, dividing it up into plots, and constituting it as The Model Town Co-operative Society. Everyone who bought a plot became a member with a vote in the Society. The plan of the town was completely geometrical. It had a series of concentric circular roads, crossed by four main roads at right angles, and smaller roads in between, all beginning from the inner circle and dividing the area into equal segments. The roads had no name, but the blocks were alphabetically numbered, so that our address was 12G, while the house opposite was 12F. To the old school of thought this was quite enough to paint on the gate. Later arrivals started giving their homes poetical names.

The big circular area in the middle was common property and traversed only by footpaths. Only thorny shrubs grew there, but it was intended to become a public park. On its perephery were marked the sites for library, school, barat ghar for housing wedding parties, and other public institutions. Only the club, the hospital and dispensary, and the women's club had been built so far. There were several private schools. Special areas were set apart for markets and shops. There were a mosque and a temple, perhaps the most attractive examples of modern religious architecture I have seen in India, and a Sikh Gurdwara. For practical measure there were also cremation and burial grounds.

On paper it looked a picture of complete equality, but Model Town already from the beginning had its distinctions. On the site of the club had originally stood a dak bungalow, and the road leading up to it was flanked by beautiful tall trees. As it was also farthest away from the main market and the road to Lahore, the areas on both sides of this road became the exclusive part of the town. The blocks diametrically opposite, clustered along the road to the city, were to a great extent taken up by shopkeepers and people who had business or work in Lahore.

Regular and well ordered as Model Town looked on the map, so were the lives its citizens lived. The transition from active working life to a retired existence was made easier by the pleasant task of first having to build your own house. One after the other, old engineers, army doctors, retired civilians and sessions judges arrived on the spot and started laying their foundations. The results of their efforts were all curiously alike, because they were all patterned on the government bungalows which had been their homes, and the dak bungalows which had been the scenes of so much of their activity. Each house was divided into two parts by a huge vestibule in the middle. On one side were dining and drawing-room and an office room; on the other side the bedrooms, with dressing-rooms and bathrooms. The front verandah overlooked a lawn surrounded by flower-beds and cypresses. Here male visitors were received. On the other side was a verandah, where meals were served except on winter evenings, and an enclosed paved courtyard, the women's domain, with kitchen and storerooms. Then there were the servants' quarters, spacious kitchen gardens and usually a small orchard.

Our house was a real work of love. All father's skill, conscientiousness and care for detail went into it. It had enormously thick walls to keep out the summer heat, and consequently it was like an icebox on near-freezing winter evenings, when father with his spartan outlook did not condescend to use the fireplaces. The house had three suites of rooms so that all the brothers, at a future date, should be able to live in it with their families, which as it happened never came to pass. Once we all three brothers had a holiday there together, but then the youngest one was still unmarried. It was typical of father's foresight that, although he sold his car when he retired, he built two garages. One of the garages was filled with beds, so you could put up any amount of people. In summer, there were three terraces for your choice to sleep on, the lower one over the back verandah, the main one, and a small terrace on the top of the barsati, a covered shelter from the rain. In its own way the house was like the British bungalows infront and grand-uncle's house at the back.

The furnishings, apart from a few sophisticated houses, were also reminiscent of the dak bungalows and strictly utilitarian. The only touch of luxury in our drawing-room was a big Persian carpet, commemorating father's Kashmir holiday. Round this carpet were arranged in precise symmetry two sofas and six chairs and in front of each sofa was a table adorned with tasseled silk net. Gärd always tried to improve it by upsetting the symmetry and removing the silk tassels, but our old servant restored the order every morning till she gave up. The pictures consisted of my brother's wedding, Ravi Varma's Shakuntala, and the Stages of Life, which Gärd recognised from Swedish farmhouses in her childhood.

In the dry climate the upkeep of such a well-built house was easy, but the garden afforded continuous interest. Here too, father's inclination was utilitarian. The few flowers in the front garden looked after themselves, but the orchard included every variety of fruit that could possibly grow in the Punjab. That was in fact its weakness, for as the few of each kind bore fruit at different times, it was not worth guarding them, and apart from the oranges, the parrots had most of it. The vegetable garden was his main interest, and in season it produced more than enough for the need of the house, and father, like a good Punjabi, looked with pride at the size and whiteness of his cauliflowers.

All the old men began their day early. They believed in exercise, and on summer mornings at half past four the circular road was full of early risers doing their 'chukkar'. Then they were too busy to talk, their minds were purely on the exercise. On cold winter mornings you heard father's alarm clock at six, and while you snuggled deeper into your quilt he was fairly running round the circle to keep himself warm. Surely the day was long enough and he had nothing much to fill it with, but it would have been against his principles to get up later. For rainy mornings he had measured up the back verandah to know exactly how many times he ought to walk it up and down.

The evening walks were livelier and reserved for talk. Father used to set out in the company of a neighbour and old friend who had been minister in Bikaner, and during the chukkar they often stopped to talk to other Rai Sahibs and Rai Bahadurs, generally enquiring about each other's health in great detail, recommending cures and comparing notes on the efficiency of their favourite medicines. They were great believers in old herbal remedies. One of the subjects was of course the pleasure-loving younger generation, who—just imagine—wanted to have a cinema in Model Town. 'Not as long as we are alive. It would only make the servants lazy and take the children's minds off their studies.' Most of them had never seen a film. I overheard someone saying in 1942, 'I believe that now they talk all the time in the films.'

But the most absorbing subject was the affairs and politics of the Model Town Co-operative Society. Having spent their lives as officials, they now all tried to run the Society office and its poor secretary, who usually never stayed in the job for long. The retired conservator of forests took him and the malis to task about the trees and road hedges; the engineers, depending upon the branch of P.W.D. they had belonged to, forced their advice about roads, buildings; canal water ditches and electricity; while the retired I.C.S. just laid the law down about everything. When the time came for the annual elections to the various offices, there was hectic activity all round. Father was seen at home only at mealtimes, and spent his day running around canvassing. But he was too straightforward and devoid of all the traits that make a politician, ever to become an office bearer. Gärd, who once accompanied him to an annual meeting, told me that he was very pleased to be asked to count the votes, and that was all his activity. She also got the answer to a question that had puzzled her, why there were ink stains all over the walls. When members got heated in the debate, ink bottles flew in all directions. She was very happy to sit in the section reserved for ladies.

Gärd actually knew Model Town life more than I did, as she used to spend some time there every year until partition. When she had been in Bombay for a few months, got acclimatised and learnt some Hindi, she went to Lahore accompanied by my younger brother, Krishan, whom mother, I think, had sent to look at his new sister-in-law. Father and mother met her at the station, and she was pleasantly surprised to find father much younger looking and livelier than she had expected. Actually, European women always found father charming, for as they did not address him with the respectful restraint enjoined by custom, he also felt at ease with them and could talk very animatedly. Mother greeted her very affectionately. Many women had asked her if it wasn't a shock to her to get a foreign daughter-in-law. In her lovely simplicity she answered, 'Isn't it better that he makes a foreign girl happy than that he should make a Punjabi girl unhappy?'

This was in August, and Gärd, anxious to create a good impression, was quite happy to go for a walk at half-past four in the morning, the only time she could enjoy some cool air. Father introduced her to his old friends and told them she was an M.A. It was a source of pride to him that both his daughters-in-law had double degrees, and he had seriously offered both to study medicine at his expense, as his ambition was to have a 'lady doctor' in the family. They politely declined, but eventually his niece satisfied him.

In the evenings, when the worst heat was over, and everybody had bathed and changed, the women used to call to see the new bride. They sat in the freshy sprinkled courtyard and each gave her two silver rupees, and complimented her on her stuttering Hindi. Whatever their own views might have been on such an unorthodox marriage, the women all did their best to put her at ease and make her feel at home. Almost every evening a neighbour, who was also a Tandon, came with her five pretty daughters ranging from sixteen to seven, all very curious about this new sister-in-law and eager to practise their English on her. In due course mother took her to return the calls, and so time passed, until I arrived for a few days' work.

Now mother got the chance to have a real marriage performed. An Arya Samaj pandit was called in, the sacred fire was lit in the front verandah, and Gärd was first purified into the faith of our ancestors and gurus, as a symbol of which she was given a sanskrit name. Then tied together we walked the seven steps. It was a short ceremony, with only a few friends and relations present, but it made mother happy. She distributed sweets according to custom. It also pleased Gärd who said a registrar's office in Bombay with two hired witnesses does not make you feel properly married, and her mother would also like to hear about the family wedding.

Two days after I left for the station, and to everybody's surprise came back. The war in Europe had broken out, I learnt at the station, so I waited for revised instructions. Next day I was off, and shortly after Gard left to visit my elder brother and sister-in-law in North Bihar. Soon after her return to Bombay we got a telegram about mother's sudden death following an operation.

Being cast in the stoic mould, father did not give vent to excessive grief, neither did he expect it from his sons. To us he wired, 'Do not trouble to come.' My sister-in-law was there to take charge. After mother's death father continued his old routine, with his trusted old servant Chatter Singh, who had been in the family for fifty years, to look after his needs. He spent some months with us in Bombay after the birth of our daughter, Maya, but apart from us and the baby he did not have much to take interest in, and missed the company of his own age. So he lived on in Model Town, and we sons took turns to send our families to stay with him. Before partition the youngest also had started a family.

Though every day was like the other, Gärd liked life in Model Town. Although she was never hurt by any social ostracism, Bombay irked her as a place dominated by Europeans, who hardly counted Indians as existing, and she felt happier in the completely Indian surroundings of Lahore. The small Swedish community totally ignored her. But from the moment she had unloaded her baggage, ever increasing as the children increased from one to two to three, on the tongas at the Lahore station, she felt at home. And when at last the cavalcade reached Model Town, people on the road welcomed her back. Life in Model Town was more self-centred than ever during the war years. Cars were laid up for lack of petrol; six miles by tonga into Lahore on a hot day was no joke, and the buses had to be booked long in advance. The Model Town buses looked like trucks, and besides their human overload always carried an enormous amount of trunks, bicycles and other heavy goods on top. The 'lorry', as it was appropriately called, had a 'purdah' section in front, and only if that was completely crammed could a woman decently sit amongst the men. Old 'Princess' Sutherland, widow of an English army doctor, and last descendant of Maharaja Ranjit Singh, was heard complaining that she could not get a seat in the lorry, when all Punjab should have been hers! The old lady had settled in Model Town and spent her days dreaming about her ancestral glory.

Model Town was not only a city of the aged, for some old government servants, who had outlived their wives and married much younger women, kept on raising a family long after retirement. Sometimes it happened that there were three happy events in the family when mother, daughter and daughter-in-law were simultaneously delivered. But the younger generation had not yet put their mark on Model Town. Its only social events were weddings and head-shavings. Old women used to come to the house to ask father's advice about a boy or girl suggested for marriage, as he had a wide acquaintance. This always pleased him. If the match came off the same old lady would in due course arrive with a big bag of sweets as a wedding invitation. Father always asked Gärd to go to these functions, not for the pleasure of it, but out of duty, adding what it was a good thing she was conspicuous as everyone would know that she had represented the family.

The two clubs, one for men and one for women, offered facilities for games, but no club life. Once some young people ventured upon something drastically new; a mixed whist drive at the men's club. This did not meet with approval particularly as it ended as late as eleven at night. Another novelty was a tea party the day after a wedding, in the last year before partition. Though there was no purdah, except in some Muslim families, there was no real social mixing of the sexes. Even husbands and wives did not always go for walks together. She would walk with her own women friends in the evening. Even young people home on leave would often conform.

So life would have gone on in a peaceful routine until the end for all these old engineers, doctors and civil servants, if they had not had to pay the price for the freedom of India. A few died peacefully before partition, but most had to start life anew, living in small flats with sons, and sometimes even, swallowing their pride, with daughters. And their wives had to leave their spacious courtyards, where they had ruled over servants and daughters-in-law, to be dependent on a son, and happy if they were a help and not an unwelcome intruder. Wherever they had to go, they were uprooted from the life they had themselves created.

CHAPTER SEVENTEEN

Partition and Carnage

Dear Prakash,
 Come and get us out before it is too late.

While the fading paper flags of the independence celebrations were still waving, the horror of partition broke on us suddenly one day when a post-card arrived from Uncle Dwarka Prashad. It contained this single line.

With my younger brother, who was also settled in Bombay, I had discounted the first rumours, while Government tried to tone down the press hand-outs. No one wanted to spoil the music of freedom still in the air. But every day the news became graver, and uncle's post-card told us that the end had come.

In June of 1947, when partition was announced, most Hindus and Sikhs had accepted it fatalistically. 'We have lived under the Muslims before, then under the Sikhs and the British, and if we are now back under Muslim rule, so what? We shall manage somehow, as we have managed before. Nowadays governments are different, they give you some rights, they have to listen to the people!' Fortified by such arguments, people decided to stay where they were and face the change.

In July things began to look menacing, but few thought of leaving. There were sporadic attacks on Hindus and Sikhs, but they were mostly looked upon as signs of another riot. The turn had come of the Punjab, where people during the war years had prided themselves on living in peace while the rest of the country shook with the ugly outburst of Hindu-Muslim violence. As things worsened, father wrote to say that he considered it pointless to leave the house. Even if there was real trouble he would be safe, because he had so many Muslim friends and neighbours. Who would want to harm an old man, semi paralysed by a stroke? Besides, he was so comfortable with his faithful Chattar Singh, who was on such good terms with everybody, Hindus, Muslims and Sikhs alike, to look after him.

In August law and order of ninety years came to an end. Elementary civil protection, taken for granted the week before, ceased. Chatter Singh felt that his own family would prove a burden if he suddenly had to leave; and to take care of father would be an added problem. So he appealed frantically to our neighbours to persuade father to go away for a while, till things improved. He was going to move his wife and children to the safety of Amritsar, now across the border. My older brother wired from Bihar that father must leave, and reluctantly he agreed, whereupon Chatter Singh hurriedly packed him off. Many others were sending their women and children and old people away. Like everyone else, father thought he was only going for a short time, till the riots subsided.

Uncle Dwarka Prashad had remarried some years after Savitri's death and had permanently settled in Gujrat. My second aunt was a very handsome woman in her youth, with long brown hair and a melodious voice. After quite a struggle she had slowly managed to tame uncle. He worked hard, and with his natural ability he soon prospered. He built his own house outside the city wall, conveniently near the law courts, where he had built up a lucrative practice. She gave him two sons and two daughters. The eldest, a girl, urged by my father, had studied medicine. She then married a dentist, and they were both settled in practice in Amritsar. The elder boy had just finished his law studies at Lahore, while the younger children were still at school.

Uncle had always been tough and fearless, and easily persuaded to fight. He had mellowed with the years as he became an elder of the biradari, a senior member of the bar and influential in municipal affairs. He was greatly respected by all communities, and most of his practice came from Muslim litigants in the district. Everyone assured him that he could safely stay, no one would touch him and his family. He wanted to believe in their assurances even as he saw the trickle of exodus gather volume. These others thought it wise to go away for a while; they would all return when everything was calm again. The thought that this was a going away for ever never crossed anybody's mind. A calamity might cause temporary uprooting, but afterwards you came back to what had always been your home.

One day, a train crammed with two thousand refugees came from the more predominantly Muslim areas of Jhelum and beyond. At Gujrat station the train was stopped, and Muslims from the neighbourhood, excited by the news of violence in East Punjab, began to attack and loot. There was indescribable carnage. Several hours later the train moved on, filled with a bloody mess of corpses, without a soul alive. At Amritsar, when the train with its load of dead arrived, they took revenge on a trainload of Muslim refugees. There was also great killing at Sheikhupura, and on the other side in Jullundur. The whole Punjab was in conflagration. Six million Hindus and Sikhs from the West Punjab began to move in one dense mass towards safety, and from the east of the border a similar mass movement was under way in the opposite direction.

Muslim friends came to uncle late one night and said with tears in their eyes that they were unable to offer him protection any longer. The family must move at once, before dawn! Dwarka Prashad now saw it only too well that they had to go away, not for a few days, but for ever. He had in fact been expecting it since the day of the massacre at the station, but the problem had been how to get out; and it was then that he had sent the post-card.

His friends rushed to an Indian military evacuation convoy that had arrived the same evening, and brought a truck. They heaved a sigh of relief as uncle and his family, with two suitcases and a few blankets, drove away. On the Grand Trunk Road their truck joined an unending line of military and civil trucks and cars, bullock carts and tongas, people on horseback, and carried on shoulders. In its long history of over a thousand years this road had never seen such a migration.

As dawn was breaking, they caught the last view of Gujrat through the shisham trees by the road; a view they had so often seen when going to the river Chenab at Besakhi. They looked at the weathered dark brown mass of the city rising as a flat-top cone. My aunt's ancestral house was in the highest mohalla inside the fortress, and she could see almost the spot from where twenty seven years ago her palanquin had descended the narrow lanes to our old house inside the Kalri Gate. She wondered what would happen to her house, to her cupboards and trunks full of clothes, linen and utensils, and above all to the buffalo and its calf that she had left tied in the yard. She suspected that in a few hours their home would be swept bare, but she was too numbed to care. Through smoking towns and charred villages the convoy moved like a long dark snake. At one time over the narrow bridge of the Bullokee headworks, where I was born, there was a convoy of over two million people seeking its way out. Through Kharian, Wazirabad, Gujranwala, Emnabad, Gakhar, it heaved forward, swelled by other convoys joining it from the side roads. After delays, alarms and rumours of attack, it reached the Ravi and crossed into Lahore. They were put up at uncle's old D.A.V. college, which had become a vast temporary camp. From here they moved on in smaller convoys, and uncle's party eventually arrived at the new frontier post of Wagah, a tiny hamlet which was now in the limelight as a scene of dramatic activity. As the truck passed the barrier into 'India', they looked back at Pakistan, their homeland which did not want them.

The truck delivered them at Amritsar, and the young Maratha major who had been in charge of their section of the convoy bade them godspeed. He had to rush back, for there were still plenty more on the other side. Uncle tried to express their gratitude, but too dazed still to sort out his thoughts, he could only recall the tense moment when they were held up at a police outpost at Shalimar Gardens outside Lahore, and an ugly crowd collected. The Maratha had leapt down from the truck, drawn his revolver and threatened to shoot his convoy out. The police pushed back the crowd and let the trucks pass. Sitting beside the major, uncle had asked him if he knew our Punjab country. The Maratha said no, but someone in his family had been here very long ago. My uncle did not know that he descended from a distinguished soldier in Bhau Sahib's army, which had tried to bar the way of Ahmed Shah Abdali at Panipat on his return from Delhi in 1761.

They landed at their daughter's house in Amritsar like wreckage from a swollen river, but my aunt's Khatri pride was fierce. After a few days' rest, for which she insisted on paying from whatever money she had on her, she decided that they must move on. The daughter and son-in-law said she was crazy. Where were they going to? Though they were now in India there was no safety on the roads. The whole of East Punjab was in turmoil. After the first taste of blood there was likely to be indiscriminate murder and looting. But she was adamant, she would not accept a daughter's hospitality.

The family was on the move again and joined another convoy on the Grand Trunk Road to Delhi. And now the rains broke, and to the hatred of man was added the cruelty of nature. Beas and Sutlej rose in an unprecedented flood, and thousands of homeless were carried away by the swirling waters. One enormous convoy had been camping on the banks of the beas on the night when the river rose in flood. The water had gone down when uncle's party arrived at the river. From a distance they saw a vast stretch of debris dotted with countless black spots. When they came close they discovered that the debris was a mass of bodies with black heads which the subsiding flood waters had left behind.

The journey from Amritsar proved less dangerous, but more tortuous, and they staggered on without knowing where they were heading for. They were carried forward on a human wave. Like a flood the mass migration deposited some here, some there, in towns and villages of East Punjab, in the hastily rigged up refugee camps, till the bulk of them reached Delhi. From here the migrants were scattered all over India, from Cochin to Kohima, and uncle and his family, for no apparent reason, found themselves at Ajmer.

In Ajmer uncle was given some work in a refugee camp by the relief organisation. He managed to find a small house, and they stayed there for over a year. But he found the work unsatisfying, and had the feeling at the back of his mind that this work was only created to boost his morale, and was in fact cloaked charity. He was constantly thinking of ways to start a normal working life, and even toyed with the idea of going into business, though this was something utterly foreign to him. He was then sixty-two, and he had not long before he stood face to face with death in another guise. He was found to have throat cancer, and he came to Bombay for consultation. The doctor examined him and told him frankly that it was a bad case, and the only thing to do was to continue the deep X-ray treatment in Lahore. Something touched the doctor in the way he walked out after the verdict, for he called him back. 'It may seem hopeless and I am sorry that I can do nothing more for you, but, you know, miracles can happen. You must keep courage, and that may help.' And in uncle's case the miracle did happen. After continued treatment the doctors told him some years later, just before the partition, that they could see no signs of the cancer, and in fact it did not reappear.

Uncle therefore did not easily despair and continued his search for a new start. And when he heard about a refugee colony in Karnal, eighty miles west of Delhi, where Government gave land and subsidies to those who wanted to settle and build a house, he took his chance and left his job in Ajmer. He built his house and set up practice again. In a short while he was doing well; in fact, better than ever. He worked like one possessed, but without joy. He was very different from our father; he was a man who had enjoyed life, loved company, and he was an entertaining talker. But when he had to leave Gujrat, something broke inside him, and his new-found prosperity gave him little pleasure apart from the satisfaction of providing anew for his family. Having twice escaped death, he came to a strange and cruel end. His alsatian bitch bit him and a friend. They both received treatment, but it became evident some weeks later that on him the vaccine did not work. Nothing could save him, and he died in agony, conscious till the last moment.

Today we have no one left in Gujrat. All the Hindus came away at partition. It is strange to think that in all the land between Ravi and Chenab, from Chenab to Jhelum, from Jhelum to Indus, in the foothills and in the plain down to Panjnad, where the five rivers eventually merge, land which had been the homes of our biradaris since the dawn of history, there is no one left of our kind.

Partition changed the course of many lives which would otherwise have run in their familiar channels. Most were lucky to find a bank where they clambered up and started afresh; but the real sufferers were those whom the ebbing currents of partition claimed again. When the turmoil was over some well-meaning but short-sighted people tried to, as they saw it, undo some of the evil by restoring abducted women to their families. With grim determination they searched for years for these unfortunate women, and sometimes with pathetic lack of understanding caused fresh tragedies by uprooting them again. Such a tragic story was told me by a second cousin of mine, Hari, a young army officer.

Five years after the partition, in 1952, Hari was posted in Calcutta, and there he and his wife, Usha, got to know a young Sikh who lived behind their house. He was a simple man, but his cheerful ways were very engaging, and they took a great liking to him. Hari discovered accidentally that the Sikh had been in the army, which made another bond between them. One day when Hari was in uniform, the man surprised him by saluting very smartly, and questioned he reluctantly said that he had done so from force of habit. He had been in a Sikh regiment during the war, served in the Far East, and joined the Indian National Army which had thrown in its lot with the Japanese. Another thing the two had in common was their love of the races. The Sikh used to come round regularly to ask for tips. He had a profound faith in Hari's inside information, and once actually did very well out of a tip.

One evening the young Sikh came with a worried look on his face, which was unusual for him, and when they pressed him he told them his story.

After the release of the Indian National Army prisoners, he had returned home to Jullundur, in the East Punjab, to live with his parents. When partition came and everybody went mad, he had also run amuck. He and a friend of his one day saw a crowd on the point of massacring two young girls. They had set fire to a house and killed the inmates as they came out of hiding to escape the flames. These two sisters were the only ones left. Their beauty, and the look of desperate fear on their faces softened him and brought him back to sanity. Without hesitation he called out to the crowd. 'Look, you have burnt this Muslim house and all their goods; you have had your revenge. All the people are dead except these two girls. Why should you kill them? I am a poor man, and so is my friend here, neither of us can afford to get married. Why not hand the girls over to us? We will convert them to our faith and marry them. Instead of killing them wastefully, you will do a good turn to two poor Sikh brethren'.

The crowd had probably done enough killing for the day, and found the argument reasonable, so they allowed the boys to take the girls away. The young Sikh took one of them home to his mother, who instantly liked her. When the girl recovered from fear she began to like the bold boy who had saved her life. They got married, and slowly fell in love with each other. Gradually memories of her parents and her former life faded. They were very happy together, and a little boy was born.

Meanwhile the social workers had got busy recovering abducted girls from both sides and restoring them to their families in East and West Punjab. Many of them were torn away from husbands they had learnt to love, from children they had borne, and handed over to parents who had given them up as dead. From respectable, married women they suddenly became unclean and outcaste, not daring to admit that during the years of 'abduction' they had been happy. But the social workers, many of them, cold, passionless women, were working assiduously, and with the aid of the police and the law tightening their net.

The other sister had not been lucky. The Sikh boy who took her away and married her did not treat her well. She ran away and with the help of the police found her way to her parents in Pakistan. She told them about her sister, and even though she knew that the sister was happy in her marriage, or perhaps just because of that, she reported the matter to the Pakistan police and gave them the address in Jullundur.

Soon the social workers in Jullundur were making enquiries, but the Sikh had got scent of it and ran away with his wife and child to Calcutta. Here he lived happily in hiding for some years, and his only regret was that he dared not go back to visit his parents. But the social workers and the police caught up with him. They prowled about his house, making enquiries from the neighbours. The poor young man was scared out of his wits, and came to Hari for advice. He wanted Usha to talk to his wife to satisfy herself that the girl loved him and wanted to stay with him. Only then would he ask them for help.

Usha asked the wife over, a pretty girl of nineteen or twenty, quiet and shy. In simple words she bore out her husband's story. She loved him and her child; she was happy, so why did they want her to go back to her parents? Her home was here, with him. She grew eloquent, as she talked about this injustice. She would rather kill herself; they would never take her back alive.

Hari and Usha were deeply moved, young and deeply in love as they were themselves. Hari had also met Usha in the mêlée of partition. They offered to hide the girl while they were finding ways and means of saving her. They approached some friends, they tried to prevail upon the social workers, and they eventually managed to get a stay-order from the court, while the law was taking its ponderous course. Meanwhile the poor youth, afraid of losing her, decided to run away again. The police were bound to get her, he said to Hari, so it would be better for them to go back to some little village in the Punjab where no one would know them, and there would be no police to shadow them. His wife was expecting another baby. Although Hari and Usha were very unhappy about it, they reluctantly agreed that it might perhaps be the best course under the circumstances. They would continue to work for her release order, so that eventually they should be able to live in peace.

More than a year later, the Sikh turned up. They found him waiting for them when they got home late one night. But he was a changed man; all his youthful exuberance had gone. Hari thought he would be happy to get the news that his wife's release had come through. Big tears rolled down the Sikh's cheeks. 'Kaptan Ṣahib, it is too late, the order is no use now.'

They had settled in a Punjab village, and things went well for a time, till the police arrived again and began to ask questions. His wife was then nearing her time. He left the little boy with his mother, and he and his wife hid in the sugar-cane fields. He dug a large pit, a kind of fox-hole he was used to from his training, and built a barricade. He made her as comfortable as he could while he lay with a gun, waiting for the police, determined not to lose her while he was alive. In the pit he delivered her with his own hands. The next day she ran a high fever, and in three days she was dead. He had not dared to take her to the hospital. He was so afraid the social workers and the police would take her away.

'Kaptan Sahib, thank you for all you have done, even though it is no use now. They will never get her, but at least they have made sure that I shall not keep her either.'

With those words he turned and walked away, and Hari and Usha never saw him again.

CHAPTER EIGHTEEN

End of Old Punjab

At partition we three brothers were already scattered outside the Punjab. My elder brother, an engineer, was working in a sugar factory in North Bihar since before the war; my younger brother, also an engineer, had joined an airline in Bombay. They had both married Punjabi girls from Lahore. Gärd and my sisters-in-law visited Lahore once a year. My brothers would join them on their annual holidays. As business took me to Lahore frequently, Gärd and the children each time stayed on for some months with father. We three brothers had bought small plots of land to build our own houses one day. Our children would probably come to Labore for their college education. They might scatter still further away in India, but Lahore would always be their home, the Punjab their vatan. The marriages in the family would take place there and some of the children might even settle back, as the developing Punjab was sure to offer more opportunities. As we made friends and formed relationships with sons and daughters of our parents' friends and neighbours, even though we did not live there permanently, so would our children inherit the family connections. And so we pleasantly planned our lives with Lahore always as the centre of it, the place where we would one day ourselves retire.

Partition changed all this. For us there was no more Punjab. Many refugees settled in East Punjab, but to us and many others, it was all over when the West Punjab went, and home was now where we earned our living. Those amongst the refugees who did not find an immediate footing in the East Punjab went all over India. One could not help admiring their courage and enterprise. Simple people, who had probably never been further than fifty miles away from their homes, set off in all directions and landed up in places they had never heard of. An old Sikh, who was our company's wholesaler in Peshawar, came to my office in Bombay because he had heard that we had offered to help settle our uprooted wholesalers and staff on both sides of the border. He walked into my office, worn out and bent, and said that he was going to forget the past and settle anywhere he could. I offered him our wholesalership in Cuttack, a town four hundred miles south of Calcutta and over two thousand miles from Peshawar.

He thought that was wonderful, just the place he would like to settle because he was sure that its air and water and business prospects were excellent. He thanked me profusely and said that he and his son would take the first train to Cuttack. But as he was going he turned to ask, 'Tandon Sahib, where is Cuttack, is it on the upper side of Hindustan or the lower; we haven't quite heard of it before in Peshawar.' He hoped I would forgive their ignorance, and it would make no difference to their accepting the offer. It did not matter how far it was but he thought he would just ask where it was.

My younger brother and I decided to forget the Punjab and regard Bombay as our home. We built two small houses next to each other, at the foot of Pali Hill in an area of largely Christian population. We had already lived in this area for a number of years and made many friends. Now, instinctively, we began to throw the roots deeper, and soon we were invited to their weddings and christenings and attended their funerals. They found our Punjabi ways, or Indian ways, as they called them, quaint. Our children went to the local schools where they learned English while they spoke Hindi at home. They never learned Punjabi.

Father divided his time among us three brothers. He stayed with my elder brother for a while in North Bihar, then sometimes with me and sometimes with my younger brother. I think he was never really happy with us because he did not like to be dependant and he always missed Lahore. He missed Model Town and the company it offered of people of his own generation, the retired Government servants with whom he had spent a lifetime of work. He missed the Punjab, its climate, the spacious comfort of his own house. He missed his old relations with whom he could discuss the affairs of their families. He used to liven up whenever we spoke about his early life and service days. He was also very interested in my career, because he said that an executive in industry was something as new today as his own career fifty years earlier.

When my younger brother was later transferred to Delhi father moved with him. In Delhi he felt nearer to the Punjab, and relations and old friends used to call on him now and then. But his life was ebbing, and he was gradually ceasing to take interest in the outside world. On the last day of 1955 the family found him unusually lively. He spent the whole afternoon sitting on the verandah in the warm winter sun, and was happy to receive a visit from his niece and her husband with their children. Krishen thought he had not seen father looking so bright for a long time. After his evening meal he fell into a sound sleep. On new year's morning, when Krishen and his wife went into his room, they saw that he had again gone to sleep after his early breakfast.

When they returned from some visits, father was still asleep. Looking closer they found that he was dead. So peacefully, without wakening, had he passed from sleep into death.

BEYOND PUNJAB
1937—1960

CHAPTER ONE

Lever Brothers — An Experiment

In 1937, with the shadow of war across Europe, I returned home after an unbroken stay abroad of eight years. There were few chartered accountants qualified in India at that time, and, as I soon discovered, the opportunities were equally few. The European firms employed their own kin and the Indians their own kith. The first were not quite ready to Indianize and with the latter it amounted to the same thing; they preferred their own, the family and caste, to strangers. At the very least, you needed an influential recommendation.

At the end of a discouraging week, I walked into the office of the international company of Unilever, and though it was nearly one o'clock on Saturday, the manager called me in and spoke to me understandingly; and asked me to return on Monday morning. When I asked him, 'around half-past ten?' he grinned. 'We start life much earlier; at nine'.

On Monday morning he spoke to me at length, probing into my reactions to my long stay in England and my return to India. At the end he asked me to go to see the Chief Accountant. The Chief Accountant was clearly having no experiments in his domain. Accounting to him was the hub of all activity, and he regarded it with a devotion that brooked no interference or innovation. In his own way he was right. The health of his company was the health of its accounts, which depended upon the unchanging sacredness of its system, the unswerving and single-minded pursuit of cash as it flowed through its veins and arteries. Each rupee, anna and pie must be recorded, extracted, translated into 'P & L' and ultimately entered in the holy horoscope, the balance sheet, which, like its astral counterpart, was a picture at a point of time that portrayed past and present and forecast the future.

Indianization, he might have agreed, had begun and he had nothing against it. Into the temples of European commerce Indian acolytes had begun to be accepted, but not into the sacred inner precincts. I had called on many of them: Volkart, Dunlop, Burmah Shell, I.C.I., Bata; the Managing Agency Houses of Bird, Gillander, Andrew Yule; and the practitioners of accounting and auditing, the partnership firms of chartered accountants. In none of these had Indianization yet been accepted as a policy. Some had taken an occasional Oxford or Cambridge Blue, the son of a High Court judge or senior I.C.S., but it was more as an adornment or concession to influence than to fill a genuine want. In the British army, after Indians had fought in it for over two hundred years, there were less than half a dozen Indian majors; British commerce, of even longer connection, had made even less headway. Neither had followed the example of the Government services. Of the thousand I.C.S. officers half were Indian. Indians might be ready to govern, but not to keep books or to sell.

Let others experiment, the Chief Accountant's attitude suggested. His own firm was welcome to make a start; but not in accounts yet. He was logical, for he opposed equally the introduction of British qualified accountants. I don't think he believed in formal professional education. You worked and trained, not read and wrote to be an accountant. The law made an audit compulsory, but he could get on well enough, if not better, without theories and academic notions.

John Rist, on the other hand, whom I was asked to see next, had been told to get an Indian immediately, and I seemed almost the answer to his prayer. They had decided to start market research into their well-known household soaps, Sunlight, Lifebuoy and Lux, and their competitors. For this a man named Thompson Walker was coming out from London in four weeks' time, and he had insisted that the one he would train and leave behind in charge had to be an Indian. Consumer research among Indian housewives could only be done by Indian girls, and an Indian had to organize it and interpret the Indian mind. Rist had been looking round but could not make up his mind. It was the beginning of a new process that led only one way, and he would be the first European manager in Bombay to try it. This seemed to fill him with diffidence, a trait, I was to find later, we shared. It was to become a bond of friendship that matured over the years. Underneath an outward poise we were both essentially diffident in the face of the new. After much covering of ground, near and far from the subject, he eventually offered me probation for six months. What did I think?

Questions surged in my mind. Were they going to put me on the same road of training as their own young Europeans? Would I, as an Indian, get the same terms and opportunities? How far could he see an Indian going—to the ultimate height? I looked over Rist's shoulders at the Bombay harbour framed by the french window at his back. It was a serene morning, washed clear by months of rains. I could see the tops of ships' hulls and their masts against the blue of the sea, and the distant hills of the mainland still green. The scene was interrupted by an occasional country boat in full white sail, its high prow swinging up and down. The rattling of a winch and the hooting of a car were the only sounds that reached us. I love the view of the Bombay harbour, much as I disliked the bustling town with its look of commercial prosperity, where for the past week I had been an intruder seeking employment, up one lift and down another. And now with an offer in front of me my spirits rose and my feelings towards Bombay softened. I would not mind working here, and in time I might even take to the city.

I never got to asking the question. I think Rist guessed what was on my mind, but he would have been equally unsure about the answer. He knew no more of the future than I did, but he dutifully faced up to it. Was there something I would like to know? I said no. I would gladly accept the job and start as soon as he liked.

There remained the question of salary. He took me into the room of the acting Managing Director, who had originally interviewed me, and had sent me to the accountant. He grinned when I came back in a few minutes looking blank, and asked me to return the next day. It seemed a pity to let someone like me go, he said. He then asked if I would forget my qualification and go into their advertising department. I said I would. I was already wondering if I had not chosen the wrong profession. I felt sad throwing away the result of many years of swotting but there seemed no choice.

He offered me Rs. 350 per month, and Rs. 450 on confirmation. I hesitatingly wondered if it could be improved because Bombay looked an expensive town. He said that they might make it Rs. 400 for a start, but could not raise the Rs. 450. I knew from advertisements in London that English accountants started at Rs. 650 in India, but this was beyond my hopes. I would have to accept. A week later I joined.

Dougal Building was in Ballard Estate, the European business quarter, adjoining Ballard Pier where the mail steamers tied. It was like all other buildings in this area, square, four storied, of grey stone, with small balconies. They all had English names. The only apparent exception was Kaiser-i-Hind, in itself of an impeccably loyal connotation.

I reported for duty on a Monday morning. When Rist was free he sent for me and briefly explained the advertising department. On market research he touched very lightly as it was equally new to him. He then took me into the main office and showed me to a desk with a heap of the quarterly advertising reports for London, and books full of specimens of past advertisements. There seemed enough reading for a week.

The clerks were all men: South Indians, if they were stenographers, Christians and Parsis, if they did general work. They all seemed puzzled at my entry, wondering who I was and what I was going to do. Sitting among them, at an ordinary desk with an armless chair, I could only be one of them. Had I been a manager I should at least have sat at the head of the general office, with a large desk and a chair with arms, a towel to wipe off sweat, and a glass of water with a bakelite cover. The desk would have had a glass rectangle, writing material, diary and a blotting pad. But mine was a plain desk like theirs; and yet if I had been one of them I would have been handed over to a senior clerk.

I could sense the speculation. Why should I be reading the reports which the managers wrote and only the managers read? Why did Mr Rist himself bring me to the office? And my clothes? The younger Europeans wore all whites, the seniors usually palm beach in light shades. The clerks wore anything that went as shirt and trousers. I still wore my English suits, dark and heavy, like the clothes of European visitors straight from the boat who had not yet been to the local tailors.

Guessing continued from a safe distance, but later that morning it came to a head. At eleven the sahibs had their tea. The office boys, who were called sepoys because their forerunners were soldiers who guarded the East India Company's offices, and who still wore some kind of uniform, took tea on trays to the managers. Everyone was anxious to see what would happen to me. I was thirsting for the morning cup of tea that the junior articled clerks used to make in my principal's office in Manchester, and I asked one of the sepoys if I could have tea too. No, tea was only served to the sahibs, and Rist sahib had said nothing about my tea. 'But', he said, 'I will bring you a cup from the Irani shop below. It will cost you one anna for a cup; two annas a day if you want it in the evening too like the sahibs'. I could, of course, go down to the shop and for an anna get a cup of tea, a bun, a cigarette, and a pice back! With all this would also go a glass of iced water, a free look at the daily newspaper, and the fan turned on for the duration.

In the afternoons, whenever he had time to spare, Rist would send for me. He preferred questions to dissertation. My knowledge of advertising had all been from the receiving end, from advertisements in newspapers and on Radio Luxembourg, but in particular from the rows of billboards that disfigured English towns and countryside, proclaiming jams, custards, soup tablets, ales and stout, and ominously, in 1937, air raid precautions. I had often indulged in condemning advertising, little realising that one day I would be earning a living out of it. As I assiduously read through the files and records it appeared to be more exciting than keeping books and building trial balances.

Rist was at that time preparing a new campaign in some fourteen Indian languages and English to create a consciousness of body odour among Indians. 'London office' had agreed to Indianizing 'Body Odour' by translating the name and the concept into these fourteen languages, and then contracting it to initials corresponding to 'B.O.' India with its hot climate must provide an ideal opportunity for exploiting the idea in local accent.

Poor Rist was to persevere dutifully and vainly at making 'B.O.' a household expression. We do not use initials in our languages, nor are we particularly worried by body odour. If you smell of sweat it is because sweat has a smell and not because you have not washed. Most people have a daily bath; from a bucket, at a well, a pump in the street, or in a river. When water dries, you sweat again, and sweat soon smells. I tried mildly to suggest that the internationalness of the campaign perhaps did not apply here. Rist listened politely, but probably considered this a part of the problem of training an Indian to appreciate modern ideas. If people sweat and smell and do not mind the smell, they can be made to mind. They could be taught to think of it as 'B.O.' and want to buy the only soap that would prevent it. Rist was totally uncynical, and to him this campaign, like all advertising, had a mission and was sacred in belief and concept. Had I expressed all my doubts he might have worked still harder to convert my pagan mind.

Settling in Bombay proved less difficult that I had expected. On arrival I had moved to some relatives in Malabar Hill. They had a large flat in Walkeshwar, an old part of the town. It was a three-storied building in stone and timber, of the kind that was being replaced by reinforced concrete all over the city, but this new development had not yet reached Malabar Hill. Its leafiness and sloping lanes were still unspoilt.

Father had assumed that our only relative in Bombay would welcome me as a guest for ever. Fateh Chand, whose wife was my aunt, was a type of which most of our Punjabi families had a specimen. Thirty years ago he had travelled to England for a perfunctory study of engineering. On his return he had joined father's irrigation department of the Punjab Government, but did little work and spent most of his time talking and eating, both in a monumental style. He was a large man with a booming voice, who at each meal carefully planned the next. He talked easily and interestingly on virtually any subject so long as one did not interrupt him or question what he said, which one was often tempted to do. Thrown out of public service for sheer laziness he had come to Bombay some years ago to make his fortune at speculation. He was convinced that with his education and reading habits he would beat those semi-literates and illiterates who had amassed great fortunes out of speculation in cotton and bullion futures and in the stock market. But he never succeeded, and in fact lost much of his savings. In the evenings his telephone rang continuously, and at first his conversation intrigued me. All he said was 'Right, right'. I discovered later that the calls were from brokers giving the latest quotations from the New York cotton exchange. I do not know when he made his bargains because he never said more than these words.

After rejecting most of his liberally given advice, the little I retained proved useful. Fateh Chand explained to me the diversity of the town, its communities and their ways, its occupations and traditions and its fundamental sense of industry. It was a town in which no one seemed to live his whole life. People came from all over India, and the world, with the sole purpose of work. Some came poor and went back rich, others just made a living, but all sooner or later left to retire wherever they came from. It was not a place where anyone put down roots. Bombay was unique among cities of the world in having the smallest proportion of locally-born pupulation. With the exception of the Parsis and coastal Christians, anomalously known as East Indians, practically everyone had come from somewhere else. But from this transient population grew in time the first truly cosmopolitan city in India.

Fateh Chand would explain all this to me, and he also introduced me to several Punjabi families, which made me feel somewhat at home. At first he found me interesting, largely because I was a good listener, but after a fortnight I think he got tired of me. One evening when I returned from the office he asked me if I proposed looking for some place for myself. I had only vaguely thought about it. Since in about four weeks' time I was going on a long tour all over India with Thompson Walker, the specialist in market research, I had taken for granted that till then he would expect me to stay with them in the customary Indian way. But people might have changed during my eight years abroad, and perhaps it was not the right thing any more. In the past, relatives stayed on for months, and it was never suggested that the stay might come to an end. I felt very upset that my desire for conformity should have been misread as abuse of hospitality. I walked out and began right away to look for a place. After wandering about for some hours I took a room in a hotel a few blocks away from my office. Late in the evening I returned to Walkeshwar and found they were both waiting for me to start dinner. Fateh Chand impatiently asked me why I was late. I told him I had been out to look for accommodation and was moving to the Regent Hotel in Ballard Estate. That was not a bad place, he said, and asked when I was going. 'Tonight, after dinner,' I told him.

My aunt was genuinely shocked, as much at my haste as at his un-Punjabi behaviour but he was not the one to feel embarrassed. With customary bluntness he said he admired anyone who did something promptly. There was very little to pack. He offered me his car and driver. Soon I was speeding down the hill to my first home in Bombay. As the car went past Chowpatty sands and along Marine Drive, my disgust subsided and I began to speculate about the future. Would she come to Bombay, would we have our own home? My thoughts ranged rapidly over Gärd, our life together, children, the firm, and my future in it. I had left her behind in Sweden, and we had agreed to decide about our future after I had settled in India.

At night, as I lay on a wire spring bed in a room with wooden partitions and sparse furniture, I tried to work out the finances of my new life. The hotel, with food and room, cost Rs 180, the extras would come to about another Rs. 50, leaving Rs. 120 out of my salary. Luckily there would be no deduction for tax or provident fund for a while. In another six weeks I would be on tour for several months, when the expenses would presumably be paid by the firm. I had never before worked on the fruitless task of keeping an account, but in my first half hour of independence I concluded that things looked uncertain. Could I possibly maintain her on this income, even with the additional hundred rupees to come? And I dared not ask father for an allowance, since he had supported me for far too long. He did not even know about my intention to marry. When should I tell him? And when should I tell the firm? I had heard that in British firms one formally went up to the chief to ask permission. How would they take it? The disturbing whirl of thoughts gradually slowed down and I went to sleep.

☆

Next day I went to the office in great anticipation because it was Wednesday, and the boat carrying Thompson Walker was due to arrive. A British business house then had its main contact with head office through the weekly mail steamer, and its whole routine centred round the P. & O. mail days. It rose to a climax from Thursday morning, when the mail came in, till Friday evening when it was posted for the westbound mail boat on Saturday. After that business returned to its ordinary tempo, quickened occasionally by a cable, till the next Thursday rush.

Rist had gone to the boat to meet Thompson Walker, and after helping him through the chaos that is Ballard Pier on boat days he took him to the Taj Mahal Hotel to settle in. After lunch Rist brought him to the office. Both were closeted together for a long time. I was anxious, because meeting Thompson Walker would mean the beginning of my work. I was also curious to know what sort of man he was. We should be spending nearly four months together organizing work that I knew nothing about and visiting places in India that were new to me.

Just as the office was closing, a sepoy came and gave me burra sahib's salaams. I was introduced to Thompson Walker. He was a youngish-looking man in his early forties, slim, with an intelligent cultured face. He spoke pleasantly and looked more like a professor than a businessman. I wanted to make a quick assessment because on how I got on with him and what I learned from him depended the start of my career. The long train journeys, evenings in hotels, places strange to both of us, would bring us together as no other circumstances could. Formal relationship must soon either give way to an easy, well-adjusted comradeship, or else freeze into something unbearable, as it nearly did in the very first town we vhis horse and rode beside the sahib, first in one direction and then in another. They rode all day till they arrived back in the evening to where they had started, and that, said this young stalwart, was all his land, if the sahib agreed.isited. There was a difference of sixteen years between us, a gap such as I had never experienced in a close relationship before.

Rist had given no signs of anything but a senior-trainee relationship; in fact, I do not think he knew quite where to place me. With his young English assistant, of my age and barely out of training, he appeared entirely at home. They were on first name terms, but with me he was formal. He let me call him sir and I gave him the normal marks of respect, but it would be awkward if I also had to treat

Thompson Walker in this formal manner. My first impression however put me at ease. He seemed informal and lively, with a turn of phrase and expression which promised much in common. We talked in a general way, mostly introducing ourselves. He broke off after a while and suggested we begin our work in the morning.

Rist had us move over to a vacant room in Henley House where the head office of the firm was located. When he instructed his secretary to make arrangements for our move it set all speculation about me at rest. Moving to Henley House and sharing an office with Mr Walker could only mean one thing. With formal politeness the secretary offered to arrange about moving my things and, as the final seal on my position, told the sepoy to serve me tea on a tray and hang a separate towel for me in the managers' toilet.

Thompson Walker and I spent most of the next few days finding out from sales managers about sales and markets for their many household products, soaps, cooking fats, cosmetics. Then he explained to me the essentials of market research, sampling techniques, drawing up questionnaires, recruitment of investigators, their training and assignments to work. He drafted an advertisement to the local English dailies, offering young, educated and intelligent woman who could talk easily to housewives temporary work as market research investigators at a daily wage of three rupees plus half a rupee for expenses.

I wondered what type of girl would apply, for I could hardly imagine that educated Indian girls would take on such unusual work. Walking about in the residential areas, calling from house to house, knocking on strange doors and engaging unknown women in conversation was something unheard of. Thompson Walker was equally curious to meet Indian girls.

Middle-class girls in India up till World War II seldom went to work, even in Bombay. The pioneers were the Anglo-Indian and Christian girls, who first took to nursing as a profession; then, in Bombay, came the Parsi girls, more westernized than the average. These girls next turned to secretarial work in European commercial offices, while the first profession the Hindu girls entered was teaching. With the spread of education among girls demand rose for women teachers, and there was no objection to teaching as it did not involve working alongside men. There were no shop girls in those days, and there are few enough even today. The few factories employed hardly any women. The textile mills took some, but only of the illiterate kind, at less than twenty rupees per month.

Our advertisement for girls with an ordinary high school education and no particular qualification or experience, at what was then a good salary, must have looked very attractive. Soon a variety of girls began to turn up, most of them with only the haziest notion of the job. Thompson Walker engaged them in long conversations to find out if they were suitable, but also, I could see, to satisfy his curiosity about their lives and background. And a lot we learned too, for most of them, once they started, were free and uninhibited in their talk. This encouraged us to believe that we need not fear reticence on the part of the housewives; in fact, we were soon to find it the other way round. But many of the girls shied away when we explained that the work meant going from door to door and running the risk of rebuffs, for a rebuff, real or imagined, is something few Indians can take. Of the four we ultimately selected one was an Anglo-Indian, two were Indian Christians and one was a Maharashtrian Hindu. They were a disparate lot, each interesting in her own way.

Nellie Thompson was of medium height, well proportioned and attractive, with a ready laughter that belied her sulky looks. She had come to Bombay from a typical Anglo-Indian colony in an upcountry railway junction. She stayed in a small boarding house for working Anglo-Indian girls in Colaba and managed to live off temporary jobs. A few years later a young English chartered accountant fell in love with her and married her. His firm disapproved of this marriage, and as was the custom in European firms he had to return home. He took Nellie with him. It was an unwritten law in those days that young Europeans in commercial firms, or in any other walk of life, were not to be seen taking out Indian girls. With Hindu and Muslim girls the question usually never arose, and it was not the done thing to be seen with Anglo-Indian or Indian Christian girls. Clandestine relationships were not uncommon, but they seldom matured into marriage. Similar prejudice existed about the community of domiciled Europeans, pure or fairly pure Europeans who had been settled in India for a generation or more.

Ada Rodrigues was a tall, well-built girl of matronly appearance, dressed in a sari wrapped twice round instead of the usual once. She was a Christian from the Mangalore coast and had three children. She had never worked before but the idea of earning some money without a permanent commitment appealed to her. She was shrewd and made the best investigator, and after a few days we made her supervisor of the team.

Miss Coutinho was a small Goan Christian girl who, I think,

needed work. She tried her best and was quite lively, but, like Nellie, felt strange with Indian women.

The pride of the team was a young Maharashtrian girl who was delicately beautiful with an equally beautiful name. She was Krishna Gulwadi, Krishna of the valley of flowers. She was slender, graceful and lively in every movement and expression, barely eighteen, but very determined. She had made up her mind to earn a living. We were both anxious to have at least one thoroughly Indian girl in the team. We should have liked to have more as the other girls, like most of their community, were not at ease in Indian speech nor familiar with Indian homes and the ways of our women. Living in their semi-western and un-Indian style they had little in common with the people. Despite all this Thompson Walker was at first not keen to take Krishna because she looked too fragile for hard work, and he also wondered whether she would carry sufficient weight with the housewives. She looked so young and dressed so well that she might find it difficult to establish contact with working-class women. She was really too glamorous to be looking for work. But Krishna was determined to get the job and she got it.

After selecting the girls we decided to spend a couple of days looking closely at the city of Bombay to decide the breakdown of its population for sampling purposes. I found it interesting to examine the social geography of Bombay and later of the many other towns where I conducted research enquiries. We were particularly fortunate in having as our guide an East Indian Christian clerk by name Misquitta, who himself had produced a small book on his community.

Bombay had sizeable communities from most provinces of India, the biggest of course being the Maharashtrians, followed by the Gujerati speaking people of Gujerat and Saurashtra, Tamils, Malayalees, Mangaloreans, Goans, Mysoreans, Telegus, Punjabis, U.P. Bhayas, Pathans, Bengalis, Nepalis, in fact, groups from everywhere except Bihar, Orissa and Assam, whose people one rarely comes across in Bombay even today. The purely local communities generally lived in the areas their forebears had founded when they first came to Bombay.

The earliest inhabitants of Bombay, when it was still a series of unconnected islands, were the Koli fishermen and the Bhandari toddy-tappers. Many of them had been converted to Christianity by the Portuguese some centuries ago, and they still lived on the coastal fringe of Bombay at Manori, Malad, Andheri, Juhu, Bandra, Mahim, Worli, Colaba and Mazagaon. There is still a fishermen's shed on the

Chowpatty sands. When Christians came from Goa, they settled in the areas of the local Christians.

The Parsis came next, with the British from Surat, and settled just outside the original fort, in and around Bazar Gate Street. Later they moved further, but they still congregate in predominantly Parsi localities like Princess Street and Grant Road. The Muslims, Memons, Bohras and Khojas, have their own areas around Mohammadali Road, Zakaria Mosque and Bhendi Bazar. The Gujeratis, who also arrived with the British, settled in Bazar Gate Street and then in Bhuleshwar. The Maharashtrians, interestingly enough, came later, after the Parsis and Gujeratis. They came in numbers as millworkers with the founding of the textile industry, and they naturally congregated around the mills in Parel. Their middle class, who entered as clerks and office workers, something which the Gujeratis, whether Hindus or Muslims, eschewed, had their homes in and around Girgaum.

The influx from South India and the Punjab began when the suburbs sprung up, and they congregated in Matunga and Dadar. The cosmopolitan areas of Bombay were Colaba, Malabar Hill, Cumballa Hill and later the reclaimed areas of Churchgate, Backbay and Cuffe Parade. Here lived people of all communities including Europeans. All through this the Christians continued to live in their ancient villages, now suburbs and part of the city.

This was the tapestry of Bombay, variegated and still existing. Its early life abounded in leaders who were Maharashtrians, Gujeratis, Hindus, Muslims and even Europeans. Starting from the mud flats of the Mahim River, at whose mouth had stood a fort since before 1000 A.D., and ending at the narrow flat island of Colaba, the city slowly spread, through reclamation, and gradually climbed up the hills.

Bombay's stratification for our market research sampling purposes was made easy by the way its communities and social classes were formed. We made little squares on a map of the city and filled in the communities, classes and the sample sizes, till the whole plan for making a thousand calls was ready. By the standards of modern statistical techniques our sample planning was certainly rough and ready.

Thompson Walker next proposed to draw up a questionnaire. It was to be a general investigation of the washing habits, for clothes and body, in Indian homes. The sales people were curious to know the answers to many questions. Since 1888 the firm's products had sold in India, increasing in variety and popularity over the years, but in spite of much empirical knowledge built up by generations of English salesmen there was very little accurately known about why people preferred certain products, what it was they liked or disliked about certain brands, their buying habits, the frequency and the quantity bought at a time, who it was in the family that chose a particular product. You could only guess why some things sold well and others did not. Market research as an aid to sales management was of recent origin in Europe; in India it was unknown and this was the first attempt, and to me fascinating.

Problems were not lacking nor were they devoid of interest. Thompson Walker and I had long talks about the Indian housewife and I would explain to him how different she was from her counterpart in the west. This bothered him, especially the answer to the question about toilet soap in the pilot survey: 'who chooses the soap you use... who buys it?' The answer for both was invariably 'the husband'. I explained that a good deal of the daily shopping was done by a man, whose word counted for everything. He decided what was to be bought. Thompson Walker accepted this with reservations. He was not convinced that the women had no say in such matters in the home. I explained that our Indian housewife always deferred to her husband, for she had been brought up traditionally to look to him for decisions. I grew quite eloquent about the classical training of the girls as future wives, the place of the husband as lord of the house, while she is its devi, grihalaxmi, the goddess of the home, demure, submissive and deferential to her master. I even quoted the immortal pair, Shiva and Parvati, of the celestial abode on the snowy peak of Kailash in the Himalayas. Thompson Walker listened to all this with a wearied look and when I had finished, said, 'Nonsense! What you say about the legendary place of the wife interests me much, but if from that you conclude that she is so submissive as to leave all decisions to the husband, you are mistaken. I bet she not only has much to say, but is the one who decides most things in the home. What she wants, like women anywhere in the world, she gets, including her soap.'

I tried to protest that our society was different. 'Maybe,' he replied, 'but I don't think it makes your women essentially different. Take Krishna, she looks as demure and deferring as the goddess of the home you are talking about, but do you think for a moment that she would do anything she does not want to do? When she marries she will be as determined a wife as you find anywhere. I have done market research in enough countries to find that women are the same all over. They jolly well always decide.'

He decided to probe into the repeated answer 'husband chooses'. He told Ada Rodrigues that next time she came across that answer she should delve deeper. Toilet soaps differ in shape, colour, perfume, emollience; there is something personal about the soap a woman uses. Would she just leave it to man to choose?

The result was funny and demolished me. At the very first call Ada made, the housewife as usual said 'husband chooses'. Ada began to probe as instructed. Suddenly a light dawned on the woman's face and she said quite simply, 'Oh, I see what you mean. My husband chooses, but of course I tell him what to choose!'

CHAPTER TWO

Settling in Bombay

Regent Hotel had a few permanent boarders like me, but most of them were people catching a boat or disembarking at the nearby Ballard Pier. I was the only Indian in the place apart from the manager and his staff. There was a sort of lounge which few ever used, and the usual meeting place was the dining room. People spoke little to each other, but to me hardly ever. Indians could now be seen in purely European surroundings, but they were looked upon only as something that could not be avoided any longer. You could not make rules against it any more. The perimeter was therefore withdrawn to enforceable limits, and in Bombay these were five places, the Bombay Club, the Yacht Club, the Bombay and the Wodehouse Gymkhanas, and the Breach Candy swimming baths. There were to remain inviolable till the end and some even beyond it. Oddly enough, the doors of homes, out of business necessity or sense of duty, were thrown increasingly open, when one would have expected that the initial meeting ground would have been the neutral premises of a club. It was a case of the club rather than his home being the Englishman's castle.

This sacredness of the club was intriguing. On the boat home I had got to know a Norwegian who had lived in Bombay for over twenty years and was his country's Consul General. Sailing was in his blood, and he spent most of his spare time in his boat. He had joined the Yacht Club of Bombay and been elected to its committee, and he told me an interesting story. The Nawab of Bhopal had sent an invitation to this club for a group of its members to sail in the lake of Bhopal. They were treated royally. There was sailing, shooting, parties and hospitality that only Indian princes could offer. Another invitation came from the Nawab which everyone was eager to accept. The Norwegian argued that they should not accept it, as they could not return the hospitality if the Nawab came to Bombay. Their rules would not permit him even to enter their premises. The other members of the committee were a little put out by his logic but, unwilling to miss the treat, they eventually overruled his objection. This club did not permit Indian guests until 1944, when the Indian members of the Bombay Port Trust threatened to terminate the lease, which they in any case did a few years later. Strange, thought the Norwegian, that these Englishmen would have happily invited the Nawab to their homes, and felt honoured by his acceptance. The club, however, was a different matter.

I could understand the desire of a foreign community to have its own club as a centre of its social life, but not the rule that debarred the people of the country from entering, except as servants. When the time came for the change, to me it made it only worse that the rule was relaxed under threat of closure. It was to take me many years to overcome my reluctance to enter the Yacht Club. Some of the British clubs preferred to close down after Independence, others were taken over by Indians, where there were hardly any British members left, and the rest began freely to admit Indians. Somehow I could never bring myself to join such a club, nor understand the anxiety of some Indians to rush in through the newly opened doors.

Entry into the European clubs even for their own people was in those days carefully graded. The Bombay Club took in mostly the civil servants and a few select British businessmen. Next came the Yacht Club which relaxed its rules to admit a little more freely the top managers of British firms. The Bombay Gymkhana took all Europeans so long as they were 'mercantile'. All the rest, the Europeans who sold over the counter in the British department stores or worked with their hands, technicians and foremen, joined the Wodehouse Gymkhana into which also went an occasional domiciled European of sufficient acceptability. The community's life ran in horizontal compartments at these four levels. The Breach Candy swimming baths were however open to all, to visiting soldiers and sailors, to the totally fair domiciled or Anglo-Indians. The only criterion applied, as they passed by the box office, was the colour of the skin. There were amusing instances such as when of two Anglo-Indian sisters, one fair with an acquired tan, and the other a natural brown, only the first could go in. In borderline cases the unerring eye of the clerk at the window, himself an Indian, quickly decided, and crises were practically unknown.

I was beginning to feel bored in the evenings. The routine of hotel and office was becoming monotonous. I spent most of my spare time in my room or walking round the blocks in Ballard Estate, with an occasional Sunday visit to a Punjabi family in Matunga, whom I had got to know through Fateh Chand, and of course to the Fateh Chands themselves. In Manchester life had been full. Stimulating company in the University Union, concerts, theatre, browsing in the Reference Library, occasional golf, week-ends in North Wales had filled the leisure hours richly. In the office in Bombay I seemed to make no friends. The English colleagues were pleasant, but when the office was closed it was all finished there. There were no Indian managers, and this seemed to apply to the whole of Ballard Estate which was almost entirely European, mostly British, with a German, a Swedish and a Swiss house. Thompson Walker, with whom I became increasingly friendly, had his evenings full with invitations from the Englishmen in the firm who would drop into our room and plan his leisure. Their coldness to me made him uncomfortable. I did not expect them to ask me, because one understood that for so long they had been complete in themselves. I therefore made no attempt to find my way in, and looked around elsewhere for company. I suddenly remembered Roshan whom I had met at Oxford five years ago. He had mentioned that he was going to join the Bombay subsidiary of a London company. I looked through the telephone book and tracked him down.

Roshan and I were together at college in Lahore. He was a year senior to me, and although we had rooms close to each other, his great prowess at sports put him on a pedestal and made him socially inaccessible to the undistinguished. From Lahore he had gone to Oxford, where again sports carried him everywhere except in the lecture rooms. Though he never smoked or drank nor talked about women, his clean looks and the Blue which he had acquired in his second term made him well accepted in all but the narrowly academic circles. I met him at Oxford during one Christmas when I stayed with a cousin in the same college. On the strength of this, I rang up to renew our acquaintance. He was a little wary, wondering whether like many others who befriended him I was looking for a job in his firm. I guessed this and explained that I had just joined my firm and wanted to meet him, just for a chat. He seemed to hesitate, but when I suggested that instead of my coming to his office he might have lunch with me he accepted.

Roshan asked me many questions about my job and the firm, my contract, what I thought of our managing director, my designation and the visible marks of my position, whether my English colleagues invited me home. To most questions I gave blank answers. I was on six months probation at four hundred rupees a month, and that was about all I could boast of. I had recently begun to get tea on a tray and had a towel with my name in the managers' toilet. I had no contract, no privileges or perquisites beyond the tea and the towel. I had not met the managing director because he was away on leave. I had not been invited to any home. I mentioned a few of our seniors' names but they did not mean much to him; they were obviously of no special account in the top shelf of Bombay. I mentioned hopefully that our numbers one and two—I was already learning the jargon—I believed were members of the Yacht Club, to which Roshan merely said that that would be so. He thought it all over carefully while I anxiously looked at his face. He was obviously asking these questions to make sure that I had started off well, and equally obviously I did not appear to have done so. Slowly his wide mouth under his long nose opened in a grin and he laughed.

'I think you have done well enough. It is a matter of getting what you can. This talk of Indianization to me is meaningless. Why should they be anxious to have Indians; they have really no need of us and they can continue to run their businesses just as prosperously without us; between you and me I think perhaps even better. Look at me, a pass degree, always barely scraped through; but of course, Oxford and the Blue make you almost pukka. And having a bright young Indian in the firm also makes a good conversation piece.' He mimicked: 'No, I don't think Indians are yet fit to hold responsibility in commerce and industry. I concede they can help in Government, and the start the army has made with them is not unpromising, but industry, you know, is different. Mind you, they run their own businesses well, but after a fashion. Our ways are different, they have a different business tradition. I don't say that that will always be so because we have already made a start. We have a very promising young man: Oxford, athletics Blue, father in senior government service. But then, such types are few and far between, and it is up to us to encourage them, though we must be careful not to hasten it; the process must take its time, it must not be rushed.'

I too laughed. I told Roshan it reminded me of the French Jew, who when asked by a hostess in London whether he came across anti-Semitism in Paris, said, 'No madam, every family likes to know one Jew who is different. I am that Jew usually.'

I had not expected Roshan to come out with these views; I thought he would be pompous, and possibly patronizing, but his simple approach to Indianization amused me. He must have thought that it shocked me mildly, for he became serious and began to encourage me. He said that with my professional qualification I had a future, because in me the firm had seemingly begun Indianization to fill a genuine need. They might not need a chartered accountant today, but such a qualification was never wasted. It was a skill that could be applied just as usefully to market research, and that was a field in which Indianization must have a meaning. If they were going to train me in market research and hand over to me when the Englishman returned home, it was not just Indianization but a new development. He himself merely provided a managerial signature and the quite ordinary responsibility that went with it. It had been a tradition in the banks and commercial houses, inherited from the earliest days of the managing agency system, that almost everything had to be signed by Europeans, in whom all authority was vested. A battery of junior Europeans was employed for just that purpose, mainly endorsing the work of Indian clerks.

He had just replaced one of these young Europeans, he explained. He felt he had no right to complain; he received a good salary, a thousand rupees a month and generous perquisites; they called him Rosh and he called them Bill and Harry, which really impressed the Indian staff. The burra sahib invited him home occasionally to parade the bright young Indian, and in the dinner conversation he used to slip in some Indian connection, he added. But what always bothered him was the technique he had had to develop in dealing with the subject of nationalism whenever it turned up, which despite their obvious restraint in his presence it often did.

Like all of us he was a nationalist at heart, but in front of them he found himself either saying nothing, or 'seeing their point', since he lacked the courage to disagree. It was a kind of schizophrenia. They, of course took his agreement for granted. A sensible Indian, educated in England must, they thought, have moderate views and disapprove of the extremists as much as they did. Their value assumption and patronizing restraint hurt, yet Roshan dared not show it.

He must have been bottled up for want of someone he could talk to freely, and admit his weakness in the face of an attitude that he disliked and yet found himself deferring to.

He got up to leave and said that we must soon meet again. His wife, Avi, would be glad to have me spend an evening with them.

With this British mark of approval we became friends. In the years to come I made a point of meeting him wherever he was posted. There was always something to learn. In his earthy way he had the habit of reducing things to their proper, often amusingly improper, size.

Roshan left a lot for me to think over. My mind went back to our fathers' days in Government service and the problems they had come up against. In the early days they were so wrapped up in their careers and so avid to learn that they accepted their position as the natural order of things. In India no one questioned the privileged position of a mentor. When father joined the service he considered the Englishmen who had trained him in the mysteries of engineering entitled to privilege. It was much later, when he was their equal in skills, and more so when the only right of a newcomer to preferential treatment seemed to lie in his belonging to the ruling class, that the injustice of it struck him. With Roshan the problem began differently. Having started off with the equality that his father's generation had strived for, he seemed to derive no satisfaction when he saw a poor justification for it, and despite the equality did not feel a part of the firm. He saw himself not as an experiment, but only an ornament. He would have felt differently had he thought he was meeting a real need.

Thompson Walker's market research survey was now well under way. For the first day or so in each locality the girls created quite a sensation. Some bold housewife would come forward and suggest that this was a foolish way of learning how people washed; if that was what the girls were out to learn, why, she could teach them all about it. Of course, she knew how everyone else washed and she could easily demonstrate it to them, so there was no need for them to walk from home to home asking the same simple questions. The girls became quite clever at dodging such women, and equally at getting the shy ones to talk. Gradually a picture began to piece together. Thompson Walker now began to plan the extension of the enquiry to the rest of India, to Karachi, and after that to Lahore, Calcutta, Madras, Trivandrum, Hyderabad, Nagpur and Allahabad. With the exception of Lahore and a two day job-hunting visit to Calcutta, all these towns were new to me and the anticipation of seeing such distant parts of India thrilled me.

Soon the Bombay enquiry drew to its end and we planned to leave for Karachi by a coastal steamer, a pleasant alternative to the dreary two-day train journey through the Sind desert. A few days before our departure the managing director, who had just returned from England, called me in. At the end he told me that as I would be accompanying Thompson Walker on this long tour they proposed to make no distinction between our travelling facilities. I would be entitled to the same expenses as the European managers. He wished me good luck and hoped that at the end of my tour they would be able to covenant me. This was a custom from the East India Company days when its senior servants were brought to India under a contract, called a covenant. The covenanted officers were a class by themselves, privileged and superior to anyone else, like the I.C.S. of the latter day, who received their contract from the Secretary of State in London.

Thompson Walker thanked the girls warmly. He took stock and felt fully satisfied with the work in Bombay, and confident that despite its difficulties market research could be carried out as successfully here as anywhere else. In fact, in some ways the task was easier. Housewives were not blase under the impact of heavy advertising. In the lower middle and working classes they seldom went to pictures or other amusements, and apart from fairs and festivals, weddings and funerals, life was unvaried. The arrival of a well dressed, educated girl asking questions about their washing habits was a welcome novelty, and they were willing to talk interminably to her; the problem often was how to get away without giving offence. With the Anglo-Indian and the Christian girls the women felt a little shy, but with Krishna they were quite at home. They felt very sympathetic to her and wondered why she had to work for her living. She was grown up, attractive, educated; why did her parents then not marry her off? She should have her own home instead of immodestly visiting strange homes. How much did she earn, they wondered, and what was she going to do with the money? Was she raising her own dowry, and if so, how much was she aiming at? Krishna gave evasive replies and got on with her work.

I began preparing for the long journey. The first thing one acquired was a bearer with experience of looking after a sahib, especially on journeys. I wrote to ask father if he could trace Shaffi, who had been with one of his English colleagues and was my only notion of a proper bearer. I recalled him from my childhood as someone who always dressed, looked and acted the part of a north country bearer. Father sent for Shaffi from retirement, but both felt that his days of active service were over. Much as Shaffi would like to serve the young sahib he did not feel equal to travelling all over India. He was however not going to let a chance go by. He recommended a relative, and this was Ahmed, who duly arrived in Bombay and reported for duty at the Regent Hotel. From then on, for the next two years, he ruled me.

Ahmed was short and dark, with a beard that he trimmed and dyed black. He wore a white turban in the traditional bearer style, low in front, moderately starched, its fold well pressed, its back-end turned up and tucked between the turban and the cap. It had none of the jauntiness of the Punjabi policemen's, the disciplined severity of the regulation army style, the rakishness of the Khasadars, the Pathan levies, the cockiness of the head office peon, the floppiness of my father's, nor had it the odd liberties that mine took when I was a boy. It was a completely sober turban, becoming a gentlemen's gentleman. The rest of his uniform consisted of a long kamiz, cut in the style of the European shirt, and a loose white salwar. He wore black shoes, whose laces were never tied because he always took them off before entering a room. In my presence he always stood slightly bent forward, with his head bowed in attention, lifting it each time he nodded in assent, his hands stretched down with the palms resting flat on his thighs, in the stance of praying. A remarkable feature of his presence was his eyes. He always agreed with whatever you said or instructed him to do, but as he looked back at you to convey his agreement his eyes, though deliberately blank, nonetheless eloquently and deliberately told you what he really thought of it. I never knew how he achieved this contradiction. His voice was equally remarkable. 'Behter huzoor,' ('Very well, sir') would be uttered in a flat, acquiescent way, and I knew at once whether he approved or disapproved. He never once gave me the chance to object to his tone or the look he gave, and yet I soon learned to know what he thought.

Ahmed had been a bearer all his life. In the early years he had served British army officers, one of whom he had accompanied as far as France during the First World War. This was the only bit of information he ever gave about himself. I never knew where he came from, whether he had a family and what he proposed to do when he retired. I don't think Ahmed loved me. For him it was rather a comedown to work for an Indian, and one of unrecognized status at that. After having served 'karnail' sahibs and 'dipity commissioners' he now had to adapt himself to a young commercial, but fortunately the work was light and he was shown the courtesy he had been used to.

I soon discovered that Ahmed had a pride in his position which bordered on snobbery. One evening the hotel manager approached me in great agitation. 'Sir, there has been a big scene. Your bearer has been most rude to a lady on your floor. She complained to me and I spoke to him, but instead of apologizing, he was totally unrepentant.' This struck me as very odd, for whatever his feelings Ahmed was always polite, and when he wanted to be rude, his politeness was icily punctilious. I found him waiting outside the door as usual. He opened the door and followed me into the room, where everything was in order for my arrival. Fresh water in the basin, a jug of hot water on the side, a clean towel unfolded, comb and brush. As I washed, Ahmed stood behind me. After a while he lightly coughed and said:

'Sahib, you may hear this evening about my wrong behaviour, for which I should like to apologize to you.'

'Why to me, Ahmed? You should have apologized to the lady or to the manager.'

'Yes, Sir, perhaps to the manager, but certainly not to the lady. Perhaps if she had been a lady, I would have apologized to her; in fact had she been a lady, I would never have been rude to her.'

Ahmed had no place of his own to stay. The hotel provided no accommodation for servants. He kept his little tin trunk in my room and his bedding rolled up under my bed. In the hot afternoon when there were no visitors about, he used to take off his shirt and lie on his bedding on the floor in front of my door, which he left a little ajar to get a breath of air in the dark and stuffy corridor. The lady in question resented Ahmed's presence altogether; place or no place, he should be seen only when serving. First she only stared at him, but one afternoon when she passed him lying on the floor fanning his bare chest, she told him to get up and get out. He protested that he was lying in front of his master's room and doing her no harm. This incensed her, because she had expected complete submissiveness from a servant. 'Jao, nanga admi. Niklo idhar se!' ('Go, you naked man, get out of here,') she ordered.

If Ahmed had been told the way he was used to, firmly but politely, I think he would have gone. But to think that a woman should speak to him like that, when really the right thing would have been to speak to his sahib! He let her know what he thought of her. He had seen memsahibs like her before, but not among the kind of sahibs he had served. She did not even have a bearer of her own: she wasn't 'pukka'. I think all Ahmed's ire at his changed fortune was vented on her.

I had never talked to the lady, who stared through me too. The smile she gave her own countrymen was the merest flicker. It was obvious that she did not relish her present circumstances; her stern hook-nosed face bore an air of permanent haughty resentment.

There was nothing I could do except gently remonstrate with Ahmed.

'Ahmed, you were rude to her.'

His answer added something lasting to my experience in man-management.

'Sahib, one does not pick on another sahib's servant; one talks to the sahib himself and he takes it up with his servants in his own way.'

More than twenty years later I recognized the lady and learnt who she was. My wife came to know her—times had indeed changed. Daughter of a governor, for whom she claimed descent from Robin

Hood, widow of a civil servant, whose forefather had been a great architect of British rule in India, she wanted to stay on in the country. With all the willpower inherited from generations of empire builders, she resisted the attempts of her only son to make her resettle in England. She returned to Bombay with her Pekinese as a stowaway; guest of two kind Parsi sisters, she refused to move from this haven. India had changed and she herself was a piece of Indian history: but India was still familiar ground compared to the England she dreaded, a country she had only seen in her youth. There she sat, eighty-four years old, small and stocky, but straight as a rod, meticulously dressed and rouged, happy still to have a servant waiting at table. To her circle of friends she was quite an attraction, for she could speak interestingly of old times, to her hosts the attraction gradually wore off and no doubt they felt relieved when her son at last managed to put her on the boat. I used to wonder what she would have thought had she recognized me.

I was always learning from Ahmed. When I asked him to do something he froze if I reminded him about it before it was due to be done. He would tell me with quiet dignity that 'he had already been ordered'. He taught me the pleasure of complete dependability. Whenever I went on a train journey I would hand over the tickets to him the day before. He would find out the station from where we left, the train time and all about the journey. Progressively, on the day of the journey, he would begin the packing. At lunch, when I returned from the office, there were still my comb and brush, the newspaper and the slippers; in the evening I would go straight from the office to the railway station and find Ahmed waiting outside my compartment. Inside, my bunk and the table beside it and the bathroom adjoining were exactly as I had left my small hotel room, complete with the book I happened to be reading on the table, open at the page where I had left it the previous night. Tea and shaving water would arrive the next morning at the halt closest to the time I usually woke up. He would order my breakfast, lunch, tea and dinner, all to be brought to my compartment at appropriate stations. But he was a tyrant. For life to function smoothly I had to be the slave of a system which he had culled from a study of my habits; where I might have taken liberties, Ahmed would permit none, and I cheerlessly suffered it.

These upcountry bearers were an institution that disappeared with the British in 1947. You saw them no more in district towns or military stations after the British civilian and military officers left. In some humble house would still hang, tattered and rusting, the head bands that went over the turban and the cummerbunds they wore round the waist, in regimental colours with metal insignia of the regiment, or the school or university colours and monograms. Most are dead, though some must live on in a village, nursing memories of the Raj which threw a small part of its glory on those who literally also served as they stood and waited. Under the shade of a tree in the summer, or warming their old bones in the benign sun of the cold weather, these retired bearers will tell their tales to the young, home from work in town and factories, about Smith Sahib and Williams Sahib, their parties and shikars, and of the power they themselves wielded when Indian of rank and wealth depended upon them for an interview with the Commissioner Sahib, which when obtained meant a reward in silver rupees.

We never had bearers, we just had servants. There was a subtle difference between a bearer and a servant which Indian masters did not usually understand. It was not the pay nor the uniform, it was the power of the class to which their masters belonged, and something more as well. It was the respect they received in the domain that was theirs which even the memsahib never transgressed; in the way they were consulted and trusted in matters delegated to them.

After acquiring Ahmed, or Ahmed's acquiring me, I went on a buying spree to equip myself with travelling kit that on the morning of my departure made a minor mountain on the pavement outside the Regent Hotel. In India travelling is a national pastime, undertaken on any pretext, and travelling light was never a virtue unless born of poverty. A message from another village that some relation is ill sets the whole family on the move; similarly a wedding. To visit a holy place a villager in the old days would walk across the whole of India, to return after months, years, perhaps never. With the arrival of railways the travelling passion could be more easily satisfied. Whole neighbourhoods would arrive at the station with mounds of baggage, beddings, pots and pans and provision—even a half-burnt log from the hearth—and sleep on the platform to catch the morning train, to bathe in a holy stream on a special full-moon day. The most unhesitating travellers are those whom paucity of worldly goods enables to carry the bulk of their possessions with them wherever they go.

My baggage was more diverse than that of the average traveller as it also contained modern impedimenta designed by generations of British. There was a large cabin trunkful of clothes for such different seasons as the frosty winter of Lahore and the perpetual summer in Trivandrum; a boxful of books and gramophone records and a player to liven evenings in dak bungalows and small hotels; an ice-box with a capacity of nearly a half hundredweight of ice, and containers for beer bottles, food and fruit; a bed-roll with pillows, sheets counterpane, quilt and blankets. Then there were minor containers for shoes, suntopees, an enamel basin and jug, and of course bundles of market research questionnaires and forms; more than enough to make a home out of the bare room of a rest-house.

Around the heap of luggage there stood an equally impressive array of hotel servants, many of whom I had never seen before. Everyone was most anxious to help, with a degree of specialization and care that was fascinating to watch. One carefully balanced on his head a small bundle of forms weighing perhaps ten pounds, another carried just my thin leather brief case, the third seemed to be staggering under the weight of the empty twelve-inch basin in its leather cover. I made a mental calculation of what was going to be the cost to me of this specialization. Apart from the table bearer I hardly recognized anyone. Ahmed had sheltered me from their none too anxious service, but now he surveyed the scene with an air that made me wonder whether he had not spread the word of departure to savour the importance of his patronage and make me pay for the minor facilities he himself had been receiving from the hotel staff.

While the bags and boxes were being fastened on the luggage carrier, at the back, on the running boards and between the bonnet and mudguards of an old Chevrolet open taxi, a stray walker on the pavement across the road stopped and watched. I happened to notice him. As the great moment came and I dipped into my wallet, which I had wisely filled with a supply of change, this man crossed the road. When everybody had been tipped he also stretched out his hand.

'But I saw you standing on the other side; you don't belong to the hotel, nor have you helped.'

He was quite unabashed. It was his bad luck that I had spotted him. He grinned and walked away.

CHAPTER THREE

Discovering India

As we travelled to Karachi in the coastal steamer, my memories were still vivid of the last trip over nine years earlier when I came from Karachi to Bombay to catch the mail boat to England. At the height of the monsoon the three thousand ton steamer, never far from the coast, had tossed and pitched in my first miserable introduction to the sea, and I had longed for the solid land of the Punjab. In the intervening years my acquaintance with the sea had grown. Numerous crossings of the North Sea and the Baltic, and trips in Gard's family yawl had at last given me sea legs. Atlantic rollers and equinoctial storms had broken my Punjabi resistance and turned it into a kind of love. If Viking blood were going to mingle with the peasant Punjabi there should be some concession to the sea, which at least had the merit of a distant horizon in common with our interminable plain.

On the first day of 1938, when I stood on the deck of the Karachi boat, watching the calm blue of the Arabian sea fringed by the palm-lined coast north of Bombay, the sea was like a new friend. In its sight I was to live for the next thirty years of my life, to gaze at it through my office window or from the terrace at home, sometimes for an answer to a problem, sometimes to share my joys and sorrows. The sea was like the dumb love out of a Tagore story who listened intently with features unruffled by words and sounds. Like her it reflected your own mood till it softened and drew peace and calmness from the vacant depths. From the brown heaving monsoon mass, when I first saw it at Karachi, to the Persian pottery blue of this fresh January morning, I had acquired a love of the sea, which was to become a part of me so that I could not bear to live away from it.

Karachi in January was pleasant. The air was cool and dry, the sun benign; its winter weather a perfect mixture of the sea and the desert, as was indeed Karachi itself. Ships, donkeys and camels made the harbour scene quite unlike Bombay's, where the West permeated Ballard Pier and the commercial area of Ballard Estate. In Karachi, the Sind desert came right up to the quayside. The stalwart turbaned Sindhis and Baluchis, aquiline and lean, struck a familiar note from the years I had lived in Bahawalpur and travelled in its desert districts bordering on Sind. From the harbour we drove along a wide boulevard through the commercial part of the town into the spacious suburbs with their low ochre-washed and green-latticed brick bungalows covered in cascades of purple and red bougainvillaeas. The boulevard ended at Clarke's Hotel, an old British upcountry hotel of the type you came across in all provincial capitals and hill stations. Clarke's, Percy's Faletti's, Spencer's, Maiden's, Barnet's, were names familiar to generations of European travellers and those like me who succeeded them. Most of them were founded at the end of the last century, usually by a European couple, as a cross between an Indian dak bungalow and a British boarding house. While some rose to the stature of a provincial hotel in England, others remained glorified rest-houses. But they all inherited from their Indian prototype the luxury of an attached bathroom, though this luxury lay entirely in its privacy, for the bathroom possessed only the simplest of fittings—a zince tub, an enamel basin and jug, water buckets and that great invention for which the Romans in Britain might well have envied the Britons in India, the thunder-box. Alongside, on a wooden stool, rested a china receptacle with a lid.

The rooms everywhere looked alike. They had standard furnishings, an iron spring bed with a cotton or coir mattress in the more sophisticated ones and a cotton tape bed in others; a chair with two protruding flat arms on which you stretched your legs, with a swivelling contraption under the right arm for placing your drink; dressing table, writing desk with chair, and a massive cupboard with old newspapers spread on the shelves. On the walls there were usually one or two old prints like the 'Highland Monarch', the 'Tempting Bait' or the 'Master's Seat'. The floors were covered with cotton carpets, durries, that harboured the dust of ages. Every morning the durrie was violently swept and the dust blew up in clouds to settle on the furniture from where it was again forcibly unsettled by a small duster tied to the end of a stick, and returned to the carpet. Some of it did escape through doors and windows but came back with interest during the day, and so this process of dust conservation went on.

The couples who ran these hotels always seemed to be relics from the past. They did not appear to know how to run a hotel, they had just strayed into it. It was a pleasant servantful life to which the only alternative was running a pub or a tea shop back home—no servants, no sun, and more demanding customers.

Once again I was the only Indian in Clarke's hotel, which was otherwise full of various Europeans, mostly British commercial travellers. There were, just before the war, some Nazi spies, observers and contact men, travelling as representatives of German firms. You could tell them by their stiffness, sometimes their duelling scars, and faraway look of rendezvous with fate. The thought occurred to one that, should things go in their favour, we might get their selfconscious haughtiness in exchange for the assured aloofness of the British. Superficially, there was perhaps little to choose, but after even a second hand contact with Nazism the thought of having to live under this race of supermen sent a shiver down my spine. The British were on their way out, with the first elected Congress governments already in power in the provinces. Even my father had seen it coming ten years ago and a lot had happened since then; but to get the Germans instead after a World War was a depressing thought that looked not far from reality when one saw these determined men taking a close look at their future estate.

Clarke's in Karachi, my first up-country English hotel, felt strange—a strangeness that took me some time to get over. I often wondered why I, who had lived in England for eight years and become integrated in their life and society, should feel strange in their hotels in India. Yet if the place had been full of Continentals, I would not have been embarrassed. The Englishmen made me feel a stranger. It was indeed curious how the British managed to make one feel positively ill at ease in the familiar surroundings of one's own country.

To my English colleagues in Karachi I posed the familiar problems. Customarily they would have invited Thompson Walker to their homes from the very first evening. It was a hospitality natural to expatriates, spontaneous and generous, to take care of a visiting compatriot who would otherwise have had little to do with his evenings. One after the other they would have asked him home, invited him to the club, taken him to the pictures, and to see the crocodiles being fed a goat at a shrine some miles out of town. But as we were staying together at the hotel, they did not know how to do it without including me, and that they could not bring themselves to do. I did not look the type who could be ignored and must have looked as if I minded being ignored.

Thompson Walker must have sensed the problems and I think he was amused. A few days later he decided to break the ice and himself threw a party. He further embarrassed his compatriots by inviting an Indian couple from the firm, Parsis, who although well connected must have been on the social fringe so far—one of those one-way traffic lanes of Parsi hospitality, cheerfully given, guiltily accepted and seldom returned.

I think Tom's invitation was attributed to his lack of understanding of their problems in the country. It was not unusual, they would argue, to see an Englishman out for the first time behaving like that. In his ignorance or insensitivity he was apt to do the wrong thing out of a fresh enthusiasm. He soon learned, if he stayed on, the wisdom of his predecessors' aloofness. The odd one who did not learn was usually sent back. But Thompson Walker was only here for a few months and therefore his idiosyncrasies had to be tolerated.

Tom was charming with women, and at the party he delighted in asking them naive questions about their social life. Did they like living in the country? Presumably they had learned the language and made local friends. They might have put him wise but for my presence. The Parsi lady was the one most appreciative of their difficulties and interjected to explain that it was not possible for European ladies to mix with orthodox and backward women who had not acquired the modern ways as the Parsis had. They often did not even know how to shake hands with men. The women of her own community, she went on, were of course different. They spoke English, used make-up, many played the piano, some even danced, and most of them knew how to eat with knife and fork. She felt much encouraged by Thompson Walker's interest and the Englishwomen's approval, but suddenly became conscious of my presence and hastily added that there were exceptions, and she felt sure that my mother was not the type she had described. I assured her that mother was in fact exactly what she was describing; she was a very simple Indian woman.

Thompson Walker roared with laughter to everybody's chagrin, and I felt almost bad for not having agreed with this well-meaning lady.

When they were leaving, one of the guests asked him if he would care to come to dinner at their club. It was a rather pleasant place and he might like to see what an up-country club looked like. Tom agreed readily, which surprised me, because I would have thought that not having been invited to any homes he would have politely declined an invitation to a club. I decided to look up some old friends of the family who had helped me eight years ago when I left for Europe. I rang them up and was asked to dinner. I had not intended to see them, though it would have meant lame excuses later, because I did not want to desert Tom since he was not asked out because of me. Now I felt let down when he so readily accepted the first opportunity to go out, without me. It peeved me, and I showed it.

Tom, though he guessed the cause of my altered behaviour, bore with me for a couple of days, hoping that it would pass off. But on the third day he thought I was going too far over too little and decided to tackle it. As we were going to be together for many weeks it would never work if small incidents like this were going to create misunderstandings. He had gone to the club because he was curious to know what an English club in India was like. One had read and heard so much about them. But if it consoled me to know, I had only missed an evening in which the conversation seldom rose above the level of the weather, dust storms and Home. 'We did not even discuss what was wrong with Indians. I noticed your impish humour with the Parsi lady. You would have had no such perverse satisfaction last night. Stop being sorry for yourself, Prakash! I know how you feel; perhaps I don't, but I do know what you think.'

It cleared the air. It hurt, but it also put the first guide post on the long path of a relationship that I had to build for myself. There would be no one as candid as Tom to help. It was a situation of loneliness at work in one's own country, and from it developed a side of my character that I can still recognize. It was hard to bear at first, but I soon adjusted myself, and accepted the imposed aloofness as part of me.

The three weeks in Karachi went by quickly. Our experience in Bombay gave us confidence. The office had advertised for girls, but the choice was limited mostly to Christians and Anglo-Indians. Muslim girls were out of the question, and the Hindu girls as yet not ready to work. After recruiting the best we could get, I began to look into the communal life of Karachi as a background to an understanding of the market.

The Muslims of Sind were an orthodox lot and among the middle and upper classes purdah was strictly observed. Few women went to school, hardly any to college. Some studied a little at home, usually Koranic reading and scriptures. Muslims from outside—Punjabis, Khojas and Kutchis—were a little more forward, especially the Punjabis, but even their women would not dream of going out to work, except the few who taught in girls' schools.

The Hindu Sindhis were of two castes, Bhaibands and Amils, two of the most remarkable communities of India. Denied the right to farm or serve as soldiers under Muslim rule, the nimble-minded Bhaibands turned to banking and business at which they got their own back by mulcting the Muslim peasantry and landlords, while the Amils with their sharp intellects served the rulers as minor officials and thus exercised considerable power. With the coming of the British, new avenues were opened to them all. The Bhaibands spread as far afield as Gibraltar, Lagos, Kuwait, Aden, Hongkong, Singapore and Hawaii, where they opened stores dealing in general merchandise, mostly luxury goods. They prospered remarkably, always returning to their home towns, where the mansions they built were evidence of the fortunes they had earned abroad. They also came back to marry and to die. Wherever they settled, the Bhaibands earned a reputation as shrewd store owners, hardworking and peaceable, but quick at making a profit. One who made a fortune in Hawaii and the West Coast of America left large sums in trust for education and scholarships. The Amils spread into professions and government service all over India, and like all good Indians they too came home, to Hyderabad, Sind, to marry, to build and to die. The Amils also liked to show their prosperity and developed overtones in dress, manner and speech—though overtones were never lacking in Sind, whether among Hindus or Muslims. Some of the most flamboyant characters in religion and politics came from among the Sind Muslims.

Karachi had also a small Parsi community of six hundred, the most advanced and prosperous of all. They were in business, stores, professions and government service, and equally—always a strong point of the community—active in civic affairs. Their leader was the agent of our firm, a venerable old getleman, as loyal to the British as anyone the Parsis ever produced. His great ambition to receive a knighthood was never fulfilled and he had to be content with the local title of Khan Bahadur, but this did not deter his philanthropy. To mark his long career of public service, he finally endowed the Corporation with a statue of himself, which was placed in a commanding position. Since he also happened to be the mayor that year, he himself unveiled it.

At eighty-six he was still going strong and had just been on a trip around the world, the high spot of which was a pilgrimage to England when he called on Lord Leverhulme and the King. I was presented to him during my first visit but I don't think I made much impression. Probably he saw no need for Indian managers. What was wrong with the Englishmen? They knew their job, didn't they? His son who was also ambitious and civic-minded looked after the agency. He too later became mayor, but his great interest was the boy scout movement, which he took very seriously, distinguishing himself as its chief commissioner. He prized both the honour and the uniform, and wore the boy scout regalia at every opportunity.

The Parsi community led a cohesive life, only regretting that they were too few to support a Tower of Silence. Instead, they had to be content with a shady little cemetery in the desert.

There was also a small group of Goan Christians, working in the railways, Port Trust, post and telegraphs, in the foreign firms, and running liquor stores. They lived a life entirely their own, went to their own schools, run by nuns and priests, and stayed in a tight cluster around the Roman Catholic Church in an area named Cincinatus Town after one of their leaders, who, unlike most Goans, had a flair for business. He had built a prosperous insurance company with branches in Bombay and Calcutta. But he came up against the inevitable problem of an Indian business: he soon ran out of relations, and Goan Christians with talent for business. He then had to make up his mind whether to go forward and engage men from other communities, or restrain the pace of his growth, and he chose the latter. In many Indian firms upon whom I had called in search of a job I had sensed the same dilemma. Well qualified though I may have seemed I did not belong to the right community. Indianization in business had not even begun amongst ourselves.

Not far removed from the Goans were the Anglo-Indian families, who, however, felt superior with their British names, a speech larded with British working-class expressions and with a sing-song Welsh intonation. On my first journey from Bombay to Lahore I had shared the compartment with a very fair Anglo-Indian, and never having met one before I mistook him for a Welshman. He was visibly pleased.

Meeting the different Indian communities, as I went about with our market research girls, was a new and interesting experience. I had only seen Indian Christians and Anglo-Indians from a distance in Lahore. There had been one or two Christians at school, but they were of the indigenous kind, wearing our clothes and speaking Punjabi, though their names were biblical—but the Anglo-Indians intrigued me. Speaking only English and living with an outward sembliance of English ways, they were yet not English. Nor were they Indian. They seemed creatures of a twilight world into which neither India nor England had clearly penetrated, though both had mingled furtively. Their girls were usually physically attractive, cheerful and hard working; their men often desiccated in appearance and energy. There was something sad about them. Their sadness was summed up by one of the Anglo-Indian leaders in the opening words of a book written as the time for the British going drew near: 'Who are they, Oh England, but thy sons!' It was a piteous appeal to parents leaving the nest.

Saddest of all was the small community of so-called domiciled Europeans, often pure in blood, whose parents had not been able to send them to England for education and thus lost them their birthright. Sometimes England was only a generation or two back, but through lack of contact, the family gradually became Anglo-Indian. The word 'home' had to the domiciled European a bitter sweetness. Cast away as they were by their own, they yet clung to their heritage and asked no more than to be sustained on the periphery, to avoid being swallowed by the mass.

Our work was smoothly completed in Karachi, and at the end of January we started for Lahore. As we settled in our compartment in the Lahore Mail, we were advised to pull down gauze blinds, glazed windows and Venetian shutters, and properly barricade the room. I protested that I wanted to look out and see the Sind desert, but I was told not to worry; the Sind desert would come to see me. And it did. When I woke up the next morning the whole compartment, floors, walls, furniture and beds were a uniform grey with a layer of fine sand. Our faces and hair too were powdered. All night the Mail had been rushing through the desert blowing up a miniature sand storm which kept it company till we entered the Punjab, where the sand changed to fine dust.

During the day, at the meal halts, we walked down the platform to the dining car while our compartment was dusted and tidied. The catering service on the Indian Railways for the upper class passengers was a remarkable organization with monotonous results. At hundreds of station restaurants and in scores of dining cars, from Peshawar to Chittagong, four course English meals were served whose English boarding-house standards were hard to beat. Thick or clear soup, fried fish or minced mutton cutlets with a bone stuck in, roast chicken or mutton, custard pudding or souffle, were the two standard menus for dinner. For lunch there was a choice of curry and rice or last night's tepid roast, euphemistically called cold meat, with thin slices of tomato and beetroot called salad. This menu was drawn up at the end of the last century when the British catering firms began their railway service, and served faithfully till 1947 when something worse took over. Thompson Walker, who was fond of good food and reviewed London restaurants for an evening paper, was greatly touched when on his last meal in the Madras-Bombay Express he read 'Roast Foul' on the menu. He felt rewarded for all the indifferently cooked but correctly spelt fowl he had consumed on India's railway system.

Train travel in India was then a complex affair, divided into eleven layers. The Europeans travelled first class and usually did not let Indians in even if there were vacant seats. Though by this time things had changed somewhat, an average Indian would still look hard elsewhere before he had the courage to enter a compartment occupied by Europeans, and never if they were army officers. The better-placed the Indian the less he dared, for fear of a snub or the remote but possible chance of being physically thrown out. As late as at the end of the last war one read of occasional incidents at railway stations. The leader of the Anglo-Indians, a Viceroy's special nominee on the assembly in New Delhi, was thrown out along with his bags at his own home town when an English army officer returning from the station restaurant discovered this unwelcome intrusion. By now the Indian railway staff had begun to feel indignant on such occasions and made common cause with an Indian. The station master would not let the train start and the officer did not care. Eventually the leader had to content himself with a long hurt telegram to the Viceroy. I don't think the British officer much cared about England's unrecognized sons.

Indians travelling first class were mostly senior government officials. The business kind and others felt more at home in second. The difference in amenities was negligible, consisting in a single cane arm chair and reading lamps above the bunks. The real difference lay in the exclusiveness and twice the fare.

After the second came the class called intermediate which catered for the lower middle-class Indian. This was more crowded, less comfortable, without fans and special lights, with hard mattresses, and you were not entitled to the full length of the bunk at night nor could you reserve a seat during the day.

Then came the fourth class called third. It was little better than cattle cars, with long wooden benches and accommodation for fifty or more, but often crowded to twice the capacity and bereft of any refinements except for one or two dim lights. At each station there was a determined invasion by those wanting to get in, equally stoutly resisted by those already in, with those who wanted to get out pressed in the middle. Men, women and children poured in through doors and windows with a diversity of baggage, and once installed they praised God. The hostility of the vanquished never lasted long but welded into a common cause as the train reached the next station.

The fifth class was the strangest. It was specially reserved for the intermediates who were neither Europeans nor Indians, the 'sons' and the professed ones. For the impecunious domiciled European, Anglo-Indian and Indian Christian of the anglicized kind, a separate compartment was provided of the imtermediate grade. When you reached the Christian end of the colour scale it was difficult for the average railway staff to distinguish them from Indians though to anyone who knew the difference was obvious. But how was a minor official of the railways to know? To him they were all Sahib. A rule had therefore been inserted in the official guide, laying down an overall qualification that the passengers travelling in this class must be dressed in European clothes. This rule created its own complications, and the story was told of a somewhat dark Christian gentleman who went to the European guard invoking his aid to remove a native who had got into the privileged compartment. The guard promised to look into it at the next station, where he found one very dark man and a fair Kashmiri, both in European clothes. He had forgotten the complainant, and without further ado he proceeded to do his duty. He picked up the bags of the protesting dark passenger and told him to get out of there and not to bother the fine gentleman. Earlier these compartments were marked Eurasian; and as that word went out of coinage they were marked Anglo-Indian. They often went temptingly empty.

For all these classes, except the Eurasian, there were feminine equivalents, but again with a subtle difference. The first and second were called 'ladies'; the intermediate, 'women'; and the third was marked 'females'. The same went for the station lavatories.

The tenth kind was a third class for troops, British in preference. The eleventh was a small wire coop protruding out of the back of the dining car right at the end of the train. In this were kept live chickens. Through a sliding shutter the cook brought out the birds to convert them into the standard dinner. The leg of goat for the lunch was, however, picked up at a wayside station.

I wonder what Mark Twain would have said had he travelled in India a century later, when travelling had become more complicated. His quip on Indian railway travel was however, as true now as then: 'The first class passengers look down on the railway staff, the railway staff look down on the third class, while the second class passengers look down on each other.'

CHAPTER FOUR

Discovering India

After twenty-four hours of steadily hauling itself up the gently sloping desert and plain that rose seven hundred and fifty feet in seven hundred and fifty miles from the sea, the train from Karachi reached Lahore. Lahore station had a character entirely its own. Its bustle and chaos beat that of any other. Upon the train red shirted porters swarmed like birds of prey and in a few moments emptied its innards of anything that looked like baggage, while the bewildered passengers extricated themselves from the melee. Hastily pointing out the number on their metal badges the coolies disappeared with the baggage and the passengers found their way out. In the porch both parties met with a swarm of tongawallas who dragged passengers and bags to their carts. How the luggage was sorted out, the coolies satisfied and the passengers got into the tongas was a miracle that characteristically introduced the Punjab. Like everything else in this vital land things somehow got done, but through what vigorous chaos!

It was my first long visit to Lahore since I left it as a college student, ten years earlier. On the first evening I went on a tour of rediscovery. There was little change in the city itself but it had developed many new suburbs, some haphazardly built slums but others well planned. I wandered through the Victorian gothic building of my old college, through the hostel in which as a freshman I had had the misfortune to be squeezed into a room with three brothers, who all stammered. Their frequent quarrels, when all three stammered with excitement, always ended up in a joint front against me. From my old room I looked down on the spot where in 1928 two Punjabi students fired the first terrorist shot, killing a young English police officer. It made a deep wound in the pride of the British, and the loyal Punjab was never the same again. Something had snapped. From the other side of the room I looked upon the Round Garden, where we sat on the grass in the winter preparing for our examinations. I walked through the gardens till I came to the massive gun, Kim's Zam Zama, that the British had captured from one of the Sikh clans. It faced the wide avenue of sophisticated shops and restaurants, the Mall Road. As students it was beyond our pockets, though once some of us did sum up enough courage to have tea at the Standard, where for one rupee you had a large spread. There I saw for the first time the strange sight of men and women in embrace gliding about to music. From the Mall I strolled to the famed shopping centre of the Punjab, Anarkali, past the shops selling fruit and spicy tidbits, and entered the city. Old Lahore inside the wall was as narrow, congested and noisome as ever. It had lost none of its fascination. I walked through the sunless lanes to the quarter of the girls, euphemistically called the Diamond Market, where painted, kohled and lightly dressed they specialised in the ancient arts of singing, dancing and love. Through the intricate maze of lanes and passages I returned to the spacious lawns of Faletti's Hotel.

During the month at Lahore, I went home to stay with my mother and father over week-ends. They had now settled in a new suburb. I thought of my student days, how good it was then to return home for holidays, never long enough to wear out the welcome. This time I ran into complications. News had travelled that I was now in a job in a large foreign firm in Bombay, and this at once made me the quarry of two kinds of aspirants, those with daughters looking out for a son-in-law, and those with sons looking out for a job. My parents felt embarrassed, though mother certainly thought that it was time for me to think of matrimony. They could not turn away friends and friends of friends who came with proposals, and yet they did not want to spoil my visit. I was even more embarrassed, for about matrimony I had made up my mind but dared not say so yet to my parents, and as for the jobs I could not convince anyone that I myself was only an unconfirmed probationer and my power of patronage did not even extend to the appointment of an office boy.

Matchmaking had changed, I found. In our circles it was no longer a deal between the parents arranged through the good offices of the family barber, in which the views of all except those most concerned were sought. The hereditary barber to the family was always asked to take a proposition to the other side and broach the subject discreetly, to save the two families the embarrassment of a refusal. It would then have been considered positively indecent to consult the boy and the girl. Modesty anyway would have prevented them from doing more than bowing their heads before their parents and mumbling 'just as you wish'. But now it was a quarter way to courtship. The family barber out, friends or relations would suggest a likely match. Often married brothers and sisters suggested someone they or their spouses knew at school or college. After discussions with the parents, some mutual friend was found to broach the matter with the opposite parents. If their response was favourable the parents would sound the children, giving details of the other family, the boy's or the girl's qualifications, his salary and prospects. If both evinced interest, the next stage was to bring them together. As yet this meeting was a mere formality, for all they could do was to look at each other shyly and make sure that there was no actual dislike at first sight. No words were exchanged, nor were they left alone. If both agreed straightaway, or with due persuasion, an engagement ceremony was arranged and in due course the wedding. Independent choice was still rare.

This was quite an advance on the time when my uncle and my aunt saw each other for the first time after they were man and wife. In those days they had to be content with coloured descriptions from their parents, and mothers in particular were adept at glorifying their choice.

In 1938 we were still at the stage of the silent interview, but as I had been abroad a point might have been stretched to let me talk to the girl. But the girl I wanted to marry I had talked to in plenty over the six years I had known her. It would have been termed by the expression that was just entering the Punjabi vocabulary, a 'lav match'. But I did not know how to mention it to my parents. Had I not promised my father when leaving for England that I wouldn't marry an English girl? In a way I had kept the promise, for she was not English, but Swedish. It was a bit embarrassing when people dropped in to look at me and both they and I had to go through the conventional motions, when only I knew that I was not available.

Those who wanted jobs were worse. Usually it was the father who came to see me to extol the virtues and qualifications of his son, insisting that there was no need for me to see him. They refused to accept my protestations that I was quite powerless. Nobody would believe that I had no influence. All I had to do was to 'speak to the Sahib' and he would immediately send for the boy and give him a job. Sahibs, they would add, used to be like that in the Punjab until competitive entrance and communal ratios came in, by which only the Madrasis, for their ability, and the minorities, Muslims, Sikhs, Christians, Harijans, for their birth, seemed to qualify. But surely it was not like that in the companies; the Sahibs would take in anyone I recommended. I ought to do something for my province which had few commercial and industrial opportunities. And then there was a long appeal to my duty to my community, my caste and my neighbours. That was the way of our biradaris—the strong and the successful helped the weak and the needy. Who else would?

And so the arguments and entreaties would go on till I almost began to see some sense in the nepotism so deeply ingrained in us. Once your loyalties to region, caste, relations and friends are accepted this becomes inescapable. Having started the admirable innovation of recruitment on merit, the British government had gradually begun to slip. Considerations of region, caste and patronage for loyalty became supreme till all the good of fifty years was undone. Agriculturists received special preference, but the most favoured treatment was shown to those whose families had rendered loyal service to the crown. People carried wrapped in white handkerchiefs general letters of recommendation from generations of high English officials. To us this system was most debasing; a sad reflection on the Raj which had to resort to such means to shore itself up.

Gradually the impression spread that long education abroad had alienated me from my own people. Whether they came for marriage or for a job, they went away disappointed.

My father was as usual very helpful. Always ahead of his time, he believed in fair opportunity and the rest left to merit. He could not understand the complex rules that seemed to favour the mediocre and protect the inefficient. In his day only merit took you further, and plenty of it could take you far. Having risen without help he did not see why he should recommend his friends' sons to me. It went against the grain.

☆

In the dining room at Faletti's Hotel, I looked forward at meals to seeing a slight pale-faced girl who sat alone. She had features uncommon to these parts and yet not unfamiliar. They were finely chiselled and surrounded by smooth black hair, parted in the middle and pulled severely over the ears. But quite unforgettable were her dark eyes of unnatural lustre, hauntingly enlarged by the deep pallor of her skin which contrasted with her brightly painted lips. She sat and stared as if into eternity, uninterested in anything around her, looking deeply into what others could not see or suspect. Occasionally she lifted the fork and held it poised in air but put it down again, and then one saw her exquisitely modelled hands, small with the grace of a waterbird in flight. But tired and transparent.

One evening I took a wrong turning in the corridor and saw a board announcing an exhibition by a painter whose name meant nothing to me. Curious, I walked in to have a look. In the centre of the room, surrounded by paintings on the walls, sat the girl from the dining-room with her usual far-away expression. Apparently few came to see the paintings. In my confusion I apologized and said I was merely going to look around for a few moments.

Like her face I remember her pictures. Their colours were bold and joyous, quite different from the popular schools of painting then reviving Indian art, which looked back to the Ajanta frescoes in poor imitation. Here was a vividness that belied her frailty. The subjects were folk Punjabi, mostly grave and demure women. Particularly beautiful was 'The Mourners'—a group of women with bowed heads covered with mantles, surrounding a pathetic figure, a bundle of a girl deep in her bereavement. No faces were visible, only the covered heads and shoulders convulsed in silent sobs.

Five years later when I was once travelling through the U.P. north of the Ganges—it was a long and tedious journey with the interminable delays of the war years—the only other passenger was a Sikh, reminiscent in dress and bearing of a Sardar of the early ninteenth century. We only exchanged some desultory conversation. Late in the afternoon the following day as we neared his station he asked me if I would like to break the journey and spend the night at his house. Without hesitation I accepted his courtesy.

As I walked into his room in the evening I looked at the walls in surprise. Between exquisite Persian carpets hung paintings by the girl from Faletti's. There they all were, with their sharp colours and all their sadness and joy. 'I have seen them all before' was all I could say. 'Yes,' he answered, 'they are my niece's paintings. This is all we have left of her. She died not so long ago of consumption. She was too young to die, but she really never seemed to belong to us.'

She was Amrita Shergill, our first outstanding modern painter. She painted for only a few years, but in that short space she left behind some immortal pictures of the Punjab, to which she added something of the Hungarian heritage of her mother. She showed the way to a new birth of Indian art which seemed to coincide with the coming of freedom, though not actually motivated by the freedom struggle. Too long had Indian art lived on tradition—freedom opened the door for new impulses from the West that led to a new flowering and made India part of today's art world.

☆

On the way to Calcutta we broke the journey at Delhi to do some sight-seeing. I had never before been to Delhi, and the first sight of the new capital left me with mixed feelings. It was a great concept, but a conqueror's, of the heart of an empire. No rulers before them had been more alien at the end of their rule than in the beginning. When next day I saw the Taj Mahal this thought stood out more clearly, for here was buried a ruler who, though his ancestor had come as a conqueror, was himself, through his mother and grandmother, of the country, and had assimilated his heritage with that of the land. But the founders of New Delhi after two centuries of connection were still alien and had come to regard any influence of the people a taint. Born of such racial aloofness, the new capital could not be expected to stir the feelings of the subjects. Yet, ironically, the architect had realized that their own contemporary architecture was too unimaginative to create a monument to their power. He therefore boldly used the materials and style of the country, a style which itself was a fusion of the indigenous and that of earlier invaders.

As I walked down the Kingsway, the widest avenue in the world, past King George's statue and the triumphal arch that commemorated the wars Indians had fought for Britain and her empire, I saw the heart of the Empire, the Viceroy's palace flanked, by the massive blocks of the two secretariats like sentinels. Built on a rise, the Viceroy's residence, known, in a colossal understatement, as the Viceregal Lodge, was suitably elevated above the city of New Delhi. On the flat land below stood the hall of the representatives of the nation, who were at the time either nominated by the Viceroy or elected by a fraction of the people. It struck me as cynical to relegate this symbol of democracy, however limited, to such an obsequious place below the throne.

The red and yellow sandstone buildings with rows of columns and Moghul arches were conceived in a grand style as indeed was the whole of New Delhi. Grudgingly I liked it all. I wondered in what style we would have built our own inevitable New Delhi, had we not inherited one. Perhaps not very differently. In fact, forty years later we added to this central complex new secretariat buildings of a similar style. As in many other fields, once our turn came we often did through choice what we before had hated the British for doing.

☆

Calcutta was an implausible town even before the war. The cream and green architecture of its spacious suburbs, so well suited to the climate, the well planned squares in the city, the wide sweep of Chowringhee facing one of the largest parks that a city could boast of, made Calcutta very pleasant, and gave it, unlike other large towns in

India, a metropolitan character. But there its grandeur ended and neglect and shabbiness took over. Roads unmended, footpaths with stone flags dug up years ago and lying in heaps, streets with garbage which brahmini bulls and pi-dogs scattered over the pavements, houses with plaster and paint peeling off, were a common sight everywhere. The city had an air of a past more affluent than the present, typified in the handsome square mansions of the old landowning families. Once these houses and their gardens must have been well maintained, but now the yellow ochred walls were mildewed by many monsoons, the green shutters cracked and warped, the gates rusty and the gardens overgrown. The houses built by the big merchants of the East India Company along the river also stood deserted in their wilderness that was once magnificent park. And yet with all its decay, the city throbbed with life. In its covered markets or in Clive Street one felt the animation and vitality. There was great activity too in the docks and the industrial suburbs, where around the workshops and factories, with magnificent managers' bungalows, there had sprung up some of the blackest slums anywhere.

Calcutta's total impression was of vitality and apathy, wealth and poverty, life and decay; here was a town without a social conscience. Its civic life had once made a great name for the city, its politicans were men of all-India stature; but they appeared to have left no legacy of running the day to day affairs. In fact one wondered whether the vision of her great men of today was ever clouded by such minor things as a clean and efficient administration. It seemed that some fifty years ago a break took place in the affairs of the city. The Scots, who had founded and ruled the town, began to mind their own business, as long as their own interests were protected, and those of the land who took over were so ready to be appalled at the injustices around them that they had continued to be just apalled ever since. The city began to go its own way and no one seemed to mind.

Perhaps Calcutta's cosmopolitanism added to its neglect. Big business, once dominated by the Scots, was gradually taken over by the Marwaris; the Punjabis seemed to be everywhere—in small business, shopkeeping and plying taxis; Parsis filled minor positions of trust; a growing number of South Indians manned the ledgers and typing machines; the Biharis pulled rickshaws, served in the police and guarded houses; and of course the Bengalis were everywhere, men of learning and culture who had delegated admirably to others the task of running their town. In Bombay cosmopolitanism seemed to work, but not so in Calcutta.

The curious thing was that everybody complained that Calcutta was not what it had been: it was becoming crowded, ill-kept, dilapidated, its slums ubiquitous, and yet nothing ever happened. There was an acceptance of the deterioration. People blamed Government and Goverment could well have complained that the people did not cooperate; everyone pronounced judgement but no one acted. One new governor pronounced the bastis, the shanty slums, a blot on Calcutta that must be removed. The press gave this much prominence, and everyone agreed and hoped that a call from the highest quarter would generate the much-needed action, but once again nothing happened, and so the deterioration went on.

Calcutta filled me with depression. It was to grip me each time I visited it in the years to come. Alighting from the train at Howrah station and crossing the Hooghly over the pontoon bridge, which sometimes delayed one for hours when it was opened to let through the river traffic, driving through the streets where cows roamed and nuzzled at the litter for possible sustenance, while graceful kites poised overhead, waiting to swoop down on some remnant of food; men in the streets bathing in the muddy water from the fire hydrants; the emaciated, panting rickshaw pullers threading their way through the stream of traffic, often hauling a whole family—rotund husband, wife and children plus luggage; skeletons sprawling on the pavements with empty cans in their outstretched hands in the hope that someone might drop a copper coin; a homeless family eating a scanty meal out of a leaf—boiled rice flavoured with a few spoonfuls of spiced liquid. Through this depressing scene the taxi honked its way. Before the panorama of Calcutta's life my spirits always sank. Yet slowly, through numerous visits, I began to like the town. Though no one did anything for its people, they themselves got much happiness out of their festivals, when whole streets went gay for a week in cooperative celebrations of a deity. They were a sensitive but helpless people, ready to laugh and willing to suffer; wrongly maligned for their sensitiveness, but rightly accused for their apathy. I never got to know them well for they are proud and shy of strangers and prefer to stick together, but once convinced of your genuine liking, the curtain of pride will drop or at least become translucent, and charm and affection will emerge, but rarely a friendship.

☆

It was a long journey of over forty hours from Calcutta to Madras in which a whole vista of Indian life slid past the carriage windows.

Through West Bengal, south Bihar, coastal Orissa, Andhra and Tamil Nadu, the train rushed through two nights and a day, carrying with it a ribbon of excitement through a quiet countryside quickened to life by its progress. In the silent night sleepy wayside stations would suddenly waken at the distant sound of the train, and as it ground to a halt the confusion of passengers rushing up and down the platform mingled with the cries of hawkers selling tea, cold drinks, sweetmeats, food and fruit. In the day the same scene repeated itself under a blinding glare, and with it all there was to me the excitement of country and people I had never seen before. The fascination of Indian rail travel has never palled for me.

Madras was as remote to us in the Punjab as 'Walayat'. The world to us Punjabis had consisted of our homeland, beyond which began Hindustan soon after our fifth river, the Sutlej. Distantly, somewhere to the South, lay Madras, which to us represented the unknown. Beyond that was the black water and then Walayat—all the lands beyond.

The people of Madras, their language, food and dress, had only a distant heritage in common with us. Between a Punjabi from beyond the Jhelum river and a Tamil from the Cauvery the links were few and not easily recognizable. Erudite Brahmins had their Sanskrit learning like the priests in medieval Europe had their Latin, but two ordinary men found little in common. Madrasis to us meant anyone born south of 'Poona—Satara', north of which was the land the Marathas came from.

Madras was like its people, simple, clean, orderly and well balanced. There were not the Calcutta contrasts of mansions and shanties, giltmirrored restaurants and beggars outside. Everyone took the air at the Marina and sucked his coffee in the ubiquitous cafes. But there were differences of a different kind, and very deep ones; not of wealth but of caste. There was Brahmin and non-Brahmin areas, Brahmin and non-Brahmin coffee houses; temples for the Brahmins and for the low-born the roadside, from where they could look in through the temple door and say a distant prayer.

It was a joy to work in Madras. A single advertisement brought a score of pleasant looking, intelligent graduate girls, free in speech, and dressed in saris, who were willing to do any work, willing to work permanently and to travel anywhere in India. We chose four, three of them sisters, two of those twins. And then I discovered that all the girls who had applied were Christians, mostly Syrian Christian—a community I had never heard of before. None of them was a

Brahmin. As elsewhere, only Christian girls came forward to work, and our only exception so far had been Krishna in Bombay and a married lady, Savitri Devi, in Lahore, who must have been almost the first among middle-class Hindus in the Punjab to leave home and work out of doors. Savitri Devi was quite remarkable. She had found herself in circumstances in which, had she followed tradition, she would have accepted parental help, but instead she went to work, despite the handicap of a scanty education that did not include English. Her husband did not work but trailed happily behind her. Later when her market research work stopped on account of the war, I felt compelled to engage him instead.

The three sisters were gems and took to work with great enthusiasm. They suggested that they would travel to Trivandrum, where my next market investigation was to be held, for they belonged to Travancore. My only problem was the twins' shyness. They were a talkative pair, but mostly talked only to each other. In a low voice they carried on an interminable conversation about seemingly nothing at all. Whenever I asked one of them a question both faces, chubby and to me indistinguishable, with huge dark eyes, would light up in comprehension, yet neither would speak first. I would repeat the question and then one would bend her head near the other's neck and both would giggle almost silently. That I could never tell one from the other did not matter because they were really one, not two. Not only did they look alike and think alike, they thought themselves one. I learned that the only way to make them talk was to let them talk together. Though they called separately on the housewives, I soon found they took every opportunity to discuss their work in such detail that when I asked a question I had to let them both answer. Nature had put them into separate moulds, but as long as they were treated as one entity there were no problems. The third and older sister was different. She had a keen mind and was an interesting talker. During our long conversations at work and afterwards she told me a lot about South India, of which so far I had been totally ignorant.

☆

From Madras Thompson Walker decided to return to Bombay and then leave for England. He felt the work we had done in the five towns had gone well, and from now on I could manage alone. I returned with him to Bombay, and saw him off with a heavy heart. For four months we had worked and travelled together, discussing much that was as new to me as it was to him, and both of us shared a keen sense of curiosity. This constant companionship had helped me to feel my way in the organization and also in the general order of things.

Free as he was from prejudices and conventions he was able to laugh and make me laugh at things that might otherwise have hurt me and left scars. When, for instance, an office sepoy brought back a small cash requisition of mine that would have been within the competence of a very junior manager to approve, with a message from the accounts department that it needed a 'European signature', I was hurt but Tom was amused, and eventually I saw the humour of it too. 'They simply have not caught up with your existence, and I bet you it is not the chief accountant but one of his Indian clerks who returned the slip, and he will take longer to accept your position than will the Sahib.'

With his sharp perception Tom saw the foibles of both sides, and as he interpreted them I began to learn the viewpoint of the British and develop a tolerance that became essential in my later responsibility. There were barriers, and some were hard to take, even though I was not particularly inclined by nature to challenge or even question them. But Tom sensed it and often encouraged me to bring my hurts to light. At first it was painful even to face them, but in a sensitive way he could be ruthless. What helped most was that he was not interested in defending anything. 'I believe you will rise in this firm,' he once said, 'and you will have twice your share of problems. It will be a great strain which you will have to take well, and as the first you will have to find your own solutions. I hope that you will let only the big things worry you and not the numerous small ones; those I would leave to small men on both sides.'

It was not easy in those days to find much in common with an Englishman in India, and neither side could be blamed. They were now convinced that they were going to go sooner or later; hopefully they felt it would be later. In the meantime, whether in industry or government, much was being done to train, to share, ultimately to hand over. They were therefore resentful of our impatience and our flat denial that anything at all was being done. There were wrongs for which they felt that they alone were not always responsible; while we were blissfully convinced that, once they left, all wrongs would overnight be put right, whether they were ours or theirs. They felt that some credit must surely be due to them; we conceded none. Few of us appreciated what it must feel like to be so misunderstood at a time when their supremacy was challenged; a supremacy that not so long ago had seemed part of their destiny and therefore unshakeable. It was a barrier of misunderstanding with a no-man's-land on either side where exploration was considered transgression.

Many young Indians returning from British universities, in their working contact with the British in India, bruised themselves on this wall of misunderstanding, sometimes suspecting insult where none was intended, and however far they progressed, the bruises usually remained. I was fortunate to have as my mentor a man untouched by the climate in India, with whom I could discuss my problems and misgivings without restraint. This must have helped give my ideas a healthy orientation and acted as a corrective, which was to be of great benefit to me in the far more delicate years to come.

I did not see Thompson Walker again, till 1949, when at the early age of fifty-three he was nearing his end. His nerves had always been in a bad condition, and much as he loved life he was convinced of his imminent end. In Lahore, he had had one of his attacks which made his legs numb and brought the fear of a creeping paralysis. Fortunately a bad influenza created a diversion, and I put him in a hospital where with rest and the care of some lively Anglo-Indian nurses he soon recovered. But back in England, his nerves gave away altogether and in a few years he retired from work. In the summer of 1949 I visited him in Yorkshire, where he lived on the edge of the moors. We spent three happy days driving through the country he loved. He took me to York Minster, to Fountains Abbey, and to an old derelict woollen mill tucked away in a hollow by the stream from which it once drew its power. For reminiscence's sake I went across the border over the Ribble River, up Pendle Hill. It was as windswept and sun-drenched as I remembered it, and there were the lone seagulls sailing in the sky. Pendle Hill had been a favourite spot during my student days, hallowed by the walks together with my Swedish wife in the summer of 1932 when we first met.

I never saw Tom again. Soon afterwards he died.

CHAPTER FIVE

Discovering India

After Thompson Walker's departure I returned to South India to start work at Trivandrum where the three sisters were waiting, with a fourth girl recruited and ready to start. This made the beginning easy for me. I appointed Sarama, the elder sister, supervisor of the team, in which capacity she worked with me for many years. She looked after the team so well that I always had plenty of opportunity to indulge my passion for learning about the people and the country wherever we went.

Sarama and I became good friends and in our free time she showed me around the countryside, explained the people, their life and their customs. She had been to school in Travancore and to Women's Christian College in Madras, which was the earliest institution for advanced education for women in India. From there she joined the Y.W.C.A. as the superintendent of a hostel, but this she found restricting. While conscientious and devoted to work she was not religious by nature and found it difficult to conform even to the light discipline of this institution. She was restless and too independent for an arranged marriage, but in those days for restless and independent women politics and social work were the only outlets. She was the first girl I met from this new class where education and independence were leading to a rejection of the past without a corresponding future.

Years later Sarama did accept an arranged marriage, for she was now unhappy at work and wanted to settle back in her village, and matrimony offered a prospect. It turned out to be a failure from the very start and she soon came back to work, but eventually she left again and disappeared altogether. Perhaps it was too early then for women to go to work in industry; and yet twenty-five years later I was to learn that women at work still did not achieve much more than Sarama did.

Trivandrum, and all Kerala, was as different from anything in the North as it was far away. The city stood on undulating ground, its residential areas scattered among groves, so that from the Observatory Hill you saw below almost nothing but tree-tops and hills. Everything had a tropical lushness and an air of perpetual summer. There was water everywhere, in ponds, canals and rivers, always densely fringed by palms.

Instead of the familiar chaos there was space and order. Small houses, well built and airy, with red-tiled roofs, each standing in its own small plot cultivated with coconut, pepper vine, jackfruit, tapioca, drumstick, hibiscus and flowering frangipani, formed a kind of urban development totally new to me. Very different too to look at were the people, so well washed and dressed always, both men and women, in clean, simple white. Even the bright red earth was different. You had to be a Punjabi to appreciate the difference. For one used to purdah, it was a new experience to see women walking the roads alone after dark, some still bare-breasted in the old way, with only the loose mantle thrown across.

Travancore was in great turmoil at the time. Here the struggle was between the people and a government that was Indian, headed by the Maharaja, though it was his highly able Diwan and the dowager Maharani who in fact ran the state. Both were of great ability and determination, with deep understanding and supposed affection for the other. In this progressive state the conflict between people and government took an almost parallel course to the struggle going on in British India. With the struggle in Travancore the British had nothing to do, and it gave me a shock to see a political phenomenon that was quite contrary to the popular belief that there could be differences only between us and an alien government, never among ourselves.

Every evening processions came out shouting 'Gandhi ki jai'. The slogans and invectives were familiar, the difference lay only in the target of the attack—curiously, always the Diwan and never the ruling family, even though they were known to support him. There were mass demonstrations, picketing and even police firing. I asked Sarama about it. She was totally opposed to the Diwan, though loyal to the Maharaja, and painted him in lurid colours as responsible for all the ills of the state. The highest literacy rate in India, the level of higher education, the best-developed public health and communications, even the growing industrialization; for all this she gave him and his government no credit, but all that was wrong was ascribed to his evil machinations. She considered her own community of Syrian Christians the particular target of his designs, because they were the most progressive and relatively better off than the rest. He was out to break whatever economic power they possessed. One symbol of their progress, a bank, was alleged to have been brought into liquidation by his manipulations. Even the police fire seemed to single them out.

Through a natural sense of justice that sought to compensate for this headlong attack, and also to gauge the depth of her feelings, I suggested that perhaps the Diwan was not such an unqualified tyrant as he was made out to be. No, she was adamant, he was bad through and through. Even the state transport service that he had organized so well was a tool in his hands designed to favour one section. Only when he went would things improve, and everything immediately change for the better, for had they not the resources, the will and the best human material? Look at the way they had spread so successfully all over India in services and professions.

The Hindus, the Nairs and the Ezhavas, all felt the same way about the Diwan though in each case there were particular factors; only the Muslims, largely in business, held nothing against him. The Nairs owned land and were a higher caste, with more education and wealth. The Ezhavas were poor, landless and not high-born. The Nairs felt he favoured the Syrians, and the Syrians that he favoured the Nairs, and the Ezhavas felt he favoured all except them, the dispossessed and unprivileged. And yet whatever the suspicions and fears, they all combined in a wholehearted hatred of the regime, and such pure hatred I had never seen before. Here was a people, I thought, among the most gifted in India, to whom nature was kind to a fault, a land where food grew around your house in sufficient quantities, a long coastline yielding much fish, a climate that varied from the tropical luxuriance of the coast to the cool but equally luxuriant mountains, where rubber, tea and coffee grew. What miracles, they tried to convince me, would they not perform once they were rid of the hated regime, once they could manage things their own way?

At work the girls came up against considerable resistance from the housewives, which, considering their general level of advancement, surprised me. Rumours went around that these girls from Bombay, who curiously enough spoke Malayalam fluently, were spies of the Diwan, paid to find out things under the garb of innocuous questions about washing habits. But the work progressed smoothly even so, and I asked Sarama to help me with a small survey of rural conditions and habits. We would motor out to some part of the country and go from one village home to another, without a set questionnaire, just talking to the peasants and their wives, or whoever happened to be at home. This was long before this simple technique became known as an open-ended interview. To me there was the added fascination of learning about a country and people that I found very attractive.

Before we finished in Trivandrum I drove down to Cape Comorin.

There may have been little in common between us in the Punjab and the people of Travancore, yet when I stood at the promontory where India literally ends, and thought of the land that stretched behind me to the frozen cave of Amarnath and beyond, I realized the common bond of shared beliefs. Two thousand miles north, in the Himalayas, I had seen thinly clad men and women from the South panting their way up the snow slopes to see the miracle of the milky ice lingam in the Amarnath cave, just a I now saw pilgrims from the North sunk in devotion here at Cape Comorin—to us Kanya Kumari, the virgin whose feet are washed by a confluence of three seas. She and the ice lingam are joined together into the unity of India.

☆

It was worth the dusty train journey of two long days and nights in the heat of May from the state of Travancore to the state of Hyderabad, to see two such extremes of Indian India. Travancore was mountainous, wet, green, clean, and its people well educated. Like anyone else, the Maharaja went to the temple every evening wearing a simple unstitched garment. Hyderabad was flat, stony, parched and illiterate. Its ruler went to the mosque every afternoon, but then all the traffic was stopped and the roads cleared of human beings. The women were heavily veiled and guarded behind high blank walls. All you saw of them was their hennaed toes. Travancore had mostly small landowners, earning at most a few thousand rupees a year; Hyderabad had enormous estates owned by landlords whose income ran into lakhs of rupees. Travancore was seething with unrest while Hyderabad lay in a medieval torpor, its many noblemen living in an isolated splendour hard to imagine. Their eccentricities were not without their humour and seemed to increase with rank. The road was cleared for the Nizam's First Lady while policemen stood stiffly to attention. The car with windows curtained would sometimes stop suddenly and begin to reverse. It rolled several hundred yards, stopped again and began to move forward; for no seeming reason. I was told that one of her favourite pastimes was to make the car go backward and forward. The First Gentleman equally sported his eccentricities, the most notable being caution in money matters. Stories went that he carried his thrift to such lengths as serving exactly six cakes on a plate to a party of seven, and therefore nobody dared to touch the plate and all six pastries were saved for another day.

I got to know a young Punjabi staying in my hotel. I had known his elder brother in Manchester, so we became quite friendly. I noticed that he did not seem to have any work to do and yet was absent for most part of the day. This made me curious, and one day he explained what he was doing in Hyderabad.

A Punjabi Khatri family had come to the state some generations ago. Of sturdier stock than the locals, through hard work they rose rapidly and were ennobled. One even rose to become the first nobleman of the court and was given the title of Maharaja and a large estate and even a knighthood by the British. Though the family was by now entirely mulki, a term used for the nationals of the state, the Maharaja Sahib stuck to one custom. He would not marry his daughters into the local nobility, because they were not infrequently an extravagant lot whose pride in life seemed to be piling up debts and mistresses; the two habits usually going together in a spiral. He therefore arranged their marriages with carefully chosen young Khatri men from the Punjab, of good stock and education and professional training. This particular young man was a prospective son-in-law. He was handsome, healthy, had finished his education abroad, was of the right height for the girl, and altogether made to specifications. Visible qualifications, however, were not enough. He had to be tested for temperament and manners, and trained to receive the title of Raja from the court, and he was therefore brought over, and spent most of the day at the palace as a member of the family, on trial.

One Sunday he asked me to accompany him. I might see the girl and give him my opinion on the whole set-up. He held out the temptation of a moghlai feast, a change from the eternal roast mutton and Anglo-Indian curry at the hotel, varied occasionally by a muddy-tasting fish caught from a pool in the garden. We arrived at the palace just before mid-day. No one seemed to take any notice of us, and as we sat on the verandah he kept pointing out the figures of the family as they flitted past, impatient to show me his future wife, whom modesty perhaps kept out of the way though no doubt she was furtively peering at us. The house was large and built in many sections, furnished in a mixture of tastes, both western and oriental. In the interior quarters there was an informal chaos of family, furniture, servants and animals, and as everybody went his own way I soon felt perfectly at home.

At one o'clock when the May heat was getting unbearable with the shade temperature nearing one hundred and fifteen, there was a great commotion, servants ran here and there, dogs barked and family members came out to meet the young Raja Sahib, the only son of the Maharaja Sahib. He rushed in and sat down in a state of collapse, wiping his face which was streaming with perspiration. When he recovered a bit I was presented to him. I sympathized with him for having been out in such heat. To my surprise he said he had been out for his daily exercise and however hot he had held out for a full half hour.

It seemed incredible for anyone to take exercise at this hour, and what kind of exercise? Even mad dogs would be indoors. And the Raja Sahib's figure did not make you think of exercise, but he seemed to assume that I of course knew all about it. His future brother-in-law took me aside and whispered that the Raja Sahib had been told by his doctor that he was putting on too much weight and needed a little exercise. This seemed a fantastic suggestion to the young nobleman who had always been helped by a horde of retainers to perform even the natural functions of life. Eventually he hit upon a bright idea in consonance with his dignity. Now, every day between twelve-thirty and one o'clock, he went out to drive his car. The driver and a servant sat at the back while he took the wheel and the car madly careered along deserted roads. He pulled the steering wheel hard from side to side and the servants clung to the straps for their precious lives. All the time he blew the rubber bulb horn and jumped up and down in his seat. At the end of the appointed time they all three returned, near-wrecks.

Soon afterwards lunch was announced, something I had been keenly looking forward to. There was a promisingly large table at which the Raja Sahib and other male members of the family sat down, waited on by a number of servants stretching in a line to the kitchens. To my astonishment the meal began with a watery soup and followed its course through indifferently prepared English dishes—mince chops with bones stuck in, fried fish, roast mutton and a steamed pudding. Instead of the famed Hyderabad moghlai cooking I faced a meal as dull as my daily hotel fare. I accepted my fate, but noticed that the family only picked at the food, which I attributed to their noble blaséness. My friend managed to whisper that the English meal was a touch of modern formality of which one took no notice; the real meal was yet to follow, and it did. As soon as the pudding was removed, there began to arrive an unbelievable succession of dishes served in beautiful Persian style utensils: pullaos and biryanis, nans and farmaishes, rogan joshes and qormas, chickens, quails and partridges, upon which the family, led by the well exercised Raja Sahib, fell to. Indifference gave way to healthy and vocal appetites, and I followed suit with my second lunch.

After an hour's relish we relaxed back in our chairs, when the Raja

Sahib suddenly announced the second half of his exercise. In the somnolent air, when all I wanted was a siesta, he called for a game of bridge, and for the next two hours we went through a slap-happy session of cards at which he displayed the gusto of his driving, with cheerful disregard for rules and conventions. At bridge I committed another indiscretion. The sun was pouring through a window and I got up to lower the blind. The horrified Raja Sahib literally shouted me back into my chair. He clapped his hands and asked a retainer to have the blind lowered. The retainer walked importantly a few paces to the window, leaned out and clapped his hands and passed on the order. It must have been relayed down the line of service hierarchy to the outhouses because quite some time later a ragged looking servant appeared, and under the direction of the senior retainer he loosened the cord to lower the blind.

In the evening I was introduced to the Maharaja Sahib, a fine old courtly figure, unaffected by time and pleasure. My friend told me that, after his fashion, and within his limitation, he still had gay evenings. His own quarters were magnificently furnished, with a delicate touch of luxuriousness, I thought, in the red velvet cushioned seat of the privy, which in the absence of modern plumbing had fresh straw placed underneath each time.

Here was a state, feudal, poor, ignorant, where progress ended with its capital city. Hyderabad itself was a relatively prosperous looking town with handsome public buildings, a variety of institutions, palatial homes and wide cement concrete roads that ended abruptly outside the city, where uneven metalled roads took over and the general ostentation gave place to poverty and squalor. And yet Hyderabad was peaceful while Travancore was seething. The great contrast in wealth seemed to excite no one's envy or protest. The noblemen of the court ruled with unchallenged absoluteness, afraid of no one except mildly of the Marwari moneylender, whom to keep quiet they also made a nobleman, at least in title. He was never sure of his money, but like the tailor and the jeweller he charged so much that even small and irregular payments were ample reward, and of course there were always the hard-pressed upon whose properties he foreclosed.

While the young noblemen were often an unattractive lot either frail or obese, extravagant, with manners whose charm was a thin veneer over deep selfishness, their young women were different. They were attractive and sensible, and combined demureness with innate self-confidence. Their education was also superior. In a special high school these girls received training in homecraft, in manners, in poise and grace. If one of them through marriage outside the state came out of purdah, it was remarkable how she would take to her new life with an assurance that showed no trace of her secluded upbringing. An English colleague, Maurice Zinkin, once invited such a couple to dinner. The young, attractive wife had just the right mixture of vivacity and poise. When they left she got into the car, took the wheel and with great ease drove away. My friend looked admiringly after her and said 'Do you know, less than three years ago that girl was still in purdah.'

*

Hyderabad had character, but not so my next stop, Nagpur, a nondescript town, except in the miracle of the monsoon when practically overnight its dusty heat gave way to cool freshness, and the burnt greyness to a luxuriant green. Here I had my first experience of a proper monsoon. After the searing heat, the monsoon came with a swift metamorphosis. I had not at first believed when someone told me that once the rains began the grass would grow knee high in less than a week.

I spent one interesting month in Nagpur, living at the railway station. There was no hotel, only a gloomy dak bungalow, but at the station I got a retiring room that was well furnished and possessed the luxury, rare for Nagpur, of modern sanitation. Through a kindly Anglo-Indian matron I managed to prolong my stay for a whole month by the simple device of buying a new ticket every morning for the next station, costing a rupee or so, and an occasional packet of cigarettes for her. The railway restaurant completed my needs and I led a self-contained life. In the restaurant I observed a custom, presumably new. I noticed in the evenings that the verandah beyond the main dining room was kept dark, as also the end of the dining room, through which some strange looking persons shuffled. They were not the type who ordinarily patronized western-style railway restaurants, but most of them were dhoti-clad, vegetarian-looking small business men. I decided to investigate and found that they came to indulge in secret vices. Some drank beer and whisky but most came to eat savoury omelettes with potato wafers, or even mutton chops. The darkened verandah of the station restaurant provided a safe place for indulging these newly acquired tastes that would have horrified their women at home.

Living in a large Indian railway station had its own fascination.

Gradually I fell into a pattern of activity. I would lean out of the window every morning, as I shaved, to watch a cloud of steam and then the metre gauge train pulling out from the platform below. The same train, its day's work done, returned to its platform as I was brushing my teeth before going to bed. In the evenings I walked about the deserted platforms and talked to idle porters or groups of villagers waiting for their trains hours hence. One interesting visitor who dropped in to my room for an occasional bottle of beer was the Anglo-Indian station master. His great worry was how to deal with the new class of politicians who frequently passed through Nagpur, because of its proximity to Wardha where Gandhiji had set up his ashram. The station master had done well under the British, whom he understood, but the coming rulers, already in power in the provinces, were hard for this simple man to understand. They wore the clothes of the peasant, but well laundered and starched. They travelled third class, but wanted the attentions and facilities of the first. If a few important ones travelled together a whole compartment had to be put at their disposal. All this they did with a show of humility, as a pointed reminder that unlike the British they did not want privileges. One did not realize it then that when power came, this expensive humility was to lead to many of our problems.

The station master poured out his doubts and misgivings because he felt that I understood his problems, which I think consisted mainly of his inability or reluctance to adapt himself to the coming order. He had to be courteous to those people but found it difficult to like them, and perhaps they did little to put him at ease. He found it natural to be civil and even deferential to an Indian like me who had stepped into the Englishman's shoes. With me he felt at home. I could sit down with him and offer him a beer and listen to his troubles. While the Englishmen kept him at a working distance, the new set left him bewildered. Pathetically he told me that he envied me, my ease with both sides, my English education and my Indian origin and ways. His was not an isolated problem; it was going to be the problem of many more than this simple station master.

For the first and last time in my life I lived in a state of expenselessness. The two rupees a day for the retiring room and the few rupees needed for food and drinks were allowed by the company, and Nagpur was the kind of town where there was nowhere to go and nowhere to spend. There were some pleasant walks during the rains along a ridge but they cost nothing. The usual clubs, the well appointed Central India Club, mainly British, and the Indian Club offered no temporary membership to an itinerant businessman like me. One evening I felt I had to spend some money, so I went to the one decent general store which also sold books. I looked at liquors, imported tinned provisions, stationery and cheap novels, and eventually walked out with a bottle of Rose's lime juice and the *Concise Oxford Dictionary*. I have since often pitied the lot of many in business in India who live in perpetual expenselessness, with every wish gratified.

☆

In the next town, Allahabad, I caught up again with my friend Roshan from Bombay who had been transferred here. After five years he was only now being tried out in an assistantship in a sub-branch office. I often visited his home and saw the life of the new Indian business executive in a provincial town where, in 1938, he still was a type unknown. In the average provincial town, apart from the mass of workmen, artisans, craftsmen, small and big shopkeepers and government clerks, there was a thin layer of perhaps a quarter to a half per cent of the professional class comprising lawyers, doctors, teachers and government officers. The few British stuck together, admitting into their company only the senior Indian government officers. The Indian professionals formed another group which even the well-to-do businessmen seldom entered, not due to prejudice but because the two were yet not miscible. It was rather a question of the influence of western education and its permeation through manners and living habits. Schooling and university education in the English language had so moulded the outlook of the professional Indian that he found little in common with the businessmen, who usually also belonged to a lower social caste. Some marked external differences also set them apart. The businessman as a rule preferred to live inside the city, he built his house in the old grandiose but uncomfortable style; he squatted comfortably on the floor and wore loose and airy Indian clothes; he spoke in his mother tongue. The professional preferred to live outside the city in a bungalow furnished with chairs and tables; his language was riddled with English; his clothes were usually a patchwork of both styles, often ill-fitting and uncomfortable besides.

Their values too had become different. One wanted money for further investments in gold, property and business—his one fling in life, when to outdo his neighbour he sometimes came close to ruin, was the wedding of a daughter or building a house, when his modesty and thrift scattered before the desire to be praised by his community. The professional had begun to regard such expenditure as wasteful, though his wife would not always agree with him. He saved for his children's education and to build a modest but modern house; and if he spent unwisely at a daughter's wedding it was only to attract a well placed professional son-in-law by offering a dowry beyond his means. In his single-minded pursuit of money, through means undisturbed by social judgement, salved by occasional prudent but conspicuous charity, willing to corrupt and to self-efface, the businessman had a secret contempt for the new professional class with their hollow pretensions, their standard of living unbacked by solid worth, their subservience in dropping the ways of their forefathers, and adopting those of the rulers only to seek favour and acceptance. But underneath it all there was also a streak of envy.

The two classes were thus apart, with hardly any social intercourse or inter-marriage. A wealthy businessman might, through a dazzling dowry, get his daughter married to the son of a highly placed professional, but in their search for a son-in-law it was unthinkable for a professional family to give their daughter away to a young businessman.

The late thirties saw the first specimens of this third class, the commercial and industrial executives. They were always sons of professionals who had not been able to get into the now saturated government services. In Bombay and Calcutta this class was becoming noticeable, but in the provinces it was still new, and its position in the social hierarchy of the district still undetermined. Through careful selection and privileges analogous with those of the I.C.S., Roshan's oil firm managed to obtain for their executives acceptance into the senior levels of the district hierarchy. Oxford education and the Blue in his case helped to give him the proper status in the eyes of British officials. Yet there was a kind of rootlessness about him and his wife. Roshan, who was basically Indian and simple, as was also his wife Avi, found it a strain to live the part of a sahib. While his Indian opposite numbers in government had through fifty years of Indianization acquired a permanence of status and could afford to be themselves in their private lives, these two felt obliged to conform to the pattern of the British, which his firm demanded. The British in his firm were themselves trying to conform to a pattern set by their predecessors in order to gain acceptance among the British officials; a pattern that lifted them out of the category labelled 'boxwallahs'. These commercial British perhaps outdid the official British just as, Roshan told me, some of his Indian colleagues in the firm tried to outdo the British.

Avi with her cynical humour told me that Roshan was often mistaken for a senior government official when he was travelling in the districts. She added with affectionate malice, 'He plays the sahib and enjoys it since he has come to Allahabad. In Bombay no one cared.'

Their living pattern seemed to have been laid down by the firm. Avi had to have an ayah, a cook, a butler, a bearer, a sweeper, a chowkidar and a driver to look after the two of them and a small child. She had to learn mahjong, acquire a taste for English food and for small talk. She made me laugh with her descriptions of their life in Allahabad, which seemed to consist of little work for Roshan and none for her except looking after this battery of servants, themselves with very little to do. Roshan's main function was to inspect the ramifications of a well organized monopoly and hers to play a role new for an Indian housewife.

To this otherwise unprepossessing town, the confluence of the rivers Ganga, Jumna and the mythical Saraswati gave some character. The rivers ran high in the month of rains. The surrounding country was a lush green with bamboo clumps and copses of stately mangoes and mowha trees. I walked about the country, talking to villagers, asking questions about their ways. The land looked rich but the people very poor. They had a drabness I had not seen elsewhere. Men and women wore white cotton that was seldom white, just a muddy grey, and their villages were mud hovels devoid of all colour. The only beauty lay in the rich crops of the flat country. This was the epic country of the Ramayana, and it was now the home of the Nehrus and many other leaders of the country.

Congress was very active in this area. One day as I stood under a tree talking to some villagers, a man on a bicycle, dressed in clean khadi clothes, stopped to see what was going on. Since he showed immoderate interest I tried to find out what he did Himself. He lived among the villagers and taught them their rights, their rights against the zamindars, the Government and against their own society when it was oppressive. I asked him how far he succeeded. More often than not, he said, the villagers did not succeed in asserting their rights, but still it was gratifying to him because at least they had learned what was theirs, when for centuries nothing but their life had belonged to them. He did not mind the many failures; the surprised chagrin alone of authority at being questioned was to him enough reward. His real disappointment, however, was the little headway he made against the excesses of the society itself, for here he was up against a blank wall and a resistance on which the appeal of nationalism made no dent, nor did society, convinced by long usage, feel any remorse. In dissuading a father from flagrantly defying the Child Marriage Act, a Brahmin from refusing to let a Harijan draw water from the well, a community from forcing a poor member to go bankrupt by giving a ritual feast, he made no impression whatever. While it was encouraging to see the way in which, once they had learnt their rights, they were willing to stand up to the police or the hirelings of a landlord, it was equally disappointing to see the way they would bow abjectly before the most unjust social dictates, he said sadly.

I wonder where that village worker is today. I don't imagine that either he or his successors pedal about on a bicycle in the selfless pursuit of teaching people to understand what is theirs. If he visits these villages again it is probably in a large car flying a flag, to ask for their votes, or to open a school. In his starched white clothes he will step forward with his head instinctively bowed to receive the garlands, with hands joined in smug humility. But maybe it happened otherwise. Maybe this one fell by the wayside in the later struggles, one of the nameless heroes who was not there when the rewards came.

On my last day in Allahabad I went by boat across the river to one of our holiest spots, where Ganga and Jumna meet. In the monsoon their muddy red waters swirled into a swift embrace and soon the two flowed together as if they had never flowed apart. As before at Cape Comorin, it struck me how moved I was by these unfamiliar manifestations of our religion, of whose practice and conscious belief I knew so little. I began to discover that rivers, mountains, trees and stones were really the centre around which our ritual revolved.

Across the river stood the large jail of Naini behind whose blank walls stayed off and on India's leaders. As I returned to the hotel through dingy and crowded streets, avoiding the roaming cows and still more carefully the frequent heaps of their droppings, I thought of what Thompson Walker had said of the Indian cities, especially those in the north: they had the appearance of the aftermath of an earthquake. A shanty standing next to a tall modern building; next door an occupied but unfinished house with girders and reinforcing steel rods sticking out; another half broken down but patched up and lived in; cattle in the streets with an air of ownerlessness; everything working in the chaos of an order newly broken. I continued my favourite walk through the railway station, over its long bridge, and descended into the green, trim oasis of the civil station with its low lime-washed bungalows and well kept gardens. The avenues of neem and hedges of myrtle washed by the rain added a clean acrid smell to the fragrance of flowering bushes. I returned to the hotel and sat on the lawn, sipping a beer. Allahabad, Naini and Barnett's Hotel, where I was staying, seemed worlds apart.

On my last day in Allahabad Avi had invited me to dinner. Roshan had asked an old friend who had been the first Indian president of a British university union. He had settled in Allahabad in a perfunctory sort of legal practice but was mostly understudying for Nehru in odd jobs, learning to be a politician, though eventually he rose to be a judge, an ambassador and a governor. There was also a civil servant.

I think Avi found life usually dull and seized upon an opportunity for a lively discussion which she lost no time in provoking. I sensed too that she was beginning to take a delight in chivvying me.

'Prakash, what did you think of Naini? Do you feel that this is where you ought to be, or are you too comfortably installed at Barnetts and would rather let those behind Naini's high walls do the job for you?'

I asked her what Roshan had said to this, for she must have put the same question to him. Avi grinned unabashed. Here was an interesting group of four young Indians, all with similar background and education both in India and in England, and each with an uncomfortable feeling of guilt. Ought he in these times to be doing something more than building a comfortable career? Even the young barrister, who was the closest to making some kind of sacrifice, was not sure whether he ought not to take the full plunge instead of skirting gingerly around. The civil servant was probably the unhappiest of the lot because he was an instrument of the authority that some Indians defied but all Indians disliked, defiance being only a matter of the degree of risk you were willing to take. Everybody, except he, could at least talk against authority; he being part of it could not even lightly indulge in that simple luxury.

Avi had us arguing in circles that widened and narrowed as the discussion became general or particular—but always around her as the provoking centre. The main theme was whether we were doing the right thing by standing aloof; did we make any contribution at all to the freedom process; did it need us all or would the country's interests be better served in the long run by having a class of us ready to take over when the time came?

My mind wandered off the discussion and I watched Avi's handsome face with its well-cut features and smooth, dark skin. Her face had the purer cut more often found in villages than in towns of the Punjab, but she had a sophistication that was uncommon and new to me. She had left Lahore and its conventional upper middle class convent education to go to an experimental school in Bengal, where she walked barefooted in its wooded estate and learned to sing and dance, and to dress in handwoven and block-printed sarees. Her figure had a sturdy Punjabi fullness. She had a better, less conventional mind than Roshan. I said to Avi:

'Why don't you join the Movement yourself? Your heart is obviously in it.'

'I would do it if Roshan was also interested. There is the inevitable jail-going if you once join, and I am not sure that that would appeal to me. If only one could do something useful without becoming a full-time worker attending meetings, joining civil disobedience marches and courting arrest. Besides, we might have to live in an ashram and "God give me chastity, but not yet"! I would find it hard to live without Roshan for long; I have not had enough of him yet.'

We all laughed at her practicalness and said we envied Roshan for her frank appetite for him. I told her that I could understand where she drew the line. She might think of it later when she mellowed down a little, though if the Movement could now draw only some of her fire it would gain quite something. She too laughed and thought we were denigrating the Movement and the part played by the many dynamic women who had thrown themselves wholeheartedly into its turbulence. When I asked whether its turbulence gave them some vicarious satisfaction, she gave me a long, penetrating look.

I went back to the hotel disturbed by Avi and what she said. If only the leaders of the Movement had not insisted upon an all-or-nothing attitude, or the Government on one of 'those-who-are-not-with-us-are-against-us'. The days of the sophisticated opposition had gone, when professional men in frock coats and hard collars could be in the Congress, and call their thinking progressive and liberal. The only real role left to their kind was taking messages between the Viceregal Lodge and some British jail in the name of negotiation and formulae. These men had neither popular following nor, since they could not deliver the goods, any influence on the government. The people now followed only those who gave their all. It could be argued that this might be a pity, as it deprived many of the chance of any personal identification, but equally it could be argued that all-outness was necessary if opposition were to be anything more than an armchair resistance.

The path of graduation from a limited self-government to Dominion Status was closed with the departure of the Simon Commission in 1930. Congress was now committed to complete freedom. Many argued that Churchil was right when he said that it was meaningless to talk of Dominion Status; it could hardly be applied to India. Australia and Canada were dominions, but with all their autonomy their peoples were more British in their love of the sovereign than the British themselves, and this to them was the ultimate, the indissoluble bond. Who wanted the King in India or who cared? What did he mean, except to the kindred souls of maharajas and nawabs? And they also would have preferred to be independent rulers, could they only be sure of their independence.

Ultimately I decided to shelve the question. I could not solve it in a hurry. Politics did not interest me at all, and short of entering politics there was little I could do. I was interested in my work, which in no way furthered the interests of the government, though equally it did not even remotely further the cause. The civil servant could sort out his worries and the barrister decide for himself. I consoled myself with the thought that Roshan and I were learning something new in commerce, something that would surely be valuable in time. The country did not need all its 350 millions. Roshan and I could very well leave it to the leaders, and, whatever Avi's feelings, I don't think either of us rated our possible contribution highly. On this unsatisfying note I left the matter, with the feeling that what I in fact lacked was the courage. That, I was sure, was what Avi thought.

Next day I returned to Bombay, exactly seven months to the day since I left on the first of January 1938. It was my longest single tour, of absorbing interest and a new education. For the first time I realized that there was an India. I savoured fully every moment of the long months.

Before my return I received a letter from the chief, the 'number one' or 'burra sahib' as they were called, saying that as he was leaving for England on his annual visit and would not be there when I returned he would like me to know that he was satisfied with my progress. He had confirmed me in the company's covenanted service—the magic word, but now with a difference. My company was covenanting its first Indian, whereas the old John Company of hallowed fame never covenanted even the British born in India. My covenant was a pale blue document containing innumerable clauses about secret processes and patents that I could put to no other use than the company's. Drawn up by some legal adviser in Liverpool at the turn of the century the contract gave away precisely nothing, but couched it all in incomprehensible but important sounding language. The one thing it did make abundantly clear was that I could be out of a job at three months' notice. Here too there were some suitable exceptions and safeguards. Had I only read it through, it made sure that I could be made to leave at once.

CHAPTER SIX

Preparing for a New Life

Back in Bombay I was told to organize another market research job of major proportions that would take me over much the same ground as before. It was to begin after the monsoon, and would last for five months.

In my spare time I decided to find a flat and make some kind of a home. Before my return from the next long tour I would also have to think of getting married, and acquiring a flat seemed a good starting point. Bombay in those days was a pleasant uncongested town, but even so I decided to live in the suburbs, and my choice eventually settled on the end of a road, on the slope of a hill, facing the sea. It was a modern flat of good design and ample space, in which every room had a view of the sea. I loved particularly the view from the verandah where a clump of palms screened the sea with their waving fronds, at its best in early dawn when sometimes a whole fleet of fishing boats, forty or fifty of them, would set sail on the morning tide. The sea, the wooden hulls of the boats and their sails were all a rose pink, gradually turning to mauve, and as the sun rose, to silvery blue. It was beautiful too on the nights of the moon when the light shimmered on the water and on the palm fronds. On full moon nights the light was sometimes so bright that you could see the blue of the sea and the green of the leaves. It reminded me of another sea far north where also the moon shone brightly on late summer nights. I was feeling restless.

My suburb stretched along the sea for two miles from a sloping headland over a valley to another hill. On the crest of my hill stood a Neo-Gothic church of no architectural beauty but with an interesting legend. On its site had once stood a Hindu temple to which people came to ask for boons. The Portuguese razed it to the ground and built a church to the Virgin Mary, but the Hindus continued to come for worship and wish. The image of the Lady was considered a sister of the local goddesses Mumbadevi and Mahalakshmi to be propitiated with a candle instead of flowers. Once a year, when the monsoon slackens its grip over the coast, an itinerant fair comes to this church. Except for the months of rains this fair keeps moving from one temple or mosque to another. In September it comes to the Mount of the Lady. The church has improved on the legend of wish fulfilment by offering wax objects to illustrate your wish. There are on sale arms, legs, feet, hands, hearts, chests, babies, anything to give form to a prayer. Poor Christians buy these from a small factory run by the church at the back and sell them to the visitors in front.

The whole suburb was dotted with small villages which in time had formed a township but in 1938 were still distinguishable and known by their old names, with some kind of separate entity. It was a charming combination of the old Maharashtrian and the old Portuguese, and equally interesting were the customs of the Christians interwoven with influence from their Maratha ancestors, then from the Portuguese, and last from the British. One day I saw a small Christian wedding procession with little dark girls in white frocks holding the train of a bride who stood beside the groom in a thick black suit. Everyone looked sweaty standing in the street under the broiling sun and I wondered what they were waiting for till I saw the local bus draw up and the procession board it, the girls still holding the train. It was very charming.

I loved my first home and the suburb. Gard was to join me here, and here our three children were born. Ten years later we built our own small house on the other hill.

In the office I now found greater acceptance. The covenanting removed all doubts among the clerks and I was now regarded a proper manager. I realized what a difference status made in our society. Whether high or low it had to be defined and named. While I was away another young Indian had been taken on, and he turned out to be someone I had got to know well on the boat. He had studied at Cambridge and was returning home with his wife. I felt happy to meet him again and have someone I could talk to freely, and I became part of their home where I spent most of my free time. We used to talk much around the topic of interest to both of us, our future in the firm and in industry in general, for we both came from the same background of professional families of whom we were the first to go into business. Arvind took a more limited view. Belonging to Bombay, he argued that here industry was largely Indian and developing fast, so that the few British firms would feel no need to Indianize, and of course the other foreign firms would take no notice. In Calcutta it was different; there industry was so predominantly British that some concession might be necessary and politic. I asked him why he had not joined an Indian firm. His father knew most of the Indian industrialists, whereas in this firm he was unknown and the future and scope for an Indian uncertain.

His family had unconcealed nationalist sympathies. His father was in the I.C.S. and had twice been made a high court judge, each time to be reverted to a less senior post in the district because in the cases he tried during one of the disobedience spells he had stuck to the spirit of the law while Government were anxious to mete out exemplary punishments; in addition, he openly had Congress friends who were sometimes in jail and sometimes out. Arvind's only sister had joined Gandhiji's ashram at Wardha with her father's blessings. I wondered therefore why Arvind had joined a British firm. He explained to me that most Indian firms were family businesses or belonged to a particular community, and it was the accepted thing that all control and privileges went to the family members; an outsider, however useful, could not normally expect to rise high, and certainly not to a top position. After the family came caste, then community and then region. When a father ran out of sons he turned to nephews and other relations. The logic of nepotism was to them impeccable: 'Whom can I trust more: my sons and those who are related and known to me, or strangers?' In a Parsi firm no one contested that the top position had to go to the family and the next senior to other Parsis. In Gujerati firms there were Gujeratis at all levels, and so on.

His wife, Aruna, was the first Indian girl I had met who had married outside her community and province, and there were not then many like her. She came from one of those rare Punjabi middle-class families that had turned Christian. In the Punjab, as all over the north, Christianity did not make much headway beyond converting an occasional poor family, but in Lahore, a few well-to-do Hindu and Muslim families had gone over. Unlike the poorer converts elsewhere they had stuck to their original names. In fact it was a mark of conversion through conviction rather than social and material improvement to have retained your Indian name instead of changing it to Daniel, Martin or D'Souza. They formed an *élite* of Lahore on account of their education and professional advancement. She came from one of the Muslim Christian families and it seemed a far cry to marry a Gujerati Hindu.

She was so unlike him. He was easy-going and good natured and nothing ever seemed to worry him. She was like the late monsoon weather—totally unpredictable; out of a clear sky would come a squall that made you think the monsoon was back, only to be followed by a sky so innocently blue as if nothing had happened. You never knew what made her happy or unhappy, but it could not go deep for she had no permanent moods. The only permanence lay in the alternation of sun and cloud; she had no middle temper. She must have been beautiful not long ago, for she was still young, but she seemed to have stopped caring. She had a round laughing face with roguish eyes, but what amused me most about her was the demureness she could suddenly switch on if one of Arvind's elderly relations arrived. She would pull her sari over her head, half covering her face; laughter went out of her voice and she talked in earnest tones. As soon as they left she returned to her normal self, angry or happy as the mood took her.

No two women could be more different, Avi and she, in looks or temperament; yet both were so different from the Punjabi girls I had been used to before I left home ten years ago. Products of convent schools, one had come under the influence of cosmopolitan Bombay, while the other was influenced by the new Bengali culture, but both had acquired a kind of restlessness. They were both always goading their men. I wondered if this restlessness did not come from a change that had led them nowhere. Their men had studied abroad and started on careers that were a natural corollary of their education; those girls had also prepared themselves and yet, just when they should have been putting their education to some use, they had married and started a life no different from that of the girls who had stepped straight out of home. It would have done them good to have worked for a few years instead of plunging straight into domesticity after an education that promised a life of equality and purposefulness, and yet led nowhere. They took a great deal of vicarious interest in their husbands' work, and the cynical thought came to me that either of them would have been better at the jobs their husbands did, for they were unusually bright and strong-willed. It was their like that found an outlet in politics and social service; they had stepped out into public life because it was the only career then open to them.

★

I began my next tour anti-clockwise round India. I started at Trivandrum where I was greeted at the station by Sarama and, hiding behind her, the twins who had lost none of their shyness. They went to work with great enthusiasm because I had promised to take them to Madras, Calcutta, Allahabad and Lahore. They were thrilled at the idea of seeing these cities, though frightened by the thought of winter in Lahore. I spent long hours giving them a working knowledge of Hindi. In Calcutta our Punjabi lady would join us to make a permanent team, trained and experienced. With the work of this tour well planned I relaxed into pleasant anticipation of renewing contacts with the towns and the country and people I had got to know. But soon the clouds gathering over Europe began to worry me in a personal way.

Gard lived on a small island in the Baltic between Sweden, Russia and North Germany. We had been writing regularly to each other, and more than a year's separation did not seem to have altered things. We had settled on letting time decide, and it did. Her letters were acquiring an urgency which the proximity of Hitler made understandable, but then she had all through been cheerfully optimistic, which I was later to find stemmed from the confidence of an infinite capacity to adapt rather than ignorance, as I then thought. Marriages between Indians and Europeans were not rare in those days, but few worked out totally well. Most were between Indian students in England and English girls. Few Indians studied on the continent or in the United States. In England, for a variety of reasons—strangeness, social awkwardness, diffidence, and straightforward colour prejudice—young Indians mostly stuck together. They lived in a society where social contacts among the sexes were normal and easy, but denied such contacts among their natural equals they found them lower down, not at the college socials but at the local palais de dance. They went out with shop girls who were impressed by their superior education and liberal pocket money, and many of the boys laid it on thick about back home, the large houses and hordes of servants. There were exceptions, but it was generally from this class of girls that our boys married. When the time came for returning home, faced with the prospect of finding a job and of giving their wives even an elementary standard of living, some lingered on, but it was then virtually impossible for an Indian to get more than a lowly job in England. The best off were the doctors who could always set up their own practice, usually in a poor locality, and do well. There was great belief in the healing powers of a dark man, which in reality was just their basically sympathetic nature and willingness to take trouble.

Those who returned home with English wives ran into many problems. In the search for a job they had to stay with the parents, who were often simple, unwesternized people. Their habits, food and way of living were so different that the unsophisticated girl found the going hard. When he got a job it was at a salary inadequate to lead an English way of life. Oddly enough, you could live as cheaply as you liked as an Indian, but to live like the poorest Englishman cost a great deal more. Even to maintain the working class English standard of two pounds a week cost many times more in India. But at least when he got a job the girl had her home and independence and the certain comfort of cheap servants and when her husband's income went up she could live in relative ease, though by then another set of problems bothered her—the social ones. She had little or no social life: the Indians she found unfamiliar, and her own kind cut her dead. Sometimes the marriages failed at an early stage and the girl was glad to return home but if it endured the early shocks she was usually happy enough in a cut-off way, showing much courage and grit. Her home was a little England, the children got English names even though they were not christened, and her intimate friends were other English girls like her. This was the familiar pattern of such marriages, and I found it difficult to convey it to Gard. The problems were all so small in themselves that I would have appeared to be evading the main issue. I think I misjudged her quite unique adaptability. A factor that deterred me—more than the traditional attitude of the European community to such marriages—was the likelihood, not to be ruled out, of the spread of Hitler and his ideals. The irony of it was that a union between one from his favourite Aryans and a true Aryan would be taboo in his race theory.

As the news from Europe became still gloomier and war seemed only a matter of time, I decided to go ahead. My elder brother had visited me in Bombay and I had casually sounded him. With his usual generosity he promised to speak for me at home. I now wrote to the chief, who I felt should know, just in case any views or feelings stood in the way. He could be lukewarm and point to difficulties. It was also painful to write to him because not so long before I had written at his wife's death. He replied promptly with an encouraging letter. Later, when I reached Lahore, my parents took everything for granted. My mother would sometimes come into my room, sit on my bed and ask me little questions about Gard.

CHAPTER SEVEN

Punjabi – Viking Alliance

Gard, at the other end, spent the year and a half of waiting teaching in her old school, on terms of uneasy equality with old masters she had been wont to curtsy to. In the summer of 1938 she went on holiday to Germany, and returned home wondering if the war would catch up with her. School had hardly settled down to its term, and it was September. That fateful month would always in her memory be linked with the awesomeness of a blood-red Aurora Borealis, on a latitude where the northern lights are hardly ever seen. In Visby people ran out of their houses to stare at the wondrous sky covered with red shafts of light, and said the red aurora was a sign of war. It was an omen no one doubted.

When the Munich crisis was over and church bells all over Sweden rang in thanksgiving for peace, no one felt more deeply thankful than Gärd. The dearly-bought peace might be only a postponement of war, but it would give her time to join me in India. The longest separation we had ever had had been hard for both of us, but in those September days we felt our own fate hung in the balance with the wider destinies. Our letters crossed each other on the way. She wrote that she was afraid of waiting any longer. I wrote 'Come as soon as you can.'

She gave notice for the end of the term. Autumn darkened into winter and the school closed for Christmas. Gärd sent in notice of her engagement to the press, bought herself a plain gold ring, Swedish fashion, and went up to Stockholm to settle her visa for India and book her passage. Getting the visa at the British consulate proved no mere formality as she had thought. Asked why she wanted to go to India, she said 'to get married there' and, requested for proof, she picked up the morning paper from the desk in front of her and pointed to the engagement column. The man's face fell. 'But it is an Indian! You cannot get a visa without permission from the Government of India'. He explained that a visa could only be granted after the authorities in India had satisfied themselves that the man concerned earned enough to support a European wife. It sounded strange to her that a marriage anywhere could be the subject of such a test, and would the British authorities in India view it unprejudiced? She worried how high the income limit might be fixed in order to exclude most cases. So, in spite of the promise of a reply at the earliest by cable, she felt thoroughly miserable and unable to enjoy her last Swedish Christmas, wondering what she would possibly do if the visa was refused, and to whom one could appeal.

She bitterly regretted that we had not got married before I left Sweden. This was something I had been against, though I had not been very clear about it. In the face of so much uncertainty back in India, determination alone was not enough, and I had left her with a future painted in doubtful colours to protect her from the shock of a possible non-fulfilment. Now when fulfilment seemed near came the maddening frustration of a bureaucratic barrier suddenly thrown up which might not be removed quickly enough before the flames of war leapt. She had no eyes for the loveliness of Stockholm deep in snow and was glad to get back to Visby where she was called back to school to substitute for somebody who was ill. This made the days pass until one morning the cable arrived. The visa was through. I had been out of Bombay on tour, and during my absence a European police sergeant had arrived at the office and asked to see the chief about the enquiry from the British Legation in Stockholm. It was fortunate that I had already asked him for permission, and though my salary was meagre by their own standards he blandly told the sergeant that I would be able to support a wife.

With this hurdle cleared Gärd booked her passage by P. & O. from Marseilles. In Sweden it is the custom for a bride-to-be to go to church on the three consecutive Sundays when the banns are read from the pulpit, and afterwards be at home to her friends who then present her with the wedding gifts. I had filled in a form declaring myself willing to marry her, but for the banns it appeared that she would also have to produce my non-existent birth certificate. So she had to forego the banns, but not the party. Her mother and the maid got busy baking all the traditional cakes and on her last Sunday at home there was a grand coffee table and another table for exhibiting the presents. For the last time she saw the old house filled with a gay crowd, everybody asking her when did she think she would come home to visit.

Gärd used to say that being bred on an island makes you prepared to go far abroad, for all through childhood and growing up you have been possessed by the feeling of being hemmed in by the sea, and a longing to get away. In the long warm summer the island was open to the world; it was a holiday resort where people from many countries came and huge steamers anchored—she once saw off Visby the black hull of the *Viceroy of India.* The children found it great fun to test their schoolbook English and German on the tourists. When the evenings again got dark the visitors left, the music in the garden cafés stopped, the promenades along the shore lay deserted and the only sound left was the murmur of the waves. Life was once again enclosed inside the city wall. The only link with the outside world was the daily steamer to the 'mainland'.

At last came the night she was leaving Visby for good, wondering if she would ever again see the towers of the city wall, the ruined churches, the red-tiled roofs of the medieval Hanseatic merchant houses, and the home where she was born. The Swedes believed at the time that in the coming war Germany and Russia would fight for the strategic possession of the island of Gotland, and feared the destruction of the city. This did not come to pass and she was to see the city again, but never her home and never again her mother. Mamma was very brave; she had never cried at the thought of her only daughter going so far away, and even at the quayside she kept her tears back, though as far as she was concerned Gärd was going to another world.

The friends who saw her off had filled her cabin with flowers. For a newly-wed daughter of the city, the steamship company would have put up coloured lights between the masts, but as it was she missed both that and the fireworks from the jetty. The bell rang the first warning, starting the long farewells of a parting by sea. The third bell went and she stood alone on the deck, the few other passengers having already retired. She saw well-known faces growing dimmer until the steamer rapidly swung round the pier. As winter darkness hid the coastline, it also seemed to engulf all that had been part of herself.

On the train journey through Sweden she stopped here and there to say goodbye. It was the most desolate of seasons, bare winter with frozen grey fields. She visited her old uncle just in time for his eightieth birthday, and when he drove her himself to the station in the dark of an early morning, ten miles through heavy slush, she knew it was unlikely she would ever meet him again. Similarly all through her journey across Europe, with the large shadow looming, the thought was always in her mind, 'Shall I ever see it the same?'

In the train to Marseilles from Malmö there were two men in her compartment. One, a retired banker, was a true globe-trotter who entertained the others with yarns about his travels till he dropped out at Hamburg. He had never been to India, because, he said, it was the most expensive country in the world for a tourist. The other traveller was a young violinist from the Stockholm Symphony Orchestra on his way to Paris on a stipend. With a couple of hours to wait at Hamburg they went out together to have supper. He was adamant that with his musician's reverence for the Jewish race he would not go into any place which bore the legend, 'Jews not wanted'. As Gärd knew before, all eating places had the same sorry tale, and eventually hunger drove them into a café where a band of faded blondes caused him acute agony.

Early next morning they got off the train at Cologne where she was spending a day. She suggested to the violinist that before his train left for Paris she might show him another Germany to take away the taste of last night. They stood in front of the cathedral and saw its immense structure gradually revealing itself in the dawn. Then they walked through the Altstadt, the old Gothic city where one of the winding alleys still bore the name Judengasse, till she had to tear him away from the sculptural abandon of the council house and rush him back to the station. In the evening she went with a German friend to the opera which had still been open to all the previous summer but now also bore the detestable legend. The young German said, 'I am sorry you should have to see this. The opera was the last place of freedom in Cologne.'

Her last glimpse of Europe was a quayside at Marseilles on a grey drizzling morning, with a grey-looking, huddled sort of crowd from which odd words in German could be heard, waiting dejectedly to be allowed over the gangway to the steamer next to hers, destination Australia. Like her, they were escaping at perhaps the eleventh hour—they to a country where they hoped to be able to live in dignity; she to a country of her choice with very vague ideas what the future would be like, but sure she would never regret.

There were very few passengers for India in the first class—married couples, some with daughters; a few single men—all of them English. In the second class there were plenty of Indian students and some European girls, perhaps travelling for the same purpose. One evening the second class passengers were invited to a dance in the first class lounge, and some turned up but very soon left. For the next invitation nobody came; the atmosphere was too chilling. The first class passengers had probably found out about Gärd by discreetly asking her table companion and decided to ignore her. It was a peculiar situation to find herself in. It is one thing to be alone in a big crowd, and it can be amusing to wander about all on your own in a foreign city. But to be absolutely alone in a small crowd, in a confined space, day after day, she found trying. She spent all her evenings in the cabin and read most that was readable in the ship's library.

Of course she was not unprepared for such a situation. She knew England well in a way, having spent two years there, if she added up all her visits to me. But most of her contacts had belonged to the student world, a world which in most countries is outside the pale of ordinary society, detached from the individual's social background; nevertheless she had heard and read of a different England east of Suez. In Sweden of course racial considerations did not exist. Marrying an Indian was more adventurous, and certainly more interesting than marrying a German or an Englishman. No one she knew had ever been to India and most Swedish people had only vague ideas about it. Indians and Europeans originally came of the same stock; there was Tagore who had got the Nobel Prize; and Gandhi: that was the sum total of their knowledge of India. She used to tell me she was often relieved that my lack of fluency in Swedish saved me from revealing my ignorance of Indian philosophy. The fact that she was marrying a Hindu and that our children would be Hindus did not seem to upset even the truly religious-minded old people, but they would certainly have pitied her if she had had to become a Catholic—a religious hangover! It was very reassuring that her father-in-law-to-be was something as modern as an engineer and I with a company whose products were well known in Sweden.

When I had moved to my flat I had sent Gärd some snaps of the house, the garden, and even my secondhand two-seater Ford. These pictures, she told me, were a great blessing, as they saved her answering so many questions. A grand-aunt, who was always something of a joke in the family, had exclaimed, 'I am so glad, my dear, that you live in a house. I read somewhere that all Indians live in mud huts!' What she had heard from me to the adverse she had never confided to anyone, or the misgivings she had felt about our future.

Whiling away time on the P. & O. *Strathmore,* she was cynically amused to imagine what her kind friends would have thought if they could have seen her in her splendid isolation. The ship's library had its limitations, and Gärd thought the ten days between Port Said and Bombay were the longest she had ever known. It was a great relief to see at last the coast of India rising out of the sea.

CHAPTER EIGHT

Starting Career

The rumbles of war came nearer, and they now came from both sides, while Gärd and I settled into the life for which we had been waiting for seven long years. The Germans had declared the Japanese 'not non-Aryans', and there appeared a growing understanding between the true and the honorary Aryans, for whom India seemed a likely meeting place. There were many in India who, despite his derogatory reference to us in *Mein Kampf* as people only fit to be ruled, dreamt of Hitler as a saviour. India and Indians had always been popular in Germany. Gärd had seen for herself how Indian students were treated and fussed over there. It did not surprise her that people in India knew little of what Nazism really stood for, when she had seen how in democratic Europe people could still disbelieve its excesses and look upon Germany as a bulwark against Communism. Hitler's pact with Russia changed this, but in India thinking was confused; our own struggle blinded us to the bigger issues, and very few clearly understood that Britain's defeat might mean the defeat of all freedom.

We argued something like this. It would be good to see the Germans and the Japanese teach the British and the other colonial powers a lesson; we would rub our hands with glee, and what came afterwards could take care of itself. It would not be our war, and we did not possess the freedom that in Europe Hitler was out to destroy. The expression, used by the British, of the choice between the known and the unknown devil made no impression. We felt instead that the unknown might hold in it a chance for the better. Besides, among all Europeans, had not the Germans come closest to understanding India? It was they who had discovered the kinship of languages and racial relationship, and we shared the emblem of the sun wheel, the swastika.

Gärd well understood our frustrations, in fact straight from Sweden she felt perhaps even more strongly the indignity of being a second class citizen in one's own country. But the idea that Nazi Germany might help us to freedom and dignity seemed to her utterly fantastic. She found equally baffling the assumed complacency of the British, who joked about Hitler being welcome to India so long as the Germans left the Breach Candy swimming pool in Bombay alone. At that time Germans, both Jews and non-Jews, were much in evidence at this treasured European preserve. The foremost topic was prohibition, just introduced by the first shortlived Congress Government, with absolution to anyone born in Europe.

When I returned home, fresh from an English university, full of the dangers to democracy and intellectual freedom, I had tried to interest an occasional Englishman I met in the subject of Nazism and Fascism. It was always received with a cold shrug, because, I think, of an uncomfortable feeling that this was not the sort of subject to discuss with an Indian. There was the stiff upper lip 'Oh we shall manage somehow,' and sometimes was added the infuriating patronage 'You Indians don't have to worry, it will be our headache. It might of course teach these Congresswallas something, but I don't suppose you agree with that crowd either. Take prohibition; you drink like one of us. Mind you, I am not against giving them power, for they have to learn; I would rather that chaps like you took it. Anyway, you don't have to bother your head about Hitler and all that, you had better think of your own problems; I mean these white topiwallas.'

One or two such conversations cooled my ardour, but I found talking to Indians no less trying. 'You are worried about the British losing and a thousand years of darkness descending? It might be a thousand years of efficient rule instead of the decay that has set in where only maharajas, zamindars and a few millowners thrive. We have got used too much to the yoke. Let us not shed tears for Britain, the Mother of Parliaments and all that she stands for; she certainly doesn't stand for any of those things here.' The rancour against the British was deep and few sympathized with them in their attempt to stem the tide.

I think it was the attitude of our leaders that put the issue in this light. The rank and file were ignorant of the implications, but even to leaders like Nehru who felt very strongly and emotionally about the dangers of Nazism, Fascism and Japanese imperialism, India's first task was to clear the British out. They did not want to compromise with one evil in order to defeat a greater evil. The common man had no idea how much greater was that other evil, and his leaders seemed unconcerned. He would have been surprised that to a refugee German Jew in India the life of the conquered seemed rather enviable. But on the whole, while we criticized the British and almost hoped there would be a war, we did not want them altogether to lose it. A close shave, close enough to humiliate them, to weaken them enough to grant India self-government was what we would prefer. So we argued while time ran out.

The outbreak of war came rather tamely. The crisis that kept rising and subsiding for once just went too far and it became impossible to satisfy Hitler's appetite any longer. There was some praise in India when Britain at last took the plunge, particularly as she was so unprepared against an enemy whose sole energy had been bent to this one purpose, and unsupported by France, who was equally unprepared and did not even possess the will to resist. We might have let ourselves be persuaded to support Britain in her ultimate stand against Hitler, had the Viceroy Lord Linlithgow not been such an insensitive person. There were at the time the first elected governments in the provinces and a central assembly of sorts; but more important, there was now a public opinion and strong leadership. Some consultation and show of confidence in our leaders therefore might have carried them along with him. But he made no attempt. Perhaps he was afraid that with the casuistry of the Congress, and the Muslim League always willing to profit by any difference between Congress and Government, he might get bogged down into arguments, clarification, terms and conditions. And sure of the control over resources, with an army whose expansion would present no problem, and backed by the ready pledges of fealty by the princes, landlords and the other honoured ones, he went ahead and committed India to war, and took a chance on the Congress Governments walking out of office. That might even suit him as he could then run the provincial governments with a more single-minded pursuit of the war effort. This is what happened and I don't think the Viceroy or his British services shed any tears over it, but a great opportunity was nevertheless missed.

For the first one year and a half the war had no visible effect on India and work went on as usual, though I was personally affected. Thompson Walker had got the firm in London to agree that I might extend my market research activities to the associate companies in Ceylon, Burma, Thailand and Malaya. This splendid opportunity was however knocked out by the war. In fact, market research in India too was soon to be wound up.

I think it is only now we Indians have begun to take an interest in the countries to the east of India. Earlier, nothing took us there. And yet to east and west, Indian communities have gone to trade and settle: in a big way in East Africa; in smaller knots in Iran, Afghanistan and the Persian Gulf. They practically invaded Ceylon, Burma and Singapore, and settled in groups of varying sizes from Dakar to California, Hawaii and Fiji. But after generations, they still regarded India as their home. Some have returned periodically to build a house, marry off a daughter, or perform some important ritual as a sign of affluence and also of sentiment. In a small town north of Bombay there is a street of vacant mansions belonging to a particular Muslim community whose affluence abroad is reflected in the size of the houses and the freshness of their blue paint. But what we lacked, and are only slowly acquiring is the understanding that comes through visits at a different level, students, tourists, businessmen looking for new venues. Similarly, all these countries know us mainly through the settlers, and that not always favourably.

The effect of this ignorance of each other did not matter as long as we were all dominated by a European power which provided us with blinkers that left only their own country in the field of our vision and maybe a tiny bit of other European countries on the periphery. It became evident later when all of us gained independence that for too long, instead of developing the natural ties of trade and culture with our neighbours, we perforce continued our dependence upon the distant European powers, regardless of whether they needed us.

With market research closing down, Rist put me into the press section of the advertising department, which had now prospered into a full scale agency with account executives, art director, press media and all other ramifications of an agency set-up. The press section dealt with nearly 450 newspapers all over India in thirteen languages, including English. The Indian press comprised then, and still does, an amazing variety of newspapers ranging from the sophisticated English language dailies that came off the rotary machines to those written by hand on waxed paper, whose copies were pulled off stones prepared for each edition and afterwards scrubbed with pumice stone and washed clean for the following day. There were dailies, weeklies, fortnightlies, monthlies, quarterlies, annuals, and some that appeared with intervals determined by the financial position of the proprietor. In the lead were a few British owned dailies from the major towns, followed by one or two Indian owned dailies, also in English, from the provincial capitals. The entire lot of between two and three thousand publications amounted to no more than two million in circulation, and a good three-quarters must have been represented by a handful.

The British dailies mostly originated from the middle of the last century, and many had had distinguished editors who had been bold, and sometimes downright scurrilous in their criticism of Government and personalities, especially the Governor Generals, but by the thirties of this century British editors had become staid and pompous.

Even in England poking fun and lampooning had gone out of fashion, but instead of developing a lively reportage and variety of interests our English papers had become dull, subservient supporters of the government reporting their news like the movements of royalty. They piously praised anyone who supported the government and preached homilies to Congress.

The Indian papers were poorly financed, but what they lacked in resources they made up in verve. All nationalist, they attacked the government on principle. Its every motive was suspect and all its actions injurious to the country's interests. The reporting was entirely political, and, as in the English language press, things that had purely human interest were firmly eschewed. Between the two there was little to choose for readability; they kept you informed of basic news at home and abroad, their one grace being a complete lack of interest in crime and scandal. For nearly two years I had not subscribed to a newspaper and only occasionally glanced at the headlines, and now they suddenly became my job.

The new work consisted in acquainting myself with the several hundred newspapers that approached us for advertising, evaluating them by studying their circulation claims. As they all needed advertising and we were the biggest advertisers in the country, all but the British papers converged on us for support, and I spent endless hours interviewing their representatives, usually the proprietors. This was the most interesting part of all. I met men from every corner of India, personalities as diverse as one could imagine, all on the same errand but each using a different technique. It took most of them some time to accept me as they had been used to dealing with Englishmen and were not sure of this new devolution of responsibility. The British newspapers' advertising managers were sure of their position and went straight to Rist, nodding to me in passing; the leading Indian papers were also fairly certain of receiving advertising and were content with an annual visit to Mr. Rist. The less important ones who came to see me optimistically gave inflated circulation figures, fully expecting a radical cut. The few straight ones usually asked for incommensurately high rates. The most tiresome were the unctuous lot who always worked for a cause. They were struggling to help the country or the society at a personal sacrifice and therefore expected, nay demanded our support, especially now that there was an Indian press media manager. A few of them were indeed genuinely selfless, and then they were modest. The aggressive lot who used their paper for political influence considered that we as a foreign firm who had no right to be in the country owed them a living. They insisted that I should support their paper by advertising all the firm's products, in large spaces and with the greatest of frequency, otherwise how were they going to serve the nation, boycott British goods and buy only swadeshi.

I learned from Rist not to take them too seriously and keep our advertising free from political bias. A paper could be as anti-British as it liked as long as it had an honest circulation. This consideration many considered unfair, since our insistence on value deprived them of support for the cause. They used to harangue me about my duty to the country when I suggested that their circulation claims were dubious. At times they almost convinced me; only I was never certain whether they, any more than I, were serving the cause or just themselves. It was my first introduction to the self-seekers who had jumped on to the band-wagon, which some of them would be steering some years hence, when they would be in a position to command instead of ask.

But the type I dreaded most was the dynamic woman social worker of Bombay. Some came quietly for help in the shape of advertising space in an annual report or brochure for a little institution among the slums of Bombay. They were interesting to talk to, modest and much moved by the misery they were trying to relieve. The ones I was genuinely afraid of, however, were the high-powered socialites who never touched a cause unless it was first blessed by Government House, where at a tea meeting called by the Governor's lady they would organize a grand fête on its gracious lawns sloping down to the sea, or an expensive dinner-dance at the Taj Mahal Hotel. With thunderous energy these women would fan out through the business houses for advertisements. A large Parsi lady, the doyen of the corps of fund raisers, one day swept into our office with protesting sepoys following her. She had the looks and ways of a dowager duchess, and when one of the sepoys pointed to me, she brushed me aside. She wanted to see someone senior, obviously a European, and before I could stop her she stormed into Rist's room. In two minutes she was out triumphantly waving a printed form and demanding that I fill it in and send it with an advertisement block to her office the same morning. She was in a class by herself, and dominated the Bombay social charities scene for a quarter of a century. Many needy institutions owe a debt to her tireless energy.

Even to the many genuine newspaper managers it was difficult to convey that we bought advertising space like a commodity or service;

that there had to be some criteria of value. The thought that they might run their publications on sound business lines, with proper investment and decent profitability, and thus offer more value to their readers, seemed irrelevant. It must always be service, however poor and inadequate. The suggestion that they might give more value to the readers seemed to make the adverse impression that I was suggesting to make the service mercenary; an idea that seems to run right through our thinking. Anything that produces a profit is bad, even though it might widen the scope of service; poverty and inefficiency are virtues because they are untainted by profit. I did not realize then that we were developing a way of thinking that was to recoil upon us later.

There was a lighter side to press work. I had to scan through all specimen copies that came to our office, and my favourites were the Hindi and Urdu magazines of the north for their vivid articles and advertisements. The stories were usually sexy, more so the pictures, but it was the medicinal advertisements that I particularly enjoyed, because they are untainted by profit. I did not realize then that we preposterous that it took your breath away, couched in a language so intimately reassuring that it made you feel almost cured as you read. They poured scorn over modern science, because western medicine could only cure one thing at a time, while they could with one and the same medicine induce diametrically opposite results. As for the mysteries of sex and birth their knowledge was boundless. There was for instance a medicine that claimed to act both as contraceptive and preventive provided you followed some simple instructions. So long as the wife took a daily tablet 'you can enjoy vigour that will leave your partner amazed, and all this without any fear of nature intervening.' But one day you decide to have a child. From then, for fourteen days, you leave the tablets and the lady alone. 'On the fourteenth day, she takes a tablet, you both bathe and anoint yourselves with emollient perfumed oils, and after following suitable instructions, exactly nine months from the day she will bear a child with the luminous face of a full moon. The whole thing is guaranteed and in the unlikely event of failure you can ask for your money back.' There were the hair oils that sharpened your memory, gave you good sleep, cooled the brain and generally toned up the system, including an aphrodisiac effect. The whole medicinal lore seemed to centre around sex, skin diseases and stomach ailments.

CHAPTER NINE

English Lifestyle

Rist called me in one afternoon and asked if Gärd and I would attend their son Tony's christening at the English church on Malabar Hill, and after the ceremony join them at a party at their new flat. It was to be both a christening and a housewarming. I thanked him with the social formula I had heard the British use: 'May I check with my wife and let you know? Later, in a busier, more senior life; it made sense, and if on occasions I ignored it I often found myself in trouble. But now our evenings were usually free except over the week-ends when friends dropped in, often uninvited.

Driving home that evening I felt uneasy. I knew I had really used the formula to gain time. I had found it difficult to say yes, as I would have liked to do, or no, as I did not want to. Had Rist invited me in Manchester I would have accepted with enthusiasm; in Bombay I hesitated and felt unhappy doing so. I had been to Rist's home once before, the evening before Thompson Walker sailed for England. I had accompanied him to Bombay to see him off, and we were going to spend the last evening together musing over our journeys. Now that the time for leaving had come he was looking forward to it less than he had expected. When Rist asked him to dinner in my presence Tom looked unhappy, and plainly asked if I could be invited too. Rist readily said, 'Yes, of course.' It just had not occurred to him to ask me.

Equally genuine though Rist's invitation was this time, to me it was not within the normal dimensions of his social world. In the two years that I had worked with him, in a society both his and mine, in which custom threw homes open to friends, friends' friends and strangers alike, Rist had not asked me home, nor had I asked him. We invited freely our Indian colleagues, most of them educated in England, but we had not thought of asking any of the English in the office. Even between Indians who had been abroad and were used to their ways, and were in fact leading an increasingly westernised life, and English who had lived in India a lifetime, there were rarely social contacts of any significant kind; only an occasional formal party, very occasional and very formal.

My introduction into mixed society at the only mixed club of Bombay, the Willingdon, founded by the well-meaning aristocrat of that name to bring Indians and English of the right kind together, was indeed an experience. Roshan had taken me to see the club and offered to put me up for membership. You walked down its terraced lawns through two worlds, each on its own side, one affluent, the other holding the power. Occasionally someone crossed over for a brief chat, but you rarely saw mixed tables. I found that as a young manager, unknown and without family influence, I would be entirely lost. Roshan was popularly sought as a partner on the tennis courts, but I had no assets of any kind to qualify me for a place in either society, so I instead joined a purely Indian club.

In this strange social equation I found Rist's invitation uncomfortable. After Gärd had joined me I had made some attempts at throwing bridges. I took the initiative, thinking that it needed one side to break the ice, and invited the managing director to dinner; later his deputy, the man who had engaged me, and some others. The parties were unsuccessful for an obvious reason, with no one to blame. The subjects uppermost in our minds and theirs at that time ranged us on opposite sides, and the relationship between the ruler and the ruled precluded free discussion, anything more than a passing reference. War to them was the war in Europe; they felt embarrassed discussing it with us because they knew we saw it in our own light, and so they avoided the topic altogether. To us politics, the formation and resignation of the first Congress governments in the states, was an unavoidable subject of conversation; but by them it was strictly avoided. There was left only the weather, which in Bombay hardly changed for eight months of the year. Social small talk at which the English excelled was also out for lack of common familiar topics, and in impersonal subjects like art, literature and philosophy few of them were interested. We thus ploughed politely through these evenings, groping for conversation and even avoiding the only subject of common interest, shop, for I was far too junior to venture on an intelligent discussion at their level.

If conversation was one problem, food was another. We would naturally have served Indian food of a festive kind, but their casual comment had made it clear that this was part of a self-imposed social taboo. The food of the country, like dress and customs, sensible products of climate and environment, they firmly eschewed. Light woollen suits, collar and tie, shirts tucked inside the trousers, heavy shoes and woollen socks throughout the year for the men; though their women, more practical had at least taken to bare legs and airy sandals. On food they were firm: 'We do enjoy our curry and rice lunch on Sundays when one can sleep it off afterwards. Our Goan cook of course does not make it quite your way, but we like it, though we wouldn't care for it more often.' Under such clearly expressed preferences arranging a menu was not easy, so we compromised on Swedish meals. The evenings were sufficiently unsuccessful to prevent repetition, and we were never asked back. This lack of response soon stifled my good intentions, but left me a little sad.

Interestingly enough there was freer mixing at the pure level of duty. Most English managers were at one time or another invited home by our senior agents and in course of time the invitations were returned with equal ceremony. To their medieval houses in the narrow lanes of Lahore and Amritsar, the simple agents invited the sahib and his wife with less self-consciousness and more poise than did the westernized type, and the sahibs also went there with greater ease. It was an equation that worked rather well.

Old Lala Ramchand, our agent for twenty-five years, played host with a gusto that I envied. He invited us and them with equally admirable unconcern though in my particular case, as I was a Punjabi, there was an intimacy of language, custom and convention that brought me closer, particularly to the women who spoke no English. The English were charmed and amused, and the parties ended hilariously with Lala Ramchand and the sahib drinking scotch in large measures while the wives in sign language or broken Hindi talked of children, clothes and their people back home. Both sides began with a formality bordering on the ludicrous; yet less of a strain than that of our party.

The special room upstairs, where Lalaji usually retreated, was refurnished with the upright wooden chairs from the shop, placed in a circle with a table in the middle. Cushions and tablecloths that the new generation of school-going girls had embroidered in designs of English cottages and gardens with 'Welcome' chased diagonally across, were brought for decor together with the permanent bouquets of paper flowers. Indian sweetmeats flavoured with synthetic essences, pungent savouries followed each other; bubbling red and green drinks with flavours of rose, banana and lemon were kept poured in glasses to prevent a break in the continuity of service; tea boiled with milk, sugar and spices was served in the flowered Japanese tea set, brought out of the glass-windowed cupboard for the occasion. There was a welcome frankness in all this; no self-effacing concession to the guests' tastes, but robust hospitality like at the tentative visit of a future son-in-law. It was pressed with cheerful unconcern for the gastronomic capabilities of the unprotesting sahib, who politely insisted that he loved all Indian food and drink in any quantity, with secret visions of lifelong dysentery. The sahib's wife was less bothered because she was soon drawn into a circle of women and could always excuse herself from eating on some mysterious grounds.

Eventually Lalaji brought out the bottle of scotch bought specially for the visit. Each past occasion had been a further education in how to keep the guest company in order to make him drink more, till he had himself acquired a taste for it, growing into a habit, and eventually quite a capacity that in my young days I learned to respect. The sahib turned with relish to the scotch after the cups of tea laced with fizz, and the evening soon lost its restraints and barriers till they parted company having well cemented the business relationship. The memsahib, who by now had exhausted all available topics of conversation, was glad to go home to her own gimlet or scotch, which Indian custom forbade her to accept at Lalaji's house.

Lala Ramchand felt equally free when he and his family visited Bombay and were invited back. He arrived accompanied by his wife, his married and unmarried daughters, sons, sons-in-law and daughters-in-law, and a few nephews who had not seen Bombay, encouraging them all to feel at home in the unfamiliar atmosphere of a Bombay flat where they sank down in low chairs with their feet out of shoes resting uncomfortably on the floor; with servants formally dressed, speaking a language of formal deference. Lalaji urged his family to try the tasteless sandwiches and weak tea. Often the hostess had specially provided Indian sweets, but Lalaji wanted his family to taste all the English delicacies, till his turn came for the scotch. After that it was as much of a job to bring the evening to a close in Bombay as it was in Amritsar. Before leaving, Lalaji would walk up to the refrigerator and open it to display to his family the type of food and drinks their hosts consumed.

The ritual of these visits was always carefully explained to a newly arrived European couple before they set out on their first trip. It gave them something to talk to their friends and to write to their parents about. But where Lala Ramchand succeeded with simple ease we made a complex failure, missing the essential point that the English were trying to avoid relationship in which they felt out of their depth. At work they felt at ease with us because they were sure of themselves. They had much to teach, little to learn, less to fear—at least not yet. At leisure they wanted to be by themselves, to take it their own way, with their own kind, with conversation familiar and of their own choosing, without the strain of topics unfamiliar or unwelcome, or of trying to impress and being impressed.

When I conveyed Rist's invitation to Gärd she was pleased. She was curious to go inside an English church, to watch a christening, to meet people, to attend a real party with cocktails and supper and see how it differed from Swedish celebrations with their mixture of strict formality to begin with and increasing gaiety as the evening went on. What should she wear for the occasion? I went back next morning and thanked Rist and told him we would be happy to come.

As the day drew near I became increasingly apprehensive. It was my first experience of attending a large English party in India starting in the unfamiliar precincts of a church. I even asked Rist quite earnestly if it mattered if Gärd wore a sari in church. Rist looked puzzled and said he did not see anything untoward in that. On the day I contrived to arrive late, and we tiptoed into the church and took seats at the back. While the guests surrounded the parents and the baby to felicitate, I led a protesting Gärd away and drove to the club on some pretext of making an urgent telephone call, and thus managed to slip in late and unnoticed as the party was in full swing. Poor Gärd was utterly non-plussed by my behaviour; but if she understood my confusion she never acknowledged it nor conveyed any disapproval. There were areas of my behaviour we left unrecognized and unexplored. She knew that the barest recognition would hurt me; so she looked away, with a naturalness that I can now only admire.

The disaster came sure and complete and in a manner I least expected. As the party progressed I began to move around, feeling freer with each drink. At the level of light conversation about the changing Bombay, its growing traffic now that there were well over seven thousand cars on the roads, its emerging skyline from the sea, the gradual change in its weather as evidenced by the lateness of the monsoon each year, its superiority over Calcutta, I began to feel relaxed. My feeling knowledge of England's North Country and people, rather purer accent and a choice of word and phrase that came from a years of well cultivated university life of leisure rather than work, brought out a side of me that had lain fallow for years. Its resurgence pleased me too, for having acquired and moulded it over eight years of an impressionable youth, I think I treasured it almost as much as my Punjabiness; I do believe in some ways more.

The easy fluency of the evening was a salve to my feelings. Rist looked genuinely pleased, and his Australian wife happier still, for their experiment seemed to be working well. I think Rist was always inwardly proud of his pioneering choice, but this evening I was to let them both down, though quite heroically and humorously.

There were present at the party an Austrlian couple, James and Sally, both artists and highly temperamental, with a full measure of characteristic Australian warmth. They had lived in Paris and in London for some years and acquired a new way of life, a kind of grafting of Chelsea and Montmartre on Sydney. When an advertising agency offered him an assignment in Bombay they took it with an innocent alacrity they were to rue bitterly, for it altered their whole life and virtually ruined it. Strangely, as it ruined theirs, it helped to shape mine.

On the day of their arrival, according to custom, their English boss threw a party to introduce them to the colleagues and their wives. Sally warmed to this thoughtful welcome and responded with a spontaneity which failed to judge the underlying staidness. The lavish mixture of scotch and pink gins before dinner, and brandy and cold beer afterwards made her feel happy with Bombay and these friendly, though rather formal people. She wanted to draw them into her warm informality and give the group a cheerful togetherness. She clapped her hands and in her rolling accent exhorted everyone to relax. Then she performed cartwheels, giving each turn her favourite variation of a dextrous pause as her legs rose vertically above her head and her blue skirt fell back like a newly opened morning glory. But instead of the whoops of delight into which the parties in London and Paris used to break here was silence, broken by 'Well, Sir, a lovely party, we must be getting along,' and before she had collected herself she stood and faced her hosts alone in an empty room—the guests had gone, the party was over!

The news soon spread, and when the welcoming round of invitation was over and there was no overlap, they realized their isolation. Genuinely interested in the country and with no inherited restraints, they turned to the Indians who were glad to accept them because though generically European they were so different and uninhibited. Some mutual friends brought them over. We found them very likeable, and before I realized it they were in and out of our house like Indian relations; but I found Sally edgy. She was sufficiently at ease with us, but the hurt of the rejection by her own people would come out in forms that concerned me. I did the wrong thing; I tried to console her.

We ran straight into James and Sally at the party, and feeling nervous myself to begin with I stayed on with them for a while. Later, as I moved about and felt increasingly at home, Sally kept fortifying herself with drinks and felt progressively worse. Once or twice she made an attempt to come close to me for support and comfort, but I was now too busy shedding my own diffidence to be sensitive to her problem. Towards nine o'clock, as the party was beginning to thin, I noticed Sally sticking close to the bar, and walked up to her. Characteristically, instead of conveying understanding, I made some facetious remark about her cartwheels. All Sally's pent up feelings rose to anger, and the anger was all directed at me and Gärd. I have never been any good at coping with women who are upset; I somehow always make them feel worse, and often push them over the edge. Sally picked up a drink, poured it down in one long gulp, and Rist's wife acted quickly. Gärd and I, James and Sally were the next moment being shown out with a we-do-understand-you-have-to-go-but-so-glad-you-came! They soon left India.

CHAPTER TEN

Facing Some Problems

In 1940 the war came nearer, both from the west and the east, and at one stage threatened to enter India. At the darkest hour our leaders decided on a complete breakaway and launched the 'Quit India' movement which burnt our boats behind us, and also the bridges in front. From then non-cooperation turned to active obstruction which gave the government no quarter and left our class with divided opinions. Those working against the regime had now the satisfaction of action; those working for it felt there was duty of another kind which in the long run would bring its own reward and satisfaction; and those like me were left just nowhere.

Earlier, in 1940, when the debacle in Europe began, I had gone on a long tour and sent Gärd to my brother in north Bihar. On my return there was a letter from her to say that she believed she was expecting a baby, and would I come and join her for a few days. She had lost one the year before and was feeling unsure. I asked Rist for a week's leave and travelled up. On the way I felt a growing determination to join up. With a secure job in an expanding firm, where my chances were getting brighter as the war progressed and took away the young Englishmen one by one, my family would consider my volunteering meaningless. Of those in India who joined the army I wondered how many did so out of a feeling of duty, and duty to whom? It did not seem to make sense to anyone that an Indian might join the British Army out of conviction. Even the British nationals usually waited till they were called up because they felt they were doing an equally important job of work holding fort in India. I therefore did not think it was worth sharing my thinking with anyone on either side, and in her present state not even with Gärd.

On the long journey back I brooded over the problem, trying to isolate my desire to join from the unsympathetic influences of the environment. Had I stayed on in Manchester there would have been no second thought; I would have joined instead of returning home, as over there I would have felt the purity of my conviction, uninfluenced by the deterring factors of what was happening in India. During the three days in the train, through the rainwashed land, I thought of Gard, her coming baby; the war that so far had only distantly rumbled in Western Europe, the growing shadows of the two hands, rising one over the eastern horizon and the other from the west, closing in a vice-like grip over India's throat. Yet thousands were being herded into jails, many of whom would have wanted to fight the war, had they been able to fight their own way, with the pride of decision theirs.

On reaching the office I asked to see the managing director. He was a little puzzled at the request and asked if I had spoken to Rist. I said, no, this was about a personal matter. I explained to him how I felt about the war; how I had felt about it ever since the war seemed inevitable. In England there had been the one side to it, but in India there were two. My problem had been to reduce what I saw in clear terms in England back to its simple one-sidedness in India, and I believed I had managed it. I had decided to leave the firm and join up. If they gave me a lien on the job I would be glad to return, but I would not insist on it. Having at last spelled out my decision, I looked closely at his face for a reaction. He laughed and said 'Good God, I don't think the war has reached the stage that it needs your joining. I think you are doing well enough in your job and we will take care of the fight.' I agreed and left the room.

In the 'Quit India' movement, two years later, I found myself uncertain and isolated again. Late one evening Chitre rang up. He was a Maharashtrian barrister, married to an English girl who had got to know Gärd. We lived not far from each other, and as petrol rationing became severer we were thrown into company in our suburb, and we met often. He was interesting till he reached the first third of a bottle, from when on he became engrossed solely in finishing the rest. She was a pleasant Cockney, full of fun and friendliness, and a wonderful cook of Indian food, which she taught me in her kitchen on Saturday evening while Chitre drank and Gärd played with their children.

Chitre wanted me to come right over because an old friend had dropped in for the night and wanted to see me before he left early next morning. It sounded very mysterious, more so when I walked into his house which on a hot October night was all closed. Chitre opened the door slightly before he let me in, and under the dim light of a shaded bulb I saw two half finished drinks. After all precautions were observed he brought out of the bedroom a sheepish looking Purshottam Trikumdas with a beard that looked as if he had just put it on. Purshottam explained that after the first outburst of violence, when he had organized sabotage in the Nasik-Poona area, he had gone underground. A close friend of ours was in charge of an important sector of power communications in the region, and Purshottam had taken a wrecking party one night to disrupt them. The police had got wind of it, and in a monsoon storm on the Western Ghats had opened fire on them. He himself had escaped and turned up at our friend's house, and was now lying under cover to take stock of the situation.

All the Congress leaders and most of the militant socialist had been caught by the police and put in prison. The communists, who could have provided some organized resistance, did not see eye to eye with the Congress. They saw the war, from the time Hitler attacked Russia, in a different light, and considered the extermination of Germany a first priority, even if it meant cooperating with the British in India; and there was some uneasy cooperation between the two, which in fairness could hardly be held against either and which both preferred to forget later.

We talked till late at night, and before leaving I asked Purshottam if the struggle needed someone like me. He looked at me kindly and said 'No. You can get up and go to jail tomorrow as a protest, but I don't think that would be any particular contribution now, if you have not been in the movement so far. No, stay where you are, we may need all kinds when we are free.' I had heard the same answer before, in an opposite context.

☆

On the promontory, at the foot of the hill where we lived, a lot of military activity began one morning, and we discovered that a transit camp for British soldiers was going to be opened. I was dismayed at the prospect of a thousand idle and transient soldiers in a suburb that offered no amenities to occupy their spare time. At a time when newspapers were full of Indian hostility to the war effort, I wondered what the effect would be upon the simple minds of those young men freshly arrived in India, when they read that people who were officially their allies openly opposed the war that they were so strenuously fighting. But our suburb was mainly Roman Catholic and Parsi. Both these communities had, through religion and culture, an affinity with the British, and the soldiers gradually began to find their way into their homes. It was interesting to watch the interaction between two cultures, of which one was a prototype to the other. Our East Indian Christian homes, rich and poor, had a distinctly Victorian or Edwardian touch. Furniture and pictures, except the religious ones, were very lower middle and working class of Britain two generations ago. But for the Indian features, the grandparents' enlarged portraits could have hung in many an English living room. Patriarchs with starched collars, drooping moustaches, sideburns and hair carefully parted and plastered, pince-nez glasses with chain over the side; stern matrons with puffed up hair, lace collars and gold chains with crosses on their ample fronts. The young soldiers gaped at these familiar but unexpected sights.

The Parsi homes had a similar flavour, but their contact with the rulers since the time of the British arrival at Surat, and their own culture overlaid with Hindu influence, further enriched by their trading contacts with China in the last century, made an interesting mixture. The Victorian fourposter beds and heavy carved rosewood furniture; the portraits of the grandparents, men in Parsi hats and closed collar coats and the women in lace blouses with saris draped over the head; prints of the British royal family, particularly one that showed three generations, Victoria, Edward and George, from three angles as you walked across the room; another happy British touch, the aspidistra on a tiled-top table; these were proud possessions of middle-class Parsi homes. Invited by kind ladies anxious to take care of the brave boys away from home, the soldiers sat stiffly sipping tea brewed with lemongrass. These ladies worked assiduously for the war effort, shoulder to shoulder with their British sisters. Out of their enthusiasm shone a deep sincerity born of thirteen centuries of loyalty to every dynasty in power, whose language, food and way of living they accepted layer upon layer in till it congealed into the most strikingly diverse culture in the country. Though an inbred community of just over a hundred thousand, they showed nevertheless amazing vitality in whatever they took to, arts, science, technology, business, politics or philanthropy. All this was of course not understood by the soldiers, but they were glad of the natural warmth of the welcome, the mere contact with a home, women and children.

Otherwise the soldiers had little to occupy them except the single cinema or the Irani teashops. The highlight was an occasional dance at the local club. Generally well behaved they walked along the sea and up the hill past our house. One day our little daughter Maya returned from her outing carried by a soldier. She had begun to talk to him and they had made friends. Between her questions in Hindi and his answers in English they understood each other, aided by the little Goan girl, Maya's ayah and playmate, who tried to interrupt in broken English. Every evening the man used to wait for Maya on the shore and see her home. He politely said a few words to us, delivered Maya and went away. We hardly knew him. At such an uncomplicated level of contact communication had no problems. Every evening he gave her some sweets from the canteen, which were not a available in the shops, though Maya hardly appreciated the difference. They expected nothing from each other, not even understanding in words. One day he came to say goodbye, as his unit was moving on.

Late one Saturday night a Punjabi neighbour and a cousin of his went with me for a short stroll along the shore. As we were walking up the slope two soldiers came down arm in arm, staggering with drink. We were not particularly in their way, though in their state and on the narrow road it was not easy to avoid them altogether. One of them shouted 'Get out of the way you bloody Indians.' I protested that this was not a nice thing to say, which seemed to incense them to more abuse and aimless hitting at us. It was not much of a fight as they were too drunk and we were anxious to avoid trouble, but suddenly one of the soldiers came lurching up to the young cousin with a particularly unsavoury abuse about his Indian origin, and hit him over the eye. The abuse and a warm trickle down his cheek made him lose his head, and he bent down and picked up whatever came into his hand, a small piece of stone, and holding it in the hollow of his hand with fingers stretched out he smashed it on the soldier's forehead. There was a deep roar as stunned and bleeding profusely the soldier slumped on the ground. His friend ran, and he got up and followed him bellowing with pain, while we walked back to the house a few yards away. Windows opened, lights went on and off, heads peered out in the dark, whispers were heard, but soon darkness and silence reigned again.

Silently I walked into my bedroom and lay next to Gärd who woke up and asked me what the shouting was about, but went back to sleep. Soon there were sounds of heavy military boots up and down the slope, and I sat up in bed and put my head stealthily to the window sill, trying to avoid the beams of powerful torches flashing in all directions. There were soldiers all over, swearing cursing and looking for murderers at the top of their voices. By now Gärd was up, but I pushed her back on the bed and whispered to her to keep quiet. Slowly the voices died, I heard the boots clattering down the stony slope, and all was still again. I wondered if they would return; I wondered if they would run amok and start a rampage. Their officers had separate quarters some distance away from the camp, and I wondered if the guard at the camp gate would hold the men back. But the silence continued and I went to sleep.

Next morning the news spread and gathered the usual momentum of exaggeration. A soldier had been killed last night; two soldiers had been robbed and murdered; some underground 'Quit India' terrorists had attacked the camp and in a skirmish with a patrol late at night they had all been killed; the camp was sealed because their authorities were afraid that the soldiers might wreak their vengeance on the population. It was a Sunday, when normally on a clear day in the monsoon the place was thronged with cars and people, but today no one came, and the deserted shore added to the sense of fear. Several times in the morning groups of soldiers came to search the road and the neighbouring compounds and went away. As the tension mounted, I became worried and wondered what I should do. It might pass off; yet if the soldier's skull had been crushed and he died his thousand idle friends might cut loose, already agitated by the hostile environment where the single repetitive slogan 'Quit India', chalked and painted on walls everywhere, was a constant reminder of their unwantedness. Disciplined as they generally were, even the regular British soldiers had on occasions wrought their ire on a village near a camp because one of their mates had been beaten up for molesting a woman. And these were volunteers who were heartily sick of India and of the war that had taken them further and further away from home, from Europe to Africa, to the Middle East, to India and on to the hell of the Burma jungles. A little defiance of discipline would give an understandable vent to frustration. I decided to walk down to the camp.

I asked the guard if I could see the duty officer. He looked at me curiously because, apart from servants and suppliers, no Indian ever came to the camp. He motioned me to a wooden hut in which I found a freshfaced young lieutenant who looked barely out of school. I introduced myself and explained that I had come to see someone about last night's incident.

'What has that to do with you?'

'I was involved in it.'

'Do you know what you are talking about? This is a serious business.'

'Yes, Lieutenant.'

He pulled out a sheet of paper and began to take down notes. I explained how I was returning home from a walk and met the two men. They were drunk and shouted at me 'Get out of the way, you bloody Indian.' I mildly protested, at which one of them charged at me and used some particularly unpleasant language. I had lost my temper and picked up whatever I could lay my hand on, and with a piece of stone hit him on the forehead.

'You are sure it was not a knife or a sharp instrument?'

'No, Officer, I was carrying nothing.'

'We sent out search parties to look for a weapon, though we did not find any.'

'You wouldn't, as it was only a flat piece of stone.'

'Well, now that I have recorded your statement, you will have to come with me to the officers' mess to meet the major.'

He drove me in his jeep to the sanitorium, and I was taken into a small room before a middle-aged Englishman of simple bearing. He dismissed the lieutenant, looked very grave and told me how perturbed he was at the incident. He had served in India for many years and knew little incidents like this could happen, particularly on a Saturday night, but conditions were different today. There was a war on, and the young officers and men who had not known India before did not understand the problems. They were sensitive about the unfriendliness of the press and the people, and hated being here. He was always glad to see them move on before they became impatient. He talked on about the India he knew and the India today he did not understand at all.

'I shudder to think of what would have happened if this had been a camp of Germans or Japs,' he said. He asked me who I was, where I worked and questioned me further about last night. In the end he seemed convinced that there was no more to this incident than what I had told him; but he must hold a proper enquiry.

'I am glad you came forward. That and the announcement of holding the enquiry will soothe the camp, where feelings, I must say, have run high. This will put the incident in its simple perspective. And would you please leave your address and telephone number. I think we will handle it all ourselves and not bring the civil authorities in.'

I felt relieved and thought that keeping the civil authorities and the police out was a better idea than he realized. In the present conditions when civil authorities were jittery the local authority might almost want to run the whole 'Quit India' movement to earth in me. And if they found that I had met a bearded underground friend, my joining the cause, that I had so long debated, would have been assumed.

Next day as I was coming out of the office I met the chief and mentioned to him about the military enquiry that was going to be held. I thought I would tell him just in case the whole thing took an unexpected turn. His comment was characteristic and amusing.

'I see you are starting a "Quit India movement" of your own.'

The enquiry did take a different turn! The major was at his desk with a captain and the young lieutenant on either side. In front stood the two soldiers, one of them heavily bandaged and looking pale and weak. Neither the soldiers nor I recognized each other, but there was no attempt at denying the incident. The major asked questions in a simple, brisk way, till he came to a point which made him suddenly look hard.

'If the soldiers, who were obviously a little high, asked you to get out of the way, what was your objection?'

'Major, it was not just that. I was not concerned with their drunkenness, nor particularly their asking me to get out of their way. I might not even have objected to drunken language; what I resent is being abused in India for being an Indian.'

'But they did not say anything like that. They merely said "Get out of the way", peremptory, I admit, but hardly abusive.'

'But, Major, they said "Get out of the way, you bloody Indian".'

'I am sorry, but this is not what your statement to the lieutenant says. I will read it out to you. Are you sure it is not what you think they said?'

He read out my statement and there was no abuse in it, merely a simple 'Get out of the way'. I looked incredulously at the lieutenant, who looked back at me blankly. The major ended the enquiry soon after that and asked me to return the next morning. He was alone when I walked in. He asked me to sit down and offered me a cigarette.

'I wonder if I could ask you what exactly happened; what the boys said to you. I have also heard that there were others besides you in the fight. There were three of you, not you alone as you have stated so far.'

I explained. We were three. I had not told the truth because I had not even consulted the others about reporting the incident. I took the responsibility on myself. I thought I should risk being able to satisfy the camp authorities alone.

'Major, conditions are sensitive today and little things can be magnified and get out of hand. I thought it worth taking the chance.'

He looked understandingly and asked me to return the next day for the rest of the enquiry. As I was leaving he asked:

'Did the boys abuse you.'

'Yes'.

He looked away. He finished the enquiry and told the soldiers that they must have drunk enough to see me multiplied. He did not mind their drinking, but they must mind their language; words and even a tone that seemed innocuous to them sounded different to people in other countries. He was satisfied that it was a minor incident, but it required strengthening the military police patrolling, especially on Saturday nights.

After the others left his room I stayed on to thank him and asked if he would drop in for a drink that evening. He said he was so weary of the mess that he would be glad to visit a home. He was pleasant company and reminisced about his service, but something I could not explain to him was the Indian attitude to the war. He looked at it as a soldier, uncomplicated by any political overtones. Hitler to him was no more than a menace that must be dealt with. He did not approve of the Russians, but he did not disapprove of Hitler and Nazism itself. He liked India, but he disliked the Congressmen. With such simple beliefs it was difficult to argue, and he did not force his point. Before leaving he asked Gard if her excellent hospitality could encourage him to inflict some soldiers on her. She said, of course, yes, send them over.

Next evening, as I walked up the steps, I saw two soldiers sitting with Gard, one of them with a bandaged head. She introduced me to them and said they had come to offer some kind of apology.

CHAPTER ELEVEN

Settling in Levers

Pettit was our Chairman for thirteen years, and when he retired in 1953 he left an organization so different that one barely recognized it, and all one saw was the change and growth that he had so masterfully induced. At his farewell his successor, Hoskyns-Abrahall, summed up his achievement well when he said 'There is not one among us here who does not owe something, if not all, to you for the furtherance of his career.' An ellipsis in it was that many Indian and European managers had failed to keep pace with him or just refused to accept him and had gone away, among them some of the ablest.

Pettit came from one of the British families settled in Argentina and was married into a similar family. Such families sent their children to England for education but many of them returned to settle. Pettit went on from preparatory school to Rugby and finished at Cambridge, after which he returned to Argentina to join the British American Tobacco Company, and later Unilever. He bore the mark of a man who has grown up away from home, uprooted at a tender age and consigned to the monastic life of boarding schools and college halls. A charming host, an entertaining companion on tours, a permissive boss, yet he had no friends and he never relaxed at work. I think his only outlet was his hay-fever, which through his early driving years was the escape valve nature provided him. As he built up relentless pressures he used to reach a stage when the fever suddenly laid him low. He came back looking refreshed and ready for a long bout of energy, when he would sometimes travel from Bombay to Delhi and back, a journey by rail of 900 miles and twenty-six hours each way, twice in the same week. At this pace he often wore out others.

I worked with him and watched the Company grow through those building years till he had reorganized it to his satisfaction; and then he did not seem to need his hay-fever any longer. Though a confident man, I think he needed concrete success to reassure him, not just the satisfaction of effort. I rather thought he lost something more than his hay-fever. I detected a growing tenseness, a little harshness, a weakening of his coping mechanisms, the denial of a catharsis. I don't know what happened to him, but I liked him less at the end, in his very successful days, than at the beginning in his unsureness.

Pettit's unsureness stemmed from a deep strength and not from fear; the winding up to meet the challenge and a tensing up to ensure success. There was in it a capacity for withdrawal, and as long as he retained this capacity he was flexible in his strength; when he dropped it he became brittle. It was then we had some conflicts after ten years of working together, and it disappointed us both. I was the loser, and yet I believe the last three years under him were a kind of detransference that I needed for my next phase of growth. Being unsure I needed the testing situation to learn by myself. Sometimes I wonder whether he did not drop me deliberately as he dropped his hay-fever; whether he had not realized that the transference had gone too far and begun to sap me; whether his plan for my future did not need a return to myself and my ambivalent basic strength with its own sureness and unsureness, trust and mistrust.

There were three of us in the company that Pettit apparently picked for growing and three more disparate characters one could not imagine, myself, Harvey Duncan and James Wheeler, and in us he put a lot of trust and effort. Duncan was a talented beachcomber who had earned an interesting living in many ports east of Suez and been through scrapes of every kind, a hedonist who never shunned any pleasure that came his way. But under his brash exterior he had an original marketing mind and great advertising talent. In fact he brought the word marketing to us; where in the past we sold and advertised, he marketed, and he made us feel very old-fashioned. Without much education or formal training he had rolled from one country and one job to another, and somewhere in China he had joined the firm. In dealing with the Chinese compradors he had learned a great deal and probably taught them as much, and shocked them with his capacity to match their ruthlessness, and he soon commanded the respect of the old-fashioned Indian traders. What fascinated me was where he could have acquired his sophisticated advertising and marketing skills, working in countries where marketing must have been a simple cadge as cadge can.

Duncan came to Bombay early in 1939, as an account executive in the advertising agency that was formed out of the old advertising department under Rist. The news came to me when I was on one of my long marketing research tours, in a letter that was characteristic of him. If I had heard that I had been fired by the firm, it only meant that my services were transferred to the new agency; we had never met each other, but he was glad to be my boss and our mutual ignorance would be an added advantage; one of these days he hoped to meet me, but till then I could keep my problems to myself because he was too busy sorting out his own. I heard no more from him till I walked into his room three months later. He was small, dapper, handsome, with brisk staccato speech and manner, and put me to work straight away, explaining his plan.

He had been consigned to the new advertising account of Dalda, a vegetable cooking fat, an unknown brand name chosen from among a whole list of brands because it sounded like a slogan. It was to be our only domestic small pack vanaspati, and he was going to make it the leading household brand in India. It was going to be the Sunlight of cooking fats. Modesty or caution were conspicuously absent from his plans, yet some years later when I succeeded him his forecasts of sales read like past history, so accurate were they. The same evening he showed his first experiment in demonstrating cooking with Dalda.

Outside the Novelty Cinema in Bombay he had constructed a small wooden stall and hired three men to run it; one cooked, the other talked, the third walked about inviting the passers-by and distributing leaflets. The cook stood behind the counter rolling out some dough which he cut up into small squares. By his side he had a paraffin stove with a deep frying-pan. He scooped out large spoonfuls of Dalda, melted them in the pan and floated the squares till they fried golden brown. The demonstrator talked about the virtues of Dalda and invited people to try it out for themselves. He asked them to take some Dalda, which they put on the back of their left hand and with their right index finger carefully rubbed into the skin to feel the grain and how it melted, and then they smelt it. He would then offer them another small lump, which they put on their tongue and again felt the grain and the way it melted. Meanwhile he kept up an encouraging patter, and when he saw a look of satisfaction on their faces he would ask them to try for themselves the sweets fried in Dalda. By now a crowd had gathered and he quickly engaged them in the sampling act. At the end he tried to sell them small tins, which many did buy and proudly took away wrapped in a coloured leaflet.

Duncan asked me to explain this curious method of testing the fat by rubbing it on the skin, smelling it and then putting it on the tongue. I explained that this was how they always tested ghee made from milk, which Dalda simulated in appearance, texture and flavour. They would find out whether the grain of the ghee was hard or soft, whether it melted easily at body temperature, how it release its aroma when melting, and only when they were satisfied with these tests did they put it on the tongue, again to test the grain and its flavour. Ghee to an average Indians has to be treated with great ritual; it is an integral part of food and religious practice; it is ambrosia, the food of the gods, and the cow from whose milk it is made is sacred. The Dalda he was trying to sell was competing with a prototype that was more than just a cooking fat. But ghee was becoming scarce and expensive and was therefore often adulterated. Dalda, at half the price, looked like ghee, felt like ghee, smelt like ghee and tasted like ghee.

Duncan's eyes lit with a new marketing comprehension as he looked at the crowd and the wrapt attention with which they went through this ritual. He had never seen anything like it. On the way back he was thoughtful; he said he perhaps needed a different marketing strategy altogether. He had not realized what a formidable competitor ghee was, and yet if the emotional attachment to it was so strong it made the task even more worthwhile. He loved the spectacular and saw his task thus. Between us began a working partnership from which I had all to gain. Pettit encouraged it.

Wheeler was the third. A simple English boy, a junior in the accounts department in London, he was sent to Bombay for six months while one of the accountants went home on leave. He stayed on for 22 years. When I first saw him waiting for the lift, the week after I joined, I thought of the favourite line of George Robey, the English comedian, 'Does your mother know you are out?' Wheeler looked barely out of school, thin, lanky, with hair down his forehead, his fists deep in his trouser pockets. Twenty-two years later when he left the Company as financial director, he looked the same except that his hair was grey. He and his wife Betty were the first English couple we became friends with and in time deeply attached to.

Pettit tried him in various places, in sales, in administration, in personnel and in accounts, and was constantly inducing growth in him; but while he prodded me and stretched Duncan, sometimes remorselessly, he was always gentle with Wheeler. He cultivated him and his wife socially and helped them in every way. I think he realized their emotional needs with a sensitivity that few otherwise credited him with. When I got to know them I discovered an aspect of the problem of an English wife. Betty was a simple girl, very English, of an environment that could never be reproduced abroad. Most others got used to the comfort of life in India, the servants, the leisure and the higher standard of living that came from the bigger jobs their husbands held, well-appointed entertainment with grace and ritual. Betty disliked it all.

She longed for her little house in London, the chores she had enjoyed doing, cooking, cleaning, shopping and looking after the baby. She resented the way of life imposed upon her with no choice, not even the right to rebel. The older wives were tolerant because she was so young, so straightforward, and they made such a handsome pair. They hoped she would settle down and see it all in terms of her husband's career. Betty gradually did settle down, and paid the price. She kept on paying it in instalments till long after it had ceased to matter.

With us Betty relaxed and spoke freely. I loved watching her face, dark with chestnut hair thick and parted in the middle, the high cheekbones, the sculptured lips and the hazel eyes that could look sullen and rebellious, yet gay when she was happy.

As I saw it, Betty paid the price in the way she acquiesced. She did not give in, she just gave up; and like a hibiscus flower, which she so reminded me of, she wilted as soon as she had bloomed. I wondered whether it would not have been a more sensitive way of helping to have sent them back home instead of building him up here; but those days the young English were sent abroad for a lifetime, and once abroad there was no choice but to make a career of it. Return before normal retirement was only considered on medical grounds, or for failure in the job. Only rarely did someone exceptionally bright or well connected, more often the latter, return for promotion.

There was a logic to the system of exile. It dated back to the days of the sailing ships, when the East India Company employees rarely returned home for leave because the journey was long and hazardous, and only men looking for a career out of England came abroad. After they had worked here a few years, the level of responsibility and the income they enjoyed could no more be matched at home. They were therefore committed to a career and a way of life from which they found it difficult to extricate themselves until they had saved enough and earned their retirement benefits. Faster communications, steamships and cables, made little difference to the basic system. They went home more frequently, but it was still a long exile.

A community in exile forms for itself a different kind of island from the one that has settled, however uneasily; and this was a community of the rulers. Uprooted from home, they denied themselves new roots for fear of becoming of the country, like the so-called domiciled Europeans, also pure in blood, but unacknowledged by the non-settled, the so-called 'pukka'.

Living thus in the artificial atmosphere of an environment within an environment, not likely to return home for at least another quarter century, they nevertheless felt the need for some kind of roots. Their brothers in the Indian army dedicated themselves to their regiments, their men and their sports; those in the civil service became committed to the peasant and, in their own light, to his welfare; but those in commerce had only their work. In the earlier years they at least had to travel a lot in the bazaars and markets, where they came close to a part of India, but as times changed most of their work could be done from the head offices and branch offices, through correspondence and agents, with diminishing contact with the world outside. They worked long hours and invariably returned to office on Saturday afternoons, even on Sunday mornings, and always on Indian holidays; not really because the pressure of work demanded it but as a safe commitment to something. There were those who amused me, like my first chief, who used to go into the rooms of his colleagues before lunch on Saturday, tell them that he proposed to return in the afternoon and how much he envied them for not having to. This meant that they also had to come back unless they found some valid excuse.

Their women similarly created their own islands, combining some mild social work with entertainment. They drank coffee and played mahjong, and took the children to the swimming pool. Some played golf, most also did some work at the European hospital, the Y.W.C.A. or a home for old indigent women of European descent. A few were really devoted to social service for which the scope was of course endless. Few did any professional work. In the evenings and on weekends the couples adjourned to the community's own islands, each 'entire of itself' but not 'part of the maine': clubs, beaches, swimming pool, golf, homes, all carefully fenced off.

Betty wondered why she had to be part of it all. It might be good for James to work here, but he would have got on at home too, and they could have had the life that was theirs.

The three of us came very close to each other in work. Duncan suggested to Pettit that with the war, marketing research was restricted, and the work I had been doing for Rist checking newspaper circulations could well rest for a while; he wondered therefore whether I could not join him as an assistant. Pettit had recently invited Duncan to move over from the advertising agency to the Company to run its marketing department. Duncan liked the idea in itself but not the prospect of working directly under Pettit. The agency atmosphere, free and easy, suited his temperament, while the discipline of a company would irk him. Besides, he and Pettit were temperamentally so different and socially worlds apart. Pettit belonged to the Royal Bombay Yacht Club, lived in a spacious duplex flat and entertained gracefully. His was a life of hard work and urbane pleasure. Duncan, a bachelor, lived in a hotel and did not care whom he cultivated so long as he enjoyed himself. He took malicious pleasure in not conforming to the image the executive of a large British firm was supposed to create. He thought over Pettit's offer for quite some time before saying yes and spoke to me about it because he wanted a sympathetic sounding board.

'You know, this is going to be the end of my career. I had hoped that I would stay long enough in this job and in India, which I like, to save something. I am tired of rolling; I not only gather no moss, but get rubbed smaller and smaller. I like doing things my way, and if Pettit had any sense he would leave me where I am. But I am afraid I have little choice; it is too early to look for another job or move to another country, so let me submit; who knows, I might even end up as a staid burra sahib, married and rearing a family. Hell,' he added, 'what will I do with all my fancy shirts and ties with my initials embroidered all over.'

His words proved prophetic. Less than five years later he left India, and soon thereafter the Company, broken in health and spirit, condemned, with all but his cynicism gone. His luck had run out. He had even for the first time in his life fallen in love, been accepted and then rejected. In those short-lived days of his love I saw in him a tenderness that was a miracle in a man so cynical. She was considerably younger than he, innocent, gold and pink, and he could not believe his fortune. But it did not last long, and the last blow was his oncoming deafness.

Years later I heard that he landed back in England and started a restaurant that prospered until he ran into competition with a nightclub across the road. This was more than Harvey could swallow. He dashed across to discover that it was run by a woman, cool, able and attractive. Soon there was a flash back to the old Harvey Gale Duncan, who had beaten fate and circumstance for twenty years from Bombay to Brisbane and Sydney to Shanghai. He put into his last marketing campaign all that he had ever possessed, and it worked. He ended up owning both Harvey's Bar and the Bamboo Club, and married its proprietress. She gave him a daughter about whom people said he never stopped talking. I never saw Duncan again; I did not want to. Some things in life are best left unrevived. Years later, someone from Singapore walked into my office. He had heard that Duncan had worked with me and wanted to know if I knew his whereabouts. The card he sent in said, 'A friend of Harvey Flash Duncan'. He genuinely believed that Duncan had been christened Flash; for that was how they had always known him.

In this year 1941, in an airconditioned office in a new building, Harvey felt ill at ease and insisted that I keep him company in this sanitary outfit, as he called it; and soon he persuaded Pettit to get me over. Rist told me one day that Pettit would like to see me. I went across, puzzled, as until then nothing had brought us together. In his large hexagonal office overlooking the harbour, I walked into carpeted luxuriance of polished teak furniture and a large glass-topped desk. Pettit himself was a large man, handsome, with iron-grey hair, immaculately dressed, with a well-intoned, well-accented voice. He walked to the door to receive me and we talked about what I did, my wife, our five months old baby, my home, my years in England and Sweden. When he had put me at ease he began:

'I hear you started some new work that has not been done before, making a survey of some several hundred newspapers in India. Do you feel that you have finished what you began? I know work is never finished, but do you feel you have taken it far enough to try something else, something new again, marketing for instance?'

I have never felt any good at interviews, so I mumbled something about not knowing how well one was doing; besides, I did not know marketing, apart from what Mr. Duncan kept talking about. He laughed.

'Well, that is just what I had in mind. Would you consider coming over to us, as his assistant? With your background, I believe you will have a contribution to make. The knowledge of the country that you have acquired through marketing research and so much travelling will be very valuable, as also your knowledge of us, our ways and methods which I think is equally of importance.'

I accepted his offer and thanked him, much impressed by his simple graciousness.

'Thank you. I am so gald. I hope you go far. In anticipation of your acceptance I have prepared a letter offering you the job at an interestingly higher salary. I believe yourshould receive the increment now rather than after you have shown your work.'

He got up and stretched himself to his full size, walked around the desk and held out his hand. I shook it. He walked up to the door, opened it for me and wished me well. I looked around the room again and left. Twenty years later I walked into that room early one morning, before anyone had come into the office, sat down in Pettit's leather chair and stared at the chair in front, where I had once sat as tense as today. The harbour was busier, the ships' masts flew the Indian tricolour, on the wall there was a picture of Queen Elizabeth; nothing had changed, only the times. I could hear Harvey's rasping voice, 'So you made it!'

From Pettit's room I walked straight to Harvey and said, 'Well, I see you did not want to sink alone.' Harvey insisted I share his room; he hated being alone and besides, he added, 'I always return late from lunch and Pettit has already begun to check on that. Now you can take the telephone instead of the poor peon, who always gets it wrong and says 'Duncan Sahib still eating lunch'.

Duncan was nothing if not consistent in his unpredictableness. On the first morning when I joined he announced blandly that he had been waiting for me to start and now he could go on his local leave, which he proposed to spend in South India selling Dalda, and he was off at the end of the week. My protests only made him laugh. He thought 'head first' was the best way of learning.

'But have you asked the Chief? I am sure he won't think much of your idea of leaving him alone with a novice.'

'The Chief thinks it is a great idea; needed no selling at all.'

'Then it is Pettit who thought of it.'

Duncan just laughed. I don't think I have ever been through a more exhilarating fortnight. Pettit saw to it that I was stretched and, through no coincidence I suspected, Duncan had left behind as much as he could undisposed. Years later I read in Philip Woodruff's *The Guardians* about a district officer who said to his assistant:

> 'This is your sub-division or your job. These are the lines on which I want it to be run. Now go and run it. If you make a really serious mistake I shall have to overrule you; otherwise I shall not interfere. If you want advice I am here to give it. If you want a definite order you are free to ask for it. But if you make a habit of wanting either, you will be of very little use to me.'

The Guardians certainly knew how to delegate.

This was my first experience of Pettit. It was also my first taste of power. I had the whole office to run the way I wanted to; utterly inexperienced, but with someone behind me who understood. If I used my commonsense and dropped in for an occasional run-through, he felt sure I would keep afloat till I learned to swim. He patiently received me each time I went to see him, but I soon sensed that he waited to hear what I proposed to do rather than provide an answer. Any mistakes I made he would be prepared to pay the price for.

My being the first Indian brought the inevitable problem of acceptance by the Indian staff. Overstretched myself and unwilling to admit it, I loaded the clerks with rather more work than they had been used to or, as I suspected, were prepared to accept from me. Perhaps anxious to prove myself I wanted quick answers to provide quick replies to anything that I was asked. Soon one of the clerks protested and said that Mr. Duncan never loaded them like that.

'But do you find the work too much? I know I have passed down a lot, but I am sure it is not more than I am doing myself. Knowing Mr. Duncan I should think he works at twice my speed.'

'Well, we are "overdead" with work since you took over.'

I felt I had to assert myself. 'If there is anything you cannot finish, I will. Please bring all the arrears to me; in fact I will also take over all the mail as it comes in.' Half an hour later the clerk walked in with two peons and placed file upon file on my desk. Some files I felt had nothing to do with me, and he must have emptied the whole office on my desk. I asked him if there was any more, and he said 'no' and walked out. I knew I was being tested.

For the next two days papers kept pouring in, and I worked long hours trying to cope. On the third day the clerk put his head in.

'Did you send for me?'

'No.'

'Oh. I thought the peon said you wanted me.'

'No, thank you. I am doing fine.'

The following day the peon came to take away some of the files. I told him to leave them where they were. That afternoon the matter came to a head. The clerk came in and asked me how long I was going to keep the files. I told him I was managing quite well and was nearly up to date.

'What are we going to do then? Every time the Chief passes by he wonders whether we have any work to do because we have neither files nor papers on our desks.'

'Well, that should suit you. You were "overdead", now you can live long, and I will do all the work myself.'

At first he frowned, and then he saw the humour of it. I laughed and told him to take all the files back, and we said no more about it.

Duncan came back from tour more full of ideas than ever. If rivers of milk and ghee once flowed in India they were now going to flow with Dalda. The population was rising fast and there was not going to be enough ghee; vegetable oils would have to take its place. But as people preferred ghee, the next best thing was to sell them Dalda, untouched by hand, sold in sealed tins, containing vitamin D....and so Duncan ran on and on. I found his enthusiasm very infectious. Here was an opportunity that would not come his way again; the chance of creating a new habit and spreading it across a sub-continent, the first branded, packaged food in a country where everything else was sold loose, weighed and taken away in one's own container. But his bold targets needed bold planning, and so he plunged himself into a five year plan that would dot every marketing i and cross every t. It was an experience to watch him at work, with his collar unbuttoned, tie loose, hair over his forehead and a cigarette drooping from his lips. He looked so different from the cool, immaculate Pettit sucking his pipe.

Duncan began to evolve what must have been the first complete marketing plan in India, divided neatly into selling, advertising and consumer promotion. He started by redesigning the pack, which was tin, and he reintroduced it in different sizes, the square 10 lb., the round 5 lb., 2 lb. and 1 lb, and a special ¼ lb. tin for sampling. He cleaned the label design and brought out boldly its main feature, a palm tree, which over the years was to become a familiar symbol, and the brand name Dalda; a household term that became generic for vanaspati. This green and yellow tin was to spread so widely in the country that you were never far from an empty one. When twenty million tins are sold in a year, among a people who never throw away anything, and much less empty tins, but put them to the most ingenious uses and make each tin last for years, a hundred million empty tins over a few years become a ubiquitous sight. This gave me later the idea of making an advertising film whose theme was the empty Dalda tin. Upon the Persian wheel in the country, rows of Dalda tins scoop the water out of the well and deliver it into the wooden channel; on the shelf of the village grocer rows of neatly stacked tins store herbs and spices; on the window sill of a small town flat the holy tulsi plant grows in a dalda tin, providing every morning a few leaves for oblation; a group of women at the communal well washing clothes and pouring water over themselves with an empty Dalda tin; villagers walking across the fields in the evening on their way home from the market, carrying tins fitted with lids and spouts to contain the oil for their lamps. In any tinsmith's shop you can see the ingenious modifications he carries out to fit the dalda tins for a hundred uses.

Duncan's new advertising took his discovery of the smell-feel-taste test as its theme, repeating itself through every medium he used, demonstration stalls, newspapers, leaflets, films, girls visiting homes. He built gay little stalls on pneumatic wheels with colourful canopies. The cook stood inside with a table in front of him displaying the tins, and made simple sweets while the demonstrator talked to the crowd. After a while they folded up and pushed the stall to the next prominent street corner. He also built motor vans with a large replica of the round tin on the chassis, and a platform at the back with a folding table top, and fittings for relaying speech and music. When the first three vans were ready, first of their kind in India, proud Duncan in his cream coloured convertible led the cavalcade through Ballard Estate with the loudspeaker pitched high to 'Marching through Georgia'. Outside the office the vans stopped, and out stepped smartly uniformed drivers, cooks and demonstrators, with Duncan in his safari outfit in front, ready to lead them into the jungles of India. As Pettit came out to inspect this guard of honour, they all stood to attention. Some of the sahibs looked out of their windows and shook their heads, but Pettit, as much a sahib, looked ahead.

Duncan then produced a Dalda film and his first cinema van. The film had all the ingredients of an Indian picture: song, dance, pathos, humour, social uplift, march of time, and coincidence. In 1200 feet it depicted the story of a father who had got his daughter satisfactorily engaged, but could not afford to cook the wedding feast in pure ghee, so he was naturally worried. As the wedding day drew nearer the budget mounted, and he wondered what was going to be the answer, because as important as the dowry was the feast, and whoever thought of cooking it in anything but pure ghee? A young relation brought the answer: Dalda; but it was to be kept a secret till after the feast. Anxiously the father looked at the guests from behind a curtain and, lo, they were eating so heartily that a new worry arose: would the food run out! After the metal plates and cups were swept clean and the feast was over the father revealed his secret, the green and yellow tin of Dalda with the palm tree. The story ended on a happy note: the young man explained that he had picked up the idea from a demonstration stall in the street and had actually tasted Dalda and food cooked in it before he recommended it. The film had a catchy theme song, which for years afterwards wherever I went to sell Dalda would be sung and whistled by the little boys who followed me. In the placid life of a village or small town the excitement aroused by the introduction of Dalda was not easily forgotten, nor the product, at least not its name. We sometimes rented an empty shop for a few days, plastered it with buntings and colourful advertising material and set up a temporary demonstration centre. The little boys would cluster around at the sound of the theme song. The news would spread and people flocked to see what had upset the monotonous tempo of their life. Children were our great asset.

It was a stiff task building a sales organization, with a network of selesmen, supervisors and sales managers all over the country. India has a long tradition of trade, of selling and distributing. Over two thousand years ago, Indian traders of the west coast, from Malabar to Cambay, traded with the Mediterranean, sending their spices and silks, textiles and timber, to a Europe bereft of luxuries. Their trading chains stretched deep inland to collect the goods, transport them to the coast and ship them for delivery in Europe by the overland route from the Red Sea. Their hundis, the bills of exchange, were honoured all over the then known world. Many amassed wealth, with which some built temples, among them the famous cave temples in Maharashtra. On a wooden beam in one of the cathedral-like temples there is carved the name of the donor, a prosperous merchant of the second century.

Trade became a caste in India accepted by the system as a hereditary right, not to be poached by outsiders. The wisdom and experience of generations was concentrated in one channel of activity, and training through childhood and youth had but one aim, to produce a trader. Even in my young days the traders had their own schools in the Punjab, where their children were taught a special script, perhaps to keep their books safe from the prying eyes of the revenue collector. The only other thing they were taught was arithmetic, largely mental, doing abstruse calculations in the head. They learned to memorize their multiplication tables from one to twenty, not only whole numbers, but by quarters, halves and three-quarters, so that a trader boy of eight could snap back the price of seventeen and three-quarter yards of cloth at thirteen and a quarter annas per yard before other children could multiply seventeen by thirteen on paper. They only went to school till the age of ten or so, and after that they sat below their father's seat at the shop, and by the age of fifteen they could confidently run the business.

While business was in their blood and opportunity for quick profit never missed, its very hereditariness was a disadvantage in the new age. Many expanded into large trading businesses and some also went into production, but with the control always firmly retained in the joint family, which alone produced the management, their capacity to adapt themselves to the new western ways of doing business was limited. It was not always easy to make them forego quick profit for a slow but long term gain. Their tradition was the pure market law, to push the price up to what the market could bear in a shortage, or down to where it would buy when there was abundance. To sell at steady prices deprived them of the pleasures of playing the market up and down. Many made quick fortunes that way, and lost them.

We had major distributors in port towns and a network of wholesalers in the country, several thousand of them. All were private family businesses with a proprietor, brothers, sons and nephews and, if the business grew large, minor relatives and members of their caste and community. Often partners came together as young men, and as they prospered were joined by their respective families, often again to break up when it came to the turn of their young sons, whom succession and not choice had brought together, as had been the case with their fathers. The fathers often saw the writing on the wall and amicably divided the business in their lifetime rather than leave it to break up afterwards. Sometimes the fathers cemented it by marriage, or brought a mature son-in-law into the firm. The older generation regarded a partnership as a sacred brotherhood that seldom broke, but with the new generation it was different.

There were many variations on the theme of family control, but seldom the acceptance of an outsider, however able and trusted, into control. It was surprising how, upon the death of a husband, the widow could step into his shoes and run the business with a firm hand. One of our big distributors died childless, leaving an aged and ailing partner and an inexperienced nephew only recently brought into the business. He had, however, a bright and competent young manager whom he had trusted and treated well; so we in the Company felt that this man could run the business while the nephew matured. To this the widow agreed, but she reacted most violently to his suggestion that he might be given a small share in the business. I went to see her to intercede on the manager's behalf and in the interests of all.

'No,' she snapped back, 'he is a servant in the business; he is not of the family and never can be. He can demand his wage and I will pay him well, but there can be no partnership between a manager and the family. He has to accept his position.'

'But what will you do if he leaves you?' I asked.

'I will come in and run the business myself.'

And she did, because the manager had his ambitions and left. She asked me not to underrate her; she would run the business with her nephew to our satisfaction, if only we gave her time. Impressed with her courage, I had no choice but to accept her. I did, however, ask out of curiosity, 'Do you know anything about our business?'

'Yes, quite a lot. I never went out, but when my husband came home he talked to me. He unburdened himself and I listened. I have no feel of running it, but I know enough about it to feel that it will not be difficult.'

She ran it for some years and ran it well. The nephew gradually took over and we did not see her again, but I am sure she never gave up interest.

Although one considered the fathers old-fashioned and became impatient with their resistance to quick change, the sons who became modern were usually a greater problem. They somehow fell between two worlds, with the advantages of neither and disadvantages of both. They lost an innate and haphazard shrewdness without gaining a systematic and informed approach. When they sat in a chair like us, instead of cross-legged on a divan like their fathers, they made themselves different from their customers, who called upon them no longer, nor did the young men take the trouble to call at their customers' shops as we and their fathers did. It was an uncertain world of transition that belonged neither to the bazaar nor to Ballard Estate. And sadly enough, while these boys tried to cultivate us socially, both the English and we much preferred to meet their fathers. I always enjoyed Lala Ramchand's parties more than his son's.

Here was, I discovered, a world within a world. Rather, there were three concentric cultures in one world, mine, Lala Ramchand's sons', and Lala Ramchand's own, with the last as the core culture. As I saw the son's problems of adjustment to a world new to him, mine dissolved; but somehow I was impatient with him though never with old Lalaji. Ultimately the day came when Lalaji retired and the business was run by the son, when we had to terminate our fifty year old relationship. It was difficult to convey to the son, while Lalaji understood, that our real problem was that the business could either be run in his own personal old-fashioned way with such modifications as we felt desirable; or entirely our way with an efficient professional impersonalness of defined systems, delegation and structure. In fact I discovered, as I learned more about the two systems, theirs and ours, that their usefulness to us lay in precisely what they stood for—Lalaji's personal credit, his knowledge of each customer's social and financial position, his inexpensive old warehouse behind the shop, the loyalty of the younger members of the family and community.

We once considered having our own distribution system, with our own chain of one hundred and fifty warehouses with staff and delivery vehicles. It was argued that we would improve the service to the retailers, and save money. The plan was all drawn up; in fact Pettit had even selected me to organize the service and run it. The idea stemmed from a visitor from London, but the story went that when he outlined it to his colleagues back in London, a wise old man who had spent his early years in business in India listened carefully, and at the end of an enthusiastic presentation made one remark:

'Do you really feel we should ever be able to do it cheaper than the man in the bazaar, or even as well? My answer is, never. There are few in the world who can beat an Indian wholesaler for cost or service.'

The scheme was dropped, and just as well. In time we improved their systems and built in refinements to suit our growing needs, but basically today the bazaar wholesalers serve as well as they have done for nearly a hundred years since Sunlight soap first landed in Bombay. After my first enthusiasm was over I began to respect their old-fashioned ways and learned to tinker with them as gingerly as possible. Old Lalaji used to say:

'Tandon sahib, tell us what to do and leave us to do it in our own way.'

In each succeeding generation of sales managers I heard the same question put: 'Would we not do it better ourselves?' and the answer was always the same: 'No, wait till you have understood the system; you will learn to respect it and not want to drop it.'

But the problem arose when Lalaji's son wanted to change it. While there was a wholeness to theirs and a wholeness to ours, and gradual change according to need was always taking place, any change that did not contain a meaning or was only part of a compromise gave a bad fit.

Lalaji was to blame for much about his son. The only boy among a number of sisters in an Indian home can be brought up with such solicitude and anxiety to fulfil his every whim that petulance is usually its only reward. I once offered Lalaji to train this young man, when he left college because his mother thirty-five miles away could not bear the separation and the thought that he was not receiving his home comforts, and her constant care. The boy felt the same way and was glad to go home. I suggested he should come to Bombay and work with us for a year, first as a salesman in the field, and gradually rise to management, on the condition however that we should pay his salary and expenses like with other trainees. Lalaji rashly agreed, but when the news reached home the mother was adamant. She could not bear another separation, and that a thousand miles away in foreign lands so far from the Punjab. Lalaji tried to persuade her in the best interests of the son, although in his heart he was not absolutely convinced either. Ultimately the mother agreed on condition that she could accompany the boy with suitable staff. I was worried at the prospect of a young Dalda salesman travelling about with mother and servants, possibly a younger sister who could not be left behind, and I soon backed out of it, to everyone's relief, not least the young man's.

A remarkable feature of the old generation of traders was their deep sense of financial integrity. With never anything committed to paper, they trusted each other for unlimited amounts; their word was a guarantee. They seldom chose bankruptcy as the easy way out; and if they were forced to accept it, sons and grandsons have been known to honour the debts. How could anyone perform his father's or father's father's death anniversary each year if an unpaid debt remained behind? Till it was paid, how could the departed soul rest and accept oblation with any sense of satisfaction at duty performed?

The first time I went on tour with one of Lalaji's salesmen we went from town to town booking orders from the local wholesalers, and all the record he kept was a pencil entry in a little notebook. In one town we met the salesman of an old British distribution firm. He carried elaborate printed forms on which he filled in details of the order booked in three copies, each signed jointly by him and the customer. I asked Lalaji's man how he managed to transact business with no records. His answer was simple: 'On trust'. But, he added, the wholesalers of the chaps with the elaborate forms might cancel their orders or refuse to accept the goods if the market in the meantime went against them. 'My wholesalers,' he said proudly, 'never!'. And indeed he was right. You can question a document, but not your own word. You have to live in a town, known to all and related to many. How could you live if your word was no longer trusted? Who would give your daughter his son in marriage? You might break your word about the dowry!

I loved working with Lalaji and his kind. Their warmth, kindness, and above all their trust, once they felt you would not mislead them, their sense of quick profit combined with genuine piety, made one cautious about the responsibility they placed in one's hands.

A harder task in a way was the building of a sales force of the new kind. For some years the Company had employed a few salesmen who travelled in a leisurely way, mostly to big towns, and booked orders on behalf of the port town distributors. Their task was simple; it usually meant accompanying the European sales managers on tour as guides and interpreters, to sell imported articles whose brand names and wide distribution had been fostered over many years by the pioneering efforts of earlier generations of cold-weather visiting sales managers. Those that still remained formed a piece of British social and commercial history. Derisively known as boxwallahs by their compatriots in the administration and the army, because they carried their samples in boxes, they used to arrive in Bombay at the end of the monsoon, and settle at the Taj Mahal Hotel.

Their daily routine was strenuous. A large egg and bacon breakfast was followed by a visit to the bazaar, which imposed a strain of hospitality in numerous cups of sweet tea or fizzy drinks. Here they worked for three hours or more, starting with the distributors and visiting in turn all the main customers. At midday they gathered at the Harbour Bar of the Taj with their counterparts from other companies for a couple of hours of steady beer drinking, followed by large pink gins before lunch. In the afternoon they slept off the strain of the morning. In the evening, a short walk along the sea, a bath and change into white shirt and trousers and black tie, and they again settled at the bar for whisky sodas, pink gins, then brandies after dinner, and ended with cold beer at midnight.

Their work in Bombay completed, they did the standard chukker to Clarke's at Karachi, Faletti's at Lahore, Great Eastern at Calcutta and Spencer's at Madras. When the heat set in, in April, they returned to Bombay to take the boat home, with the customary joke that the best view of Bombay was from the aft of a boat. It was a hard life that killed some while young; but the consistent superior quality of their products and their orderly, planned selling methods made what they sold into household names. As their business grew their firms set up branch offices in India, and then they came for two and a half years' duty and six months' home leave. They now brought their wives with them, and the pattern of life became less hectic.

Our Indian salesmen were trained under these free and easy itinerant managers and followed in their footsteps with corresponding success. They too were usually a hard-living lot, and like their English managers posed a problem when men like Pettit introduced new marketing methods, imposing new disciplines to which neither were used. They now had to submit to a thoroughly regulated system of travelling and work. Fixed itineraries were drawn up for each salesman taking him around his territory in a planned way. For every tour, arrivals and departures, number of days in each town, order in which the dealers were to be called upon each day, sales targets and display material were planned in advance, and the progress had to be recorded, day by day and town by town. The managers were asked to make random checks, which left little scope for doing things your own way. I ran into my very first problems with one of these rugged salesmen.

Gopi, a favourite of the trade and the Company, was an individualist to the core. He liked to be left to get the best sales out of his area. The new form-filling and working to schedule irked him, and he accepted it with transparent hostility. To me, inexperienced and raw, fell the task of training him, and Pettit set it in his usual way. On a visit to Gopi in Poona he took me along. In his presence Gopi was at his best. He went from shop to shop introducing his burra sahib, drawing an effusive reception from each shopkeeper, selling as much as he wanted, each dealer playing up to the occasion by showing just the right amount of resistance but eventually accepting what Gopi thought in his sales wisdom would be best for him to buy. Pettit was most impressed, but in the middle of the morning he suddenly decided to leave me to continue the selling and took Gopi away to another part of the bazaar.

I had never sold anything in my life. Left with a handcart full of Dalda tins, some advertising material for display and a quiet little man from our wholesalers, I set to my task with more resignation than courage. In the first shop I entered I thought of Gopi, how he virtually took over the shop, conveying a complete sense of assurance about what was good for the dealer and generously waving aside his protests. To some he would say, 'No, you try and sell this first and next time I will give you more'; and to others he would equally blandly sell more than they wanted with the assurance, 'I know what you can sell; all this Dalda will go in no time and you will be running out of stock before my next visit. What sort of a salesman will you call me if you have to disappoint your customers?' I tried to remember Gopi's ploys but my tongue was tied when I approached the shopkeepers. After some inconclusive sales, hot and sweaty as the morning advanced I took off my jacket and tie and at least tried to look like a salesman. Just as I was arranging some Dalda tins on a shelf and dusting them to make their labels shine, Pettit returned. I think the sight of me moved him. He told Duncan afterwards that he was impressed by my literally having rolled up my sleeves. I had not sold badly, but more important my daily sales report was neatly filled in and the advertising material properly affixed in prominent positions at the proverbial eye level. Gopi looked displeased at this display of a gentleman salesman in shirtsleeves, which he considered affectation.

A few months' later I came over one hot June midday to meet him on tour. At the wholesaler's I was told that Gopi had left the previous evening, contrary to his new itinerary. So I took the next train to a town seventy miles away, drove straight up to our wholesaler's shop, and was informed that Gopi was resting at the hotel. In some temper I reached the hotel and woke up Gopi. He blandly told me that he did not feel like working and wanted to rest. To my protest that he could not play about with his itineraries, he replied that he could always finish his job in half the time that these new-fangled disciplines demanded. He added archly, 'But would you like to go selling, Sir, as you did in Poona?' I said I would and told him to go back to his rest.

Rarely had I felt more nettled. I went back to the wholesaler determined to get even with Gopi, who had added a calculated piece of insult by suggesting that he might accompany me after all as I had no experience of bazaar selling. With the salesman's daily report folded under my arm, I set out from the wholesaler's godown with a handcart full of Dalda, determined to sell it all. I worked till late in the evening, selling for dear life. At nine o'clock, as I trudged back to the godown, I had exhausted the handcart stocks and made a record sale of over two hundred and fifty rupees of Dalda. As I reached the hotel I saw Gopi sitting cool and fresh on the lawn sipping his beer. All my meanness came out as he enquired how I had fared and said he was feeling fine now and would go back in the morning to finish the day's work.

'Well, Gopi,' I said, 'I have sold all the bazaar could buy for weeks to come; but you can try your luck.'

'What did you sell?' he asked.

'Over two hundred and fifty rupees worth, but maybe you would like to teach me what a lot more you could sell.'

He raised his eyebrows. That was a lot of vanaspati for those days. He realised that I had been as mean as he had been to me, and in fact saturated the market.

I tried hard and in different ways, but I never succeeded with Gopi. There was a watershed between us; between the old, leisurely though hard-selling days, and Pettit's new methods, where the whole operation depended upon a system. A journey cycle, as it was called, put on a schedule a whole month's work for a salesman. This Gopi found irksome, like some of his sales managers. It deprived them of the freedom they were used to, but there was no doubt that it produced better results.

The clash came soon. I had sent Gopi to the north to develop some new markets. Working so far from home did not suit him, but even more he disliked having to introduce himself to the new disagreeable system. When few days later I met him he said he was returning to Bombay for a short rest.

'With whose permission?' I asked.

'Oh, in the usual way. I have worked for several weeks at a stretch and I think I will go home for a while, but if you like I will wait till you have finished your tour.'

I thought I might as well grasp the nettle now as later. Gopi was undoubtedly pushing the point further each time.

'I suggest you return to Bombay tonight. I will finish the tour alone, and please report at the office next Monday. I will have a word with the Chief about it, but so far as I am concerned you can consider yourself through with us; at least with me.'

He was taken aback and protested that it was no insubordination, he merely wanted to go home for a few days. This was the way he had always worked and he saw no harm. I felt some remorse, but I had had enough of Gopi. His influence on the younger men who were being broken into the new ways was disruptive. On my return to Bombay I reported the matter to Pettit who had been expecting some such thing. He realized that I could not manage Gopi and it was best to give me my head through my first crisis. He listened with his usual patience and left me to decide. Duncan was more positive. In the office there was much talk and open hostility, but eventually Gopi left. He tried to make up but I felt I must decide now, once and for all.

Many years later, a large chauffeur-driven car sped past me and signalled me to stop. Out of it jumped Gopi. Balding, portly, suave and effusive as ever, he greeted me like a long lost friend and thanked me for what had turned out to be the beginning of a prosperous career.

Among the new and younger types, too, there were problems, largely cultural. The new ways clashed with our inherited ideas, which though rating the craftsman high, did not value labour. Pettit insisted that the salesman's job was a whole from the moment he entered the shop. Most of the young men, to begin with, disapproved of the very idea of walking beside a handcart or carrying the handbag that contained the report forms, samples, a pot of glue and a stapling machine, a duster and a wet sponge to clean the fly-blown unsold tins; but when it came to the chores of putting tins on the shelves and cleaning them, or stapling and pasting the advertising pieces, they positively rebelled.

One of them, whom I was training in the bazaar on his first day with us, remarked to one of the older sales managers that he would rather work as a coolie than be our salesman. The old manager looked pleased as he secretly agreed, while to me there was no argument about it.

'Don't you like working like a coolie or do you find yourself not up to it?' I asked.

'Well, just to show you, I will work for a month, if only to prove that I can do it, and then I quit.'

He went back to work and stayed with us for twenty-three years. He rose to head our best branch and took great pride in showing the young salesmen the dignity of labour.

CHAPTER TWELVE

The Raj System

With the turn of the tide of war, as the Japanese were at first halted and then gradually began to be pushed back in the Far East, and the Germans in North Africa, the conclusion became obvious and a matter of time. In India there was a kind of stalemate between the Government and Congress. All our leaders were in jail; the top leaders were all put in the same prison, the fortress of Ahmednagar, except Gandhiji, who was lodged in an extraordinarily ugly palace of the Aga Khan, outside Poona. Either the Government was facetiously generous in allowing them to live together like one of the many evacuee governments of the time, perhaps naively believing that with nothing to do they might break the impasse, or it might have been to facilitate negotiations when the moment came.

So the leaders sat in idleness, planning and dreaming of the future, of an India free and ruled by them. They would undo the trends of a thousand years of history, of domination and exploitation, when the interests of the masses were excluded by the needs of dominion. They made a post-war, post-independence plan that would quickly and dramatically get India out of the morass and put her on the road to industrialized affluence, welfare, and international equality and influence. They would build a socialist society, with the state in control of key functions. They would write a constitution combining the best of all political systems. While they veered towards the system of the Western democracies, their economic thinking leaned towards the socialism of Russia, in which they saw fulfilled their aspirations for a non-exploiting, progressive society of heavy industry and cooperatives.

I used to get into arguments over this. Everyone agreed that all that was wrong with the society and the economy was the British. In subtle ways, sometimes openly and sometimes covertly, they thwarted all progress. Openly, they were not interested in the effective spread of education, in improving communication, in industrializing; subtly, they kept choked the mainsprings of progress: the social change so necessary to encourage economic growth. All our ills, social and economic, were either of their making or encouraged by them. If the Brahmin did not accept the untouchable, it was because he was not made to; if the trader profiteered during the war it was because, as Nehru said, he was not strung from the first lamp-post; if the Hindu women did not enjoy all the rights of man and more, it was because there was no legal statute to permit it.

To an extent this was so. As rulers they were not particularly interested in waking up dogs that had slept for so long, but what one doubted was the calm assumption that the moment they went and we came in, the society would suddenly wake up and dramatically set about to undo all evil, and usher in good with an unerring instinct. It was difficult and sad to argue with this naive optimism, such arguments always left the impression that those who did not share this optimism almost did not want it to happen; as if there were in them an underlying opposition to the coming change; something which did actually exist in the minority communities.

Among the Christians and Parsis of Bombay and elsewhere, who had accepted the British as their special protectors and acquired cultural affinities with them, there was open fear of change. With exceptions, they were unhappy at the possibility, now increasingly a likelihood, of the British going. It was argued that they were afraid of being deprived of their privileged position, which I think the British had given them out of a genuine desire to encourage the underdog, though also of course to ensure their loyalties, to create small islands of agreement that could always be relied upon. It was understandable that the minorities did not want their islands to be swamped when once the support of the British was withdrawn.

The minorities misunderstood their position. All they would actually lose were the excrescences, the relatively unimportant trappings of their British connection, but these they seemed to value because they set them apart from the rest, which was just what the rest resented. They had nothing to be afraid of as minorities, even with the alien qualities that distinguished them. A group remained a minority only as long as it resisted assimilation and retained its distinction. In the case of the Christians, they were all Indian, mostly of relatively recent conversion, only set apart by their faith and their names, and the distinctiveness of a closed endogamous group which imitated the British. The Parsis were ethnically different, though over the 1300 years of their domicile in Western India they had married and intermingled. While adopting Gujerati language, food, dress and customs, they had sufficiently altered these to give them a Parsi touch.

It was in the end a plain fear of the dominant Hindu community not giving them a fair deal just because they had been the favourites of the British. In identifying themselves with the rulers they had to an extent to disidentify themselves from the rest of the people. Their attitude had acquired some of the aloofness of the British, and some visible mannerisms deliberately cultivated struck us as somewhat ludicrous. Personally I found them a little pathetic and felt sad that they should have so isolated themselves as to become afraid of the mainstream. I was equally sad at the attitude of the mainstream, which did not have the bigness to let the little streams run their own course until they felt comfortable about returning to its bosom.

I felt sad too at the abundant complacency which claimed that everything was wrong with everyone else, with the British and the minorities, with those Indians who saw anything good in them or anything but good in us; that as soon as the dark curtains of British rule lifted there would be a bright vista of a long straight road to progress. I had once got into an unhappy argument a few years earlier about the British and the Germans. Nothing was right with the British; everything was understandable about Nazi Germany.

In the Company we began to plan for the time when progress could again be resumed, unhampered by all the restrictions that the war had piled up. I had the feeling that, necessary as it had been to restrict during the war, there was something inherent in the character of the British administrator, who was essentially unsympathetic, often hostile, to trade and industry, and had always regarded business with distaste. His model was the English county gentleman, and in the earlier days he often came from a county family, a second or third son coming to India in search of a career that combined adventure with sport, power and profit. To this kind, business was an unattractive profession with which you did not soil your hands.

On the other hand, the Indian trader, usually also a money-lender, had ways that endeared him to no one; but whereas in the days of the East India Company the factors, and later the administrators, had shared his exploitation, and therefore tolerated and encouraged him, the new civil service was not dependent upon him for trade or revenue, and was openly contemptuous of him. I think the neglect of India's trade and industry through these valuable fifty years was largely due to this attitude.

The administrator was basically a law and order man, and his efforts were mainly addressed to the interests of the villager, as he saw it, in maintaining peace, land records, title deeds—things the peasant had not known for centuries, with some attempt at development in irrigation and communications. There was a list we were made to learn by heart at school: Blessings of the British Raj—peace, post, telegraph, roads, schools, hospitals, canals, and I think one or two more like that; all of them useful innovations by themselves, but most of them hardly touching the villager. He had no one to correspond with; normally no place to go, except the nearest small town market; he was illiterate; and the nearest hospital was in the district town, twenty, thirty or fifty miles away, with no means of getting there. With the exception of the Punjab and some relatively prosperous irrigated districts here and there, this was still the picture of most of rural India a hundred years after the Queen assumed power and the insignia of Empress of India. The villages stood still. There was no attempt at giving them communications or a voice. No roads led to the village, except the tracks made by bullock carts, nor was there a post office, school or dispensary. The villager was left in an idolized splendour of isolation, at the combined mercy of the past, the monsoon and the money-lender. The monsoon was often fickle and sometimes failed, and with it his slender livelihood; but the past never failed him in the comfort it gave through familiar ritual and ceremonial, though its demands at births, weddings and deaths could be exacting and onerous. And this is where the money-lender came in 'to help balance the budget'—a money-lender's advertisement I saw in Boston many years later.

The administrator genuinely loved the peasant, but I do not think he understood his real needs. These were simple—they felt need for credit, constantly needed to maintain life, honour and death, even the memory of death; and the unfelt, but more urgent need for education, though on the surface he seemed content with the learning contained in his cumulative racial memory and his ritual. The administrator helped him with neither. He tried later to do something about credit by discouraging the money-lender and opening some cooperative credit institutions, but these were so hemmed in by his love for rules and regulations that the illiterate peasant preferred the money-lender's high rate of interest on loans given at the moment and on word of mouth to the irksome form-filling of the cooperatives. The new regulations meant to curb the money-lender only managed to increase the cost of the load, and so the administrator neither provided the answer nor an alternative to the peasant's need for credit.

When later the trader and the money-lender became industrialists the old mistrust continued, augmented by the fact that he often openly allied himself with nationalism and supplied the Congress Party with funds. The rising voice of the legislatures and the press achieved a few gains for the nascent industry in the way of tariff protection, but the administrator did little to encourage it either directly or indirectly by providing even the elementary infrastructure. Right up to 1947 two of the most industrialized cities, Bombay and Ahmedabad, were not even connected by road.

The trader, never loved, began to be thoroughly disliked during the war when he exploited the law of supply and demand to the fullest. Where there were shortages he charged whatever he wished, and where the supply was adequate he waited to sell till the prices went up. He became almost whimsical towards the consumer, and many times one walked out of a shop feeling sick at his cynicism, as when he would raise the already extortionate price just because one protested.

'But only a few days ago you charged me less, and the price has not gone up since.'

'No', he agreed triumphantly, 'but the price goes up right now. I asked you two rupees; and if you still want it, it will be two rupees and a quarter. If you don't, it will be more when you next come for it.'

Complacent in the assurance that he would always get more and more for his stock, he felt reluctant to part with it. It was bad business to sell to-day unless he charged the premium that he would get tomorrow.

The administrator passed laws and made rules, and made them yet more stringent when they did not work, till a maze of regulations spread across everything. There were prosecutions for refusal to sell, and I was flooded with telegrams from wholesalers in the lock-up, praying me to get them released, because they had refused to sell in retail and under our instructions sold Dalda only to selected retailers on a planned quota. Pettit rushed to New Delhi and persuaded the Department of Civil Supplies to issue a special exemption to our wholesalers so that we could continue orderly distribution, but I found my problem was how to get the administrator to accept it in his district.

One realized the immense power the administration gave to its men on the spot. This had been its tradition, and the secret of its success. If the man out on the limb chose to go his own way he could go pretty far before he was pulled up. When he proved right he was regarded as an eccentric, and if he was wrong he was only moved. One of our wholesalers in Ferozepur was locked up for a few days for refusal to sell, and in spite of the letter from the Company he produced quoting Central Government's exemption, the English Deputy Commissioner refused to withdraw the prosecution. To save the poor wholesaler I travelled all the way up to Ferozepur to call on him. This was my first experience of dealing with a British administrator.

Whether he behaved as expected of him or was like that by nature, his curtness was disconcerting. He spoke of the traders and their untrustworthiness and how, if he had his own way, he would put them all behind bars, for nothing would teach them to drop their anti-social ways but the plain fear of being treated as common criminals. He sounded very frustrated and this I could understand. The war had placed upon him burdens of a new kind, to which was further added the general political sensitiveness and the rising communal tension in the district. He now had to deal with an unfamiliar set of problems arising from the new civil supplies department, which mostly meant keeping a lot of dishonest traders in check; a new function he least relished.

I explained to the Commissioner how our system was designed to ensure as equitable a distribution as was possible under conditions of acute short supply. Compelling a wholesaler to sell to all and sundry would only mean that stocks would immediately be cornered upon their arrival, whereas we tried to distribute them to a selected list of retailers on a pre-determined quota with a fair chance of their being sold to genuine customers. Prosecuting the wholesalers for refusal to sell under the Act would produce no more Dalda nor channel it to the right people. That was why we had obtained a special sanction from the Central Government exempting our wholesalers from section 9 of the Anti-Hoarding and Profiteering Ordnance under which this man had been prosecuted. We had convinced Government of the need for the exemption. To my passionate arguments his reply was simple and curt.

'That may be so in New Delhi, but here you have to convince me.'

'I don't know how to convince you then.'

I was up against power, delegated to the end of its limits. His action would be supported all the way, but it would as surely be defeated by the Court; though only after a protracted and costly case. The system had a strange ambivalence; it gave the executive naked and arbitrary power, but also provided a check through the judiciary which was independent and often suspicious of the executive. Both sides had equal freedom. The exercise of power could always be turned back at the boundaries of justice, but until then it would be a law unto itself, sometimes lawless in the law it tried to enforce. I remember a story my father told me—how a man who felt aggrieved said to a minor village official:

'But surely there is the Sirkar!'

'Sirkar, who is the Sirkar? Here I am the Sirkar.'

The Deputy Commissioner had told me just that. The chain of arbitrary action had continued down the ages from the Moghuls, the Marathas, the Sikhs, to the British, and we did not then realize that one day we might be adding our own links.

The administrator sat in his chair in his airy brick-built office, dealing with just another situation; he was always preventing people from doing wrong or punishing them for doing it. There was nowadays nothing constructive left; the interest of the pioneering days had gone, the excitement of breaking new ground, opening up new areas to peace and order and to development. Now he was desk-bound, attending to stacks of files, coping with an ever-growing multiplicity of new departments and legislation, mostly of a negative kind, controlling transport, food and supplies, prices and procurement of food, controlling nationalism.

He looked at me wearily. I could understand his distaste for the business he came across, but I felt hurt to be included in this distaste; that my attempts at developing a modern idea of integrity in trading mattered so little to him that instead of praise I was met with suspicion. Back in Bombay I heard the wholesaler had been released, and there was a touching telegram of thanks from him.

Some years later, travelling in the Punjab with Maurice Zinkin, who had been in the I.C.S. and had joined Unilever after 1947 and returned to India, I related this story to him. His reaction was sharp and unequivocal.

'Of course he was right! The exemption New Delhi gave you neither altered the rule nor directed him in any way. It was given for you to produce before a local authority for their consideration, but as long as the rule remained it was up to them to decide in their own right. The letter was not a directive to the Deputy Commissioner and did not bind him in any way. Right or wrong, in the exercise of his judgement, the power and discretion of the man on the spot always remained his. His decision could be examined by the authorities, and he could be criticized for a wrong judgement, but not stopped from exercising his discretion.'

Maurice went on to add, with his characteristic verve, that the day the power of discretion of the man on the spot was interfered with would be a sad one for the administration. I confess I did not see it that way then, and few did. Later, years after the administrator had lost power and a political system had taken over, I realized the significance of what Maurice meant. The politician naturally preferred the discretion to be his.

Later another case came up that had its lighter side. An English district magistrate in the U.P. was trying one of our wholesalers for a similar offence. As usual I wrote him a letter explaining our distribution system and enclosed a copy of the exemption letter from the Central Government. It had worked in most cases, but this magistrate regarded my letter as contempt of court and ordered that I be produced before him under an arrest warrant. I was saved by a technicality. Recently one of the U.P. High Courts had decreed that a stormy petrel of Indian journalism, an Irishman, B.G. Horniman, be produced for contempt for writing a prejudicial article. He was the editor of the *Bombay Chronicle*, and the virulence of his pen matched a fellow country man of his from another age, William Hickey of Calcutta. Both usually had the English as their targets. Horniman had settled in India, was violently anti-administration and lost no chance to advocate Indian nationalism and flay the Government. In this case an amusing situation arose. The British Chief Justice of the Bombay High Court, though he no doubt had his own views on Horniman, refused to let the summons be served on the grounds that the Chief Justice of the U.P. had no jurisdiction over a citizen of Bombay. The British judiciary had often refused to uphold the British administration, but this was a rare instance in India of a British judge protecting a British citizen against another, equally senior British judge. This case came to my rescue, as the Government advocate reminded the magistrate that under this judgement in Bombay he had no jurisdiction over me. But the magistrate was not to be thwarted. He passed another order that I should be produced before him the next time I entered his district.

☆

The war was nearing its end, and Unilever decided to send a rather remarkable man to India, Roger Heyworth, youngest of three brothers in Unilever, all of whom rose to its board, the eldest becoming its Chairman. Roger, as he was known to all, had spent some time in a Japanese camp in Hongkong, where he had landed from Singapore on the day the Japanese occupied it, and had only recently been released on exchange. I think they sent him to India to get a feel and a measure of the Company and the country, as it seemed obvious that the end of the war would mean a transfer of power and a considerable growth in the country. For this task he was well suited, as he combined a sharp intellect with an intuitive and sensitive understanding of people. He appeared more at home in Bombay in a week than I had found some Englishmen do after a life time.

He sent for me one day and said he wanted a general chat. This in itself was something new, as indeed was everything else about him. Although the office was air-conditioned he had taken his coat off, loosened his tie and unbuttoned the collar. He sat in his chair with one leg over its arm, with the shoe laces untied and the shoe dangling off his foot. He half got up and waved me to another chair and we sat away from his desk, near a window, from where he could look out at the Bombay harbour. He was strongly built, of medium height, but the thing you noticed immediately about him was his large head, with thinning hair neatly parted, big round eyes behind glasses, and a friendly, high-pitched laughter that was very infectious and disarming.

'Talk to me,' he began unexpectedly.

I began to talk about Dalda and the general situation in the Company and the country.

He interrupted me, 'I know all about that, I want to hear you talk, and his face burst into laughter. I discovered how he mixed encouragement with crispness. Slowly I began to describe how we had worked on Dalda, the early problems of introducing a substitute fat in homes that had always used, almost with reverence, ghee; how Dalda's strong and logical appeal cut into a tradition for which we would not be forgiven for a long time to come; for the more logical and successful our advertising, offering the purity and economy of our vegetable fat in place of the often adulterated but always expensive ghee, the less they forgave us their own acceptance of this logic. It was our most interesting social industrial phenomenon of the century, and while I was glad to be associated with it, there was occasional embarrassment.

'Do you mind it?'

I said yes and no. I found the work exciting and satisfying because the field was so open to new marketing in India that any effort brought quick, almost disproportionate, returns. I enjoyed the travelling that took me to all parts of the country. On the other hand, people still wondered why I sold Dalda instead of being in Government or politics, because particularly Dalda was not regarded a respectable product. My friends, and even people I barely knew, asked me to put them on our Dalda quota list, but always with a patronizing air—'You know, we have to use Dalda nowadays; you can't get pure ghee any longer and it is so expensive.' To them from ghee to Dalda was a come down, but even the Dalda had to be sought as a favour.

'Would you rather have been working for Government?'

'I don't think so.'

'Because it is British and not your own?'

'Yes, perhaps.'

'You would rather not have been working for a British firm?'

'I don't know.'

The conversation changed facets fast, and was full of surprises. He seemed to be doing a quick reconnaissance and wanted an approximate idea of the heights and hollows. He was utterly candid about what he wanted to know and spared neither my feelings nor his own. Surprisingly I found my customary reticences dissolve before his ruthless curiosity. I cannot say that I enjoyed it; nor did I find it irritating. Instead, I learned something new, that purposeful curiosity combined with sincerity, such as he conveyed, did not hurt but brought candid answers. His questions went like the probing hands of a surgeon which passed over the body lightly, but pressed whenever he wanted to know more, making a mental note to leave anything that needed a deeper enquiry for a further session; and it was clear that there would be more sessions like this. I did not mind the prospect and perhaps even relished it.

On the next occasion he went straight into an after-Indian-freedom-what session. He agreed with me that the stage was past for Dominion Status, and that the question whether we would leave the British Empire would be a matter of our choice and not Whitehall's.

Anything less than complete freedom made no sense to him, even from Britain's point of view. India's economic problems were too great for Britain to meet without India's support. We should tackle them ourselves with any help that Britain could give and India might ask.

He laughed and went on:

'Not only can't we do it, but I don't see why we should take any responsibility for your problems, and all the blame that will go with all the mistakes that are bound to be made. I think it will be in Britain's interest to give you the kind of freedom you want. Once having decided, we should not hold back but meet your wishes all the way.'

That struck me as a curious attitude, for everyone else advocated hastening gradually, in slow deliberate steps, to make sure that the country was ready at each stage—the sort of thing that made one very impatient; and here Roger showed impatience in the reverse direction. He went on to say that he saw it in practical business terms. British interest was no longer imperial. Right now they had to concentrate on the war, with Indian help or without it, but once they had finished, their interest in India was going to be purely commercial and industrial; a frank return to the original trading connection of the Company's days. Britain would gain more that way than by hanging on by the worn out strap of power. What did I think would happen to British business in India after independence?

I expected that that would depend upon the safeguards built into the instrument of transfer of power. British business had already been expressing concern that the transfer might lead to discrimination and interference with their freedom to operate, and had suggested a commercial treaty of safeguards with sanctions.

This Heyworth pronounced to be nonsense. A commercial treaty whose only purpose was to safeguard the interests of one side after its imperial connection had gone was worthless with or without safeguards. A foreign community could only continue to conduct its business with the goodwill of the host country, and there was a better chance of such goodwill if no pre-conditions were laid down. If British business had a contribution to make, it was sure to be welcome. He laughed, 'Of course, no matter how well we behave and whatever is our contribution, there is no certainty that you will always know your best interests.'

I saw why his brother had chosen to send him to India, a country soon to be free to mould itself its own way. Roger Heyworth could convey the right picture. He started from the simple assumption that India had to be free and would be free—what would she want to do once she was free; who would be the new administrators and managers, what is their mettle, their fears and aspirations? He would take a close look at the business and its environment, and what might be done to attune it to the future.

He explained to me another day that he saw the business with Indians in charge of it; but not Indianized merely to satisfy Indian sentiment. It would be a pity to be dictated by a Government about what was in the best interests of the business. Governments are often poor judges of industrial problems, and in their enthusiasm to industrialize rapidly they can think of costly but unprofitable ventures. The firms would have to insist on their right to decide; otherwise they had no place, no value.

India, he thought, would be right in expecting them to help in her growth and to enter new fields that required skill and investment and involved a measure of risk, but assuredly a delayed return. For this they should try to create areas of understanding with Government and it was imperative to develop men in the business who would be understood and trusted by the future Indian leadership.

He spent a lot of his time in New Delhi meeting government secretaries at all levels. He was fortunate in getting to know Maurice Zinkin, whose brilliant and effervescent mind was just what he needed to sharpen his ideas on. Maurice brought him into contact, especially socially, with the circle of British and Indian government servants into which businessmen, British or Indian, were rarely admitted. Quite different personalities, they had yet much in common, especially their ideas on India, her development and the place of the new professionalized business in the society after the war. Not long afterwards, when Independence came and Maurice Zinkin left the Civil Service, Roger Heyworth persuaded him to join Unilever in London and return to India two years later.

The process Heyworth began with me, Zinkin continued. I find it difficult to describe it. I think they were both trying to persuade me to accept the responsibility that circumstance had brought my way. Roger sensed my reservations and my holding back, despite my complete commitment on the surface. He sensed that underneath I was trying to evade the logical consequences of the process I had accepted implicitly, and that unless I accepted wholly it would not work. He was right in the way he visualized the future of the business and the scene around, and also in his insistence that my commitment had to be complete. He sensed too that emotionally I was not ready yet to give such a commitment to the business.

I had sensed it too and it had worried me. I did not know with whom to discuss it. Inside the Company I felt alone because my Indian colleagues were all junior to me and they had their own doubts and anxieties, and discussing my problems with them would have made them even more uncertain about themselves. They looked to me for strength, and had they sensed that I had my own hesitations they would have felt let down. The first wave of Indianization had suffered a setback, when nearly twenty Indian managers had left, some because the war offered better opportunities and others because they did not fit in and the Company let them go. But the effect was a generally lowered morale, which I would have accentuated had I displayed my own lack of commitment.

Now I could no longer avoid facing up to my problem. With Independence things began to move fast, and I drifted into deeper commitment and a greater unhappiness. Roger Heyworth must have watched me like a doctor a patient moving towards the crisis of an illness, about which he can do very little except watch and hope. I did eventually pull through after a long struggle, on occasions very painful, over the next ten years, but Roger Heyworth died, and though he set me on my path he was not there at the end.

CHAPTER THIRTEEN

End of the Raj

The war came to an end. I was in Calcutta at the time, staying at the Grand Hotel, which was full of American officers on leave from their outlying units. I had seen few Americans before the war brought them in large numbers. Apart from the Ludlow jute factory in Calcutta, Firestone, American Express, Union Carbide with just a small Ever Ready torch battery plant, Dodge & Seymour, an early import house, and the assembly plants of Fords and General Motors, there was hardly any American business in India, though there had been early trading with America back at the time when ships from New Orleans used to bring ice as ballast to Calcutta, to take back tea, jute, indigo and other commodities. The arrival of ice was an event in those days that involved much social activity among the parched British community of Calcutta.

There were of course a number of American missions, one running the well known Forman Christian College at Lahore, another the Woodstock School at Mussoorie, and a number of small schools and hospitals all over the country, of which the one at Vellore was famous for its surgery. The total American connection was small, both in size and impact, but from a distance we admired them, if only because they had no empire and wanted those who had one to liquidate it. Of course, they had also fought the British and beaten them, but one did not really think of America as a former colony, nor their war as a war of liberation; it had been their own government after all, though in time they found that the King behaved like an absentee landlord. Today, while Hitler was trying to win an empire, Mussolini and Hirohito striving to expand theirs, and Churchill trying to save one, Roosevelt, it was common knowledge, would have liked to see the whole iniquitous institution dissolved and freedom given all round.

The first American soldiers began to arrive in India late in 1941, and our first impression of them was their informality which made them so unlike the British. As I saw them around the country, in trains and hotels, I wondered what they would be like as rulers. We could only judge by what we saw; their informal ease, their shock at what they saw in India and impatience with her rulers for leaving it at that, and their own thoroughness in organizing and getting things done. Judging by all this, one concluded that they would at least be more efficient in their exploitation.

Their officers and men went about similarly dressed, to us indistinguishable in language and demeanour, while British officers and men patently belonged to different worlds. Their crumpled beige uniforms, unpolished shoes and forage caps placed anyhow upon the head, their loose build and easy gait, left epaulets the only distinction. But the greatest surprise which finally brought to an end a British sartorial custom of two hundred years, was the sight of them going about under the blazing sun of their first summer in New Delhi in light cloth caps instead of solar topees or pith helmets. At one time the British used to wear spine pads, huge helmets with a thick khaki cloth hanging from the back to protect the neck, and still soldiers and civilians alike wore their topees which the town Indians copied. When the Americans appeared with virtually no protection everyone predicted that they would die in their thousands long before facing the enemy. But they survived their first summer, and the topee did not; others began to shed this ugly headgear and soon it was a part of British history.

Strange was also their early generosity. They did not understand the value of the rupees which when translated into cents made everything it bought seem ludicrously cheap. This often made them look more foolish than generous. Coins less than a rupee they usually gave away, as they could not be bothered to count parts of a cent. Many stories went round. A tongawalla protested at the fare an American soldier had paid him. After some bargaining the American gave him more and walked away, but the man ran after him and shouted: 'Amreekan Sahib, why aren't you taking your horse and tonga away; you have paid for them, though it was less than I asked.'

The British generally disapproved and thought them brash and ignorant while the Americans did not conceal that they thought the British had done a poor job in India. They criticized them openly for the poverty, illiteracy, poor communications and general inefficiency—presently more blame than the British deserved was laid at their doorstep. The British were on the defensive when they talked about the problems they were up against instead of frankly admitting that they had come here to trade, and ended up with an empire at their feet. The day was yet far off when the Americans would acquire their own burdens abroad and carry them with great earnestness.

We still saw America only in the image of Roosevelt, who stood out as the shining knight in the cause of freedom for all, who disagreed with Churchill and included India in the Atlantic Charter of four freedoms. Our admiration for the Americans was genuine and deep. Roosevelt held his own against Churchill and sent one of his roving ambassadors to India, the first of his kind to visit us. He came to study the general situation, but unfortunately then all the Congress leaders were in jail, and he could only meet British civil servants and a few Indians to assess feelings. The British felt that this move added insult to injury.

At the same time there was a good deal of sympathy among Americans in India for the British, because of our leadership's call for complete non-cooperation with the war effort. They could appreciate that we might not want to fight the war for the British, but they could not understand why we were fighting the British themselves, when war was being fought against two ruthless enemies who, if they won, would give us no quarter. The Americans themselves had kept out of the war through its crucial early period, and only joined because the Japanese drew them in, but at all times it had been obvious where their sympathies lay. I do not think they understood the accumulated strength of our feelings.

As individuals they were friendly and informal, anxious to start conversations and to be invited to Indian homes. But they were up against a barrier when it came to their custom of dating. At that time it was unthinkable for Indian girls, even in the cities, to be familiar with men and go out alone with them. For dating, the only girls available were the Anglo-Indians and a few westernized Indian Christian girls. In Calcutta, which was their base, the Anglo-Indian girls had a wonderful time. They forgot their traditional loyalties and dropped the British officers and men in favour of the Americans, who had more money and better goods in their canteens and, what counted more, were genuinely warm and generous and showed no trace of embarrassment when taking them out. The British officers felt and could not help showing a certain discomfiture when seen in public with an Anglo-Indian girl. The girls sensed this, though maybe they did not mind, but with the Americans they could now feel at ease.

Yet it is surprising how few marriages it led to, considering the many that took place later in Japan. The girls in Calcutta came of partly European stock, always spoke English and dressed in western clothes, which made for ready familiarity. Yet the relationship seemed to remain at the simple level of having a good time. The girls were used to this from the British with whom affairs had seldom matured into marriage. There must naturally have been some to whom

Luckies, Mars bars, black bras and bourbon were not enough, in whom deeper feelings were evoked than a leave weekend's excitement. Maybe it was the very veneer of western manners that kept the men off marriage, while Indian girls, had the opportunity been there, like the Japanese might have compelled in them a more lasting desire. There must have been many sad instances though of genuine disappointment, like a pathetic letter by an Anglo-Indian girl I once read in a Calcutta newspaper.

The American soldiers certainly livened it up wherever they went, and made the Chowringhee of Calcutta a more cheerful place than it used to be. The shopkeepers loved it; the rikshawallas loved it; the waiters and hotel servants loved it; and so did the families who received them. The shopkeepers displayed their goods to catch the eyes of this new type of customer to whom buying was habit rather than a need; the rikshawallas held long conversations with them, each side eagerly expressing their own views without understanding a word of the other, and in their happy moments a couple of soldiers might install the riksha pullers in the cabs, get between the shafts and race each other. The waiters loved serving them because there was always a laugh, a friendly word, an incomprehensible crack and a generous tip. As visitors to a home they made friends with the children and treated the older people sentimentally like their parents back home.

There was a sergeant called Solomon, Solly for short, whose visits to a family I knew were the event of the week. The drawl of his language and his sunny disposition made him welcome. One evening Solly looked slightly morose and explained that he had had an argument with one of his officers. My friend, who was a reservist major, was mildly shocked, and Solly added that he too was shocked with his captain.

'All I said to my captain was "Gee, captain, I don't like your attitude".'

'You don't like my attitude, why?' asked the captain.

'I didn't like the way you spoke to my mate there, just because he asked for leave when he was not due any.'

At this, Solly went on, the captain got mad and bawled at him to mind his own business.

'You see, captain, that's why I don't like your attitude.'

And having registered his protest, Solly walked away with disgust written all over his face. He had so wanted to bring his friend along that evening.

I was in Calcutta when the news of the bomb came, and the word atom acquired a new meaning. The reports of the havoc that challenged creation itself held such surprise and shock that one could not take in its enormity. Before the Japanese could even separate the dead from the living what had happened, down came another bolt from the sky, this time mainly to satisfy the scientists' curiosity about the device's behaviour in its capacity for destruction when it was exploded in mid air. At last the scientist gained an upper hand over the military man who had so far consulted him, used him, but kept him at a distance.

I used to stay in the Grand Hotel where most of the rooms were reserved for American officers. With the news of the bomb, my friends asked if I would like to move out and stay with them. I said I didn't think it necessary. Next evening the news of the surrender came and the hotel all but went up in flames. Men fifteen thousand miles from home, some since three or four years, burst into an orgy of drink and noise to express their pent-up tension. As I lay in my bed that night with the door bolted, it terrified me. They leapt in the air and banged on all the doors, they yelled and hurled imprecations, they beat a tattoo on cans and buckets with pieces of broken furniture as they ran down the corridors. The next morning I moved out.

The end came with unexpected swiftness. The Japanese war machine was after all intact, and we had expected a long bitter war of attrition with the Japanese pride yielding ground literally by inches in a long struggle from Assam to the Solomon Island, over hundreds of scattered islands to the heartland. But in less than two days it was all over. One wondered if the thing would ever have been dropped, not once but twice, over the enemy in the west, over a white populace; whether there is not a kind of impersonality where people of colour and creed different to one's own are concerned.

*

Our own problems were not long in starting. A relatively small but testing situation arose with the trial of a group of officers from the so called Indian National Army. They had defected during the war and joined Japan. They could not be called traitors to their own country because, although the Viceroy had declared war on behalf of India, Indians had never really agreed to it. On the other hand, they were volunteers who had taken an oath of allegiance to a distant king who was their supreme chief, and under military law they were traitors. Out of over one hundred thousand officers and men, the British Government decided to try three leaders, all Punjabis: a Sikh, a Hindu and a Moslem!

When the empire fell like ninepins in Burma, Malaya and Hong Kong, large numbers of Indian troops, who had borne the brunt of the attack, were captured by the Japanese. There were in these lands also large numbers of Indian settlers, and stories came of the often unashamed preoccupation of the British civil and army authorities with saving their own civilian and military units and letting the devil take the hindmost—in this case the Indians. Two roads led out of Burma to India, the more comfortable one was reserved for the British, who were well provided and cared for as they retreated, while the Indians were left to fend for themselves on a trek that later became known as the Burma Road and stirred the conscience of the world.

Among the Indian soldiers there was great bitterness and this the Japanese exploited, helped by Subhas Chandra Bose, a former President of the Congress, who had made a dashing escape from British surveillance in his house in Calcutta, through the whole of North India, Afghanistan and Persia, till he reached Germany. From there Netaji, the leader, as he became known, had been taken by submarine to Japan, where he announced the formation of an Indian National Army, with himself as Commander-in-Chief. He travelled to Singapore, which had the largest concentration of Indian prisoners of war, and persuaded some of the officers to join him, soon followed by other ranks in large numbers till a sizeable army was formed, which should one day march into India with the Japanese to free the Motherland. The part it eventually played was insignificant, but it acted as a boost to India's morale, and when the British decided to conduct the famous I.N.A. trial popular feelings rose to a high pitch.

Of the irony of this strange drama which they played with such sad perfection, the British surely cannot have been unconscious. It was as if some intuitive sense of history led them to 'beat retreat' before lowering the flag a year hence. The Empire's Consul, the Viceroy, himself a famed soldier, cannot have been unaware in the hour of victory that the sunset was coming with tropical speed, when he decided to hold the trial at the very Red Fort of Delhi from where the last Moghul Emperor, Bahadur Shah, was led out a captive in 1857. It became a test case, Nehru put on his barrister's black robes after many years, but the man who ably fought the case was Bhulabhai Desai, the leading advocate of Bombay and a member of the Congress. He held that under international law, if a country had undertaken the responsibility of defending the citizens of another country and failed to discharge this duty, the loyalty of these citizens lapsed and they had the right to defend themselves as best they could. The British, he averred, had failed in Burma. He was successful in his argument and the three accused were released on discharge from the Army.

The British seemed to indicate through this acquittal that they were passing on the ultimate and the larger decision in this case to Indians. They showed a rare intuition; for a year later when independent India was fighting its first own war in Kashmir, the Indian Army flatly refused to take back one single I.N.A. officer, despite all the covert pressures from the Congress leaders. The men whom Nehru and Desai had defended as heroes; men who had broken their sworn allegiance to answer a call to higher duty, to serve their own motherland rather than the country that held her in bondage: all the rhetoric of the trial failed to move the Indian Army General Staff, many of whom had personally known and served with these men. Nehru and his colleagues having won the trial had to accept defeat in the implication of its result; and it was to their credit that they did not make the issue public, or press it beyond a seemly point. The feelings of the men responsible for the new army had to be respected, and their feelings apparently were very strong.

Once when I was travelling to Bombay from Madras, a young Maratha captain got into my compartment. He looked strained and nervous. We had a night's journey ahead; he began to talk, and we talked till late into the night. He had been to Sandhurst and joined a cavalry regiment before the war. His regiment was sent to Malaya, and when the Japanese invaded from the north they were one of the first to take the shock. There was really very little fighting, he told me; they mostly retreated, lost their units and rejoined them till they reached the sea and could be pushed no further, and there they all fell prisoners to the Japanese at Singapore. He spent the rest of the war in a prisoner-of-war camp in Singapore and shared a cell with a Punjabi officer about whom a legend had grown.

Life in the camp, he said, was hard and one's main consideration was how to spend the least energy to be able to survive on the meagre diet. However, they were more fortunate than the many who were sent to the Siam Railway or to the Solomon Islands, especially the latter from where few returned. He described life in the camp, the interminable hours of waiting for nothing, lying in their bunks staring into space, punctuated with incomprehensibly brutal treatment by their captors, so senseless that it could only be explained, he thought, by the scant value the Japanese attached to the life of anyone who chose to be taken prisoner.

But there were lighter moments. His cell-mate, on a morning of particular boredom, wrote a skit in verse on the Japanese officers. A few days later, when the Maratha was alone in his cell, a Japanese lieutenant and some soldiers entered without knocking. The captain got up to attention, but the lieutenant pushed him aside and without a word they proceeded to turn the cell inside out, searching their few possessions, their clothes, and tearing open the partitions. After a half hour they walked out. Apparently the camp authorities had got to hear about the poem and were determined to get hold of it. When his mate heard of it he was most amused, but the Maratha was relieved to hear that the poem had been lent to an Indian medical officer the same morning.

Some days later the cell-mate called out that he had a new idea for a verse. The Maratha jumped out of his bunk, put his hands around the throat of the verse-writer and threatened to choke the idea out of him, for if the Japanese heard of another poem they would raze the camp to the ground.

His anecdotes, though amusing, gave glimpses of the suffering he must have gone through. There was no trace of bitterness in him and he regarded the Japanese with amused contempt. They had given his cell-mate a really bad time, seeming to pick on him with unusual hatred; maybe it was his appearance that irritated them. He had a tall, robust Punjabi build, a large cavalry moustache and an overbearing manner, all of which seemed to make the small Japanese want to slap him. They often did, and things worse than that, but nothing broke his cheerful arrogance.

After the surrender the Japanese guards went round to the same Indian officers asking for testimonials certifying how well they had been treated:

I asked the captain where he was going, and his answer was short and clear.

'On a very painful mission to New Delhi, to testify against some old friends—the I.N.A. undertrials.'

'Really. Poor chaps. I suppose you can understand their position,' I said.

'No. Unfortunate they no doubt are but there can be no sympathy for them.'

'But I thought they displayed great courage in resolving their conflict.'

'No. There could be no conflict. I am afraid I can only see it in my own simple light. They were men who had joined voluntarily, and as officers no circumstances could absolve them from their oath. Even if we assume that they were mercenary soldiers, they still owed allegiance to whomever they agreed to serve.'

'You wouldn't consider taking them back?'

He replied quickly, 'There is no room in the Indian Army for them and us.'

☆

Things that were simmerings now reached the boiling point with the Indian Navy mutiny in Bombay. Communal tension also soon broke its banks. The whole country was restless, and the British realized that freedom could not long be postponed. The mutiny was an ugly signal which they were quick to recognize. Everyone looked to Nehru as the man of the hour.

I was on my way back to Bombay from Bihar, where I had visited my elder brother. My younger brother had recently married my sister-in-law's cousin and the bride had been on a visit to them. She was now returning with me to Bombay where they both lived with us. We were in an airconditioned coach, which had a series of compartments connected by a corridor. At Allahabad there was more than the usual commotion of an Indian railway station. A crowd converged on our coach, and when the excitement died down I discovered that Nehru had boarded it. After the train started moving I walked up the corridor and found him sitting in a four seat compartment. I had never seen him before and felt an urge to talk to him. Back in my own compartment I wrote a short message on the back of a visiting card.

'Panditji,

'You don't know me, but I have a great desire to meet you. Unfortunately your compartment is full and I am wondering if you would consider it impertinent on my part to suggest that you might walk over to our compartment at the end of the coach. We would feel honoured.'

I rang for the attendant and asked him to take it to Panditji.

'Who?' asked the Goan attendant.

'Pandit Nehru.'

'Who is he?', he asked innocently.

'Haven't you heard of the great leader, Pandit Jawaharlal Nehru?'

'No. I know there is some big Indian, not a sahib though, travelling in the end compartment, because there were many people at Allahabad to see him off, but I don't know who he is.'

'Never mind, take this card and give it to him.'

Afterwards I felt foolish and regretted my impulse, but soon there was a knock on the door and Nehru put his head in and said simply, 'Did you send for me?'

I got up in great confusion and said, 'Well Sir, that is putting it very graciously; do come in.'

He came in and sat down, and talked in a shy, hesitating manner. He asked me about my family and my work. I reminded him of the somewhat caustic remarks of his book, *Unity of India,* about the luxurious airconditioned coaches, with the privileged few sitting in cool comfort behind blue glass windows. He blushed at this and said that he did not like travelling in such style, but the train was full and there was no accommodation anywhere else. He did not like airconditioning anyway.

'You see, I had a message only this morning from Sardar Vallabhai Patel asking me to go to Bombay immediately in connection with the naval mutiny, so I took the first train.'

After a short while he got up and said that he must go back and do some work; he was trying to finish a book. As he was leaving, my young sister-in-law asked him if he would sign her autograph book. I felt embarrassed and apologized, hoping that he did not think we had asked him to come over merely for this. He laughed and said, 'No I understand. Children are like this,' signed and went out.

Soon afterwards the press published correspondence between Jinnah and Gandhiji, who had invited Jinnah to meet him, suggesting that as Jinnah was travelling from Calcutta to Bombay, he might consider breaking journey at Wardha, which was on the way. Gandhiji added that he would normally have travelled to Bombay or Calcutta himself, but he was not keeping good health and would like to avoid the journey. Jinnah replied curtly that he would be pleased to see him, and his address was Mount Pleasant Road, Bombay. I thought of Nehru walking up to my compartment on the train.

Independence came sooner than we expected. Mountbatten, from the moment he landed, showed that he was in a hurry to give India freedom without any qualification about membership of the Commonwealth or a commercial or political treaty. If Indians could get together and work out a formula, they could have independence any time and on any terms, but the formula should be acceptable to all parties. The Muslim League flatly rejected joint independence and pressed for a separate state of Pakistan. Feelings ran high; there were riots in Bengal, then in Bihar, followed by West Punjab, and as the flames rose higher Mountbatten suggested dividing India into two independent states of India and Pakistan. Reluctantly Congress accepted it, and naturally Jinnah. One felt there was no alternative to the division.

After months of rioting, the news came as a relief. Mountbatten and the Indian leaders were going to speak on the radio, and on my way back from the office I stopped at a shop to listen. Mountbatten was crisp and clear. He would have preferred a united India, but there was no choice, and, the job done, there must not be any regrets; one had to look forward. Jinnah was never in any doubt about the outcome, the only just solution, and he was glad the others now saw the sense of what he had been advocating all along. Nehru, emotional, stirred to the depths, decided to look ahead.

As the fifteenth of August drew near, despite the rumblings in the Punjab, our spirits lightened. We Punjabis accepted partition fatalistically. After centuries of change, this was just another turn of the wheel of fate. For nearly a thousand years we had lived under Muslim rule and we would do it again, this time in the shadow of India, whose secular strength would ensure justice to us in the Muslim state. Thus reasoning, the members of our families left across the border looked to the birth of the new state neither with joyous anticipation nor with craven fear, but with sober realism tinged with sadness. We and they would in future belong to different nations, for there was no doubt that the Muslims, having won Pakistan, would make the new state a strong independent reality, as distinctive in personality as possible, in a conscious effort to break all visible links with India. I kept thinking of an Urdu poem we read in school about the long-necked birds, the koonj, that each winter fly high all the way from Siberia, seeking the sun of India. Once when the flock was flying eagerly towards home, a hunter took an idle shot and wounded one of them, and left it wounded where it fell. The bird bid its companions fly on and leave him, hoping one day to rejoin them, though he knew in his heart that there would be no reunion.

About the only cheerful day that year was the fifteenth of August. Bombay was happy and festive, as I had never seen it before. The new tricolour in saffron, white and green with the blue Ashoka wheel fluttered in millions, from every window, lamp post, tree, tram, bus and car. Everyone was out in the streets, gay, happy, confident. The price of freedom, those left behind in a foreign land, were forgotten for the day. There were meetings, long speeches, pledges and confident predictions by the political leaders, who promised Rama Rajya, accepted by the masses with thunderous cheers. Nehru stood above the main gate of the Red Fort of Delhi and spoke to a multitude stretching as far as the eye could see. The next day, Mountbatten drove from the Santa Cruz Airport into the city, the first and last Englishman to receive a hero's welcome in Bombay.

On the third day the monsoon that had long withdrawn returned in cool and nourishing torrents, and on the fourth day, as the colour ran out of the paper flags, all cheer vanished as news from the Punjab began to pour in. First in West Bengal, then in East Punjab, next in Rajasthan, then in the U.P., an upheaval began that uprooted nearly fifteen million people. In a few weeks took place the largest migration history has ever known. How many of those who left their old homes never reached the new will never be known. Who was there to count the dead? Not the law for there was none left; nor the relations, for they were fleeing. Like a string of Divali crackers, where one bursts after the other, this fire raged on till it enveloped the whole North, from Peshawar to Dacca.

There was no end. As the religious frenzy slackened, war broke out in Kashmir, where even before the two armies had sorted themselves out of the one force they were engaged in fratricidal combat. But as the snow on the mountains paralysed the two armies, and the people in the plains wearied of hatred and slaughter, a man walked up, bowed with joined hands and extinguished the life from lips that barely had the time to call on God. Even hate recoiled at what it had done and averted its face. Peace descended.

A month or so earlier a man had sent his card in to my office. He was the editor of a newspaper in Poona. I supposed he had come to persuade me to advertise Dalda in his paper, but he seemed too proud to sell. He said he ran this paper to advocate a cause and not for a living and the cause was a Hindu India. He asked me if I was a Punjabi or a U.P. Tandon, and when I told him where I came from be became very eloquent. He talked at length and with feeling about the injustice to the Punjabis, for whom, along with the Marathas, he had great respect. They were the fighters of India, who had taken the shock of every invasion and were the last to be overcome by the British. Right through history the Punjabis had kept their entity, faith and customs, but to-day for the first time they lay broken. The land that had been theirs since the dawn of history, the flat fertile soil between the rivers, was no longer theirs, and no one, except some abducted women, remained behind.

Words poured from him like a torrent. He was a small man, muscular and trim, with short cropped hair and intense dark eyes that shone with sad anger.

'It is strange,' I said to him, 'that I as a Punjabi should feel less strongly, and less express my feelings, than you from so far away.'

'Yes, I do feel very strongly.' And he walked out.

On the evening of the thirtieth January, as I walked up the sweep of steps to our veranda, Gärd told me she had just heard on the radio that Gandhiji has been assassinated. My immediate reaction was a silent prayer that it may not be a Muslim. When the name was announced of a Brahmin from Poona, I remembered it. It was the newspaper editor who had been to see me.

Two months before Partition, we three brothers had managed with some difficulty to persuade our father to leave Lahore where he had lived alone since our mother's death. Each of us and our families used to visit him and keep him company in turn, and he was loath to leave his home. But when his close friend, a Pathan neighbour, told him with tears in his eyes that it was safe no longer, even for a lone old man like him, he moved across, and with him our last link with the Punjab broke. Seventeen years later I visited Lahore for three days, but alive though it was, it was dead to me. In its reincarnation I did not recognize it.

I tried to forget by sorting out the debris left by this overwhelming tide. There were salesmen and staff, the Dalda wholesalers and their men, all of whom had moved to this side. Daily I received pathetic letters from their friends and relations, wondering if I knew what had happened to them. I spread the word as well as I could that on crossing over they should contact us, and we would do all we could to help; they should rest assured that they would be provided with jobs as soon as they had recovered enough. I made the same offer to our Muslim wholesalers who had moved or were hesitating. I would help with the exchange of their business, the premises, their houses and furniture, and even their Dalda delivery trucks, the horse carts and hand carts. In the end it worked out well, and each man and his family was as comfortably settled as times permitted.

One day, dictating the answer to an anxious letter from the parents of a young salesman who was by now overdue, I told my faithful secretary Ramachari to vary the end of the letter to express a fervent hope that the boy was now safe and well. Something in the hunch of his shoulders as he left my room made me call him back to read the last sentence again. 'Sir, the last sentence read, I fervently hope the boy is now safe in hell!'

I had not realized the bond we had built with our Dalda wholesalers till a tragi-comic incident occurred. Our wholesaler in Sialkot wrote to me that all was going up in flames and they must leave. He had sent his family to this side for safety, but a letter had just arrived that a Dalda consignment was on its way. He would remain behind to honour the documents, pay in the needed amount into the bank, and then leave, but would I in the meantime try to stop the railway wagon with the Dalda at Amritsar before it crossed the border. He was anxious for the documents not to be dishonoured, and equally that a good twenty tons of Dalda should not reach the other side. I managed to stop the wagon at Amritsar, where the wholesaler reached a few days later. Contrary to all practice, I told him that he could receive delivery and sell the Dalda in Amritsar itself, which was not his territory, in any way he liked. I heard subsequently that, homeless and penniless, he had sold the Dalda tin by tin in the bazaar at Amritsar at whatever price he could get and begun life again with several thousand rupees in hand. Years later when I met him at Meerut, where we had settled him, he embraced me in the Punjabi fashion of greeting a long lost friend, with his arms around my shoulders, and said:

'That was the only time we both disobeyed the "system." I literally auctioned every tin while telling the people openly what had happened, and, as there had been no Dalda in Amritsar for weeks, they cheerfully paid me whatever I wanted. They really gave me a new start in life. And,' he added softly so that the others did not hear, 'I took your name with each tin.'

My English colleagues in charge of the other marketing divisions, maybe partly because British sympathy at this time seemed to lie more with the other side, thought I was going to unnecessary lengths.

☆

The Company was fast taking new shape, and the effects of Independence were soon to be felt. I had already been asked to take on additional responsibility, and an Englishman had been put under me, the first in the Company to work under an Indian. The Chief followed up with an invitation to dinner at his home, and this set me a problem. I thanked him and said I would let him know. The next day I conveyed our regret on account of a previous engagement. A month or so later he invited us again. This time I thought it over for some days and eventually wrote him a short note explaining that, while I deeply thanked him for his invitation, I must be honest enough to say that we could not accept it—I hoped he would understand. He never referred to the matter or showed any reaction; he discreetly ignored it.

All kinds of testing situations arose. Another English colleague had invited a visiting Indian scientist to lunch and asked me to join them, but forgot to tell me where the lunch was. I waited in my room, and at about a half past one he rang up wondering what had happened.

'Aren't you coming to lunch?'

'I have been waiting here because you never told me where.'

'I am sorry, it is at the Yacht Club.'

I froze at this. Recently the Club had relaxed its rules and Indians could now enter as guests, but this I could not bring myself to do. He guessed the reason for my hesitation and added.

'It is now open to Indians, so be quick and join us here.'

'I am sorry, most sorry, but I cannot come.'

'You mean you don't want to come.'

'Yes.'

He rang off, and never referred to it again. I felt doubly upset at this irony, upset because in the past there had been places in India that were closed to me only because I belonged to India; and perhaps more upset that they were now open; upset that the Chief should for years not have felt that he ought to invite me either to his business lunches or to his home, and when he did I should feel that I must say 'no'.

As I was the senior Indian in the firm, overtures came from all directions. Would I consider joining the Gymkhana Club? Would I join the European Hospital Benefit Scheme? This was a scheme started by the European residents of Bombay since Government's St. George's Hospital had lost its European semi-exclusiveness after Independence. Pettit explained the scheme to me, saying that it was common for expatriate communities to start their own hospitals to provide the standard of medical services to which they were accustomed at home, and to satisfy their desire to be tended in an illness by a compatriot doctor. On the other hand, they did not want to make their hospital exclusive, though naturally it could not cope with accepting all and any Indians. They would therefore like to evolve a scheme under which the European firms would become subscribing members and receive a special rate for their European and Indian managers and their families. It would of course be open to other Indians of suitable kind. The firms that became founding members would each have a representative on the Board of Trustees, who had to be of European birth. He was anxious to invite Indian managers in the Company to join the scheme subsidized by the Company. So far, those of us who so chose had in the past carried our own medical insurance, but he now proposed to start a medical benefit scheme within the firm.

I reacted with what was now becoming my expected style: a 'no'. I agreed that since St. George's was opened to the public it was necessary to start a new hospital for the European community with standards that the private and Government hospitals of Bombay did not have or could not afford. I also appreciated the desire to be treated by one's own; in fact in England I had usually myself turned to an Indian doctor. Medical care in Bombay was no doubt expensive and any assistance the Company could offer would be welcome. But while I approved of the idea of providing the Europeans in the Company with their own hospital, I could not see the relevance of sharing this facility even with select Indians. I would personally prefer to choose where to go, and even use their hospital if my doctor so suggested, but would not accept a medical scheme that tied one down and left no choice. In fact I wondered why they needed to ask any Indians to join the scheme. A European medical welfare plan, to be run by Europeans for Europeans, was quite justified, like their right to have a school for their children, or their own recreation ground. Generous though the offer was, I was sorry I could not accept it.

In the other case I was not sounded directly. There was now someone else in the firm who was more amenable. Though the Yacht Club only admitted Indians as guests, the Bombay Gymkhana had opened its doors for membership to some Indians working in European firms, because with their own numbers diminishing they needed support and they probably also wanted some mild Indianization. It was suggested that our managers might be given the facility of joining a club, preferably one offering sports facilities, like the Bombay Gymkhana. I kept away. I still remembered how a friend of mine who was invited to play in a tennis tournament at the Gymkhana had found his clothes removed from the dressing room on the Secretary's orders. Even as a guest player he could not use the Club's amenities.

I felt I was becoming negative and was far from happy. Although I searched deeply into my motives, I found there was no rancour or desire to get even; but that there was hurt involved was as clear to me as to them. Any attempts I had made years ago at socially integrating myself were long forgotten by either side, and the balance we had reached over the years was now being upset with indelicate haste. Things could have been left to slide into a new harmony; there was no need to Indianize social relations so hastily.

Independence had certainly changed overnight the equation that had been progressively moving in the same direction for a hundred years; in fact, from its inception it had carried within it the momentum of change. The tempo had varied; some times it dawdled and at others it rushed, but always inexorably forward. There were always the same things said by each generation: it is going too fast, 'they' are not ready for this yet; while we said, it is not fast enough; but all the same the movement continued in the direction envisaged by Macaulay. When Gandhiji appeared on the scene he disclaimed the idea of change in measured doses, to which the liberals of the early Congress had agreed; he asked for change, complete and without commitments; without preparation. If you wait to prepare to hand over, there will always be good enough reasons never to hand over.

But that was change in terms of political and power relationship; interestingly, no one referred to social relationships; the sensitive ones did not ask for it. Why then this sudden desire for throwing social bridges—where was the need? The Europeans in business had inherited from the British in the services a pattern of relationships that was aloof and self-contained; in fact they had followed it even more meticulously; possibly because Indianization had begun the last in business. A balance had been reached that I saw no immediate need to upset. The administration had gone; did the removal of support imply to European business a vulnerability and need for protection through cultivation of social relationship? Did this sudden discovery of the need for social contacts imply a fear, a mistrust? Was the onus put upon us to respond and to reassure? I believed this was so, and in my negativeness I was evading this onus.

There was a senior director in the firm of great character and lovableness, which stemmed from an indeterminate past that stretched from Poland and Germany to Holland, Britain and India. From Poland he had as a child moved to Germany; as a youth he had worked for a Dutch family of margarine manufacturers, and he had come to India in the early twenties to represent them. Vanaspati, vegetable ghee, had then begun to be imported from Holland and Belgium, and it was he who first organized the sales all over India. He travelled extensively, building the network of distribution that I had inherited. He had never really belonged anywhere, and each of the many languages he spoke had the accent of another, but he was essentially Jewish, with the deep sense of humanity that only someone like him could possess, who had been uprooted so often and never known a permanent home. Before and during the war he had helped an endless number of refugees from Europe; some he had helped settle in

India; others after a time went away to England, Australia, Canada or the United States. He was simple and humble, and looked at you with deepset eyes that reflected a history of suffering.

He sometimes took me home to lunch, and maybe aware of my possible future, he would drop in at my office and talk discursively about the past of the business, how he had set it up and the problems he had faced. In me he sensed an understanding and love of the past, and he talked to me about his own life and work like a kind of folklore. From him I acquired a feel about the vanaspati business. Where Pettit gave me the order and system of a modern business, and Duncan its marketing flair, Leser taught me the core of humanity that a business ought to have, making each one a person to it. In my youthfulness I often defied him and wished to deal with someone harshly when I thought this was just. He would walk into my room with a knowing smile on his face, and begin by saying. 'I have heard about it; I know how right you are, but...' I often gave in. He never made me feel in the wrong, only made me understand that where there was justice there could be compassion too; my own upbringing, my father's austereness, had contained little compassion, only justice.

Leser had watched my growing restlessness in the new circumstances, but had wisely refrained from discussing it. I now felt the need to talk to him and he put me at ease; he said he had been waiting, hoping I would come and talk. I did not have to say much. As I began to explain my feelings I looked out at the harbour, and watched the ships that now flew the new tricolour from their masts; it was strange to see this rebel of not so long ago fluttering alongside some of the oldest flags of the world: Swedish, Dutch and British. I looked at Leser, to whom no flag meant more than its nationality.

'What should I do?'

'Forget the past.'

'But I am not trying to remember it. I am doing nothing about it.'

'No, but you are holding it against the future. And that distorts the present.'

'What should I do?'

'Just what you are doing now. Bring your hurts into the open; they will heal. If you keep them hidden in the dark they will remain tender and suppurate.'

'But why can't I be left alone; I am not letting anything interfere with my work; I am friendly, courteous; I don't demand any new privileges; I don't want any updated equality; I am content with the gulf as it has existed in the past; in fact, I want it to continue as it is, I don't want any bridges. Mr. Leser,' I said with my voice slightly raised, 'all I ask for is to be left alone.'

Leser looked at me and said patiently: 'You cannot be left alone. How can you be left alone? You may be called upon to run this business one day, and it will be a much bigger business than it is today, and part of a world mainstream. It will be far more complex, and many of its complexities will be the makings of your own people. So you can't escape the future, though you must escape the past.'

He got up to go and put his hand over my head as if to bless, and walked away with infinite sadness in his form, saying very softly, as if to himself 'What have we not gone through and what have we ever held against anyone; and there is no end in sight yet—perhaps there never will be.'

I walked into Chief's room that afternoon and asked him if he and his wife would come to our new house to dine with us. We had just completed the house and they along with the Lesers would be our first guests, which would be most fitting.

☆

Things went well for a while. There was a lot to do in those early years of Independence when there was optimism abroad and a will on all sides to achieve. It was a period of new adjustments in the business, in industry, in the country and in the world. Roger Heyworth, it appeared, had carried his sensitive understanding back to London, for a new pattern seemed to be emerging. Its special feature was the appointment of an Englishman of a type unusual for India. His appearance and name alone distinguished him from the rest. He was tall, lean, with an ascetic look and gentle, almost clerical manner. He spoke to everyone with grace and diffident dignity, and treated even the sepoy outside his room with a self-effacing courtesy. A.J.C. Hoskyns-Abrahall, in both name and manners, left people puzzled, but I soon sensed the purpose behind his appointment. His total oppositeness to any Englishman we had ever had in the Company seemed justification in itself in the new context of things. He not only had no commitments to the past but a marked unconcern with it; nor did he display any particular interest in the country and his environment. His aloofness interested me as perhaps part of the new pattern of the uncommitted executive type coming to India for a few years to do a specific job of work, and then return to his career and life at home, unless he was wanted elsewhere for another job. His ability marked this assignment as an interlude and a step in the progress of his career, so different from those in exile in the past, sent to serve a lifetime in a foreign country, where most of them could only run down in the skills they once brought, and eventually fall back on a form of proprietary rights, waiting for an early retirement.

Watching Abrahall I wondered whether the thesis that the growing speed of communications between India and England hastened the end of the British Empire did not acquire a revised truth. The soldiers and clerks of the East India Company had had to be tempted to settle in this country, marry and learn the language, to make their exile bearable, but when ships became faster and did the journey of months in days, the expatriates began to regard themselves as belonging in England—not in Anglo-India—visiting India on short assignments, doing jobs that Indians were being trained to do and acting as leavening as long as the connection was to continue. Abrahall seemed to me an example of yet a new thinking, part of a process that was to become known in Unilever as 'isation'. The true significance of this process came to me many years later when I taught International management at an American University. Whether he himself realized it or not, Abrahall was the first catalyst of the new kind, a role he filled with an attractive weariness, for whatever its historical importance the whole process appeared boring to him—yet, or perhaps because of this, he seemed the man most fitted to play the role. As a true catalyst he did not himself seem involved in the process. Having been torn away from England, after spending the war years in Canada, he could not have cared whether he was made a part of the process in India, Malaya or the Philippines, and this very unconcern made him in my eyes the most suitable as a catalyst. His modest but unmistakably able ways conveyed to me a sense of the new order, a new kind of assurance.

I do not know in what terms I was stated to him as a problem, but he seemed fully conscious of it and made no attempt to hide it. His attitude was healthy and seemed to convey that while he would be glad to provide me with a new kind of background, he would have to leave the rest to my good sense; and if he was not going to rush me or upset me in the process, he was not going to particularly upset himself in the process either. All this I sensed and was at the same time deeply impressed with the simple sincerity behind it. I began to respond, and occasionally even gave him a glimpse of my problems as I saw them. He sensitively refrained from taking any more interest than I permitted him and seemed content to let me handle things my way, well or badly. We were indeed soon to run into a problem where he left me to test my own feelings.

As part of the new form of training Unilever sent us two young Englishmen. One of them, John Defrates, had done his spell of national service in the Navy, then read literature at Oxford and brought to business a very sensitive but cynical mind which in no time created a poor impression upon his somewhat teutonic boss. Dubious from the start about young Defrates' business acumen, matters came to head when he found him quoting Shakespeare in an official letter to a merchant. Though the subject of the letter was the purchase of groundnut seed and oil, John's reference was amusingly relevant. What upset his boss was that John was neither bored at his work nor facetious or flippant, but perfectly natural in quoting what he thought was an apt reference at that point in the letter. The boss was clear that John would never make a good businessman, at least not a serious buyer of commodities. Pettit on the other hand felt a responsibility towards his charge, and while he agreed with John's boss he felt that he ought to be given another chance. He got the idea that it might be a good test for us both if he attached John to me. He would be my first expatriate trainee, and a problem at that. So he called me in and explained his feelings that though young and wayward John was able material that he would like to see developed, and he felt that I could do it. He knew that I would try it with an open mind because, if anything, I would be amused rather than appalled by John's informal approach to business. I said I would be glad, in fact, welcome the chance of taking over the rest of John's training.

I think John too was amused by this challenge to us both and displayed much keenness in dealing with it. He turned to his sales training in Dalda with an earnestness that I did little to disturb for fear of encouraging a 'relapse'. He travelled assiduously through the hottest months and the monsoons, sharing the life of the salesmen, scrupulously consuming all the sweets and coloured drinks that the Dalda wholesalers placed before him. They also took to this fresh-faced young English sahib because there had never been an English trainee before. Pettit was pleased with the change. And then the blow fell on poor John. He was dismissed and paid his fare back to London.

I had felt that I was fighting a losing battle, but the more I realized it and the harder I argued his case, the less chance John had of success. I later wondered whether, left to fight it himself, he might not have served his interest better.

John was very interested in the country and soon made many friends among the younger Indians, and informal by nature, he fell in with the Bombay film crowd where he met Maria, a beautiful girl from Goa. She worked in the films in supporting roles and could with equal ease play the vamp or a simple country girl singing and dancing to Goan folk tunes. Maria was quite the opposite of John—he was serious and scholarly, she was full of laughter and fun, with only a Goan convent school education. She was essentially simple and very affectionate, and this must have fascinated John's sophisticated mind. A few years earlier Maria had married an English pilot who flew Dakotas for an Indian airline, but they had not been married long before he crashed and was killed. Maria who had just had a baby was thrown back to work to support herself. John fell in love with her. Maria tried to discourage him but with doglike devotion he followed her everywhere. Gradually she thawed and eventually agreed to marry him.

John immediately went up to the Chief and told him of his intention to marry, and if this was not enough surprise, he added that the girl was Indian and worked in the films. It was pointed out to him that he was still under training and ought to wait till he was confirmed. This John considered irrelevant and said so, which did little to assuage feelings. He did not see what difference a few months' waiting would make. If the idea was to give him time to change his mind, it made him only more determined. He explained to me later that he thought he was being dissuaded not so much from marriage as from a marriage that was disapproved of. Had he sensed approval he might have waited, but now he saw no reason why he should wait at all. He went ahead and got married. The Chief never acted emotionally or hastily. He casually broached the subject with me once or twice, and my reaction was equally casual. If Defrates wanted to marry this was his business. One day I was called to a meeting to discuss the Defrates' affair. I was asked how I rated his performance and I said it was good.

'How would you regard him in comparison with his Indian colleagues?'

I thought the questions were leading up to Defrates' confirmation and said simply that while John was excellent and better than most Indians, there were nonetheless some whom I would rate higher.

'In that case is it right to confirm him?'

'Why not' I said astonished.

'You know it is our policy to Indianize, so that a European we employ must be equal to, if not better than the best among the Indians. It would otherwise not be fair to them, nor do we want less than the best Europeans if they have any justification to be here. You yourself, surely, would agree with that!' I did not.

'If we accept that, few Europeans in the Company would have the justification to remain in India.'

He asked me what I thought of the marriage, and I repeated my views that it did not concern me nor the Company. She was a nice enough girl, and I did not think John's marriage would make any difference to anyone.

'But do you think she will be acceptable to Indian society?'

'Yes.'

'Don't you think there may be a prejudice among his Indian colleagues against a girl who works in the films?'

'No, I don't think so; in fact they have a lot of Indian friends both in the company and outside.'

At this stage he rang up the amenable soundingboard. This was an Indian whom I had introduced to the firm, impressed by his apparent qualities till I discovered to my chagrin that he was utterly self-centred. Worse, to further his interests he had developed a complex style of feigned independence which somehow always let itself be persuaded the way the right wind blew. With Pettit he practised this with consummate skill. I never knew whether Pettit saw through it, but he certainly used it to his advantage.

While we waited the meeting broke up for a few minutes. Abrahall and I walked up to the toilet. He had kept out of the discussion and left the argument to me. He now said somewhat warily:

'I did not realize you felt so strongly on the subject.'

'Yes, I do. You are right, I do feel strongly about it. We have talked about injustice to Indians, and I would not like to see the first Englishman working under me treated unjustly.'

We went back to the meeting. The amenable soundingboard was asked the question how Defrates' marriage would affect his relations with his Indian colleagues.

'Well, Sir,' and I guessed the tactfully chosen words that were to follow, 'Mr. Defrates' marriage is naturally his personal affair but it would be understandable to think that his Indian colleagues are likely not to approve of this marriage. After all...' and he continued carefully to suggest the prejudices that I knew did not exist but were calculated to suit the situation.

'How would you compare him with his Indian colleagues?'

'I believe, Sir, that he is an able man but there are a number of Indians who are as able and abler. I would say that good though he is he is not among the best, though I must admit I have not had much contact with him at work.'

'I agree,' I interjected. 'I don't think you know anything about the quality of his work. I do and I think he is very good.'

The meeting was closed at this point. It was decided that we think it over, though there was the point about the problems the marriage might create for Defrates with his Indian colleagues!

I knew Defrates would go, and a few days later he went. He did not seem to mind very much and thought the whole episode unnecessary; at his age he could surely decide when to get married and to whom!

CHAPTER FOURTEEN

The New Raj

There came a crisis, my first in business, and a kind that the new life was not to lack later. Some rats had been fed in a research laboratory on a diet containing vanaspati but deficient in vitamin A. It was said that their third generation lost hair and went blind, and this was attributed to the vanaspati. A question was asked in Parliament, and the minister confirmed that the laboratory had found this to be the case. There was immediately an uproar and a demand to ban vanaspati and permit only the sale of liquid oil. Government averred that in some shape, as margarine or shortening, oils were hydrogenated all over the world, and nowhere had scientific opinion suggested banning hydrogenation as a health hazard. The Government instead referred the matter to a committee of scientists, who in turn sent the brief to a number of laboratories to conduct prolonged experiments on animals, children and adults to test the comparative nutritive value of ghee, vanaspati and groundnut oil in diets equal in all other respects. An anxious year and a half followed, in which the many who opposed vanaspati kept up the attack. Ban it now, they urged—why wait; at best it will never be proved the equal of ghee.

In all my years with vanaspati there were always problems, and I often wondered why. Here was a product, wholesome, economical and fulfilling a need; yet always under attack, in which the public that wanted it and the Government that should have provided it both joined. I sometimes wondered whether it did not suffer from the fundamental ambivalence of being wanted, and hated just because it was wanted in place of something else. If, perhaps, as in Europe with margarine and butter, there had been an open choice between ghee and vanaspati—ghee in abundant supply, cheap and of good quality—vanaspati would have been treated on its own merits, accepted or rejected. As it was it was the other way round; the ghee they wanted was scarce and bad, and the vanaspati they did not want was abundant and pure. The problem of vanaspati was therefore created by the very solution it provided. It was not the problem of a suspect food, for it had been pronounced wholesome by science all over the world, but a deeper problem of a society unable to face the hard choices before it, and settling for the soft options. Instead of ensuring good ghee, a formidable task since it was part of the yet more formidable problem of an inefficient agriculture, or accepting and encouraging vanaspati, since it at least provided a working alternative, the course suggested was the softer option of banning vanaspati on the ground that its absence in itself would solve all the problems of ghee. The vacuum of demand alone would provide the needed stimulus for ghee to become pure and abundant.

It was the soft option solution suggested by the protagonists of many causes. Ban the manufacture of mill cloth and the dying handloom industry will automatically revive, and so will the decaying rural economy. Let us go back to the legendary days of peace and plenty by just walking out of the present and setting our face against anything that symbolizes modernity; discard machines, industry, science, medicine, urbanization, and all the complexities that they characterize today, and revert to handicrafts, handloom, ayurveda, and the simple past. Another aspect of the soft options was the naive faith that legislation alone could solve a problem. The more intractable the problem, the more sweeping needed to be the legislation, the higher the penalties, and the stronger its enforcement. To smother the cause that needed to be tackled was evading the hard choice; that the problem remained was the fault of someone else.

Because the problems remained unsolved, compromises had to follow. Panditji, when pressed by the cow protectionists to ban vanaspati now, stood his ground and said that it was for the scientists to declare the results, and if they found vanaspati harmful he would not hesitate to ban it, but if they found it harmless no action would be called for. The scientists experimented for nearly two years and ultimately rediscovered what scientists had discovered elsewhere fifty years ago, that vanaspati was harmless; that it was as assimilable and digestible as ghee and the raw oil it was made from; that like its source, groundnut oil, it lacked vitamin A, but when the diet was reinforced with this vitamin the growth rate of children and animals was comparable with those fed on milk fat. The Indian scientists recommended however that vanaspati should be made to a melting point corresponding to body temperature, 37 degrees centigrade, so that it would have the maximum digestibility, and that it should have vitamins A and D added to it.

This verdict did not satisfy the opponents, and innuendoes were made about vested interests influencing the scientists, and the interests of the cow, dairying, agriculture, and the whole rural economy of India sacrificed to keep this nefarious product going. The attack came with renewed fury, this time on a moral plane supported by religious arguments; and now support came from a new quarter.

Gandhiji had once written an article in his weekly, *Harijan,* saying that some friends had drawn his attention to the harm vanaspati did to dairying and the cow, that it was an imitation product at best, and made no contribution in the process of converting oil. He thought there was a point in it and left it at that, a thought to be examined objectively and fairly. But the inheritors of his tradition saw it in emotion alone. To them no examination, no proof was necessary; vanaspati should just be banned, for they were convinced that this was the key to the whole rural problem of India. They fervently believed that unless vanaspati went no start could ever be made to solve it. The decks had to be cleared of the excrescences of industrialization; in the place of the loom, the charkha; for the modern oil press, the kolhu; for alcohol, nira; for vanaspati, pure ghee.

Mashruwala, one of Gandhiji's closest followers, had remained at Wardha, Gandhiji's last ashram, and continued to run the *Harijan* after the teacher's assassination. He picked up the controversy and gave it a new angle. Gandhiji had believed in always distinguishing between truth and falsehood, non-violence and violence, reality and imitation. Mashruwala concluded that vanaspati not only did harm to the cow, but was a spurious coin that drove out the good currency, ghee, and in imitating ghee it contained a falsehood. It must therefore be banned.

Coming from Wardha, in Gandhiji's own paper that had for years been his means of thinking aloud and conducting a dialogue with the world, this pronouncement on vanaspati was *ex cathedra.* Government felt embarrassed at the charges levelled at them of trying to please the industrialists at the expense of the poor millions. Their embarrassment was indeed acute because not so long ago Panditji had assured Parliament that this was a matter for the scientists to decide. Having got their verdict he was now being pressed to ignore it and take a contradictory stand. Government eventually gave in and decided to refer the whole issue to Public Opinion.

This was the first time such action had ever been taken, nor has it ever been done again. Parliament referred the issue, to ban or not to ban vanaspati, to all the States' governments, leading municipalities, chambers of commerce, institutions of national and local importance, political and religious associations, and to members of the public at large, to express their opinion. It was an extraordinary spectacle. Anyone could express an opinion and send it to the Parliament

Secretariat, with or without giving any reasons in support. The Cow Protection Society—Go Seva Sangh—exhorted people to save Go-Mata, the Mother Cow, and called upon the country to raise its voice against vanaspati.

Never before had a product, a plain cooking fat at that, acquired the prominence of a widely debated national issue. There had been doubts in other countries about the effect of margarine upon butter, and where an agricultural lobby was strong, as in U.S.A. and Australia, some restrictive legislation had been passed; but these were countries with abudance of butter and an affluence that could afford it. But here was a case of emotions stirred in a society that was short of everything and could ill afford to spurn even an ersatz product.

As Pettit was the chairman of the Vanaspati Manufacturers' Association and had to lead the defence of the industry, I was drawn in, and I threw myself in with unusual zeal. My duty apart, I felt I was fighting a modern cause against the old and outdated. It was a crusade against the fantasies of those who wanted to merge in the timelessness of India and resurrect a past which could never be made to live again. They talked from the highest level about traditions, heritage, glory, the kingdom that was Rama's, the Vedic Age of milk and honey: all this would return if only we pressed the button of bans—ban vanaspati, ban sugar, ban longcloth, ban tea, ban alcohol and restore the pristine and viceless past. I felt moved too by the ease with which we slid into a compromise. Our scientists knew all about the work done abroad, but they were told to satisfy themselves. Despite the pledge to abide by their findings, the matter was now turned over to the most amorphous of all judgements, public opinion, for how could it be gauged or quantified on a national scale, short of a referendum? And so a most confused public arguments began.

The Cow Protection Society, with the tacit support of the party in power, began its campaign in right earnest and held an Anti-Vanaspati Day with meetings all over the country protesting against hydrogenation and demanding the ban. Whatever an average individual's previous views, the moment vanaspati was termed the enemy of the cow it became anathema. It was no use arguing that ghee was ghee, it came from the cow, but as there was not enough of it why should vanaspati be blamed for trying to look like ghee, if people wanted it. Nevertheless, fight we must and we did against such archaic sentiments.

I travelled everywhere organizing our salesmen to approach the trade and their associations, prominent citizens, especially doctors and university teachers, and canvass members of the public for signatures; but no matter what we did, each editorial in the *Harijan* undid things. Danger to the cow, when spelled out by Wardha, made the case for vanaspati quite hopeless. A thought came to me in the last resort. I suggested to Pettit that I would like to go to Wardha and meet Mashruwala himself for a heart to heart talk. He was taken aback by this suggestion, and characteristically wanted to examine it appreciatively but critically.

'What do you hope to achieve?' he asked.

'Well, Sir, I realize the strength of his convictions and the depth of his emotions. Let me analyse them. His opposition to vanaspati is an article of a whole faith whose fabric cannot lightly be tampered with, nor can he let go a single strand. He believes in a return to the village as the focus of economic and social growth; to him the towns are unnecessary and evil excrescences. The villager cannot be left in splendid isolation and it is the responsibility of Government to help him, but in the process he must be saved from the contagion of modern economic and industrial beliefs, large scale production, mechanization and corporate effort. His old tools may be improved in a limited way, like the old charkha has been changed to the amber charkha, and his old hand and bullock press to the more efficient kolhu. He should also be given certain simple amenities: his village should be cleaned, his roof repaired, roads built, a new school, a dispensary, but preferably of the old ayurvedic system of medicine, a drinking water well; but no attempts should be made to introduce either machines or the products of machines into his village. I cannot ever hope to change such basic thinking, but I want to try and isolate vanaspati from at least its most rigorous aspects.

'I also realize the risk, the big risk, of my very logical and rational arguments rebounding off his mind and in the process starting something new and far worse. He may conclude that the industrialists are now trying to influence him in the way they had worked on the Government. In fact, he can draw conclusions worse than that and may feel spurred in his crusade to make it an even larger public issue than it is at present.'

Pettit looked at me seriously, but it was like him not to turn down a proposition that showed a promise, however fraught with risk it appeared. Coming from me, in this particular instance, he was intrigued too.

'Do you realize the zeal of the man, the strength of his conviction, the deep honesty behind them, and what your approach may mean to him? It is not just a case of nothing lost if you fail but, as you say, giving an altogether new twist to the controversy. If he is unconvinced and, what is worse, misunderstands your motives, it could blow up into something serious. He is a most honest man, and I deeply respect his motives, but this makes him as an opponent the more serious.'

'Yes, I realise all that, but there is still the chance that I may persuade him that he may do no more than agree to differ and leave it at that, and that alone may bring the controversy to a rational level.'

'Good luck', said Pettit, 'Go and see him.'

I wrote to Mashruwala the next day and asked for an appointment for the following week. He wrote back cordially inviting me. It was the month of heavy rains, and as the old Dakota tossed about in the upper monsoon layer, I sat looking out of the window into the turmoil of clouds. Down below, through occasional openings, I could see the wet green Western Ghats, their deep canyons full of swirling streams. The green was such as I had never seen anywhere; at places I could count eleven shades of it, the greens of the grass, the rice fields at different stages of growth. There were really only two colours, the brown of the water and the green of the growth, but within them the subtle variations turned into a riot of colour. But in all this turbulence there was a soothing restfulness.

In pouring rain I took a taxi from Nagpur to Wardha, some thirty miles away, and as usual on such occasions my mind went into a restful blank in which my thoughts about the meeting moved about like wisps of fog. I arrived in Wardha ahead of time to look around the ashram. In the monsoon green, its neat cottages looked beautiful, with their small gardens well tended. The inmates of the ashram moved about quietly and there was an air of restraint and tasteful calm. Gandhiji's own small cottage was as he had left it, in utterly simple taste. The whole place had the air of an idyll.

At one end of the ashram was a village which I decided to look at. The contrast was striking. Here, after many years of contiguity and close contact, the village lived as it had a thousand years ago. The poverty was understandable, but not the squalor and neglect which a little self-help could have corrected. The roads were dirty with sewage running through their middle, the homes were uncared for, the roofs unrepaired, the garbage unremoved, and there were no fruit or flowering trees; it was like any other village.

For nearly two decades the mainspring of India's rural emancipation and reconstruction had flowed past this village, whose men and women daily visited and worked in the ashram; yet the impact cannot have been much or it had already worn away. The two communities had lived side by side, one deifying the other, preaching its future glory and rightful place; the other seemed to have looked on apathetically. I wondered whether this was significant of the sheer magnitude of the villager's problem or only proved how theoretical was the interest of the ashramite. It could be that the planners had found the resistance to change insuperable; maybe with the passing of Gandhiji, when the villagers no more found themselves in focus, they just lost interest in the effort.

I arrived at Mashruwala's house and was met by a small, thin, gracious man. He thanked me for coming all the way to meet him, and I thanked him for receiving me. I explained that I was not an industrialist or capitalist, just a working manager with a point of view on industrial growth. He sat down on the floor and began to spin. I sat next to him, although he had offered me a chair.

'Mashruwalaji, what have you against vanaspati?' I began by asking.

'Everything', he answered. 'You begin with raw groundnut oil that people have eaten for centuries, but go and refine it, hydrogenate it, take the colour and taste out of it, and then add the colour and taste of ghee. Why don't you leave the oil alone and let people eat it the way they have always done.'

'I would agree with you,' I said, 'If there was any compulsion attached to it. But people still have the choice; they can still buy the groundnut oil, and most do; they don't have to buy vanaspati. There are lakhs of housewives who buy some raw oil, some vanaspati, and some ghee, each for a different purpose, and in exercise of free choice. Each product has its own use, the ghee for flavour, the vanaspati for general cooking and oil for frying. Given ghee at the price of vanaspati they would naturally not buy the latter, but that is out of the question. Why then do you object to this choice before the housewife?'

'Our objections are many. First, and to me very important, vanaspati is the product of machines and I object to machines. Oil and ghee are simple products of nature, processed by hand with the aid of the simplest tools that a villager can make, the press and the churn. They are part of the villager's self-contained life. I do not see the need for taking the oil away to a factory in a town, processing it and bringing it back costlier than it left.'

'Do you know, Sir, I am watching the charkha on which you are spinning and I am reminded of the contraption my mother used to spin on. It weighed over twenty pounds and was a cumbersome thing; it took a lot of effort and produced a meagre amount of yarn. Yours is light, efficient and almost a machine in comparison; in fact, it is a product of modern mechanical thinking. But supposing someone said to you that he could attach a small motor to it so that it could spin twice as fast and produce twice the yarn. When my mother's health began to fail at a young age and she could no more spin enough yarn to clothe us and make sheets and towels for the house, would you then have objected to a charkha that went as much faster than yours as does yours from hers?'

Mashruwala looked thoughtful and I could sense his mind balking at the question.

'No, I don't think I could object, so long as the machine is designed to provide occupation to an individual and improves his productivity.'

'Then I think you have conceded industrialization, because this is exactly how the process began. Iron tyres round wooden wheels, a steel shaft and greased hubs, and one day a small engine in the chassis. From your own loom to the village weaver, to a loom and weaving shed with several men employed in it, to steam and power and the automatic loom. I cannot see how and at what stage you can either stop or reverse the process.'

'Does that mean that industrialization is inevitable and that we have to go through all its evils?'

'Inevitable it is, if you want to live as part of the world society. To print your *Harijan* you need machines, and you need machines to carry it to all parts of India. It is not inevitable though to bring the evils of industrialization with it; we know enough to avoid them; but is the poverty and squalor of the cities really so much worse than that of the village next door? Is it primarily the creation of machines any more than in the villages it is the creation of their handicrafts? No, I think squalor in India has something to do with history and geography. It begins at its worst in the north and changes as we go further south. Villages can be poor but clean, just as I have seen industry in Scandinavia free from its ugliness in Britain.'

We discussed industrialization for a while, and his fears were naive. Like his master he wanted time not to move beyond a point in the past and the problem became serious because many who shared the belief now had the responsibility of running a Government with their minds split. The half-clad needed cloth that only the mills could produce in plenty and cheap, but the expansion of mills had to be banned to encourage the amber charkha which could not possibly cope with the demands of such a multitude. Similarly they wanted to ban the efficient extraction of oil from the seed in favour of the wasteful village presses.

'Sir,' I began again, 'if vanaspati and oil are available side by side, and people have the choice, why should you object to some preferring vanaspati, especially as it serves in place of ghee that they cannot afford?'

'Because vanaspati is a deception and a delusion. The woman who buys it is in fact only buying oil which is made to look like ghee, and she is deluding herself. If she cannot afford ghee, let her accept the truth and buy oil, not deceive herself by buying something spurious.'

'But she knows what she is buying. She knows vanaspati is oil, and not ghee.'

'I would still feel it my duty to prevent her from committing this untruth. T- imsa, untruth is violence.'

priving her of a satisfaction?'

ecause it is being falsely fulfilled.'

is stage Mashruwala's wife entered the room with two cups of milk and after serving them quietly withdrew.

'I noticed that your wife wears gold bangles, presumably because they give her some satisfaction.'

He flushed and interrupted me, 'Well, I would rather she didn't. I don't believe in gold and ornaments, but you know what women are.'

'Yes, and I agree with you, though I think she has the right to the satisfaction of wearing jewellery. But supposing her maidservant wanted the same satisfaction but could not afford gold and therefore took brass bangles to the goldsmith and asked him to gild them. Would you object?'

'Yes, I would. I think she should wear brass if brass is all she can afford, and not make brass look like gold. It is self-deception.'

'I think now you are being unreasonable. She knows full well it is brass, and yet you would legislate that no one should be allowed to make brass look like gold, even when it does not deceive anyone and is honestly sold as gilt brass. I think it is you who are being "violent" in imposing your opinion on others. And I think this is just what you are doing with vanaspati. You may like oil, but there are many who don't like the taste of it and therefore prefer vanaspati. For you to ban vanaspati would only deprive them of a choice and force them to use the oil they don't like.'

I continued, 'You are right to demand that the adulteration of ghee should be stopped, with vanaspati or anything else, as much as passing off gilt for gold, but to ban vanaspati is like banning brass itself. Even to insist that vanaspati should not look like ghee, that it should not be given the flavour and colour to make it resemble ghee, to me would be wholly unjustified, but we may have to accept it because rather than accept the ban on vanaspati we would accept a ban on colouring and flavouring it.'

Mashruwala looked nettled by my argument and somewhat taken aback at the accusation of being violent. I was feeling frustrated by his unction and the implied sanction in an attitude that decided what people should eat, wear, adorn themselves with, and was ready, if they persisted in disagreeing, to ban the means of indulging their taste. He would prohibit or restrict liquor, coffee, tea, vanaspati, sugar, textile industries, horse racing, cinema, import of books, export of monkeys, fertilizers, vivisection, vaccination, all modern medicine: the list ran on interminably.

And yet when I looked at him, frail of frame and weighing barely seventy pounds, racked by asthma, there was in him a light of conviction, and a courage cast in the mould of his frail master, who had stood up to the mightiest opponent anyone in the world had ever known.

On the way back in the taxi, through the wet night, a sadness came over me. The task done, the freedom won, masters of our own fate, were our energies now going to be bent to build with tools of yesterday, to preoccupation with the means and unconcern with the end? For years now the controversy was running its arid course about how to revive a dying past and the glory of a mythological Vedic age, while the real problems of the cow, milk and ghee, the village and its agriculture, were barely tackled, in the vague hope that once industry was banned a large enough market would be opened up to revive the countryside and set right its problems.

'Vanaspati may be good or bad for health, but none can deny that it is a corruption of morals. Along with textiles, sugar and other industries it has created vicious economies by making the utilization of food crops and maintenance of milk cattle less profitable than the cultivation of cotton, groundnut, sugarcane, tobacco etc., and thus bringing about deficiencies. The fundamental issue is moral.' (The *Harijan)*.

'The cow-centred civilization of India' was what they wanted to revive,

The public opinion poll proved inconclusive, though we managed to get a greater weight than the opponents of vanaspati. But the whole thing was meaningless. The bill was ultimately withdrawn upon the promise of the Prime Minister that a committee would be appointed to suggest suitable methods to stop the adulteration of ghee. The *Harijan* wrote:

'Nehru gave three assurances: that ghee was much adulterated, that Government were anxious to put a stop to it, and that experiments carried out on hydrogenated oils had shown that they were not harmful. He turned down the demand to ban the production of vanaspati because Government were quite clear and convinced of the fact that the use of vanaspati was not harmful to health. By repeated scientific tests and research it had been found that nobody suffered from it, although vanaspati and its like was used by 75% of the people the world over. He continued that Government would instead control the production of vanaspati so that it contained vitamins A and D, sesame oil to make adulteration of ghee easily detectable by a commercial test; and take the colour and flavour of ghee out of it.'

Mashruwala was angry and said that 'such arguments convince none, deceive none. They indicate that both the scientist and the statesman act in collusion with the industrialist and simply create an estrangement between Government and the people.'

On 9th September 1956, three months after the bill was withdrawn, Mashruwala died. An article which appeared posthumously summed up his simple and sincere mind. In reply to a question someone had asked about the so-called soya or groundnut milk, he had replied:

'If the preparation of soya or groundnut milk becomes an industry; if they are manufactured and canned in factories and sold in markets, it will surely be as harmful as vanaspati. But if people prepare and consume them at home, it stands on a different level. Just as there is no competition between groundnut oil and ghee, similarly there, need not be any between payas (soya or groundnut milk) and milk.'

For some curious reason he wandered away in a rather different vein about milk.

'It is difficult to determine the precise effect of milk on sex-impulse. All that we can say is that milk and ghee are animal products; also that those engaged in cattle breeding and dairy industry frequently come under the disturbing influence of sex acts of animals at an impressionable age. This cannot be helped. Even otherwise they are not immune from such impressions, because they are frequently around in nature. Efforts have to be made to maintain purity of mind in spite of such influences.'

'One cannot say definitely that those who take vegetable diet exclusively, even abjuring milk and its products, are immune from passion. Sex is a very subtle impulse and to a certain extent assisted with age, and what we consume through our eyes, ears and skin touches also. Diet regulation and discipline in self-control are helpful in overcoming passion. As a Hindi poet has said, "A sadhu living in a forest cave wearing bark of trees, living on fallen fruit and leaves, and sleeping on bare ground may be harassed by sex passion." But diet is a helpful factor and may not be ignored.'

CHAPTER FIFTEEN

Unilever Accept Change

Geoffrey Heyworth was an even more remarkable man than his brother Roger. Unilever had steadily grown from a national to a European business, and its overseas units changed it into an international business, but it was under the fourteen years of Heyworth's chairmanship that it strove towards becoming multinational. I watched this process of growth from a junior distance, when its unfolding had only a limited significance for me. I could not become international in the exact sense because the absorption of men from the regions to the centre and their projection to the international scene had not yet begun. To feel international in a country ruled from outside had no meaning, but after independence it was of one's own choosing how close one wanted to feel to the rest of the world; and it is easier to feel close to others when you feel their equal. As the years progressed after independence I could sense this weight of inequality shedding, and curiously the process in my own case was accelerated by the vanaspati crisis, because here was a problem of our own making and our own tackling, for which we could no longer blame the alien.

Heyworth felt that to cope with size and geography, as Unilever sprawled further over the world, you needed delegation to the ends of the limbs, and this could best be done if the overseas units were manned by executives carefully selected, trained and groomed, who must ultimately be nationals of the country. It became imperative as national aspirations required a sensitive understanding of the many new complexities. The process became known as 'ization', a generic simplification of Indianization, Ceylonization etc. The older Lever men shook their heads and doubted if it would ever be possible to train locals to take over complete responsibility. There were natural limitations which no amount of training could overcome, at least not in the foreseecable future. In this there was a certain amount of cynical truth, for limitations one had, but when they were levelled as inherent and irremediable and therefore a kind of genetic bar, frustration and apathy set in and soon the 'limitation' became real; only to prove the point. Heyworth now wanted to hasten the course of 'ization', and in this he was helped by Desmond Bonham-Carter, who on his very first visit to India set a new pace.

Bonham-Carter was a big man, over seven feet in height and proportionately broad. His presence in the Company could not help but be noticed, and he took care to let it be known what he hoped to persuade our Company to achieve. 'Ization', he let it be known, had to be rushed and chances taken to complete it in five years. He seemed to pick up where Roger Heyworth had left. I invited him home one evening and decided to let myself be checked over, which he did without hesitation. His style differed from Roger's, for though equally direct he was sometimes deliberately unreticent and made calculated leakages of plans and information to check your reactions.

We talked about the new Administrative Staff College started at Henley to bring together experienced men from industry and government in Britain to learn from discussion and mutual experience. He felt that its benefit should be spread over the Commonwealth countries and someone from our business in India should be sent. I saw something of the hospital scheme of Pettit in it.

'Why?' I asked. 'You have started the institution to train British executives, and it would be a pity to share such a valuable facility with foreigners. I hope one day we will start a similar college in India to train our own executives.'

I was wary, and in this cold and prickly tone the conversation went on. I think he tried to find out what made me react this way to his overtures, as it certainly was not a lack of interest or commitment in my work.

An invitation to Henley was therefore sent to Chandy, another senior Indian in the company whom I greatly admired and who seemed better integrated than I, at least on the surface. But Bonham-Carter was not easily deflected; there was soon an invitation from him suggesting that I might join a Unilever course called the Executives Management Conference, to be held at their training centre in the country. To this satisfaction, if not surpirse, I accepted it readily.

I returned to England after seven years. The last time was in 1949 when I went on a training visit to Unilever for three months and stayed on to spend another three months in Sweden where Gärd joined me with our three children. Sweden, of course, had not been touched by the war, but England was then still very much a country of shortages and damage. In 1956 England was back to normal and on the way to its new life of affluence, but it had changed from the country I knew in the thirties, a different England, better in many ways, though not in all. Bonham-Carter was pleased I had at last decided to come over, and particularly wanted to see me after the course to hear my reactions. I missed Roger Heyworth, who had suddenly died the year before in Ceylon. He had been to India with his new wife, Gerda, whom he had known many years earlier, and married after his Danish wife left him He looked happier and more relaxed than I had ever seen him before, together at last with a woman he must always have loved; but it was not to be for long.

The course was held in an attractive country house with pleasant grounds. The small group of about fifteen people consisted of directors from various associated companies from America to Australia; men mostly of a high calibre. The leader was an Australian accountant with unorthodox ideas who liked heresy of any kind. He was acid and provocative, and a complete iconoclast, and set a leisurely pace and gave us plenty of time to think and relax. There was a constant exposure to facets of Unilever I had not known. The chairman, vice chairman, the Dutch chairman and members of the board, heads of divisions, scientists, production men and specialists came in a constant stream to talk to us. We questioned them freely, occasionally with unmerciful criticism.

The strand that ran through was delegation, which the chairman had preached and wanted the organization to practise. The rest was new techniques the organization was learning to adopt. I listened a good deal as it was my first experience of living and working in an international group with such breadth of experience, and slowly a realization emerged. Here was an institution, in its own way unique, that had an opportunity to bring together a diversity of cultures and sub-cultures and unite them through a common purpose of commerce into a flexible yet strong framework with a total corporate personality. Similar attempts were being made in the new international agencies to create world departments and international secretariats, but the problems of the two were different. The international corporation usually had to work under constraints, especially in the newly independent nations, and yet make a profit, whereas the international agency, though equally faced with similar environmental problems, was distributing largesse; besides, their organization structure followed more the bureaucratic pattern of governments. The same internationalness made one efficient and lively, and the other inefficient and dull. I was to learn the answer some years later.

After the course I went to attend a Unilever annual conference at Brighton, where one hundred and fifty of the top management in the U.K. and Europe, and those like me who happened to be visiting, assembled on a Thursday evening for a forty hour brainstorming, with the whole board, Dutch and British, as interested spectators. Through the next day, till well past midnight, the discussions went on. Once the chairman came in, shuffling on his two sticks, modest in a presence assured and felt. In a few minutes the discussion took a new direction, and perhaps because of my presence, but largely because of his own interest, we began to explore the internationalization of the senior talent. He was a man of few words, and these were mostly monosyllabic grunts, but the crystal clarity of his mind and the way it pursued a thought were interesting to watch.

Saturday morning we relaxed while the board went over the reports. I went for a walk by the sea, and remembered coming to Brighton many years ago. The recall brought back a lot of things I wanted to remember and some that I did not. I realized that a recontact with the past was not possible. I had tried it on my last visit in 1949 and failed miserably. I had then attempted a reunion with my old college friends in Manchester, and found that I could not transcend the barrier of the intervening years. The war had changed too many things, and in my ignorance too often I touched spots that hurt. What had happened inside this small circle seemed to mirror what had happened to England herself, once the most stable society in the world. From the patronizing and comfortable Britain of 1929, stern in its confidence and oblivious of the first gathering clouds, to that of 1949, anxious to be left alone while trying to readjust, I perceived the difference.

I was almost afraid of picking up the old threads because of my experience in 1949. A people we had known to be gracious were raw at the edges, and one no longer dared to agree with them, even occasionally, when they indulged in their old habit of self-disparagement. I remembered asking a waiter at tea, on the boat train to Holland, whether the one lump of sugar he had placed between me and a man sitting opposite was his or mine. He flared up and told me that I did not realize there was rationing in the country, that there had been a shortage of sugar and of many other things. However, he added, I could have it. But there had been the lighter side to life too, when in an obscure little restaurant in Soho, to which I had been referred by someone who knew, I was served a steak, my first in London for three months. I had asked for the menu, and an absent-looking Slav girl stared at me uncomprehendingly and said. 'No menu.'

'Then what can I have,' I asked.

'Only steak'.

And when the bill came, I innocently said.

'But I did not have one, never mind two, bottles of red wine.'

'No, but you had steak.'

Only too true, I admitted.

Somehow it was not so much the young who were sensitive as the old. The young had lived through it for ten years and it had become a way of life, a hard way but one to which they had become accustomed. If there was a restaurant where you could get a steak on the sly, they did not mind telling one about it. My embarrassment was with the older ones, to whom this was a come-down in life; the common things of the old days were scarce, available only at a price.

By 1956 things had changed vastly, but a mark had been left behind; or perhaps I imagined it. Our connection also had been broken for nearly ten years, and every now and again we made independent little noises about the Commonwealth. On this and on my many following visits I never travelled out of London. My work done I would take the first plane back to Bombay. Strangely I felt ill at ease in an England that no longer ruled us.

From this morning walk by the sea I was nearly late for the plenary session. There was a free discussion on some critical issues, and on international management the chairman drew me in. I said a few words but I was more interested in listening to the heartbeat of one of the world's largest organization. The general tenor of the debate seemed to be an underlying fear about the organization's capacity to sense the change in time and overcome it.

Around the isolate manager the discussion also revolved at some length. Was there room only for organization men? Who was the isolate and what were his problems? There was general agreement that while his sheer ability put him way beyond his colleagues, what isolated him from the rest was usually his intolerance of the less blessed, as also of organizational formalities and channels of communication. He went ahead and did things, and wanted the rule swept aside if it thwarted him. It was in his nature to experiment, often regardless of cost; he was incautious and tentative, and failure to him was of little concern. And yet all agreed that the organization must encourage him and that there must always be enough of his kind around.

A year earlier I had been on a board in Bombay selecting trainees, with Hoskyns-Abrahall in the chair. Among the group up for the final interview was a conspicuously able young man. At the group discussion he stood out in sheer ability and maturity well above the rest, whom he seemed to irritate. He was impatient with the speed of their reasoning, and would often become apathetic until some argument attracted his attention and he joined in, only to disrupt the group again. At the individual interview, he was equally brilliant, but he also managed to irritate some of the board.

After the interview we broke into a lively discussion. All were full of praise for the boy, quite the best mind we had come across for a long time, and yet the same question came to all of us: would he fit into the organization? If he managed to irritate some of us, what about his colleagues and subordinates? He was able, highly able, but would he make any effort to tolerate the less able, or accept genuine disagreement? In an organization like ours it was mostly a matter of team-work where the individual's achievement was rarely entirely his own. And yet we all felt we were letting talent go; there should be some way of fitting him in; it was almost a reflection on the organization to turn him down. We decided to ask him back to the board, something we did not often do. The boy returned, cool, almost contemptuous. Abrahall in his mild, scholarly way said:

'You know, we have asked you a lot of questions, but it did not occur to me to ask you if there were any questions you wished to ask.'

'No,' he replied coldly, and looked straight at Abrahall, 'I have nothing to ask though I have something to say. I do not think you will select me, I am not your type.'

'Yes,' said Abrahall simply. 'I think you are right. I am sorry because we are very impressed with your ability.'

'I know, you really want someone else, able, but more likely to conform.'

Shortly afterwards he was offered a Rhodes scholarship to Oxford.

The conference over, I returned to London, to Unilever House for a day, and after a brief visit to Rotterdam, introducing myself to the Dutch side of business, I flew back to India. The whole of Europe was under a blanket of fog, and having just managed to take off at Amsterdam the nearest we could land was at Nice, after trying Rome twice on the way; and from there on to Istanbul, Karachi and Bombay. On the long journey home I tried to take stock.

The Dutch plane, decorated for Christmas, was a last contact with Europe. I felt I was returning to India recharged, though with the core unchanged. I lived in two worlds: the outer shell world of England, Unilever, the western executive; and the inner core world of the Punjabi in me. Looking into the limitless space outside the small square window of the Constellation, I tried to examine my problem. I had perhaps let the two concentric worlds move in contrary directions and created friction. While the outer world was essential to progress, I needed the inner for harmony; if only I could make the two move freely, independently of each other and therefore without friction. But this visit had made a difference. While it had given me a clear understanding of Unilever and brought me closer to a large number of its senior men, it had at the same time sharpened my individuality. Could I be a part of it and yet remain myself?

I watched the Dutch cabin staff trying to create a festive spirit among a planeload of Dutch families returning east, tying bright pinafores on the little Dutch children and setting them to help; I looked down on the sundrenched Middle Eastern landscape below, wondering if a harmony was ever possible. As the valleys below filled with a deepening darkness while the last light of the sun hung around the plane at its height, there were two worlds, the plane flying purposefully, disembodied, through space, and the earth, below, moving unconcerned.

A few days after my return Bonham-Carter visited Bombay, and suggested that I talk to our management about my visit to Unilever. I saw a challenge in this and accepted it. I talked about the England I had seen, so different from the one I had known, and the Unilever I had not known before in the new international dimensions it was trying to organize. Bonham-Carter listened with interest, and must have sensed a change in me which was really a successful readjustment, with the core still firm. I wondered if he did not prefer it this way to be of any use to them.

About this time the company was reorganized. As the result of a suggestion from the Government an Indian equity company was formed and some shares put on the stock market at the end of 1956.

It was a momentous step by which the three almost independent companies were merged into one. I reminded Abrahall of a breakfast conversation in 1947 at the Cecil Hotel in old Delhi when he had asked our English Delhi branch manager what he thought would happen to our business when Independence came. The manager began a long account of the problem that we would have to face with an Indian government that would be unsympathetic to foreigners in general and to British business in particular. He felt it was but natural that having obtained political independence the country would discriminate and eventually want to get rid of British business altogether. I disagreed and said that all this was unlikely, but what would happen was that 'India' would have to come out of the brackets. This is just what happened nine years later, when Hindustan Vanaspati Manufacturing Company and Lever Brothers (India) Ltd. became Hindustan Lever Ltd. Abrahall had then laughed and said that that would be no bad thing, much to the disgust of the manager who was not amused.

As chairman of the new company, Abrahall set about the task with meticulousness. The new board had five Englishmen and three Indians, and Abrahall thought that I should give up vanaspati and return to head office to exchange jobs with Maurice Zinkin. After nearly twenty years in marketing I felt awkward at the thought. Maurice had combined marketing research, with which I was of course familiar, with planning, economics and statistics, and the intellectual that he was he had set a standard of advice that being unacademic myself I could never hope to maintain. His new book, *Development in Free Asia,* was perhaps the best contribution to the problems of a developing India, and his observations are even more apposite today than when he made them in the early fifties.

I had no confidence that I would make a success and asked Abrahall the reason for the move. Had I failed at my job? Abrahall of course politely refuted this and said that I had done well in the past and would no doubt do so in the future. It took me some years to learn that in a crisis, if one is diffident one makes all the calculations against oneself, to the extent of giving oneself no quarter. I later saw men much stronger behave in the same way, and the effort it took to convince them that by thus writing themselves off they were being as unfair to themselves as to those who had probably decided it in their interest. I learned too that a little lifting of the fog around such decisions—perhaps some calculated thinking aloud—can help.

Abrahall wanted the board to operate as a team; left to ourselves in our own functional spheres, he wanted us to consult and decide jointly on all company matters. I found his patience and permissiveness helpful in my growth as a board member. My experience at the Unilever course had so enthused me that I suggested he might ask Bonham-Carter if my name could be put up for the Advanced Management Programme of the Graduate School of Business Administration at Harvard University. I felt that my educational and working contacts abroad had been entirely with England, and with the wave of new ideas in management that were now spreading out from America, I would like to visit that country, preferably on a course like this. Unilever usually sent two executives to each of the spring and autumn sessions, senior and handpicked men. Bonham-Carter responded quickly. Yes, he would put up my name for Unilever's approval and Harvard's acceptance; the standards set were very high though.

CHAPTER SIXTEEN

Ahmedabad

Soon after I succeeded Maurice Zinkin, an institution in Ahmedabad invited me to their annual conference to give his customary talk on market research. My only experience of public speaking had been long ago in the debates at Manchester University, usually more effervescent than serious, but in my fresh enthusiasm I accepted this invitation, the first of its kind.

I found Ahmedabad a strange city. I had been there several times selling Dalda, but this visit after a gap of some years evoked in me an interest in the town that was to last for many years, an interest from which I gained a great deal, but at a price. The first thing I noted was that large sections of the old city wall were being demolished. It was an unplastered wall of unusual beauty, built from brick treated specially to give it a good finish. Sad as it was, it was a sign of the city's improvement plans of the kind that one was becoming reluctantly used to. Civic improvement in India was taking its toll of old beauty; in fact, 'beautification' began to mean replacing a harmony in brick, stone, timber or tile with a disharmony in cement, concrete, steel and incongruous colours.

As I looked at the beautiful main gate facing north, from where the city for many centuries drew its power, I thought of Akbar standing before it with characteristic regal risk. He had heard barely four days ago that the governor of the south western provinces was plotting against him, and decided to teach a quick lesson to his and others who might harbour any ambitions. With a few horsemen he rode day and night from Agra to Ahmedabad and arrived at this gate unannounced. The governor was so shaken by the news that he rushed to the gate and fell at the emperor's feet. Having made his point, Akbar said no more about the suspected treason; merely let the man, as indeed the whole empire, ralize his omnipresence.

The town came into prominence when some of its Jain families more than a century ago started a modern textile industry. A plant was imported from England and brought in bullock carts from the coast. The first venture failed, but others succeeded, and by the latter part of the nineteenth century Ahmedabad had a flourishing textile industry, second only to Bombay. The leading Jain entrepreneurs then also spread to Bombay, which because of its port and cosmpolitanism grew rapidly, while Ahmedabad remained just a large textile centre. Undisturbed by the competition that other communities from outside could have offered, these Jain families who controlled the textile wealth intermarried and became an endogamous group, like a large single joint family in which the wealth accumulated and circulated centripetally. Away from the city and the mills, across the river, they built their palatial homes, emulating the style of architecture and living of the neighbouring princely families of Gujarat and Saurashtra.

A new impulse came when Gandhiji built his first ashram on the banks of the river Sabarmati. The mill-owning families began to wear khadi and became discreetly nationalistic. The contact with the new movement benefited them in many ways. Gandhiji's mediation gave them such peace with their labour as no other town in India ever experienced; swadeshism gave protection against imported cloth. His influence also made their self-interest enlightened, although they did not rise to emulate the philanthrophy of their Parsi neighbours.

After Independence and the death of Gandhi and Sardar Patel, their interest in Congress waned and their influence ceased, which even the formation of their own state of Gujarat did not revive. Perhaps they expected the newly arrived political masters to consult and defer, but these new men did not have Gandhiji's gift of making use of all and making each feel big, as if he had been allotted a special task in his plan of things. The mill owners began to concentrate in a new direction; they tried to make Ahmedabad a centre of culture and education, and with their wealth they opened many new institutions; and to attract attention to their institutions they held conferences to which they invited people from all over India. A real feather in their cap one year was an inauguration by the Duke of Edinburgh.

It was interesting to watch the composition of the people from Ahmedabad at the conference. There were among them three distinct types. The elders of the community, the heads of the mill-owning families, managing agents as they were called, were portly gentlemen dressed in immaculate white khadi caps, long coats and high dhoties; one was the president of the Mill Owners Association, the other the mayor, the third the chairman of the institution which had organized the conference, the fourth, remarkably similar to the others in appearance and ways, was the leader of the local textile labour union. They all made speeches extolling the virtues of modern management, the need for adopting new technologies, and the value of a happy, well cared for worker.

Next, there were their sons and nephews, all dressed in dark American suits, educated at Harvard, Columbia, Michigan, and occasionally in England. They were the top underlayer of the managing agencies, often mere boys in their early twenties, always identifiable by their curious use of the first person possessive whenever they referred to anything to do with their organization—it was always 'my factory' and 'my factory manager'. There was that unmistakable aura of confidence and proprietariness about them as noticeable as the self effacing air about the third category, their hired professional managers, the technicians and even the research scientists, who invariably came from other parts of India. I wondered why this was so, and could only surmise that the local youth of the cotrolling families always worked in their family businesses and preferred to start as directors, well above the top rung of the professional ladder, while the middle-class young men of Ahmedabad preferred to start their own small business.

I was impressed though that these family heads, men of another generation, brought up in different traditions, could so welcome new ideas and encourage their young to adopt them. They patronized education, science, art, architecture and dancing, and endowed well. There were research institutions for textiles, physics and psychology, a design centre, a Tagore theatre, a private dance academy, all in the style of Le Corbusier, whom they had invited to design a number of buildings, including the house of one of the well-to-do young.

The Family homes were what one would have expected. On the first night we were all invited to a party by the doyen of the managing agents' corps. His was a large palace set in virtually a cultivated forest, in which were dotted the homes of sons and daughters. They lived like a brood in separate nests but comfortably close to the parents. The marble entrance hall of the main home had an office with clerks and janitors on duty, and a telephone switchboard. The living rooms were of mixed Western and Indian design, and the whole effect was of well harnessed wealth. On the terrace there were little earthenware oil lamps, a design on the floor of coloured flour in religious symbols, and in the centre an open log fire. Servants went round with sweet and spicy drinks, and after two rounds had been served soup arrived in tea cups, and a vegetarian buffet dinner was displayed in mixed Western and Indian style. On silver trays there were curries, curds and pickles, and on Royal Doulton china salads and stews. Within the hour, by nine o'clock, the party was over. A hundred or more of us all left together. The following night there was a party at the next senior home, that was similar in all ways, but on a reduced scale.

On the last day we all went to lunch to the doyen's son, and here was an interesting evidence of change in one generation. He had built his house outside the parental colony, and though large by all standards, it was modest for the family, but its interior was a wider mixture of America, Britain, Scandinavia, Japan, Gujarat and Moghul, with a touch of South India. The spacious living room was air-conditioned and divided into three styles; one was Indian with large white cushions on the floor and bolsters against the wall, another Scandinavian with low modern chairs, tables and bookshelves; the third was the dining section of American character. Raw silk curtains, abstract paintings, modern European ceramics and glassware, Japanese drawings of lobsters and horses, Indian rural pottery and woodwork, a sitar next to a hi-fi. Bach, Bismillah Khan and West Side Story: with all this it was still a liveable room. There were the same soft drinks, followed by soup, Indian food, a variety of salads and gratins on china with abstract designs, and then an abrupt and early farewell.

As I went from one party to another, eating the same food and meeting the same people, I was puzzled by all this hospitality, showered on strangers with faultless impersonality, part of the pattern of self-imposed duty. Nothing was left uncared for; there was a tea party too on the last evening on the lawns of the Corbusier headquarters of the textile industry, where for the first time the protocol was relaxed and there were some men who looked as if they lived within the city wall.

The conference progressed like all conferences in India I have since seen, except that this one tried all things. There were keynote speeches, votes of thanks, talks, group discussions on the stage, seminars in separate rooms, presentation by the seminar leaders, open discussions, a plenary session, a summing up; but in its rhythm it had a euphonic quality in which the views expressed were all in complete accord. The occasional difference was quickly harmonized, and the whole thing progressed like a melody in which all the right notes were struck. Human relations must always be good, and having accepted this simple truth the conference proceded to trace variations on the theme. Examples were given of how production increased because Ram, a good manager, understood the problems of his group of workers, after production had declined because Sham, a bad manager, had not bothered to understand his workers. Syndicates of young men, who had worked on such problems since the last conference a year ago, now came forward to corroborate from their experience the goodness of the Rams and the badness of the Shams. Speeches were made with much unction on how the man, worker and manager, should be understood and made to feel wanted, delegated, consulted and promoted. The unction was transparently sincere; but I could not help wondering how much of its was practised; for in such a highly structured and stratified society democratic management could hardly have arrived except in theory.

My own performance was dismal. I had come earnestly prepared about the latest in marketing research, its new directions and likely future trends, but the chairman of the session debunked it all, greatly to the delight of the audience. In his summing up he agreed that the new marketing research theories and practice had a lot to say in their favour, but in real life there was nothing to beat the hardheaded and sound judgement of the experienced man. With much humour he made whatever I had said sound good theory and no more. At first I felt angry, but I soon saw the funny side, for after all he reflected my own reaction to the heavy doses of management goodness that we had received for three whole days. he belonged to an industrial family from Delhi and had a robustness which found the earnestness of the locals heavy going, and when he got the chance he spoke out.

The conference ended aimlessly amidst general euphoria; everybody agreed it had been a great success; we must all meet again; so much had been achieved and the good work must go on. As I looked back it struck me that though it had been a conference perfect in itself it had not been a learning experience, there had been talking for its own sake, an exercise in the statement of the desirable, a search for wisdom and the truth; once the we-all-must-have-good-human-relation-in-industry was established as the truth, it had been enunciated repeatedly, like the name of God in its different manifestations, and pursued with the veneration of devotees. There had been no room for disbelief or questioning. But practice—well, that was another matter, a personal affair, like religion outside the temple. The contrast between this and the Unilever Conference was revealing; one was brisk and hard-headed, out to get results, the other got lost in perfectionism.

On the last evening as I was walking across the lawn in front of the auditorium, a woman whom I had seen a good deal around the conference and who was obviously one of its leading lights, walked over to me and asked me what I thought of it. I made some non-committal remarks, and she invited me over for a cup of tea. She lived on campus in one of the faculty bungalows. The interior was a less expensive version of the doyen's son's house, with the same self-conscious taste, a mixture of the many countries visited on conferences and delegations, with Indian art revival thrown in. I wondered if this was not the coming style of the professional Indian's home. But her home had a pleasant understatement, helped no doubt by her smaller means.

We discovered we both came from the same part of the country, the same professional Punjabi background, though her essential Punjabiness must have given way to later influences. We had been to the same college but afterwards our paths had taken different directions. After an early, tragically-ended marriage she returned to studies and set her face against matrimony, taking a professional career instead. She had become attached to one of the Families, to which the group reacted in an interesting way. They closed the ranks around the outsider in an attempt to dissolve the problem, but the outsider seemed not content with the acceptance, she continued to remain both in and out, a constant challenge to the Family's capacity to absorb.

Till late into the night we discussed the subject of the Family, the Institution, the whole culture of Ahmedabad. She explained to me the system of a joint family converted to industrial management, but without losing its essential core. The power centre was very much the head of the family; the sons a board; the mother and the daughters forming a shadow bord; the close relations and elders a consultative committee: all forming a tightly-knit in-group in the larger group of the Family that through inter-marriage and inter-investment had become powerful and monolithic. A young man from abroad had once married one of the daughters, but he soon left his wife and a blonde child and went away; and another daring youth from the north also came and went; and both daughters merged back into the family and lived in their separate nests in the wooded estate. This outsider was given the same choice. For a while she also lived on the estate but she would neither go away nor be assimilated.

'But how have you managed to stay so close to the family and yet apart for so long?'

'I think because I have always stayed at the edge. Everybody outside thinks that I am a part of it and yet those inside know that I do not belong.'

'Why did you decide that way?'

'I don't know.'

A withdrawn look came on her face, of someone unwilling, incapable, of facing a problem.

The family reminded one of the Rothschilds: cultured, cohesive, with their heart in money.

I soon found myself becoming compulsively attached to the whole scene: the city, the Family, the institution, her. Here I came across the first ferment of Indian management. Elsewhere, the Marwaris of Calcutta, the Banyas of the north, the Chettiars of the south, wherever industrial wealth had accumulated, the new processes of production had left them untouched personally. They too had endowed institutions, but in an impersonal way, uninvolved, and distant; nowhere as in Ahmedabad was there the same air of an institutional life, rooted and strong.

CHAPTER SEVENTEEN

Harvard Business School

Bonham-Carter confirmed that I had been accepted for Harvard in their spring term of 1958. Would I spend a few days in London on the way, and a week in the United States to get 'acclimatized'? I had never been to the States and had known barely two Americans in my life. I had seen them during the war, but from a distance. One had heard and built up many generalizations about them; and the whole photo-montage whirled round as my Constellation winged its way slowly through a heavy February night over the Atlantic to a dawn over hundreds of miles of frozen land, till we landed at New York into the insulated heat of the glass and chromium airport.

New York airport, the drive to the city, the city itself, the Lever office, a quick visit to Chicago and Washington, a snowbound weekend in Connecticut and ultimately a day-long train ride to Boston, ending at the Business School campus, was a week packed with impressions as never a week before. As I lay on a narrow bed in a tiny monastic cubicle, with an adjoining study, shared by someone in another cubicle who called himself my canmate, I felt about as low as on the first night at school. I discovered next morning that I had eight more canmates, and the can was the toilet facilities shared by the ten of us. We were going to live a life together, at work and leisure, for thirteen weeks, and at the end of it stand smiling together and be photographed. We would collect in the evenings, and do our homework together, throw parties to other cans, go to each other's homes for the long week-ends, sometimes a thousand miles away, and of course call each other by first names from the moment we met. This of course created a problem with my name, but they soon solved it by dropping its last three letters. The highlight was the last week, when wives moved in to Boston and each can became a large, happy and more united than ever group, that vied with other groups in who looked happiest.

I found the average American modest and gentle, anxious to be liked and most pleasant to work with. In discussion, he seldom disagreed clearly, and even plain speaking was uncommon, unless it was of the we-are-losing-the-heritage-of-the-founding-father type. The discussions ran at an even tempo, with much humour, but an idea had to be sold carefully, never slammed down, and much less put under the skin. One's appreciation of things American had to be clear, simple, straightforward and not wrapped in humour, at least not of the dry or barbed kind. Sophistry and cynicism had to be carefully avoided, equally any visible manifestation of intellect or philosophy, of which they were highly suspicious. Modesty was a cultivated feature, carefully worn and always becoming, so that one had to take care not to be even humorously immodest. Intellect was well concealed, for the 'egg-head' was suspect, and even the use of an uncommon word, however succinct, was shunned. But one could not help but greatly admire their extreme practicalness. The discussions were always relevant and produced results, avoided generalization and verbalizing, two much feared words. There was thus seldom any attempt at evolving a principle. Philosophy was a word used only for their belief in free enterprise and the American way of life. Anything that transgressed these bounds smacked of heresy.

A stimulating experience I found were the joint classes on labour relations that we held with a similar group of trade union executives, also going through a course in management. Interestingly, it was the union men who first cowed the executives. Their very presence and their belligerence seemed to make the executives lose their breezy confidence. The union men sensed this and pressed their advantage; but soon the executives also swung into action, and every day the two sides were ranged in pre-selected positions in the case studies, the executives always supporting the actions of the managers and the unionists the men.

The professor sometimes used my non-commitment when controversy flagged. I had mentioned to him one day that I would like to ask the union men, particularly the German, their views on co-determination. He agreed, but saved it for an occasion of his choosing. One day when the union men had got the executives on the run he turned to me; and there ensued a revealing discussion.

'Prakash, you wanted to know about co-determination. Let us ask what the class thinks.' And he turned to the executives. Few of them had heard of it or ever imagined such heresy could exist. He turned to the German union man and asked him to explain. It had begun in Germany during the reconstruction, to stimulate the interest of the men by involving them in the operation at the policy determination level. Workers' representatives thus worked with the directors in the process of decision-making and shared responsibility.

'What do you think of it?' the professor asked one of the American executives.

'Nothing', was the bland reply.

'And you,' he turned to one of the union men.

'Not on your life.'

I had expected this from the executive but not from the union man.

'Well, that is a surprise,' I said to the union men. 'I would have thought you would welcome it. For days now you have been talking about the responsibility of management to produce more in order to give more to the men. You have blamed them for pretty nearly everything and under all circumstances, and asked for more and more. Now when it comes to sharing the responsibility to produce that more you chicken out. You disappoint me, but perhaps you don't.'

The executives went into hoots of laughter and the union men into loud protests. The professor smiled as if he had expected it. When the furore died down, the union man began to explain.

'You've got it. We want more and more, but we don't want to have anything to do with how the more is produced. That is the job of the managers. Haven't they been talking about their prerogative to manage? So let them keep it. They have been trained to manage; it is therefore their responsibility to manage. I am not so sure that we would manage well; we wouldn't know how to, but even if we did, once we are inside the board room and share in management we shall have lost our strength to bargain for more. No, theirs is the job to produce more, and ours to demand an increasing share of what is produced; and if it hurts them, we don't care; they must learn to live with it and be more efficient. If in the process of meeting our increasing demands a firm goes to the wall, then it deserves to; someone else more efficient will pick up the assets. It is not our responsibility to keep the inefficient and the outmoded alive; they should give way to the more justifiable.' And as a last fling the union man added, 'And if we ever take over we will take over the entire outfit, and there will be no co-determination.'

My thoughts turned to the Indian scene where many such issues, large and small, were examined through a haze of sentiment. In fact, co-determination like other ideas ahead of our capacity to absorb had already reached India and was picked up by those in power who seemed to feel that they were setting the world an example.

To the other courses, finance and accounts, business policy, and administrative practice, one responded according to one's interests, but a number of us subscribed optionally to one on public speaking and listening. A private individual, who ran it as a business, had evolved some basic rules and practices on clear speaking and good listening. I had noticed that most American executives were poor speakers; they took the merit of short sentences too far, usually punctuating them with ahs and I-means, and found it difficult to speak freely for any length of time, particularly if depirved of the opportunity to lean on humour. This was in marked contrast to most Indians who are facile speakers; perhaps too much to the other side.

Our course aimed at developing consciousness of one's style of speaking, to the point of being able to hear oneself speak. In the playback of our own speeches, we became aware of our shortcomings, especially the difficulty of how to begin a speech and the yet greater problem of how to end it; but the second half of this course, listening, proved even more difficult. I had never given any thought to listening as an art or a discipline; I had just listened and thought no more about it. And yet when we were put through various exercises we dolefully learned that if we were poor speakers we were poorer listeners; we who prided ourselves as executives in attentive and patient listening would have been shocked, had we been told at the beginning how little we heard and, what the course did not directly bring out, how much we interrupted in a discussion.

This course was thought-provoking. If the average American, whom I had found an attentive listener, took in, as we were told, only twenty-five per cent of a speech, how much did an average Indian listen? In our society, as the listener ascended in importance, his degree of listening descended. The young, the subordinate, only listened; the old or important only spoke. Those who believed themselves wise felt it their duty to instruct, and this they performed remorselessly, forcing the less wise to listen dutifully. As soon as someone tried to talk, the wise man would think he recognized what the other was going to say, interrupt him and continue, brushing away any faint attempts by the other, even at trying to convey that that was not his point at all.

In our young days this applied to our elders, who spoke with the fervour of mentors while we listened; and today it goes for our leaders, who regard it their duty to talk, thereby solving all problems. In the British days the press used to report that a delegation received a patient hearing from a Governor or a high official; today it is the delegation that gives the leader a patient hearing. There was a case of an eminent minister who had invited a group of us from industry 'to instruct him' on some issue. He began by modestly referring to his ignorance and how necessary he felt it to learn from us. As one of us started to explain, the minister seemed to feel instructed at once; he cut in and spoke for the next twenty-five minutes, interrupting himself now and again to say that no doubt we agreed with him. The meeting ended cordially with the minister thanking us all for a most useful meeting from which he had learned so much.

It is our tradition to learn by listening. Villagers, and town people, will sit for hours to hear a discourse by a learned man, never questioning, never questioned, often absorbing very little, but simply lapping it up. I remembered what Aldous Huxley had once said on this point; how little Indians listened to even their venerated leaders. He had once been to a meeting that Gandhiji was addressing, where people had come from miles, neighbouring towns and distant villages for the darshan and hearing him. And yet when he spoke, people talked with each other, walked up and moved about, women suckled their babies, children ran about chasing each other. Hardly anyone listened; and yet this was no lack of veneration; they had had his darshan.

The society has lost its earlier tradition of the guru-chela dialogue, of discussion, an interplay between the speaker and the listener. Today, speaking is the prerogative of one and listening the duty of the other. To me as an Indian here was a new definition of listening; listening cultivated as much for the benefit of the speaker as of the listener. Here was something we needed to acquire, a culture of listening unrelated to age or seniority. It could be the first stage of a truer contact between our leaders, who have the knowledge, at least the power, and those of us at the receiving end; between the leaders and the led, a contact today sadly lacking.

As the course drew towards its end the working morale weakened. We began to miss the can discussions and sometimes even cut classes. The week-end parties began earlier in the week and lasted longer into the nights. I liked the men in their relaxed moods; they were communicative; they talked about the country, about their families and their work, and rarely had I met men more easy to converse with once they had dropped their executive formality and stopped playing a role. Life became happier and rowdier as we approached the last week, 'the week of the brides'. The night before the wives arrived there was one last fling when the din of empty cans, beer bottles, drain pipes, fire alarms, banshee howls in the early hours woke up the undergraduates. Next morning the men woke up to face the brides, and moved into hotels. The nightly parties were now just cheerful, the husbands enjoyed themselves soberly.

Early one morning I took the plane to New York, having quietly warned the Dean that I was going to miss the last day, the graduation ceremony and the ball. He looked disappointed, but I could not take it; I find it difficult to face farewells, mass farewells at that.

I returned home via San Francisco and Manila. As the plane flew for long hours over the wastes of the Pacific, with a short break at Hawaii, and a little walk to stretch one's legs near the signal hut at Wake Island, I dozed, looked out of the window, drank at the bar below, and tried to wrestle with my impressions. I never thought I would return to the U.S. again, and yet chance and a deep attraction brought me back first with a group of Indian marketing executives; next to discuss with Harvard the new business school at Ahmedabad; and then to teach at Los Angeles. Each return made me want to return again. In Bombay someone asked me if I could have settled there. 'Yes,' I said wistfully, 'if I had been ten years younger.'

*

Back in India, I looked at things in a new light—of a managerial answer for all problems. The case studies at Harvard, spreading over a wide area of technical and human problems, gave on the feeling that all problems could be solved if only we approached them unemotionally and managerially. I remembered how one of our canmates, when in our first can group discussion we had got bogged down, had brought an inscription and placed it on the table. It said: Are you helping solve a problem or becoming part of it? Our endless discussions in India, always looking for a perfectionist solution and criticizing anything that fell short of the ideal, reminded me now how much we had become a part of the problems we had set out to solve. And yet 1958, when I returned from Harvard, belonged to the years which marked, despite all our complaints and dissatisfaction, much achievement. We were drawing towards the close of the best of the Nehru era. The heavy public sector industry that he had founded was coming to the end of its long gestation. The big dams and multipurpose projects, at one time over twenty in building at the same time, were nearing completion. There had been a big wave of industrialization in private industry, and things were manufactured that we had not dreamed of a few years ago. The many new universities and national laboratories had taken education and research to all parts of India. Excellent institutions of technical and general teaching were springing up everywhere. Schools, hospitals, roads, communication and air links, the large new townships, and all the new growth, reminded me of the spurt of a hundred years ago in our land of five rivers, for then there too had been sudden growth of a new kind.

Today in the whole of India, growth was at its most spectacular in the new Punjab. Mutilated and truncated only a decade ago to less than a third of its size, it had already rebuilt with unbelievable energy. It looked as if the shock of partition had given it a new vigour. Without moping over its losses, even bothering to think about them, Punjab set to building as never before. Wherever the displaced Punjabis went, whether to settle elsewhere in India or in their new homeland of East Punjab, they became like a new people, regenerated and confident. They set up as small entrepreneurs wherever they went, but the best job they did was cultivating neglected lands wherever they found them in north India. They adopted modern farming, with tractors, trucks and tubewells, and discarded the bullock cart and the Persian wheel. Cut off from the old home in West Punjab, I got a vicarious pleasure from visiting East Punjab every winter when the fields were at their fertile best. I would look again at the green of the wheat, the yellow of mustard, red of the rai, and the blonde plumes of the sugar cane, all waving joyously in the benign and pale winter sun, and return recouped to Bombay. Born and bred on the plains of the Punjab I had to return to them off and on to stand life in the crowded island of Bombay, though its open sea did compensate.

This nostalgia, prodded by Maurice and Taya Zinkin, persuaded me even to try and recapture in writing our family's life over three generations, from the time the British came after their last battle in 1852 outside the city walls of Gujrat, till they left in 1947. It was to be a record of the time since my grand-uncle went to school at Gujrat, later to return there to start as a lawyer, until the time when my uncle, also a lawyer, had to flee from Gujrat in the chaos that followed the Partition. The British had come to a Punjab in a time of chaos, and with the irony of history left it in the same state. I had begun my writing a couple of months before I left for Harvard, and on my return I picked it up. I found it an absorbing occupation to leave the present for the past, to exchange my life in a British firm with my father's in the British administration. It also, I think, helped sharpen my perceptions of the India around me.

After eight years in England and twenty years with an English firm, the break at Harvard, short as it was, seemed to change my direction. In the brief spell of three months I seemed to have given myself to this American experience as if I were looking for a new orientation. This came from two directions. Harvard had unset me from an English,

European orientation, in which I had become framed, over to something seemingly much wider and less settled. It was closer to India, with its unrest and state of being than to Europe, especially to England, which seemed "become." On the other hand, writing took me back, far back into the Punjab that had become smothered under subsequent layers. I felt myself stretching forward. I also felt as if I were stretching backward into the past.

CHAPTER EIGHTEEN

Business Management

Back in the Company, I began to take stock of myself. In its own way the visit to Harvard had been my second moratorium after an interval of twenty-five years. As a student in England, after finishing my degree at Manchester, I gave up work for nearly two years. Apart from a half-hearted attempt at economic research, I did nothing more serious than go to the library and to concerts, walk through the northern countryside, play golf and take an active part in the Union debates. It was a life of idle exploration, in a vague pursuit of excellence, which a woman psychologist at Ahmedabad called by this important-sounding name of moratorium. Having lived through such a one herself, she said it was a kind of flight that sometimes occurred in those who were overstretched and in need of rest or readjustment, though she said that I was otherwise mentally offensively healthy. I had entered university at the age of fourteen and finished a second degree at twenty. Both were of mediocre achievement, but the effort must have drained me out, particularly as the latter had also involved a process of adjustment to a life in England, so utterly different from life in the Punjab. The moratorium was also aided by the arrival of Gärd on the scene. We both left off our studies to do nothing together, visiting Sweden in the summer and at Christmas.

The visit to Harvard, away from responsibility and routine, was the first pause from my work, and I dissolved the problem I had taken with me. A few months earlier I had suffered my first setback in the firm. So far I had been progressing unchecked, and no one junior to me had gone past. Whatever my prospects, I had felt satisfied that I had moved steadily forward, along a line that pointed upwards, but suddenly I came to a halt on level ground. An Englishman, David Orr, eleven years younger than me, of great and visible promise, was made vice-chairman. Under normal expectations, he would remain in front of me as vice-chairman and chairman, for another seven or eight years, by when I would be due to retire at fifty-five. To discover that one had been suddenly written off was quite an experience. I tried to analyse it.

'Ization' had been the policy, declared and pursued. The number of expatriate personnel had been reduced and they no longer formed the management structure, only providing special skills or time till an Indian was ready. It could therefore only be that while retaining the control they did not feel secure with an Indian at the top, or that I had not made it—something, I could accept, but not believe. Such a problem is bad enough in itself, but infinitely enlarged by one's inability to check one's own analysis or conclusions. I have never turned to others for advice on matters that concerned me alone, but I felt that in this case I needed to know the answer. I decided to ask the chairman. Knowing me, he was surprised, but glad that I had decided to talk to him. To my question he replied simply, 'Well, it is a "no" this time, but there never is a "no" for ever.' And with this characteristic mixture of humanity and taciturnity, his watery blue eyes conveyed understanding.

A quite remarkable man was Steve Turner, the chairman who had succeeded Hoskyns-Abrahall. No two persons could be so unlike each other. Of humble origin and self-taught, he had joined the firm very young, taking a degree in chemistry at evening classes. Aloof and cold, he went out of his way to be alone, but not really liking the loneliness he punished himself at work, and drank. His formidable character seemed to consist of two layers, the top one, hard and impenetrable; the one underneath, malleable and soft, but, unable to find an outlet, in a constant state of flux. Like a volcano, the hard crust kept the heaving core firmly inside. A generous man and excellent company when he so chose, it was in keeping with his whole make-up of cultivated contradictions to cover his perfectly valid instinct of kindness, for he was essentially a kind man, with a gruff manner and a speech clipped into icy precision that at first used to frighten me and later pushed me away.

He had been manager of the vanaspati plant, where during the war and for years afterwards production of Dalda was never enough to meet the demand, and he was constantly under pressure from me to produce more. With nothing in common between us, either socially or at work, the often uneasy relationship between a marketing and a production man, especially under conditions of stress, was escalated by lack of personal warmth between us. I convinced myself that he disliked me as an ignorant nuisance. It came to a head one day when I rang him up with some usual demand from the marketing side, and probably went about it insensitively. Instead of appreciating his difficulties I made light of them, and when he protested, I was not understanding. His reaction was out of proportion; his sarcasm, of which I had had some taste before, was devastating; seething with indignation I rang back to tell him that if he was going to behave like that it would be the end of any contact between us, and I put the receiver down, trembling with shame and anger.

My anger I could cope with, but I could not understand my feeling of shame. I began to unravel the tangled skein of my emotions, and a light came on a problem of long ago.

On my arrival at Bombay by a P. & O. ship after an absence of eight years, I had shared the belief of each generation of Indians returning from England that the attitudes of the British had changed; that having lived among them for some years as an equal one had acquired acceptability; that during one's long absence things had moved forward at home to equality between the races. Yet one soon found the same wall, the same gulf. Eight years earlier on my way out, I had heard the legend that on the journey westward the air changed as the P. & O. ships steamed out of Port Said into the cool Mediterranean. The tensions relaxed, the English faces softened, little conversations began, and even the dance floor became hospitable. In reverse, when the eastward bound ship sailed down the Suez, the two groups fell apart, and in the Indian Ocean the gulf widened.

At eighteen, straight out of the simple Punjab, I had not understood what the watershed of Port Said meant. I was just as shy of talking to them before Port Said as after; but on my return it was different. Eight years among them had changed me, and the P. & O. ship did not look frightening any more. I met them unselfconsciously, neither belligerent nor over-compensated. I moved among them as I moved among Indians, but things became strained as we neared Bombay, and broke into splinters at the Bombay harbour. A small incident was enough to unsettle me. In the customs shed, where typical Indian chaos prevailed as passengers and porters rushed in all directions, I stood for a moment not knowing my next move, and in the short moment a voice rasped behind me, 'Come on, get a move on or get out of the way; don't just stand there.' I turned around to see an irate Englishman glowering at me with an impatient contempt I had not seen before. Typically dressed in a cotton jacket, with the collar of the white shirt over the lapels, khaki shorts and long stockings, his pale face under a topee looked peremptorily at me. I moved away mumbling an apology. The whole scene flashed back twenty years later as I heard Steve Turner's voice on the phone, 'Make up your mind, and let me know what you want'.

☆

My mind then strayed back to ten years ago, when Pettit had suggested appointing an Englishman under me; the first experiment of its kind in the firm. This Englishman had come to India before the war and was well ahead of me. During the war he had served with the Indian Army and retired as a captain in a distinguished Gurkha regiment. Upon his return to the Company, Pettit had decided to put him under me, which was an even more trying test for him than me. He rightly regarded me as his junior and, worse, someone who had gained at his expense by staying back while he had served. It made it even more galling to him that he should have been picked for the experiment when there were others, younger and less senior. I do not know how Pettit put it to him, but when I spoke to him he was plainly dissatisfied. I tried to rationalize that it must be a temporary posting to familiarize him with the quite significant advances we had made in marketing, where the whole scene had changed radically during his absence. I was sure he would not hold it against me that he would be learning from me. I was in no doubt of their intention to move him up to higher responsibility as soon as he had caught up with things, and new openings appeared. But he was not a big enough man to realize his long term interest, and working under me worried him considerably. As a first experiment it turned out an unhappy failure for both of us. If I suffered from excessive anxiety to make it easier for him, he suffered excessively from anxiety to make it clear that he thoroughly disapproved of the whole unnatural situation. He felt it the more acutely when I first visited him in his branch. In the head office he could reasonably ignore me but in the branch he had to display me as his chief before his men, and in the bazaar to his wholesalers and retailers, who were traditionally used to seeing an Englishman as the boss. After all, India was not yet independent and, except for a few civil service secretaries, Indians were rarely seen above Englishmen. The whole thing preyed on his mind till he could take it no longer. On this visit to his branch we travelled together from Delhi to Lahore, where before the work was finished he informed me that he was leaving before I was due to take train back to Bombay. With nothing else to do, I asked some of his men to stay on for an informal discussion, men I had known and trained when I was their manager for the branch.

On my return to Bombay I received a curt note from him protesting strongly at my behaviour in talking to his men in his absence, and went on to preach some elementary management principles. It irritated me, but I decided to take it no further. On his next visit to Bombay I told him I was sorry if I had upset him, but his letter had hurt me.

'Good,' he said firmly, 'I am glad because it was meant to.'

Soon he got his chance and was given independent command in a neighbouring country. To this opportunity of building a new company in a new country, with everything in his favour, he brought the same small mind and was a sad failure.

Pettit seemed undaunted and, not content with my first failure, persisted in training me in the art of handling English subordinates. He soon gave me a much bigger problem, where I failed completely. On his visit to England he had selected a young man who had been a salesman before the war. In the Royal Navy he had risen from able-bodied seaman to the rank of lieutenant-commander, and then re-joined the Company as a van salesman. A man of much enthusiasm, Pettit told me, he must have considerable character because he had also done rather well as a boy scout, and risen to high rank in the movement.

Carried away by Pettit's description, I built him up before my managers, who were frankly disappointed that I had not selected one of them for the job. I explained that on the first occasion we wanted the new job of General Sales Manager, in charge of the entire sales operation, to be defined by someone of experience who would bring new thinking from Unilever. The men accepted this and promised me their cooperation, and in fact began to look forward to his arrival. I arranged a special conference to launch the new man, for I was anxious to succeed this time and retrieve my last failure.

The evening before the conference, on my way to dinner at our local branch manager's house, where all of them were collecting, I called in at the Taj to meet the young man who had just arrived. Excited, I rushed along the corridor and knocked at his door. As I entered and introduced myself, a wave of fear swept over me. I sensed failure again, surer than before.

The men, waiting at the party, asked me to tell them all about him. This was their first English boss, for they had all joined during the war and only served under me. India had been independent for a year, but that year had been an age. The accepted supremacy of the Englishmen had just vanished. The natural order of things until yesterday had ceased to be. Any Englishman from now on was going to be judged only by what he had to offer; and to command respect he had to visibly demonstrate his skills and communicated them to the Indians who worked under him, so that they could learn and take over. He came as a trainer and catalyst and not just to fill a quota percentage; this is what I had conveyed to the men. What was he like, they anxiously asked me. I tried to described him in the most generous light possible. He was a simple man, essentially practical, self-made and with the confidence and ways that go with it. He would offer drive and competence, and perhaps a contrast to my impatient imagination that more often ran away with things. On the whole they would find him less strain than me and easier to work with. The more confident I grew in describing him the more dubious they looked. Self-contrast and self-deprecation were not natural to me. However, as the party warmed up they cheered up too in a trust that took no time to be shattered when the conference began the next morning.

In his simple cockney he talked to them like men lined up on deck or a troop of boy scouts and gave them a pep talk to get on with the job; he would always be behind them; they could count on him; he did not believe in any highfalutin marketing ideas and big words; he was a simple salesman, out to get results. He got carried away and promised to put the Company right; in this, of course, he expected all cooperation from them and support from the top. Let that be made quite clear, for he was a straightforward man and believed in calling a spade a spade each time. I squirmed as he laid it on thickly. The men fortunately found it difficult to follow his unfamiliar accent and expressions, as well as the directness of his language, but they sensed clearly enough that he was a new kind of Englishman. They had never heard anyone talk like this.

I faced the problem non-plussed. No good at sharing problems, I could not go to Pettit and admit it; and he, blissfully ignorant, did not sense anything; instead he kept emphasizing the virtues he had seen in this man when he interviewed him in London, and his enthusiasm here, and I kept agreeing. As time went, the men chafed under his sergeant-major handling, and he sensed and resented it. He expected me to underline and applaud his approach, which I could not bring myself to do, and I found I was pressed between him and the men. Neither understood the other, but both sides wanted my support against the other. I could honestly not support him any more. I had given him all the support I could before he arrived, and for a while afterwards, and he would still have received it had there been anything to uphold except a tragic and pompous ignorance. The men looked at me resentfully as if to say, what are you asking us to accept?

He was sincere in his own way, and had sensitivity of a kind. He sensed all that was going on around him, the total lack of acceptance, but had no understanding of the cause, and therefore did not know how to cope with it. Almost unlettered, he resorted to his only strength, the determination of a losing boxer who puts his head down and lashes out blindly. He lashed at me, at the managers, the men, at the wholesalers and the dealers. He also found himself isolated from his compatriots who felt let down and ignored him, and the fact that his Indian managers noticed this made it all the worse for him. Six months after his arrival I was due to go to Unilever for a three months' training visit and then on a three months' holiday in Sweden, and during my absence he was going to deputize for me. This, I felt, would give him the opportunity of running things his own way, long enough to work out his own style. It actually proved fatal. He exercised his freedom the only way he knew, in an up-guards-and-at-'em way.

Pettit left him alone, there was little in common between them, and as can happen among the English, they spoke what to an undiscerning Indian seemed two different languages. Pettit's well modulated drawl and this young man's half eaten words, with either the beginning sucked in or the tail bitten off, came from different worlds altogether. In the firm, as was usual those days, after Pettit's Rugby and Cambridge and Abrahall's Charterhouse and Oxford, there were either the grammar school or the secondary school, but here was barely the elementary school. The difference between him and Abrahall was even greater, and yet he seemed to feel more at ease with him than with Pettit, and certainly more than with me. I began to understand this. Pettit had in him more than the characteristic English administrative distance. His aloofness lacked the humanity of Abrahall, whose distance could vary; it shortened when you needed closeness and lengthened when the need was gone; while Pettit's was a permanent distance, the same under all circumstances. I think it was Abrahall who first saw the problem and began to shorten his distance to this young man. But he also saw that it was an untenable situation; the man's capacity was well below the minimum required for the job. On my return Abrahall spoke to me and wondered whether I would confirm his observation; he also wondered why I had not mentioned anything to him. I found it difficult to explain my reticence. I did occasionally go to him with minor personal matters but on all major issues I kept my own counsel and dealt with them as best I could. Used to my ways, Abrahall shrugged his shoulders and left it at that, but decided to talk to Pettit.

Pettit wrote to London that the young man did not fit into the Company and should return home. Their reaction was curious. They said that he had been sent on a considerable promotion, which the attendant risk of a career closing behind him if he failed. From his senior position in India they could not very well take him back to where he was before leaving, and there was no question of giving him a promotion upon an unsuccessful return, so it was best to let him go. In any case he was now an employee of ours. We protested that he was their man, not engaged locally, so as an expatriate he should return to them and then they could do what they liked. Later his old boss in London remarked lightheartedly to Abrahall that his posting to Bombay had been a solution of their problems.

I now had to my credit two failures, leaving me more confused than ever on how to make a success with English subordinates, which apparently I must inevitably learn to do if I were to acquire larger responsibility in the firm. I could not see where I could have done better. Had I discussed the subject with someone, I might have understood it differently, but how could one discuss what was a kind of racial problem with one of the race itself.

My father had mentioned to me how once, at the end of a hot morning's inspection tour, his chief on arrival at a canal rest house after a few moments of courteous conversation took leave of him but asked his subordinate, an Englishman, to stay for a drink. My father, a reticent man, gave me occasional understanding of his relationship at work. I was a little surprised when he related this incident, for he was a man without rancour and never one to show hurt. The incident returned to me over the years, for instance, when I noticed how at the end of his monthly meeting Pettit used to take only the European managers out to lunch, and once when Duncan suggested that he might invite others, he gave an embarrassed, 'No, it would become too many'.

Here was an international firm whose own men abroad were part of its own design but had to remain out of the local pattern. In Ahmedabad I saw the same phenomenon. Despite the introduction of the latest technology and management theory, members of the family were treated as enclaves, subject only to their own laws, rather like the old rule that an Englishman in India would only be tried by an English judge. Similarly, though Indianization had proceeded at a rapid pace, the problem of an Englishman remained theirs; it did not become ours. Long after, when there were very few of their members left, this attitude still persisted. Their own kith and kin were still supra-environment. This lack of mutuality created a constraint quite different from the constraints inherent in work itself.

This was just one of the things I had learned at Harvard: that in any situation a manager is faced with constraints, social and environmental. These are stronger constraints than the operational ones and do not respond to his personal efforts but have to await the slow change in the environment itself.

Harvard wiped away the cobwebs from my mind and filled it with some fresh thinking. I learned to accept limitations, whether they were my own or imposed by the organization or of the environment. I would never achieve what my colleagues from U.S. companies could achieve; I could not even match my English colleague on the Harvard course, who like me worked in an overseas company. I had asked him one day:

'Where do you think you would like to go in the Company; how far do you think you will go?

'The vice-chairman of my Company soon, then its chairman. One day I would like to be on the overseas committee at London—yes, I would like that very much, having been overseas so long. After that the Unilever Board—who knows!'

Yes, I agreed, why not. His ambition more or less began where mine, only by a stretch of imagination, might end. For him it was a matter of calm assumption.

☆

Now, Steve Turner received me back warmly and shortly afterwards offered me finance directorship which I accepted happily. It was, ironically, a return to my original field into which the Chief Accountant twenty years ago had refused to take me. He was right in a way; after so many years my qualification was meaningless. The new job brought me into contact with all sides of the Company.

The fifties were also an interesting period for the start of new management thinking in India. The first waves of this thinking came to us from England because of our closer contacts and the new work that was going on in the Tavistock Institute, but America was soon to swamp it all. India was fertile ground; our enthusiasm to listen to anything new and our ability to turn it into an intelligent discussion gave to the men from American universities and foundations a happy feeling of having come to the right place. Young Indians were now going in large numbers to business schools in the States, as their elders had gone to Cambridge and London to read law or economics; and while the fathers had entered the services or the Bar, the sons were entering industry.

In my first enthusiasm from Harvard, and possibly because the acceptance of my limitations in the Company gave me the need to expend my excessive energy elsewhere, I became quite engrossed in this management movement. The Harvard course in speaking and listening, and the many new ideas the other courses had poured into me made me into an enthusiastic speaker, with some modern managerial experience to offer, which was more than one could say about some others who became professional at management without having managed. The professor at Ahmedabad kept inviting me back, and we began to work as a team. Her academic output was sparse, and she was unable to communicate with more than the smallest group; yet with her forcefulness, which she sedulously kept covered to fit in with the gentler beat around her, she found that I responded to academic stimuli and perhaps provided a vicarious expression of her complex personality and circumstance.

I got carried away by the fascination of this process of change, sparked off by Harvard, by her, and by Maurice Zinkin, a most remarkable man. I think he saw in me the new stage of the British connection with India, the growth of professional management. As a part of this phenomenon I appealed to his deep sense of history. He began to work on me, to bring something dormant out of my mind. I think he sensed the resistance in me too, but he was a determined man. It was as if he wanted to achieve something in me before he left India the second time, having been uprooted suddenly at partition from the civil service to which he had offered his all. From a fine Jewish rabbinical stock, he had a mind of rare speed and versatility, with a projectiveness that wanted always to begin with the answer, a conclusion, a thesis. Let me suggest a conclusion to you and you can demolish it, but in the process we will trim it down to greater relevance till we have reached a conclusion pure of the irrelevant, was his approach. But my Hindu mind seemed to him unconcerned with the conclusion, and after laboriously reaching one, it could, to his astonishment, start all over again because it had seen something new. This frustrated him, and he worked hard to curb and discipline my mind through the year he worked under me; a year of much agony for both of us. But I learned rapidly, and this gave him great delight. I began to project and hypothesize and pay attention to synthesis; at the same time as the professor in Ahmedabad worked on my mind not to be afraid of examining experience and subjecting this to the harsh light of conceptualization.

Maurice Zinkin believed in the mission of the British. Their old role as the welders of India into a modern state was finished voluntarily, but he saw a new role for them. This time British industry, without privilege or power, would offer values and a system of professional management to help create an industrial state. As in the old political state they had developed cadres of administrative and political leadership, so they would help to bring up a class of managerial leaders without whom modern industry would not grow. He put me in the front row of this new generation of managers. We would discuss the subject and its historical background at length.

Three centuries earlier, while many nations competed for the prize of trading with India, as the most determined and disciplined, the British had won. They opened small trading stations and manned them with their soldiers while the traders spread into the hinterland, looking for any opportunity that came their way. Their purposeful base far away was the East India Company, whose only aim was profit. Their masters were hard-headed businessmen, and the men they sent out provided the earliest examples of what management today talks about, delegation, initiative, judgement and quick decisions. A year's distance away from home, these men decided first and consulted afterwards, and any approval or disapproval of their action two years later was only of historical interest. The masters loved a formidable language. 'Tremble ye' was how one company director began his letters—but the men on the spot anything but trembled and did what they thought best, though always taking care to feign humility in their reply.

From this prototype came the administrators, rulers instead of traders, who governed tracts of land and populations sometimes equal to their homeland. Allowing for the times and for their paternalism, which saw their task as of guardians, they did a good job. They were benevolent and interested in the people, and strove to remove the oppression of centuries, but no more. Trimmed of its excesses, time once again stood still. The rapacious officials, the thugs, the roving bands of adventurers went, but the peasant continued to till his land with the wooden plough and scatter his seed and reap his poor harvest. Here and there water was brought in canals and wrought a miracle of lush crops, and a well fed peasantry, but elsewhere the grinding poverty remained. But out of it all came something new that was less noticed than the law and order so lauded by the rulers and the ruled. This was the new class of Indians who were taught to administer, admittedly always under the rulers. But progressively the column above the Indians shortened and they rose higher and higher in the hierarchy of administration.

Maurice Zinkin and I had interminable arguments. As an historian he was a romanticist, lacking in objectivity when it came to the British connection with India. I, on the other hand, was always rejecting, perhaps because he pushed me too far. This rejection I applied to the firm, which also, I argued, found Indians useful. There was no duty or trust about it; it was good self-interest, neither to be decried nor unduly applauded. I did concede however that whether in government or in business, something did distinguish the British from the other Europeans abroad. How often must I have hurt his feelings, never meaning to but always managing to. His belief in the British connection bordered on the religious. The process of Indianization, he believed, was inherent in the Raj and had transmitted itself to its commercial and industrial successors. There was never any expediency about it; it was just that the administrative concept of the British could only work through delegation and trust. This always led to the logical conclusion that the man was built up to a point from which he could not but reach the top. Each next step might be denied him from the time it took the administration to adjust itself, but the final plunge was always inevitable.

But our discussions were not always about the firm or the British; we often talked about the social and economic side of India. The political side he seemed to leave increasingly to his wife, Taya, whom he was grooming as a journalist. Physically and mentally restless, Taya was suited for journalism. She was an indefatigable traveller, persistent, and like her husband she also began with a conclusion, which she however mostly managed to prove. If not, she lost interest and turned to something else. Both were equally and passionately interested in India and always trying to discover what made it go. In me they discovered, to theirs as much as to my surprise, that although I had lived away from the Punjab for so many years my roots were still strong and fresh. I yet maintained a sensitive recall of the Punjab where I was born and brought up as a child, the Punjab since vanished in the debacle of partition. I shared the cumulative racial memory of its lore and custom. It was they who between them made me write a book.

I was very diffident about writing. I could explore and project in conversation but the discipline of writing I found difficult to submit to. Maurice and Taya insisted that I try it because what I remembered about the Punjab, they said, was not commonly remembered and would soon be forgotten. Social history to Maurice was background to history and gave the historian the dimension that contemporary records otherwise lacked. Social history made the past live again in its men and women, their way of life and customs; no serious history is possible without it, he argued. Used only to commercial correspondence and reports, I felt uncertain of writing for print, but under their combined pressure I offered to write one chapter on condition that they sent it to their publishers and obtained their opinion. If the publishers saw a book coming out of it the effort of continuing would be worthwhile.

To my surprise I found I wrote easily, and enjoyed doing it. The past began to live with the clarity of today; its earliest memories were neither vivid nor dim, they were just natural. They came out like old books and toys and clothes discarded long ago and stored in a cupboard. They still lay there neatly stacked and locked away, and it was beautiful to take them out again and examine them with the detachment of intervening decades, without any trace of self-consciousness or attempt at reinterpretation through today's mind. I lived them again, the village, the medieval walled city, the life in its homes, births, marriages and deaths: the memories all had the evocation of when they were and not of a past.

Peter Calvaocoressi, a partner of the publishers, perhaps more encouraging than critical, wrote back that while the style was discursive and he did not want to curb it, he could perhaps suggest that some discipline might be applied to decide upon a format. On second thought, he preferred to leave me alone, but they saw a book in the few pages I had sent.

A book eventually came and was well received, in both its English and American editions.

I suddenly felt freed of the past, the firm, and my anxieties for my future in it. Although the authorship gave me neither prospect nor income, it gave me a feeling of independence. A creativeness appreciated, a creation however small upon which a favourable judgement had been passed by the many reviews it received, made my relationship with the firm appear in a different light, almost irrelevant; their appreciation as important no longer. Withdrawal came easily to me; and with it came a peace of mind and satisfaction, a new calmness in which success in the firm mattered no more.

I had been working hard on the book, on my growing extra-mural interests, and at my new responsibility in finance, determined to give it all the devotion that I had given to Dalda. In a particular fortnight I neglected a cold and a flu, till one day after speaking at a seminar, followed by lunch, as I walked out of the hotel I felt dizzy and unsure of step, with a tight feeling in the chest. I asked a passer-by to hold my arm and walk with me to a nursing home that happened to be only a hundred yards away, and there to the astonishment of the nurse in the reception I gave myself up. I asked her to tell the doctor on duty to look me up when she was free, preferably not before long, and inform the specialist who gave me my annual check-up that I was here.

Through the many checks and consultations that followed, I dozed through an uneasy half-slumber, uninterested in their subdued discussions. Through sedatives, light food, long hours of sleep, and idle gazing through the window at a rusty shield bearer with abundance of yellow flowers, I let the strain of months and years evaporate, leaving me cool and light. I refused to see anyone or received messages, flowers or books. Gärd came once a day but stayed only for a while because she found me absent and uninterested even in her company. After ten days I went home, and spent another week in a shack on the coast, where I also did nothing but sleep or gaze at the sea through the casuarinas. As I lay down on the warm sand and looked at the blue sea, extending in an eternity to meet the blue of the sky, the problems of twenty years, so alive till yesterday, were no longer part of the present. They became petrified in the past, and where only yesterday they had squirmed and writhed, today they were set and inert. The whole past of twenty years showed softer contours, as if a rare rain had suddenly washed away its harshness; its landscape no longer appeared so inhospitable. But I now realized how much despite this seeming inhospitableness the past had nourished me, what my years in the firm had done for me though really it owed me nothing except perhaps the compulsions of circumstances. Both I and they had given our all, though each side felt the other was holding back. And then it grew on me that I had really received more than I had given; perhaps I was the one who held back. But did it matter any longer, now that I felt freed? The new freedom came out of this past, as a gift for the future that was all mine to determine.

RETURN TO PUNJAB
1961—1987

CHAPTER ONE

Unilever

Lever Brothers of Port Sunlight, near Liverpool, had exported soaps to India since 1875, and had built up their business over the next half century till Sunlight soap became a household name, synonymous with soap, as later Dalda with vanaspati, the vegetable cooking fat. They appointed distributors in the port towns of Bombay, Calcutta, Madras, and Karachi, Indian and European merchants, and through visiting salesmen and through new forms of advertising and sampling they built up a wholesale network that reached every town and village, whose cost was usually paid out of the resale value of the empty wooden packing cases. In the 1920s offices were opened in the port towns, followed by setting up companies and factories which in the 1930s became fullfledged manufacturing and marketing operations, fed with new systems and policies from the UK and the growing international operations. I had joined them in 1937, and after many interesting years, when I travelled extensively and learned about the India of villages and towns, I became a director in 1951; a member of the first board of the new Hindustan Lever in 1956, and vice-chairman in 1960. In 1961 Steve Turner, my chairman, had a heart attack, and as it became clear after a few months that he would have to return home, they invited me to London for discussions, which turned out to be the ritual of my hastened appointment.

Sitting at Unilever House in the room of Robert Siddons, member of the Overseas Committee responsible for India, I looked across the Thames, shimmering and busy under a bright June sun. On the other bank the city rose from the warehouses and municipal office buildings, the Royal Festival Hall tucked among them as a contrasting contemporary note, through the hazy roof-tops to the green hills of Kent. It was a view similar to the one I had looked at in their Bombay office, across the harbour to the hills beyond, when John Rist offered me the job in 1937. Robert began a little selfconsciously

"Prakash," he said, "we don't think Steve Turner can go back to India after his heart attack; and we would like to offer you the chairmanship."

"Thank you, Robert, I appreciate the trust."

This embarrassing ritual over, we began to discuss the details.

In the evening, Andrew Knox, chairman of their Overseas Committee, asked me to a drink at the Liberal Club. He was the last of his kind in the firm. At fiftyeight he had already served it for 42 years. His father before him had moved from the church to join Lord Leverhume in the early days of the business and merged into the legend of the founder. He left behind him his son Andrew, whom the founder must have trained with some personal care. Andrew had graduated through the ranks of service at Port Sunlight, near Liverpool, the home of the business, at London in the new grandeur of Unilever House, and had for many years visited India every winter—a cold weather bird as they used to call the visiting businessmen who came from Europe at the beginning of winter, travelled through the country doing business, and took the P & O mail boat back as the summer began. He became very deeply attached to India, and the Indian business in his eyes could do no wrong and deserved the best. I felt it an honour that he should have been associated with the decision to appoint me their first Indian chairman.

As we walked along the Embankment, he talked about his past and the Indian business. He told me how it had been threatened with extinction when the Swadeshi movement's boycott of foreign goods brought it to a stand-still in the 1920s, and yet that threat gave the business its new foundations. From an indenting business, whose port town distributors of Bombay, Calcutta, Madras and Karachi placed orders on Port Sunlight for distribution in the hinterland, over the next quarter century it grew to be one of the largest manufacturing houses of India; and with all this Andrew had been closely associated and responsible.

In the Liberal Club we were settled in deep leather chairs that could not have seated many Indians in the old days, and he lifted his glass and took the plunge.

"Prakash, we will have to say Prakash and Andrew now, for times have changed. In the old days we could have been Tandon and Knox, and got along pretty well, but today they will think we are not getting on well with each other if we continue to use surnames."

He relaxed. He had got over this onerous duty and now turned to our working relationship.

"It will be for you to keep us in touch with the business. I would like it to work in a way that if someone stops me in the corridor and says, 'What is this we hear about India,' I should be able to say, 'I don't know, but if there is anything to it, we will no doubt hear from Mr.

Tandon, and I will let you know. And if we don't hear from him, then it will not be worth bothering about.' We would prefer not to ask but let you tell us, how much and when you think necessary. There will of course be times when you will want to consult us. After all, it is not the same as working in London, where you can telephone or just walk across to Unilever House. Though you can phone from Bombay, somehow the distance makes it sound like a crisis, which can be misunderstood. So you will have to take most of your decisions by yourself, but when you do want a personal consultation—well, just put on your coat and hat and fly over."

Andrew went on to warn me about the problems of the Indian business, and seemed to come out with pent-up feelings.

"Like too many things in India, things seem never to get a move on. There are always things happening the one way, to slow down; much less happens the other way, to speed it up. And there is always one more good reason that no one else had thought of before to make the government people take another look, just as something is getting done. You have an able government, but the ability seems to go into making more and more rules and producing more good reasons not to do things than anyone else I know of. It all baffles us. We get an interesting picture from here of our operations in many countries, new, developing, developed, old. Few I know have your ability. In South America, Africa, the East, near and far, few I have greater respect for, but you must learn to move faster, at the speed you are capable of, and not always be holding yourselves back.

"I wonder sometimes what stops you. It is not, as in some other countries, a lack of liking for business, for business is in your blood. Nowhere have I seen anything like your wholesale business which for so little can do so much. At less than one per cent they will store, finance and deliver across distances, in dilapidated trucks and bullock carts, but always you can rely on them to do the job. And yet something seems to stand in the way. Our business is sound and well founded and has the capacity for much greater growth.

"And yet while your government is restrictive it is also permissive. In the end you get your way, depending upon your perseverance. But let me not blame your government, for there is a lethargy within the business too. Even after your government has sanctioned you a project, and we have approved of it, you seem to take ages to do it. What takes nine months to build elsewhere takes you five years. Look at your office building that you began over three years ago; I wonder if I will ever enter it in my working life."

Andrew was in a relentless mood. In the past he had discussed these issues with their own chairmen, but that was not the same as talking to me; I was both chairman and Indian and could be held responsible for the sins of both the company and country. It was for me to put them both right! I considered this a tall order but I preferred to listen. This was Andrew's day; it was their day. In the afternoon, passing the office of Bonham-Carter on the floor of the Unilever directors, I had knocked on his door. It was only a few years ago that I had made my coldness to Unilever clear to him and had turned away his feeler about my visiting England to attend a course at Henley Staff College. As I entered his room he rushed across like an eager giant and shook my hand up and down and said "Prakash, this is a great day for all of us—for Unilever, for the Indian company and for me." It was their day, for their experiment with "Isation," meaning indigenising managerial talent up to the highest rungs of the ladder, bore its first significant fruit; my own feeling I would analyse later on the long flight home.

There would be many hours to think alone. I let Andrew say all he had come to say. He was not talkative by nature, and he was a good listener, but whatever he had to say he said, without apologising for length or bluntness. He told me that he did not believe in dressing down a man in the newfangled way, used by some of his colleagues, of inviting him to lunch and letting him eat the food like poison till with the coffee they smoothly began to take him apart. "No, I call the man and tell him across the desk what I find wrong with him, and what he can do to put himself right with me. In the end they have been grateful because this leaves them with their self-respect. It also puts a little fight into them, if they have it in them," and so Andrew went on.

He warned me that my problems would be more with my own people than with them. They found Indians very sensitive and not an easy people to deal with. I remembered what an English writer of the twenties, Edward Thompson, had once said—an Indian is quick to register disappointment but slow to register satisfaction. Gard, my Swedish wife, used to remark that nobody ever seemed to acknowledge wedding presents, or open a gift for a new baby; they just put it aside impassively without a word of thanks; yet a guest could make a blunt comment on your hospitality. A country cousin who paid us a visit remarked upon our home-made ice cream, "In our Bahawalpur there were two kinds of ice cream—the four anna kind and the two anna kind. This is the two anna ice cream."

"We can deal with each other with a directness that we cannot use with you without risking a hurt," said Andrew. He gave me the example of his difficult relations with an English colleague, Paul Addis, whom I knew as an interesting man but not easy to deal with. They did not care for each other, and in the end hardly spoke to each other, which could not fail to be remarked upon in the company. So one day Andrew said to him, "Paul, you do not like me, and I have no great love for you, but it is not fair to the organisation because people are beginning to talk about it. We have to get on with each other." And they did, and even got to like each other, much no doubt to their mutual disgust.

I thought this an extreme example, but Andrew was an unusual person. He was a small, simple man, of a kind I had met in North England in my student days, direct in speech, manner and look. There was a completeness to him that made him totally predictable. He had one set of beliefs, a single faith, one manner, and was totally devoid of mannerisms. I have known him sad, overcome, happy, joyous, but always the same Andrew. His Scottish blood made him the warier as a Lancashireman. He would give when he believed it right, the right amount, no more and no less. I remembered him pulling up a waiter in a West End restaurant. "No, my lad, you put the change down and I will decide what I give you."

We had two drinks and I went my way, thoroughly clear on what was expected of me. With Andrew at least I would never be in doubt. After my farewell visit to Unilever in London seven years later he wrote me a note to say that though I hadn't said anything at our last meeting, he felt that I was leaving with something on my mind. I replied that in leaving the company, to join a state enterprise, I felt what an Indian bride was traditionally said to feel when she leaves the shelter of her home to venture into an unknown world, not knowing how the new world will treat her. To this he replied:

> If you feel that you have left home, I suppose I may claim to be one of your step-parents. An honourable position, and if you feel you need a word of encouragement, or even just a passing word of cheer, I hope you will always feel able to write 'home' to.
>
> Yours,
> Andrew

CHAPTER TWO

The Last "Viceroy" Levers

My salary was fixed at a level to last me for ten years. It was modest by private industry standards in India, and carried practically no perquisite. Robert Siddons and I discussed plans for the new board. They thought that, on account of a big programme for many new projects, I might keep Jim Davies, the technical director, as vice-chairman. I agreed. I also accepted the idea that like the vice-chairman I was before him he should continue to keep his own department. Robert added that Lord Cole, the Unilever chairman, had hoped that Jim would keep the technical side, for without it he and I would get into each other's hair. Just then, Klijnstraa, also a giant of a man, a Dutch member of the overseas committee, joined us. He disagreed and put forth rather a novel view. As the first Indian chairman, I was likely to be called upon by the government and the community for many extramural commitments that I would not be able to refuse. He thought that for this I was also suited by nature. With all the new projects, Jim Davies would not have the time to be a real vice-chairman to me. So he must be kept free of all direct responsibility and concentrate on being a vice-chairman, to enable me to be the kind of chairman Klijnstraa thought I would have to be.

This altogether new idea had a logic that had just not occurred to us. Except at the Unilever centre, at the very top, this had not been tried in any company around the world. Till not so long ago a chairman regarded himself as running the business, instead of directing it through his board of directors. To have both a chairman and a vice-chairman with no direct responsibility in a company that was after all not so large by world standards, was indeed new, and I found myself with an equation that was to have a profound effect on my life inside and out of the firm. One word launched me on a type of a career I had not visualised. If the firm after my departure thought it an experiment of dubious value, and one they never repeated, it certainly enabled me to work out things in a way that gave me much unexpected and worthwhile experience.

In the evening there was a small dinner party to which were invited members of the overseas committee and a few others whom I had known in India. Like all parties at which Andrew Knox was present it was over early. There were no speeches; they just wished me well. That night I took a midnight BOAC Comet to Bombay, the beginning of an interminable series of Bombay-London-Bombay flights, always Air-India on the way out and usually BOAC returning home—a kind of ritual gesture. The two airlines were interesting in their difference, one friendly, colourful and informal in the mediocrity of its food and service; the other impeccable and coldly efficient. Not infrequently the young Air-India hostesses and stewards would ask me about one or other of my children at college in Bombay; the English hostesses and the usually elderly and thin-haired stewards made you feel you were at the Savoy—you had paid to be there and you would get your value, with little extras thrown in if a uniformed airline personage saw you up the gangway. Air-India tried hard, but its boys and girls, used to servants in their homes, never learned to serve formally; they did not object; they just did not know how to. But it was their enthusiastic amateurishness that made the service attractive. On this occasion I was glad to have taken BOAC; I needed to be left alone, to sort out myself, and there were none better than the discreet English staff to trouble you the least once they realised that that was how you wanted it.

I have always enjoyed flying, more so since the planes began to fly high and non-stop over long distances. Detached from earth, sheltered from its ever-insistent communication systems, high up there in the safety of withdrawal, I feel complete in myself; a feeling I can only experience in some inaccessible valley in the Himalayas. I am happiest alone, with myself; and up in the air there is a feeling of primeval aloneness. Nothing can happen except a sudden end, and time is whole, even though brittle. In this peace through a night and a day I sat with pencil and paper, and thought. Writing, even jotting an odd point here and there, puts order into my thinking, as much as a tidy surrounding does. Order does free my thought!

The company had decided on a large number of projects. I began to count and it made an impressive list. New detergent powder plants and modernisation of the old soap plants, more glycerine capacity, new poultry and cattle food plants; a new nickel catalyst plant, a new pea and food dehydration plant; a new research complex, a new plant for fine chemicals and perfumery, a new dairy and milk processing factory ringed with fifty milk collection and chilling centres spread over a radius of fifty miles; expansion of all four vanaspati factories and a host of minor improvements and plant changes all over India; and a new head office building. It was a programme running into many crores of rupees, and yet money was no problem—we had enough reserves—the problem was only one, government permissions, permissions, the many, many permissions, just to be permitted to grow.

Why should permission to grow be the problem, when growth was what every Indian, and the government, wanted so passionately, I asked myself. Could one not visit New Delhi and proudly announce to those to whom the power to grant growth belonged one's intention to grow in a really big way? One would arrive with an armful of plans and put them down on the table, one upon another, in a sizeable pile. For one company it was quite formidable, especially as an earnest of the intention of a company that was foreign and wished to stay and identify itself with the country's economy. My spirits rose at the thought that as the first Indian chairman I would start at the threshold of so much development, the most extensive and diverse ever in the history of this company, or many other Unilever companies, or other companies in India then. I was fortunate to inherit the blueprints and all the spade work that had gone into them, the financial and the technical planning; my task was only to clear with government the formal sanctions, to arrange for the small amount of foreign exchange involved, and to start. But I felt diffident. I had heard enough of the impermissiveness of government, not just towards a foreign firm but to industry in general. As a matter of principle, industrial growth seemed to be carefully pruned and curbed.

I began to delve deeper into my doubts, both to rationalise them and to find an answer, because already I was beginning to get worried about government's general attitude to industry, especially in the private sector; and why would not such a negative attitude attach itself one day to the public sector, when its turn came. There was a basic lack of permissiveness, and an imperative of control in the attitude, and little regard for growth in reality, though much lip service was paid to it. I could sense that perhaps increasingly our problems would be outside the firm. Inside, we had strong skills and structure, and a capacity to maintain a forward thrust; but all this could only be geared to growth if the environment permitted it. If at each step red lights went on, and each clearance made a time-consuming process, progress would be slow. There certainly was no smooth track laid in front of those who wanted to grow fast, with green lights all the way, even once the starting semaphore signal dropped. And why, when the whole time we passionately wanted development and growth? Like a gum boil my tongue went round and round it, unable to cure it.

Stepping out of the plane at Santa Cruz airport, Bombay's June heat and humidity, built to the pre-monsoon crescendo, hit me in the face. The air was like steam and carried the mixed odours of the buffalo stables of Andheri and the suburban shanties that were built on the marshes of the creek, where the tidal water mixed with the refuse from the slaughter house and the open drainage had churned into a stagnant black liquid that seeped and oozed out of thickets of lush grass and mangrove swamps. This was the early morning smell before the sun rose to bleach it out and the breeze from the sea aerated the atmosphere. The terminal building was a chaos of officials, forms, declarations, certificates, stamps, methodical searches, including an account of where each one of the past seven days had been spent; but it was a highly organised kind of chaos in which no control was missed out. Each authority, health, passport, prohibition, customs, foreign exchange had to be fully satisfied, and each authority in turn had to fully satisfy its own Audit, for whose each sustained objection a new control was introduced. As I was being shepherded out of this maze by an airline official I saw Gard, my wife, at the other end of the hall, looking eager and questioning.

Driving home on the new highway, the early morning defecators, each with a water can, made usually from an empty Quaker Oats or Dalda tin, made a strange sight for an international city. In our school English they were "answering the call of nature," an imagery understandable where nature called you out of the village into field or forest. Used to it from childhood in the open countryside of the Punjab, where after the cutting of the crops little privacy was left, the sight did not repel me much; but it did not belong to the modern cosmopolitan city known as the Gateway to India. An American architect, Louis Kahn, who designed the impressive Indian Institute of Management's campus at Ahmedabad, raved over it. He called it the daily communion with nature.

The state authorities felt ashamed of this sight, next door to their international airport, to foreign visitors their first introduction to the country. There were protests from the tourist department, the Rotary clubs and the elegant citizens of Bombay, less for the lack of elementary sanitary facilities for the poor shanty dwellers than for its closeness to the airport. Plastered cement walls were erected on both sides of the road to hide the hutments, and painted with cheerful folk pictures. So the gregarious defecators, who ejoyed the sight of the traffic, moved to the road side of the walls. Here and there, wherever there was enought space left newcomers put up more tin sheds and gunny sack huts to take advantage of the wall. Next, the municipality built some latrines with flush that nobody used, and at last everybody gave up, except the shanty dwellers. They continued to treat the area as their domain and to sit there every morning, preferring to face the highway and see the traffic go past.

Tired suddenly beyond words, I remembered Hoskyns-Abrahall, an earlier chairman, when he had succeeded Pettit as chairman, telling me how different and suddenly alone he felt the first night after he took over. Every problem of the day before assumed different proportions because it was now entirely his. In the middle of the night he woke up oppressed, palpitating, in a sweat, andsent for the doctor, who shrewdly gave him a sedative and sent him back to bed. He had been standing in for Pettit during his leave abroad and managed it pretty well for two months, and yet when the letter came from London informing him that Pettit would be leaving India and they would like him to succeed, something happened, something changed. Till then all problems had ultimately been Pettit's; now they were all his. Something suddenly snapped—the dependence; the lifeline broke and he was all by himself.

Some years earlier, at a seminar, Abrahall had remarked in his characteristic shy manner, how a man at the top would dearly love to know how he was doing, and yet, he thought, it was a temptation he must resist. He must choose loneliness if he chose the top. He had to be his own best judge and worst critic.

An indifferent sleeper normally, the very first problem I faced contained its own remedy, Gärd told me afterward that I had slept, but for a short break or two, for twentytwo hours. I woke up tired no longer, no longer diffident, confident neither—just cool. Nor was I ever to experience tiredness again, nor elation or depression; just an aloneness always. On this even, detached note I was to continue for many years.

I was gradually to discover the deep anxieties that must have surrounded Turner, my predecessor, in steering the business through the currents. While he was ready to discuss his plans with us on the board, and in fact he kept us meticulously informed about his discussions with London and New Delhi; not even with me, his vice-chairman and likely successor would he ever share his doubts and hesitations, fear and anxieties, which the job, I was to discover, never lacked for a day. He shared things at the surface, but the shocks and tremors underneath he absorbed alone.

To each of his plans for growth, questions were put, motivated partly by the embarrassing position government found itself in on account of opposition to us by a leading Indian competitor, Tatas, who had gathered the smaller manufacturers into an association whose task seemed only to oppose Levers. They began in the middle 1950s to complain against its size and growth and advertised in the press about "the foreign firm" that should be stopped from growing further.

This anti-Lever campaign was carried to the press, the public and government, sometimes in a quite bizarre form. Naval Tata, a charmingly colourful personality, in a dramatic gesture hired a Dakota and with his staff set out on a tour of India, holding meetings with vanaspati and soap wholesalers, pleading with them not to patronise that "foreign firm." He invoked the "swadeshi" spirit and quoted Gandhiji to boycott foreign products, even though they were now made in India. It had no effect on our sales, but he did get government worried enought to begin to raise objections to our plans for growth.

Of Naval's "Bharat Yatra" we heard some vivid descriptions from salesmen and wholesalers in places like Patna and Amritsar, where a top class Bombay Parsee, his Bombay Hindi laced with Parsi, Gujarati and English, was something outside their experience. In later years, when we became good friends, Naval Tata and I had a good laugh about it.

In spite of all this effort, I think Tatas did our business no harm, nor did their attacks in the press take any customers away. People in India were, if anything, on the rebound from swadeshism. After years of shortages of imported consumer goods, with shoddy but expensive substitutes, people were glad to buy anything of quality, and they were not interested in the finer distinction between made in India by a foreign or an Indian firm. The foreigner gone, boycott of foreign goods as a political protest had meaning no longer. But they did start something which was in time to grow bigger than they could ever have imagined—an economic outlook whose independence was close to xenophobia and isolationism, which was to shrink our industrial and technological contracts abroad. When world technology began to travel freely across frontiers, we treated it warily; and while Russia signed an agreement with Fiat we terminated it. Our terms to foreign investment became stricter and frankly uninviting; we grew firmer in our belief that the answer to gaps in our technology was not to learn where we could but to learn it ourselves, even at the cost of some delay and outdated technology. We must discover the wheel by ourselves. Something else also came to the surface.

To protect Indian industry, duties had been progressively increased since the 1920s till there was virtually a ban on imports, and industrial growth was planned in such a way that no new production could be sanctioned if somewhere else there existed unutilised capacity. When Turner sought permission to expand, they demurred on the ground that the industry had enough surplus capacity which ought to be used up before they could allow us to put new capacity. It was a new economic logic of the convoy; the fastest in an industry must wait till the slowest caught up with it.

Tatas were no ordinary firm, not just a big industrial house; they were an institution of a kind that probably existed nowhere else in the world. They had pioneered India's industrialisation and struck new trails in virtually every direction—steel, textiles, chemicals, electronics, consultancy, insurance; they even started perhaps the first airline in Asia. They were patrons of science, culture and social uplift; they had been in the vanguard of our nascent political life and contributed an early president to the Indian National Congress, and also the first communist member to the British Parliament, Saklatwala of the Tata family. Their prestige and influence was enhanced by the fact that they had not shied away from political protest at a time when protest was uncomfortable for a firm dependent on a foreign government. When at last we had our own government, one of Tata's early acts was to protest against a big firm growing bigger, little realising that here they began something that eventually was to rebound on size itself. They set in motion a bias against all large and successful industry.

I think there was also the reawakening in us of a feeling that I think is perhaps always close to our otherwise quite friendly approach to the foreigner. An Englishman who came to Bombay from Indonesia in 1955 told me that he was struck by the absence of such hostility as he had felt in the streets of Jakarta, where the foreigner got sullen looks and was even edged off the pavement. I explained how in the worst days of the "Quit India" movement in 1942 Englishmen scattered in remote places felt safe. Even in the parts of Bihar, where for sometime British law and order had ceased to exist, there were no cases of British families attacked. Rare even were cases of insult to an individual Englishman in public, let alone injury. The insults were usually their prerogative. The freedom movement seldom took a violent edge despite the provocation of the opposing might.

With independence, no longer voiceless and choiceless, we began to develop our own new relationship with foreigners. Politically, we opened missions all over the world; socially the very British and the Europeans who had kept their distance in the past were now glad to be made welcome. The Indian young, always venturesome, now began to pour out in thousands as students, doctors, nurses and workers in any capacity where they could learn or earn better abroad. But all the same, while extroverts abroad, at home we became defensive and sensitive, almost unconsciously at least mildly anti-western, with a patronising attitude towards Africans and fellow Asians. As I once told a foreigner—in India we are freely critical of all we do, but don't you ever agree with us there? As years passed and lakhs of Indians worked and settled abroad, and remitted hundreds of crores home, our regulations became progressively tighter about the few hundred foreigners who worked in India, mostly in some multinationals, and the small fraction of the inward remittances that they and their firms remitted out.

Steve Turner was caught between the growing pressure that customer demands placed upon his production capacity and government's pressure not to permit him to expand. It was the kind of situation he was not cut out to meet. He cultivated no personal equations, as is the common approach in India, with our competitors, or with government secretaries and ministers, with whom he could have talked things over, explained his case, and come to some kind of compromise, as we always do in the long run. Lord Heyworth, the Unilever chairman, when he visited India in 1957, went all out to meet Tatas, to understand their point. He spoke to J.R.D. Tata, and wondered whether the line adopted by them would not in the long run harm the interests of private industry in general. It could be Tata Oil Mills against the larger Hindustan Lever today, but inevitably this line would extend to the smaller companies versus the larger; and if Levers were "monopolists" today Tatas would be the "monopolists" of tomorrow. Did they have a basic faith in enterprise and competition? And why could they not do better? There was no mystique in our success. Tata, cool and logical, a modern executive of the international kind, saw Heyworth's point, and the pressure did begin to lessen, though the line stuck with the authorities and was never to be loosened again. It began its own chain reaction that only went the one way; ending twenty years later with the main activity of the large units in soap industry being taken away from it and reserved for the small producers, at least in a government industrial policy statement.

Steve's departure was marked by a simple farewell ceremony. I made a short speech, some others spoke, and he replied briefly. It was an occasion of pure sadness; few ever expected to see him again. But the directors' farewell party at his flat that night was a cheerful affair. Here he let go, and so did we all. He was totally relaxed, his acid wit returning as the evening wore, and he was genuinely carried away by the occasion. Next afternoon the directors and wives bade him a final farewell in his flower-filled cabin on the Italian boat. This was the real occasion—a touching end to his twenty years in India; an end to an era; a transfer of power of its own kind; the departure of the last Unilever viceroy

When I saw him next year in London at his only home during many home leaves, Hotel Coburg in Kensington, I realised that he had made up his mind to go. Shortly afterwards, having dinner with our research director, Varadarajan, one evening at the Coburg, he collapsed and passed away quietly. Unilever telexed me in Bombay to ask if I knew of anyone in England outside the company who should be informed of his death! I remembered he had a sister somewhere.

The day after Steve's departure from Bombay I walked into the office building that I had first entered over twenty years ago. The doorman, a Sikh ex-havildar, gave me the smartest salute ever, the liftmen beamed and stood aside, the sepoys bowed, the clerks stood at their desks and smiled sheepishly, and as I walked into the board room, where the managers had assembled for my first "prayer meeting," as we called our weekly early morning chit chats, they stood up in discreet applause. Having reached as far as I could, I realised how deference and seniority go together in our society.

Uncertainly I walked up to Turner's chair and thanked them. I felt strange to be at the end of the board table over whose full length I had hesitatingly moved up over the years. I thought of ten years ago, when I was first placed on the board; twentyfour years had gone since I had stepped on the first rung of the ladder! Steve's departure left me feeling like an uncertain ship's captain on his first voyage in command after the pilot has left.

From the board room I walked to the chairman's large hexagonal office. Its French windows and balconies looked over the Bombay harbour with its docks and ships, and a blue expanse of the bay. I looked across the desk, at Steve's empty leather chair, the dark brown carpet, the glass shelves with samples, the full-length portrait of Lord Leverhume, the founder, in his baronial regalia, made to look very patrician by Laslo. On another wall was Queen Elizabeth, with a "Portia look." Laslo and Annagoni had both done a flattering job. Should I take them both away or add Gandhi and Nehru? Eventually I hit upon the idea of giving them both to my Welsh vice-chairman. It was a custom left behind by the British to hangd the portraits of the emperors and empresses in all government offices.

I pictured my predecessors, Shaw, my first managing director, sitting in this chair and telling me that the experiment they were starting could only go one way, to the ultimate in Indianisation; the subsequent interviews, once to mumble a few words of sympathy over his wife's death, and next seeking permission for my own marriage, as was the custom those days in British firms; the more necessary in my case because the British Legation in Stockholm had enquired of authorities in Bombay if I was in a position to support a European wife. A British police sergeant had called on Shaw who, pre-warned, gave me a "clearance" On another occasion, moved by Hitler's mounting success in Europe, I had felt the urge to join the war; but Shaw had laughed and said that although things were going badly they would manage to win in the end, as they always did; there was no point therefore in my joining. And later, being called by Pettit, his successor, when he gave me my first chance in marketing; I thought of his constant encouragement over the years, as if determined to prove his point that I would make it, often in face of my awkward and resisting ways.

I went back to my vice-chairman's room and I sat in a reverie, looking at the past and peering into the fog of the future, till Mrs. Aga, the redoubtable Parsi lady who looked after administration, came in to ask when I would move into my new office and whether I wanted any changes made. Changes, none, I said, and I didn't think I would like to move in yet; I preferred to take some time to adjust.

Banerji, our chief medical officer, had nursed Steve Turner carefully during his last months in India. I called him to say that he was going to have a tougher job with me, for strains and stresses were going to be even severer. I would do all I could to help him. Banerji took it all very seriously, and through the years we guarded my health together. At first I used to feel self-conscious walking frequently through the office to his room, wondering what the staff would think. "What's wrong with the chairman; always going to the doctor?" I would drop in for a check and chat, and it developed into an interestingly casual relationship, good-humoured but with an underlying seriousness. He never made me feel watched, and I never kept anything away from him. I encouraged him to develop a similar relationship with others, the older men, those under special strain, but he found this less easy. Most people, he said, were on the defensive and regarded it as an intrusion. Some could have been the gainers. Banerji in fact taught me to come to terms with the stresses of the job, the long hours of work, the busy social schedule, the hardships of travel in a country where a flight to anywhere mosty starts at dawn, and departures rarely on time, when there began the era of interminable strikes and delays, until a determined chairman of Indian Airlines, Pratap Lal, put things right a decade later.

I envied the executives in the West their shorter hours, five-day week, regular holidays and, most of all, the relative lack of their environmental strain. Their stresses were from within the organisation, not from the problems of their society. They led an orderly existence with work and leisure in separate compartments. The telephone did not ring early in the morning and late in the evening for a business call, nor did people come to their house to "pay their respects," really to seek favour. It was a habit cultivated under the Raj, and the British in their turn had acquired it from the Moghuls. It still flourishes; some administrators and many heads of family business still hold "durbars" at home, especially on Sunday mornings. It all adds to the strains, especially the new undelightful habit of holding seminars and conferences over the week-end to "save" working time.

CHAPTER THREE

New Delhi

I envied the chairman who came from outside, a stranger to all, unknown and untested; free therefore to create new relationships. In an organisation like H.L.L., which did not rely upon hierarchical assertion of authority, the chairman was just one of the directors, primus inter pares, with no powers of his own. He was only the chairman of the board that decided collectively all matters of importance. But to have been one of them for so long and one day to be their leader is not easy, even though fortunately for me I had superseded no one. To assume leadership in a discussion revealing differences that could sometimes be quite sharp, and try to obtain an acceptable decision or, failing that, create a decision acceptable to all, was not easy at the beginning. Fortunately, the system of having a vice-chairman who, other things being equal, would succeed the chairman, was a useful institution. There was no break and no guessing. A year of vice-chairmanship and six months of acting during Steve Turner's illness had besides given my colleagues and others a feel of me, my way and style, so different from Turner, and especially my idiosyncracies.

My first problem with them came soon enough, and appropriately for the Indian scene it was in union relations. There was trouble in one of our factories, where the union president had assaulted a worker, who had openly disagreed with him. The factory manager wanted to take the obvious action of dismissing him, but the state government intervened and the labour authority concerned asked us to let him off with an apology, making it known at the same time that if we insisted upon dismissal, the man might well be reinstated by them on appeal. I favoured accepting the man's apology and issuing him a warning; for to have him reinstated would visibly weaken our authority. My colleagues all felt that no such flagrant indiscipline can be conducive to peace in a factory, and if the state government interfered—well, never mind, we will have at least made our own stand clear.

The board discussion went with positions hardening, and while the directors were on one side, the vice-chairman sensibly kept neutral, seemingly to protect my position. It was a Saturday afternoon, and eventually I decided to sleep over it and resume on Monday. Jim Davies, the vice-chairman, followed me into my room and spoke plainly but with much understanding.

"I see your hesitation, Prakash; you don't want the state government to reverse the decision since that would undermine our authority within the factory. I personally would take a chance, at least letting it be known that dismissal was our straightforward answer to indiscipline. If we are overruled, let us be overruled; but let us not take less than the right and deserved action. However, the main thing is to act. Further discussion will only show our own internal division, and such things get known. Give your decision. They will take it; they would have taken it this afternoon, had you ended up with a decision."

"Thanks, Jim. I needed that plain speaking. I found it difficult at our very first disagreement to overrule them all."

They had anticipated my decision to accept the apology and received it gracefully. No one demurred; they all understood. Curiously, the union man completely misunderstood it and started boasting about it. Before long he repeated himself and left us with no choice. I was not worried about being overruled this time. He tried hard for years and brought pressures to bear, but we refused to take him back. He had had his chance.

It was nothing if not a blunt board, of determined personalities. The two Englishmen were experienced, out to maintain the highest production standards, and themselves highly disciplined men. If at first they tended to treat me as almost a part of their Unilever job abroad to bring up the new chairman, they were sensitive enough soon to realise that I was conscious of it.

I had next to start dealing with the great problem that was to be my major preoccupation, dealing with "New Delhi," as the administration was referred to by business in Bombay. A new, quite complex relationship between government and business had grown over the years, ever since the British government first began directing industry during World War II, and business began its new dependence upon government decision for its growth. Before the war Delhi had no importance to us, when we had just a small warehouse. Our sub-office in Lahore was moved to Delhi during the war, as we found a growing need to call at the central government secretariat, at first to get an odd import licence or arrange for supplies to the defence, and later to discuss price controls as they assumed importance. In 1944, planning for the post-war brought in a new government policy to plan and control industrial growth; and the Delhi office acquired an important new role. Pettit, our chairman, deeply involved in getting a share in this growth, sometimes travelled twice in the same week to New Delhi, a train journey of twentyfour hours with invariable and interminable delays caused by the heavy troop movement.

After the war, New Delhi became also the businessman's capital, where lay both patronage and permission, and as the first air services began their regular schedules, executives soon found themselves taking permanent suites at Delhi hotels. Some companies rented bungalows, called guest houses, where the visiting senior executives stayed. As planning and development regulations proliferated and began to cocoon industry, a stage was to come when for allotment of raw materials, for installing plant, shifting an existing one to a new site, for launching a new product or even a new size in a package, capitalisation of reserve, bonus issues, new issues, debentures and large loans, staff retrenchment, import of a foreign technician and his terms, appointment of directors and their terms, import of knowhow, process technology or a collaboration, taking a young trainee fresh from college if he happened to be closely related to a civil servant; for all these and most conceivable things, one had to ask New Delhi. It was safer in fact to ask before acting at all. As the administration expanded to cope with its ever-growing task, procedures grew proportionately more complex, till the whole system was like a honeycomb. Permissions naturally took longer, and so did the executive visits, and the Delhi offices grew ever bigger. Interestingly, it was not only private industry that opened representative offices in New Delhi but also the state governments and public enterprises, because their problems were not dissimilar basically—dealing with procedures and delays, and obtaining sanctions from the central government. The system had at least the merit of impartiality, for it dealt as slowly with its own state governments and public enterprises as it did with private industry and public at large.

Dealing with New Delhi posed me a delicate task. Large companies had developed their relationships in different ways. Some had a Delhi director, usually chosen for his capacity to foster contacts; others went a stage further and appointed a retired I.C.S., whose junior colleagues and subordinates would provide convenient contacts for some years to come. He would also know well the anatomy of decision-making and be able to forecast the course of the File. Some companies showed a predilection for employing politically well connected sons and nephews with easy access to power. The interesting, if not cynical part of this whole process was that mostly everybody got what he wanted, but it had to go through a long-drawn drill that satisfied a series of impeccable desirables in planning and procedures. If the request did not fit in the frame, this added to the time; but little was ever denied; only everything went slower, and like a sluggish stream less water went through. There were of course those who got more and sooner through their own devious ways. In fairness, the large international and the Indian companies of the professionally managed kind did not ask for more than what was their due, but matters that had been theirs to decide at their management's initiative and discretion were now subject of prolonged negotiations. The time that should have gone into policies went into procedures. Growth was thus painfully slow.

What made it more complex was the fact that all ministries worked independently of each other, without a system of coordinating people's problems that concerned more than one of them. Where the ministries should have done their own inter-ministerial clearing, they expected you to go from ministry to ministry to get each clearance. At the end of the labyrinth, there was always the risk of an unexpected innocent casual comment on a file which could freeze things, because no one would act finally until the road was cleared of the block, no matter how small or irrelevant.

I had only a distant acquaintance with this system and its culture. I knew no one in Delhi. I had met one or two secretaries through Maurice and Taya Zinkin (he, first an I.C.S. and then with Unilever, and she a prominent journalist), but so casually as not to be able to claim their acquaintance or even ring them up. To approach a secretary is not like approaching even the most senior executive in Bombay, or anywhere else in the world, you don't ring and just get through; you explain unconvincingly instead to a suspicious personal assistant who you are, what your business is; and if he does not recognise your name, the answer is invariably that the secretary is at a meeting, which in fact he is for most of the day, or he has just left the room, or he has gone to the bathroom, you are informed with perfect candour. If you leave your name and ask to be called back you wait in vain; and so you keep trying, adding to the assistant's frustration and yours. But if it could take a week to contact someone on the telephone, it could take months to get a reply to a letter. Sometimes you did receive a prompt acknowledgement that the matter was receiving attention, and that usually was the end of the matter. There was a strange unconscious cynicism to it all. No one therefore approached this way. The companies developed their own contacts at different levels, between their Delhi representative and his personal assistants and the secretariat hierarchies. It was a curiously self-defeating process that helped no one but wasted a lot of time on all sides. The personal secretaries defended the secretaries from the barrage of visitors, who in turn argued that nothing moved unless they met the secretaries themselves; and so everybody met them.

With such utter dependence on New Delhi, and my utter innocence of its cocooned culture, I wondered how I would ever make any headway with my long list of projects, each needing more than one sanction. Perhaps I should also go in for a retired civilian or someone with a name to represent us in Delhi; a key to open doors. But my instincts held me back. Somehow it did not seem to fit in with our own style of management. I decided to leave the matter alone and feel my way through, even though Unilever told me that in their Pakistan business they had taken on for this purpose a couple of prematurely retired English I.C.S.

With much trepidation I decided to take my first plunge into New Delhi and start the round; little knowing that New Delhi was to swallow me slowly until I would belong there. The first secretary I chose to meet was K.B. Lall, because I had heard so much about him from the Zinkins that I felt I almost knew him, and from their description he appeared for a civil servant to be somewhat of a character.

Lall was then joint secretary in the ministry of commerce and industry. A Srivastava, he belonged to the Delhi Kayasth class, whose remarkable history ought one day to be told. A business caste, it comprised a large number of families—Narains, Lalls, Bahadurs, Dayals, Sahais, Srivastavas, Mathurs—all closely related through marriage, sharing wealth and influence and notoriously nepotistic. Settled in Delhi for centuries, they had made their peace with each wave of invasion and each new dynasty, serving it in business and at court, with a loyalty that was total while the dynasty lasted, and upon its eclipse as total again to the successors. They let the wave submerge them, but when the wave had passed and calm returned, like little rocks they came to the surface and reoccupied their traditional positions. The new dynasty needed money to pay troops, fight wars and build new forts; business had to flourish to provide taxes and levies. The need was mutual. The Kayasths formed the financial system that could only be destroyed at the king's own peril. They no doubt had their ups and downs, but they bounced back each time and survived the violent change from the Moghuls to the British; and they held key positions in the New Delhi of independent India in their traditional network.

He was a handsome greying man in his forties; with an odd mind that could be mercurial and ponderous, and a mobile face which could suddenly set when he was interested in what you said or when he came close to a decision; and yet he was curiously ponderous. Through the discussions he kept up a jovial facade of cultivated nonchalance, punctuated with much deliberate laughter and a complex, sometimes forced humour, whose best part was the barbs he threw around. I explained that I was new to the job, new to Delhi, new to everything, and in my newness quite diffident. As I always played the cards facing up, he could rest assured that my demands would be few and reasonable, and my advice, if ever sought, objective. Perhaps something touched him in my open diffidence. He said, "Remember, you may find us indecisive and dilatory but, compared with the British civil servant, with us you enjoy an advantage that is most worthwhile. When my British counterpart in Whitehall makes up his mind, it is made, there is no further argument; but when we decide, if the decision does not suit you, you will always come back—and the door will be open." And then he laughed "We remain indecisive even after we have decided."

Lall was an interesting mixture of a modern British trained civil servant, impeccable, suave, competent equally at procedure and solution, with the administrator's gift of lowering his antennae to what he found imprudent to perceive and always determined to get what he wanted. He had the Kayasth flair for business and results, with the curiously complicated mind that in face of a straight solution took a deliberately cautious detour. An interesting trait I was to find commonly among administrators—almost an instinct to make a detour and leave no traces behind. This contradiction between their capacity to perceive and to react, and much less to commit, I found, seemed a product of an alien training grafted on an Indian mind; of a pragmatism shot through with philosophy and flexible values. I suppose this flexibility was a quality of ours that suited the British, who themselves were adept at its use.

I began to understand their systems and how they operated. I found that the administrators, the Lalls included, were masters of power but slaves of their own system that was basically suspicious and untrusting. Where this extraordinary system had begun and how it would ever end, was to me, as much as to them, an everlasting source of wonder. What E.M. Forster had called "the maniacal suspicion, that besetting Indian sin," had so percolated down the administration that we considered it a legacy from the British, part of their mistrust of their Indian subordinates taking advantage of any permissiveness. This was however facile since we preserved it with tenacity and made it even more rigid and pervasive than what they left behind. It must too have belonged to us. In many years in Delhi I was to ask this question again and again. There were many ingenious but unconvincing answers that left even the administrators themselves unconvinced. A section officer in charge of a few clerks was the first level to "note". The simplest form of hierarchical life, totally innocent of the technical, financial or any other issues of a problem, with only a knowledge of precedents and a great adroitness at the cautious but negative supposition, was entrusted to analyse and comment on a case complex far beyond his comprehension; and he could cast it in a mould that could not be broken even by the secretary. This was something no one could explain. They all complained about the tyranny of the system, but they all accepted it helplessly. It was not that they had become desensitised; it was worse—they had accepted it as Sindbad's old man—like poverty and dirt in India, with the resigned acceptance that "they shall always be with us". There was no fine impatience shown, just complacence. "It cannot be changed."

One of its more trying characteristics was also its eel-like capacity to slither even out of its own decision through a series of qualifications. Having once announced with great flourish that to stimulate production a twentyfive per cent expansion could be made in a firm's licensed capacity without government's sanction, provided there was no foreign exchange or substantial imported equipment involved, there came a clarifying and circular letter, that

> Expansion of capacity of existing units within certain limits has to be interpreted in the context of each specific industry and should not be understood as overriding all other considerations of policy. It is not the intention to relax all controls over expansion of industry.

The positive flourishes were in the brave announcements; the negative whimpers followed in the clarifications.

From the lowest level the file progressed upward, acquiring notes at each level, but as it rose up the ladder, even an innocuous twist in an earlier noting could damn the case in a way that the highest with all his power and conviction might not be able to undo. An innocent doubt cast, a sceptical question placed gently under the skin of the case; and no one could afford the risk of overruling, just in case the decision were to go wrong and a subsequent audit or a parliamentary committee wonder why this decision was taken without first dispelling the doubt which had been posed. The fact that out of a hundred decisions this was the only one that went wrong would be totally irrelevant, because they were only examining this particular instance of failure and not the many successes. It was no valid argument that this one failure was compensated many times. Why this fallure; why was notice not taken of the caution, the doubt, the question; and the questioning could be relentless. It was no answer that anyone can raise a doubt; that anything in retrospect could have been done better. It was a system that could only breed fear, caution and delay.

The system could also be made to work flexibly. The higher-up could call the lower down, and carefully plant ideas for the note—and then each stage would echo back, and one heard what one had tuned in for. Each stage built the case in a given direction, precedents that suited were quoted, exceptions cited and a welter of favourable arguments put forward, with usually, for abundant caution, some suitable but easily disposable doubts subtly cast, out of which the high-up chose the ones that suited him: and he wrote out his own "balanced" note.

On my return I discussed it with my colleagues and we all felt that despite our innocence the right way with New Delhi was to deal direct, to convey the convictions behind our aims and efforts, and for this Chandy, our legal director on the board, was well suited. But after only a few months, towards the end of 1961, Chandy left to head the new Indian Institute of Management at Calcutta. His experience in industry as an analyst and adviser, his intellect, and his pedagogic style made him an ideal management academic, better than he was to fare as an operator later.

Chandy's unexpected departure was a great loss to me, and left a gap that had to be filled quickly. I decided to try and experiment and send a young man, Aspi Moddie, who had joined us late, after a wartime career in the army and then the new Indian Administrative Service.

☆

As a district officer in Bihar Moddie made somewhat of a name for himself as a young man of unusual initiative and thrust. He had turned up in my office one day in 1952, a small compact man in his early thirties, with a cultivated crisp style. I asked him why he wanted to leave the administration, and he gave me a list of reasons, mainly centering on the difficulties of working in the districts under the new political masters. Stories had already begun to be told about these rulers, and the ways of personal rule of some.

These were early days of power, and the imitation of the earlier rulers varied from the naive to the ludicrous. There was one minister who sent in advance the programme for his visit to a district town: arrival at the station at 8.15 a.m., garlanding; reception at the town hall at 9 a.m.; and so on through the day. A police friend, who gave me the story, said it was good to have plain instructions so that the police were lined up and the garlands, kept moist in a basket, as the minister beamed and said they shouldn't have taken all the trouble. There was another who got upset because the red carpet was not long enough. The arrival of public figures with a cavalcade of motorcars, with the national flag fluttering at the old British circuit house, where police presented arms and took up positions to guard, struck familiar chords. Inside, delegations waited with petitions, complaints and offers of fealty; and for favours from the district authorities.

Moddie's young ideals were shattered. He saw interminable delays, red tape, hesitation and, at the political levels, much more. Some of it was endemic in the administration, but, he said, a new hesitancy was creeping in. The administration had always been slow, running at its original mid-nineteenth century speed, but, backed by the system, it could be decisive, as long as it acted in the desired direction of subserving the broad interests of the Raj. Now the system itself was tending to become intangible and amorphous, depending on the whims and interest of an individual minister. The supplicants in the circuit house would ask him to intercede with the administrator to release a man from jail and arrange for the criminal charge pending against him to be dropped, or to allot a scarce rationed commodity, sold at a premium in the open market, to someone who had no right to it. Such waywardness confused the administrators. When Moddie once said to one of his seniors that he proposed to act in a certain way, his senior agreed and told him to go ahead, but added that if there was disapproval from the minister, Moddie would have to square it up himself. I told Moddie to go back, for his reasons for leaving were not good enough. The new era was not even five years old, much change had to take place, and not always for the better, but to quit soon was a hasty decision and a kind of withdrawal in face of a problem. He ought to give it a trial for another six months. Half a year later Moddie came back, determined to resign.

Moddie, an ideal choice for New Delhi, did well in creating an understanding between us and government. He was different from other representatives in that he played his role in a low key; did not throw parties; and relied upon the strength of our case, neither giving nor receiving favours. His old Bihar colleagues, of whom there were quite a number at the centre, felt at ease with him in his new role.

About Chandy's replacement on the board, Unilever in London suggested that on the assumption that I stayed as chairman for ten years till the retiring age of sixty, would I like to project how I saw the board manned over the decade, and my likely successor. We had tacitly agreed that there would be two expatriate directors out of the usual strength of eight, and an Indian chairman, and preferably the vice-chairman Indian too. With these assumptions, I prepared a plan for ten years, ending with who might succeed me as chairman; someone who would have to make the board in about 1965, be vice-chairman in 1968, and chairman in 1971, upon my retirement.

A ten-year exercise of this kind was like playing a chess game, moving pieces forward and off the board till a winning piece reached the top, or, like snakes and ladders, some would fall away and some lag behind. It was an exciting thought that the one who made the board in 1971 in my time, and succeeded me, might, all things being equal, remain head of the company till 1981; and the likelihood that one of those we would place on our "A" list, the pipeline to the board, before 1971, would be my successor's successor from 1981 to 1991! Thus in 1961 I was looking ahead thirty years to a time when I would certainly not be around; but whatever the shape and activities of the company then, the promising men would be trained in all kinds of testing situations, exposed to the latest in technical, financial and managerial ideas all over the world, attending courses wherever advanced thinking was offered, and always be kept in line with the finest of their international collegues, men running similar companies around the globe. Some day, in a world government they could move with complete ease from one country to another. It caught my imagination to be the architect of such a plan. There was always of course the risk that men so well groomed would be tempted away. Some of the best among them did indeed move to government, where their special culture must have been an asset valued.

The discussions in London brought forth a droll point. Ernest Woodruffe, later chairman of Unilever, asked:

"Supposing, Prakash, you were run over by a bus tomorrow, what should we do?"

I proceeded to explain the possible immediate and the subsequent moves.

"But supposing your successor got run over by a bus the day after?"

I explained the next set of moves. The exercise had so absorbed me that I must have done some hard thinking even at the subconscious level. We laughed when I said that we might leave it at the second catastrophe and not strain the law of probability too much.

Seven years later, when I asked hurriedly to leave three years ahead of time, I suggested that Vasant Rajadhyaksha, who according to plans was to become vice-chairman just then, and chairman in three years, could be made chairman right away. The ten years plan was compressed into seven, but it worked.

To me, this exercise had a special interest, because succession in India is a delicate subject, usually avoided till events overtake and something has to be hastily done. I think it goes deep into our culture. When we were children, any hint of a guest's intention to depart was hushed up, something that must not be discussed. It was met by a family chorus: "Don't say anything like that. Haven't we made you comfortable in our poor home?" His bed roll would be unpacked as ceremoniously as he had packed it, and the guest would shamefacedly have to wait for another chance to get away. It was the same with an allusion to death. A sensible man might want to make a will, or some arrangements with his sons about the division of the property in the event of his death. This would lead to loud protests from the family, asking him to take the name of God and withdraw his words. So the subject was closed and, instead, when death came there was the usual bickering that often broke up hitherto united families.

CHAPTER FOUR

Unions

Nineteen sixtyone was a wonderful year for India, the last of the halcyon years of the Nehru era, when everything went well and all the first fruits of the post-independence effort and planning began to ripen. The planning; the Nehru permissive policies of secularism, democracy and industrial growth, created a world interest, intellectual and material in seeing an underdeveloped nation's bold experiments succeed. The upsurge in growth when the new planned projects were coming out of gestation into production, the dams, steel plants, heavy engineering works, community development, institutes of excellence in technology and management, the chain of national science laboratories, new universities in towns that had barely possessed an intermediate college, two peaceful elections involving more people than the world had even seen at the polls; it all gave the country a sense of initiative and confidence that it had not possessed for a thousand years. Industrial growth boomed, Indian and foreign enterprises stood in queues for permission to expand, start new plants, new joint ventures, pouring in any amount the venture could absorb, with the public oversubscribing share issues fifteen to twenty times. Indian young went to foreign universities, and were often snapped up by their well endowed faculties and international agencies on the look out for talent.

I learned to shuttle between Bombay and Delhi by the new Viscounts that cut the journey from the train's twentyfour hours, the De Havilland's eight, the miracle of Dakota's five, to less than three hours. A pressurised cabin, hot meals, and conditioned air made the journey pleasant. Each time there was a round of the ministries, finance, industry & commerce, food & agriculture, planning commission, petroleum & chemicals, giving clarifications, offering assurances that the project would hurt no one else's interests, raising foreign exchange. This was at the central level; then there were the state governments for sanctions for land, water, effluent, plant, buildings, boilers, raw materials, excise, sales tax. Then there were the financial institutions to get the accommodation that government had agreed upon. I had made a long checklist to score off the things done, and indeed the list began to shorten.

This was also the year of a new long-term agreement with the union.

Of late the unions in India had taken a leaf out of the freedom struggle to press their claims with protest, boycott, hunger strike and demonstration. The old slogans of Down with the British, Quit India, injustice, all were revived, but less tolerant and less peaceful, relying on invective, calumny, with sometimes plain or filthy abuse added to the repertoire. There were pen-down strikes, token or relay hunger strikes, where each person went without a meal, gate-demonstrations, processions and marches. The unions called them "peaceful" while they relied only on shouting abuse, yelling and cat-calls, and there was no physical attack on management or facilities, although the borderline between peace and violence was always thin. Here again, like the satyagrahas, there was occasional violence, and a stage was reached in the late 1960s when, rather like in the 1942 Quit India movement, violence often became open and widespread. Even the term peaceful had its subtle and not so subtle nuances. A dense crowd in a manager's room, equipped with a loudspeaker pitched high, blaring abuse, and forcibly placed close to the manager's ears, hour after hour, refusing to allow the manager to visit the toilet, was called peaceful. It had its own name of "gherao"—to surround! The aggrieved protestors of course demonstrated in relays to maintain their own comfort and spirit.

Over the years the trade unions had evolved a classical course for a strategy and tactics of protest, which followed in essence the style of satyagraha campaigns. This in fact was to become our national style of protest over any issue on which anyone disagreed, individually or collectively, with an organisation or the state. The unions perfected it with great masterliness.

A campaign always began with a letter from the union president to the chairman, following the pattern of the letters to the viceroy from the Congress in the old days, conveying his deep concern, which in turn reflected the deep concern of his followers, in the sincere hope that the issue would be resolved immediately through the chairman's personal intervention. The letter always ended on the note that much as he would like to and was trying to restrain the rank and file, he was afraid that unless full satisfaction of their just demands was forthcoming, rightaway, they would be compelled to resort to direct action—another phrase borrowed from the political past—for which the management alone would be held responsible; he, the union president, having tried his best to avoid a clash. The letter often contained an in-built wish-fulfilment of rejection, based on a demand pitched impossibly high with the solution demanded peremptorily; sometimes giving a few days, even a few hours, in which to concede everything. Short of total acceptance, the door was shut. I once received a letter at midday giving me till four O'clock to concede all demands, and another at three regretting my callous dilatoriness! Punctually at four hell descended in peaceful protest, though I did have the satisfaction to know that with equal punctuality it would be over, at least for that day, at five, to enable the demonstrators to go home. Then there would begin a slow build-up; a gate meeting, some meetings with the management, inconclusive from the very start, and then the sudden declaration that despite all efforts negotiations had broken down because of management's intransigence, leaving the leadership with no choice but a peaceful struggle. There were now lunchtime gate meetings, black mourning badges, refusal to accept the morning and afternoon cup of tea, a pen-down strike for ten minutes at stated intervals, a silent stand-up protest at the desks, and whatever else the leadership's ingenuity could muster as weapons. The fairest management was lumped together with the unfairest.

There was the lighter side as well. We had an Englishman on a two-year spell to organise our new cattle food compounding business. Robinson was a charming, old-fashioned young man, of whom the best description was the Edwardian Robinson. He had Edwardian ways, manners, appearance and already a cut of clothes that was later to become the rage. The story spread that one afternoon, when the staff in the main hall was in the midst of a silent stand-up protest, standing among them most solemnly was Robinson, his head bowed and hands folded as if at a graveside. Just as his tea tray arrived and everyone stood to attention and bowed with folded hands in protest, new to the country Robinson thought that somebody had suddenly died, or may be it was the anniversary of some tragic event; so he hastily followed suit. To his dismay everyone began to titter, but he let it pass as another incomprehensible custom to which he really could not subscribe. Mourning was mourning, even though he had seen a Hindu funeral with clanging cymbals and bells and strangely cheerful singing. Well, thought Robinson, it takes all sorts to make the world!

On another occasion, some years later in the State Trading Corporation of India, I had invited some pressmen to lunch, and in the meantime there had blown up a flash protest over some minor issue. Late at night I received a letter by a special messenger.

> It is most unfortunate that despite our just demand for the withdrawal of management's unilateral action, you have not acceded to our request and even thought it fit to ignore it and throw a luncheon party, on Monday the 7th at a hotel. We strongly resent this callousness, and have decided in our own humble way to observe a mass hunger strike in the office throughout the office hours on that day. So, while you will be at the luncheon party, we will all be foregoing our lunch in the office and even be skipping our tea and snacks as a mark of our heart-felt protest throughout the day, with prayers for a better understanding to dawn on the management.

Each protest meeting rose to a higher key, with varying attempts at negotiation, and soon the "struggle and fight to the end" was announced. Even though we never had a strike and always managed to reach an agreement, for the union basically trusted the management, which because it was fair could also afford to be firm, a struggle nevertheless had become a ritual that had to be performed, because the gains at the end had always to be "won" by the leadership, which had to prove itself; otherwise someone else took over promising more drama and a better struggle.

The struggle contained an ingenious array of weapons that brought out the Indian love of drama and pageantry—wedding, funeral and a mohalla quarrel all in one. There would be a cheer leader who had to prove his capacity to coin rhythmic and alliterative slogans; there would be banners, placards, cartoons; often a effigy to be burnt like Ravana at Dussehra, a mock funeral, marches along thoroughfares to attract public notice. As one went further north the proceedings became lustier, bordering on bawdiness and reaching out into pure mudslinging.

A competent Punjabi union leader could organise a "siapa," the old Punjabi custom where a death was celebrated for several days by women collecting in a circle each morning, stripped to the waist with uncovered thighs, following the siapa leader's rhythmic, doleful chants and beating of breasts and thighs with both hands. A good, experienced leader could raise it to a crescendo when women became black and blue, but dutifully returned the next morning. A real siapa was usually reserved for a young death, especially a son. The union siapa was for the management, usually the chairman.

Yet pure hatred or pure violence was rare, at least in the Punjab. There was an underlying good, robust Punjabi humour, and a basic kindness in the mutual relationship, nor was the respect, provided one commanded it, ever really lost; and as if to reassure management, throughout the struggle odd individuals would drop in too tell you that what they said was not necessarily how they felt. But this was not so in the East, where the flame of hatred could burn fiercely, with none of the innocuous ribaldry of the North. Violence was always there close to the surface; and the protest had altogether different political and emotional roots. An English manager was bodily lifted and thrown into a furnace.

The abuse, filthy or otherwise, hurled by the union at management was in interesting contrast to the language expected from the management, which must be impeccable. Our branch manager at Delhi, once conducting a disciplinary enquiry, when asked by the union representative for yet another adjournment, said, "I am afraid I cannot go on postponing the enquiry interminably. If Mr. X has not been able to prepare his case despite the ample time he has had, this is his funeral. I propose going ahead with the enquiry." We paid the price. The enquiry officer was accused of prejudice; he had used unpardonable language; he wanted to see the poor man dead and his funeral taken out; he wanted to destroy the union. We were taken to court, and even upon appeal we lost. We had used intemperate language! And this, after all the union cursing and mock funerals of the management!

My first long term union agreement took more than its normal course. It was a trial of strength over heightened expectations from the first Indian chairman. The charter of demands was a document of such perfection that due in January it was not ready till July. It was a model of welfare that absorbed the entire company profit before tax, leaving the management with the challenge to start all over again to rebuild the profits. In the interminable list of demands nothing was missed out except payment without work. This in any case was not necessary because legislation permitted a person to be away from work with pay, on half pay, and without pay for 180 days every year; and meanwhile he could work elsewhere.

The whole system of confrontation and struggle seemed out of place in the context of our poverty and needs. Perhaps it was necessary once when management were ruthless, but it was unseemly and crude as a weapon. Now when in India we had perhaps the world's most protective legislation, and when for a company like ours the difference in the take-home pay between me and my driver was barely three to one after tax, what we needed was something else that would, at least for some years, put the collective shoulders behind the wheel. Negotiations, yes; tough and as hard as they could be, with much homework to challenge management. I remembered the union leaders at Harvard, with whom I had shared a course in advanced management, how they poured over company financial statements, working out profitability, cost and resources, employed ratios to see where there was room to get more out of management. They did not rely on slogans and lung power but backed their struggle with knowledge and cogent argument. How much easier, I felt, was management's task in India in one way, yet more difficult in another. But again these demonstrations had a lighter side.

The factory union was trying to force us to take back some workers who had rushed the security personnel at a shop to force the unwilling workers inside to come out. They sent notice that they would march in a procession to our suburb and hold the usual "peaceful" demonstration outside our house late in the evening, allowing for the time it took me to get home; and could I please cooperate by being in. The personnel director felt that this must be discouraged, and I ought to stay away that evening and inform them that I refused to cooperate. Reluctantly, because I felt that it might be misunderstood as shying away, I decided to go to an evening cinema show. My wife was both amused and delighted because it must have been years since she had seen a film in my company. So with a feeling of having been trapped I sat through the film which was actually quite good, with Ava Gardener to look at. The demonstrators had meanwhile checked on me and decided to call it off; but next week they sent word again. This time I told personnel that I must face it and get it over with.

A strange sight met me when I reached home. In the quiet, leafy lane at the end of our drive the usual peace was shattered. Some bewildered children had collected to look at the crowd, while the frightened neighbours had shut their windows for safety but had their noses pressed to the glass panes. As the car swung in, the noise subsided dramatically into hushed silence. I decided to leave the car and run the gauntlet by walking up the drive. The crowd separated politely; I waved and saluted with joined hands, forced a smile and went on, apparently to their surprise. It was only when I reached the top of the flight of steps leading to the house that they recovered, but decided to stop the demonstration. They asked Bakshi, our driver and almost a member of the family, to convey to me that they would like to send up a delegation. I said I would certainly be glad to meet them, but there must be no more than two or three representatives, and I would be equally glad if they chose to continue with their demonstration. No, came the answer, they did not wish to shout but would rather discuss.

Slowly, looking shy and awkward, came a long line of a dozen men and women up the garden steps. Apparently they had not been able to keep the number small. We all sat solemnly, not knowing where to start. They looked at each other like shy school children. Eventually I opened the conversation. We discussed everything of the subject, around it, and far away from it. Conditions in the factory, piled up problems, rising cost of living, inflation, and everything else connected with life and work came up; and as I was quite relaxed and in no hurry the talk went on for well over an hour. Particularly lively was a Christian girl from our suburb. Finally we shook hands and agreed that while the matter would be examined carefully, we were all behind the firm despite such differences as were bound to arise now and again. But the aftermath was unexpected and amusing.

These were days of prohibition in Bombay, and ours was a suburb of Christian and Koli fishermen, notorious for illicit distillation and bootlegging. Most of the demonstrators were people from the locality who had found it convenient to join the procession on their way home. As our discussion went on, the crowd below who had agreed not to shout became restive. Some of the locals invited others to visit the neighbouring huts for a drink, and in the hour or so of waiting they drank quite a lot, so that when they reassembled to hear the delegation's report, some of them were quite high. As the delegation had not much news to give, the followers began to barrack them, and there was a free for all. Disgusted, they began to stray back to the huts, and decided in future to resort to the more conventional and convenient form of half an hour's demonstration at the factory gate.

My first encounter with a colourful union personality came a few years later, with George Fernandes, the rising star of Bombay, who was to succeed the strongest leader the city had known, S.K. Patil.

George Fernandes had been trying to take over Bombay factory union, which was one of the few in the main industrial area of Sewre that he did not possess. Our Bombay factory union had a varied career, having tried every political shade, even complete independence. Starting as an in-company union, it broke away because its over three thousand workers could neither be led by the four hundred clerks of the head office nor lead them, and tried in turn socialists, communists, and Congress.

Under the Maharashtra government rules a new union could not be challenged by a contender until it had a year to prove itself, but George Fernandes was much too impatient and regarded it a meaningless formality because he was convinced that if a poll were taken he would win hands down. He was nothing if not confident; and when the time came, he indeed did win. After that there was no holding him back. He started firing one broadside after another. He picked up something quite small and made a big cause out of it. He wrote me brief staccato letters, tuning up the urgency each time. There was danger to peace, threat of a complete breakdown, and if things went out of hand, which he was convinced would happen very soon, the responsibility would all be mine. He built it up to a crescendo and delivered an ultimatum. He and I must meet to save the situation from blowing up—again the responsibility must all be mine. It was becoming such a familiar phrase. I wrote back and invited him over the following week—perhaps he would have a cup of tea with me.

George Fernandes walked into my office briskly, self-assured, a handsome well set man. He looked surprised at my office. It was a bare room in cream and light mauve, a bare desk, with none of the usual excrescenses and appurtenances denoting the busy importance of the chairman's office. Besides, I walked up to meet him in a bush shirt and chappals, which seemed to surprise him the most. I took him to the low chairs by the wall and asked him to sit down.

"You are surprised at my dress and the office, Mr. Fernandes?"

"Yes, I expected to see one of those large offices, with a couple of peons outside, and you in one of those Bombay Chairman's dark suit, collar and tie, and a patronising manner. Instead, your office looks simple and you look so relaxed, dressed just like me."

So I told him how I learned to wear bush shirt and chappals on my visits to Delhi in the summer. I discovered when I passed the guards outside the ministries, that if I was dressed in the usual Bombay businessman's suit and tie they invariably stopped me and asked for my permit, but if I was in a bush shirt they took me for at least a secretary, if not a modern deputy minister—so they saluted and let me pass. It was besides the most sensible dress in the hot weather. At home, I said, I always wear kurta pyjama, and that is even more comfortable. He asked why I couldn't wear it at the office too. I said I had often thought of it but rejected the idea, for a practical reason. Our staff here, in contrast to other offices, was reasonably well turned out; if not smartly, at least neatly and tidily. What I am afraid of was that once I wore something as informal as kurta pyjama, it would be a signal for them to come dressed anyhow, and the imaginable variety could be quite something—pyjamas, maybe striped, dhoti, mundu, lungi, shorts, jeans; in fact it could be pure sartorial chaos.

Fernandes laughed and conceded that at least it was not snobbery on my part.

"Mr. Fernandes," I said, "I am glad to see you; I have heard so much about you; please tell me which unions do you control in Bombay?" He laughed self-consciously and said, "It would be easier if you asked which I don't control—I have all the government offices, central and state, transport, oil industry, rubber companies, dock workers, taxi drivers, hotels and restaurants...and now yours, as I told you a year ago when you preferred to stand on a legal formality."

"I appreciate that, but let me assure you we will observe the seme legal formality in your case, when the time comes!" This in fact we did because a new union followed after he left Bombay for Delhi.

He laughed again. He explained to me that what gave him power with Bombay labour was that he could speak fluently to them in Konkani, Marathi, Gujarati, Hindi, and English, which no other union leader could. They felt at ease with him.

"Tell me, how do you manage to control such a vast spread—an empire, I was going to say. I am quite interested in how one runs an organisation which most of the time lives to struggle."

I told him about my experience at the Harvard Business School, where the second line of union leadership, handpicked by their organisation in USA and Europe, were trained for three months, mostly in financial, production and marketing management, and industrial relations of course. The idea was to give them a thorough grounding into general management, both to run their own organisations better and also to understand how their adversaries ticked. "I often wonder," I added, "how much easier is the task of managers in India, where they are never challenged by equal or superior knowledge of the law, or financial analysis." Instead we have only demonstration and attrition, which does get something but not nearly enough to force the management into greater efficiencies.

We discussed generally the need about training, whether of men who manage a company or a union, and I suggested we might run a training course for one of his groups. He thought it was a good idea, but who would pay for it? I said, of course it should not be misunderstood as charity or, worse, an attempt at indoctrination. If he felt it would do his men good, the union had to pay for it. That was worth thinking over, he replied, but suggested we get down to the crisis at the factory.

"That, Mr. Fernandes, I suggest we leave to your union men and our personnel management. I don't believe in looking over the shoulder of our men, as I am sure you don't either. They are negotiating; but if there is an occasion when you would like to discuss an issue directly with us, the personnel director and I will be glad to have a chat with you and your colleagues. But as things are, why don't you let the men sort it out. My door is always open, but let us confine our discussion to general matters of policy or to insuperable problems."

He went to see the personnel director and remarked to him, "Whew, that was sophisticated."

Next year Fernandes got elected to parliament in a most dramatic victory over S.K. Patil, the veteran of Bombay, who had spent vast sums of money, even on an airplane with streamers, while Fernandes knocked at each voter's door. He shifted his activity to Delhi, where somehow he did not make his mark. I met him at a Rotary meeting in Bombay and asked him about it, and his answer was interesting. "In parliament today you need to behave in a special way to make your mark. If I really do my homework and study a subject to make a well reasoned, thoughtful speech, then all the press will report is, 'Mr. Fernandes also spoke.' But if I fulminate and accuse, refuse to sit down and generally display much agitation—well, the next day in the press Mr. Fernandes will hit the headlines. Our press, the readers and even my colleagues are only interested in display and excitement."

I found this strange coming from George Fernandes, because I thought he would be good at this, and enjoy it, but apparently it was different. He loved excitement, crowds and battle; but there was some innate niceness in him. Excepting once, when a strike got out of hand and the men rushed some expensive and complex atomic power generation machinery, and in the subsequent police firing some ten men lay dead, his struggles those days were always surcharged, but clean and peaceful. His greatest triumph was the first Bombay Bandh, when he brought a bustling city of eight million people to a halt. Nothing stirred, except the police on duty, and the demonstrators. Everything came to a standstill. What it achieved was another matter; but it proved his power. He was tough but avoided rough tactics; he fought clean, and managed to keep the Bombay strikes orderly. Of course Bombay had a tradition of decency, but his power at one time was so absolute that he could have changed it any way he wanted to, and make it into the nightmare that Calcutta became for some years.

After his spell in parliament he returned to Bombay and tried to stage a come-back. There was the old verve and fire, but not so the old sure touch. His attempt at politics had unsettled things. He needed a clear task in front, not the amorphousness of our politics; he was a very clear cut man, who I imagine found it difficult to align, unalign, realign. His own splinter group of the socialist party of course was too weak to give him strength in a country where all trade unionism is politically based. I wanted very much to get to know him personally but my normal hesitation stopped me—my fear of cultivating someone who might mistake it for trying to create a para work relationship for its usefulness to me. He was still young and who knew then where his ability and courage would take him.

As the year 1961 came towards its close, everything in India somehow looked good, especially to me. Perhaps the exhilaration of tackling my problems by myself gave it a more shining edge. But it was indeed a year of success: Nehru's India vindicating its stand on secularism, neutrality, democracy and planning. There was of course a cloud the size of a hand over the Himalayas, but with our friendship sworn and resworn of a brotherhood of two thousand years of history, of a peaceful border, everyone felt sure that only the ignorant or the politically perverse could suspect the Chinese of hostile intentions. The rumours about Aksai Chin and the Chinese building a road were dismissed. A junior army officer who asked Krishna Menon, then the defence minister and the co-architect of our foreign policy, whether irrespective of our relations with China we could, purely from a defence angle, leave such a long border untended, drew a wrathful harangue on history, neutrality, British imperialism, and American perfidy and many other things the young officer ought to know better.

By autumn as my affairs were going fairly smoothly, I decided to take my annual holiday in Kashmir where the family used to go every year. It was a little late in the year but we decided to try it as a change from spring and summer.

CHAPTER FIVE

An Indian Road

Since 1953, we had visited Kashmir every year for our annual holiday. From the very first we did the journey of fifteen hundred miles by road, an experience which was a great education, especially for the children. It was a spartan life on the open road, with very early morning starts, sparse meals, and nights in lonely dak bungalows, whose only inhabitants were usually the lizards, and for neighbours jackals. As the children began their schooling in Mussoorie and Dehra Dun, the journey became nearly two thousand miles and covered quite a part of India, containing a variety of people, towns, countryside, flora and fauna that showed the diversity and unity of India. And over the years, as we repeated the journey, we saw two sides of India, one growing and one static.

At a lonely spot, somewhere in north Maharashtra, where a road took off to a small town eighteen miles away, an enterprising person had installed a Burmah-Shell filling station, open 24 hours. At night the man slept on a string cot with a hurricane oil lantern by his side, getting up hastily at the sound of a truck drawing in. During the day he maintained the place, cooked his food and passed the time chatting with the truck drivers.

Soon, someone else saw a chance and arrived with a bullock cart loaded with bamboo poles, matting, some rickety wooden benches, pots and pans, and set up a cook shop. First he provided only hot syrupy tea, but as his business grew he also gave a simple meal of chapatis and dal, to which he soon added vegetables, and eventually a meat dish. Now he was serving compete meals, and one day an impressive signboard went up declaring that it was "The New Highway Hotel & Restaurant—Hot Vegetarian and Non-Vegetarian Meals. Rice plate is ready." You could also get hardboiled eggs, biscuits and coloured aerated drinks, and for the drivers who wanted a few hours sleep there were charpoys in the open, under the stars at night, and under the neam tree during the day; a hand pump for water, and a dry privy. The "hotel," with the stress on the first syllable, had come a long way from the original tea stall.

When the Malayali vulcanizer in the next town heard about it he sent his assistant to explore, and soon he too arrived with a truckload of tyres and tubes and vulcanizing outfit. Along the thousand miles from Bombay to Agra, vulcanizing was synonymous with Kerala. The vulcanizer could do almost anything to a tube and a tyre, except make it; and if a truck had needed a job done at night he would gladly get up from his sleep. He never complained if the truck was in a hurry, but of course grumbled if he was awakened in the name of emergency and the driver then went to sleep at the "hotel" for the night.

The filling station progressively turned into a garage with cleaning and servicing facilities and some spare parts. Before long a young mechanic from a neighbouring town offered to work on his own at the garage. The garage men welcomed it as it gave one more reason for the trucks to stop. The drivers were pretty good crisis mechanics themselves and could do virtually anything with wire, string and Sunlight soap, which, mixed with some grit and dust, did an ideal job with leaking petrol pipe joints. In fact, they only overhauled on the roadside, whenever there was a total breakdown and the truck just stopped; preventive maintenance was not in their vocabulary. Then they would put some stones around the truck, left exactly where it had broken down, often in the middle of the road. The driver would look philosophically under the engine hood or underneath the chassis, and decide on the course of action. He would leave his mate, usually called the "kleender," to guard the truck, and thumb a lift in another truck to the nearest filling station, there to discuss it with the mechanic who returned with him for a further examination. If the breakdown was serious, they would proceed to the nearest town, buy the needed spares, and perhaps bring a more knowledgeable mechanic, and the three of them would get down to the job, sometimes taking the whole engine away for a complete overhaul.

The repair completed, the driver started up again, with no more thought for maintenance until the next breakdown which, if the signs were strong, might be attended to at a proper garage, but usually had to wait till the vehicle packed up completely. The anticipation which could have avoided the breakdown was not in his nature. The very couplets in Urdu or Hindi that were calligraphed on the back of the truck, with gaily painted festoons of flowers and scenes of lakes, snow mountains and pine forests, summed up their fatalism. What could happen when God cared; no storm could blow out the lamp He protected. "May you with the evil eye have your face blackened." Added to this were friendly gestures—OK, Bye Bye, Tata; Use dipper at night; God protect; We shall meet again. They were totally nerveless drivers; Aldous Huxley called them the most unmechanical in the world. They always grossly overloaded their trucks, they drove them hard and tirelessly for days and nights, they ate and drank heartily, and rarely could one travel for more than one hundred miles without seeing a wreck, not infreqently two trucks in a headlong collision, lying in the most preposterous positions. There must have been a deity for drivers who protected them from more wrecks and casualties. And indeed along the roads there were small temples where truck drivers prayed for their little deserved safety.

The hotel "sublet" a corner to a pan-bidiwalla who prepared the pan and sold bidis and matches and also kept some popular soaps. In due course a kirana merchant joined the community and sold a variety of foodstuffs, soaps, hair oils, toffee and biscuits, fruit juices and other things that passing motorists and bus passengers might be tempted to buy.

Apart from the Shell inspector, some salesmen began to visit the community, the first among them, as always, the Brooke Bond man with the tea-stall variety of tea, which could be brewed over and over again, the strength of the brew ever improving; the Wimco man with matches, and then the Sunlight man.

In a few years I saw this outpost transformed into a flourishing community of shopkeepers. After ten years it was a small township of a few hundred people. It could not be termed a village as no farmers lived there; it was a small township of shops and services, dependent entirely on the road, and on their initiative. This is how one saw growth and "urbanisation", the catalyst a new road, a cross-road, a T-junction; buses and trucks; a filling station: the rest could be left to the enterprise of small men, who came up like mushrooms overnight. They needed no help; only an opportunity. These were men whose earlier generations had gone to many parts of the world.

Like all new growth in India it was haphazard and unsightly, with and air of transience, but this was misleading. It arose out of poverty and reflected the best these people could do out of their meagre resources, but one could not mistake the initiative behind it, the upward thrust of the seed to the surface of an inhospitable soil.

In contrast, the green, well tended housing colonies of the new public sector factories along the road made one wonder. There villages were suddenly lifted into urban standards, comparable in amenities with anywhere else in the world, with schools, hospitals, clubs, swimming pools, shopping arcades, community centres, wide well lit roads fringed with lawns and trees. Might it not have been better, one wondered, if so much money had been dispersed over many times the number of people in the shape of opportunities, where the small entrepreneurs could have been left to sort out their own life for at least one generation, until their productive capacity had acquired its own momentum; new life for them, and new employment to others? The haphazard growth bore no comparison to these colonies, but it was self-created and self-sustained. Each lakh spent on it would have multiplied faster than the crores spent on the ravenous colonies. But I suppose it was a question of priorities as one saw them. New growth could of course also have come from surpluses produced by these new ventures, but in those days they rarely produced a surplus; mostly they drew in more and more funds to keep them going. If one petrol pump and the passing trucks could create so much employment, how much more would the saved crores have done. Roads and trucks were the fastest catalysts.

When the road left Maharashtra to enter Madhya Pradesh it not only changed its rutted, ill maintained surface, but also its character. It crossed the Vindhyachal, which divdes the Hindustan from the Deccan. In the hot summer, the landscape had a rugged grandeur of scrub covered hills, gnarled thorn and teak, and dry riverbeds. The drab colour was shot with the blaze of flowering trees of the early summer. Undulating valleys and plateaus alternated for several hundred miles, till the road dipped down into the flat and uninteresting alluvial plain of the north.

On our return in July, the dry and dusty land was transformed. The sky was now a washed blue with fat clouds moving north to their annual rendezvous with the Himalayas. Sometimes they moved like lazy groups of soldiers, sometimes like the vast expanse of an attacking army, eagerly awaited by the soil for its liberation. At the violent beat of the rain the dry earth sighed with hissing steam and softened to the onslaught, and soon innumerable gurgling little streams gave voice to her satisfaction. The sunburnt land was now a happy green. All the watercourses were rushing to merge into rivulets and rivers, and ultimately into the sacred Godavari or Narmada, or the Chambal, which empties into the holy Yamuna, and finally into the sea. One or the other of them was bound to be in flood and to have washed over, if not swept away, the bridge. No matter how high and strong the bridges, the rivers each year kept trying to crush them in their furious loveplay; and of course some of the bridges, the way they were built by the contractors, were always willing to give way.

Feast or famine was the fate of the land; rivers dry or swollen, earth scorched or lush, scrub or crops, mud huts or palaces, straggling pi-dogs or bounding deer. Violent contrasts, also among the people.

On our way north in the heat of May, the road used to be gay with wedding parties, going from one village to another, women and children packed into bullock carts, and the men walking. Before the rains break there is not much for the farmers to do, so there is leisure to celebrate. The people of the fertile plains are of the sturdy Jat or Rajput stock, the men in red turbans and the women in red and yellow. But sometimes we met a different kind of wedding party. They were the forest people, the Bhils, of a different racial origin, the earliest inhabitants of the land. Small and lean through endemic disease and chronic malnutrition, but wiry and sinewy, they were beautiful. Their graceful small-breasted women, walking behind the men, were decked with jewellery of brass and copper, occasionally silver. The men wore their hair down to the neck, and each carried bow and arrows. I took these to be mere symbols, but when I stopped a Bhil and asked him, he shyly told me he could use it. To demonstrate, he held himself as taut as his bow, pulled the string and let go the steel-shafted arrow. It flew with a fine zing and hit a hard dhak tree, where the head dug deep. He pulled it out and let me feel its weight. It was doubtless a killer. I asked him if he would sell me his bow and arrows, and in my indiscretion I offered a fair sum, but he politely shook his head. A bystander explained that a Bhil's weapon was part of his male pride, which money would not tempt him to part with. With a smile the man walked away.

We came across a strange Indian dream in the forests at Shivpuri, a small market town that a maharaja of Gwalior had tried to develop into a summer resort. This platean was much cooler than his capital in the plains, with stray showers in the dry weather. In the forest he had laid our roads, built a palace, villas and offices to accommodate his court and retinue. There was a lake with a boathouse, gardens and a family temple. But the maharaja died before his dream materialised. Most of the buildings were never completed, some were ready but never occupied. Strangely the forest people have not availed themselves of the magnificent accommodation at their disposal, whether from fear of ghosts or awe of the old rulers.

By strange coincidence we once passed two royal elephants going down the road. A prince of Iran had been entertained to a tiger hunt, and for a day this modern Fatehpur Sikri had come to life. At Sikri the shrine Akbar built is still worshipped, and at Shivpuri the temple built in memory of the maharaja's mother is the only place alive and maintained. In the evenings hymns are sung, and villagers come to pray.

For some twelve years we did our annual pilgrimage to Kashmir, usually going up in the heat and returning in the rains. We never rushed the hot part of the journey. We used to set out before the first light of dawn, stop at midday for lunch and rest, start again in the afternoon, and look for a quiet dak bungalow before dark. We would settle in for the night, organise a meal, and then go to sleep in the open, a lovely sleep in the cool night air, where the only sound was some jackal's far off cry.

Through the years we evolved our own gradation of the bungalows; our five stars were those way down the PWD rating, where very few people ever stopped. They were built of brick and tile, always clean and had bucketfuls of cool well water, and the chowkidar was visibly pleased to have guests. On our black list were the new garishly painted cement concrete bungalows in district towns, generally dirty, and if they boasted about the so-called modern comforts, these were usually out of order. It was in any case difficult to get in at the bigger places, were the rooms were occupied by government officials, and often by some minister holding his local durbar; in fact all such bungalows along the road were shut to the public when a minister was expected. Then there would be police guards outside.

The narrow strip of road rolled on for a thousand miles to Delhi, through the vast and timeless landscape, broken by clusters of mud huts, with thatched or tiled roofs, small temples and mosques, old congested cities, ancient forts, palace ruins far from anywhere. But there were also new townships with suburban housing and all the signs of growth, ugly but alive.

Away from the towns, in the fifties, the road still teemed with wild life. It was not uncommon to see neelgai, wild boar, big herds of deer. But sadly India's freedom began to take its toll. In the British days gun licences had been issued sparingly, and while hunting had been the preserve of a few, maharajas and high officials, at least wild life was spared. Freedom brought indiscriminate freedom to kill, until Indian wild life is nearing extinction. It is lucky that the peacocks are held sacred, and still cross the roads in early morning, rending the air with their raucous love calls.

Sometimes by the road we saw small encampments of a few families with carts, whose shape strongly resembled the ancient fighting chariot, heavily studded, but no horses. They are like gypsies, and live like gypsies the world over, parking their caravans near prosperous habitations and playing their trade of iron smiths. They keep their possessions in the chariot, which has the superstructure of a small tent. They live in the open, build little mud ovens and create a kind of permanence that has no real permanence. Any day they will suddenly move on, leaving behind some debris and cold ashes. How they pulled their heavy carts away always puzzled me.

They are known as Lohanas, from loha, iron; and legend has it that they came from Chittor in Rajasthan. When Chittorgarh fort was taken by Akbar, after a long and bitter siege, their ancestors left and vowed to wander about and not to return until the conquerors had left Chittor. The Moghuls went, and the British went, and the government of the new state of Rajasthan in a flamboyantly imaginative gesture decided to fulfil the old pledge. Some hundreds of Lohanas were collected at the foot of Chittorgarh. Led by Nehru on horseback they marched in procession up to the fort and were ceremoniously conducted into their ancestoral home. Two pieces of fractured history were joined together; but when the speeches and celebrations were over the Lohanas took again to the road that had been their home for twenty generations, to the only life they were familiar with.

After Delhi the road got slightly wider and acquired a more prosperous look. The fields were better cultivated, the people sturdier and better dressed, but the greatest change lay in the absence of bullock carts, in the number of buses and trucks, and of course the number of wrecks; in the numerous tubewells and the tractors. The wedding parties here went in buses or in trailers hitched to tractors. You rarely saw a horse. All the main towns had new roads bypassing them, but I liked the feel of their vital chaos. The inner cities had remained unchanged, but with the population increased ten and twenty-fold they teemed with people and traffic. I always feel good, probably because I come from there, to drive through the Punjab and feel its vitality and progress. The way it lived still had some of the old timelessness about it, but not the way it worked. In the two hundred and fifty miles from Delhi to Amritsar one saw more that was new than in all the thousand miles to Delhi.

One also saw the unmistakable sign of the widening base of bureaucracy and regulations along the road. In the twelve hundred miles from Bombay to Pathankot there grew in fifteen years some hundreds of road blocks holding up the freight trucks—a new source of revenue, some going to the state but much shared along the line. The transporters overloaded their vehicles dangerously as they moved contraband stuff like wheat, sugar or cement from a surplus to a scarcity area. This has to be "regularised". It still moved, but to mutual interest of those who moved and those who regulated and, it was said, those who legislated. There were also points that checked licences and permits, and others that only checked who passed. The arm of regulations reached out with an insatiable appetite. But here, too, initiative was at work, and the important check points also became growth points, with filling stations and shops that took care of the checkers and the checked, on the implicit understanding that the trucks were held up long enough for their business. One wondered how long the system would endure before the roads became fit for any Indian to travel and transport freely. The Grand Trunk Road was the road Kipling's Kim travelled on, where he saw the nefarious and colourful activities of his time; and the road was still full of interest.

One learnt as we travelled along the road how people in towns and country reflected their position in society through their hours of work. In the summer, by seven in the morning all those who lived by the sweat of their brow were at work; by eight the small shopkeepers had lifted their shutters, and well before nine all shops and businesses were open; but it was only after ten that there were signs of the rulers stirring—the government offices, post offices, and later the nationalised banks and insurance offices. Anything to do with administration did not really settle down to work before half past ten. It was in the reverse order in the evening when administration stopped work between four and five, shopkeepers by eight, while the toilers were at work till as late as they could earn some living. In the winter administration's hours became shorter still and much time was spent in front of the offices basking in the sun, sipping tea, while the supplicants waited patiently, trying to hasten the process by some other means than their patience.

This road from the coast to Kashmir was an education in itself. In its variety of climate, from the coastal damp heat to the snow peaks; of the vegetation, from the thorny scrub of the Vindhyas to the juniper and dwarf birches; of the people, from the small compact Maratha farmers to the large bearded Gujars, it presented an interesting vertical cross-section of India. To me, perhaps only too conscious of the power of New Delhi, the abundant signs of a powerful administration, slothful and wasteful of resources, was a marked contrast to the enterprise of the people with meagre means.

CHAPTER SIX

Kashmir

After Amritsar one becomes conscious that the border with Pakistan was near. East Punjab was now like the North-West Frontier of the old Punjab. There was a military presence about. After recent harvesting the fields were empty, for troops and tanks to conduct their spring manoeuvres. At Pathankot, now a garrison town, one at last left the plains of India and began to climb into the Himalaya along the three hundred miles road to the valley of Kashmir. It ran almost flat till Jammu, skirting the foothills and crossing innumerable dry rivers, which could in a few hours become raging torrents. From now on one never got away from the consciousness of a neighbour. The road often overlooked the contiguous neighbouring Pakistan districts in which I was brought up, and evoked the nostalgia in me that not many miles away was what will always remain home, though unreachable and closed to me for ever.

The road from Jammu to Kashmir, the only link then except an uncertain daily flight, was a miracle of engineering tenacity. Like the trucks on the Bombay-Delhi road, it used to breakdown a number of times every year; each time it was hastily repaired to resume the impatient piled up traffic at both ends. At every major breakdown there was talk of a new alignment which would avoid the crumbling mountainsides of the first range and build on the safe rock of the inner ranges. Each year the engineers, a bit too pleased with the tough repair job, no doubt ably and speedily done, seemed to begrudge the trouble of having to start on a new road altogether. The road was really an old bridle path that at best had been good for tongas; the real road had been the one from Rawalpindi to Srinagar. Upon Pakistan's attack on the Kashmir valley the bridle road had been hastily made serviceable for heavy military traffic, and when peace returned there was too much spent on it to discard it. There had in fact been a third road, the one used by the Moghuls, which went up from my home town of Gujarat to the Pir Panjal range above the Kashmir valley; but this too was left behind in Pakistan.

From Jammu the road climbs to about four thousand feet and then descends to under two thousand. Once again it climbs tortuously to seven thousand feet, and then promptly dips down to two thousand;

once again it climbed to nine thousand, to descend at last to the five thousand feet high valley of Kashmir. The last climb through the bleak Banihal pass, closed in winter, was discarded when the Germans built an all-weather cement concrete tunnel four thousand feet below.

Nothing was ever again quite so exciting as our first sight of the Kashmir valley in April 1953, when after a freezing night in a now abandoned bungalow we drove through the short brick and wooden tunnel near the top of the Banihal at nine thousand feet, and saw the wondrous valley deep below. The sun rose on the huge snow walls on both sides of the road, and on the inundated rice fields below, which were glittering silver and blue. But for the clumps of trees visible, it would have looked like the vast lake that it once used to be.

In April the road was crowded with convoys of army trucks, and Bakarwals driving their goats up to mountain pastures. Bakarwal means a goat-man, and his cousin, the Gujar, is a cattleman. Both are Muslims. In winter the Gujars and their animals huddle together in low huts made of stone and mud, cut into the hill slope which makes the back wall. From above you hardly notice their grass and poppy covered roofs. In summer they drive their cattle up to higher pastures and live in tents under the pines, with pine twigs for mattresses. It is lovely when the sun shines but miserable in the rain. Their clothes are dark and drab like their mud huts, but their hawk-like faces are handsome. So are their women who wear sombre but harmonious colours, usually black and dark red—and embroidered long kurta, flared salwar and sturdy spurred shoes like their men. Their quaint red and black caps with long ear flaps down to the shoulders seem relics of the helmets the men wore as warriors long ago. Their hair style of innumerable intricately woven plaits is not conducive to frequent washing.

There is something sad about the Gujars, as if the memory of their lost glory had stayed with them. Once they came from the plains of Central Asia as proud conquerors on horseback and formed a dynasty. After them is named the present state of Gujarat, and also my home city in West Punjab. Driven away from the plains of the Punjab by subsequent waves of conquerors, they went with their herds into the mountains of Kashmir, but their language they kept, a melodious Punjabi, purer than that spoken in the plains today.

The Gujars are a hospitable people and will unhesitatingly offer you their bread of the sweet maize they grow on the hillsides. They never beg, and once at a Gujar camp when a woman came up to us and begged, the Gujars hurriedly said "She is a Moghul." Her ancestors must have been camp followers of Jehangir or Shah Jehan, when their huge holiday camps moved into the valley but she still did not belong and the Gujars looked down on her for her lack of pride.

When the "Lion of the Punjab", Maharaja Ranjit Singh, conquered the valley, many Sikhs came to settle and did well for themselves, as resourceful Sikhs always do. Later the British took Kashmir, and as they considered it of no use to them they sold it to the Dogra Maharaja of Jammu for a paltry sum. A certain number of Dogra Hindus speaking a Punjabi dialect came with the new dynasty as civil servants and soldiers. Karan Singh, the son of the last Dogra maharaja, became the first head of the new state of Jammu & Kashmir after independence, and there the dynasty ended. He took a Ph.D. and became a plain citizen, and a minister at the Centre for many years.

The Kashmir Muslims themselves live in the valleys, as farmers, traders and artisans. Men, women and children all wear a loose wide-sleeved embroidered robe, reaching below the knees, over the baggy salwar. It is a comfortable dress in all weathers, for in winter they pull in their arms for warmth, letting the sleeves hang loose, and even carry inside their robes their individual central heating, the kangri, a little basket with a few live coals. For holiday their best robes are in brilliant colours with rich embroidery. The Pandit women used to wear a dress very like the habit of European nuns, though in bright colours. The colour is disappearing and now you but rarely see some old woman in her traditional dress; young Hindu women have all gone over to the sari, and the middle class Muslim women to the salwar kameez. Some of the gaiety of a Srinagar Sunday seems also to be gone.

On the first warm spring Sunday all Srinagar was picnicking in the Moghul gardens by the lake, Nishat, Shalimar and Chashma Shahi. It was still too early for the tourists. The plains' people have a lesson to learn from the Kashmiris. They sit there quietly on the lawn and enjoy the sunshine and the flowers, the playing fountains and the birds, without making the raucous noises so familiar elsewhere in India. They open their wicker baskets and make tea in their samovars, and eat their hard biscuits and whatever they have brought, and when they leave they put every scrap of paper and waste back into their baskets and leave nothing behind on the grass; litter and noise are always the contribution of outside visitors. The emperor Jehangir, who built the gardens and planted the majestic chenar trees, would be pleased to see how well the Kashmiris maintain them.

The Kashmiris are handsome and fair, with the charming courtesy of speech and manners that is the heritage from the Muslim rulers. They are also very hardworking, and utilise all resources of soil and water. Every little patch is cultivated; every stream is diverted into laboriously built little channels; every man, woman and child toils in this market garden that is the valley. Women and children gather the lake weed, and on a floating mass soil is heaped and vegetables sown. As one crop follows the other more soil is formed. These are their floating fields, patches that are sold and bought, and it is a curious sight to see a field towed away by the buyer. Eventually they anchor the fields by planting trees whose roots will reach the bottom, and in this way the lake gradually shrinks. As elsewhere in India, the pressure of population is eating the environment away. The Woolar and Dal lakes are now only half the size of what they used to be, when I first visited in the 1920s, and in a few generations this unique heritage will be lost to reclamation.

To the small valley of Pahlgam, where snow peaked mountains slope to the confluence of two streams, come every year people from all parts of India at the time of the festival of Raksha Bandhan in August. Rich and poor, city people and peasants, young and old, and a gathering of sadhus, throng the single street of the town and the forest paths. They bear the features and garments of wherever they came from, Kohima or Kanyakumari, Cuttack or Keshod. They are mostly Hindu, with a sprinkling of tourists of other faiths. They have come together for the Amarnath Yatra; most from faith and religious fervour, others for adventure and the beauty of the trek. And one morning a mile long caravan begins the arduous climb through the woods noisy with the chatter of the descending Shishnag river.

Walking or clutching their ponies or carried in litters, the pilgrims arrive at their first stop, a little plateau called Chandan Wadi, valley of sandalwood, though only pine grows there. On one side is the snow bridge, and the many who have never seen snow rush down to feel it. The children throw snowballs, till hunger drives them to the cook shops and then cold and fatigue into the tents. A whole little town of shops and tents exists just for one week in the year.

Next morning the procession winds its way across the snow bridge and up the arduous thousand feet climb of Pissu Ghati, and you are in the region of the birches, shimmering silvery trunks against the blue sky. On the tissue thin flakes of their bark, bhoj patra, the holy Vedas were written. The chill gets stronger, the birches become smaller and give way to tiny juniper bushes, until you reach the tree line. Then nothing breaks the contour of the overwhelming landscape. But along the path now blooms the miracle of the short mountain summer, poppies and irises in yellow and blue, and a gay carpet of a hundred kinds of tiny flowers. The only inhabitants are the shining black ravens, and the whistling little marmots who sit on their hindlegs and stare curiously at the invasion of their domain.

The second camp site overlooks the awesome green Shishnag lake. The pious bathe amongst its ice floes, but most shiver even over a wash in the stream let which trickles past the camp. Plains' people huddle together to keep warm at twelve thousand feet. By now strangers have got to know each other. Kerala folks join Punjabis, and in Hindi, or English they talk about the journey, their homes and their daily lives, discovering the common heritage of an ancient land.

The air gets thinner and colder, the path more fearsome, hanging on to the rock over abysses of two thousand feet. The third night is spent at Panch Tarni, five icy streams that defy bridging. Next morning, the day of the festival, the pilgrims have only a few fairly easy miles to the famous cave. Here at thirteen thousand feet is their destination, a long way from anywhere, accessible only for three months in which spring, summer and autumn are hastily compressed before the snows close in. Inside the enormous cave, in the soft colours of opal, pink, blue, green and mauve, the sacred ice lingam stands perfectly formed. Its sides melt smoothly into a hem of ice, which the pilgrims cover with wild flowers. Some feel a mystic ecstasy at the sight they longed to see, others are struck by its strange beauty; but in all there is a feeling of purity that cleanses the soul. And they hopefully look for the legendary pigeons said to be incarnations of Shiv and Parvati.

Here is the unity of diverse India. Here people meet, some in faith and others to find solace and inspiration in the vision of their origin and the majesty of their God. But here too, alas, a mountain road is making its way inexorably forward, and soon cars and trucks and buses spewing smoke will shatter and pollute the peace and clean air of the mountains and valleys, and the annual yatra will become a return day trip. We shall have progress.

In Kashmir's mixed population of different ethnic groups, the oldest are the Kashmiri Brahmins, whose learning and culture goes back into centuries to beyond the old sun temple of Martand, near Srinagar. After the Muslim waves of invasion, as Kashmir changed hand from one dynasty to another, they lay dormant for centuries, until in the British days they came into their own again, and spread into Punjab and U.P., always in letters and professions, and politics. After independence they rose higher in their stature and have provided talent and leadership.

Curiously, those who were converted to Islam shared none of their characteristics. Where the brahmins went for erudition, the Muslims went for farming, cattle herding, and handicrafts—something to do perhaps with the caste origins. Even under the Moghuls, Sikhs and Dogras, it was generally the Brahmins who were prominently the officials. It is a curious quirk of the indestructible caste system of ours that through a thousand years of Muslim rule, the Brahmins who remained Brahmins, refusing to take the softer option of embracing the conqueror's religion, willing to suffer indignities, managed to retain their pre-eminence in an order which failed to lift the hewers of wood and drawers of water, the tillers and the artisans, above the stations to which they had belonged in the conquered society before they had adopted the rulers' faith. They were then, as today, where they were before. It was the same under the Sikhs and the Christian British, as under the Muslims. It is the same in the Punjab, the "kami," meaning literally the worker, actually a term for the helots of the society, be he Hindu, Muslim, Sikh or Christian, is still where he always was, unless he can get submerged in the urban anonymity of a modern profession. In the most tolerant society of them all, the Sikhs, where all are equal before the Guru, the Harijan converts are still referred to as the Mazhabi Sikhs—Sikhs who merely adopted the religion.

While the Brahmins stuck to learning and profession, the Kashmir Muslims are among the world's greatest arts and crafts workers. European travellers introduced them to some new crafts, papier-mache, crochet, crewel tapestry, petit point, but all continued in the traditional patterns the Moghuls had brought them, the Persian delicacy in colour and line, in painting, embroidery, and wood carving. But though great artists in wood, they are no carpenters, and their furniture is always poorly joined. Even their character has the great natural naivete of the artist—euphoric, often unpractical, always optimistic but bound to tradition.

Their tourist department was the most likeably euphoric of all, making the tallest promises and giving the shortest measure of reality. They were full of plans for making their tourist paradise—never tired of quoting the couplet attributed to Jehangir that "If there is a paradise on earth, it is this, it is this, it is this." My managerial mind was fascinated by their plans of new roads, bridges, resorts and playgrounds, ski slopes and cable cars, modern centrally heated winter hotels. One was always asked, "How does Kashmir compare with Switzerland; is it not far more beautiful? We will make it even better than Switzerland." As we always came fully equipped, and needed only a couple of bare rooms, we resisted the attractions blandished by the Director of Tourism—"This time you must stay at our latest Swiss chalets, which beat anything they have in Switzerland." It hurt him that I would rather take a permit for the old forest bungalow in the pine wood. To please him, we went once to a Swiss chalet, prepared from experience for the worst, and it was worse than we had expected.

The wooden huts had only a borrowed shape in common with their Swiss prototype; all else was indigenous talent. They did not even have the utilitarian beauty of the old forest huts. The natural deal wood, which Kashmiris usually leave unpainted to acquire a satin smooth patina with age had been garishly painted. No hinges or locks were properly fitted, broken windows had not been replaced because of the administrative problems involved. The boasted "sanitary" had not yet been fitted but was lying on the bathroom floor. For some reason the job was left half done. The forest and the stream which had to serve instead for the basic needs were a good ten minutes' walk away, as the huts had been built in the middle of the marg, the meadow.

To us who knew our Kashmir well it was a strange sort of progress from the old timbered huts built by British forest officers. They built them inside the forest, protected from cold winds, near a perennial spring or a stream. Given a slope, there could even be running water in the hut. The rooms were small and cosy, easily heated by the open fireplaces. No lack of fuel! At dinner time our cook used to place the utensils on the glowing embers from where we helped ourselves, and in the apple season for dessert we roasted apples in the ashes. But in the Swiss chalet, exposed to the winds of heaven, there was not a single fireplace. Somebody hadn't noticed them in Switzerland, or they were centrally heated. On a rainy day it was miserable. There were not even enough lanterns, because there was supposed to be electricity for which there was only the wiring so far.

Such signs of "planning" were fast multiplying all over Kashmir in the fifties, as money poured in to raise the standard of the people and of the tourist amenities. The waste was impartial—the locals got no better deal than the tourists. More lakhs were budgeted than were spent, and more lakhs spent than actually put to work. To make up for the lack of results, more plans were made and more budgets prepared. I also spent time looking at their industrialising process, where also large amounts were spent on new plants and projects. Some never worked, others fitfully, but there was no dearth of optimism. The whole face of Kashmir was going to be transformed!

Many years later came a team of management experts. They left an elegantly bound and phrased report, which advocated management accounting to men who had still to learn their debits and credits; information and control system and modern communications to a system that ran on dog-eared files with white flaps forever swelling with notings as they travelled up and down; organisation structure, performance budgeting and appraisal; finally a suggestion to start a cadre of committed and competent managers. This report had not visible results, except that the brain behind it got an invitation to Harvard to propound on the growth, constraints and solutions to problems of a developing society, and ended up with the UN, doing good to other developing countries.

With each year's journey, from Bombay to Kashmir, I learnt more about the contradictions between the vigour of unplanned initiative and the often weak results of planned growth. It was the difference between a sturdy weed and a wilting overbred plant. One saw the usual waste of planned effort and the careful husbanding of the small self-created opportunities. While around that multiplier of non-directed growth, the filling station, there had grown a thriving population, the well-planned factories and their manicured estates had a forlorn look of low activity.

These were early days though for drawing conclusions. Why casual seeds brought growth, but careful sowing a constant drain on resources that bore no fruit? Likewise, the village community hall, opened by a minister, often remained unused, while the villagers congregated outside the tea shops, listening to their radios and making their own comments. And yet to tackle such a vast problem some such planning was perhaps necessary, if only to provide the road, build trucks, import and discover our own fuel, if the road T-junction was ever going to sprout. The question was how to marry the old sturdy initiative, ruggedly individualistic, with the discipline of modern planning; not to make one exploitative and the other ineffective. Would we learn this with time?

Kashmir was full of new government departments and their outposts, departments for sericulture, flood control, improved agricultural practices, co-operation, animal husbandry, poultry farming, industrial development, fisheries, soil research: all meant to help new growth in a society, static and impoverished for centuries; but all a fairly resultless paraphernalia. Many years later, I was invited to work on a committee to review Kashmir's development of the past twentyfive years. As I listened to the problems, there was a familiar ring to it all. Were solutions always to be so far behind!

Kashmir was really a compressed version of our problem of institution building everywhere, and a blown-up version of Delhi then, where budget-oriented institutions sprouted and flourished in a breathtaking variety and silent contribution. Where a hospital would have served, there was sponsored instead an institution for the study of the history of Indian medicine. It also served?

CHAPTER SEVEN

Government and Business

1962 was my first full year as chairman of Hindustan Lever, and with the union contract behind me I devoted all my attention to New Delhi. If government was difficult and ponderous Unilever were sensitive and suspicious. If government felt they were doing the company a favour to accept its plans to expand, Unilever did not see it that way and felt instead that the price for that favour was unfair and high—and so between them I was like our dhobi's proverbial dog that belongs neither to the house nor the ghat.

Negotiations with New Delhi dragged a lengthy course, while the file moved from point to point, backwards and forwards, occasionally only forward. Then it went to the ministries in the state capitals concerned—U.P., Bengal, Madras, Maharashtra. In our rounds of the ministries we sometimes passed the same point again and again, till like the bullock at the persian wheel, we were familiar with each point of the circle; but at least the bullock's eyes were mercifully covered so that he could not get dizzy. The negotiations took nine years altogether.

A trip to Delhi always began with a sick feeling deep inside me. The single daily Viscount left at dawn, after a restless night when I thought of the early morning alarm and what new problems were in store during the day—some surprise, a setback. Would one be down again to the bottom of the snake, and slowly start moving again in the hope of striking the lucky bottom of a ladder?

Befittingly, Indian Airlines had then also started their delays through strikes, go-slow, and technical troubles which were to add hours of philosophical waiting at the airport to the waiting for the file. The reasons for both could be equally trivial. I once sat for three hours at Palam, because an air-hostess on the inward flight had "insulted" the pilot who reprimanded her for not serving his tea promptly. He refused to fly back unless she apologised or was offloaded. The girl said she was busy serving the passengers, so why should she apologize; and if she was offloaded the other girls would join her. The girls became adamant and so did the pilot, as one waited patiently. Ultimately they had to collect a new crew, and hours late we boarded the plane wondering if the offloaded captain, his mates and the girls had all collected their overtime, and whether these hours of argument had been clocked into their month's flying hours.

These were also the years when the pilots, who would not have soiled their hands with carrying their own cup of tea, were declared "workmen" by a court and given all the privileges of workers under the Industrial Disputes Act. They could even ask for a living wage, a charming euphemism for a wage and perquisites many times higher than the highest wage in the civil services; much in tax free perquisites, denied to others under the tax rules. Soon they learned to work to rule, which was worse and meant yet more delays. As a class of prima donnas one began to find them an unlovable sight, associating them always with predictable delays for unpredictable reasons. The engineers had not yet learned to be workers; but they soon were too. The only heroes were the least privileged commercial staff and the passengers. Even the loaders had their go-slow tantrums.

In Delhi the next morning Aspi Moddie would come to my room at the hotel which was my second home, and give me the latest intelligence about the file. "Ramachandran" his personal assistant, had his antennae out and had learned from "Ramaswamy," the personal assistant of a minister's secretary, that according to the information he had received from "Ramadurai," the personal assistant of the secretary in another ministry, that was where the file was now taking rest. After a noting by the under-secretary the file had gone to the joint secretary, who was waiting for the return from tour of the additional secretary, before it would go up to the secretary. The noting could raise a new issue that could be as frustrating as it could be ingenious. It was no use asking to be trusted, for trust was not what the system was built upon. It was best in such cases to go back to the questioner and appeal to his superior knowledge to guide us. He knew so much and we so little; we, who after all, were only the investors risking capital, but he was guiding the nation's economy.

Sometimes the objection was trifling; then it needed the most careful consideration, at least one had to be wary and treat it gingerly for fear of upsetting some seriousminded but limited enthusiast. With one such I had a harrowing experience trying to learn the first principles of financial management and marketing, which he propounded generously for my benefit. It was difficult to reason with him and impossible to argue; something one learned with some difficulty was that one could not afford to argue with a bad idea. Although one continued to agree in a choicelessness, one had to remain persistent in its non-acceptance. He who had the power always knew more; it was like our Punjabi proverb, he who had the stick, his was the buffalo.

I pondered over this system that the "heaven born" ICS of the nineteenth century had left behind, which Kipling lampooned, and the administrator today, a century later, abhorred, but helplessly. The only strength seemed to lie in its predictable negativeness. Time as a cost in rising prices and delayed production was not its concern. Spawned a century earlier, it had not learned the cost of delays in an era of inflation, where prices of equipment rose monthly. Yet one could see the administrator's point, because a decision taken quickly could have laid him bare to suspicions of undue haste. Why was a decision taken as hurriedly and why was the file so slim; what was the motive behind it all? There was no national crisis, no emergency; why then this unseemly haste? The onus to prove innocence lay on the poor administrator who had acted with speed.

There were those in industry who met the system's hurdles in subterranean ways through their Delhi representatives, working quietly and assiduously at all levels to ensure the smooth and speedy passage of the file. I heard a conversation in bits and pieces of the greatest businessman of India, known for his industrial empire and political power, talking to a minion, one of the many men he employed solely for this task of smoothening the path in front of the file. I had taken Lord Cole, Chairman of Unilever, to meet him, and as he spoke to us in English, he kept up a steady conversation on the side with this man, in a dialect of Hindi that I could at least make sense of.

"When is he arriving?"
"I see, by the 7 o'clock flight."
"Will you meet him?"
"So you have it arranged; and the file will be on his table tomorrow."
"Do you think he will decide tomorrow?"
"I see, you have it settled."
"Do you think there is likely to be a hitch?"
"Well, I know you will manage it."
"Or, else, let me know, but soon?"

Of the same businessman, someone told me later that where it took us many years to get a licence it would have taken him as many months; and then he had the theoretical right to block our way, because he had been granted licensed capacity that would, under our system of planning, take care of the market. Whether he went ahead to build that capacity, and how long he took over it, was not relevant; he could thwart competitors of today or tomorrow. It became known as pre-empting capacity.

As was usual with the system, something that K.B. Lal had tried to teach me but I had by now despaired of, the break always came, but unexpectedly; what had become a tangled skein suddenly showed signs of untangling. I got a message that L.K. Jha, previously secretary in the commerce ministry and now secretary in economic affairs in the ministry of finance, had called an inter-ministerial meeting to discuss our proposals all together to finalise everything; and would I attend the meeting. I was suddenly so elated that I forgave, even blessed, the system, its years of delays, and in my euphoria felt as if the system was deliberately designed to baptise one's proposals through an ordeal to ensure that we made no mistakes in a haste, and chiselled and honed each proposal to trim it of all unnecessary cost.

L.K. Jha, known popularly as L.K., a custom with the British, who did not call their Indian colleagues by their first names, as they found them difficult, or because calling them by the first name would connote an acceptance of the ultimate familiarity which they preferred to avoid. A tall handsome man, he made his presence felt from the moment you entered his office; a man remarkable for the quality, rare among Indians, of being a good listener. As I got to know him over the years I admired him the more. I could ring him for a ten minutes appointment and take literally ten minutes sometimes even less. With none of K.B. Lal's expansiveness and bubbling humour, Jha got down to business straightaway, and his face literally moulded itself into all attention. As the presentation came to its first important issue, one of his eyes opened a shade wider and fixed itself on you with compelling attention. At the end, he would sum up his understanding of what you had said and give his views openly and tersely; there was never any equivocation.

He belonged to a pre-war generation of ICS, each of whom was an individual, though they all had the stamp of a basic prototype. Dharma Vira, Bhoothalingam, Dandekar, Ranganathan, Lall, Shankar, of the ones I got to know well at work: all men of great ability and competence but each a character by himself. They were the system's rare problem solvers. Interestingly, one could tell them apart from the type of professional executives in industry, especially the multinational, and yet they were essentially professional executives from the same Indian matrix. The difference lay in their wide powers and authority that went back to the time of the Raj. They were the givers, and everyone else, even the highest in industry, were always supplicants. You were conscious of their power as you entered their large offices past obsequious entourages.

As I entered the meeting, there was a bevy of secretaries. I was alone, and it perhaps gave me a subtle advantage. I felt a little nervous as a supplicant asking for economic grants. How easy life would be, I felt, if one stopped growing and profited from a stagnation which assured you the comfort of shortages and high profits. Jha came straight to the point that our projects were all growth promoters and foreign exchange savers, but we were a foreign company, repatriating dividends, and government would like to take this opportunity to ask us to dilute our foreign holding and increase Indian participation. No doubt even the reduced equity would mean a higher profitability on the whole, and no diminution in Unilever's earnings or control. He would therefore make us an offer: government would grant our proposals to expand our existing plants and set up new ones, in return for reduction in our Unilever's shareholding in favour of the Indian shareholders. With great punctilio he corrected himself—he meant, resident shareholders. An Englishman resident in India had rights equal to an Indian shareholder, he added with a sardonic humour, because we who owned properties in most parts of the world were soon to pass a law restricting foreigners owning it in India. I agreed on the percentage, and Jha was glad. The formalities of fixing a price of the issue to Indian shareholders would follow in due course, though he thought the price of the shares might be around thirtyfive rupees. I returned to the hotel where I began typing out a letter to Unilever. A major catastrophe followed. My letter alarmed Unilever.

Recently I met a senior civil servant, Bhoothalingam, who began to reminisce over the beginning of Indianising the capital of foreign companies. Government had picked on two of the largest British companies in 1955, both Anglo-Dutch, Shell and Lever, and approached them to convert themselves into Indian public limited companies with a small Indian shareholding. They were both alarmed, but while Unilever agreed Shell refused, saying that they could make better use of their scarce capital elsewhere in the world. Bhoothalinam wondered what the shape of the foreign oil companies might have been had they accepted the offer, which government then genuinely saw as much in the interest of the Indian investing public as the foreign companies.

On a subsequent visit to London I asked John Hoskyns-Abrahall, who had been chairman in India at the time, and now was on the Unilever board. Yes, he told me, H.V.R. Iengar, commerce secretary, had called on him with a proposition from T.T. Krishnamachari, his minister, suggesting that Levers might consider going Indian. They had done well out on the country and had a good future, but there was a rising national sentiment that wanted to see foreign companies in India adopt an Indian look; and of course for their future prosperity they were dependent on the government for import and other licences and permits, he added significantly. Abrahall heard this proposition, hitherto never dreamed of, with great aplomb, but he confessed that "you could have knocked me over with a feather." He thanked Iengar for a proposition that displayed such solicitude for Levers!

Later, I asked Lord Heyworth, then Unilever's chairman. Yes, he remarked, it was the first proposition of its kind to them from anywhere in the world, but as he told his colleagues, it was a sign of the times, and if similar propositions were going to come from other developing countries, it was time they examined its implications. The Dutch chairman saw it otherwise; if they entertained it from India, they would receive them from all the developing countries. No, it had to be turned down firmly and clearly to nip such economic nationalism in the bud. Heyworth countered that if such propositions were indeed going to come from other countries, then India was the best country to try it. The experience alone would be worthwhile. They would always be reasonable in India, which was more than he could say of many others.

I asked David Mudie, chairman of Shell in India. He had had a similar offer from Iengar and had recommended it to his headquarters in London. Whether it was the Dutch or the English, the proposal was turned down flat; they would take their money elsewhere! Mudie agreed that had they accepted, who knows but the course of events might have been different; as it was, their expansion and diversification was doomed for ever. In fact government began its own oil company that grew rapidly, as Shell, Esso and Caltex stagnated and were to be all taken over twenty years later.

The reply from London was unexpectedly sharp and brief. Jasper Knight, finance director, accompanied by John Short, senior partner in Cooper Brothers, the Unilever auditors, was flying to India immediately, and would I please arrange meetings with government. They were deeply concerned at my recommendation.

The idea of Knight's visit without consulting me seemed to take things out of my hand; but that Short was joining Knight to emphasise the "shareholders' interest," to me added only a ludicrous touch to the heavy-handedness with which they had decided to handle the situation.

My first reaction was to tell Unilever to handle it all themselves. I would be glad to withdraw altogether to save them the embarrassment of having to undo my tacit agreement. Admittedly it was tacit and subject to their concurrence, but nevertheless it was an acceptance of government's viewpoint by the man on the spot, who could have disagreed with government but did not, or played it safe and not reacted at all, which also he did not. It might be better under the circumstance for Unilever to go back and recommence negotiations alone on the track that suited them. I was filled with a cold disgust at this over-reaction. They could at least have discussed the matter with me, or asked me to "put on my hat and coat and fly over to London"; but to send a team over seemed to be unnecessary at this stage. It had the implication that London felt alarmed at government's proposal and, worse, that I showed little or no concern by my ready agreement, without putting up a fight on their behalf. And if this was how I began, where would I end. Somehow when I imagined these discussions, the wisdom of Andrew Knox seemed to become illusory; the trust, the delegation, and all the theory one had heard and discussed at the conference in Unilever and outside seemed remote.

A quiet exit from what seemed an unpromising beginning was tempting. But a withdrawal was all too easy; also a soft option, when one had been trained on hard choices. It was understandable too if they felt diffident. They had long considered me something of a problem in view of my internal struggle of conflicting loyalties, even though they had "found my conduct always quite unexceptionable." In retrospect I could understand why London now suddenly took fright. The doubts about me that they had waived, when they handed the company to me, must have been revived in a suspect situation. It was early days for Indianisation, and they could have waited and had one more expatriate chairman, and yet they had preferred not to, and appointed me; but this crisis must have reawakened their fears of me, who after all was not one of them.

I decided in the end to handle it coolly, and telexed back welcoming the visit—it would give Knight an opportunity to meet government officials and get a personal feel. Such problems might arise again in the future; it was best therefore to meet this one with all possible care.

With Knight and Short we got down to discussions straightaway.

Knight was wary and defensive, and Short trailed behind him like Stan Laurel. At the first opportunity I tackled Knight. I said I could understand Unilever's anxiety, but did he really feel that their interests were not being looked after by me in a way that would inspire confidence. He admitted they had got that feeling and thought it best to be open about it. They did not much mind government driving bargain on equity, but very much to be asked to shed their equity at such a low price. At this rate, each time they wanted to expand they would have to lower their shareholdings, each time at an unrealistic price, so that theoretically they could be totally dispossessed at a throwaway price. This was totally unacceptable to them. And, he told me frankly, they did wonder whether I felt the way they did. He had brought John Short along, as they had many thousands of shareholders all over Europe, and now in America; and thought their auditors should be included to represent the shareholders' interest. He hoped I agreed with him.

Yes and no, I said. In the West they would never be asked to dilute their capital, and therefore this sequence of actions would not follow, but this was India, where it might be different, but not mulcting or confiscatory. It was still a profitable investment for them, but they would have to adjust themselves to the aspirations here that were both political and economic, with a touch of emotion thrown in. They might come across the same in some other developing countries, but with less reasonableness and security. I went on to say that government reasoned that expansion would bring them—I somehow could not say "us" to Knight because his attitude made me feel an outsider—more profit in total than before, so that equity dilution would mean no loss, in fact an expanding gain in the long run; and to shareholders in India a gain that was theirs by tradition of the market. I felt convinced that government would not have given this deal to another company, and there had been cases of a foreign company recently accepting a much lower price than ours. I thought that in their best interest they should accept; otherwise my fear was that a reopening might harden positions. I could however assure him that if that was the position they adopted as the fairest, I would be with them, with my weight behind it.

The round of discussions began disastrously. At the very first meeting with the controller of capital issues, Venkatachalam, after hearing Knight's arguments, both exploded. The controller proceeded to explain at some length a jumble of financial reasoning, and this particularly galled Knight. There followed a heated discussion.

While Knight quoted the securities Exchange Commission of the USA and the City of London, the young, eloquent controller quoted from Amercian text books on finance; and while he raised his voice, Knight's quivered. We met many others but made no headway. I let Knight handle it his own way. At the end, I told him, with a touch of unkindness, that he should by now know government's views and it looked to me like retrieving a lost position. He would have to leave me to handle it. Knight and Short left at the end of the week in disgust, and I returned to Bombay and wondered how I would be able to retrieve it.

On his return to London Knight wrote Jha a tough letter, expressing his disappointment, and ended on a clumsy note that if there were no agreement on the issue, Unilever might have to reconsider its policy of further investment; a situation they would greatly deplore; and some foreign companies they knew were already reconsidering their position. Had the letter been addressed to the young controller it would have torn the whole thing, Jha, more polished and cooler than Knight, a seasoned civil servant, who years later as our ambassador in Washington with skill and patience performed the delicate task of handling an angry Nixon and his administration over the third India-Pakistan war, and later as governor of Kashmir helped Sheikh Abdullah's return from exile, ignored the letter and instead discussed in a practical way where we were going next. This experience must have helped him years later when he was appointed on a small, select UN committee on the multinational firms, and in fact met a Unilever delegation.

My trips to Delhi began all over again, and I started with the broad shoulder of L.K. Jha. He was very understanding and felt that our agreement on both the extent of Unilever shifting their equity shareholding, and the price at which we should offer it to the Indian shareholders, should stand. Eventually we all agreed, and I put the details before a special meeting of the shareholders in India to get their imprimatur on the agreement. This was a delicate job, for even if Unilever held ninety per cent of the shares, using a brute majority would have created a new crisis. The press, stock exchange and the shareholders already considered the price of shares too high and forcing a vote would have won us only a hollow victory. Somehow it went through at the shareholders' meeting, but not without protest.

The year was coming to an end, and it appeared as if my problems might at last soon be over. My love of results had made me introduce a weekly profit and loss account, ready every Tuesday afternoon. The results for 1962 had been mounting steadily, and production, sales, profits, went up and up. In a developing country good results give one a satisfaction all its own. With this alone, I felt I could face the angry shareholders. And then out of the clear blue Himalayan autumn skies came the bolt.

I was in Srinagar relaxing for a week-end with Ernest Woodruffe, the Unilever's vice-chairman, and his wife Enid. They had only recently been married and came to India virtually on their honeymoon. Gard and I accompanied them to Delhi and beyond. At Srinagar he told me one evening that he had heard the news that China had attacked India. Our first reaction was that it was no more than another border skirmish; someone's picket had pierced too deep; but it turned out to be much more—a short but full-scale war, of a kind that was to become typical in this part of the world in the years to follow. It brought to an end the first era of Independence.

CHAPTER EIGHT

Indians Wars

1962 became a testing year for the country, when the uninterrupted progress of many years came to a watershed. It marked the beginning of the end of the Nehru era. A good neighbour foreign policy with China, sedulously built on honest trust, gave way and there followed a short, sharp war that was a galling traumatic experience.

For many years we had pursued a policy of critical neutrality in the West, an appreciative neutrality in the East, and an uncertain attempt at leadership in the third world. In the early fifties the world had taken some notice of Nehru's political stance and held him in respect. Even China changed its attitude radically since the Korean war, when it had called India the lackey and running dog of American imperialism. In a world where no one had trusted another, without a powerful country behind him, in fact about the poorest in the world, Nehru backed his leadership with only a moral authority. This was something new and messianic for the head of state without conventional strength, with only courage and integrity. To the West, Nehru combined a Western intellect and sensitivity with an Eastern message of peace, and he was heard by those who were sick of wars and had the guilt of colonialism. They needed a neutral friend, a bridge to the Communist world, and an example of modern state to the developing world, to whom Nehru was a beacon to independence. We also felt a pride in the friends Nehru made abroad, and the return visits of leaders of states. Bulganin and Khrushchev, Tito and Chou En-lai, and the pleasant irony of fate, the Queen of England, who but for the changed course of history would have come as empress of India, and certainly not received the spontaneous welcome she now did.

One of those who influenced Nehru in his predilection for neutrality was the first Czech ambassador, Bohuslav Kratochvil, who came to India in 1949. Returning home from England on the Jal Jawahar, the first Indian-owned passenger ship on the U.K. run, we got to know him and his wife, who came, I believe, from the Masaryk family. They had both been in German concentration camps, but talked very little about this experience, from which she seemed to have recovered well, but he only partially.

The assignment to India, a welcome break, was to a great extent a step into the unknown, and through me Kratochvil sought to get a feel of the new India. He asked me questions on Indian history and on policies. He wanted to knwo about Nehru, and for this he had a source in the author Reginald Reynolds, member of a pacifist group going to India for a conference, who twenty years earlier had spent a year in Gandhiji's ashram and conveyed the famous letter to Lord Irwin, the viceroy.

A European intellectual and a socialist by conviction, Kratochvil was on a mission to the world's largest nascent democracy, which had also chosen socialism. He felt that his own country, European in its industrial and social culture had something to offer India as a bridge to the Eastern bloc, while India held the promise also of a bridge for the Czechs to the Western bloc. The two sides of Europe could not stay divided for ever, and socialism was bound to spread over the West, though probably not in its eastern form. In case of a confrontation, India would be trusted by both sides to help towards a disengagement.

In New Delhi, I dropped in on them occasionally, and he sometimes visited us in Bombay. The two of them enjoyed a way of life they had not known for years. Bohuslav told me how he had got close to Nehru, with whose intellectual make-up he had much in common. He talked about the fast-moving events in a world that was forming new alignments, and the role that India and Nehru ought to play. The new American hard line was distasteful to European mind, while he could understand the Russain hard line as a reaction, though perhaps not necessary, to the war and to American policies. No one else had the strength to stand up to America, he argued.

Slowly there came a change. Boha was not so sure of his ground any more; he no longer seemed acceptable to his own government. Prague had sent a new man to the embassy, whose only functions seemed to be to watch the ambassador. Kratochvil made his decision, and told Nehru that he was going to quit his post to settle in England, where he hoped he might have a better chance to serve his country, than if he had asked for permission to stay in India, which also might have embarrassed Nehru.

Boha, his wife and child managed to leave the embassy unnoticed, and we saw them in Bombay, and waved them goodbye from Ballard Pier. The news of the first defection of a prominent East European broke soon afterwards, and the press swarmed upon them when the ship reached Aden. In London he settled into a small job, and there he eventually died in relative obscurity, one of the endless stream of men without land that one war after the other leaves behind.

Kratochvil, I believe, had an influence on the shaping of Nehru's policy of neutrality, which he ultimately did unsuccessfully try to modify. Perhaps Boha on his side felt too intellectually committed to be an apostate, even though the system in the end rejected him.

1962 was one of our last great years of the Nehru era and a culmination of all he had sedulously built over fifteen years. It was the year when his three policies—democracy, secularism, planned growth—were seemingly all bearing fruit. In fact, his every success had begun to raise the expected question of who would succeed him—a healthy sign. He must latterly have been asking that question himself, for in some moments of loud thinking he expressed a desire to retire, which however went no further, but this did not stop people from asking the question.

Some years earlier, in 1953, I had met Louis Fischer, the journalist who had written an engaging book on Gandhi, and he told me that he had just received a cable from his New York paper saying, "Cable two hundred words after Nehru what?" He explained to me that if when the time came for Nehru to go, democracy had taken the roots in India he thought it had—after a Roosevelt a Truman, after a Churchill and Attlee, and after Nehru someone very unlike him, unspectacular, uncomplex, with no flair for international affairs, or imagination for great projects, but someone who would get on with all the day-to-day matters, the little things that Nehru was not interested in. Without realising he outlined the type that in fact did succeed—Shastri.

Democracy had indeed taken the roots that Fischer hoped, as the test of the subsequent three wars, droughts and famines, two rapid successions, and the Emergency were to show. Whatever the occasional problems that religious differences might have created Nehru had firmly headed us off a theocratic state, the basis on which India was partitioned. Industrially the many projects in the public and the private sector were coming out of their gestation. Industrial growth reached eleven per cent, for the first and the last time. There was confidence abroad that the road we had taken, neither to the extreme right nor to the left, was leading us somewhere. Many who watched China and India must have felt gratified that the Indian path too was leading somewhere.

But something had already begun to happen. Our policy had begun to waver and reactions to contradict each other. In 1956 there was an expected reaction over the Anglo-French action in Suez, but Nehru unexpectedly held back over Russian action in Hungary. Over Tibet there was an ambivalence, torn between historical logic and his political emotion. He seemed to throw away Tibet and lower India's northern guard, as if to prove that Tibet's neutrality was a creation of British imperialism. There were other growing ambivalences too that could not be sorted out, presumably because while logic pointed to one side or the other, emotions took him only to one side, the Eastern bloc. After Tibet followed the Chinese movement in Aksai Chin, which we generously tried to ignore, or settle through negotiations, as we had always advocated, which did not work in the face of new and hard realities. In the end we had to face a war, which we were pushed into by the Chinese on the one hand and our advisers on the other, one military and one political, Krishna Menon and his amenable and overpromoted military chief.

We knew the Chinese very little. The only ones one had ever seen outside Chinatown in Calcutta were cloth peddlers on bicycles, who disappeared during the Second World War. They had never featured in our school history, except Hiuen Tsang and Fa Hien, who travelled in India centuries ago. This historical brotherliness made no impact, and it would have been better if the new Chinese friendship had been put to the people on some other basis, such as community of interest, a good neighbour policy, with a people also making a heroic effort to rise out of centuries of poverty.

The rupture caused considerable bewilderment, more perhaps to Nehru and Krishna Menon, the leadership, than to the people. They said our patience with the Chinese was wearing thin, and despite our friendliest persuasion and repeated demands they were nibbling deeper into our territory. We were now told that our brothers, disciples of Buddha, seemed only to understand force, for once when one of our pickets deep in Ladakh stood up to them they retreated. And if they continued with their unheeding policy we might be pushed to act—with our forces limited in comparison and concentrated against the wrong enemy, our men with inadequate equipment, sometimes tennis shoes and first world war rifles. In the meantime we prepared erudite notes proving our claim to the usurped area, quoting shlokas from the Vedas, and relying even on the old British claim, the MacMahon line, in our favour. But nothing worked, neither erudition nor the protests, nor the heroic sounds. In the end an inexperienced, quixotic staff chief threatened to throw them out. He rushed to the area to assume personal command of troops. That worked in a way, because the Chinese struck, and hard, and like the hordes of Jhengiz Khan swarmed down the passes and rolled us as far back as it suited them. We were outmanned, outgunned and outflanked. And as swiftly as they came, having achieved whatever they had set out to, they declared that they were going back.

Reactions differed, but their common denominator was—and they whom we called brothers! It perhaps did not occur to us that the faith in "two thousand years of friendship" was of our own creation; a faith we had foisted on them; that in their realism, the Chinese should not have been expected to overlook their own interest merely because we had cast the mantle of brotherliness, "bhai bhai," upon them.

We are emotional; forever looking for objects of fixation from whom we expect a lot. We give what we can, but we certainly expect all, and we are soon disappointed and disenchanted. I don't think we realise enough how much our society conditions us to expect and receive. Our caste and joint family system build in us some fundamental rights irrespective of our capacity to return. Once, sitting next to an English visitor in a plane, I asked him how he regarded us. His answer was curiously direct. "What one does for you, you regard as your right and accept casually; what one cannot do for you upsets you greatly. One is judged not by the lot one may have done but by the little that one may not have been able to do. If you only occasionally showed some appreciation for what was done; sometimes even generously ignored what could not be done—better still thanked one for at least trying—what a difference it would make. If only you had a simple common word for thanks; you have to say it in English." We both laughed.

To our credit, we soon bounced back, and the memory of it began to fade, quicker than similar incidents in many other parts of the world. We are not good at nursing grievances. Joint family living teaches you not to sulk for long. After all, the loss of a distant stony territory in the frozen wastes of the Himalaya; a mere speck compared to the fertile plains of Pakistan in the east and the west that we had left behind, was soon forgotten. And with adherence to our own logic we even kept supporting China's entry into the U.N. Had China but made a bold conciliating gesture we would have been "bhais" again.

One did wonder though whither our neutrality led us, for at one stage we had cut relations with a billion people in the world. Where others, who strongly, even violently disagreed with someone, yet maintained a reasonable contact, we broke off with China, Taiwan, Pakistan, Portugal, South Africa, Israel. Instead of a sense of tolerance and benign patience with all points of view, agreeing with some and disagreeing with others, but taking sides with none, neutrality led us into a phase that otherwise was not in our character nor belonged to our history. We have not held the past against others. Even when the British left, we parted with almost lachrymose ceremonial, adopted and even improved on the trappings they left behind the viceroy's palace, complete with his ADCs, bodyguards, the London coach and horses, bugles, the Last Post and Abide With Me. In starched immaculate whiteness, the new rulers learnt to walk stiffly past guards of honour. There was no rancour against those who till yesterday had been called oppressors and exploiters, and their conduct as rulers we now often treasured and faithfully followed. How could we then not be friends with a third of the world's population? Why did neutrality, which should have been benign and tolerant, make us brittle like the western people, who have a capacity to see things in stronger lights, where we manage to forget and compromise? We have in the past minded our own business, but now neutrality led us into a self-righteousness where those who did not see it our way were in the wrong.

There was some overreaction for a time, some necessary and some avoidable. Some who had approved of Nehru's policies for fifteen years now found them all wrong; some began rushing in small circles as if preparing to fight the war backwards. Nehru soon fell ill, and typically one realised only from a photograph in a London paper that the illness was serious. Our papers said the day after his stroke that he was taking the slight illness as an opportunity to rest after months of overwork and strain; he sat in the afternoon sun and relaxed. The shock was great, for all the architects of nascent India, he was the second greatest and now the only one.

The Chinese went back, presumably their objective, as they saw it, achieved. And left at that it would probably have done the country and its economy no particular harm, if only having failed to react in time we had not overreacted afterwards. If the brief invasion gave a jolt to our ego, economic overreaction affected the foundations of new growth. This, some argued, was just what the Chinese had hoped and expected us to do. Their calculation might have been that it would not only bring India down a notch or two in the estimation of the world, especially of the developing nations, but also make us tie our economy in a knot. We went into a phase of brahmanical self-mortification, self-denial and deprivation. Instead of strengthening the economy as a base for a stronger defence we began to tighten up things, and an impermissiveness took over in the name of austere use of resources. Just when we should have relaxed to produce more we closed in. The finance minister was given the task to raise the necessary resources for doubling the defence expenditure; and he sat to work with a characteristic singlemindedness. Instead of spreading the burden over two or three years the budget came on the economy like a sledge hammer.

☆

This was not our only war; there were three more, all with Pakistan. We Punjabis had accepted Partition in disbelief. Only when the flames began to singe us personally and mass evacuations began, from mohallas to city centres and then to large evacuation camps, where they herded groups into guarded trucks, did we come to regard it as a reality. The convoys moved towards the main artery of the Punjab, the Grand Trunk Road, for countless centuries the path of invaders' sword and torch. And now the ancient road was full of soldiers ferrying their own across the new border.

When all this was over and twelve million people were evacuated to their new homes, as the flames began to subside and the strangers settle to a new life, there began our first war. The Grand Tunk Road was full again of military convoys moving to and fro, this time defending Jammu and Kashmir against Pakistan's so-called raiders, whose first waves as they broke into a chaos of rape and loot, were followed by professional armies. Then a real war began, with the bulk of the men on both sides again Punjabis. The ceasefire came after a nearing eighteen months of fighting in the high snows of the Himalayas; at times it was the highest war ever fought.

When the war ceased, once again came renewed activity of new roads and canals, and in the sixteen years of peace Punjab's face began to look different. Many of the new farmers had left behind the lands that the new canals and their effort had enriched in the districts of Shahpur, Sargodha, Lyalpur, Montgomery, Warburton, named after the founders and guardians of their new canal colonies. Their grandfathers, who had been tempted away from their farms in East Punjab over a half century ago, with the promise of as much land as they wanted in the new canal colonies, had marvelled at the combination of virgin soil and flowing waters. Today the refugee grandsons, back on the old soil, marvel at the new canals from the Bhakra dam. When the water flowed for the first time through the new brick-cement and polythene-lined Nangal canals, the refugee farmers danced with joy. But old people who had heard of the succession of upstream power stations feared that the water had lost its power to nourish the soil, when the electricity, the "bijli," had been taken out of it. By the 1960s, the Punjab was again flourishing agriculturally and producing surpluses of wheat, and even rice, of which it was very proud. It was once again the granary of India and inevitably its sword arm and its history's no man's land.

In 1965, in the pleasant month of December, my wife and I returned to our Punjab. We were invited by the Pakistan Lever company to visit them for a week. Relations between the two countries were steadily improving, and the many Punjabis who had visited Lahore and further, had returned full of praise of Pakistan's achievements and the untouched beauty of Lahore. The Harvard group of economists went further and found more right with Pakistan than with India. Its industry, agriculture, exports were doing well at a time when India's pace, after the China war, was beginning to flag.

From Karachi, where at eighteen I had first seen the sea and sailed to England, we took a train to Bahawalpur state, where I had grown up in the medieval rule of a Nawab, in whose capital city the roads had been closed and men warned to stay indoors when the heavily veiled royal ladies were driven from one place to another in equally heavily wrapped up Rolls Royces. In Lahore, Aziz, an old trainee from the Indian Company, now a director of the partitioned company, and his wife provided us discreet company, ready to look the other way if something attracted my reminiscent gaze.

One evening I left Falleti's Hotel and walked into the Lahore I knew as an adolescent—by the Mall with its untouched late nineteenth-century buildings, mixture of late Persian and British colonial, past the old bronze Sikh gun and the statue of Lawrence. The inscription that he was willing to serve (or was it to govern) with both the pen and the sword was in the early days of national awakening read as a blunt reminder of the conquest. I walked through the Gol Bagh, laid out in a circle, where out in the sun or under shrubs and trees one studied during the cool months, up the slope past the Victoria Gothic of Government College, from where I had seen the hockey players leave for the Olympics at Amsterdam in 1928. The world championship gave them no great thrill, for the world did not know then how to play hockey. Many of them lived to see the day when an Indian team could not even get into the finals. At the Shahalmi gate I left behind Lawrence's British city, and entered the old city ascribed to Rama's son Lava. The ambitious young widow of Ranjit Singh, Jindan Kaur, had literally handed over the keys to Henry Lawrence, without a fight. I found it to the credit of those whose Lahore it was today that both the old and the new part were left untouched, and had escaped the ugly growth that was enveloping the Delhis of Shahjahan and Lutyens: the pseudo Man Singh—Lutyens pompous-looking ministerial bhawans, and the mohalla-like cement plastered nagars lacking the beauty of the old brick mohallas. Here in the old Lahore, no modern traffic entered the narrow bazars and lanes with their overhanging carved wood balconies. From the busy streets and mandis I nostalgically walked through the famous Hira Mandi, the Diamond Market, a little early though in the evening for its bright lights and painted faces and kohled eyes. The Pathan, Kashmiri, Dogra, Chamba, Kulu, Sindhi and pure Jat Punjabi girls were still busy with their toilet after the siesta that refreshed them for, hopefully, a long night of song, dance and love with the old, the young and the adolescents. Through Lahori gate I walked through Anarkali, the busiest, most prosperous bazar of Lahore, with its brightly it shops, stores and restaurants; it was still the great attraction of all Punjabis. And I walked back slowly by the back of the Mall to Faleti's.

Next day we drove to Gujarat, eighty miles from Lahore, where I went to school and college. Around the old walled town time had stood still. Apart from some new suburbs the town was untouched. We stopped at the gate from where a narrow lane went to the mohalla and the lane in which we lived. Some doubt, discreetly encouraged by the man who accompanied us, prevented me from going inside the city, and after literally doing the Punjabi proverbial ritual of touching Gujarat we returned to Lahore.

From the Grand Trunk Road, through the sunset dust I caught the last view of Gujarat through the shisham trees by the road, a view I had seen so often when going to the river Chenab at Besaki. I looked at the weathered dark brown mass of the fortress in the city rising as a flat top cone.

Pakistan was busy with its forthcoming elections and it all seemed peaceful. It came clearly to me that partition was for ever; there was no going back. All I met and saw made it clear that the new Punjab was a purely Muslim Punjab, in which its Hindus had no place.

The skirmishes on the border of Rajasthan in the early summer months of 1965 seemed an ordinary affair. We did not realise that it was a prelude to a full-scale war. After the rains the border between our Punjab and Jammu and their land was aflame again. It was serious this time, with squadrons of tanks and planes and army divisions engaged after the fashion of a blitzkrieg. It was strange to hear from the security of Bombay in the news the old familiar names of canals, villages, towns and suburbs now pounded by tanks and planes. Shalimar gardens, Ichhogil canal, associated only with picnics by flowing water; the banks of the river Sutlej, where people used to collect on the bacchanalian spring festival of Besakhi; their reed marshes, home of water birds, were now the graveyards of disabled tanks. The war seemed such a desecration of a peaceful countryside. The heroic announcements on the radio that our brave troops and their tanks led by a Punjabi general were reaching the suburbs of Lahore gave me a sick and hollow feeling deep inside. Would he shell the city, the Mall, the Government College, the mohallas and mandis? When he was forced back over the canal it would not have made sense to a Bombay man if he had heard me say, "Thank the god who looked after Lahore."

As if all this was not enough, there was a third war five years later, in 1971, and again the borders of Punjab and Jammu were a battlefield. Again tanks and planes pounded our villages and towns.

These recurring short wars did however not leave scars behind, and we did not make vendettas out of them. They did drain precious resources that should have gone into growth, but nothing held back the Punjab.

CHAPTERS NINE

Shareholders

On the first day of March 1962, I was flying back from Lucknow to Delhi with Aspi Moddie. The budget had customarily been presented on the evening of the last day of February. The headlines screamed. I read fast through the Finance Minister's preamble with an apprehension that built up to a crescendo as it came to the crunch, the new taxes.It was a tough budget that in the aftermath of the Chinese war raised large resources in one full swoop. I skipped the personal taxes, quite unconcerned about how it might affect one personally, and ran on to the corporate taxes, making mental calculations at a furious rate. All I could say audibly was, Oh no! The profitability of the business, built with such loving care through the year, my first full year, adding each week's figure to the last—it was all shattered; it lay in splinters, and I wondered what it would take ever to restore it. The answer seemed hopeless.

What Morarji Desai had imposed on personal taxation was probably a worse blow, but that seemed not to matter; what mattered was what happened to the company one was responsible for. My mind momentarily wandered back to the utter surprise of a shareholder at the last annual general meeting when he discovered that I (or the directors) did not own a single share in the company. "But what is your stake in the company, Mr Chairman, if you own nothing of it?" I now sadly recalled my answer—my professional pride in seeing the company and his interest in it prosper. I do not think he believed me, any more than did a minister I worked under some year later, that one could be devoted to an organisation, it's growth and profitability, with a professionalism that excluded one's own interests.

As I grappled with figures and their impact, a horrible thought came, at first slowly and then in a blinding flash. The thirty-five rupees as a rights value of the shares that I had fought so hard to get from government, and which we were now going to offer to the Indian shareholder, was now history, it was no longer fair nor relevant to charge it in the new circumstances. In fact the stock market would take a dive and make its own judgement during the day and place a much lower value on the shares. Indeed share values dropped, and precipitously; so that by the evening the stock exchange had to be closed.

At Palam I met Ravi Bhatt of the Unit Trust of India and asked him if he understood the full implication of the new surtax. He was not too sure but, always an optimist, he did not think it would be too bad. He was to prove wrong. Back in my room at the Ashoka, which I had only left a day earlier feeling generally satisfied with life, I returned to the fray, Was growth, I thought to myself, for ever going to run against a strong headwind, when surely it should have had the wind behind it. Will one be fighting for it all the time? But there was no time to philosophise, and so Aspi and I began to figure out the future, and like after a flood or fire one had to make a quick beginning somewhere. We felt the first and the right thing was to immediately withdraw the rights offer so that the shareholders would be left in no doubt. We had many thousand small holders who had implicit trust in us, and if approached even now at thirtyfive rupees, many would take up their rights at that price despite the changed circumstances, trusting us to have offered them good value. Many would not even read the market quotations, and even if they did, the uninitiated would think we were expecting our shares to rise, and therefore offering them not a bad deal. We then poured over a long coded cable to Unilever stating our views, and sent it off.

London reacted quickly and well. There was no delegation flying over this time; instead in a long-distance call Robert Siddons said they were as shocked as I was, and would I come over to London to discuss. They were not agreeable to my suggestion to withdraw the offer, since it would look a weakness on our part, both in the eyes of the government and the shareholders, as if we were loosing faith and courage. I was satisfied that at least on this occasion they were asking me to put on my hat and coat and fly over! All right, I told Robert, I would be over next week, as soon as I had worked out the implication of a new plan, and sounded New Delhi. Back I went to L.K. Jha and placed my views before him. To go to the market with thirtyfive rupees under these circumstances would be immoral. We must withdraw it and there after we would return with a new plan as soon as things settled down. In the meantime we would like to clearly state our intention to go ahead with the core of our expansion plans, though in a phased manner.

Jha liked the idea; and I assured him in a letter the same day that we had hope and faith that despite the burdens arising out of the emergency and new taxation we could press on with our plans to show trust in government and the economy. We would go right ahead when many were understandably hesitating. He also liked the financial arrangements I suggested. In principle he was agreeable; but of course he had government to consult and I had Unilever. In my heart I forgave the system for my past experience of it; even blessed it for such decisiveness.

I took the midnight Air India to London where there was more than the usual driver with the Unilever placard in his hand waiting at the exit of the air terminal; there was a young man who wondered if I could go straight to Unilever House for a meeting they had fixed for 11 o'clock. It was now half past nine. After a night flight of fourteen hours, the idea of meeting straightaway was sensible. I could get the preliminary round over with, and sleep the evening and night through. Through that day I realised that whatever my intellectual ability for a top position, my capacity to take strain, physical and mental, at least was a qualification of some order.

As it was, I felt more and more alert as the day progressed and we decided to talk things through, so that I could see the Special Committee of the two chairmen, George Cole and Frits Temple, and the vice-chairman, Ernest Woodruffe, the next day, and leave the day after. Andrew Knox, chairman of the Overseas Committee, with a personal knowledge of India extending over forty years, agreed that we must go ahead, but he was sad at the turn things had taken. "It can only create more problems for you," he added wisely. "You are over-reacting, and maybe you should not oblige the Chinese by acting this way. Anyway I am sure the Special Committee will accept your proposals, particularly as you have cut out the frills and dropped some of the projects like buying a biscuit company."

If Frits Temple had expected all this when he questioned Lord Heyworth's judgement seven years ago, at least he did not say, "I told you so." Lord Cole was anxious to go ahead; compared with some on his old African beat, this was still reason. If Unilever had any reservations about going ahead exactly as was originally planned, something in my earnestness to find a way that suited both Hindustan Lever and government must have made them withdraw these. Jasper Knight was silent this time while I was vocal and insistent.

I left the next day on one of those midday flights from London where the plane raced away from a sunny Europe into the night in the East. In early March the days were still short, and by the time we had lunch, heading for the first eastern stop, it was already dark. Soon there was tea, then drinks, and then dinner. I always set my watch to my destination, which while it makes time irrelevant for many hours is in tune with my disembodied state of mind; in any case time has no meaning when it is changing every half hour.

I felt sad this time at leaving Europe, which after its difficult early post-war years was now in a state of great vitality and growth. I had never seen it with so much confidence; a long way from the Europe of the great depression, Europe sliding into a war it did not want to fight but could not avoid; Europe after the war still in a state of trauma. Now it bustled with healthy activity, with its back hopefully forever turned to wars, and coalescing instead into a common market. It was in an exhilarating mood of expansion, and affluence, whose ill effects had not hit it yet. While we too not long ago had been full of optimism and expansion, we were now suddenly, after the Chinese "incident," as it was by now called, in a "Johar" mood of economic policy. Now should have been the time to build eagerly, freely, confidently; instead of piling up new restrictions, quotas, cutbacks, and throwing ashes in our hair. Europeans, the victorious, the vanquished and the neutrals alike were hitching their wagons to racing stars, while we were digging into earth instead of building towards the sky. The Nehru era early confidence now gave way to gloom; and he himself must have felt distraught and confused. The only one who looked confident and purposeful in midst of all this was Morarji Desai. He had his brief, and as a man upright, austere, severe and with a streak of the self-righteous, he went through the process with visible satisfaction of "It hurts me more than it hurts you boy."—"Later, Nehru blamed me; but this was his brief to me, and I did it. Why could he not have told me otherwise", he said some years later when he was out of power.

In Delhi on my next visit Aspi said there had been new trouble. Someone had twitted Morarji Desai in parliament that as an instance of the havoc his budget had caused, the chairman of Hindustan Lever had dashed off to London to tell his principals to drop all expansion plans. When I went to see L.K. Jha he said, yes. Morarji Desai had misunderstood the purpose of my visit to Unilever in London to persuade them not to proceed with the rights issue. He thought, as someone challenged him in parliament, that I had gone to ask Unilever to withdraw all plans for growth and expansion in India. I decided to see Morarji, and asked Jha if he would mind my telling the minister that I had seen him and he had agreed with my plans. Jha said, he would not mind.

Morarji's personal secretary, Tonpe, one of the kindest, mildest of men, with long and great loyalty to his chief, saw my predicament and arranged a meeting at practically no notice. He said I could have precisely the time it took Morarji to go in his car from his office in parliament to the Congress House where he had a meeting; and as Morarji got into the car, Tonpe hustled me into it. Morarji sat in a corner, withdrawn into himself, engrossed in his file. Never had I felt anyone so remote a mere foot away.

"Yes, what have you to say."

"I will wait, Sir, till you have read your papers."

"No, I can do both, read and listen to you. Go ahead."

It was a disconcerting experience to talk to such a forbidding presence; if in its remoteness it could be called a presence. His face had a granite calm and his voice was cold and resonant. There was something compelling. You could not but help admiring him at least for being all of a piece.

> "I came to see you because I believe there was some misunderstanding about the moves I made..." I began.
>
> "No, there is no misunderstanding about it. You are entitled to act as you think best, but don't come to me for anything. I will have nothing to do with it."

I persevered.

> "But this is exactly the misunderstanding. You have a feeling that I have acted wrongly. If you knew the position correctly you would not think so. What I did was the right and the only possible decision in the interest of our Indian shareholders. I have discussed the matter with your secretary and he agrees with me."

He suddenly turned away from his file and looked at me with the first flicker of interest.

> "Oh, you have spoken to Jha, and he thinks yours was the right step?"
>
> "Yes, sir, he would be glad to explain it to you."

Morarji's reputation for being inflexible had also admitted his administrative fairness, and those who had served under him had always spoken highly of his decisive and trusting supportive nature. To one who had never met him before, this was not visible in a flash. The car reached his destination, and as I left him he almost smiled. He said that he would have a word with the secretary. I gave myself a sixty-forty chance, because although he had heard me he was not known to change his mind easily. I decided to leave it all alone and await results. A couple of days later, I was at a farewell party at our vice-chairman Jim Davies' flat, when there was a call from New Delhi.

> Prakashji, this is Aspi here; I thought I would mention to you that I have got an appointment with Morarji Desai tomorrow to follow up our case and see if I can clinch it. Do you mind? I think I can manage it.

This shook me, since it was quite contrary to my intention of leaving Morarji alone, in case he felt I was pressurising him. Moddie's quick follow-up might irritate him; and yet I could not say no at this stage. He sounded so rearing to go, and I did not want to hold him back. I had to decide quickly.

> Yes, Aspi, by all means—and good luck. I am sure he will listen to you.

A triumphant telex came from Aspi the next evening saying it was all settled; we could go right ahead. I was glad it was all settled; more glad that Aspi had done it. That night I slept long; in fact good sleep was becoming a habit with me as stress mounted. Next day, as I took stock of things, what a victory, I thought, to be allowed to grow!

My day of the final test came when I had to put it to the shareholders for approval at a special meeting. We had expected a stormy meeting but never so stormy as it turned out to be. Our new building, Hindustan Lever House, had its own auditorium, which was packed to overflowing, and in the front row were all the familiar faces of the professional shareholders, who went from one meeting to another. They were mostly old Parsis with a few Gujaratis to whom this was an occupation in an otherwise dull retirement. At most places they had a big tea, at some a gift or a gift coupon of the company's products. There was one among them who was always against every thing we did, and I had to be very careful with him. He could hit out at any level that suited him, and many a great chairman had fallen a victim to his ingenious, well timed blows. We had crossed swords before, but fortune had not favoured him; especially on the occasion when he complained to the local Company Law Board that he had asked me a very reasonable question which I had most unreasonably ignored. Shamdas, our company secretary, and I swore he had never asked it, because I meticulously noted and answered each one of the over one hundred questions over the three to four hour length of the meeting. And then something dawned on us! We always invited each shareholder to come to the microphone, but on that particular occasion the man had thanked politely and said that he was all right where he was. And that was the ruse. This was before the days one heard of bugging, but how I wished we had had the whole auditorium wired. Shamdas was however not to be daunted and rushed back to replay the tapes on an off chance, and returned triumphantly to announce that the tapes had picked up what the shareholder had said—and he had not said it.

There was tension abroad, and as I walked up to the dais and looked at the familiar faces in the front row and bowed to them their smiles in return were wan. Speech followed speech, each battening on the criticism of the one before. Some old Parsis waxed eloquent and their refrain was, how dared this foreign firm have such disregard for India, today when the empire no longer existed and Britain ruled neither the waves nor India; how had they dared first to exploit India and then mulct the shareholders—such treatment of the poor, underdeveloped and down-trodden was ugly imperialism and a new economical exploitation. And so the speeches went on.

Only two persons were silent, my special shareholder and I. I said I was in no hurry and would like everyone to have his say, at any length he liked, because the subject was so important that I did not want discussion curbed. Eventually, after many had spoken twice and thrice, they demanded that I answer. I turned to our shareholder and suggested that surely he also had something to say. He said, no, he would rather hear me reply to what had already been asked. The general strength of their feelings, in his opinion, must have registered well enough on me by now. This brought great applause. Without saying much he had said enough.

I felt it ironical that at last having persuaded first Jasper Knight and Unilever, and then government and my friend the controller of capital issues, and last Morarji Desai, I had now to face the shareholders' suspicion. How isolated one can be! Unilever felt that I had let them down; Morarji felt I had let down the national cause in an emergency; the shareholders made no bones about my joining Unilever's "exploitation." Unilever had of course sent me the proxy if I had to decide by putting it to a vote; but this was what I dreaded most. Failing to convince the three hundred shareholders present, having them unanimously voting against the resolution, and then to call for a poll and use the brute strength of the ninety per cent to carry the resolution and the day, seemed wrong.

I got up on my feet of lead and began to explain that Unilever had made their own gesture; they had not taken up their due share of rights, but they did not see why the other shareholders should not pay a fair price, especially at this juncture, so that the money received would strengthen the general reserves of Hindustan Lever in which they too had a stake. In fact, it would be improper for the present shareholders to deprive the future shareholders of a fair price and accretion to reserves in their own selfish interest. The gain belonged to the company and not just to those who happened to be the shareholders today; a company was in perpetuity. I went on to explain the whole record of Hindustan Lever, an enviable one of growth and fairness. We the board members had voluntarily refrained from ever buying any shares because our inside knowledge would place us at an advantage over the shareholders, which we did not consider fair. With this record of company's behaviour and performance, how could one be so misunderstood! I ended by saying that if today they were paying a few rupees extra, they would gain that and much more through future return on an asset so greatly expanded and strengthened. I was confident of our future and their share in it. In the end, after four hours of discussion, I appealed to them to combine their strength to support the management and not to mistrust it. I then put to a vote the motion to make the rights issue at the price fixed by government, though the shareholders had thought it high.

There was complete unanimity, except for "the" shareholder who alone refrained; and while normally many don't bother to raise their hands, tonight a forest of hands went up, when I asked—"for." As I walked out of the hall, an old Scotsman, who was the head of our firm of solicitors, came up to me and said very kindly—"today, the mantle of that great chairman of Bombay, Sir Purshotamdas Thakurdas, should fall on your shoulders." I felt touched but embarrassed, because I felt I had really pulled out all the stops.

CHAPTERS TEN

Maya

Nineteen sixty-four was the year our eldest, Maya, who had now finished college, got married. Child of mixed parentage, she was a girl of some originality.

When the children were small my wife had been anxious that they should grow up as ordinary Indian children without any feeling of being different from other youngsters because of a foreign-born mother; and in this she succeeded well. In the early years, before we moved into a house of our own, we shared the ground floor of a rented house with a Punjabi couple whose only son was like a fourth child with us. Their house was always full of Punjabi relations with children. Our own home too was an open house, Indian style. The top floor was occupied by the owners, a joint Muslim family where the children were also welcome. None of the women of the house spoke English. Gärd spoke only Hindi to the children, and she further had the Scandinavian notion that they should not be sent to school at an early age. This was regarded a strange notion in a country where children are doing spelling and sums at the age of four. Therefore, when she took them to Sweden in the summer 1948, only Maya, seven, who had been to convent school in Bandra for a year and had learned English as another language, could communicate with strangers. All three nevertheless played happily with Swedish children, and soon picked up Swedish. At the end of their five months' stay they were fluent, but back home they forgot it just as quickly. Gard saw no point in keeping up a language that was not likely to be of any practical value, but would make them feel apart. Besides they had now to learn English, once Hindi was firmly established as their own language.

Schooling in India was a problem then, and in other ways it still is. Most good schools in a town like Bombay were run by Christian missions, and although India was free, their education was not yet geared to this fact. Geography still started in them with the British Isles, and in the history books "we" meant the British. The Indian schools on the other hand were either in Gujarati or Marathi, which made it difficult for children like ours to move from one part of India to another. When Maya was nine, we decided to send her to Woodstock in Mussoorie, of which we had had good reports. It was a co-educational school, founded in mid-nineteenth century for the children of American missionaries, and had a reputation for good academic standards and American Protestant upbringing, strict and reformative, yet sufficiently secular and permissive in its own way. Generations of American children from all over India and neighbouring countries had studied there. I once met an American who fifty years earlier had gone there from Malaya, a fortnight's journey by rail, road and sea. With the advent of international air traffic children came to the Himalayas from the oil fields of the Persian Gulf. In the cold and snows of winter the school was closed for three months.

A confident child, Maya was to begin with quite excited about this new adventure, and all the new clothes she was getting. She had never had so much at a time, and was particularly entranced with all the woollies. Woodstock had no uniforms, unless you counted blue jeans with patched knees, still outside Maya's experience. Into her black japanned tin trunk went clothes and toiletries and a generous supply of goodies. On the day before leaving Maya said she didn't want to go. "Then," said Gärd, "we unpack the trunk and lock up the woollies you don't need in Bombay." This made Maya reconsider her decision. The brothers teased her, but were told to mind their own business until their time would come, when they would be snivelling like babies.

Next day at Bombay Central station we saw Maya, with an eye firmly on her trunk, bravely getting into the bogey reserved for the Woodstock party. We waved her off, and she joined the boys and girls who were to be her companions for two days and two nights in the train, and for many years at school.

That was the end of the Maya we knew, and as the Frontier Mail pulled away and her face faded into the phosphorescent darkness of the platform, I wondered whether separating the young from home was really an intelligent form of upbringing.

The decision to send her away to school was largely mine. Gärd, not being Anglo-Saxon, did not believe in boarding school education; she saw no sense in separating young children from their parents. But like so many of my incomprehensible actions she accepted it patiently. It was a British institution that served their need and culture. In India the British had built schools in the salubrious mountains, though they had always preferred, if possible, to send their children to England, even though it often meant lifelong separation in the old days. There are some pathetic references in the diaries of mothers quietly pining for their young, whom they met years later as grown-up strangers; the joy of their childhood denied. The system eventually developed into a caste distinction: to the hill schools in India went the children of those who settled, then called Anglo-Indians, those of mixed descent, then called Eurasians, and the children of British soldiers. Only during the 1939-45 war did they send their children to school in India, for obvious reasons. These hill schools became schools for Indian children, run on British public school lines but learning to gear to life in India, after a fashion.

The reasons weighing with me were the climate, and also the problem of daily commuting by bus or train from our suburb to one of the good schools in the city. There were convent schools in Bandra, and Maya had been to two of them, but their methods of teaching seemed oldfashioned and uninspiring. To be fair, it was a period of transition, and the new idea of secularism demanded some adjustments, while these schools provided an education that centred round the Bible and Britain.

Gard readily saw the benefit of Woodstock's higher quality of education, and from her own experience thoroughly approved of co-education. But there were risks involved, for although Woodstock provided for Hindi and Indian history for the Indian pupils, the upbringing was really meant to equip the children for life in America. It was no more secular than Catholic education; some teachers were broadminded and with some interest in things Indian, others very rigid in their faith.

Maya took to Woodstock from the beginning, her mind opened wide to their teachings and their ways. She was thoroughly happy and made good friends with clean, simple American girls and boys. She seemed to be developing very well in these surroundings. But as she entered her teens I began to notice a change—a growing alienation from Indian culture. Her accent, outlook and ways, her conversation and interests began to point in one direction—to a continuation into an American life. It would have been hard to define what Indian culture was then, or today over twenty years later; but whatever it was, Maya was growing into a pure American girl, whom nobody would have called Indian. And she was changing in a very natural way, smooth transition from childhood into her early adolescent personality. This new personality was naturally moulded by Woodstock's environment. She was growing like any other girl at Woodstock, and most other girls were American.

American culture, as I was to discover later for myself, has a stronger pull than any other. I have known Indians who have lived in England for a lifetime, and yet their ways and accent have remained Indian. They could return to India and remain unnoticed, but not so those who had lived in America. American culture is infectious and insistent, so easy to acquire, for it permeates so easily. It is a culture generous in giving itself with none of the involuntary holding back of the British or the European. Two years at Woodstock had more influence on Maya than the British style public schools on the Indian boys who were sent there. Many considered me somewhat like the British, even in my emotional make-up, with an open withdrawal in face of emotion, and a self-control that to many bordered on unconcern, if not callousness. With most people I worked or dealt with there was a gulf that only I could bridge, not they. Perhaps I was built that way, and eight impressionable years of my youth in England merely accentuated it. And yet while the stamp of this culture on me was one of cold aloofness, on Maya the American stamp was one of warmth and open friendliness. It jarred, at times, but never froze one out. So why should I grudge Maya gaining the stamp of a culture foreign to India when the one I had acquired was equally alien, whatever their comparative merits or demerits.

I questioned myself what was I really afraid of? Was it of her leaving some unidentifiable Indian culture to adopt an identifiable American culture? And was there an Indian culture; and what was it? The question baffled me. We spoke not even a language of our own except to illiterates and to children ; to anyone even moderately literate we spoke in English; and even when we spoke in an Indian language, our speech was spattered with English words and whole English sentences. Particularly did we need English to express emotions or sophisticated thinking. We did not lack expressive equivalents in our own language, but speaking English we used Punjabi and speaking Punjabi we used English; so much so that a stranger could easily get the gist of the conversation.

What else did our culture contain? Few ever read books in any language; sadly, few ever read. The popular reading outside an English daily used to be Reader's Digest; now it is also Time magazine, possibly the Economist or an Indian weekly; but it seldom goes beyond current affairs. In arts, painting had changed from the revival of the Ajanta, the Rajput and Kangra styles to the European impressionists, later to give way to the non-objective and the abstract. Sculpture was confined mostly to making diminutive statues of Gandhi, complete with glasses, and later Nehru, to fit a small crowded city's main chowk, to suit the modest municipality purse. The most charming of all was a diminutive statue of Lal Bahadur Shastri, himself of small stature, with a garland around his hand and a Gnat aircraft over his head, commemorating no doubt his 1965 Pakistan war. Sometimes, to give them durability, like the Gandhi statue at Juhu Beach of Bombay, the statues were covered with aluminium paint. Indian upper class homes at the time were dull imitation of Europe; the renaissance of Indian handicrafts was just beginning; all else was Swiss cuckoo clocks and Japanese calendars.

What was the Indian culture that Maya was losing? Under the British, the middle classes had acquired a patchwork culture reminiscent of E.M. Forster's description of Indian guests at an Englishman's tea-party. European dress, he said, was like leprosy upon them, a patch here and a patch there.

Our culture, so called, has always baffled and also bothered me, especially as I have lived and worked in an international environment for most of my life. By nature a good learner, with a high degree of imitativeness and an approach bordering on perfectionism, when I went to England at the age of eighteen I gave myself over to their ways without hesitation or reservation, and without any judgements passed, as most foreigners living abroad do. I was going to live there for many years, so I decided to like their food, manners, music, arts; in fact I adopted everything, for better or worse. In the end, I could not see any trace of an Indian left in me. Upon my return home, it so happened that I joined a British firm of the north country, where I had lived my youth's formative years consequently I fitted in with them like a glove. Even my Lancashire accent, before I lost it, made some of those from Warrington and Liverpool feel homesick. But then a change came, after Gard came from Sweden to marry me. I split myself into two, the half that worked with them and the other that withdrew inwards.

As first Indian manager among a large number of British, I stood out. While at work, I learned fast and imitatively, absorbing totally their approach and style; socially I was completely out of their life. In the office my contact or familiarity with my peers was confined to work, with a few pleasantries occasionally exchanged. This enforced isolation was hopeful in its own way because it helped me to take to the learning process with an obsession, and to recrystallise in me what had originally been Punjabi but had become diffused through the years. Born and bred in the heart of the Punjab, the West Punjab, that was all the India I had known. Now living in Bombay and travelling extensively gave me my first introduction to India. Punjab was not India; it was history's no man's land. It only vaguely shared India's culture, its culture was mainly one of survival, at which it was adept, rising to any kind of heights only when laid it low. I think some such atavistic change began in me again. Inside the international, British exterior I began to revive the Punjabi core.

Had I not worked in this foreign environment but joined government or an Indian firm, I believe I would have developed differently. Instead of the two clear halves, I would have developed a melange of the kind E.M. Forster described. I would have acquired the fluent capacity to have English and Punjabi weave in and out in the same sentences like colours in the bleeding Madras cloth, and an approach equally confused, as I was to find years later, when I joined government business.

Maurice and Taya Zinkin, who had lived in India until Partition, when he left the ICS, and returned after he joined Unilever, in their inastiable appetite for knowledge of the country and people engaged me in long conversations, in which they remarked that I displayed some sensitive though instinctive understandings. Around my Punjabi core I had apparently acquired some knowledge of India, which they seemed to find interesting and of a taexture better than that of the usual westernised Indian. On Punjab they found it of special interest. To Maurice, who had begun his career in ICS in Maharashtra the Maharashtrians were the finest people of India, with the austerity and keen mind of the Jews, a brahmanical tradition that went with his own rabbinical inheritance; but as he got to see the Punjabi through my eyes, and learn something about them, he grudgingly began to admire them too, though at a safe distance from the Maharashtrians.

In discussing the Punjab and the Punjabis, I discovered that I had inherited a memory, for after all I had lived there barely for the first eighteen years of my life, and that mostly in lonely canal colonies and in small towns; nor had I read anything in Punjabi. Watching people and their customs, the ritual at birth, marriage, love and death, their lives of selfless, generous help and vicious intrigues, I must have learned and absorbed some deep impressions as a child and boy. I felt too that I had inherited a cumulative racial memory of sort. Maurice and Taya began first to suggest, and then to insist, that I write it down before my own memory dimmed and the knowledge died with the present generation, whom the great Partition had already exiled to all parts of India. How much would Maya, Manu and Gautam know how their father and his father and his father had lived; of the world they were born to, now totally erased by a wholly Muslim Pakistan.

My mind was confused over this problem of Maya's Americanisation and de-Indianisation. Unfortunately for me the Americanisation was more obvious than the de-Indianisation, because while the one was clear the other was not so clear. I also asked myself whether in preventing Woodstock and its American culture permeating Maya's mind, I was also not keeping out their values which were wholesome and better than anything our Indian schools' environment could then give her. Just as the thousand years of Muslim rule had atlast begun to produce a common Hindu-Muslim culture, the British had arrived with new and totally unfamiliar concepts. While through the thousand years of a hard Muslim rule we had managed to keep our essential core, under the benign British we began to lose it and turn into a hotchpotch.

And so my thoughts oscillated—what I thought was not good for Maya had nothing wrong with it by itself, and what Maya should have in its place was unidentifiable and had really nothing better to offer.

When I broached the subject with Maya she reacted sharply.

"Why, why should I change my school? I am happy, I have good friends, I am doing well at studies, the teaching is good. What have you against it?"

I said I had nothing against the school. It was a good school, she was doing well, and her friends were all nice.

"Then?"

"Maya, it isn't easy to explain, but I will try."

I explained how I felt about her avid absorption of American culture, which was making her a product not fit for the Indian Soil. She would thrive if she went to America like the other girls. But when she left school one day to return to the Indian environment she would have to readjust herself, and this readjustment would be more difficult and painful the longer it was postponed. She had gained much from her school, and these foundation years would prove useful to her, but she now needed an Indian orientation. She should move to a purely Indian school, such as the Maharani Gayatri Devi in Jaipur. This had originally been a school for the girls of the Rajput princely families, but was now under a new English principal a good public school for Indian girls.

Maya kept asking me what was the American culture she had assimilated that I objected to, and I did my best to convince her that I was not prejudiced, but the American ways—let us forget culture—she had assimilated were so different from our own ways that she would stand out like a foreigner. Perhaps in a country with its own well defined culture one could be bi-cultural, as many Europeans were. There were Dutchmen in Unilever as British as they were Dutch. But our case was different. Today our Indian culture, however one would define it, had not the strength to withstand something so dominating as American culture, and in Maya's case, she had not yet found an Indian core.

Reluctantly she agreed to give the new school a trial. As she was a little late for the term I took her myself by train to Jaipur. Something of a hedonist, she enjoyed the luxury of airconditioned travelling as a start to a new life. She would be ahead of the other girls who had not had her experience of international surroundings. The principal, Miss Lutter, extended the unexpected courtesy of meeting Maya at the station. She had understood her predicament and went out of her way to put her at ease. I went to the hotel, and Maya with Miss Lutter to the school in her charming old Austin Seven.

Next evening I went there to take her out to dinner. Maya ran impatiently to the car. In a long red woollen coat, blue shirt and white salwar, and her dark brown pigtails plaited with black cords, she looked so different. She talked excitedly about the school, the different systems, and how the girls were awed by her experiences.

Maya stayed there three years and finished well, topping in Rajasthan in the Senior Cambridge examination. For this she got a gold medal, endowed by a local businessman, which she complained was wafer thin.

Twentyfive years later she wrote to me from Washington that, excellent though the schools were there, she wanted, in view of her own experience, to send her nine year old daughter Ayesha back to school in India. She felt it was the best thing to do.

With her brothers, Manu and Gautam, there was no such problem. They both went to Doon School at Dehra Dun, which had only Indian boys, and they grew as purely Indian boys of their kind. Maya after the college at Bombay married a Punjabi boy, as an interesting coincidence, from Gujarat; their home in fact had been in the next *mohalla* to ours. He worked with an American bank and later joined the World Bank in Washington. Manu after a commerce degree in Bombay went to London to do his articles for chartered accountancy, but quite unlike me, he did not like England at all. With hundreds and thousands of Indians now living in England, he detected a clear race prejudice, understandable but no more tolerable for that. Gautam joined the army in one of the old cavalry regiments. They both married Punjabi girls.

CHAPTERS ELEVEN

Hindustan Steel

Hindustan Steel, India's first and largest public enterprise, started in 1961, was having teething troubles. Its new, dynamic minister, C. Subramaniam, felt that they should have a professional manager on the board, and asked me to join as a non-executive director.

Hindustan Steel was my first experience of serving on the board of a major public sector company. The steel company was India's biggest industrial complex in 1963, running four large steel mills, which specialised in a range of products, coal and iron ore mines, and a fertiliser plant. It was large by any standards, with the added complexity that the plants were built in collaboration with four countries, Russia, Krupps of West Germany, a consortium in the United Kingdom, and one in Japan, with sub-contracting in a number of other countries for quite sizeable contracts. Each was responsible for a turnkey job to build and hand over a going concern. If to all this industrial and cultural diversity were added the naivete, indeed utter innocence of anything to do with steel or management, of some of those from our side who coordinated and ultimately ran the mills when they were handed over, confusion of a rare kind can be imagined. In fact, a story I heard, which I considered apocryphal, turned out to be so true when I checked, that one's mind boggled at the reality.

Our chairman, retired from the civil service, went on a visit to the USA, where he was invited by the U.S. Steel. Its president, as the head of the world's largest steel company, decided to take personal note of the visit of the chairman of the developing world's largest steel complex. He specially arranged to fly with him in his private plane to one of their plants to create an opportunity for a personal chat. It is said that no matter how much the American probed into Hindustan Steel's working he drew a blank from our chairman. He was genuinely interested in the working of a steel complex in a country like India, of its technologies, one at least of which was among the latest; especially as talks were going on then about the next and largest plant to be set up with U.S. collaboration. Our chairman, neither a steel man nor particularly sensitive to the new technologies and their operational performance in the environment of India, gave short, simple answers. Fortunately he did not talk authoritatively about things he did not know, a not uncommon feature of ours. Exasperated, the president gave up, with a polite remark, "Mr. Chairman, you are the most relaxed chairman of a steel company I have had the pleasure of meeting."

"Yes, yes," said the chairman happily when I asked him about this incident, "he really was very impressed with my calm, relaxed way; he expected I would be tense and overwrought like the highpowered American top executives. I am, as you know, a very relaxed person." And, as if to illustrate it, he sucked at his briar pipe.

Those responsible for negotiating and planning were drawn from the administration. They came from the Indian Civil Service, the Indian Audit & Accounts Service and the Indian Railways. The ICS men led the teams, helped by the finance men, whose knowledge was not really in finance but in audit and control, in rules and regulations. The technicians were railway men, mechanical, electrical, signals and construction engineers. There was occasionally a metallurgical scientist and someone from industry. I think there were emotional blocks in both government and private steel industry. The latter had two plants, one of them particularly successful. Government, setting up in competition with the private sector, was not anxious to learn from it, nor were the private firms anxious to teach. It is interesting that we asked private industry abroad for help, but not our own.

I think the sensible thing would have been to do a clean job, like the British government, to nationalise the two private steel firms, Tata and Indian Iron, learn to run them well, use them as nuclei, expand and diversify, and then build new ones. This ideological contradiction stemmed from our tendermindedness, which always creates problems. Or else, we should have given the private plants freedom to expand and diversify, to stand or fall, in competition with the public sector plants; this too would have made sense, but letting them exist without the freedom to thrive did as much harm to HSL as to Tatas and Indian Iron. In fact, Indian Iron so declined that government had to take it over fifteen years later, instead of taking over when it was in full health. Fifteen valueable years were lost through this tendermindedness at a great cost.

The men who did come from the private steel plants were not always the best, and working under civil servants, unappreciative as well as oblivious to their skills and contribution, the best mostly left in disgust.

To man the new mills, we sent hundreds of young, freshly graduated engineers to the USA, the UK, Germany and Russia for periods of nine months training with their steel companies. They went from shop to shop, mostly observing, and came back as steel men to run our shops. I met a group in America, and I gathered that they had done a poor learning job. After joining the board of Hindustan Steel, I met them later in the shops, at work and in the evenings in groups socially. They were generally a keen bright-eyed lot, anxious to prove, perhaps more than to learn, but always very anxious to please and impress, that fatal characteristic of ours at all ages and levels. I have always longed to see in an Indian subordinate, but seldom seen, that steadfast gaze, open and direct, combined with a capacity to listen intently and appreciatively; a gaze returned directly with the answer that has within it a capacity to agree without ingratiation, or to disagree with courage, politely but firmly. During their training abroad they were full of euphoria, straining at the training leash that held them back, rearing to go and prove themselves. I found this attitude disquieting; it forebode neglect of training that would create problems at the coalface. Also I heard, vaguely and politely though, that they combined their desire for an early return with a characteristic capacity for travel; they were always visiting their friends or relations among the vast numbers who live or travel abroad. Given affluence and freedom to travel, no Indian will ever stay at home for long—he will always be visiting holy places, or friends and relations, and of course today, "going foreign". I could well believe that with the discovery of the long week-end, easily extended through a small request, some took their learning process in a relaxed way.

In the UK I doubt if they learned more; in West Germany it must have been a bit better; but the best job was done by the Russians, who put them to work as soon as it was possible, and let Russians stand by, teach and watch. And there was nowhere to go in Russia anyway.

At Rourkela, I met many of them at the club in the evening, and they displayed a touching concern for opportunity to show their paces, held back by the presence of so many German technicians. If only the foreigners could be sent back, they would get on with the job and show what they could do independently. The Germans were "experts" away from home, the boys argued, not among the best—why should the best be sent out who had their chance at home. No outsider could have had the feel they had for their own plants in their own country. And so they talked with great fervour and conviction. I liked their enthusiasm, but the rest left me unimpressed. No matter how keen our own young Lever trainees—a far more carefully picked and trained lot—I would have felt alarmed at the idea of their taking over things at so immature a stage. The irony was that here from top to bottom all were inexperienced. No one had ever made steel before. But what bothered me more than their inexperience was their xenophobia combined with a lack of humility to learn, when neither inexperience nor ignorance of steel making was their fault. One was worried by their refusal to realise all this. Their confidence did not impress, as would have done a certain becoming diffidence.

I then went up to the German superintendent, a large cheery man whose very appearance extruded a steelmakers' masterly confidence. "Yes," he said in answer to my question about the plant and the boys. "It is a fine plant, the latest in world steel technology, the LD process, one of the first outside Europe. It is a very sensitive process, fast and economical, and with it goes the rest of the mill which specialises in flat products, not the simple billets, bars and rails, which of course makes it the more profitable. It has therefore to be run with great skill, and its most important demand is maintenance. Both these are matters of experience and care. The boys are a fine lot, keen and intelligent, and I have no doubt that in years to come they will make good steelmen, but you do need experience of more than a few months' training. They need to work hard at it; steelmaking is an exacting task, a little neglect, there can be a snarl up and a whole line has to be switched off. The workmen too are new and they have also learned their skills on this plant. Many are not far removed from the village and their familiarity with machines is recent. For skilled trades we have especially some fine Punjabi Sikhs and Malayalis, but the labour from the neighbourhood is unskilled. The boys have therefore a double job, of learning themselves and teaching others."

The German superintendent knew the feelings of his Indian colleagues and anticipated my next question. "Yes, they can do the job, even now if they like. We shall be gone soon; sooner, if they wish; and even sooner if we had our way," he added with a tinge of sarcasm. "Rourkela is not a place that enamours us. We are comfortable here but our wives are lonely; there is nothing for them to do all day, the same movie house, the same club, the same swimming pool, the same faces. Of course they do manage to keep themselves busy; German women will not remain idle. They have organised some activities and run a school for our children, but they miss home; we do too, though work keeps us busy, sometimes round the clock. Yes, we will soon leave, because jobs are easy to get at home—in fact all of us were tempted out of our jobs because Mr. Krupp personally regarded this as one of the first major prestige projects abroad. It was good for the new Germany's image, and I think we have done a good job; it will now be up to your people to show that they can complete it by making the plant run well and produce the products you so need for your development."

The German showed neither anxiety about remaining here nor impatience to return home; he seemed imbued with only one idea—to leave behind a job well done. The Indian engineers began to collect around us, but he spoke on, unperturbed, as he had no complaints, no blame. One could however sense a little sadness at the lack of at least some appreciation, instead of the anxiety to see them go, which also carried the implication that they were here in plush jobs with nothing to offer that the locals could not do. To the German steelmen, with generations of skills behind them, with a dedication to work, this must indeed have been gall to swallow. Three years earlier I had done a fortnight's sponsored visit to Germany, starting from Frankfurt, going through the densely industrial belt and ending at Hamburg. Because of their Indian connection at Rourkela, Krupps paid special attention to our Indian marketing team of ten. At Hamburg, I stayed behind for a few days with the Unilever headquarters for West Germany, the largest and the most prosperous in the Unilever group in Western Europe. In December 1960, Germany was fully restored and affluent, and while the new affluence had brought Italy, France and especially England frequent strikes and a growing desire to take it easy, in German factories and offices work was still worship, Nehru's slogan that remained only a slogan in India, hardly ever practised. At Unilever's Hamburg office the working day was eight in the morning till six in the evening. "Lunch break—no, we eat our sandwiches at the desk." The German superintendent at Rourkela saw no signs of hard work, often not even a moderate amount.

In the early sixties we were already taking it easy; in fact—when did we not, except during the three fortnights of the Chinese and Pakistan wars. Offices opened at ten, officers strolled in up to halfpast ten, the clerks slightly later; then the cups of tea and coffee; in the evening the exodus began soon after four in the afternoon. The workmen emulated this.

The Russians at Bhilai, also their biggest prestige project abroad, were different. To meet the board and local management, they arranged a party that began Swedish style with just one drink as we congregated at seven, and the next five hours at the table. So unlike the habit we picked up from the British and improved upon, of drinking on an empty stomach for so many hours that most people say goodbye as soon as they have finished dinner. Here, like in Sweden you never drank alone; someone toasted you. As is customary among Russians, it was a stag party and the drinking perhaps unusually heavy, but with food it did not appear burdensome; both time and liquor flowed smoothly and fast. The conversation was mainly through interpreters. Some of our men had picked up quite a fluency in Russian, but the hosts preferred to use their own interpreters, including a particularly charming girl, the only slim Russian girl I met. Someone told me that she use to joke about it—"Which Russian will ever marry me, I am not even 140 pounds?"

The Russian superintendent was not unlike his German counterpart, large, bluff, competent looking; but with no conversation. Here our men did not talk leave-us-to-do-the-job and expressed no anxiety to take over. The number of Russians was large and continued to remain so. I believe they deem this necessary even today. They did not attempt to mix and certainly not to fraternise. They mostly lived at Bhilai Hotel, belonging to the plant, a family per room, entirely to themselves. No questions were asked, no answers given, and no discussion. Nor were there any inter-personal problems. The Russians came to do a job of work and would stay as long as they considered it necessary. This seemed to continue fifteen years later. They took their own decisions. And Bhilai production-wise has been the most successful of all the plants, even allowing for the fact that it is of simple technology.

At Durgapur there were very few British left after the construction stage. They lived a life apart, like their governing predecessors before them, which had meant some recrudescence of the old social problems of real and imaginary affronts, an aloofness misunderstood all over again—though I gathered the fault partly lay with a pompous and status-obsessed man we had appointed from our side. The British, like the Germans, decided to leave as soon as possible, not to overstay the welcome, and to escape operational recriminations of which there had been enough already. Oddly enough, when C. Subramaniam took over the ministry he made the bold decision to keep Douglas Bell as general manager of Durgapur for two years longer. Bell was given two men to groom, and asked to recommend one of them to succeed him—of course we chose the one he did not recommend; and when the plant ran down, Bell was blamed roundly for having flogged the plant to show near-capacity production during his own stay. This I could hardly believe of him, for like his Russian and German counterparts, he was a steelman and shared their feelings for the plants. He was a Scot, born and bred in steel, handpicked for the job by the British consortium and knighted after he left—a small consolation for the criticism we gave him gratuitously and in good measure. I talked more freely with Douglas Bell than with the formal German; with the Russian, one had no contact, but they all represented a fine dedication to steel, and to their respective plants. The type of successors we hastily bred were naturally different, but I wish I could have found in them the basic quality of steadfastness and strength that living with steel, had built into their foreign counterparts. In any case none of our three plant managers was a technician.

To my first board meetings of Hindustan Steel I went most carefully prepared. I ploughed through the voluminous agenda that kept pouring in, first in Bombay, then the papers waiting at the HSL guest house in Calcutta, some more on the company plane waiting at Dum Dum airport to pick up the visiting directors, another lot in the car waiting at Ranchi airfield, more at the Ranchi guest house, and the last instalments on the board table, where papers kept arriving through the meeting, and the last minute supplementaries were placed on the table after the agenda was finished. It all showed a tremendous but suspect keenness to finish as much business as possible till the meeting next month. After a while I saw in this enthusiasm also a bad habit, and came to the conclusion that whether the board met weekly or annually the agenda papers would still have arrived like the irregular and ever-swelling course of a mountain stream. The agenda itself consisted of papers of varying sizes, quarto, foolscap, double foolscap, some pages folded upwards, other sideways, and yet others folded upwards, sideways and at the corners. And then I wondered whether the bad habit had not a method in its madness. I did wonder too whether there was not a gamesmanship in it—to send the agenda items inversely in their order of importance, placing some important items last on the table, after the meeting.

The text of the agenda was typed downwards, but the statements and tables in all directions. Truly breathtaking was the mass of facts and figures. The introduction to each case reached as far back in times as possible and pursued its slow course until the present. References, cross-references, correspondence with the ministries, state governments, contractors, management and others were carefully reproduced. Dozens of columns and hundreds of figures filled the statements, but never an attempt at evaluation, assessment, statement of alternative or recommendations; only at the end there was the charming euphemism for indecision—"The Board may kindly decide." The board had always to do everything with kindness, be kind to be informed, be kind to consider, and the ultimate in kindness was to give a decision. It was the same amusing culture of the Indian Airlines where everything, including its frequent delays, was announced for the kind information of the passengers. Thus did the East India Company, literally translating a customary courtesy from Persianised Urdu, refer to itself as kind, generous, honourable, gracious, the fountain of everything, bahadur—the brave. The same spirit still endured in generous references to the board—the board would kindly recall that they were pleased to consider this matter, and they kindly decided and directed. The directors were however addressed as plain Shri, with no reference to our personal courage, achievements or attributes.

As a classical touch, the agenda's some hundreds of pages were pierced and joined with a string in candy stripes, and the whole thing tied on a flat board with side flaps and grey-white tapes, no longer red. I was not surprised when next year I began to receive similar agenda from the venerable Reserve Bank of India; but receiving it in HSL on matters relating to the LD steel process, R & D, or the purchase of a new executive plane, it looked anachronistic. Besides its antiqued appearance, its wealth of facts and figures was more than I could assimilate, despite all my love and familiarity with figures. As was only to be expected, the agenda set the tone for the board meetings, which could seldom rise above its own detail. There was little chance for policy discussion.

What puzzled me in my first experience of working with a government undertaking was the whole new world of non-management. Brought up on systems and predictable behavioural patterns, I was astonished to see a world of non-systems. The agenda served as an introduction, but what followed was sometimes bizarre. At one meeting the chairman read out a letter from the secretary in the steel ministry suggesting that the board might consider passing a resolution along certain lines, adding however that it was not government's intention to lay down what the board should decide, nor did they wish to direct it in any manner. It would nevertheless be advisable, without treating this letter as a directive, for the board to resolve in the manner suggested, exercising of course its own judgment and prerogative to decide. The chairman explained that government had actually powers to issue directives in the name of the principal shareholder, the President of India, but in this case and many others, it appeared that government would rather tell us what to do than formally direct us to do so. The secretary wanted us to treat it as advice and not a directive, but to act as if it were a directive, so that while we decided in our own best judgment, it should be in the way government had decided. And, finally, the letter ended with the request that the chairman might let him know that we had done so. I asked the chairman to tell the secretary formally that we had indeed done so; and also assure him that we appreciated his concern for our autonomy as a board. The chairman laughed wryly, and said, "Join the public sector," he added, "You will enjoy it hugely." It was the secretary who received his reward by being elevated to a highly decorative post where he did nothing ever right and nothing ever wrong; he just did not do anything.

The chairman and the board could not do much without consulting the ministry, which took an all-pervasive interest in the company. It was always argued by the ministries' men that as they were responsible to parliament, they had to know what went on, and to guide the board in a way that prevented trouble with parliament. Parliament of course treated the ministry and the company alike. The company was therefore at the receiving end of both, and both were as free with advice as with criticism. The administration and the legislators could as easily deal directly with HSL's units, sub-units and individuals. They could make recommendations for jobs and contracts, demand information and little facilities and generally act as privileged persons.

I became quite engrossed in HSL, and was asked to draw up plans for a management information system and a new corporate plan. I suggested that the three main steel plants be made into subsidiaries of a holding company to be formed out of the head office at Ranchi. Each plant company would be a corporate profit centre, responsible to its own board, whose chairman would be the plant manager, and he would also be a member of the holding company board. Finance, R & D, senior personnel, dealing with central government buying abroad, and such matters would be handled by Ranchi. It was received with great enthusiasm, but while the chairman was sympathetic, somehow it got nowhere, and I realised that to them, bred in their administrative systems, it made no sense. It was perhaps regarded as fanciful; such a system might work in private industry and suit international companies, but here they were up against local circumstances—and Audit. And how would it help produce more steel, or solve labour problems.

As someone new to administration's culture, I could not understand how they expected an industrial undertaking, run wholly on administrative lines, ever to produce results. The two cultures were quite different. Outdated enough in its own sphere of administration, it was a worse misfit in the job the new enterprises were set up to do. The railwaymen, the civil servants, the audit and accounts men, men of competence in their own fields, all brought their own manuals, forms, filing and noting system; a system that had been evolved a century earlier as a foundation for districts and centre relationships, to the steel mills. HSL thus became two worlds, the one that adopted the new technology, and the other that controlled everything through an antiquated system not suited to industry. The two worlds blamed each other—the managers felt they were always being thwarted, and the administrators disapproved of the liberties taken and the corners cut in the name of more production. Both were right in their own ways. The difference came out at the board meetings in mutual recriminations. If the finance men ever had a point, it was lost long ago. If the production men had one, they never seemed to make it, they only argued like the young engineers at Rourkela—leave us alone! That controls of finance and freedom of production could be made to work jointly never occurred to anyone. Each fought his battle for his own base line. This permanent schism's only victim was HSL, and any risk-taking or venturesomeness that it might have evolved.

With the sudden departure of Subramaniam, the minister, who was infusing some life into HSL, to the Ministry of Food and Agriculture, where his drive was equally needed and where he did indeed give a push to the new varieties of wheat, HSL began to sag. With a characteristic kind of imagination, the minister, the secretary, the chairman, and the plant managers were all changed at the same time. This was not a conscious clean sweep but just a coincidental routine change, to which no one gave any thought. And once again, the new men were not steelmen. They put Banerji, plant manager from Rourkela, as vice-chairman, to act as chairman indefinitely. He didn't know whether he would be confirmed as chairman or sent to the New Delhi secretariats. I called on the new minister to offer my services in case he wanted to consult me on anything. I suggested that he might visit Ranchi and meet the board to acquaint himself with our problems. His eyes lit for the first time and he said he would very much like to visit a plant and address the workers; as for the board, yes, he might meet them too, but he showed no enthusiasm.

I wondered later whether I was right in not accepting Subramaniam's offer. As I outlined my plans about reorganising HSL, he listened with interest and asked me if I would take it over. I felt embarassed because I did not wish to be misunderstood for the interest I took; in any case I explained that it was too soon for me to leave Levers. As their first national chairman, I had the task of grooming an Indian successor, who was being put through a number of forward moves to be matured and prepared for the top. To leave at this stage would compel Unilever to send out an expatriate chairman, which both they and I would consider a pity. Subramaniam understood, though he asked me later if I would take over the Bokaro project, the largest steel plant that was going to be built with Russian help, after the American collaboration failed to materialise.

It was sad to see HSL decline when it was so close to success; to see this great dream of Nehru, an international venture with so many industrially developed partners in the world, shrink into a sick and limping reality.

In 1968, Chandy became Chairman of HSL. Chandy faced the accumulated problems of nearly four years of neglect, an administration of minimal cooperation, a restive parliament, and a hostile left political group that one would have imagined close to him emotionally and ideologically—something that must have pained him more than the rest. Labour problems became acute, through bitter inter-union rivalries, and a management demoralised by the constant political and labour pressures which became truly cruel at one stage. No one helped; many hindered. Each time I met him he looked a sadder man, his ulcers worse. Ultimately, after three years of heroic effort he threw in the sponge and left. There was no introspection into why had he failed, what had gone wrong, what could have been avoided. There was another reshuffle at the top, but things were no better. In 1961, the first year of HSL, India made a total of 3.1 million tons of steel, in 1970, 6.1 million tons and 6.4 million tons in 1975. Against this progress, a brave minister made a statement in 1975, brave even for him, that India shall make 100 million tons by the year 2000!

A solution, simplistic, caught everyone's imagination in 1971 as a panacea to the ills. The new minister, Mohan Kumaramangalam, one evening over dinner outlined his plan of a holding company, The Steel Authority of India, whose chairman would also be secretary in the ministry of steel. It would hold shares of HSL and its subsidiaries and also in the two private steel companies, to the extent that government financial institutions had given them loans. I thought it was a good and a bold idea, provided the systems' weaknesses were now removed and not allowed to bedevil the new set-up, as was done to each reorganisation in the past. I had doubts though about his second idea. Combining chairmanship and secretaryship would no doubt shorten the organisation links, but while solving one problem it would make another. A secretary in a ministry is a permanent civil servant who guides and serves the minister in his dealings with public, parliament and cabinet, and also coordinates tasks that concern other ministries, which for steel were many. Directly and indirectly he has to deal with ministers of finance, home, petroleum and chemicals, labour, planning, foreign trade and commerce, supplies, railways, transport; almost everything except perhaps health and family planning. Looking after the minister through three sessions of parliament lasting nearly seven months, each with an avalanche of questions, and attending the many parliamentary committees, coordinating with other ministries both at the centre and in the states, attending numerous meetings; would all this leave the secretary-chairman any time to run the largest holding company, a vast agglomerate? And in the end what matters is the freedom he enjoys, whether he is a chairman or secretary-chairman.

I suggested that the secretary could fall between two stools and make neither a good chairman nor a good secretary. Besides, the two jobs called for rather different skills—one of industrial management and the other of administration in a political set-up. And if the idea was to stop the secretariat interference this could easily be done by just stopping it. An understanding could be reached that the chairman would consult the secretary and seek his help, but he should have direct access to the minister. In fact the three of them could work as a team—the minister, the secretary and the chairman. However, I wished him luck. Whether the idea worked well or not, Kumaramangalam's successor unceremoniously, without a review or analysis, dismantled the whole arrangement because he did not like the secretary-chairman. And his successor changed everything again.

CHAPTER TWELVE

A New Indian Business School

Ahmedabad played quite a role in my life; an unexpected one, through a deep personal relationship that developed both with the city and with two remarkable intellectuals, Vikram Sarabhai and Kamla Chowdhry. It began with an invitation from them to the Ahmedabad Textile Industry's Research Association's annual conference on human relations in 1956. It was the first of the kind, I believe, in India, where one met some interesting personalities in the teaching and practice of management, human relations and social sciences, from India, the UK and the USA.

Vikram had founded ATIRA as the first institution that was a marriage between industry and science, with the new feature of making it inter-disciplinary. It had, besides textile industrial research and development, divisions for statistical quality control, marketing research, industrial relations and financial management. Vikram was perhaps the first institution builder in India who looked at things in more than the single dimension of the core activity and its disciplines. He made things multi-dimensional, where others saw them on a single flat plane; in fact I had to remind myself that Vikram was basically a physicist. The Physical Research Laboratory that he had founded at Ahmedabad was the only place where one recognised him as a physicist; elsewhere, a manager, a humanist, a new type of world citizen, was what one saw in him.

He was of medium height, unusually light skinned and grey-eyed for an Indian; what attracted you right away as you met him was his large head with a boyish face, and a sincerity that shone through, and an openness of a rare kind. He at once engaged in animated conversation, making whatever you said sound interesting to him. Whatever the subject, his interest was genuine and deep; and if it was unfamiliar he listened avidly to learn. He was at the same time rather naive, especially about people as people; he judged them as he saw himself. He lived only for whatever he had taken up, his world was his own world, to which no one was barred but which few entered deeply—I could only think of Mrinal, his wife a dancer, and Kamla, an academic—for the rest it was full of his own activity, like an antechamber always full of people, from all over the world.

Vikram was so much essentially an institution builder that I wondered if he could have been a researcher, unless it was that like many of our real researchers he too went the way of administration. His interest in research had overflowed into building an institution around it to encourage the growth of the subject and the men, rather than a personal contribution to the subject and its knowledge. I do not think he added anything himself to physics, industrial research or management—he had not the time—but he widened the horizons in those areas, and of the men who trained and researched in them. It is significant that in the plethora of instituions we have built in India since Independence, his were among the exceptions that flourished; textiles, management, space. Into whatever he built he also conveyed his own characteristic refinement and excellence, whether a personal relationship, a building, or its landscaping. You could see his hallmark.

Vikram was a restless man. His mind and body never stood still. They raced together towards a rendezvous with fate until his body could keep pace no longer and they both stopped. He died young and suddenly, but to me expectedly. He reminded me of the opening lines of a novel, "Appointment in Samara," of the slave who one morning at the market met Death, who pointed its bony finger at him and said, "What are you doing here?" The slave rushed home to his master, who gave him his fastest steed and bade him flee as fast as he could. The slave rode hard all day. Exhausted, he arrived at nightfall at Samara; and as he alighted from his foaming horse, Death walked up to him and said, "Ah, this is where I was expecting to meet you. I could not understand what you were doing in that other town."

Vikram's not untypical schedule could take him literally to Boston, Berkeley, Paris, Vienna, New Delhi, Srinagar, Gulmarg, Bombay, Ahmedabad, Cochin, in virtually one itinerary over three weeks, attending conferences, seminars, lectures, negotiations. I would see him in a huddle with his assistants at an Indian airport, in between a domestic and an international flight, receiving reports and giving instructions, with his secretary taking notes. At a management programme at Srinagar, Kamla would receive a call from him late at night to say that he had just arrived from Harvard and was on his way to Ahmedabad; he was thinking of flying over to Srinagar for a day to discuss what the Business School faculty had suggested, and what Ken Rice had to convey to her from the Tavistock Institute in London. Vikram and Kamla, each eminent in their own field, physics and psychology, had joined together to make a pioneering pair in the nascent area of management, which owes them much. But they were yet more remarkable in their togetherness, which was rare then in India and, in its refined sensitiveness, always will be.

A number of groups were involved and supported the new venture. Vikram, the builder, was backed in Ahmedabad by the elitist millowning, inter-married group led by the doyen, Kasturbhai Lalbhai, who had great affection for Vikram and backed anything he built in Ahmedabad. Abroad, Vikram had full support from Ford Foundation and Harvard. Through him they knew Kamla, and they began to respect her in her own right and admire her for her personality. They undoubtedly made an attractive pair of intellectuals so well in tune. In government all doors were open to Vikram, and support was easily forthcoming. So he had everything his own way, and the usual difficulties that were the bane of institutes in India never posed any serious problems to him. Vikram's problems, if any, were of his own.

Vikram had much in common with Homi Bhabha, also a physicist, and it was a coincidence that fate cut both down as they were entering their finest hour. Bhaba had introduced atomic energy to India, and Sarabhai, his successor, was launching her on a space programme. In a country abounding in planners and visionaries they were rare as men who also achieved. Would Vikram have agreed to explode the atomic device, I often wondered, though he did help produce a feasibility report, as I read later. A mutual friend said that Vikram had been morally opposed to it.

Vikram and Kamla fitted perfectly like the tenons and mortises of a dovetail. He spoke freely and was projective; she was slow and had to carefully define her thoughts before she expressed them, and then only hesitatingly, withdrawing from each answer. He could think on his feet while her voice dropped when faced with an audience of more than two. He was always advancing while she was withdrawing. She had to feel wholly at ease, almost at a level of intimacy, before she would project; he was at home anywhere.

Kamla, a Punjabi Khatri from Lahore, was a product of Shantiniketan, the sylvan university founded by Tagore, which she attended at a time when Punjabi middle class girls traditionally went to the McLagen, Queen Mary or Kinnaird of Lahore, all Christian and British, and never ventured into co-education. Only a few of a daring, nationalist, aesthetic kind had begun to go to Shantiniketan. There, instead of learning to play harmonium and sing as a qualification for matrimony like other Punjabi girls, Kamla learned sensitivities and aesthetics, with singing, dancing and flute playing. From there she went to Calcutta University, and then at twenty she married a young ICS of her own choice.

And thus she would have dipped into a placid life of children, relatives, affluence and domesticity, ending up as a secretary's wife in New Delhi, in a cream coloured bungalow with a large unkempt garden in Akbar Road, but for the tragedy that befell her only three months after her wedding. It was one of those senseless murders, typical of the West Punjab. Her husband, in his first spell as a magistrate, was trying someone in his court, who when he realised that he might be convicted, naively thought that by removing the judge he would put an end to his trial. So Kamla's husband was murdered; and her honeymoon barely over, she returned to Lahore, to lifelong widowhood. She was not even twentyone. Slowly she picked up the threads of her life, convinced that there would always be a tear in her eyes—an old woman had prophesied this—she joined my old college at Lahore. From mathematics at Calcutta, she turned to psychology and did a good master's degree, and decided to continue at Michigan, for a Ph.D. The war had just ended, and she made the long journey, her first abroad, on an American troopship. Her stay in America and the subject she studied moulded her into a new and unusual personality. Living in a world of men, with a subject that developed an intense maturity of mind, she had neither small talk nor time for any but serious company; and yet with it all she was deeply feminine, and wanted always and only to be treated as a woman, even when one could understandably have treated her as a man, at least in an argument. She would withdraw in hurt. Working among men on equal terms she still demanded the conventional privileges she was entitled to as a woman. She wanted an unequal equality.

I saw Vikram and Kamla together at conferences, and there appeared always a perfect rapport between them professionally, an aura of deep relationship. His colleagues in science, in India and abroad, accepted Kamla, as much as her colleagues in human relations and organisational behaviour accepted him. Together, they dreamed up the new institution of management at Ahmedabad they would produce together, and how they would rear it and watch it grow. Their conversation was always around human relations and management, seldom on current affairs or people, except about their colleagues and men in their fields.

When on the death of Homi Bhabha, Vikram succeeded him, Kamla began to work on the organisation growth and structure of the Atomic Energy Establishment, to study what contribution Bhabha had made; and out of this she evolved the interesting thesis that unlike all others in India, who built institutes and manned them, Bhabha built institutes around men. If he got an outstanding man in a discipline, he gave him a new department, with freedom to build and develop it as he liked, and left him to recruit his own men. This is how she and Vikram too had built.

At my first ATIRA conference in 1957, I was vaguely conscious of Kamla's form flitting apparition-like in the aisles, but seemingly an important part of the conference; her name I vaguely recognised from the tragedy I had heard about her. With one shoulder bent, her head at an angle, bag and papers under her arm, she moved around organising the conference through remote control. The only time she appeared openly was to nervously climb the steps to the platform and make an announcement. In the afternoon the conference broke up into study groups, and at one of them I saw her with Vikram discussing with a small group their experience of the recent visit of a textile team to Japan. She sat with her legs folded up on the chair, listening intently, while he talked freely. Although never categoric he was always sure of himself, in a nice way. She sometimes underlined him, and occasionally she would give him a different direction, which he seemed to like. His face would soften with that rare smile, when Vikram was at his handsomest, and he would look approvingly at her and pursue the new line. She seemed to be his monitor; and so long as she listened silently he felt he was on the right lines. After each day Vikram would go to Kamla on his way back from work, and they would together go over the day's discussions and decisions, and plan the next. In the morning, whenever in Ahmedabad, he would drop in for a coffee before he began his day.

The Indian Institute of Management was Vikram's brainchild, supported by Douglas Ensminger, the director of the Ford Foundation, who had first mooted the idea of management education in India. He had suggested to the Indian and the US governments that two institutes of managements, along the lines of the American business schools, might be formed in India. Two professors, one from Harvard and another from Chicago, came out to survey the scene. They were an odd pair with an odd music hall combination of names—Miriam and Thurlby. I was invited to a meeting in Bombay in 1957, where they met a number of executives and academics; and I was not surprised when Douglas Ensminger later told me the gist of their report, that what India needed was not business management education at this stage, but plain education! They were right in their own way, but they ignored the simple fact that the process of growth is not so orderly and logical, or sequential; Indian Airlines, as an example, could not have awaited our perfecting the bullock cart!

Next year Dick Miriam taught me at the Harvard Business School. Undoubtedly brilliant, he was most staid in contrast with the other professors, some of whom were positively colourful and taught the ordinary prosaic subjects of managements vividly and with verve. One incident illustrated well the reputation he had acquired, which had given him the affectionate nickname of the Iron Duke, well justified by his austere exterior. While discussing the area of the president and his company, we were on the case of the president of a medium-sized company that had gone badly wrong. These case studies were post mortems of past situations from which we drew lessons for the future. What had ultimately happened to that president or the company was not considered relevant. In this particular case hardly anyone of us could see anything right with the president. At the end of the class, one enthusiast, whose sense of justice had been outraged by this unanimous criticism, began to plead for the president. The man was no fool, he said, he knew what he was doing, and although his first failures were obvious, they were but teething troubles of the change he was introducing. We must not judge him in a conventional manner; events were bound to have proved him right. The president's lone supporter held us in our tracks, and many of us began to retrace our steps and agreed that there was perhaps something in it after all; perhaps we had gone too far, and we all began to atone for our harsh judgment.

As the Iron Duke was leaving the class, the enthusiast called after him and said, "Professor (he was the only one who was never called by his first name; to call him Dick was unthinkable), as this firm appears to have been from the Boston area, do you know what happened to it?" This was a bold departure, as it had been made clear to us that the identity and the fate of the companies that chose to remain anonymous should not be established. The large corporations cases nearly always carried their names, and their fate everyone knew, but smaller companies usually chose anonymity. As a case was discussed purely as an objective intellectual exercise, the outcome really did not matter. The professor turned round with a look of surprise and more than his usual severity, but then gave a faint smile. "Oh yes, I knew the man. As the case showed, things became so bad that the firm had to wind up and," here he paused dramatically, "the president could not take it—he shot himself." And with this the Duke walked away imperiously.

No wonder, I thought, the Duke felt we in India were not ready for the sophistications of management theory and its teaching. Vikram Sarabhai and Douglas Ensminger were persevering however and got out a very enthusiastic person, Dean Robbins of University of California, Los Angeles, and he put in a glowing report, based on which Douglas and Vikram approached Harvard. They sent out a team of their own, consisting of Dean Fox of their foreign operations, an equally remarkable personality, Robert Austin and Harry Hansen, who was later to take the India Project, Vikram and Kamla asked me to join them in the discussions, as I had spent three months at Harvard's Advanced Management Programme. I had become rather attached to the school and in return got quite liked by the faculty, and meeting some of them so soon again, and in India, was a happy reunion. While they were attentive and formal with Vikram and Kamla, they felt free with me. They were impressed with a lot of what they saw and recommended the India Project, but mentioned some of their reservations to me.

Vikram and Kamla worked feverishly together, drawing me closer to them as I too began to work with them. In 1963, Kamla, as our first senior professor, went to Harvard to the Advanced Management Programme to learn something about their business academic culture. Harvard asked me to visit them for discussions after Kamla finished her course in May 1963. After the Chinese war, and its aftermath of the hard budget, I accepted the invitation readily, as an interlude between the past problems and the new crop that was now coming up thick and fast.

The fortnight I spent at the Business School campus, where I had stayed five years earlier, was a watershed.

My first visit to the USA in 1958 to Harvard, followed by the publication of "Punjabi Century" in 1961 with three editions in quick succession, had left me slightly puzzled. Reasonably confident in my relative ease with marketing, first helping build Dalda, and now entrusted with Hindustan Lever, I had however always been diffident about my intellectual capacities, which I rated ordinary. Nothing in my academic record ever pointed that way. At Harvard I did well, but that I attributed to an exotic presence among the hard-headed American executives of one who mixed easily and held his own equally in the mornings at class discussions and in the evenings at the bars. That many leading reviewers in England, USA and India considered the book worthwhile was something I could as little understand as the readiness with which Vikram, Kamla, and now the Harvard faculty, accepted me. Academic acceptance inspired me, but made me feel uneasy. Nevertheless, I looked forward to my visit to Harvard, especially because Maurice Zinkin was also attending the course, and in the "Brides' Week"—the last week of the course, when the wives joined—Taya was sure to turn up.

As I flew over the Atlantic on a mid-May afternoon, the Boeing travelling into the sun at half the speed at which the sun receded, the afternoon stood near still, sandwiched between the sky and the sea, both intensely blue. Hindustan Lever, Government of India, licences, permits, budgets, air dashes to Delhi, in and out of the pseudo Man Singh—Lutyens—Le Corbusier government bhavans, with pompous exteriors and unkempt interiors, where files moved like snails and "sheep in sheep's clothing" flitted from meeting to meeting—all these nightmares dissolved as the Boeing flew in clear sunlit silent space, and I made good use of the BOAC bar.

Many years later, when I joined a bank, whose entire operations were confined to India, I realised how much these international contacts, academic and business, had helped me to maintain the optimism and determination with which I tackled things in an environment so discouraging. Through the years these contacts built for me an interesting life in which business and academics alternated pleasantly and stimulatingly. The day they stopped I would scarcely breathe; though in the end fate unbelievably took me to academics as a full-time occupation, with stimulating international interludes.

At New York I spent a couple of days visiting Levers, and meeting the Burkharts, the chairman of the American company, and his wife, Fran, who had visited India the autumn before and got caught in the midst of the Chinese invasion. Of all the wrapped around glass buildings in Park Avenue, Lever House, the first of its kind in America, was the only one I found attractive. Those that followed spent more money with less taste. It was built by a Unilever American whizz kid. Unilever, in its early beginning in America, could only have chosen Boston as the rightful place on the Atlantic coast, nearest to Liverpool, as staid and stately; and for years they had an American in charge of their business whose portrait and name, Francis Countway, lived up to one's imagery. While the business ran reasonably well, it never rose to be one of the giants as it did in Europe; in fact even in my days it was mediocre, something that always touched Unilever's pride at its tenderest spot.

After the war, so the story went, and not too apocryphal, Unilever bought a successful competitor, the Pepsodent toothpaste company, mainly, it was said, to buy the young genius who ran it, an architect turned marketer. Charles Luckman turned the American Levers inside out. Coming from the West Coast, Los Angeles, he had no sensibilities for the East Coast. One of his earliest decisions was to move the company from Boston to New York, a decision he might have got away with had he implemented it with a little less than his characteristic brashness. He built the Lever House in Park Avenue, and organised the move in a way that left a scar on Boston for many years. The Bostonians thought it an unforgivable insult. On a Friday evening there were two kinds of envelopes waiting for the employees—one containing a ticket for a special train to New York, and the other a farewell cheque—so the story went.

Years later I went into a restaurant in Harvard Square for a coffee. I had forgotten to take off my class label bearing my name and Hindustan Lever. The waitress caught on to the name of Lever. She told me that her sister used to work for Levers in Boston till they moved to New York; but the tone of pure hurt and anger showed how raw were her feelings still ten years later. The Time Magazine that had portrayed Charles Luckman on the front page as an English firm's discovery of an American prodigy, not so long after had to run another story to explain his departure.

I arrived on a sunny mid-May afternoon. I drove from Boston airport to the Business School, where they had thoughtfully provided me with a room at Hamilton Hall, where I had stayed five years ago at the Advanced Management Programme, and where the current session was just finishing. No sooner did I finish my unpacking than Maurice Zinkin arrived.

Unilever's decision to send Maurice to AMP interested me because, as some of the professors were to tell me, he ought to have entered the Business School as a teacher. Bob Austin, one of their lively intellectuals, told me they had been learning more from Maurice than they could ever have hoped to teach anyone. And yet Maurice was always humble and said he had learned a lot. He began to tell me that from what he had learned there was something that would interest me and would be a useful concept in India. Harvard, he said, sets out to teach you to shun soft options and take the hard choices. He went on to the case method of study, where you analyse a situation that was live once, often cases where an organisation or its head had gone wrong because they had followed a soft option, and sometimes cases to do with change and innovation. "In India," said Maurice "you do it all the time; but what is worse, you make a virtue out of a soft option.Worse still,you then pursue it with unction and get involved in proving your point instead of dropping it when you realise that it does not work."

This was typical of Maurice. At any time he could engage in the earnest discussion, oblivious to circumstance. We had not met for quite some time, but before even exchanging the commonplace news about the families, he was off on his fascinating thesis, and as I always enjoyed listening to him on any topic, he warmed up.

"Of course, we are no better than you. We share these dubious qualities of unction and the urge to compromise; but there is a difference. We were not always like that; in our pioneering days we took the harder choices with a perversity. You cannot afford the soft options, and God knows we too cannot any longer. This was a characteristic of Nehru. A product of early European liberalism and later Fabian socialism, he got carried away by hard words but took soft actions. Your well ordered society, assuring a place for everyone, has a gentleness about it. I wish you could learn that to be a little cruel is to be a lot kinder, sometimes."

Maurice suddenly remembered that some AMPs were having a party out of Harvard and he and Kamla had invited me to join them. They would be just about gathering in the lounge for the Happy Hour—the Harvard euphemism for the early evening drinks. We went down and Maurice introduced me to the group, much the same as my batch of 1958. There were the executives, defence officers, some Europeans, Latin Americans and Asians; all friendly, earnest, relaxed. In the midst of it, Kamla arrived in an old-bronze colour sari and a simple silver medallion, excited, flushed, and ran up to embrace me.

"Mr Tandon, so you have arrived. Here have I been telling all my friends that one of our directors is coming, my boss, also a friend, and you never even wrote, not a line, not a word, not a sign; but typically male, you write to Maurice, not to me." The AMPs all gathered round Kamla, impeccably wrapped in well ordered elegance. I looked her up and down. I had never seen her so sure, so confident, as she consciously bathed in the adulating gaze of the rugged middleage American executives, to whom the novelty of Kamla appeared not to have palled over the familiarity of three months. But it did seem that they had not seen this side of Kamla before—the self-conscious gay abandon of a dancer walking on to the stage, expecting applause. She took off her glasses and looked at the ring of men with that fetching intent look of a shortsighted person.

Someone asked her what she would drink. "No," she said categorically, "Mr Tandon is going to mix my drink, and he knows the exact proportion." This was the gimlet I had once introduced her to. They were all intrigued by her new vivacity.

The AMP party was typical of American executives on a stag evening out. Cheerful but restrained, in good taste but expensive; and it finished early. I walked back with Kamla, who had the solitary honour of a small apartment to herself. She spoke at length about the course and her colleagues, the professors, the teaching method of case study; and also of her problems with one or two of the men, whom she liked, for whom she was something different and new. As a psychologist, Kamla was sensitive and understanding, and people got close to her quickly, and she let them, though she would repel them firmly but gently if they came too close. As the only woman among a hundred and fifty men leading a monastic campus life, mature but at a watershed age, many wanted to be close to her, and in the case of one at least she had had to be firm with herself too, she explained, and tell him not to be carried away by her novelty. In the fortythree such programmes that Harvard had held since the war began, originally to familiarise selected defence officers with business administration, she was the first woman. She spoke far into the evening. Cooped up on the campus for three months, she had a lot to talk about. Although Vikram had been here a week earlier, she seemed to want to unburden herself in a different way.

Next morning we began our discussion with the faculty about our new school at Ahmedabad and its first programme, which we hoped to organise in January 1964, followed by the first post-graduate two-year programme in July. She and Vikram had already recruited some Indian faculty, who were to join the school when it began. I was very impressed with the amount of preparation Vikram had been able to manage during his few brief visits, helped of course by Kamla, with his usual capacity for getting things started.

An interesting problem that came up in our discussions was the general feeling I had gained from the junior and middle managers in India that the enthusiasm with which they took back the new ideas and techniques they learned abroad or at courses in India was soon dampened and put in its place by the attitudes of their seniors. The enthusiasts were told to get back to their work and forget the new-fangled notions, which might work in business abroad but certainly not in India. This was particularly so with private firms and, then, the public undertakings—the former because the control lay with the family, while in the latter control and audit in the all-powerful system imposed a skull cap on innovation and change.

This resistance to change was a problem then and still is in a society that wants change with such virginal expectancy, and resists it when it comes with equal stubbornness, yet always convinced in its ambivalence that the fruits of change are withheld by all else but itself. I have sometimes wondered whether there is not a death wish in us. As Patrick Moynihan, when America's Ambassador at New Delhi, was to put it many years later, "I think, with all your talent and capacity, you have just taken a vow to poverty." But these contradictions in our society were then just dawning upon me.

Out of the preception of this common problem of the Indian managers we evolved a new training concept of a 3-tier programme, to which we would invite middle, senior and top managers from an organisation, and, if the organisation was large enough, from the same division. This was to become Kamla's famous Ahmedabad 3-Tier Programme at Agra, to which have gone a hundred managers each year over the past fifteen years.

The campus was now closed, and in the glory of a New England spring I spent a peaceful fortnight, mostly in the company of Kamla and the faculty, with meetings during the day and invitations at night to someone's home, among the innumerable people Kamla knew, in her own right and through Vikram. She appeared well thought of in her area of human relations, and I had the chance of meeting some well known personalities, Fritz Roethlisberger, Abe Zaleznik and Erik Erikson. I listened intently to their discussion on the latest thinking and practices in organisational behaviour and behavioural sciences in general, an area that I had of late begun to grope in, untutored and unlettered, as a reverent novice. Kamla had already begun to discern a pupil in me, and to instil confidence she began to tell me that if I lacked theory I had something not unvaluable to offer—experience, of which, she felt, I seemed to have made some intuitive use. I had of course read some textbooks on psychology, personnel theory and management, but when I heard Kamla and her colleagues I was enthralled by a knowledge that was new to me. Perhaps my modesty in theory, combined with confidence in practice, made an unusual and attractive combination for Kamla, because I found her increasingly interested in me, and conveying this interest to her colleagues. Now and again she would become impatient when I defended a practice that she questioned. "Don't be afraid of exposing your experience to an academic examination; it helps you, and it helps us, to separate the grain from the chaff. And, please believe me, you have some grain! Vikram, who began as a physicist, has developed great insight and, I would say, competence in his field, to which he was new not so long ago."

I left Kamla reluctantly, wondering what it would be like to meet her at Ahmedabad, away from the Boston spring, the mirror calm Charles River, the ivy covered halls, the stimulating evenings with the faculty, and walking back in the light green nights in the peace of the campus. We travelled together to New York where I left her at the Ford Foundation headquarters, and she disappeared into the swirl of Fifth Avenue's humanity, her sari a small gash of colour.

I did meet her some weeks later. Travelling on the early morning Viscount flight to attend the Institute's board meeting at Ahmedabad, I heard a tired voice say, "Hullo." She had just arrived by the connecting Air India flight from Europe and looked as travel-worn and crumpled as only Kamla could just as only she could look fresh and crisp.

"See you at the board meeting."

"Yes, Sir."

*

I entered 1964 with some confidence that after passing through three years of hard weather, things could only be better; and during these years I had learned to feel at ease with my three masters, Unilever, shareholders and government. Their interests should really have been identical at least in a professionally managed company: the growth and diversification of the company, with good profits for one and abundant taxes for the other; and no profits syphoned out for family and friends. In fact government's share of the profit by way of company tax alone, ignoring the many duties and taxes on the side, rose to two-thirds and more; the shareholders and the reserves sharing equally the remaining one-third. But even with their four times bigger share than the shareholders, government seemed not to be satisfied; in fact one saw signs of resentment against profits as just profits, no matter how honestly they were earned and how much they served as grist for growth and, of course, the ever-growing administrative mill. It was a curious and incomprehensible ambivalance that wanted growth without the surplus to feed it. Its roots were interesting to unravel, as we seemed to be raising a new economic culture striving to bear fruit from no seed.

Kamla organised the first 3-TP at Jaipur early in 1964. Its participants came from medium and large private and public enterprises, and a few also from the central and state governments. Kamla asked me to give a talk, and the theme I chose came from a discussion a little earlier at the Planning Commission to which its new head, Asoka Mehta, had invited me along with a number of others for a free and frank discussion on how to accelerate growth in the economy. Many views were expressed at the meeting, centering mainly round freedom from the many restrictions upon growth; the complex and cumbersome licensing procedures that not only took years to grant permission but always tried to whittle down the demands. It seemed that if you were willing to accept a smaller expansion or a smaller new venture you stood a better chance, and also a chance of an earlier disposal of your case. One got the impression that the processors and recommenders of a case made it a point in their favour, and the applicant's, that he had been persuaded to accept smaller growth. Growth that should have been poured out in ladles was doled out grudgingly in spoonfuls. I added that fundamentally profit to government was a dirty word. Asoka Mehta reacted to this and in a public lecture shortly afterwards denied that profit was a dirty word. I pursued this topic at Kamla's programme.

"Service, not profit," was the constantly preached motto of our leadership; but service out of what? We needed surplus to plough in for new growth; this leads to size; and we did not like surplus and we did not like size. Surplus and size amounted to success. To us success was always suspect. Profit honestly earned was as much frowned upon as that dishonestly come by. Profit had become synonymous with profiteering; size with exploitation; and success with something anti-social. With such counter growth attitudes, how could there be growth? Even the existing small growth had begun to decline and would soon disappear, giving way to a stagnant economy in rapidly rising population. We therefore not only needed positive pro-growth attitude but an intolerance of the anti-growth attitudes. Its proper distribution was a matter for the leaders; its creation was the task of the managers.

On the flight back from Jaipur to Bombay I saw a headline in a financial daily analysing the performance of a hundred large companies, and Hindustan Lever was declared to lead in its return on capital employed; the most efficient user of capital. The irony of it struck me immediately. Already the previous year's budget had introduced a new tax which in a capital-scarce country hit those harder who made higher profit on a given capital employed than those who made less. The least efficient got away altogether. I put my worry into a letter to Andrew Knox. I said this might, on the face of it, be considered a great compliment, but I feared it would be the beginning of new troubles. We had been singled out; our size and success were already held against us; now our profitability would make us the bigger target. In fact, the headline talked about giants in industry, when the biggest could not even then have figured among the first five hundred firms in the world. Interesting, I thought, that in Hindustan Steel I had felt sad because we made no profits, in Hindustan Lever I was sad because we made profits. Andrew Knox wrote back with his characteristic understanding—yes, he said, he was glad we were efficient, but unhappy that what should normally have pleased me should instead be a new source of anxiety, in an atmosphere already replete with worries.

Our public relations department under Chandy had recently prepared a press campaign explaining the role Hindustan Lever played in the society; its theme was "Hindustan Lever serve the Home." It was a well designed campaign, in a reasonably low key, but I was unhappy with the idea itself. I had watched the Burmah-Shell campaign a few years earlier—"Burmah-Shell, in India's life and part of it," how Shell kerosene and candles lit the village huts and its fuel oil and lubricants helped move the wheels of industry, and my reaction was that even as a company whose products reached every nook and corner of the country, it should perhaps have literally hidden its wax candle under a bushel. These were the years of great institutional campaigns the world over, but in India I could not help thinking that it was better for a private firm, and an international one at that, to keep a low profile. Product advertising, Yes; the company's achievements, No, in an environment almost hostile to growth, size and success.

The first 3-TP ended well, an experiment worth continuing. Kamla's and Vikram's plans were working out well, with me on the periphery, for the new post-graduate programme, building the new campus, forming a team out of the new faculty. One day Vikram made me a proposition. Dr Jivraj Mehta, recently displaced from the first chief ministership of Gujarat, the first chairman of our board, was now going to London as our High Commissioner and had therefore resigned. By tradition such posts belonged to chief ministers and politicians; why pick on me, I asked, when it was suggested that I accept the chairmanship. I was neither a public figure nor a politician, nor at the helm of a large business family group; I had none of the usual qualifications. "We need a professional manager," said Vikram smilingly.

Kamla said, when I consulted her, "Accept it, you will like it and you have something to offer."

This was my first position of responsibility outside the firm, apart from some board appointments in the public sector that I had just accepted. In the unfamiliar academic world Vikram's and Kamla's support meant everything to me. I accepted the chairmanship and served for five exciting years full of problems.

The Institute's early problems were many. The first was to lay down certain academic workload standards with the first group of students, who were used to an academic laxity that bore no relationship to the rigours of the Harvard Business School standards that we were trying to set. Used to earning a good second with a quite light workload of barely twenty hours a week, with a short spurt as examinations approached, now exposed to a seventy-hour week with regular assignments and tests, they broke down soon after the first term began. They struck. The assignments were too many, the examinations too hard, the question did not stick to the books, the professors were heartless and unsympathetic; the whole system was unfair. It must be changed. These were the early years of student protest, which did not have anything to do with principles. This kind of performance was becoming the new style at the universities, and was tolerated in the name of justice and freedom, and supported cynically by some political parties. It struck at the roots of the academic system and was to grow to a stage when the right to pass examinations became as if a part of the fundamental rights the constitution conferred on every citizen.

At Ahmedabad there was a large number of subjects, compulsory and optional, and their study was based on understanding rather than learning by rote. This meant a mental concentration and a form of discipline they had not been used to. The case study method was in itself a new and absorbing experience in participation between the teacher and the taught. It demanded careful preparation before class so as not to drop out of the discussion. The teachers drew knowledge out of the students instead of drearily pouring it in during long lecture hours; and tested you while you were learning.

Manu, our elder son, who was then at the Sydenham college of commerce in Bombay, considered the best of its kind in India, was surprised when I described to him our style of teaching at Ahmedabad. "What, interrupt a teacher in class?" This wasn't done even if you found it genuinely difficult to follow the teacher. I related to him my own first experience at Manchester University, the thrill when I could put up my hand and stop the dean of the school, no less, and say, without even a by-your-leave, "Could you go over that again, please!" And when I interrupted him twice over the same point he asked me to see him after class, and he would run through it with me. Somehow our sense of hierarchy prevents us from participating even in the process of learning.

They expressed their resentment by boycotting classes, demonstration, shouting and generally disrupting. Their behaviour followed the students' protest strikes during the early days of the freedom movement. I wondered whether Gandhiji had realised what he was doing when he taught my generation to refuse to receive education at the hands of the British. Did he visualise the time when a few unprepared students would rise from their seats in the examination halls and shout for justice, disrupt the examination, and cause other serious students to lose valuable months of work; when for one English professor then shot there would be countless Indian teachers stabbed; when protest on patriotic grounds turned into prurient attempts to pass examinations through intimidation. Through the years when student unrest spread and first affected the universities and then the new institutions of excellence, such as the Institute of management and of technology, and ultimately even the Nehru University, it never came back to our institute, even when Gujarat University broke out in the worst riots ever of Ahmedabad and toppled a stable state government.

I suppose Gandhiji had hoped that protest, as a weapon, like the sword would be hung or turned into ploughshare. Instead it turned arid and destructive, and became an almost daily affair at schools and colleges, as much as in factories and offices, and in the streets. It was to take its greater toll of the quality of education. At an engineering college in the north, one of the striking students' demands was to be given a degree automatically at the third attempt.

We had a young faculty, barely older than the boys and girls, mostly just out of their doctoral programme. Kamla, fortytwo, was the oldest of them; they were all a young and youthful lot, and there was no generation gap. The faculty were besides men and women of qualifications that merited their intellectual leadership of the young students. Their teaching style was new and their minds fresh; and they were a dedicated lot of teachers, not just men who waited for a better job or to get into one of the civil services, and regarded teaching as something better than just waiting.

Fortunately the faculty at Ahmedabad held firm. Gradually the students too saw the meaning of the new system, and realised that you did well if you worked steadily and intelligently. The case study method was in itself a new and absorbing experience in participation between the teacher and the taught, you were tested while you were learning. After the first tantrums of the kind they had brought from their old colleges, the IIM students settled down to hard work, frequent examinations and academic disciplines of a peaceful campus. It was not luck alone; many factors contributed.

I wanted IIM Ahmedabad at least to try to avoid a common mistake of the academic institutions in India, which becomes their biggest problem; one that turns most of them into arid administrative bodies rather than institutes of research and academic excellence. Sponsored by government they are cast in the image of government departments—their staffing patterns, rules and procedures, designations and hierarchy, all unsuited to academia or research; and for that matter even to modern administration. Administration's typical staffing pattern of a high tail to teeth ratio permeate into our institutions and laboratories, with the result that with rising cost, more and more is progressively spent on clerks and peons than on teachers and researchers. To support non-academic and academic personnel many typically absorb two-thirds to three-quarters of the total budget, leaving a meagre proportion for the faculty; and this non-academic expenditure rises fast with inflation, soon to cut further into what is left available for the faculty.

It goes back to the Clive culture, where as a young writer at £10 salary per annum in the East India Company at Madras, he wrote home that even at his junior level whenever he went out he was accompanied by an entourage of ten men, otherwise the natives would not consider him a person of any consequence. This tradition they inherited from the Moghuls; part of it we inherited when we were free.

Industry too was beginning to take notice of Ahmedabad, and a new practice began of personnel recruitment teams visiting to get a feel of the calibre of teaching and of the students, a new breed of potential managers. The students became conscious of the demand, and the higher than usual starting salaries that were beginning to be offered to them. They therefore concentrated on their studies, and as soon as the final batch was out and was snapped up at premium salaries, their successors needed no further urge to make the best of their two years. Their inhibitions and rough edges were soon knocked away, and work became their avid and only pursuit. They found the faculty led them well and teaching was good, and so they settled down to their task.

A problem that loomed large was the appointment of a permanent director in place of Vikram, who was honorary and part-time, and Kamla who deputed for him without the strength of holding it in her own right. It was a weak arrangement altogether. The board was divided over it, and Harvard rather unhappy. Some thought Kamla could be the permanent director and others opposed this completely. I was surprised at Harvard's opposition to having a woman director in principle. They were quite clear that a woman would not be able to run an organisation that needed not only academic strength, which they conceded she possessed, but administrative strength, which they felt she did not possess, nor would probably any other woman. I felt they were prejudiced on this point, although I did concede that Kamla was not outgoing enough and did not have the kind of firmness she would need in plenty to deal with a young and ambitious faculty, some hundreds of very lively students, industry and donors, especially the Ahmedabad group, and government. Each one would be as supportive as the director was clear and firm in pursuing the objectives. There was besides a large building programme for the new campus, involving large sums, many hard decisions and much fund raising. The whole thing was literally a man-sized job.

I had been surprised when I first went to Harvard how rare it was to see a woman student or faculty member at the Business School; and their answer was that business management and its teaching was not a woman's job. Among the three thousand or so alumni of their Advanced Management Programme for senior business, defence and government executives there had never been a woman, until Kamla attended it in 1963. Women and negroes you rarely saw at the Business School. On top of all this Kamla was as feminine as she could be, withdrawing and shy, confident only with a few with whom she felt completely at ease, with no flair nor visible liking for administration. But she had her point of view. This was a man's world in which the so-called male quality of firmness was at a premium; when applied to an institute it had no meaning, especially if it took precedence over academic qualities. In other words, the selectors would consider it quite proper to appoint a retired civil servant, as they were wont to do in India, who was weak academically, rather than to choose a woman academic who was weak administratively.

Vikram felt acutely unhappy through all this. I think he had almost built the institution around Kamla. In the Textile Research Institute, where they had worked together, she had made a contribution by introducing social sciences into a purely technical research atmosphere, thereby giving it refreshing new directions towards human relations and also marketing and consumer research. Here they would work together to build India's first business school. He had great faith in her capacity to give this institution a culture of business education, new and different to the usual family business culture of private industry and to the administrative culture of the nascent public sector. They had discussed this at length between themselves, and at Harvard, MIT and Stanford; and now that their dream was taking shape, a wall of prejudice was rising against Kamla on his account. She was a woman and a woman whom he admired. This was enough for those who could not believe that Vikram could be objective in this regard. He dutifully carried out the board's desire to look for another director, and even contacted an ICS man, then an ambassador, who at the end of his posting, and uncertain what offer government might make him, showed interest. Vikram asked me to talk to the board, and they were immediately taken in by a name of such administrative distinction. I wrote to him and we corresponded desultorily, but soon government's offer of the governorship of a state settled his vacillation, and he wrote back to express his perfunctory regret. The challenge of an academic assignment that he had talked about evaporated quickly. I was relieved, for if there could be a choice between a governorship and the chance of a lifetime of building a new institution of this kind, his rejection was the institute's gain.

There were others who tried, many retired administrators and generals, who all felt that their experience was close enough to business administration. As I resisted each case, word went round that first Vikram and now I were stonewalling for Kamla's sake. Comparisons were made in favour of the sister institute at Calcutta, where Chandy had been appointed director two years ago. Vikram got discouraged and stopped taking interest; he felt unbelieved and therefore unwanted. He also felt he had let Kamla down when he did not resign from the board. She felt the same way about both of us. Whatever I thought of her administrative capacity, the fact was that I rated her academically high enough to accept her as a director; and if the board could accept a civil servant whose only merit was administrative experience, surely they could have accepted one with only academic strength. But she felt that neither Vikram nor I was willing to make an issue of it. Only through such strength displayed could the principle have been established. Vikram withdrew, I felt I had to see it through; but it was a duty that had ceased to be a pleasure; and I began to think of leaving as soon as the appointment was made.

Ravi Matthai appeared over the horizon. He was young, only thirtyeight, had worked in industry, and under Chandy's influence moved from industry to teaching at Calcutta. With a clear, thrustful mind he made a good leader, and his high values assured me that there would be no compromises with the institute's growth. He took more than a year's persuasion, because his heart, he said, was in teaching and research and not in administration; that was why he had left industry. While he had transparent integrity, I think he was mistaken about his desire for teaching and research, for when he was in a position to do both, he did neither. He was too restless and lacked the necessary perseverance for research at least. He was really an institution builder, and that is where we were lucky. Ravi made two points clear—that he would not remain director for more than five to seven years, and that I should stay on for another two years, at least till I had completed my five-year term. Leaving administration to go back to teaching was, I felt, a healthy principle in academic life. As for the second condition, I was reluctant to stay any longer than he needed me to find his feet, which should not take much more than a year; I was prepared to leave even earlier. I did not want to breathe down his neck; used to being an active chairman I did not relish a purely decorative capacity, especially now that the building job was over. I would prefer to fade out. Ravi seemed genuinely eager to have me stay; and there was besides one delicate task to accomplish, to build a bridge beween him and Kamla and get them to work together.

Ravi had his doubts whether Kamla would accept him as the director and give him the much needed help. He would understand if she kept aloof but it would make things difficult for him. Kamla on her side was also a reluctant partner in the new setup. I was afraid she would withdraw into her shell, and Ravi, finding her uncooperative, might throw in the sponge. In fact both expressed to me in the same vein their anxiety to leave if the new arrangement were not to their liking. The prospect of both of them leaving and thus being stranded was a nightmare to me. Instead the least expected happened. I managed to bring them, so close together that I could soon tell that I was needed no longer and felt uncomfortable staying on. They worked like the team that she and Vikram had been at ATIRA. While the Calcutta Institute now began to develop its own problems of politicisation, Ahmedabad, once set on the new course, went from strength to strength, until it could afford to shed its pioneering generation and take the change in its stride.

I stayed on a while, because the board insisted that we create a convention of a five-year term. In due course Ravi stepped down when he felt that his task was done, but stayed on to teach. His succession must have pleased Harvard's keen desire for faculty democracy; the faculty were asked to choose their next director and did so; they chose someone quite young, Samuel Paul. The connection with Harvard had matured and was shed, and Ahmedabad turned to wherever it had something to learn. Vikram died suddenly. Kamla left Ahmedabad for ever.

Vikram's end came suddenly. I was staying in Bangalore with Air Marshal Mehra, head of Hindustan Aeronautics, who told me that he was going next morning to meet Vikram at the airport. I said I would like to go too, as it was a long time since I had met him. At the airport we were told by the station manager that the special airforce plane bringing Dr. Sarabhai was due in another hour. Mehra asked in surprise, "Is he not coming by ordinary flight?"—"No Sir, a special plane is taking his body to Ahmedabad." It was a strange way to get the news of a friend's death.

A new, younger generation took over the reins, competently and securely, which is something rare in Indian institutions. In my last year, at the graduation ceremony, I watched Ravi Matthai deliver the valediction, and while he was speaking with his characteristic youthful verve, I passed a small note to our chief guest. "In a little way I feel I have achieved something—to have left a young successor first in Hindustan Lever and now in Ahmedabad, both barely forty years." She smiled knowingly; for she was a young prime minister.

☆

As I began to pull out of Ahmedabad, I became more involved in the public sector, in many of its new industrial units, the Reserve Bank, government committees on diverse subjects, from railways to foodgrains distribution and the national system of budgeting, and into other management academic institutions. Klijnstraa's prophecy that I would receive heavy demands to serve government proved more than right, and I willingly accepted the demands for it widened my horizon. Unilever however were generally unimpressed by these extramural activities.

I also saw growth's almost imperceptible first decline. When it stopped altogether for a while, I was part of the system. I perhaps saw things a little better than many others around me, the regular administrators, few of whom were sensitive to the production process. Time and the unresult-oriented system seemed to have blunted their sensitivity. Also, from both sides, from their own caste system and that of their British predecessors, they had inherited a distaste for business and a suspicion of profits. They could place crippling constraints on production without the least feeling or regard for consequences. An administrator, whom I was once meeting on behalf of a manufacturers' association to solve a difficulty that his department had created, announced on the spur of the moment that he would ban a small pack, in the interest of economy. To my reaction of disbelief, he said "So what, it may deprive the industry of profit, but we are not here to ensure its profit." What about the demand for that pack, production, employment, consumers, taxes? I asked. But I found I was only provoking him to go ahead; which he did—in the name of economy, national interest, consumer with even the poor man thrown in! The senseless step he took was not reversed till some years later.

Working with government, and in its public enterprises, helped me at least to understand and thus bear better the burden of their decisions in industry, which would otherwise have sometimes baffled and frustrated me. Many were the times when I would return to my own office from New Delhi, lean back in my chair and feel how good it was to return to an island of predictability like a fine ship whose systems and men were responsive to the smallest touch on its wheel. There would perhaps be a board meeting, with an agenda of ten points, each explained in a brief paragraph, even a single line, together with a single sheet showing the month's results, instead of the public enterprises' voluminous agenda running into two hundred pages and more, and saying very little.

My own base was strong and secure, with Ramaswami as vice-chairman freed completely of day to day responsibility. Older than me, he had seen all rungs of the ladder and knew the business thoroughly. An understanding developed between us that I could think and act as boldly as I liked but always secure in the knowledge that I would feel the restraining touch of Ramu's hand on my back, if he detected an indiscretion or haste. Free of direct responsibility, he made an excellent sounding board and a filter; altogether an institution that I found very helpful.

Ramu had a keen sense of humour and proportion. Once at a board meeting, when there was a prolonged deadlock over an appointment, some considering the man able while others felt that though able he was unsuitable because the man under him would chafe under his ways, Ramu ultimately broke it by remarking, "Well, let us take a chance; he is capable and that is more important than his personal angularities," and he ended, "what if his men will find it difficult to stand him; have we not stood Prakash for years?" There was loud laughter, a complete thaw, and we went on to the next item on the agenda. On another occasion, a young manager rushed in with some news from Delhi that looked quite bad. We dicussed at length its implications and our chances, and slowly it began to look not quite as hopeless. At the end Ramu remarked, "And when in the past have we not been able to solve a problem; so we will this time." And he added philosophically, when the young man left the room, "It is the young who are the pessimists; we have faced and survived too many crises not to have become optimists."

With Hindustan Lever, after we had adjusted ourselves to the ravages of the post-China budget, in which there were gradually relaxations, I felt time had come to take a close look at the organisation. The last major reorganisation of the company had taken place in 1943 when, in the middle of the war, it was decided with rare insight to look ahead to the end of the war. In 1964 the company was doing well and in good shape, perhaps the best time to consider a reorganisation, though little did I realise, when I began the exercise, what a long, difficult task it was going to be.

CHAPTER THIRTEEN

Los Angeles

Los Angeles, where I spent the spring quarter of 1967 on a Regent's lecturership of the University of California at Los Angeles, to take a course in international management, was quite an experience, especially as a continuation of my Ahmedabad experience, which in fact had emboldened me to accept teaching. In the post-war period, multinational firms were assuming much importance in the business schools, and my personal contribution could perhaps lie in the leavening of experience I had gained in one of the oldest and the biggest, and my gain in an academic examination of my experience.

It was quite an experience to meet my class for the first time. It had a sprinkling of foreigners, a Mexican, a Chilean and one or two others. I had always been impressed with the industriousness of American students, and Anant Negandhi, an Indian member of the faculty, had told me to load them from the very beginning without compunction. I found that they worked assiduously at home and in the library, helped by their girl friends, whether students or working girls.

They surrounded their keenness with an air of an almost studied informality that took some adjustment. Their clothes, always informal, sometimes bizarre; their language with its drawl unclipped and leisurely; sometimes a foot dangling over the seat, a paper cup of coffee and two little mountains of buns on the desk: when you entered class you wondered whether you had not by mistake come to a football club meeting. It certainly held no promise of future well groomed international executives in dark suits and airconditioned, wall-to-wall carpeted offices. The greeting, Hi, to the chairman of Hindustan Lever, would have delighted a hundred young managers back in the company.

The class never lacked interest; their reactions were always lively and sharp. In the first week, when we were discussing the reactions of an international executive to a foreign culture, the question arose whether he had any right to pass judgements upon it and, where he disagreed, to try and alter it. An American student reacted strongly, and said that if he did not try to change it he had no right to be there; he was there only because he had something to offer, mainly in the way of change, the need for which he was better able to see than a local. But if, in the name of tact, courtesy or respect for local mores, call it what you like, he shied away from his duty, then he was of no use to that country. And as an illustration, he concluded "If I have a new idea that works on my mind the whole morning and I get steamed up enough to rush into the boss's room at midday to work it out with him, and then I am told that the boss is out to lunch for four hours—well, I have a right to get mad and want to change the working hours." At this obvious reference to a Latin American country, the Mexican boy reacted immediately and violently. "Hell," he said, "this is the damn ugly American we don't want out there. What right has he to change our long lunch break. We work long enough; what if we enjoy our lunch and siesta in a leisurely way instead of this son of so and so's hurriedly munched sandwich and coke? No, we don't want him or his change; the Ugly American!" The class approved uproariously, but the American protested loudly that the days of siestas and mananas were over; they certainly didn't go with business schools.

The first rumblings of an overture to the coming student problem were already in the air, and were noted by the sensitive; they were of particular interest to me as a comparison with our own student unrest. Student informality was already testing the outer edges of tolerance. When the spring rains were over and the sun shone, I saw at midday on the lawns a weird spectacle of chaos in colour and sound. There was a band of boys dressed in anything they could think of, each with an instrument that he thought could make some sound, kettles, cans and pots. The result was a cacaphony to whose underlying rhythm they swung and swayed. Some teachers protested but it went on. It was also the time when doubts were openly cast on the Vietnam war, and there was a story in the press of CIA infiltration in the Peace Corps in India.

I was introduced to some of the Punjabi settler families who farmed in California. Their fathers and grandfathers had come early in the century, and some of them may even have belonged to members of the Gadar Party, the first rebels of India whom the British expelled. They were mostly growing vegetables or fruit, and stuck to the ways they had brought with them. At a party one night I sat next to a Punjabi lady whose dress and every gesture was preserved from the day she left her village in Majha or Malwa of the East Punjab. She talked quietly, with the hem of her diaphanous *dupatta* drawn discreetly across half her face, in a gesture that seemed so far away from home; a gesture that even the girls in her village practised no longer.

Her *salwar kamiz* and her black *gurgabi* shoes were in harmony with everything else, and must have been imported from home. She began to tell me her story. She was a widow.

When she was a girl in her early teens, *Sardarji*—following old custom, she could not use his first name—had come to the village. She was produced before him, and as he approved she was given to him in marriage. They told her later that he was a big farmer in California, in *Amreeka,* where his father, the elder *Sardarji,* had settled many years ago, which of course meant nothing to her. She went with him on a big ship, and they settled on the farm, where she looked after the kitchen in Punjabi style. They had no children; *Sardarji* was a bit old, but she was otherwise quite happy, because it was a plentiful life, and she never had to be economical, not that she wasn't. Some years later *Sardarji* died. After the mourning she had to decide whether to return to her village or stay on and run the farm. It was a big farm of two hundred and fifty acres, many times bigger than you get them in the Punjab. There were two Mexican helpers who had their cottages on the farm. She did not know any English and they did not know any Punjabi. After thinking it over for a day or two, she decided to stay—it was too far to go back. For some years she had been running the farm; it was her home now and she had never been back. I asked only one question.

"How did you manage to get work out of the two men, not understanding each other?"

"There was no difficulty. I put them to work and they worked. And now they understand a little Punjabi."

She turned her face and pulled the *dupatta* across in the self-conscious gesture I had not seen for years, as I looked at her still handsome head in unconcealed admiration. What a people!

Towards the end at Los Angeles a message came from Moddie to ring K.B. Lall, secretary in the ministry of foreign trade, at Delhi. I could not understand what he wanted of me 15,000 miles away. KB could be droll, but this was incomprehensible. I managed to reach him, working forward half a day in time, and though the line was not very clear I caught his unhurried voice that came to the point in a gentle detour. He was glad I had now had experience in teaching, having done my job with Levers. Six years of Levers' chairmanship of course meant that it was perhaps time to leave and do something else. As my precious dollars ticked rapidly over the long distance, KB seemed in no hurry to get to the point. Having served the private sector for so many years, he went on, it was time I perhaps thought of something else, such as the public sector. Having just touched the subject, he went off at a tangent and wondered whether after manufacturing I might consider planning as a possible area, though of course there was steel and heavy engineering, fertilisers and chemicals, even food. And if I did not feel interested in planning there was international trade—STC, for instance. And there he stopped; he had pointed to the perch he had chosen for me, and I knew it.

My heart sank. STC, the State Trading Corporation of India, the dread organisation of the public sector, always under fire from both industry and government, and now in trouble with parliament. Accusations were always flying freely over its head; incompetence at buying and selling and corruption being among the milder charges—a serious one of late was breach of privilege of parliament, for which the chairman was going to be arraigned before the privileges committee of the house. Planning, however ineffectual it might have become of late, was at least peaceful; international trade was risky but exciting.

STC had been in trouble ever since its inception. It dealt in the most scarce, the most sensitive product in India, foreign exchange, where the open market rate was way above the official. Companies wanted it to import valuable plant and raw materials, the public wanted it covertly for their little luxuries in life, women wanted it for gold and diamonds, and men for liquor and gadgets. They all wanted it for the craze that was travel to the west, for numerous, often unnecessary trips round the world, to bring back trunkfuls of nylons, georgettes, cosmetics, cuckoo clocks, Dresden shepherdesses, colourful prints of sylvan peace, anything that could be had at home in better taste and at cheaper prices, had they but had the appreciation of those who came to India to buy its products of tradition. The junk that covered the walls and shelves of the newly rich homes was always the bad sign of well financed travel abroad.

STC was the gate to foreign exchange for the many who sought it by under-invoicing their exports and over-invoicing their imports, apart from those who genuinely needed it and earned it by exporting in order to earn their imports.

My mind raced along as K.B. Lall spoke, with now and then his highpitched laugh that was its own commentary on his own humour. I said I was returning to Bombay shortly and would come over to Delhi for a chat. Yes, that was a good idea, he thought; his characteristic response whenever he wanted something his way, and rang off. I rang the operator to find out the amount because I had put the call through from a friend's house. It was not small, and STC seemed to have begun already to exact its toll of me.

The tests over, the boys were feeling relaxed and began to drop in more often for a chat about what they were proposing to do in life. Their interest in the subject of international management had marked most of them for a career in the American multinationals, and indeed some had already been invited for interviews. Somehow they appeared reluctant to join large corporations and said they would prefer to join some international service agency and work in India, Africa, and South America. They said they were averse to the very idea of large corporations, and talked about their exploitation and predatory methods in their neighbouring vulnerable countries. They did not even relish working for their government, at home or abroad; they would prefer an international agency, non-profit-making and unbacked by a war-machine. I asked one if he had discussed the subject with his father, and he answered in mild disgust that he had not; he knew exactly the advice he would receive, to join a big corporation that pays well, and offers a good career, with rapid growth; he knew all the jargon of success as the old man had seen it in his time. He was looking for satisfaction and not for money or success. No, it was no use talking to fathers; they just saw things differently. Generation gap as a phrase had just been discovered, but as yet there was no rebellion about it. In 1967 I found that America was just beginning to simmer—Vietnam, blacks, student protest, Chile, Nixon, CIA were all at early stages of the obsessions that they were to become later.

A refrain common among the young was their growing mistrust of the old; at least it came out strongly to me that they no longer looked to their fathers and teachers for advice. Their professors they felt had not enough time to devote to them and to their problems; severor producing and consulting. Competition was becoming they were busy for attaining full professorships, deanships, and for getting known at home and abroad. They all tried to get called to Washington, Taipeh, New Delhi, Tokyo, and while there was an impressive vitality in it all, it left the students unmoved because it deprived them of the time that by rights they felt should have been devoted to them. Wherever they turned, from homes to the society, and now to the universities, there was an unconcern; at least so they thought. I was particularly interested in this, because the problems of our young, so politicised, were so dissimilar.

As a stranger, I could only ask a question here and there, more perhaps for my own interest than of help to them. Not understanding fully, I could do more harm than good with advice.

My last experience in this fantasy town was a dinner at the School at which the Dean especially asked me to sit next to a valued patron of theirs. She was a widow, grey and well groomed, with a limited range of conversation but unconsciously uninhibited. She lived in the favoured Bel Air area, through which most of my generous friends had driven me. Their commentaries differed, but they all agreed that it must represent more money per square mile than any other residential locality in the world. It was indeed an extraordinary area whose opulence had long gone past two tennis courts, two swimming pools, and two cars. It was on a scale much larger, though as ostentatious as some of the new areas of New Delhi, proudly called colonies and enclaves. No one had invited me to see one of these fabulous homes of the American maharajas, but I had heard that inside too they made interesting use of fabulous sums, again in the style of our new rich. I therefore listened with great interest to her description of her home.

Her house apparently was indeed different. Tennis lawns, swimming pools, greenhouses, all these things she took for granted, and she talked mostly about its interior, which had been done by a great decorator. She looked at me and guessed that I was an oriental, and she began to describe her bedroom which was different; it was an oriental bedroom. Of course I would know what an oriental bed room would be like. I volunteered that it would be a room with low divans, carpets and rugs, low furniture and cushions, but I said I would let her describe it as it must have some rare features. She very coyly told me that her bed was on a platform, and there was a step to it so that one had to step up to her! Isn't that cute, she said, this oriental ritual. I took fright at the thought that I might after all be invited to view the interior of a Bel Air home, and made a hasty retreat from the subject to look helplessly at my wife who had no idea of my chagrin. I went back to my steak, systematically finishing it. She looked at me, my plate, and then at her own plate, on which the steak lay barely touched; and to my second but touching surprise, she said, "Would you like to finish my steak? I loved to see you eat yours." And then she blushed and mumbled an apology. Not at all, I told her, I would certainly have finished hers too; their steaks were really so good, but unfortunately I had two square meals that day, for someone had invited me to lunch. I begged her not to feel embarrassed about it because I appreciated her gesture. She must have thought I had overdone it because she turned to the other person on the side and lost all interest in me. I only hoped that I had not let down the Dean.

My last evening was spent at Anant Negandhi's and his German wife Erni's place. They had invited a number of young Indians from the university and outside, and a discussion began on a subject that was to come up again and again on my subsequent visits, of the prospects of their return home one day; the question was when and to what. I looked around at the group; some were assistant professors, some held fellowships, others were working with firms in the area. Many had been home to bring back brides from their own communities, often through advertisements in the daily newspapers, sometimes finishing the whole operation in less than a fortnight's leave from work. Parents must have short-listed the girls, with details of education, dowry, family and whatever precise specifications the American-educated young man had laid down as the minimum; in accordance perhaps with an evaluation system with cut-off points. One sees such couples on Air-India planes, the young man unmistakably Indian American, and a self-assured bride looking forward to her new gadget-filled home; their acquaintance developing over the long flight. Some marriages do not work out, especially if the boy had been attached to an American girl and had succumbed to parental pressure, but mostly they settle to a comfortable Indian life abroad. One now also sees on the Air-India flight old parents and widowed mothers travelling out to visit their sons. In due course the boys send for their younger brothers for advanced education in the US having already helped them with their university education at home. The brothers too sometimes settle down; and I even came across a father who so liked it that he too settled and developed a good business in Indian condiments and spices.

I felt that not many seriously meant it when they said they would return home; some of course would try, but be back again. Those who married American girls sounded more keen, but they were relatively the quicker to return. At the Institute of Management at Ahmedabad, although we offered the work environment they had hoped for, also comfortable houses, those with American wives all went back; perhaps because the cord with America had remained connected.

Even in my limited experience I could feel in those days the pull of this environment; and if you had the sheer merit of many of these boys, it was always tugging at you to stay. It is not without significance that when after two hundred years of connection, the British took from India in the last twentyfive years many hundred thousand of semi-skilled and semi-literate workers to do their unwelcome jobs, like cloak room attendants; the Americans selected during the same twentyfive years many thousands of the best from among those we sent them for advanced education. They were no simple Indians who had left home looking only for a living; they were from the cream of Indian universities. The first ten, it was said at one time, of those who passed out every year from an institute of technology went straight to American universities, where they were first turned into some of their best finished products and then kept back. Each one of them was a potential catalyst in India, where growth would have been the better sparked by them. Those comfortably ensconced in India, especially the politicians, sometimes talked of a spirit of sacrifice that ought to make these men return home to develop a truly Indian science and technology, and at other times menacingly of cancelling their passports, but not of what we had to offer them; how we could interest them with academic challenges and opportunites instead of the administrative frustrations.

No, I said to these young Indians at the end, they should try to feel comfortable with whatever they decided to do. If they decided to return, then they should stop making unfavourable comparisons and take India as it is; and they would soon fit in. And if they did not find the opportunity they were looking for, then they should make up their mind to stay here in America, but in that case they should regard it their home. They should not run down America to prove that it was not its attractions that made them stay. For the peace of their mind, and in fairness to the country, they should accept it with grace and realism. America had given them everything and held back nothing; it had in fact served them better than its own minorities. They should give it credit for the frank appreciation of their talent. In return they owed their country of adoption something at least, the loyalty they held back, and which interestingly enough they also held back from India. To prove to themselves that they always wanted to go back to India, they ran India down more than it deserved, and they certainly never praised America as it deserved.

Anant Negandhi was a rare example among them of someone who had made up his mind to stay; and I seldom heard him talk against India or against America. He was pleased with both. One had given him his first chance, and the other his second. By all means let Indians in America keep their roots fresh. Many of them would visit India periodically, but America was their home; and if emotionally not quite theirs, certainly their children's.

I laughed self-consciously and said that I had made the Gettysburg speech that one of them should have made. I admitted that I was only too conscious of how easily one could get related to this society; nowhere else do you get assimilated so soon, provided of course that you don't hold back, but give yourself to it.

CHAPTER FOURTEEN

Leaving Levers

On my return to Bombay I plunged myself into the five-year plan for Hindustan Lever. Prepared mostly in my absence, it was a thorough and polished effort that made only one major assumption for fulfilling its ambitious targets—to be permitted to grow. It made the minimal demands on public funds, foreign exchange or Unilever help; its accent was on research and development and import substitution. The new research and development laboratory, the recent reorganisation, and the growing cost-consciousness, would assure a high rate of growth, despite all the constraints, if only these became no worse. Research was led by a young able scientist, Varadarajan, whose rare passion was the profitable application of science to industry.

I went to talk to K.B. Lall, who remembered how I had called on him six years ago to discuss our plans then. He lost no opportunity to press his point and said, "Ah, this is the time you should leave; don't have the vanity to do two plans; leave your successor with something to do, as did your predecessor." I explained that I had no one ready, though we had someone in mind. Rajadhyaksha was going to be made vice-chairman the following year, and would be groomed to take over on my retirement three years later, in 1971. It would not be fair to leave at this stage and force them to bring in an expatriate chairman. However, I offered to help STC with advice, but at this he laughed. He said it might work in Levers, but it would not work in STC, because their government culture was different. Advice from outside would make no difference; they would listen but go on as they were, with the possible danger that they might even turn my advice to their advantage to do what they wanted but ought not to do. And yet if I sat in the chair they would do as I bid; if there is one thing they do understand, it is orders. I saw his point from my experience in Hindustan Steel. They seemed as incapable of using advice as arguing with an order, good, bad or perverse. It was an interesting culture of total deference to power.

K.B. Lall must have thought it over however, because on my next visit he suggested that I talk to STC about their organisation structure. The minister had plans which he could not put through because in its present shape they both doubted STC's capacity to carry a much bigger burden. He had therefore made an appointment for me to meet the chairman of STC.

I would not have been surprised if he had deliberately sent me to bring his point home; so abortive was my visit, in an almost ludicrous way. A clerk met me to say that the chairman had been called away to a meeting but had left word that I might meet one of the managers; I was therefore going to be led to the head of their economic division. My disappointment somewhat lightened at the thought that at least they had such a division. The important gentleman who received me began by describing himself, a barrister-at-law, who had held various important posts in government, and now headed this big department. I discovered however that despite its name it consisted of a large number of clerks and managers, and the head of the economic section was a graduate in chemistry. Their only economist had left in disgust soon after joining. The department assisted the chairman in answering parliamentary questions, and currently in his problems with parliament itself; it also controlled foreign offices and their postings. The ultimate prize in the corporation, as a reward for good service, was to be given an important division, however unrelated to your past experience, or a posting abroad, which this gentleman himself was hoping to get next year for his last three years of service. Instead of posting the younger men abroad to bring back their experience to the headquarters, they mostly retired at the end of a posting abroad.

He looked blankly at me when I asked him about their plans, or any changes they had in mind. Why should they want to reorganise or change? As for planning, government made their decisions for them; so really government should plan. He turned happily to describing his job and brought out a pile of studies of various countries that he had prepared for exporters. I thumbed through some and found them simple accounts of geography, people, production, imports and exports. He told me that they had been found so useful that they were going to be reprinted. As he seemed quite uninterested in the purpose of my visit, I thanked him and left, and complimented K.B. Lall for really understanding his STC. Having persuaded him and some others that while glad to serve the public sector I was not, at least yet, ready to join. I returned to my own problems in Levers.

A recently introduced reorganisation of Hindustan Lever, with a far reaching change, accepted readily in Bombay and Madras, with surprisingly only a token opposition in Calcutta, then in a real industrial turmoil after its first communist government came into power, ran into considerable trouble in Delhi. There one way or another it continued for many years, even after I left, and the matter was taken by the Delhi union as far as the Supreme Court, and lost there. The proximity of parliament created its own pull on industrial relations, to keep even a non-issue alive, which elsewhere would have been resolved. Politicians would be invited to become presidents of unions, address conventions and meetings, ask questions in parliament at each session, lead delegations to a minister, and get some of the capital's numerous press correspondents interested. Under the patronage of a political personality, there were many means available to keep a problem alive; while a question in parliament could be arranged for the asking, sometimes without first ascertaining facts.

Though this reorganisation, a feeling began to grow in me through 1967 that accumulation of Hindustan Lever's internal and external problems was once again making Unilever somewhat sensitive. After the two difficult years of 1966 and 1967 of bad monsoons, the economic situation worsened in the wake of a big devaluation in 1966, and the first of a series of recessions set in. Government promptly introduced tight controls, and as a result our profitability fell. Unilever appeared to feel that my growing involvement with government, while it might have had some limited value, was resulting in my handling our own problems with government with less directness and vigour. I was too close to them to press our claims at the risk of upsetting them; I was also spending too much time with government enterprises and committees, and my three months' absence at Los Angeles, for something that had no direct relationship with their business, were all indications to them of my diminishing interest. Hoskyns-Abrahall, in charge of India, once asked me how much time did I spend with government and when I said about one-quarter, he was surprised, because they were under the impression that it was more than half.

A small but interesting problem, which delicacy prevented me from discussing with them, was my feeling about the growing lack of interest among the Unilever young to come and work in the Indian business. Two directors, and an odd specialist we might need for starting something where we had no experience, was all we needed. In fifteen years, when the business had grown much in size and complexity, the number of expatriates had dropped from over fifty to a mere four or five. Unilever were keen to have a couple of their promising men on our board, but it was becoming increasingly difficult to bring out men who were interested in the country, and would regard India as more than an interlude that furthered their career. At their level they had not only to be really able, but they had to demonstrate their leadership over men nearly always older than them, and usually no less able. They also had to be liked, and to be liked they had visibly to like working in India. We made it easier for them to go home every year on leave; and there was of course the spreading knowledge in Unilever that those who made it in India had a good chance of making the home board. Somehow this seemed to add to the intolerance of at least some for having to make it in an environment they did not like. The congestion and climate of Bombay, the unfamiliar and seemingly unnecessary problems of business, the struggle always with raw material shortages and production constraints, were enough to fray a national's nerves, but to them even the greater glory of Unilever appeared not a good enough cause.

At the beginning Unilever would arrange for me to meet the man and his wife, and usually an ex-India hand would do some gentle selling beforehand; but usually it became a process in reverse, the couple, especially the wife, interviewing me instead. Some took a chance and decided against India, secure perhaps in the feeling that if they were good enough to be tried in India they would still be tried somewhere else. I had one dour unhappy person who, had it only been realised, was obviously going to be ultimately unhappy anywhere. Another liked India perhaps even less, but he took it more shrewdly; both however were never really part of the business, and one could not even derive advantage from their not being a part of the scene, because they were not objective. I somehow got the feeling that they were enclaves that Unilever were not willing to discuss; in fairness though, and this was more likely, they had not given much thought to it; at least they never discussed the subject with me and I left it alone.

Seven years' stewardship of the company was also perhaps long enough in itself, and a change was needed for Hindustan Lever's sake, for Unilever's sake, and for my sake. I was becoming increasingly conscious of how easily the answers came to me, the facile temptation to repeat what had worked once. I remembered the remark of a professor at Harvard that a management will tend to do in the future what it thinks it has done well in the past; and in that lies a danger. If I stayed longer there was both the danger for me of getting stale, if I had not already become so, and of building up a feeling against them; they who had always been supportive and constructive. There was besides the danger of my justifying those feelings in an unfair way. The more I thought about it, the more I came to the conclusion that time had come for me to go. There was on the other side the insistent call of the public sector that I seemed no longer willing or able to resist. I was forming an attachment that was pulling me towards it; knowing though that it was not going to be an easy master to serve. K.B. Lall had guessed well.

Just then a small incident, of no particular consequence in the normal way, conveyed to me that they were becoming edgy; and in retrospect that perhaps I too was becoming edgy. With no one to discuss the problem with, I thought, perhaps brooded over it for some days. At a Board of Trade meeting in Delhi in January 1968, on an impulse I sent a scribbled note to K.B. Lall to say—the answer is yes. Back came a note from him that this was very good news; when? As I left the meeting before it closed, he followed me out and wanted to know more about it. I explained that I was going for a week's holiday to the Kulu Valley, where I would have plenty of time to think over the decision that I had made only a few minutes ago. He readily agreed that we would discuss it further on my return.

It snowed all week at Kulu, so I had plenty of time to think over the decision. It seemed best, all things considered, to go. I was interested and curious to work in the public sector. Later that month I was to visit London on Andrew Knox's retirement, and that would give me the chance to talk things over with them. He was leaving the company after fifty years of service, and a great meet had been arranged of all the chairmen of the companies that he had been associated with, and as India had always been his first love I was given the honour of making the farewell speech at the banquet. Before leaving I asked K.B. Lall if I could return via Moscow to get some feel of what it would be like to deal with the most important customer of STC, Russia. He thought it would be a good idea to visit the STC office in Moscow and the commercial section of the embassy. This step, taken purely out of curiosity, took me still further towards the final decision. News also came from London that with the departure of Andrew Knox there would be changes in the overseas committee, and Hoskyns-Abrahall would also be retiring. In Hindustan Lever, the vice-chairman, Ramaswami, one of the directors, was due to retire two years ahead of time to make way for Rajadhyaksha to become vice-chairman. The year 1968 was picking up well after the last two bad years, both in the economy and in the firm, and this was reflected in the results of the first few months. Thus wherever I looked I saw signs that this was the best time to go. Let Rajadhyaksha take over as chairman and deal with the new overseas committee, and make this equation. Let him start up the plan, with good results in his own first year.

On the Monday in early February, when the conference began in London, I wrote a brief note to John Abrahall saying that in this year of so many changes it might be well for Hindustan Lever too to have its own change and begin with a new leader. This was perhaps the best time for me to make a new start. Government had been making repeated offers; I would like to accept one of them. I left the note on his desk. When I walked out of the room, that was the moment of leaving; not when I actually left half a year later. I went back to the conference and joined my colleagues from many parts of the world, some of whom I had known over the years, as our careers went in their upward curves, meeting them at courses and at Unilever House, reading about their careers and the progress of their companies. As I sat among them, part of them and yet a part no longer, a nostalgia came over me. But when I thought of Rajadhyaksha and his young board, whose average age would drop to below forty with the departure of Ramaswami and me—the new chairman himself barely forty—it seemed indeed the time to go. For many years I had been helping the young to rise, so that anyone who had merit got his first shot of senior responsibility in his early thirties, and had a chance to make the board in his late thirties or early forties. The logical consequence was for the old to retire voluntarily and before their time.

At lunch John Abrahall walked straight up to me and said, "Well, that was a surprise." Next morning he, Andrew Knox and I spoke about the timing of my departure and the succession. I thought how fitting that I should be discussing it with Abrahall, who was the one sent out to India over twenty years ago, soon after the war, to start the new process of Indianisation, with instructions no doubt to identify and train the first Indian chairman. The process by now was so well set that I had no hesitation in recommending Rajadhyaksha, even though it meant promoting him straight from being a director. Abrahall wondered vaguely whether I would stay on for a period as president or something to see the transition through, but I told him that in joining government it would be best to make a clean break, for both government's and the firm's sake. There was certainly no point, they agreed, in bringing a chairman out for three years; the process of Indianisation at the top having started, there was no point in even a temporary deviation. Rajadhyaksha would no doubt make as good a chairman now as three years later; he had the qualities that inspired us to trust him with the responsibility now; that in itself would bring the best out of him. If ever I admired Unilever it was in such moments of trust and decisiveness. I reminded them of the succession plan that we had discussed seven years ago; at least it had worked on this occasion, in its first major test.

Later in the public sector I missed this more than any other tradition of the firm. There top positions could remain vacant for a year and more, and the process of selection was long and vacillating, and sometimes the final selection incomprehensible, even perverse. The appointment of even a selection committee for the public sector did not work too well. Planned succession seemed alien to the culture, and consequently also a continuity in policy.

Through the week of the conference I began to feel the excitement of a new career. I thought of a new life with its unfamiliar challenges. I would miss, from what little I knew about the public sector, the order and predictableness of the system I was leaving behind. I had worked nowhere else, and the culture of the firm was all I knew. I realised that the doubts I had lately begun to harbour about Unilever were merely my way of pushing myself into a decision to leave; I was now sure that in fact neither they nor I really felt that we had had too much of the other; although it was time anyway for a change. K.B. Lall would have won anyway. Looking around at the group of chairmen at the conference, each one of them well selected and groomed with meticulous care, among the best executives in the world, I wondered how much freedom would one enjoy to develop such talent, with care, consideration and feelings for the person. This was one thing I was going to miss in administration. Aspi Moddie told me later, "You will find that in it man does not matter: the designation, the rule, the file; all but the man."

A few months earlier, Andrew Knox had taken farewell of the Indian company in Bombay, where he had broken down. I wondered therefore how it would go at his final farewell, and as I spoke I found it more difficult than I had expected, because I was saying my own farewell too, but Andrew must have understood my feelings. He and Abrahall were men I held in great regard, men so different in appearance, ways and style, but both men of pure values.

CHAPTER FIFTEEN

Moscow

I took the Aeroflot flight to Moscow the next morning for a week to a world quite unknown. With Unilever, and later with STC, I travelled to many countries, in all continents, but to each new country one could extend some pre-knowledge, culled from books, newspapers, films, people, so that one could build up some familiar expectation of the new country; but not so with Russia. I had seen perhaps a dozen Russians, spoken to one, and known none; and this for someone who had been brought up in his youth in Europe, and revisited it many times. Even in Sweden, that had become my second home after I met Gärd, you never met one, even though they were neighbours. One's total contemporary knowledge came from their propaganda literature, a Unilever buyer who had been there to discuss a sunflower deal, Wendell Wilkie's account in "One World" of his visit during the war, and some contemporary literature and music.

The air hostess gave a monosyllabic reception, and when I asked if I could sit at the back, she just said, no, and I discovered that that was where she was going to sit herself much of the time. After we took off, I asked her if I could have a drink, she said, no, and as an afterthought, added, later. Much later, after she had served the crew and eaten herself, she asked, "you eat," and added generously, "drink?" I consoled myself with the thought that she and the crew were at work, while I was doing no work; perhaps therefore she had the right approach to serve the workers first; besides, it was a change from what might have happened with a friendly and voluble hostess on a long flight with no other passengers in the forward cabin. I saw the sense of it. It was the same democratic reluctance to serve at the hotel, an old-fashioned place called the Peking, which, I was told, could neither have its name changed nor receive a facelift while the relations with China remained as they were. It had the familiar ring of experience of our own state-owned hotels and public service counters.

As it was Saturday night, and though it was past midnight; I asked the young man from the embassy who had met me at the airport, if I could take a walk in the street. He offered to come out with me and explain things. The night was cold, though I was informed that for the first time in weeks the temperature had risen to a mere minus twelve; but there were a lot of well muffled men and women walking in the streets with an air of nowhere to go. He explained that government had recently declared a five-day week, but as there were few private cars, no tradition of a week-end, and few restaurants and bars, people just walked about. He added, government ran into an interesting problem that it had not expected. With little to occupy the long week-end the consumption of vodka went up. The strong impression on me of that night and on the following days was one of a European city that affluence and its concomitant noise, fumes, cars, neon signs, advertisements, crammed shop windows, the total nervous rush and bustle, had passed by, leaving a simple calm behind. The few shop windows, the goods and food in them, people and their figures and dresses, the few cars; everything had a functional look about it of a no-nonsense and no-frills, no-glut and no-waste society, whose decision makers saw things simply and austerely.

On Sunday morning, I walked about the streets again. The air was crisp and clean, and there were fewer people, even fewer cars, and even more calm. I later went to our commercial counseller's house, in a block of flats built for embassy staff. At the entrance there was a Russian guard, who opened the gate and let you into the privileged and protected enclave. All foreigners lived thus, I was told, on their islands, whose drawbridges were lowered in the morning and lifted at night; the single gate guarded during the day, with all communications for all services, except their daily shopping, channelled. A few blocks away there was a large building that ran along the entire length of the street, called the Friendship Street; this building was practically deserted ever since most of its inhabitants, the Chinese mission, had left. The mission had been built and the street specially named in the first euphoria of friendship, the time we were also *"bhaibhai"* with them; and then it must have burst with activity, but now it stood in silent protest. I walked about this suburb in the cold undisturbed air, and I thought if only Moscow, the capital of a very large country with a relatively small population, could stay that way and escape the kind of affluence that its leadership was already threatening it with but never seemed able to achieve. If it had only twelve gas stations, it also had so much less gasoline in its air; and yet they proudly told you that the Plan promised to begin pouring thousands of new Fiat-made cars into Moscow. An endearing explanation you could offer for being late was the heavy traffic.

On Monday morning I went to visit my first Russian public enterprise, which had bought its first consignment of detergent powder from Hindustan Lever. The deal was interesting, because we had never met Russians before, and the negotiations were like bargaining, with bids and counterbids, and new conditions introduced every now and again, sometimes quite incomprehensible to us. We showed them some of our brands and asked them what brand name they would like, or did they not believe in such a bourgeois practice. No, they must have a brand name—Umbrella; and when we asked for its equivalent in Russian, they said, simply Umbrella. They asked for the panel on the side in English, but not the Hindi on the opposite side, to remain. They also wanted to retain both the women on the panels, in the dress and in the saree. It then dawned on us that with good old universal advertising sense they were trying to give the pack an imported and exotic look that would no doubt make it a fast seller, and fetch a good premium. The Russian text was to be featured as a concession to explain the use of the product; otherwise it was to look strictly imported and foreign.

We entered the building through a security area and were taken up to a small room where an elderly officer and his interpreter met us. I did not know the ritual, so after the greetings I asked if he knew our product and if he would like to tell me about it, how it reached, the quality, packing etc. He said that their president was busy, so he could not see me; and there was nothing he had to say about the product, but apparently he knew a lot, and loosened up the moment I suggested that I could take it that they had no problems. I had assumed that as this was the first consignment, they might have had some trouble.

At this his face lit and he set forth volubly. There was nothing right with the product, its quality, cartons, outer packing, delivery schedule. Apparently, as with us, the way to a Russian heart was through an invitation to complain. I kept nodding my head, as he complained volubly, the interpreter barely able to keep pace; at least I had got him to talk, and this so surprised him that I expected him to come forward with a big claim. To anticipate such a move, I apologised for all that had happened. Under the circumstances it was as well for us not to receive another order, because we were short of the product in the home market and had only entered into the contract for our government's goodwill sake. We could sell all of it and at a much better price than they gave us. My helpful advice was that they buy it in Europe in future.

I do not think he was sufficiently senior, and was sent because no one's time was worth the meeting with me; but at my unexpected reaction he seemed to take fright. He excused himself and left the room. He returned with a smile and was glad to inform me that the president had unexpectedly become free and would be glad to see me. They had done an excellent deal, at prices far below Europe, and paid for in non-convertible rupees, while we had to pay valuable exchange to import the raw materials.

From the small windowless, bare room he took me to a large handsome office with a view over the city. The president was a well dressed and impressive looking youngish man with some goldplated teeth; he walked across the room and took me to the conference table. He was expansive in his manner and conversed easily and amiably, through the interpreter of course, about our product, western Europe, Unilever and the current market situation. I was back in the familiar multinational world. He could have been an executive in Shell, Philips, Unilever or Tatas; but he was unusual, I found later. We did not discuss detergents much, and of course he had let the little man go; there was a more important looking man there instead. Eventually as I was getting late for a lunch appointment, I asked his leave. He got up, took me to the door and added happily that we would be meeting later as he was coming to our cocktail party. At the party he walked straight up to me and started an animated conversation, and I realised that he was speaking freely in English, without an interpreter. I discovered too that at parties only the ministers had interpreters.

I spent an interesting evening with the family of a young Swedish journalist, who had spent almost a decade in Moscow. There were some other European journalists too. He said the same thing; how much they had changed. Yet they knew no one they could claim to know. And never to be out of someone's sight; from the maid at home allotted to them, to the man who sat at the drawbridge, to the one who issued a permit to go twentyfive miles out of town; they were all solicitous but watchful. They had got to know a lot of people, but no one to whom they could say "drop in." They could, but there was a whole process behind the acceptance, and often someone else also came along. It was not only a different way of life but a different people.

It was facile to judge. One looked for the landmarks one knew well around the world, but these were different people; bred and brought up differently. I met one young recognisable kind of couple, casual, bantering, with a light touch, but even to them one could not say, "come and have lunch!" I soon stopped looking for familiar landmarks, and that made it easier.

After some illuminating discussions with our minister at the embassy, Damodaran, and sightseeing through Air India, always a friendly outpost abroad, a look at Lenin, fresh-faced and roseate, as if he had died yesterday, a variety show at the Bolshoi, and the famous Working Restaurant for a vodka and caviar dinner, where couples danced sedately to a band literally from the 1930s, I was put on the midnight Air India plane from London, for the journey from the snow of Moscow to the summer of Bombay. Well muffled, under my new beaver hat, as I climbed the gangway in a long queue and stood in the freezing wind, while a much better muffled Russian policemen stood inside the warm cabin, examining each passport for the last time with great care, I knew that I was going to return. In dealing with the Russians there was the familiar prospect of many things in common.

K.B. Lal was pleased with my visit. A satisfactory report had of course already reached him from Moscow. We began to plan together for the many details involved in joining the public sector at that time, for someone from the private sector, and a foreign firm at that. His complex mind would not envisage anything simple; he had to devise a strategy. He had rightly expected the STC trouble to rise to a pitch during the budget session of parliament, and he wanted to move with finesse. Just before his ministry's grants would come up for discussions, he would announce the appointment of a committee to review the working of STC, with me as its chairman; with of course a hint thrown to the press that I was likely to take over the corporation later. He would thus gauge parliament's reaction during the debates, both to the committee and the rumour of my appointment. One morning I found a telex message on my desk—"The following message was received for the chairman this morning from T.T. Krishnamachari—'Prakash please do not commit suicide. T.T.K'." The message amused me, it pleased me, but coming from T.T.K. it intrigued me as well. As Nehru's finance minister, he had found the STC; in fact he had been the architect of the public sector, the instrument of Nehru's socialist dreams. He was once agent of Levers for South India. That he should take so much notice of a three line announcement in the press and telephone our Madras office from his home in the country, not with his characteristic half congratulatory half deprecating message but with something so sharp, disturbed me. I sent a message back thanking him and making some crack about the slow death of the private sector that he had already ordained. But one day this message was to put me back from the furthest edge of desperation.

The STC Review Committee's terms of reference were wide enough to give me the unusual experience of first suggesting all the change I could think of, then an assurance of it being accepted, to implement it myself and finally be responsible for results. K.B. Lall would certainly make it possible to do whatever I thought worthwhile. On my own farewell visit to London in May, I decided to combine it with visits to STC offices in Tehran, Beirut and Rotterdam; and if my one visit to the head office could have served as a gentle warning these foreign offices were enough to bother the stoutest heart, so ill-organised and purposeless were they.

The Unilever farewell was a gracious affair to which they had invited some whose acquaintance I had cherished over the years, and many with whom I had worked in India, and others I knew on the Dutch side at Rotterdam. Lord Cole, chairman, gently stilled a past controversy and said—Prakash was a patriot to whom India's interests came first but with whom the Unilever interests were always safe.

Back in Bombay I said farewell to the company, in which there remained very few who were there when I joined it thirtyone years ago. Next evening I took the Frontier Mail to Delhi, a train journey that I used to do so often in the past. I thought it would be relaxing to take the twentyfour hours trip in air-conditioned luxury. As it turned out, we ran into floods and the journey took three days and three nights.

I fell back in the enforced but relaxed idleness to think about Hindustan Lever, a foreign firm, a multinational as they call them now. The picture as it pieced together was of light and shadows which mingled into an experience that had been worth having. To be the first and to be sensitive had made it the more difficult, especially in a period of political transition, when to work for your own was considered better than to work for the rulers. Fortunately, I did not see it that way, because all our own that I had approached for a job thirty years ago had not been interested in other than their own kith, kin and caste.

Levers had in a way been a continuation of the process of my maturation in England. Matured in the Merseyside business and social culture, Levers was its comfortable extension. In a multinational, I was its first experiment in grooming a national head of one of its largest business, and I saw the business developing, together with my own development, through distinct stages of our mutual growth—from dependence through independence to interdependence. From the time in the 1930s when it was all a one-way traffic—home mail, home policy, even home advertising material, a "European signature" for all sanctions—we moved to the stage when one felt we ought sometimes to disagree if only to assert ourselves; finally to a well balanced though not always smooth relationship. Moving from one stage to another had its problems and conflicts, but somehow we each managed to get to the next stage, creating new relationships of a different texture in which each unit does what it can do best, but relies upon the centre for what its world experience has taught it to do better.

Leaving Hindustan Lever ahead of my time to join the public sector, and Chandy's earlier example, set a kind of pattern that my successor, Vasant Rajadhyaksha, the chief economist Nath, the director of research, Varadarajan, soon afterwards followed, beside many others. It proved a good matrix to train and send out men in their own right as professional managers. Curiously, the multinationals were generally more successful at this than even the professionally managed Indian firms, and more so than the family firms, whose family men would not venturee out and whose professional men were not given the confidence. Even today, fifty years after the process began in the West of family-founded firms being run by professional managers, in India there is scarcely a large firm which is not headed by someone whose name is the name of the firm—Tatas, Jains, Sarabhais, Kotharis, Mafatlals, and several hundred others. And today most multinationals in India are headed by Indians.

I wondered how much trust the controlling ministries would give one in a public enterprise. Would they appreciate independent thought and action, divergent from their own: Would I be allowed to mould the new organisation the way I would want to, and would the environment, if not permissive at least be tolerant? Would it permit me to derive the same satisfaction that my last assignment did, where with all the problems of change I managed to change but, more important, leave a successor behind who while improving and filling the gaps would not proceed in desperate atavism to demolish all that was left behind, in trying to prove himself. So often had I seen in public enterprises new brooms sweep out much good and bring in nothing better. Rajadhyaksha was a different type, with the quality of personal warmth, which the organisation would need above all, after my coldly impersonal drive for efficiency. And while grooming him I had left behind Thomas, who had left the company a few years earlier to join his family business and, predictably, returned. Someone had asked me how his colleagues would react, and I said, badly at first, but the organisation would gain a likely chairman; and he succeeded Rajadhyaksha. In fact he went further and was appointed to the Unilever board.

CHAPTER SIXTEEN

State Trading Corporation

STC, India's first international trading corporation, was set up by Government of India in 1956 at the request, first of the Chinese government and later the Russians, when they entered into bilateral trade agreements with us. These were based on inconvertable currency accounts, and known as the Rupee trade; in fact a barter trade. They both agreed that their state enterprises would feel more at ease dealing with a state enterprise in India than with the private trade. A running balance was maintained, and the surpluses on either side could not be converted into free foreign exchange; they were carried forward and offset by further trading. The Chinese agreements came to an end with the war in 1962, but the Russian bilateral trade has continued, considerably reinforced by other East European countries joining in, till it formed a substantial part of Indian imports and exports.

We imported whole plants for the new public enterprises, defence equipment, chemicals and pharmaceuticals, ships, power plants, but no consumer goods. In exchange we exported commodities, tea, coffee, cashewnut, jute, textiles, railway wagons, shoes and light engineering goods. It helped both sides in a way. It enabled the communist countries to find markets for products which were not sophisticated enough to find access to the European markets and buy in return our commodities and other products without having to use their hard-earned foreign exchange, which they could put to use for more sophisticated imports from the west. The benefit to us was an access to plant and equipment for which we did not have sufficient free foreign exchange, of which a good part was spent then in importing foodgrains from U.S. Mutually beneficial, it meant perhaps a greater gain to them, if only because of their superior trading strength, helped by a touch of euphoria on our part, and a naivete among our administrators turned traders, a class which at home they scorned traditionally.

In course of time, the Russians were to hold it against us that through our trade plans we "forced" them to trade through the STC and did not give them the freedom to buy and sell freely through private enterprise, as did America, West Europe, Japan and others.

When I pointed out that they too channelled all our trade through their public enterprises in Moscow and did not allow us to deal with their republics or states, they simple argued that that was their system. We had to deal with their monopoly enterprises in Moscow but they wanted the benefits of competition in our open markets. In course of time, even though they dealt on a state to state basis with us, they nevertheless appointed their own Indian special agents in India, whom they paid commission for a service performed that we could not visibly see.

This system of Indian agents for the Russians was also the manner in which large corporations and consortiums, especially in the aid-giving developed countries worked in India, more so when their aid was tied; and we were just as vulnerable. Their "cartels," operating sometimes only where we were concerned, could spread their influence around the world, so that no matter when we made a bid to buy, within a country or around the world, we came across "understandings" on prices. These cartels argued that they were forced into it because they were forced to deal with a state monopoly. Whichever way we looked at it competition was only for the strong and equal. The interesting thing was that these developed free enterprise countries' monopolies had as strong agents' lobbies within India as the socialist countries, but with a difference—the Indian "intermediaries" of the developed countries were usually a very sophisticated lot, often retired defence officers, whose strength was quite visible at the lavish parties they threw, with a bevy of those who mattered invited, and the telephone calls they could arrange from above at the opportune moment. The agents of the East Europeans were usually unknown parties.

Placed in such a sensitive position, dealing often with the seamier side of international trade, STC could please no one. It was always criticised by private industry, public enterprises, press, government, parliament, Audit, intermediaries, state enterprises and cartels abroad; it could never be right. Ill equipped professionally, with an archaic administrative and financial system, it had much to be blamed for, and it was understandable if a state of paranoia and perversity had entered its soul. Into its office, if it could be called that, I entered one monsoon morning, anxious and unsure about what was in store for me.

B.P. Patel, my predecessor in STC, was relieved when I arrived. He hoped to take some leave, and the next parliament session, starting soon, would now not be his worry. The breach of privilege issue had been settled, and the committee had absolved him. He looked somewhat embarrassed when I asked him if I could drop in the next morning, and wondered if I could make it after midday. I gladly agreed and suggested that if it suited him better, I would take over on the following day. He jumped at the idea and thought that to be ideal.

Alexander had earlier negotiated my salary and terms, with instructions from K.B. Lall that government would be willing to consider a salary higher than the maximum of the scale for civil servants Rs 4,000. We both agreed that it was not worth making the exception. In fact, the paradox was that on my STC salary after personal tax, which then touched 97 per cent, house rent, provident fund and other deductions, I owed some money every month for the privilege of working for this public enterprise. And my total personal income was of no great magnitude.

Next morning, Patel, looking well pleased, handed over charge, a ritual from the British days, and we both signed a statement to the effect that he was handing over and I was taking over. As a modern touch, there was a photographer present who made us shake hands.

I looked around my room and at the Muslim graveyard outside, one more depressing than the other. The main office, through which I was formally taken around on another ritual, the inspection tour, was a slum of dirt, disorder and unbelievable chaos, with stacks of floppy files to the ceiling, rickety glass and wood partitioned private offices, ink-stained desks and collapsing chairs. The whole office reverberated with the noise of people talking loudly across their desks, or standing around in groups, bells ringing to call peons, who took their own time to respond as they too were busy conversing and doing nothing somewhere else. My office was at one end, secluded from the rest by a vestibule and a small office for my staff of eight, two peons on morning duty and two in the afternoon, a personal assistant, a personal secretary, a stenographer and a filing clerk. My office was enormous compared with the small pigeonholes outside, and it was full of furniture; a large horseshoe desk and a big swivel chair, a conference enclave, and walls lined with shelves and covered with charts, all with coloured lines going upwards and bars getting taller. On the floor there was a wall to wall carpet and many smaller ones on top. In one corner there was a screen hiding a basin, a bucket of water and a jug, a towel stand and a soap dish—another distinct British touch from earlier centuries.

I called for the two peons and started sending them out loaded with books, files, charts, furniture, rugs, pictures of presidents and prime ministers. They asked me what they should do with it all, and I told them to take it anywhere. An hour later my room was sparsely furnished, its walls bare, and I sat back exhausted. I vowed to give STC a new modern office, decent for people to work in. My office would be quite small, with no desk but just a few low chairs, no carpets and raw silk curtains to fade and acquire dust, but instead grass mats and bamboo chiks, handloom tapestries and hangings with simple themes. The last touch would be to panel the walls with stained strips of wood to prevent dirty marks. This eventually was to become the style of all STC offices in India. It was simple, cheap and of a purely Indian decor.

The curiosity aroused by the mounds of furniture on the landing was fanned into utter disbelief when I declared that I would need a staff of no more than one, a good stenographer, and they saw me carrying my own papers to another room, taking my own telephone calls, making my own coffee from a thermos flask of hot water and a jar of instant coffee powder. I announced that anyone wishing to see me could walk in without an appointment; that I did not wish to receive a file but only a note stating a problem or a proposition, the alternatives and the recommendations. I was determined to do away with the anachronistic remains of the Moghul-British style, so carefully woven into our own.

There were certain expressions of basic equality that I missed in this environment, such as a senior manager saying to me on the telephone, "Yes, I will be over, but could it be in about fifteen minutes because I have a visitor with me?" No, in this culture even a director would drop everything and leave the most important visitor alone to come running. And for someone to say, "well, I am not so sure that I agree with you on that," was unimaginable. The disagreement always came, and in good measure, but only after you left the organisation, and then everyone would hasten to assure your successor that he never agreed with your policy, the boldness with which he had disagreed and how he was made to suffer and pay a price. There was, while you were there, an atmosphere to total agreement and deference, in which people went wrong with fatal ease and slipped into a feeling of infallibility, just as there was a total disavowal after one left.

The organisation was like a steep pyramid in which all matters for decision went up in a straight line to the apex that was the chairman. Down the line there were powers delegated to different levels, always jealously guarded by those who possessed them, and yet to the decision itself they somehow always managed to bring in someone else, preferably their senior, to share the burden, just in case anything went wrong. All decisions had a chance of being questioned one day, and in retrospect a quick bold decision could prove fatal. I was shown a circular that among other things advised decision makers to look carefully at a decision taken faster than at the normal speed. There could be a ground for suspicion. And yet many patently suspect decisions were taken, but so well camouflaged in rule and precedent that you could do nothing but in your frustration admire the ingenuity in the way the game could be played. The new head of administration, I discovered, distinguished himself in interpretation of the rule. Describing their library, consisting of a few thousand volumes, mainly government publications and fiction, he mentioned proudly that it had a staff of four, a senior librarian, a junior librarian, a clerk and a peon. I asked about the volume of work and found that on an average eighteen books were issued and received in a day. "I suppose," I said, "the work of our library had increased so much that you had to add a junior librarian." "No, Sir, we had to recruit a senior librarian, for there was already a junior librarian." I asked him how he managed to make a case for that. At this, he went out and proudly brought back a file on the library and showed me the pages that made out in serious perfection a case for strengthening the library staff. Corporations have to have books for reference by their staff, to enable them to keep up to date with the growing knowledge in their areas...at the same time it was necessary to provide the staff with general reading matter to improve their minds...the library was started with a meagre few hundred volumes but now it had grown to some thousand, thus showing a many hundred per cent progress, which is expected to continue...therefore, in prudent anticipation of yet further progress, it is recommended that the library staff be strengthened...

"But you must have had someone in mind for whom you wanted to provide a job," I hazarded as a bold guess.

He grinned knowingly. "But, Sir, all posts are created and filled in accordance with proper procedure. I know my rules." He seemed to be proud of his capacity to legitimise an illegitimate request, and equally to refuse to budge a hair breadth from the rules, when it suited him or someone.

And how well indeed they manipulated things, I discovered later. There was a system, for instance, for providing for sub-standard and unqualified protégés by taking them on temporarily, for which a separate rule relaxed the qualifications required for permanent employees. Both rules, perfectly valid, could be used as one wished. There was however no limit to how long a person could remain temporary, and a justification could be made time to time to continue the post, but only on a temporary basis. The person was given excellent reports for two or three years, and then, with as much insistence, it was recommended that a permanent post be created, and the temporary one was made permanent on the strength of his length of temporary service and good reports. Another person, who had no influence behind him, and was taken on temporarily, merely to circumvent the need to make out a case for a permanent post and seek the necessary sanction, could remain forgotten for years.

We decided that in future there should be no temporary posts created; people should only be taken against a justifiable need and through the proper selection procedure of qualifications and tests. In any case we were grossly overstaffed, especially at the clerical and peon levels. As for the existing temporaries, we decided to waive the entrance qualifications, which none naturally possessed, but to subject them to some test, though of a standard lower than the normal; and as a further concession we gave them up to three chances. One by one, all those who took the tests passed. Some preferred not to take the test but to leave, but ultimately we were left with a girl who failed each time. There was pressure from all quarters, including from a minister, to confirm her. I spoke to the personnel manager about her case, but what I discovered shook me.

"Can't you do something to close the chapter of temporaries; there is only this one girl left. Could you not give her some simple test that she could pass?"

"No," he said, looking acutely embarrassed.

"Why not," I pressed.

"Well, I will tell you the truth. The girl is barely literate so she cannot pass any test. She can read and write a little Urdu, but even in that I doubt if she could pass a test. For the past two years she has been coming to the office and spends her time knitting and talking. Everybody likes her, they understand her position, and she has been receiving good reports, so that in the normal course she would have been confirmed on the strength of the reports."

The place was full of persons placed by someone, somehow. It was the haven for those who could not qualify for entrance into the government services, where quite high standards prevailed and the competition to enter was stiff. It also proved a temporary haven at all levels for men on deputation from the ministries, till their turn came for promotion in their parent department. Here they could get a deputation allowance, and good reports; there was besides the much coveted foreign travel. I was reminded of a story that Bhagwan Sahay, who was then governor of Kashmir, told me. He asked me if it was true that I was joining STC, and when I said, yes, there was some talk of it, he said that it needed tidying up because it had become the refuge of those with influence who could not get in anywhere else. He had met someone at Delhi airport who was anxious to shift from a distant posting in Rajasthan to a more congenial place like Delhi or Srinagar. Bhagwan Sahay tried to put him off, as he considered him useless. When the man realised that Sahay would not help, he said in disgust that if there was no other place then he would have to get into STC; and he did.

Those who came in through the backdoor, in course of time developed their own vested interests, and demanded that the later deputationists be sent back, and we accept no one from outside. The most strident, not unexpectedly, were those who owed their own entry to influence, including a woman, who later led them. There was also a demand, at almost my first meeting with the officers, that I should introduce merit as a policy in place of seniority, as must have been the case in my old company. I agreed that I was brought up that way; but I asked whether in their culture they were ready for merit. They protested loudly that they were all in favour of merit, but a senior man, who was retiring soon, disagreed with them. He said they were not at all ready to accept merit in reality; it would be a case with them of merit when they have it and seniority when the other man has merit. He was right, I was to discover.

Upon joining it was suggested by the cabinet secretary that I should call on the prime minister. In the brief audience she gave me she mostly received little notes and scribbled back on them. This was a habit she shared with important persons in India; they usually go on with their work as they receive you, taking telephone calls, reading files, receiving their staff, and asking you to go on with what you have to say, which in my case was very little. She expressed the hope, as I was leaving, that I would introduce merit into the corporation; but she added that I would not find it easy to do so. She recalled an interesting incident that characterised a kind of approach to merit. When appointing someone, whom everyone considered suited to the job and had the right merit, she was reminded by a senior colleague quite earnestly that, "Madam, there could be other more important considerations in life than merit." She added with a smile, "one does not even know where to begin answering something like that."

I discovered that it was always the case of the rule when it was in their favour, and exception when the rule was against them. This would be understandable were it not for the protests that always came when someone else gained in the way they had tried to. Their pragmatic acceptance of really big influence however was interesting. The one who had it was envied, for the source and strength of influence was known to all. Curiously, it was better tolerated when it came from outside and especially from a high quarter; but any exercise of it from inside was regarded as unfair. That you could not resist pressure from outside was understandable—and there was always a give and take—but that you exercise it yourself, when no pressure was extended in favour of someone was not acceptable.

One of the first to call on me was the Russian trade commissioner, who had also joined the week before. He said it was a pure courtesy call, and as both of us were new to the job he would leave the business side to another occasion. I recalled my visit to Moscow and suggested that there must surely be some problems. It worked. He had come with a long carefully prepared list, and he went through it with diligence. It seemed the way to a Russian heart was through an invitation to complain. How very like us, I thought, for never did I discover from our own industry delegations anything but a meticulously drawn up list of all that was wrong. I suggested that all he said must be true if they as customers said so; but we must have a system to solve their problems. We would hold a monthly lunch meeting with the men concerned from both sides, with an agenda, and we would begin the next meeting with a review of past progress. This surprisingly simple kind of solution worked with both sides; and, as the trade commissioner said, not so much for the problems it solved at the meeting, but for what the staff on both sides settled in anticipation of their coming meeting.

K.B. Lall kept a close eye on me and made Alexander my wet-nurse. He was to see that with my private sector training I did not leave my decisions unrecorded and unguarded, so that years later they might be questioned. If there was no record to show how a particular decision was taken, the justification could go by default. The noting system could cover even a perverse decision with a lengthy recitation that at its weakest must at least admit some argument, whereas a good bold decision, poorly or simply recorded, stood no chance. I found too that the notes were made with such precision that they could begin with "the meeting was called by the Secretary in the Ministry of Foreign Trade on Monday 1st July 19 ...at 4 p.m., in the office of the Secretary at Udyog Bhavan, New Delhi, at which were present the following persons. The Secretary opened the meeting by stating...." I was informed that someone got into trouble because he had been unable to prove in his defence that his action was decided at a meeting, because no time and place of the meeting could be proved from the note he prepared.

At the beginning K.B. Lall used to often ring me about some good idea or another, and as he found me completely open to new ideas he felt encouraged, till I had to tell him one day that his ideas were generally good, and I was always a ready buyer of good ideas, but at this rate he would find me no use to him. He had brought me over to bring my ideas and not only for trying out his own. He laughed and saw the humour of it. He said he took the point readily, and must try out what I had to offer. From then on he began to listen to me, and would sometimes ask what my manager's mind would think of one of his own problems. I learned a good deal from him, especially from his capacity to look at a problem from its political and administrative angles. He would impress upon me that while we could not ignore in our society a century of good administration, at the same time, even though the political side of decision making was as yet relatively new, and sometimes immature, we have to learn to respect it and help it develop. Administration and politics were at the base of our Indian society. He was more understanding and genuinely tolerant of the politician than other administrators. He saw their foibles but also our need of them. He had genuine regard for the ministers he had served. For Dinesh Singh he had a special regard; he thought he was a gentleman and generous at heart.

My first experience of "Audit" was instructive. On the numerous checks made on an enterprise, Audit was a feared name; and yet not without its humour, if you could rise above your suffering. The audit men would arrive and begin a minute examination of all actions taken, decisions made to buy and sell, all contracts entered into; and as the audit took place usually three to five years later, sufficient time had elapsed to enable the auditors to show in retrospect that some at least of the myriad decisions taken were either wrong or could have been taken better. Then, why were they not? After the war between India and Pakistan in September 1965, when the field of action was Kashmir, the civil road traffic between Srinagar and Jammu had been disrupted at the time when the autumn walnut crop was ready to move down. Someone decided that to help the farmers, who usually owned a few trees each, STC, the only commercial organisation available to government, should buy up as much of the crop as possible and sell it in the Indian market. Of course in the bargain it was made to buy at a high price, to give the maximum help to farmers. It was therefore left with large stocks that it had to sell at low prices, and thus lost money. That the main purpose of timely help was served was of no concern to the young audit team leader. No, he said, why was the crop bought; was it bought in the ordinary course of STC's commercial operations? Was the price it paid and that at which it sold both commercially sound? The answer was an emphatic and honest no. Then why was it done? I explained that it must have been done under instructions from above. Were the instructions received in writing, and if they were, before taking action was the commercial unsoundness of the operation pointed out to the authorities concerned, in writing, and were clear instructions sought to proceed nevertheless? Was it also made clear in writing that there was going to be a loss, and the nature and likely extent of the loss, and was written sanction sought for it, and received? STC was an autonomous corporation, and its management surely must be expected to either act with commercial soundness, or seek clear instruction not to.

I put myself in the shoes of the man who had acted. If he had dotted all the 'i's and crossed the 't's, so meticulously pointed out by audit now, it would have taken months, and he would besides have been regarded as a pretty poor specimen of a trader! And I was amused too at the thought that some administrator would commit himself in writing to buy and sell with such patent commercial unsoundness, lose money, and take upon himself the risk of inviting the very audit questions that STC were now facing. He must have been wise enough to ring up someone in STC, and possibly followed it with a letter that left STC to decide—of course in the way that he meant it to! I remembered the letter of the Secretary to Hindustan Steel!

"Tell me," I asked the Auditor, "during the emergency of the war, is this the way you would have acted?"

He tried to equivocate. "Your question is theoretical; my task is only to point out, and it is for management to send its own explanation. I am not passing the final judgment."

"But you are exposing the management to the risk of being questioned by parliament, and do you think this is how STC will ever run as a modern, international trader, who will have to buy and sell on snap judgments, and yet be unafraid of buying badly if the market should go wrong?"

He was unmoved. He put in his audit para, though he did admit to me naively that he had to think of his career; objections sustained would go to his credit, and if not sustained at least to his watchfulness. And we—well, they all managed to explain things away; I need not take it too seriously!

Audit was like an angry and punishing god, who always found something wrong and breathed hard down those who had strayed from the straight and narrow path of the rule. What mattered to Audit was the rule, not even honest result. You could produce more, save more, spend less, earn more, but all that Audit set at nought if in so doing you had broken a rule. Utter lack of initiative and complete failure to reach goals was irrelevant, in fact you could feel righteous even be blessed for being mindful of public interest, so long as you stuck to the manual. Audit seemed to have spread such fear through the cumulative administrative memory of generations, reinforced by parliamentary control since Independence, that whatever innovation was suggested, the invariable reaction was—Audit will not allow it; questions will be asked. Always out of that memory a case was recalled where someone had broken the rule and lived to regret it.

Some years later, STC was caught doing in Andhra just what the young auditor had suggested it ought to have done in Kashmir. During my absence abroad it was asked to buy the left over unsaleable varieties of a tobacco crop in sufficiently large quantities to make a big impact on its prices, to please the local electorate in the elections due shortly, and to start doing it in a big way in three days. The exercise was meant not so much to favour the farmers, who had sold their crop already, as the politically influential tobacco traders, who wanted STC to buy it at inflated prices. Someone in STC agreed but asked for written instructions, because commercially it was not a particularly sound proposition, and added that at the quickest it would take a week or so to send men to that distant part of India and organise the operation, which covered a large area and involved many crores. There he went wrong. Did he mistrust those who gave him the orders, to want them in writing? Was this the speed at which the premier trading organisation of the country moved? Could he not act first and ask for instructions later? He did in fact act; the crop was bought, the "situation was saved"; but the instructions never came, and the man was called uncooperative, unimaginative and was transferred from the STC. As we rued our fate I remembered the young auditor.

I discovered that the questions Audit asked paled beside the questions that poured in daily when parliament was in session, for which a manager and a small staff were specially appointed. The questions covered almost the entire range of activities, and certainly kept the corporation and its management on its toes, though at some cost. Many of the questions were directed at me personally—my educational qualifications; my private sector past; my travelling abroad, its cost and the export orders I brought back; my relations with the ministry and its secretary, names of the foreign journals to which the corporation subscribed since my joining it, were some of the gentle ones and easier to answer.

A few months after joining, I put in an interim report of the Review Committee, and some months later, the final report. K.B. Lall said government would accept all the other thirtyeight recommendations, but not the one which suggested the appointment of a vice-chairman, who, apart from taking much routine off my hands, could provide succession, which is always the bane of most public undertakings. K.B. Lall was certain that this particular recommendation, logical though it was, would not find acceptance. When I pressed him he said that no minister with power to appoint would let pass the opportunity to appoint a chairman of his choice. Whatever the reason, STC thus took a year to find the chairman after I left, and it was common for public enterprises to have board and chairman's posts lying vacant for long, when retirements were known years ahead.

The sensitive and generous support I received from all of them, Dinesh Singh, K.B. Lall and Alexander from the start had perhaps proved costly, for it created a feeling lower down that it was at the cost of the power that they would normally have exercised over STC. The way power in this system is both diffused and concrete is interesting. It is exercised along a queue and not jointly in groups; and there is little participation, though some consultation. It is exercised under the rule and not towards a result. Even were it obvious that it would not produce the desired result, in fact possibly even a wrong result, it had still to be exercised in a given way. This was where my young auditor came in; he would object to not sticking to the rule, but not to lack of results. A man's job was to do a job, unconcerned with achievement.

I began to understand the soft options and the hard choices of a politician; the harm that can come out of the former and the good out of the latter. Curiously, in this culture there could be much tenderness towards a person, someone quite undeserving, but organisations somehow were regarded inanimate and did not evoke any sympathy, and could even be treated with callousness, without any regard for their growth or wellbeing. An organisation could be punished, it could not protest: if it ran down or collapsed—well, another could be set up. There was a curious lack of sensitivity towards the organisation. Was it, I wondered, because the administrators were for ever moving from one area to another, never staying long enough anywhere, and thus failed to acquire feelings towards organisations; or were they no longer trained to develop feeling, perhaps not even for administration itself? Were the new political masters without any feelings themselves for administration, and uninterested in keeping its edges sharp? Were the politicians or the administrators interested in training the young in new traditions and morals? The insensitiveness with which some politicians could run down the administration and the administrators, even their own men and organisations, and intrigue against them—their very wards with whose welfare they were charged, the contempt with which they called the administrator a bureaucrat, whenever they did not like him, it was all truly amazing. The men on whom they relied for their own success were the men they ran down. As a result the shrewder among the men were soon following the new mentors. Many young men used to come and see me to discuss their problems which they could not discuss with their own seniors, who did not, or perhaps could not, train and build the young with the care and sensitiveness that they themselves had received. My advice was always the same—keep your own cutting edges sharp for the day you will be in a position to cut well with them; don't let them become blunt through frustration, for one day you will be in a position to effect all the improvements that you advocate today.

☆

We developed a board like a constellation—stars of different magnitudes and all moving in the same direction. Fernandes, who was already in the STC, was a man of remarkable drive and optimism, whose hero was Tipu Sultan, on whom he wrote a book. He had unbounded imagination and the courage to break new ground, and was my early ally in change, Ramachandran, from Post and Telegraph, was cautious and austere and provided a ballast. I used him for trade with East Europe, on which he was experienced, and Fernandes for new ventures like engineering exports. The next to join was Bhalla, from Indian Audit and Accounts Service, mild, willing to learn, and made his finance division absorb all the new systems and ideas needed to convert it into a modern management accounts unit, which helped STC to take the burden of its growth.

Sarin, who next joined, also came from Audit and Accounts, and had worked in the public sector for a number of years. He had just returned from a year of Harvard, and had perhaps the clearest and toughest mind of them all. Nath, a Ph.D. in econometrics, came from Hindustan Lever, where from economics he had moved to buying and then to marketing. A young man by name Misra came from a small British firm.

They formed as good a board as I have seen anywhere, of men so disparate and yet well combined as a team, with basic value systems and no particular interpersonal problems. The total board, which had in addition representatives of various ministries, was also harmonious, and gradually delegated many of its powers to the working directors.

Soon after joining STC in 1968, I had outlined my plans to the ministry to leave the corporation for three months in 1970 in order to accept a teaching invitation at Berkeley. It would be useful to let the corporation run on its own momentum, and on my return I would be ready to start grooming someone to take over, but in any case I would like to leave at the latest at the end of four years instead of the contracted five, preferably earlier.

Before I left early in October 1970, there was a short, sharp staff problem. It began with the new system of taking in a dozen or so management trainees every year to provide fresh blood. Added to it soon was another problem, the anathema of Indian labour, the computer. Our growing volume of international contracts and backup suppliers' contracts had to be put on a computer to process the large amount of data generated. To this there was a violent objection. As these problems were being resolved in the ordinary course, the newly active officers' association got involved and the issues became mixed up.

The officers' associations, comprising the junior and middle ranking manager, were a new phenomenon, peculiar to the public sector, originating vaguely perhaps in the ICS Association, which was however a gentlemanly annual get-together, more like the regimental reunion dinners, at which some reference was made to the state of the service.

These new associations flourished rapidly in the public sector. Officer staff felt they were being increasingly pressed from below by the increasing belligerence of the labour unions, who demonstrated with violence. The unions were encouraged by political parties and so always won their point, and no action was ever taken against their misdeeds. From above, the officers felt unsupported. They began to feel isolated, and were often humiliated by the men, while senior management could not help them, particularly as after each strike there was a standard clause in the agreement that there would be no victimisation, which in effect meant that no action could be taken for the most flagrant breach of discipline or insults to officers. Management was usually helpless, either because it was weak or was under pressure from the top to settle, as it was a foregone conclusion that management must give in, in the name of justice. The officers therefore began to seek protection in organising themselves, and they too turned to the politicians for support; and soon they were also demanding and protesting in the same way as their men had demanded and protested. There were enough men in their ranks who had been promoted from below, with experience in demanding and protesting. There was at first some hesitation among the directly recruited officers about whether and how to protest, but soon the men who had come up from the ranks took the lead in establishing new methods of demanding and protesting, till some of the officers' "charters of demands" read like the workmen's union manifestos, as also their protest slogans and their method of delivery.

Things in STC had been simmering for some months, the officers not quite knowing what they wanted except "justice and fairness," generally meaning more and quicker promotions, with as little induction of officers from outside as possible, and a straight line automatic promotion by length of service. They were led by a redoubtable lady, quick, intelligent, in size and proportions a natural leader. We would often have chats on merit, on which we both agreed; but pressed by her followers for seniority she had to support this too. She suggested to me that I should follow the example of an earlier chairman, whom she regarded the best chairman STC ever had. He believed in both seniority and merit, and at the same time, so that if he felt that the tenth man on the seniority list was the one with merit he would promote all ten. The nine senior to him were happy to receive the promotion, eight of them unexpectedly, and the tenth he put where he needed the merit. Thus he made everybody happy. She waited expectantly for my approbation; instead I made some trite remark like, "What about the organisation?"

Leaders of the staff association and the union decided to throw in their lot with each other, and as this was the week before I was to leave for Berkeley, both sides must have felt that this was the right time, and hell was let loose, both at the office and upon my house.

In the same week our younger son Gautam, a young cavalry captain got married, and we were holding a small reception at our house. The union men arrived in several hired trucks, just before the guests were due, and lined up in front, complete with the large, lugubrious Punjabi drum that is slung from the shoulder and beaten on the sides with two sticks. With great Punjabi lustiness they beat the drum to a dirge that invoked death for me, followed by rhythmic beating of their breasts in a Punjabi siapa, as if their wish had already been fulfilled. The invocation for my death would start again and be followed by the dirge: all this to add their own contribution of a funeral oration to the felicitations that the young newly-weds were expecting from the guests. In between there would be protest passages about management trainees and the computer, and then they switched to English, lacing it with much abuse and invective. My wife and I came out to present ourselves, because there had been a telephone call from their president, a member of parliament, to warn me of the demonstration. He had genuinely protested, he told me, when he learned about the wedding reception, and had made them agree to disperse as the guests arrived. It might however be helpful, he suggested, if I went out and met them for a moment so that they would feel rewarded for being noticed, but of course I must ring back if they did not look like keeping their promise. He had also taken the precaution of asking the nearby police station to send an officer and a posse of police just in case things got out of hand. As we appeared there was a shout that rose to a crescendo, and happy, laughing, transformed in a moment from demons to children, they broke off. Their cheer leader came forward to shake hands and now offered congratulations to the young couple, after having earnestly wished Gautam paternally orphaned. It was no different at the office. There was much shouting, yelling, musical instruments and drums, and muck dumped on the board floor, all of which puzzled the foreign visitors, and particularly those from the communist countries.

Everybody had made his point. The next day an agreement was signed. It was all over. When I reached office, the whole place had been cleaned up, the broken plant pots replaced, and the dignified calm of an international trading corporation had descended. And the victorious lady gave me a disarming smile. The leadership proved itself once again by successfully leading them through a struggle to the end, including a morcha—they had led a sortie and infested my house.

I went to say farewell to K.B. Lall, and he asked me what had happened. I explained that it was an expression of a protest against me alone, for the two years of strain that the organisation had been through, the change I had introduced, and the pace I had stepped up before going away for three months. They had accepted it all with more willingness and grace than I would have expected in many other organisations, but a point had to be made, and they made it, and I heard it. The organisation could freewheel for a time, and I did not think he would have any problem in my absence. This had been a protest against me alone.

☆

Berkeley was one of my moratoriums, and a recharging experience. The student unrest, whose first signs I had seen at Los Angeles three years earlier, had burst and reached its peak in the spring quarter of 1970. In the autumn quarter, when I joined, it was quiet and calm.

I was received at Berkeley by two friends I had made in New Delhi, Alice Ilchman who came in 1968 as director of the Berkeley group at Delhi, and her husband, Warren, who had taken a year's sabbatical. They introduced me to a big group of their faculty friends; in particular, Philip Lilienthal, director of the University of California Press, his wife, Sally, a sculptor, and Leo Rose, the specialist on the three Himalayan Kingdoms of Nepal, Bhutan, and Sikkim (the latter has now progressed to the status of a state). Philip had taken a chance on publishing a new edition of *Punjabi Century,* following upon its earlier editions from London and New York.

Berkeley's rise in the post-war world had a special significance for India, because it had trained the largest number of young Indians of any university abroad, especially in science, and still the largest contingent among its foreign students came from India. Many Berkeley scholars had worked in India with an interest that matched and exceeded the interest the British once displayed during their connection. If the British had worked hard on their Gazeteers, the Americans took up such narrow subjects as the growth of the families of a small Punjabi village over a hundred years, as they spread all over the world. I asked this particular young scholar why he had chosen this village, and he told me that he had married one of its Sikh girls who was researching around. Another was doing research on the Gadar movement, before the first world war, a subject little worked on in India, and he had built a whole library on the subject. A third spent his young life, that he ended abruptly in the U.P., working on Munshi

Prem Chand and translating his works into English. But this scholarship was now on the wane because our new rules progressively froze them out. When I visited Berkeley two years later there was only a trickle of exchanges left, and their scholars were turning to Africa, China and Russia. The British, French and Germans had lost interest in India many years ago, the Russians were never interested, the Chinese were cut off from us, and now we decided we did not need the American scholars.

There may have been political and rational reasons for our academic isolationism of the late 1960s, but to me the interesting part was perhaps the envy of our own academics, who began to feel that the American scholars were intruding on their ground, with vastly more funds. But were many among our academics really interested in research? This was a question that was never examined. Few academics in India produce, and as a whole they hardly ever suffer from the threat of "produce or perish." Much teaching is still from books only, and the output from our institutions of excellence is sadly small. And when they do produce, it is mainly a collection of articles or readings. There must, of course, have been Americans who descended on India without much feel for their subjects, or much scholarship, but with ample funds; but there were many more whose contribution was real and substantial on subjects that did not seem to interest our scholars, at least then. In the end, what put the lid down firmly was, I believe, the rule that a student coming to India to research for a degree from his own university abroad should not only work under an Indian faculty, but that their veto could debar his own university from awarding him a degree. We also began to ban entry on one ground or another. A brave young diplomat tried to get permission for Stanley Wolpert, the author of the banned "Nine Hours to Rama," professor of Indian history at Los Angeles, to direct the Berkeley group in Delhi, but failed. Even his sensitive book on Morley, sympathetic to India, did not move the authorities. Wolpert was told that he was of course always welcome to come as a tourist. There was much talk of their anti-Indian writings, their lack of understanding and misrepresentation of India, and of course the CIA, now charged by the American press with infiltrating the Peace Corps. Was the truth perhaps that having received so much aid and food over the years, the sheer weight of gratitude had somehow to be compensated, and we perhaps over-compensated.

Towards the end of my stay, young Indians began to drop in with the expected question; but this time there was a difference. Many had settled down or were in the process of doing so, and there was less talk of going back; others, and a much larger number this time, who were planning to return, had decided to start their own businesses, and were saving enough capital and looking for some process collaboration. What worried them however was the talk they heard and reports in the press and speeches about delays and the graft needed to get through the maze of permits and licenses. For a license to produce, to acquire land, to get power, water, telephone, finance, raw materials; for every step forward they had to pay. But there was nevertheless greater confidence among them, and the problems they took as so many challenges.

CHAPTER SEVENTEEN

Portrait of a Minister

I was in Moscow in the summer of 1970, staying with D.P. Dhar, our ambassador, when the news came of a major cabinet reshuffle, and I found a change in my own ministry, the third in two years. The new minister was L.N. Mishra, whom I had never met. I therefore asked Dhar how I would find him as my minister, especially after Dinesh Singh and Bhagat, with both of whom I had got on well; both predictable men, though at varying depths. He smiled. "You will have no trouble with him at all. He will always have a big hug and a broad smile for you. There may be a message to give help here and there to someone interested in an import license or a job; and so long as you help you will have no problem. None, at all," he added with emphasis. It was my first experience of dealing with a real politician. Not a regular civil servant, and unused to dealing with political personalities, I was diffident at the thought of having to learn to deal with my third new minister in two years. I felt uneasy starting on the journey home, afraid that in my relations with the ministry I would now have to cope with political factors, something I found unfamiliar and distasteful. I had come to STC to offer my managerial skills and not to cope with politics for which I was plainly unsuited. As it turned out, while I found it somewhat difficult, but less than I expected, to deal with Mishra, I was always in a state of silent conflict with his in-group, whose non-standards and non-concern with international trade was accompanied by some involute ways.

On return to Delhi there was a message asking me to meet Shri L.N. Mishra, the new minister for foreign trade, for which would I make an appointment through his personal assistant. In this environment no one at a level senior to you would ring and introduce himself, or send a short note with a word of welcome; the custom was to leave it to the personal assistants to arrange for someone's presence. "The honourable minister will speak to you," would be the peremptory demand of his secretary over the telephone.

Early next morning I rang up Harish Sarin, secretary in the defence ministry. I asked him what he thought of his old minister, and he described the man and his style with his characteristic clarity and forthrightness. Harish had learnt something about me from his younger brother, Mahesh, who after a particularly rough passage in two public enterprises had joined as one of our directors, and seemed to have settled well. Harish told me I was not going to find the going familiar or easy, for of all the ministers he had worked under in his long years in Delhi, even including Krishna Menon, Mishra was the only one with whom he did not know how to build an equation. "I don't think I ever satisfied him," said Harish, "I wonder if I would even know how to. He is warm, effusive; but let not that worry you. With your lack of understanding of our administrative and political ways, with your sensitiveness and your management style—well, you will find it, let us say, interesting; and I wish you luck."

Apprehensive, I walked into the minister's room, where I had so often breezed in confidently in the past, during and before STC. Mishra was of medium height, round, with a short thick neck accentuated by a closed collar coat, and a tooth-brush moustache. He gave me a wan smile as he half rose to offer a soft limp hand. He received me without any special warmth, and began to question me perfunctorily and absently, while he talked to his deputy minister. I explained a little about my background; that I had only been in STC for two years and was not a regular public sector man. He cut me short; he knew all about that, he said. How was STC doing?

"Doing reasonably well," I said. "It could be better but of course it has been growing fast."

"Have you any problems?"

"Not particularly; and if I did I would try not to trouble you with them."

"Oh, why not?"

"Well, they would be for me to solve, and I would not like to worry you."

This seemed to puzzle him.

The conversation continued desultorily for a few minutes and then he waved me out, and continued to talk with his deputy. It was one of the very few business conversations we had of such length. With the same sick feeling in my stomach that I had walked in, I walked out, bracing myself for an unfamiliar kind of experience ahead.

I went into K.B. Lall's room, and with his usual cheeriness he asked me to tell him how the first meeting went. I said, badly; I had left him unimpressed. I don't think he needs a manager; he needs a minion, a tool for I don't know what. Lall became serious and asked me to sit down. He could guess how we had reacted to each other, he said, but one had to realise that here we had a new sort of person to deal with. He would not have Dinesh Singh's ways, and considering their backgrounds one would not expect them to have much in common. He would be different also from Bhagat who again, though unlike Dinesh Singh, would allow himself to be persuaded, if one disagreed with him convincingly enough. Here was someone who would be determined to have things his own way. Recovering his cheerfulness, he added, things will undoubtedly be different, but we must wait and jump to no conclusions. If I was depressed, my curiosity was also aroused at this new challenge of the public sector.

Dinesh Singh was basically shy and somewhat unsure of himself. Product of an old U.P. family, Doon School and the Indian Foreign Service, he had the merit unusual in our seniors and mentors, especially politicians, of being a good listener. He both spoke well and listened well, with sensitiveness to a word or phrase that made me feel greatly at ease with him from the start. He was however deceptively mild and could take a hard political decision.

Bhagat too was gentlemanly, well read and willing to listen.

A few days later Lall said to me with a touch of seriousness, instead of his customary facetiousness, that I had been right, my first meeting did go badly and I certainly had not impressed that minister. I was not alone in this; he too was having problems. The minister wanted K.B. Lall's additional secretary transferred—right away. K.B. had tried to explain that an official could always be transferred—it was the prerogative of a minister—but when an official had a good record a hasty transfer could cast an undeserved shadow over his reputation, apart from leaving him discouraged. One should find a suitable place for him first and then make the move, rather than removing him from the job summarily. The desired end could be achieved without causing harm to the individual. But as Lall had expected, this did not work; the man was transferred, and so was he himself not long afterwards. Although he put on a brave face, I knew that he was hurt and disappointed, particularly as there was emerging a new group in the ministry who had begun spreading the whisper around that it would next be his turn to move; that it was now the turn of the Brahmins in place of the Mathurs.. A number of secretaries were also moved around at that time, on the ground that they had been in the same ministry for too long. Lall had been in the ministry for over ten years, except for a three-year break as ambassador at Brussels, to Belgium and to the increasingly important Common Market. In the defence ministry, to which he was now moved, he succeeded Harish Sarin. The latter had been there for over twenty years. It made sense to introduce new blood, given good administrative reasons, but many would not see it that way. I wrote a letter congratulating him. I was very sad to lose him; after all I had come over only because he had asked me to. I was certain that he would bring fresh air into defence and would soon be immersed in a job so entirely new to him that he would be glad of the change. In any case, I added, it was time he moved because the answers and solutions were coming far too readily to him. But, under it all, I knew that while as a man of much strength of character he would under most circumstances have taken his transfer well, in this particular case there would be left a nagging doubt in his mind that though defence might need him, he was certainly being rejected by foreign trade's new minister.

When I suggested to him that perhaps the minister might want to shorten my tenure and select a person of his own choice, he reacted right away. "No," he said, "although I do see your point, the organisation needs you for some time yet. In any case, it is best not to suggest it because he will most likely take advantage of your offer. He must already have someone in mind. Let us leave it over till after you return from Berkeley, and I will support your other suggestion to test out Praxy Fernandes, one of STC directors, to act as chairman." It appeared the minister did have someone in mind and felt thwarted that Fernandes' recommendation had already been made. I believe he wanted it to be withdrawn and to make his own recommendation. There was an impasse, but through Lall's insistence Fernandes acted as chairman from the start although the official confirmation did not arrive till near the end. As it cannot have added to K.B. Lall's acceptability with Mishra, and it must have been one more reason for his own departure, I was a little surprised, and touched, that he should have so perserved.

Upon my return from Berkeley I found STC in good shape. Despite some differences among the directors the team and the systems had worked well. Praxy had proved a good leader. Although in his first big command his "up guards and at 'em" approach had not been quite the style of the others, he was dynamic and well-meaning, and all went off well.

Just as we were starting my first committee of management meeting a telephone call came from the minister. After a perfunctory notice of my return, he told me that he was fed up with Fernandes, who refused to do what he had asked him to. I said I would look into it and report back. It was a case of a promotion sought by someone, denied for good reasons, but brought to the minister's attention as an injustice.

Praxy's problem with the minister during my absence was interesting as an example of how we can be carried away by a story of injustice without knowing or finding out the other side. A young man in STC had approached the Chief of Army Staff, under whom he had served, and asked him to speak to the minister of a grave injustice done to him, an opportunity denied because of a bad annual report, which had been given deliberately after the good one he had received the year before. General Manekshaw must have spoken to the minister, who spoke to Praxy. Praxy tried to explain, but no one was interested. Since no action was taken, the young man must have reminded the general, who prodded the minister, apparently adding that the minister's writ did not seem to run far in his own corporation. Praxy contacted the general and tried to explain, but again with no success. Everyone was convinced that there had been injustice, and it had to be put right. By now the young man, the chief of staff and the minister were all feeling frustrated. I must have arrived at the flash point, when I took the telephone call from the minister. I told Praxy not to worry, I would see the general myself. He grinned with relief.

It was strange, I thought, that such a small matter could ever grow big enough to engage such senior attention.. Praxy was generous to a flaw, and though a man of clear likes and dislikes he was just and fair, and had in this case gone out of his way to help. And yet no one believed him, the acting chairman of one of the largest corporations of India, or even asked him for the facts; so convinced was everyone of injustice.

I decided to see Manekshaw, soon to be the hero of the third Pakistan war of 1971. Fresh and trim, immaculately uniformed, he received me openly, without condescension, but with his own touch of drama. I said I had come to see him because Fernandes did not seem to have been able to convince him that the young man had not been unfairly dealt with. The general declared himself convinced that an injustice had been done, because he knew the young man was good material. The same man who had given a good report the previous year had now given a bad report, which looked like deliberate downgrading. He spoke crisply and confidently, as he had no doubt about the only version he had heard. I said I could appreciate how he felt about injustice to others, as he had once himself been unjustly treated. If this surprised him he did not show it. In fact, my heart had gone out to him when during Krishna Menon's regime in defence he had been nearly asked to leave the army on some spurious and naive grounds that he was overly British and therefore of dubious loyalty to India as a soldier. I suggested to Manekshaw that I would send him the confidential reports of the man for the last two years. I would then come back, and accept his judgment. "Fine," said the general, "that is good of you."

I had read the two reports, written by the same man, and found them entirely fair, consistent and sympathetic, bringing out both the strength and the weakness. The earlier report had also touched upon the weakness.

I saw Manekshaw again a few days later. He received me with much warmth this time and said he had read the file, and agreed with us. He was sorry that the young man had not responded to what we had tried to do for him. He would say no more. I thanked him for his generosity. I would still help the young man because he was indeed good material. "With all the regard and respect he has for you, it might help if you speak to him," I suggested. "You bet I will," replied Manekshaw.

As I shook hands with him, I added that he had acted just as I had hoped. I had a young son in the army, and I felt reassured. At this he seemed surprised and pleased. It was encouraging to think how little it took to change the environment, in which far too often the judgement was handed out with the charge.

I explained to the minister that I had spoken to Manekshaw, who was now satisfied. The minister was satisfied too, so long as he would not be reminded about it. Soon, he stopped sending men for favours because the men he sent were usually not the kind who made the grade. He realised that I was not prone to asking for or granting favours; though I don't know whether he appreciated such independence. It seemed out of place in an environment in which, like a joint family grid, favours done and favours asked were a natural exercise of any power one possessed. He must have had demands on him all the time. Relations and friends, and other who need little things, and increasingly the not so little, always turn to whoever has the capacity to favour, for a job, a promotion, a transfer, to withhold the retribution of the just consequence of a wrong action, to grant a contract, a licence, a permission out of turn and at the expense of someone else. For a whole range of favours, whose common denominator is always a preference shown, people ran to members of the power grid to put in a word to someone, if that someone was higher than them, to speak to him if he was below them, or just tell him if he was well below, and if he was too far below then to have him spoken to. There was a well defined and demarcated system of hierarchy in the method of approaching, which had been refined into an art. The telephone call, the personal visit, if the matter was very important, and sometimes even a dinner invitation, were all well timed, neither too soon nor too late. Equally, persuasion was well balanced between a hint and a demand, sometimes a feather touch and sometimes the sledgehammer. The timing was usually flawlessly coincidental. The message would come just as the file containing the case reached the table. In such cases the help of someone lower down had of course already been invoked to create the coincidence. The personal assistant of one would ask the personal assistant of the other when the file would be put up, and upon the tip-off arrange the phone call. It was not unknown for a senior minister to ring up someone for the appointment of a peon or watchman.

There were usually two styles of approach, the simple and the sophisticated, the direct and the indirect. The simple, direct approach, common among the politicians, high or low, could be utterly direct and simple, depending upon the power he backed it with, and consisted of just asking for something to be done, exactly in a certain way, with no quarter given and no reasons accepted for your inability to do it; these were merely regarded as excuses. "You didn't want to do it and you have not done it; you could have done it if you had wanted to do it!" The sophisticated approach, exercised by some, usually the administrators, was the gentle approach of leaving you to decide—but, of course, in a certain way; their way. In between the two were the personal styles and nuances, but in the end, if you joined in, they all added up to a plain give and take, a mutuality of interests, a candid sharing of the fruits of power in a net of self-help. There was Mishra's in-group: if you joined it, pressure did not need to be exercised, because you were a part of it and had accepted it as a way of life; you did what you were asked to do and in return asked for what they could do, each unto the best of his ability, which meant to the outermost circumference of your power, and even in the penumbral region beyond. In the circumstances, the desire for the justice that everybody wanted was self-defeating. They were all seeking justice, removing injustice—like poverty. It was argued that if you left it to merit alone, and did not take the precaution of shoring it up with whatever influence and power you could muster, no matter how strong your own case, someone else's might have been leavened with influence, and together the combination would outweigh your merit alone.

There were exceptions. When I said farewell to Dinesh Singh, as I was leaving for a trip to the East and Australia, and he was on the point of being transfered, though this I did not know, he asked me if I would look at a young man in the ministry whose chances in the government setup were limited. I said, "Yes, we would be glad to look at him, but may I suggest that while we would feel glad to do what we can, I hope we will not be made to feel bad if we are unable." Dinesh never sent him or anyone else.

On the other hand, a member of parliament, who kept ringing me, always before I was awake, about a young man who had applied for a job, flared up when I told him that another thousand boys had applied for that job and were taking the tests; all had a right to be considered. What more than his right was this boy asking for, he thundered. In a free country had he not the fundamental right to employment, which even the constitution assured everyone; was he not merely demanding his right to a job; was he not qualified for it; by what justice could I deny him that right? Men like me had no sense of justice, fairness, national feeling—and he enumerated all he felt I lacked. Men like me should not be where we were; we still clung to an antiquated, slavish past. I had no answer to his logic; besides he was privileged, I was not. And his patience seemed exhausted; mine could not afford to be.

In the midst of our new management trainees selection scheme, for which a refined, modern three-tiered system had been introduced, Mishra rang up Mahesh Sarin, in charge of it, and said, "What is this newfangled scheme you have introduced? What do you need—first class graduates, sportsmen, with extra-curricular activities; how many do you need—ten? I will send you ten with all these qualifications—no, I will send you twenty so that you even have a choice. What more do you want? I don't see the point of all this fuss and expense!"

The way a favour was asked certainly had its own logic, presented irrefutably.

There was of course the lighter side too, as when a minister, not known to me, rang up and spoke most affably.

"Ah, Mr. Tandon, how are you."

"Well, Sir, and you too, I hope."

"No, haven't you read in the papers; I had a severe heart attack, very severe, and I only came out of the hospital yesterday."

I politely apologised and agreed suitably.

"Yes, and as I left the hospital, the doctor told me to be more careful in every way."

I was now beginning to guess.

"He told me to ride in a very smooth car, not our Ambassador; the jolting would not be good for me."

I now knew just what was coming.

"A friend advised me therefore to go in for an imported car—what is its name, Mercedes or something. Will you please see to it that the STC releases a good recent model."

To the politicians and businessmen of a kind, an imported Mercedes was the symbol of power and success. The politicians got it through the exchequer at a favoured price; the businessmen bid for it through their firms at our auctions and paid lakhs of rupees. The poor man died soon afterwards, even with the well sprung car.

Lalit Narain Mishra, my minister, a middle class village brahmin, whose upbringing and education must have given him a directness, but not scholarship, was purely political, suffering few inhibitions. His likes and dislikes were never in half measures. Placed in a job, next only to foreign affairs in sophistication, his foreign trade portfolio demanded an understanding of the world of business and international trade, while his own horizon spanned from provincial politics in Patna to national politics in Delhi, and to the commerce and industry of Coimbatore, Surat, Ludhiana and Kanpur. Bombay and Calcutta he did not care for. Into this world, like the depths of the seabed, no light of the wider world penetrated. He was elemental and earthly. It was as interesting to see him at a meeting with politicians from his home as with a foreign ministerial delegation on international trade. At the ballet in Moscow, he yawned through the Swan Lake and left before the interval. He was essentially a Bihari living in India, now drawn to an international trade scene, with no concessions made to what was not Bihari. A man all of a piece, his grain ran consistently and predictably one way. He was truer though than some other sophisticated politicians.

Slowly he granted me an easy familiarity. I would see him with or without appointment, but we did not discuss the intricacies of foreign trade; and looking back I cannot even recall whether we discussed trade at all. The meetings were usually to convey some information he wanted from my side, to explain something. Sometimes I asked him to desist from something, to go easy with STC. He seldom sought my advice, but he always listened. I would occasionally tell him about the results, and he was content to know that everything was going well. He wanted, above all, no problems in STC, and once when we had some staff trouble and I wanted to take clear and firm action, he told me to go ahead so long as I could contain it. "Bhai Tandon, peace buy karo," was his simple advice to me, "Make sure they don't take a procession to parliament or to her house." He seemed however to like his relationship with me, and showed almost visible pride in the presence of some colleague in my partly familiar but impeccably correct and circumspect manner, implying both respect and equality. It was an unfamiliar combination to him, and he seemed to like it.

But there was a court. His bulky soft figure, especially when he sat with his legs drawn up on the sofa, dressed in loose starched kurta and dhoti, was like a zamindar rajah, an interesting contrast to Dinesh Singh who was a zamindar rajah but played a changed role. Having lived as a boy in an Indian state, Bahawalpur, medieval except for the Rolls Royces, I could understand the culture of a court, where people moved in convolutions, which mostly achieved so little that they appeared to be made for their own sake.

Trusting in his own way, at least when things went well, he seemed by nature to put more trust in luck and omen and in lesser men than in a confident self-reliant course. Among themselves, his in-group were a disparate lot with talents that, had they been used to help him grow into a bigger man, might have taken him further than to his early abrupt end. In a modern language these men practised an old art of statecraft, in which the world of international trade played no role except to provide a good life at home and abroad. The trusting way in which he let himself be influenced and even moulded puzzled me. According to an apocryphal story, he was asked once to cut someone down to size. He obliged, and afterwards asked if they were satisfied. He was assured that he had done it extremely well. "But what had the man done?" he enquired naively. In my own presence he once remarked, as if tutored, "Yes, yes, we will have to provide for some direct control over STC, for the time when Mr. Tandon is there no longer." It was a hint I was supposed to take while I was there.

Curiously, Mishra was a good friend of Manekshaw, presumably since his days in the defence ministry, and they both had an easy familiarity that superficially lacked logic. Theirs was a case of differences reconciled; something common among us. Mishra seemed to like calling Manekshaw Sam and Manekshaw calling him Lalit, both slightly mispronouncing. The trim, moustached, heavily British-accented general, who could have fought at Balaclava, Oomderman, Amiens or Chhamb, and the soft Maithili politician, on first name back-slapping terms, was indeed a combination not easy to understand. I saw it as the contradiction common among some of our public men, who often contradicted in behaviour what they expounded; and there was, I think, also our propensity towards synthesising our contradictions. Mishra was an old type in a new situation and Manekshaw a new type in an old situation. And yet the two were so utterly different that they hardly seemed to belong to the same country.

I was reminded of what a Yugoslav had once said to a young man at the Indian embassy at Belgrade, when they were entertaining a visiting group of politicians. He had always wondered whether in India we had two different kinds of people. "They don't dress like you, they don't look like you, they don't talk like you, they don't eat like you, and yet they are Indians and so are you."

Perceptibly the pressure mounted on STC, and I could feel the growing effort needed to protect it. It began with a whispering campaign that STC was becoming too big and complex, and its present autonomy ought to be curbed for its own sake. Government, ought to have a greater say in its day to day affairs. A note was prepared to effectively control it, through the device that all contracts above a quite low value limit should be negotiated with the concurrence of the ministry, whose representative should be associated with all negotiations at all stages. This did not strike only at the root of STC's autonomy but at any speed and flexibility it had acquired lately through its reorganisation, especially when dealing abroad.

A New York oilseeds broker told me that STC had in the past always paid more because a firm abroad had to take in a cushion to allow for market movements during the fortnight it took it to decide, where others decide in hours. "When STC decides to buy 'quickly' on a Monday, by the time the office has prepared the note and cleared it through finance it may be Thursday, at the earliest. Then, as the message is sent by telegram, because STC does not even possess a telex, we receive it on Friday, when again no broker will quote readily without a cushion because he does not know how the markets will open after the weekend, and add a little more again because there are more procedures to go through."

Since then STC had acquired a telex and a speedy system to decide; and a branch office in New York: and now to have to refer every transaction to the ministry and associate its man, who for his own safety would understandably take all the precautions he considered necessary, would mean an even slower process of buying than the one that used to prevail. It would be back to before square one.

A question that someone had asked me at an early stage in STC, at a manager's conference at Srinagar, began to return to my mind. How much of what I built would last? I began to wonder now whether anything one builds and grows that the soil and environment will not accept, can endure? And what could STC alone do in face of such opposition to change? This question was often asked me as an early change agent in the public sector; some were convinced it could not be done, others wished me well; few indeed had shared my quiet optimism, certainly not those who loudly proclaimed their faith in it. The pious and vocal advocates often took up safe perches, and from there passed judgements on the public sector.

Out of the blue, late one evening, seemingly well timed, someone rang up to say that orders had just been signed to relieve me of two of my directors, because they had not exercised their option to stay permanently in STC or return to their government departments. The third was on the list; the fourth Praxy Fernandes, had already wisely decided to return to government. Thus I would be picked clean of my team, so carefully built, and in return have one of their choosing imposed upon me. It was an effective way of emasculating STC; first its power to decide, and now its leadership.

I rang Mishra immediately and said I was coming over to see him. He replied, uncertainly, that he hoped not over this matter. I said, please, it is over this; and in a few minutes I was in his office. He did not quite seem to know how to cope with a situation that I was convinced was not of his making; nor perhaps to his liking, though he visibly disliked some of the directors. I met him several times that week till he decided to say yes to me. I think we were both defeated in our own ways. I certainly felt defeated and was convinced that I was needed no longer; a rot had set in, whatever the ostensible reason he was proceeding to dismantle the board for faults that were in fact its strength.

Next week, the crisis over for the time, I wrote him a short letter addressing him for the first time by his first name, in my own hand, to say that I had tried hard to satisfy but had failed; I had done my best by STC and by him; I would appreciate if he would now let me go. There was no rancour in my resignation, only a touch of deep sadness. I wished him well in his future and in his own career. I do not know if he referred the letter anywhere higher, and was told to stay his hand, or felt in his own interest that my departure should not be sudden, and I should stay a while longer; but he rang me up with great effusiveness, anxious that I should stay. I said, yes, for his sake, but only for another two months. He then wrote a warm letter, also by my first name, and thanked me. I warmed up towards him. If the in-group was thwarted, he at least went up in my estimation.

Two months later, after running in the year's results, seemingly to his satisfaction, I left. He arranged one of his weekly officers' meetings for the day I left and made a warm reference at the end of it to my departure; and within his ministry and outside he asked people to suggest a "new chairman like Tandon." I thanked him.

A week later they struck at all three directors, and then at STC. News came daily in the press about all that was wrong with it—a sudden and complete disavowal of what was after all the ministry's own corporation; a public excommunication of its own child. The profits duly audited and approved by both the external and government's own auditors were considered suspect. Someone was even sent to Bombay to look for incriminating material against STC, preferably against me. The press built it up and made it worse by suggesting that the directors should be taken back. I remembered the words of Praxy Fernandes, later to become the Director General of the Bureau of Public Enterprises, and one genuinely devoted to the cause. "No, Prakash, I cannot stay in STC; who knows what will happen one day when you have gone. There is as yet no basic security." He was not the kind that looked for security in the ordinary way; and yet his deep emotional faith in the public sector, for which he was well cut out, could not give him the confidence to stay and make a career of it. I could only repeat to him what I had once said to someone in Unilever, that Rome began to decline when its young patricians refused to live on their estates but wanted to run them from the security and comforts of Rome itself.

Curiously, despite the seeming irrationality of it, I found faith to impel me to persevere with the public sector. It was there, it had a future, and someone had to serve it; otherwise it would not have a future, it would not even be there. The early days of Indianisation in a multinational had not been easy; and it was early days for professional management in the public sector.

Mishra had something in him that, despite the worst storm ever faced by a minister in parliament, had the makings of something bigger than what some of his wellwishers would have him be. He was essentially a gentle and superstitious man, but with the great asset of determination. He hitched his wagon to the star with unshakable faith and fidelity, beyond which he had little to offer. His ambition was to serve. And who knew what the distant future might have held. So long as his patron saints and the astrologers were happy, he was content to serve and wait, propitiating them and the gods, both of whom ultimately cast him aside. He moved on and moved up—and beyond! His violent death brought surprisingly little comment which understood the man. Beyond some trite sympathy and condemnation of violence, no contribution was recalled, as if none was found. Some recognition came later in the changed ambience of the Emergency, when an attempt was made to place a mantle of martyrdom on him. He left behind a big question mark, and on my mind he left more than a scratch.

On my arrival at Bombay in January 1971, from Berkeley, I had called on Ravi Hazari, deputy governor of the Reserve Bank, one of those many new excellent choices by government from academia. He asked me if I had had enough of STC and would consider moving to banking. I laughed with surprise but told him that the answer was a clear yes. What a difference from the last time! I told him the story of K.B. Lall's approach. He said he wanted me to go the Punjab National Bank, not because I knew anything about banking, but because it was time they had a manager in banking; at least tried it.

⭑

Looking back, STC's vivid patches were more varied. The problems in STC, quite contrary to the bank later, had all been across the boundary; within, it depended entirely on whatever momentum it could generate. As my first experience of an Indian company for me to mould, it gave me the feeling of having been raised like one of those venturesome horse regiments of the 18th and 19th century—Probyns, Hodsons, Skinners—to do a frontier job. In the years before or after me it received little praise from parliament and press. Praxy Fernandes, who stayed in it the longest, a student of Karnataka history, biographer of Tipu, who could himself have played the part of Tipu, Duplex, Clive with perfection, summed up its spirit. B.P. Patel, my predecessor, a Gujarati patedar Patel, gave it the thrust that the organisation founded by the Kayasth K.B. Lall had needed. These two had been outstanding personalities as chairmen, with some political and administrative interludes.

STC's problems abroad also were not light. Some friendly nations offered credit on easy terms and received back through tied sales more than they could ever hope to receive on sales for cash. Competitive bidders had "understanding" among them; cartels hemmed one in from all sides; whether the bid came from east or west, whether from a free or controlled economy; a price had to be paid for being new and inexperienced in the world market, especially wherever there was aid attached. As someone quipped—if aid comes, can strings be far behind. As if all this was not enough, some private traders in India would fly over and undercut export quotations with suspicious abandon; or get appointed as representatives of foreign exporters, really performing no service and merely adding to the import cost, but giving their principals the assurance that they were fixing things in India on their behalf. The ways of the intermediaries could be devious and unsavoury, and some at least showed visible signs of power and influence. The bevy of administrators and politicians they could muster at their parties was difficult to believe.

Countries of different political hues were all grey in the dark of this world of international trade. But the only and the best way to learn was through experience and jolts; and at this the men of STC showed uncommon courage, never sure they would be backed if anything went wrong.

Altogether it was an experience and a gain that was mine, in no way diminished by the frustrations, but the more worthwhile as I looked for no career reward, nor had I any ambitions or expectations. My only hope each time was to get by unscathed, which I nearly did not in STC, but for an intervention at the very last moment of my endurance, generously given, neither expected nor owed. With my voice trembling for once I had pulled out before P.N. Dhar, the telex message from TTK, "Prakash, please don't commit suicide," I had carried it till then like a charm in my wallet, and at this darkest moment it worked. My gesture surprised me. Back home, late in the evening, he rang—"I went after you, Prakash, but you must have literally run out of my room, because I lost you. Instead I went to see her, and if it is any consolation to you; Prakash, she was very upset." I said I was touched. Next day the hounds were leashed.

Why did I not leave in time, knowing the risks surrounding me and the STC? Why did I let K.B. Lall persuade me to come in the first place, and then not leave when I wanted to? Later he wrote me that in retrospect he was wrong in dissuading me, but had thought of the organisation first. He agreed that I should have left when my instincts told me to; and even if he felt I should stay on, no one else would have shed tears at my departure. I recalled also the words of P.N. Haksar, to whom I went for advise, that Girja Shankar Bajpai, his guru, had told him when he joined administration, "Young man, one luxury you can no longer enjoy is to choose your boss; you serve whoever he is." I think the reason for not leaving earlier lay in me and not in them.

The same tenacity that made me stay with Levers, in its early years of Indianisation, when the going had often been hard, made me stick to the public sector in the early years of its professionalisation, in whose future as in that of Levers I had faith. Perhaps it was also faith in my own capacity to make some contribution; or perhaps, just that having got my teeth into something I did not easily let go; or some plain weakness in me—I didn't know; but soft options I had always shunned as also the sanctimoniousness of those who judged but would not serve. I was ready to go through more, and moved to banking in the public sector. Kamla's words kept coming back—now my only contact with her—you will look for problems, only to be able to solve them.

The public sector was all an experiment worth something, though at least then I could not have said worth what. It took me back to the Punjab, later also to Ahmedabad, and gave me a spell at Boston to teach a course in management of public enterprises.

CHAPTER EIGHTEEN

Punjab National Bank

As I entered the dining room on my first day at the Punjab National Bank to meet my senior colleagues at lunch, I felt I was back in the Punjab of the 1920s. Time here must have stood still. Someone was addressed as Panditji, someone else as Lalaji; others were Sharma Sahib, Verma Sahib, Chopra Sahib, Kapur Sahib, Brara Sahib, Soneja Sahib, Prasher Sahib. There were all the Sharma, Verma and Arora sub-castes of the west Punjab. Men who had worked together, since they were fresh out of college, at branches at Lahore, Amritsar, Sargodha, Khanewal, Hoshiarpur and Phagwara addressed each other with formal courtesy and gravity. An exception was the exotic presence of a Vora Sahib, but a Gujrati Vora, who after years appeared still to feel a stranger. The food was the same simple middle class Punjabi food, Arya Samaj priti bhojan, not rich or too spiced, a dal and a vegetable, with the fruit of the season. They all ate heartily and were mostly overweight; and one by one, as they finished, and before the toothpicks were passed around, they expressed loudly their appreciation with the ritual of a grace. The thin one, Lalaji, bantered about the fat one, Khanna Sahib, in what sounded as the daily routine. The only variation from the daily Dayanand Anglo-Vedic College menu was fried fish for Panditji, his only concession to non-vegetarianism was pomfret fish, but only fried.

As I listened to this conversation I was back among the ghosts of my father and his friends, dressed, eating and talking in a manner that had not changed in half a century. To test more firm ground under my feet, I asked if they went for a morning walk before getting ready for office; they all did. Emboldened, I asked one more austere looking than the others whether he was out well before the sun? Yes, he replied, by six in the winter and five in the summer. Another made sounds, wanting to be asked, and said that at that time he would be back from his walk. Then the conversation expectedly turned to their alimentary system, its behaviour since last discussed yesterday, with much familiar advice exchanged. About their working system and the whole institution, I could gather, there was a timelessness, only broken when Walker Sahib came from the old Imperial Bank for a few years and made some changes.

In the afternoon I took a walk around the office and felt as depressed as I did in STC on the first day. The place was full of desks, files, cupboards, peons and clerks; a milling crowd on the landings and the staircase on the way to the canteen, from which ill-clad boys rushed up and down the stairs precariously balancing trays of food all day long and spilling tea and gravy. The canteen and the conveniences next door emitted mixed odours. The stairwell of the building had a single volume of sound that reverberated round the walls continuously. From this organised cheerful chaos I walked into my office, a large pompous room with grease-stained upholstery, a carpet that harboured the dust of many chairmen's feet, and a large kidney shaped table piled high with files, masses of paper strung together by a thick thread with steel ends piercing through each piece of paper. This time I knew where to start.

I sent for the architect and suggested that he cut my room in half, and ask STC if they would sell my old furniture to the bank at its written down value, because no future chairman of theirs would ever use it. We reorganised the executive wing into smaller offices and refurnished them in my STC Indian style. The change however left the general manager, known respectfully as Lalaji, untouched; he still had his large office, horse-shoe desk, buzzer for the peon and other symbols, including his late hour of arrival at the office, in keeping with his past habit and position. A peon awaited his arrival to open the car door and carry his slim briefcase. I found these old-fashioned symbols charming since they appealed to my sense of the past, and also as some kind of cushion against change. For an old institution it was useful to leave at least one familiar landmark, a rallying point if the wind of change blew too hard, and something to revive after I left.

Starting in 1895 as the premier Punjabi commercial institution, it was founded by the nascent Hindu reformist movement of Arya Samaj and later became part of the new nationalism. It withstood many crises, especially the failure of a locally owned British bank, Alliance Bank of Simla, in the middle twenties. With a Punjabi sturdiness it grew stronger with each crisis, as if to prove the point that nationalism had an economic strength as well. It was one of the three pillars of the achievements of the Punjabi middle class society, the other two being the Dayal Singh Majithia Trust which ran a school, a college and the famed English daily, *The Tribune*; and the Dayanand Anglo-Vedic chain of schools and colleges, especially their first schools and colleges for girls. Interestingly, one sprang from the Brahmo Samaj of Bengali import, and the other from the Arya Samaj that came from Kathiawar. The Punjab National Bank and *The Tribune* belonged to my earliest memories. Coming as chairman to the bank of Lala Lajpat Rai and Mahatma Hansraj gave me its own satisfaction that was quietly different in quality from the STC and Hindustan Lever, and with it the familiar feeling of the Punjab.

I had my first introduction to the bank the week I joined Levers in Bombay in 1937. Its branch manager rang me up and wondered whether I would drop in. Impressed by such flatteringly early recognition of my prospects, and the likely persuasion to bank with him, I called on him. I discovered to my amusement that what he had in mind was something totally unexpected—an offer of matrimony with the daughter of a very respectable and affluent customer on whose behalf he was approaching me. Considering one disappointment enough for him, I opened an account.

More than half of the bank's assets were wiped out in Partition, but its chairman had shrewdly moved in good time the head office from Lahore to Delhi, in teeth of opposition from the Muslim-dominated government of the Punjab, and then only by moving the High Court. As if reinvigorated by the shock of Partition, the bank grew even stronger and now began to move to every nook and corner of India, changing from a Punjabi to a national bank; its very name National now acquired a new, bigger meaning. Yet the same chairman, scion of one of the founding families, who had effected the move, for reasons of his own, secretly sold the bank first to a Rana of Nepal, and then to a Marwari group. Between the two ownerships innovation was neglected, and the bank began to fall. It even missed the opportunity to follow enterprising Punjabi emigration, and never opened a single overseas branch.

The remarkable inherent strength of PNB, that Ravi Hazari of the Reserve Bank had mentioned, I realised at my very first board meeting, which was to be the last meeting of my predecessor. To a massive agenda of hundreds of pages, so like the public sector, a massive discussion did justice, and the directors, Punjabi and non-Punjabi, argued with familiar Punjabi vigour, and took the management to task with great Arya Samajist rectitude. As the chairman was the only member of the board from the bank, he tried heroically to defend management, but mild by nature he stood the ground mildly. This only egged on the directors, who kept saying that they had heard these explanations before but nothing ever happened. There was much iteration and reiteration of lapses that continued despite the chairman's assurances, one particular director kept repeating. Occasionally one of the managers in attendance would try to explain something, but soon had to retreat as he was easily proved wrong. With such thorough discussion of the faults of management once a month, I thought management would have very little chance to go astray, and yet the discussion gave one the impression that despite the board's assiduous efforts, the management had learned nothing and forgotten nothing. I could also gather that each member of the board specialised in some area in which his criticism made a particular contribution.

I was interested to see how after the chairman's last meeting his colleagues were going to bid him farewell, but they spared him thoughtfully. It was an austere affair, which after two soft drinks and a buffet meal ended at an early hour. I had served on many boards, but never seen such severity and lack of colour in an evening's enjoyment, where even public enterprises were learning fast.

The internal systems and non-systems, were reminiscent of STC, the chairman-may-kindly-decide kind of decision making, the board-may-kindly recall. A loan proposal could begin at a distant branch and end at the board months, sometimes a year, later; and then the decision took as leisurely a pace, to percolate down, unless the customer was influential, when things moved fast. There was little modern planning, budgeting or appraisal, mainly reliance on accumulated experience and wisdom. For planning, the environment was left to sort out the uncertainties of its own creation. There was expectedly no telex. Before nationalisation, the whole thing had worked well to serve the interests of those who owned and those who were close to the owners; whatever the quality of service to the general public. With little knowledge of the workings of commercial banking, I used to be puzzled at first by the number of customers who made losses or at best poor profits in industries known to be profitable. When I shared my apprehension with my senior colleagues that our money could not be safe, with such companies, I was assured that it was perfectly safe as they would never let us down; but of course one had to take a "practical view" of how they made losses; this was their business. I was to discover why. It was not uncommon for customers to borrow money from the banks for a business that did poorly, while the directors made personal gains that they invested elsewhere. A remarkable example was a small company with capital and reserves that stood wiped out by accumulated losses, whose director had taken a loan from the company of twice the total capital, repayable after thirty years, in the year 2001, at an annual interest of 2.5 per cent per annum, when the going bank loan rate was round 15 per cent. Equally common were boards packed with father, wife, sons and daughters, both major and minor, and near relations. Why the family members, even the young, I really understood when one saw them fly in parties and stay at luxury hotels at holiday resorts—to hold their board meetings.

Bank nationalisation wanted instead the importance of the small man to be built up; small and poor farmers, artisans and rickshaw pullers, and the very poor workers on the edge of subsistence: they were all to be helped with credit, on cheap terms, and without an emphasis on security. This was a much harder task. The first problem for the banks was to seek them out, then to offer them credit that was not to be mistaken for charity and spent on ceremonials, but on building assets and creating an income, and then to recover dues. These men would have to be coaxed to come into a bank branch and, be faced with multifarious forms and signatures or thumb impressions when the local money lender lent on trust, any time of day and night, but of course at his own rates.

There was also soon to spring a class of middlemen who offered to solve the problems of the branch managers, hardpressed to produce rapidly rising percentage improvements, by bringing in filled-in forms in shoals. The branch manager hoped to be transferred by the time recoveries became due and a problem; while the debtors who actually received little or no money had in any case little or nothing to return; and the intermediary usually disappeared. The begining was not easy, especially in a system in which work even at the senior levels was an easy virtue, starting the day after ten and ending before five, interspersed with numerous cups of tea and coffee with friendly customers.

There were two schools of thought in the bank towards the change I attempted—the many who, with a Punjabi resignation born of strife and change, felt that like other changes in the past this too would blow over and it was best therefore to simulate interest; and others, also with a Punjabi characteristic, to whom change appealed and who responded genuinely. To the first the new regime of rule, discipline and initiative was irksome, for it deprived them of their comfortable world of give and take and flexibilities at work, which gave them personal power and patronage. To them initiative lay in running private businesses and insurance agencies on the side, to stop which was an infringement of their fundamental rights. I was told a story of a manager who hired a motor rickshaw. When he asked to be taken to the

Bank's head office, the driver said, "yes, and to the fourth floor." "I suppose you even knew where I sit," said the manager. "Yes," replied the driver proudly, "I also work in the Bank. I sign the muster roll every morning and then go to my own work."

Soon after I joined I got an excellent opportunity to delve into the problems of banking. The National Institute of Bank Management, which I had already begun to cultivate as my academic mentor like Ahmedabad, under an able biologist turned bank management educator, Niranjan Mehta, called a conference of the chairmen of all the nationalised banks, to which were also invited the finance minister, the governor and some of his deputies from the Reserve Bank. Nationalisation of banks called for a far-reaching change in the system, and Indian banks were not prepared for it. The finance minister, Chavan, was therefore interested in hearing about their progress with the objectives of nationalisation, but the bank chairmen seemed preoccupied with their major problem, the attitudes of the unions and officers' associations, which were leading to deteriorating customer service, growing indiscipline, a poor day's work, and subsequently rising costs and falling profitability. The banks had indeed made much progress with the new tasks, but unless, they said, they could cope with the problems of staff, progress would be limited. The minister asked what would be their suggestions in this regard; and they replied that he should talk to union leaders and prevail upon them that now that the ownership of banks had been taken out of private hands to the public, they should be more cooperative. Chavan agreed, and gave his inscrutable smile that always conveyed different things to different people; they read it as they wanted to.

The bank chairman were in fact a competent set of well trained men. They had built up a system of banking that was safe and solid, and could be envied by many developing countries, but somehow while banking was ahead of Indian industry in the 1930s, after the war industry went ahead but banking fell back. The leading groups that controlled industry also controlled banking, and while in industry many innovated, diversified, introduced modern management, research and development, they left their banks alone, so long as they provided their own industries with the needed money at cheap rates, among the cheapest in the world. When everything else was scarce and expensive, money was abundant and cheap. Banks continued to run as they did before. Despite vast growth they retained their simple old methods of bulky ledgers and signatures and counter signatures. The Reserve Bank of India, and following its example most commercial banks, did not even have a separate personnel division till the 1970s; and the myriads of transactions continued to be manually handled. For a paper to move from one desk to another in the same room, one relied on peons while customers waited patiently. A cheque from another town would take three weeks to cash, when the mail took a day.

But if the banks did not change and modernise, their men did. They organised themselves into modern strong unions, while the officers formed their own associations, a subtle social difference in names, and both demanded modern benefits from old-fashioned banks. They were well directed, but not so the bank managements, and so while the union, and in the wake the officers, won all the benefits they asked for, management got little in return except a diminishing output at a rising cost. Instead of better terms leading to modernisation of the operations, to reduced costs and improved service, it led to the opposite and wrong solution of engaging more and more men and letting the existing service deteriorate. In fact management became just a holding operation. Soon the banks were charging the customers more, giving them less, and paying a lower return to the new owner, the government. There was a familiar public sector ring to it all.

After the conference finished, a bank chairman invited me to lunch to meet a great union leader, Prabhat Kar, the master of all All India Bank Employees' Federation. The lunch was long and voluble; as one problem was explained another was posed. The union leader explained in vivid terms that the main problem was management, the lack of it in the system. The banking system in 1972, in its over 15,000 branches employed over 250,000 of whom one-half were under thirty years of age and had joined since nationalisation in 1969, and the clerks were mostly graduates. It was the single largest graduate workforce in the country, and the largest single-product industry. These young came from an environment of protest; they had always protested, and demonstrated, and had always won, at home, at school and at the universities. Their demands had been varied; to get a teacher changed, an examination postponed, a test made easier, results relaxed; and if their efforts bore fruit, as they seemed to be doing at one stage, to have the whole system of testing scrapped, with freedom to attend a class or not, study or not, with a degree assured at the end. There was even a slogan, no degrees, just jobs.

He continued, and I listened in fascination. From a background of vast unemployment, banking gave these young suddenly, a well paid job for a relatively light day's work, backed by a very strong union whose demand had gone far beyond the need-based wage to what he called a "fridge-based" wage. To make these young work and to train them to become useful productive bankers, he regarded as being the job of bank management. It needed two things, management systems and management skills; and these he was not sure that the management themselves possessed, or in what measure. Most managers had themselves risen from the ranks, with little input of management knowledge, with only simple experience. They were hardly in a position to guide and train. What role his own powerful union could play, he did not touch upon. And then he addressed me directly.

"From what I have heard, you have not come to your bank just for a job but, to use your own language, as a change agent. But you will face a big problem; you must begin your change at the top, and that is where you will face the most resistance. Those at the top are the non-change kind, otherwise there would have been no need to bring you in; they could have done it. But they don't think they need you, and they are not going to be happy with you; you have been imposed upon them. They will join with the men below, with us, and try to sabotage all you will try to do; and whatever you manage to do they will try and undo after you leave. Let me assure you that we shall not be your problem; it will be they, the managers. We would like change, but we cannot help you."

I so much wanted to ask why, but decided not to. He enjoyed the audience I provided, of a kind he probably did not often get, even among his peers. Through big puffs at his cigar, which he cynically added, his friends, the bank chairman, kept him provided with, he watched me with interest and a benign smile. He certainly guessed the problem but gave no solutions. Had I asked him, his answer would have been that they would have their own solutions the day they ran the banks. Nationalisation to him was only a half-way solution and a stepping stone to the larger aims of the party to which he belonged. He ended by talking a little about himself, and of handing over soon to younger men, but this with no great conviction. I left him with mixed feelings. Here was another task to be performed in perpetual strife and confrontation, and little help from either side.

I could see soon where Kar's strength lay. Walking through our largest branch in Delhi, on the ground floor of the head office itself, before four o'clock one afternoon, I found men happily playing games in the office. When I asked them about it, they said that this was customary, and in any case they had "finished their work for the day." This very branch had asked only a few days earlier for more staff to clear some arrears that had accumulated over many years. Both men and managers accepted this as the normal situation. The union leaders shrugged their shoulders and said it was management's task to get work out of men—without of course adding to their already "heavy burden of workload"! The manager pleaded helplessness; at the slightest show of discipline men would shout and rave. It was Dickensian. The result of all this was not without its humour. In some branches men went home in the early afternoon, having of course finished their allotted work, collected their overtime also for the day, and then went to afternoon pictures. Some came back from their mythical sick bed, or annual leave, to collect overtime, euphemistically called "contractual" overtime.

But there was the cheerful side; if there were many internal problems there were few pressures from across the boundary. Perhaps these were early days for bank nationalisation, but I had never seen such permissiveness in the public sector. Parliament was benign in its interest, and dealt mainly with the ministry, and the ministry seldom bothered the banks, nor did the customers often go to government or members of parliament for help. For once, all my problems were my own and PNB's; for us to create or solve.

The new board reconstituted under the Act of Nationalisation came at the end of 1972. Its fourteen directors were to represent government, Reserve Bank of India, depositors, small industry, medium industry, big industry, scheduled castes, economics, handicrafts, progressive farming, officers' association, staff union, and one, in my case, who represented his own influence, and was supposed to have been connected with the highest. The chairman and an executive director were the only employees of the bank representing management. The post of the executive director was not filled in any bank; as someone put it, for the benefit of the chairman, to save him the presence of an impatient crown prince, a common feature of the public sector, encouraged often by the politician. To this perfection of boards' organisation, the board wanted to add one more touch. In order to provide adequate guidance and control over the day to day management of the bank, in addition to its meetings every three weeks, it wanted to divide itself into subject sub-committees that would meet in between. The board, entirely of outsiders, would then decide policy, and its sub-committees implement and manage. This I had to oppose.

Dutt, the most prominent member of the board, was a civil servant, the most sensitive of Bengalis. He had been told by his earlier chief, when I was about to join, to try and understand me by reading my books, which he dutifully did. Baxi, then secretary to government's department of banking, had somehow decided that the chairman of PNB should be a Punjabi, with a feel for the Punjab that I had displayed in the Punjabi Century; and Dutt was entrusted with the task of inducting me into the era of post-nationalisation commercial banking. A man of quiet courage, he would rise to his full height when someone suggested compromising with what he considered wrong in principle. In the administration's ambience that sometimes demanded acquiescence, preferably active, and at least passive, he could oppose without fear of consequence.

Chadha, representing the union on the board, was also a remarkable man, whose farsightedness surprised me; for union leaders are men of the moment; essentially vulnerable men, they are expected by their followers to produce results almost day by day. They must constantly be in the thick of a fight, or else someone else will step in to show that he is a better fighter; so that even when there is no fight the leader will have to make one. Through sheer habit, and for self preservation, the leaders became more like guerillas than warriors; shrewd calculating men of immediate tactics; attack all the time and at unexpected spots. The whole thing had thus developed into an arid struggle that continued for ever, beyond the victories, with corporate national goals the inevitable casualty. But Chadha could ask himself a question. He had a fierce Punjabi pride in PNB, and in nationalisation, to whose ultimate success he was genuinely dedicated.

Ahluwalia, representing the officers, new to the process of unionisation, had an idealist's approach to all problems. He always sought an immediate and a perfect solution and would not settle for less. He was always deeply concerned about injustice, so that anyone could gain his sympathy and support if he could talk enough about injustice but he too looked ahead, at what could be the ultimate consequences of unionisation reaching upwards. Would it mean splitting an organisation into three irreconcilable forces? As time went, more and more men would come up from the ranks; where would then their loyalties lie as they rose up? In the face of the prospect of a split of such a crude nature, the top began to think in terms of some process of participation that gave them a common purpose.

These three men showed a deep permanent interest in the board; the others came from their own busy functions and went back to them, including a delightful personality, Ramji Kak, whose contribution belied his hedonist appearance. I called him our director for socialism, for he always delivered, whatever the occasion, an impassioned plea for the socialist objectives of nationalisation. No common man himself, he spoke eloquently on the common man's behalf at each meeting; for the rest of the meeting he puffed at his cigar and waited for lunch. The progressive farmer Bhargava's sole interest was in his own area, while the dean of the faculty of management at the agricultural university in Punjab, Kahlon, spoke mostly to the point, and on his subject, agriculture, but always willing to resist any transgression of management principles, which to my joy he always defended, although perhaps he taught me the fundamentals of management a bit too often. He was a good ballast against any extremes. The one representing industry, Mahajan, had his practical way of saying that it was all very well for them to meet once in three weeks, tell the management what to do, and go back to their own jobs; someone had to run the bank for the other twenty days. And one of them, virtuous and upright, meant to be influential and helpful, and suggested naively that I should talk to him the day before the meeting and he would smooth the way for me.

It was my first experience of a non-working, entirely outside board, with only me representing the bank, and two who represented sectional interests within the bank and were able any time to confront me with inside information that always left me vulnerable. It was an interesting if not an utterly confounding situation, in which I was in the weakest position and not infrequently in a minority of one. Some well informed member could always bring out some detail of a lapse from one of the eleven hundred branches and the matter would be built up with righteous indignation into violation of rule, principle, justice and equity. Having served as chairman of such different kinds of boards as of Hindustan Lever and STC, Vanaspati Manufacturers Association and the Institute of Management, I was at first bewildered by the responsibility placed at my doorstep. There was nothing done that could not have been done better, at least differently; why was it not therefore done that way? Long speeches would be made, delivering judgement and charge both together, calling upon management, really only me, to pay more heed to their advice and benefit by it. To someone who had spent a lifetime in professional management, their frequent enunciations of management principles was not without its irony. I had constantly to learn sucking eggs.

With nationalisation, the officers' association was starting to flex its muscles, and I perhaps helped it in its process of maturation. It was management's own creation of a buffer between itself and the union.

Its early presidents were amiable senior officers, and to its gentlemanly annual conventions the chairman and senior managers were invited to "give their blessing," until one leader, frankly political and ambitious, and another an idealist with a morbid concern for justice, took over. They overthrew the seniors and started on a tough line. Their first growls were misread by a wishful conviction that they were going to be overthrown by the rank and file, who surely would not approve of their new belligerence, but when the increasingly awkward spectre could not be wished away, and these highly paid officers began to demonstrate and shout "murdabad," the senior managers formed their own association, to which the officers' association at first reacted violently. Later, with a practical wisdom, the association saw an advantage in accepting it, provided the dividing line for membership was drawn in their favour. Between their two leaders and their daily broadsides and broadsheets, first against each other and then me, I was sandwiched; each wanted support from me and condemnation of the other, and when they did not receive it they both went for me at the same time as they went for each other. Thus only I knew where I stood—that I did belong nowhere. The rest, including the top, had a sneaking sympathy for one association or the other. The senior association died a natural death, for the true answer to the problem posed by the officers lay in facing it and not in circumventing it by creating a new force to oppose them.

I gently warned the association that in their enthusiasm to strengthen their ranks, while demolishing a past they did not like for its favouritism and nepotism, its leadership should not set itself up as the new fountainhead of power, offering favour and protection to those who came under its wing. Their president had come storming into my office one day asking for a transfer to be cancelled, because the man concerned was his local organiser; and he stormed out when I refused to interfere in the transfer made in the ordinary course. His favourite phrase with me was "co-operation or confrontation," both defined by him, in his flexible way; but there was always something predictable about him so long as one looked at his interest and not for consistency. He had an attractive smile, but whenever I saw it I knew I was being asked to concede or had conceded something unreasonable; his frowns I found more reassuring.

The staff union was strong and more confident. They could afford to leave me alone for a bit to let me get ahead, because the change I made would affect the management first, while their own interests were secure within their own strength. Their president, unlike the officers' president, had no advice to offer me, nor any expression of fears, expectations or support. To him I suggested what I had suggested to George Fernandes some years earlier, that he and I should let our staff negotiate and conclude, but we should meet occasionally to discuss policy issues or remove any serious roadblocks. With him, as with Fernandes, both generous and concrete men, it worked well.

The union president made the unusual suggestion that the whole promotion process, based on seniority alone, be overhauled to give the young a chance to rise rapidly on merit; a suggestion I had never heard before or since from my union leadership in India. We worked on it and arrived at a new promotion policy. Where it took clerks usually into their early fifties to become managers, under the new formula we devised they could compete for a management post within six years of entering service. That the president showed the wisdom to recognise the impatience of the young and got them to pay the price of competing for self-improvement, was as remarkable as it was encouraging to me to press ahead with the change. There was some opposition; someone took it to court but nothing came of it. The policy stayed, but it was abolished soon after I left.

The union president asked me one day about my plans. I told him that I hoped to use the first of my three years for rapid change, the second to freewheel and consolidate, and the third, if the organisation and the board had not built up too much resistance to me, to lay the foundations for a totally new style of management. He said he would wait and watch for the first year, which he scrupulously did. At one stage he wondered though whether I was not going too fast for an old and set organisation like PNB, but I assured him that I was keeping a finger on its pulse; I was trying to be both a surgeon and my own anaesthetist. As luck would have it, although it did not appear so at the time, the organisation developed problems at so many points in the second year, almost like antibodies to change, that there had to be a forced freewheeling instead of the controlled one that I had hoped for. Maybe, as in STC, it was the consequence of the too rapid change, but everything happened together; and I let it in the hope that things would clear up for the last year; and again, as luck would have it, they did.

The union president fell ill seriously and was laid up for almost a year. A dominant personality, his withdrawal from the scene created a vacuum both in the board and in the union; but out of it came also a remarkable experience for me, a rare personal relationship. First, out of courtesy, then out of curiosity, and later out of pure interest and a new involvement, I began to drop in to see him in sickbed. He was at first courteous and wary, but slowly began to talk about the bank problems, the slackened pace of change lately, and how much of it would last after I left. In fact, he had heard that someone, conservative and opposed to change, was already trying to make a bid to succeed me, and was at the back of the new problems. He and, as he put it with unconscious self-importance, the "progressive forces behind bank nationalisation" had opposed him successfully when he last tried, and would oppose again. He also talked about the banking system and wondered what nationalisation had achieved in reality; they had begun with such high hopes of a new economic order, but now the system was reverting to what it was. They had met the minister and the prime minister, and she had asked for a note; but nothing came out of it. He despaired of nationalisation, and felt the more depressed that what little the PNB had achieved lately might also be wiped out. One day I asked him if I could also think aloud, and at some length. Niranjan Mehta, the director of the National Institute of Bank Management, Zarin Dastur and Mrs. Chari, his PNB watchers, were present and encouraged me to open up. I posed a large open-ended question.

"You, as a union, are powerful, and I believe that your all-out support hastened nationalisation which might otherwise not have taken place, or at least been delayed. Since then you have gained more strength and more concessions for your men, who are now the highest paid in industry and government, for work that is relatively light. No one can move one of your men even from one desk to another a foot away; many build their own homes, after which it is impossible to move them even from one branch to another in the same town. In a small district town they get more money than the young civil servant who comes out of the pick of the universities and is on the move every three years; much more money than the young army officer who is moved practically every year, and for years is posted at heights from where he visits his family only once a year for two months. In PNB I had to ask Sam Manekshaw to get some young prematurely retired officers to open our new offices in the distant mountain places, to which every one in the bank had refused to go despite the generous pay and allowances. And your organisation protects and cossets your man till he has lost the basic desire to work, even to progress. Many refuse promotion to avoid transfer, and certainly a promotion that means responsibility. The system costs the customer more each year and gives him less, not even normal courtesy; and he is choiceless.

And when management protest you regard it as victimisation, transgression of rights, undemocratic. It is all rights and no obligations.

"Management cannot cope with the problem because, I think, they are themselves not trained as managers should be; after all they have risen from your ranks—but do you ever give even your own men a chance when they rise? While the officers are going to solve their problems by following in your footsteps and organising themselves into a strength of their own, what will the senior managers do? Will they also organise themselves, as they tried to do? And will having three unions—staff, officers, managers—solve the problem; or will it ultimately be left in the lap of government, whom you blame for inaction?

"But why always expect government to do something that you won't do, but can do? Government should ask you a question. Having got nationalisation what have you done about it? The banks are yours; you are on the boards, staff or managers; it is for you to make what you want to of banking, and no one will stand in your way.

"Socialisation of banking ought to have happened, but just to happen was not enough; it had to be the means to some end, and that is service to the society of a kind that it certainly has not been. Your senior colleague told me a year ago that change will only come when it is accepted at the top; the top say that it has yet to be accepted lower down. Both expect the other to change first, but resist when the other tries. Yet where change is concerned there is no top or bottom, it can begin somewhere; but it must be accepted by all who believe in it. At least in our bank it has begun, and if at the top they have not accepted it, have your men? They all, managers, officers, men, want change, and they all fight it at each step."

There had been a lot building up in me. I laughed and told the president that I had been waiting for a chance to express my feelings; they were in the nature of a protest; everyone else protested; it was time I protested too. He looked thoughtful and said I had given him an idea. For a man trained and brought up only on confrontation, on whose face I had seen pure hatred and venom pour out when addressing a union meeting, a curious softness appeared.

Next time I called, he said he would like to pursue the subject. His union colleagues had often wondered what I meant by the change I spoke so much about. Would I talk to some of them, if he arranged a meeting? I reacted with alacrity. I would go further, and arrange a seminar, to which I would bring some of my senior colleagues. We would survey the bank operations over the last few years, and have an open discussion about what were our strengths and weaknesses, and where were we going and should go. Banking is unlike any other industry in India, because its operations are so decentralised. Our own 18,000 men are scattered over 1100 branches, each an island entire to itself but no part of a main. No circulars can make the small group at the branch in Peo, the last town on our northern border, frozen for more than half the year, feel a part of the chain unless we make its each link feel it has its own strength and yet is dependent upon all the other links. If ever there was a case for participative movement, it is in banking.

We held first a seminar with our management, another, after some tantrums, with the officers' association and then with the union. After that suddenly problems descended thick and fast, to which all of us, I, the officers and the union contributed.

Government, also my senior colleagues, had been urging banks to do something about the falling discipline and the rising cost of overtime. Overtime had become a "fixed" obligation of management; so much had to be paid every month for, in effect, a twentyfive hour week. Wherever this habit took root, it inevitably affected customer service and discipline. In my last year, I decided to deal with it amidst immediate cries of injustice and rights violated; rights wholly irrational that once established could not be waived. Also, within the union, at the prospect of participation, some deep inner personality conflicts rose to the surface. The officers' leaders first tried to take advantage, and then, as the staff turned upon them, backed away.

In Delhi there was a prolonged struggle for half a year, when the old familiar demonstrations were held, some gheraos made to build pressure behind the demand to revert to the old overtime. At one particular "peaceful" gherao of a manager, more men than one would have thought possible were packed into his small room. Surrounded tightly, and listening to obscenities was the mildest part of his ordeal, which they kept on in relays through the sweltering, suffocating May heat, till their "shocked" leader arrived at midnight to relieve the siege. Then the victim was allowed his first drink of water and visit to the toilet for seven hours—shades of Siraj-ud-Daula! He went home and next day to hospital with a severe heart attack, his health shattered for the rest of his life, but he was luckier than one of his collegues who in his gherao had earlier slumped dead in the chair. My own gherao a week earlier was a pale shadow in comparison, relying only on shouting imaginative accusations, with derisive references to my foreign car and my foreign wife; and praising their own courage, solidarity and strength with much conviction. For months there could be no talks held on participation. Whatever the cumulative past sins of the management, and they must have been many; in the years after the unions were formed and acquired strength they were more than paid for by this generation of hapless management. Gradually, after simmering for some months, the troubles began to subside and the problem was ultimately resolved.

As the time for me to leave came nearer, I made it clear that I was not looking for an extension. In December 1974 I went to see my minister to sek his permission to leave at the end of contract in the following July. I had about three months' leave due to me, and this I would like to take before retiring. In this environment this was something unheard of. Seeking extensions was a great pastime, and at the least one tried to get one's accumulated leave refused. This gave the politicians, in whose hands the patronage lay, power over the men during the last few years of their service, when retirement began to cast its shadow, for they could grant extensions and even new employment. It tended to affect, sometimes even vitiate, the men's power to decide, and opened the way to an unhealthy use of their gratitude. The men could not be blamed, for retirement at an early age of 58, fit and able to work for many more years, with family responsibilities usually at their peak, at a pitiable superannuation of about one-quarter of their retiring salary, with all facilities gone, posed quite a problem to them in an age of inflation.

Ironically at the same time as I was trying to get my release, a senior secretary telephoned to ask me to receive a tribal group. He was sure I would find them interesting visitors; and I did indeed, when half a dozen handsomely built men of dark satin smooth skins walked into my office, complete with feathers, spears, cowrie shells, wild animals' teeth and tusks. The leader soon got down to the point; he wanted a letter from me on the bank letterhead, a "testimonial," and next proceeded to tell me that I had "luck on my forehead." As he looked at my grey hair, he brightened at the clue, and said I was going to get an extension of at least one year! Everything would be alright!

In their anxiety men consulted astrologers, and propitiated both politicians, gurus and gods. Whether consciously or unconsciously, the system added to the dilatoriness in succession, and there were cases of bank chairmen asked literally after the last minute, to stay on month by month, and even for years. One bank chairman, for whom I had arranged a farewell lunch, was utterly surprised when I told him on the phone that the ministry's secretary, who was also invited, had rung up to ask if the lunch was still on, for it had just been decided that he was staying on for a year. As it was, he stayed on for two years more, and each time the news reached him on the last day of the year's extension. At last he retired, and two years later was back again. I wanted the PNB to be spared this fate; also the fate of STC, which was in no man's land for over a year.

With the union problems out of the way, the organisation was now on fairly even keel and showing signs of picking up its interrupted progress. As the time for my departure came closer and my intentions to leave became clearer, I even detected a softer light falling upon me from the eyes of the board and even the officers' association's leadership. Suggestions came from both the union and the association leaders that I might accept to stay longer to complete the experiment. Things were at last running smoothly, and with a new wind behind the sails we could all combine to achieve much more. I told them that these encouraging remarks were perhaps the very sign that it was time to leave; if they felt I should stay longer, then it was time to go.

The union and the association then suggested that we at least wrap up the participation experiment and bring it to something concrete. I agreed, and we organised a preliminary meeting of the three groups, union, officers, and managers, at which a steering committee was appointed to lay plans for holding a convention upon my return from leave and before I left. We all realised that the experiment was so big and amorphous, that we could do no more than show courage in embarking upon it. There would no doubt be many problems, but at least PNB with its change was better placed to try it.

We held a participation conference in Bombay at the National Institute of Bank Management, who had adopted us and our experiment. There were nearly a hundred persons from all parts of India, representing the federation, the association and the management. There was much hard discussion and questioning, but a general agreement on the need to experiment. As the conference drew to a close all differences seemed to dissolve, and there was reminiscing about the past three years and what we had all learned. Much irritation and needling I had caused when introducing change was remembered, but reconsidered in softer tones; my past forgiven and their future welcomed. With a Punjabi lustiness even three cheers were raised. Many rose to a bigness and sentiment I had not suspected.

Alone in my rooms at the Delhi Gymkhana next night, I looked back over my last three years with PNB. What had I received, what had I given? After four years of STC and thirtyone of Lever, and the eight in England before that, I had needed the three years of this Punjabi bank to bring me back from fortythree years of exile from the Punjab. I had got too far away from it. Perhaps the men, officers, managers, directors: all had helped to re-teach me my Punjabiness. Chadha, the union president, a Punjabi Khatri turned a radical, had at last accepted that I had feelings for the bank; Ahluwalia, the association president, a cross-grained Jat, at last editorialised in his association's journal that it was the end of an era that had meant something to the bank; Kahlon, who always said at least what he meant, and usually a lot more beside, had looked straight at me and said he was going to miss it all, including me; Dutt, the civil servant representing the ministry, a support in my moments of despair, the most discreet of them all said nothing but conveyed much. Among the managers, some whom change had infected remained discreetly silent and at a distance, wondering whether they would soon be recognised as change's agent; others smiled knowingly—like all change this too would now blow away.

Lala Lajpat Rai, Mahatma Hansraj, and many stalwarts of the Punjabi society, with Arya Samaj and its new nationalism as their background, had founded and nourished the Punjab National Bank, until some fear, perhaps personal calculations, led to its surreptitious sale to men who kept the Punjabi facade to serve their ends. After they had been swept away by the new wave of nationalisation, to be chosen from nowhere, with no experience in commercial banking, was but an honour I highly regarded.

Yes, I had gained a lot, but then I felt I had also given something in return, unstintingly, a professionalness to an institution which for 80 years had grown as a personally managed domain of one family or another. Times were changing, and nationalisation had given a new content; and in introducing me into the bank someone must have felt the need to cross its traditional sturdiness with a new but a Punjabi management strain. Many of its systems and the ways of its men were truly old but, charming though some were by themselves, out of tune with the time. A simple old branch manager in a small town said to me, "Tandon Sahib, you have done wonders—Kamal Kar ditta—you have even given us a new language; what we called a loan department we now call credit administrashun deveeyan. Vaqia he Kamal Kar ditta!" I laughed self-consciously, but saw his point, because with the new names came new demands and new ways. Credit had to be administered; not just a loan given.

In PNB you could tell what came from the periods of the Lalajis,

Sethjis, Walker Sahib; so why not something from Tandon Sahib. I had my doubts, though I had begun to feel part of this history, a short period but compressed and vivid. This brief, atavistic connection with a Punjabi institution had in its own way meant more to me than any time with STC and Hindustan Lever, and a wrench of an unfamiliar kind. Repelled by its near century-old crust, I yet came close to its core that was alive and vital, the core of its men.

And thus after three strenuous and seldom peaceful years, I left the bank. I knew there would be many changes, rejections, much unctuous disassociating by some with the past to express fealty to the future. This was our Punjabi way. I remembered as a boy my father being transferred from Lyalpur, where the new incumbent, an Englishman, arrived the day before, and how the whole staff disappeared on a salaaming pilgrimage, some doubtlessly even conveying that fate and sarkar were kind to have sent them a sahib again. As a people we were good at adjustment, and I chuckled equally at my experience in delegation with a very senior division head, whom I had made chairman of an important committee. Reading the minutes once I asked him about their line of reasoning for the decision on an issue. He immediately retracted and said, "No, huzoor, I entirely disagreed with the committee; I entirely agree with your honour, but then the committee members would not listen to me. Now I will go and change the minutes and tell the members that both your honour and I disagree with them all. That will teach them to listen to me in future, and I will always consult you in future before the committee meets." I gave up teaching him delegation!

As with Levers, on leaving PNB I refused to take the bow with the customary Bharat Darshan. On the last day, after my last board meeting which Subramaniam, finance minister, attended, I hastily emptied my room and asked them to sell the simple furniture they had bought from STC, a few low chairs but no desk, in turn to my next employers. To the old general manager's large office, kept vacant, the old furniture was moved back in anticipation of the new chairman's joining the following day. There was a desultory farewell function, and a press conference to announce the half-year results. A seasoned journalist, Chopra of the *Eastern Economist,* had said to me three years ago, after I joined the PNB—"Why don't you go and teach and write? Probably it will last even less here than it did in STC." At this press conference he reminded me about it, and I told him this time I was going to take his advice.

I said an apologetic and self-effacing farewell to the board and the new chairman, a bustling and cheerful moon-faced Punjabi, who uttered some extrovert words about my contribution and what I was leaving behind. I could only mumble—"Well, thanks, but please don't hold it against me." The point went past.

And so till deep into the windy monsoon night I relived the PNB and my life with industry for nearly forty years. I remember also my father's career that finished forty years earlier and had begun at the end last century; so varied in their own ways, and yet so alike. He left as the shadows cast by the British were lengthening; I began when the sun of the Raj was setting into the dawn of an India independent after a thousand years. It was full of frustrations, full of interest and full of hope, if one had a faith that drew its sustenance from far in the past and from the distant future.

CHAPTER NINETEEN

Return to Punjab

My fresh association with the Punjab became even stronger after I left the Bank. Invitation to join the State's new Planning Board, some research projects on its development and, what touched me most, joining the University of Punjab as a senator, professor and dean of the faculty of management, meant frequent visits that refreshed my roots. I discovered a new Punjab; its vitality and activity reminiscent of the early days of my father's career, nearly one hundred years ago.

I was sad that he died when the new Punjab was young and struggling against the heavy odds that Partition had set it. He had migrated to Delhi, but for some years he had not been well enough to move freely; in any case there was no one he could have visited in the Punjab because all our relatives were refugees on this side. He had heard about the new Bhakra Canal and the luxury of its full cement and polythene lining; of crops that grew in areas that were once arid and parched; wheat, sugar, rice and groundnut in an unimagined abundance. He did not live to see the green revolution arrive a decade later.

I wonder what my father would have thought of the new dwarf foreign wheat compared with the tall Punjabi wheat that waved so gracefully in the wind; or of rice cultivation, making the Punjab the largest exporting rice state in India, larger than the traditional areas of Tanjore and the Godavari delta. How would he have reacted to the old sight of the well and the Persian wheel under a shady tree with its musical sound giving way to the hum of the tubewell; the complete disappearance of the bullock from cart, well and plough; the spluttering sound of the truck and the tractor instead of the affectionate swearing and cursing of the bullock driver; mud houses giving way to houses of cement and plaster with tall radio and television masts; houses moving out of the village into the farmers' fields; the Jat's long kurta, turban, tehmad and spurred gamashahi shoes exchanged for nylon bush shirts, trousers and plastic chappals? Along the three hundred miles of the Delhi-Amritsar Grand Trunk Road one seldom saw a bullock cart, a plough, a horse, or a Jat walking.

So the Punjabi farmer, unconcerned with aesthetic feelings, rushed ahead with his passion for productivity and prosperity. When he first saw the new wheat, he would pay fancy prices for the seed, equally willing to steal, to have his fields flourishing with the visible symbol of progress and high yield. He educated himself in the balanced use of inputs, water, fertiliser, pesticides and weeding. He learned how to cost them and calculate the return, and alter his mix to maximise it. He learned to handle and maintain the tractor and farm equipment as if he was born to it. His appetite for life grew with his affluence, which he loved to display. On Sundays, the town squares were full of the tractors and trailers of villagers visiting the cinemas. He would appear at the bars, his pockets bulging with hundred rupee notes, and order the most expensive scotch, and with a touch of contempt mix it with cheap beer. The farm labourers too had acquired expensive tastes, and apart from relatively high daily wage, with full meals, they wanted a bottle of whisky in the evening—though they were content with the Indian variety.

While the farmer produced and progressed, the planners and academics argued over what he should and should not do. They developed a schism over his mechanising agriculture. In some areas high yields and increase in crop intensity through mechanisation had created a greater demand for labour, such as in the Punjab, while in other parts mechanisation had displaced labour. The more vocal among the planners therefore insisted that mechanisation should be discouraged, and without consulting the farmer put a ban on import of combine harvesters. The ban affected mainly the successful Punjabi farmer, who had the highest yield and crop intensity and was also the biggest magnet to "guest labour."

Father had witnessed and participated in the first miracle of the new canal colonies started by the British revenue officers and engineers, which made men from the east of Punjab move to the deserts of the west. This time one witnessed an even greater miracle, worked by men displaced and broken, who had brought with them only the bundles that those who drove them away allowed them to carry. These men fought hard, helped by equally dedicated district officers and engineers, who settled them, built roads, rail links, canals and a new capital in the feverish speed. The same government worked as hard to help the refugees in eastern India, but results were different.

My grandfather had seen the beginning of a new Punjab. My father saw its flowering and collapse. I witnessed its rebirth and new vitality. In just a few years there was no one called a refugee. What will my father's twenty-five grand and great grand children see?

In Faridabad, a new township built specially for refugees, and now the largest centre of big and small industry in the Punjab, I decided to build a house. The inhabitants of Faridabad all came from the old Frontier Province district of Dera Ismail Khan. Distinctive in dress, language and appearance, they were still quite uninterested in the local Punjabi population thirty years later. Their grandchildren born in Faridabad referred to some of their playmates as "Punjabis," vaguely proud of their different homeland and distant origin, their Pathan Punjabi accent still intact. At the golf course, they earned some pocket money as caddies and agewalas, and it was a mark of shame among them to lose a ball. They would spend hours, sometimes days, to find a badly driven ball from the undergrowth. "Where is Langoori," a boy nicknamed after his prowess at climbing tree like a monkey, I asked one day. "Oh, he dare not show his face Sahibji; he still has not found Chadha Sahib's ball since yesterday," was the contemptuous reply. They still retained their violent temper. In a fight his brother got so mad that he cut Langoori's foot with a knife, and he now limps forever with an amputated foot.

Punjab's politics reflected our vital chaos, and after a succession of mild Hindu chief ministers, the state was firmly and well managed by a Sikh, reminiscent of Ranjit Singh, the last Punjab King. He was a ruthless builder, who wanted only results and got them. His education in America had developed him into a product of the earlier American style. He built agriculture, industry, education, while his sons built lucrative cinema houses and in keeping with the way of the sons of our public figures, proved his undoing. He was killed in revenge on the Grand Trunk Road by someone whom the sons had allegedly wronged. He went unmourned, but remembered as a legend for his firmness, something the Punjabis love. He was what one calls a Male Man, Nar Admi.

The new city of Chandigarh, designed by LeCorbusier, the father of futurist architecture after the First World War, was a bold experiment, both in founding a new city and giving a foreigner a free hand. Next door, an American dam designer, Slocum, a self-taught man, was invited to build a dam, then the world's highest, from which water and power would flow to give energy and nourishment to the new-ploughed land. The new University of Chandigarh was perhaps the best endowed in the country, designed by a brother of LeCorbusier, Jeanneret. Nehru's vision was a great support to the Punjabi passion to build big, as if in revenge to build bigger than what they had left behind.

Out of its vital chaos I came and to it I returned.

EPILOGUE

Into our long line of Punjabi Khatri blood, kept pure through strict rules of caste and sub-caste consanguinity, entered the Swedish Viking from an island in the Baltic. But, almost atavistically, the three children of this distinctly mixed marriage, all brought home Punjabi spouses, two Khatri and one Sikh Jat. As said in the prologue, the Punjabi saga as it was first written, spanned four generations from 1849 to 1975. But since then much has happened in India and in Punjab, which is once again in its familiar state of flux.

Return to Punjab, the last volume of the trilogy, ended with the Emergency, an ironic conclusion to the tryst with destiny Nehru had ushered in on the midnight that ended a millennium of alien domination. The Emergency was surprisingly brief, and contrary to what many of us had expected. India was led back to democracy by the one who had led it away. I was in a small coastal town in France, on a brief interlude between the Punjab National Bank and the National Council of Applied Economic Research, taking stock of a move into yet another unfamiliar area. The BBC news sounded grim: arrests of the entire opposition; the army and police swarming the streets of Delhi; press censorship, expulsion of foreign journalists; all one had associated with the swift coups in South America, Africa and Asia, but never thought 'could happen here'.

A month later, at a conference at the Australian National University, Canberra, I met Anthony Low, Vice-Chancellor and Indian historian. He asked me how long I thought the Emergency would last, and to the commonly shared fear that it was there for ever, he shook his head. No, knowing the roots democracy has taken in India, he thought, Mrs Gandhi would behave for a while like a disgruntled Viceroy who, fed up with the opposition Congress, would arrest them all, and impose Governors' rule in the provinces. Everything would run peacefully for a time, but soon the Viceroy would begin to miss the very democratic process that had been assiduously fostered. He would send an Indian emissary to meet some Congressmen in jail, then let out one leader for negotiations, and eventually release them all. There would be discussions, civil disobedience would be withdrawn, elections would be held and, behold, the Congress would be back.

The analogy was apt. First, at the end of 1975, Parliament's term was extended to avoid elections and if there were murmurings in the Party, no voice was heard. The only voice that had but merely questioned the need for the Emergency (ironically, that of a Sikh) was never heard again. A year later, to the chagrin of some seniors, a bill was again introduced to give the Government a further extension, but within the month, elections were announced, unexpectedly and dramatically, in a seeming desire to gain legitimacy, especially in the eyes of the outside world. Anthony Low had proved right so far, but would she win and be back? Few doubted that she would not; the apparatus would see to it.

I was in Boston for a quarter's teaching in the spring term of 1977, and I could not believe the news as it came in one evening. The Prime Minister and her son had both lost their seats, and the entire election! I remembered the words of Swaminathan, former cabinet secretary, now election commissioner, that the elections would be totally fair and normal. In the whole Hindi belt the Party won but one seat. How right Swami had been, and how prophetic Tony Low! The next day, the *Boston Globe* asked me to write about it. I reproduce some extracts from the article I wrote:

> In Paris, on my last evening, I went to an Indian party, of men working in different government agencies. All cautious, each asked others what they thought of the Emergency; each in turn deferred to the next. Finally, they turned to me, the oldest of them all, expecting a lead they had all ducked. Yes, I said, I will react.
>
> I am not political, I began, in fact I am apolitical, my mind is purely managerial. It looks for an analysis, an analogy and a solution. The analysis is simple. For years we have been dissatisfied with a lot of things—foremost with the arid politics of perpetual confrontation; everyone seems against everything.
>
> For years we wished an end to chaos and willingly promised to forgo some rights for some order and sanity, for an end to how a whole town of 10 million could be held to ransom by whoever chose to call a strike, for whatever cause was going. Cars, buses, pedestrians ceased to move, and were attacked, vehicles were burnt, because someone had tried to go to work, something had moved. In steel, railways, buses, airlines, docks, everyone struck for less work and more pay.
>
> And where did it lead us: in a quarter century our income per head improved by half per cent a year, and that too was sucked out by the privileged and the organized.
>
> The Emergency puts an end to all this and a new chapter begins. What that chapter will bring, one cannot say. There have been many such

> drastic changes in many countries, and each time there were some dramatic pronouncements, some quick improvements—trains and planes ran on time, work began on time, the administration was polite, the streets were swept.
>
> The Emergency has gone, and with it Indira Gandhi. A question we might ask is whether she was carrying out somehow, unbeknown to her, the cumulative will of a democratic people looking for a catharsis. Long tired of incompetent governments, they asked first to try total rule, and when that did not work, they asked, and she took them back, to the democratic process which, with all its faults, they felt worked better than authoritarianism. She declared and held honest elections, received a clear 'no', and after the verdict went.
>
> It is good to live in a country, however poor, which has deep democratic instincts; but if Indira Gandhi has something to learn (and she has paid the price), so has the new government; and more so the people, for it may not work so well the next time. Governments must in future be honest and competent; and people must realize that a democracy only thrives if with rights there are also obligations, and a basic discipline. Perhaps the last years were the greening of India.

A decade later we ask the same questions, seek the same solutions, and get the same answers. Have the basic truths been learned? Are governments clean? Is the administration responsive? Does the press know the limits of freedom, beyond which it is licence? Is industry, seeking for itself the freedom to grow, conscious of consumer rights? Have tax evasion and funds in foreign havens grown less? Are state governments and their leaders more concerned about their own needs and welfare or the people whom they represent? How much has it all changed or is it a case of ... 'the more it is the same?'

What gives one hope, of course, is that while of late there have been problems of growing magnitude, the country's healthy democracy has been externalizing them instead of suppressing them. Better some effervescence than the apparent calm of our neighbours, where problems are no less but remain internalized, and fester.

I am reminded of an evaluation of our democracy by Louis Fischer in 1952 or thereabouts, not so long after Independence, when he mentioned to me that he had just received a message from his editor: 'Cable two hundred words after Nehru what.' I asked him what he proposed to say, and prophetically like Tony Low, he said to the effect that 'When the time comes for Mr. Nehru to go, if democracy in India has taken the roots which I think it will, after a Churchill an Atlee, after a Roosevelt a Truman, and after Mr. Nehru someone quite the opposite. With none of his, stature and charisma, none of his flair for international affairs, and great projects, someone who will however get down to the day to day chores for which Mr. Nehru has no time nor an interest. Grateful as the British were to Churchill, a Churchill to follow him was not what they needed.' Twelve years ahead of the time, he drew a pen portrait of a Shastri, who was not even particularly well known at the time.

But we cannot afford the luxury much longer of refusing to learn from even our own history. Al Beruni warned us 900 years ago, at a time when admittedly our knowledge was at a low ebb; Churchill's prophesy that India would descend into chaos, was a warning too, had we read it that way instead of as wishful thinking. In our struggle for Independence, it suited us to misinterpret history, and thus misperceive British motives in regard to some important national issues. Maurice Zinkin, a colleague in Levers, a student of history and formerly of the ICS, said back in 1951 that Nehru's sense of history was unreal, influenced more by the euphoria of coming independence and suspicion of British motives than the hard realities of the Indian situation, whether India was governed by the British or the Congress.

In the years that followed, Nehru appeared convinced that the British wanted Tibet to be independent as part of their imperial design to keep it as a buffer against any Chinese expansionism. He must, therefore, have readily agreed with Chou En Lai, and given him the impression that he would not actively oppose Tibet being their's, especially as part of the new, progressive communist regime. He therefore lowered his guard, of which China took the fullest advantage. And today we are in a situation where they claim the entire length of the Himalayas. The British calculation, if it was imperial, was for the protection of their asset, India, which, once it reverted to us, should have been protected with the same wariness.

It was euphorically argued that once India was free, we would undo the provincial structure introduced by the British, to suit their administrative convenience, and return to our ancient political entities of the Maharashtras, Uttar Pradeshs, Madhya Pradeshs and others, whose names sounded more Indian and sonorous than the United Provinces and the Central Provinces. We perhaps missed the new logic, of creating modern inter-regional, inter-lingual states; instead, we opened the Pandora's Box of linguistic, regional and religious nationalism. Nehru did see the danger soon enough and suggested zonal-regional structures, but it was not pursued vigorously enough. What might have been well left alone, once awakened, acquired an inexorable logic of its own that rejected the logic of size, numbers, viability. It is axiomatic that once emotions take over, there are no bounds to unreason.

Viewed constructively, the desire for linguistic autonomy has behind it perhaps only the need for autonomy. Historically, with its many cultures, ethnic and sub-ethnic, India has run best with a centre strong against outside aggressiion and assuring an internal integrity, but permissively federated, with much autonomy where the individual units are concerned. The Mauryan empire, our first empire, when India was the largest it ever has been, ran well while it formed a strong, protective shield against external enemies but left its distant parts relatively free. It began to crack up when it became overcentralized and placed an intolerable burden (of its vast armies of soldiers, informers and functionaries) upon an economy that could no longer support it. It then fell to an internal usurper and not before a powerful aggressor.

Today, our central planning spreads into all spheres of activity, into the furthest corners of India; as does our labour, industrial and fiscal legislation that is the most comprehensive in the world, and therefore the most complex: both combine to deprive all activity, private and public, of whatever initiative they have and absorb every ounce of the country's resources which are then directed by the centre into areas that produce poor or no returns. The consequent overdependence of the units upon the centre for subsidies and subventions creates a petulance in the centre-state relationship that breeds an assertiveness, which is mistaken and dubbed antinational, which it eventually may become once frustration sets in. This is perhaps the problem of Punjab, developing from the earlier demand for the Suba to a demand hovering somewhere between provincial autonomy and India's own desire once for dominion status, and then that of a republic, with the difference of the new factor of fundamentalism thrown in.

Punjab is a challenge to statesmanship, bigger than any the British ever faced; however the country today does not have the benefit of Nehru's capacity to act when something went wrong, his flexibility to avoid a fracture, the dispatch with which he adjusted. He preferred some form of continuity to a dissolution, which he tried to avoid at all cost, and shrewdly managed to.

Habib-ul-Rehman, an early trainee of ours in Levers during the war, and later chairman of Pakistan Lever, asked me a question in early 1983, just as Punjab was getting restive. How did I see the problem, and how would we handle it? That, I explained, depended on how our Prime Minister saw it fitting into a political strategy. But I could say how it should not be handled: the way Pakistan handled East Bengal, by losing its temper and flying to a military solution. Instead, we should be patient and cool, and especially attempt to discover how the whole issue was rooted in larger problems. Shortly after, I was asked to speak on Doordarshan about the Punjab problems: I felt that we might look at its three possible roots.

Its historical roots lie in Sikh history. Moghul repression forced the Sikhs into an entity. What began as a sect, seeking freedom to belief and practice, was driven into militancy. Once forced to fight, it gained under one determined leader an entity, and under another an empire that extended over the whole of Punjab, Kashmir and Afghanistan. The empire began with Ranjit Singh and ended with him. In the ten years after him the British annexed Punjab, taking advantage of the internal dissensions among the Sardars and their misls. The Punjab School, as the dedicated band of British officers was called, under the leadership of the two Lawrence brothers, Henry and John, and the personal direction of Dalhousie, did a remarkable job of conciliation and rebuilding. As the last defeated people, the Sikhs stood by the British in 1857, when with Meerut in the north, Cawnpore in the east, Jhansi in the south, even a threat from the west would have sealed their fate in Delhi. Perhaps this was because the Sikhs did not want to save their erstwhile persecutors, and restore the Moghul empire. And through the next century they continued to stand by the British and helped in two wars; they had their differences, mainly on the recognition of their rights, and they always won.

In the crisis of Partition, which created the biggest migration in history, they suffered the most and yet were the first to recover. In Independent India the Sikhs were equally successful, and in the three border wars and the green revolution, in which they led the country out of its ship-to-mouth food crisis. Against this background of three centuries of strife and success, it would have been surprising if the issue of their separate identity did not arise, once the linguistic states of Andhra, Tamil Nadu, Maharashtra and Gujarat had emerged.

Within the community, given its success and affluence, a new way of life was becoming apparent. Punjabi young men and women were taking to change with great speed, and at a cost to their tradition and orthodoxy, that must have disturbed the traditional and the conservative. One had begun to wonder whether with discarded outward symbols they would not soon merge back into the stream they came from. There was little difference between a shorn and bareheaded young Malhotra or Bhatia Sikh or Hindu. The visible symbols gone, faith and ritual alone would not sustain the entity the Sikhs had so carefully fostered and developed, since the last Guru. Many Hindus went to the gurdwara, believed in the gurus, were intermarried, and cremated with the same ritual and custom. After all, the distinctive symbols had only come with the last Guru. With Islamic fundamentalism so much in the air, a revival of Sikh fundamentalism was only to be expected.

Second, the economic root. This was perhaps a repetition of a policy error of the British in Punjab, logical in itself but not in the best interest of Punjab, and especially the Sikhs. The British developed the state as the sword arm and granary of India, and let industrialization pass it by. After Independence, the Indian Government helped Punjab generously with the rehabilitation of its people and its infrastructure. Like the dedicated administration of Dalhousie a hundred years earlier, Nehru chose the best men, from as far as England, France and America, to build the new Punjab, its capital, universities, canals and dams, rail and road connections. The Sikh farmers, displaced from the jungle lands they had converted half a century earlier into India's best corn fields, reciprocated with diligence and enthusiasm. They reclaimed and cultivated the tiger-infested Terai and the *banjar* areas of East Punjab into lush wheat, rice, sugarcane and mustard fields, when the refugees further east went back from the Terai and Dandakaranya to the security of Howrah railway platforms.

They were thus ready for the Green Revolution, when it came. It brought mechanization and new inputs, and crop intensity, which while increasing the demand for farm labour from as far as Bihar, Orissa and Andhra, to sow, weed, harvest, thresh and store, required only one son to help the father run a small or middle-sized farm. Traditionally one son had gone into the army and, of late, one abroad, but with immigration discouraged and the army looking to the "non-martial races" to get a national mix and balance, these options were cut short or limited. This is where industrialization would have helped.

Private industry, especially after the first two border wars, shunned Punjab as a border state; this belief was encouraged by the Government's own policy of taking its new public enterprises everywhere else in India but the Punjab. Punjab was considered too affluent (by relative standards) to need further encouragement; besides it had its prosperous small industry. Left to themselves, the Punjabi's enterprise and manual skills had indeed developed small industry, but these produced mainly ancillary products; the state needed large industries to provide them a market. A small part of the huge investments made in public enterprises in other regions (where they only returned losses) would have multiplied more successfully had they been made in the entrepreneurial soil of Punjab.

Along with the other professional members of the Punjab Planning Board, one often suggested that Punjab's high rate of growth had been sustained by the Green Revolution, which had now run its course. In future, to maintain such a rate of growth, the state needed to diversify its agriculture and industry, especially to provide employment to the farming young. Instead of adding to the large national buffer stocks of cereals, we suggested the state should encourage the farmers to grow oilseeds, fruits, vegetables and dairy products which add higher value than rice and wheat at procurement prices. In Delhi, a hundred miles away, all packaged butter came from Gujarat, many hundred miles away. Punjabi farmers had therefore a large market at their doorstep for milk, butter, ghee and cheese. No, Tandon Sahib, would say the Chief Minister, we Punjabis are bred on these products; we should never let an ounce leave our Punjab. That we could grow twice what we needed to consume, cut no ice. In industrialization, we advocated was not steel and aluminium plants but industries that produced the inputs of agriculture and processed its outputs. None of these measures were implemented to any great degree and in the underemployed young, with spare energy (that should have gone into industries and services) and among their successful migrant cousins (who sent home large sums and duty-free tractors) new ideas began to germinate.

The third root, we should look at for clues to the Punjab problem, is perhaps the Zionist. The Jews and Arabs had co-existed peacefully for a long time in a Muslim world. Indeed the only persecution of Jews was in Christian Europe. It was only because of the affluent and successful Jews of Europe and America (who in the liberal 19th century had come into their own) that the world's superpowers accepted the concept of a Jewish homeland in 1919. It was this that led to Palestine, where in the British Protectorate Jewish talent settled, with generous financial backing. In due course, as the time approached for the ultimate British withdrawal, the first Arab-Jewish riots started in 1929, and two decades later the protecting power left Palestine partitioned in the style of Ireland and India. In this Zionist movement and its successful culmination perhaps lies a root of the new demand in Punjab—for a homeland in which history would restart where it had left off in 1849.

But Punjab must be seen as one of the challenges that was inevitable when we opted for democracy; we must persevere with it; and the question to ask is if not from history, how soon will we learn from our experience? In our democracy, with our genius for compromise, all problems are solvable, provided our public leadership understands them. We must learn that our society, like others, has undergone a fundamental change in the past century. Where societies were traditionally governed, they began to be administered in the 19th century, and today they are managed. Public well-being depends upon a sound management of national resources by public leadership (which consists of the five sectors of a democracy—the political at the top, the administrative, economic, academic and defence—of which the last-named, by democratic convention, does not participate in public affairs). How successfully will our society grow and develop, and be able to solve its problems, will depend upon three factors—the professional excellence of sectoral leadership, a common perception of the tasks, and the extent of coordination among the sectors.

If we examine one of the sectors of democracy, a sector I have been involved with for decades, our economic leadership is basically good. In economic management, industrial and trading, the penetration of modern management has been extensive in the professionally managed firms; in these firms the level of management practices and the quality of managers is as good as anywhere in the world. There are today 24 Indian managers working in the various companies of Unilever (of which my old firm, Hindustan Lever, is a part), in South-East Asia, Latin America, Europe, Korea and Japan, and the demand is growing for higher levels of responsibility.

On the other hand, the family-managed concerns remain anachronisms, where the modern management practice of separation of ownership and management has not reached; fathers, sons, daughters, sons-in-law and daughters-in-law are still the bosses and take all decisions, with succession provided strictly through chromosomes. There are sometimes retired administrators, bankers, and generals on the boards of these companies—some serve on 25 boards but they only lend their name and influence while the family decides. With growth, much capital has been inducted from the public into these companies and the family share has often been reduced to a few per cent, sometimes under five, but still all control lies with the family. The process of a divorce of capital and control passing into the hands of the public and managers which began in Europe and the United States in the 1920s and was completed by the 1950s, has still to begin in India; where most leading conglomerates are still headed by scions of the founders. While some firms have accepted modern management, few are truly professionally managed.

In the public sector, owned and controlled entirely by the state, the politicians and administrators, the public has neither ownership nor control. As a concession to socialism, it is called the public sector, though the public has no say in it. Even to suggest that it might be thrown open to public shareholder, owning equity and choosing directors, is considered a return to capitalism. With low public accountability, therefore, the state sector loses money, except for a few units that enjoy a monopoly and can administer prices on a cost plus basis, without looking for cost economy.

Our administration is professionlly manned and managed, with its men selected by merit and excellently trained for the tasks they have to perform. Like professional managers, they are propertyless managers, whose personal stake in their function is purely in exercise of their skills, with a pride in their professionalism. Ranking, for over 150 years, among the half-dozen finest civil services in the world, of late under the impact of rapid change, its performance has been lacklustre. This may be attributed to two causes. As Lord Fulton pointed out 20 years ago in the case of the British civil service, so with us in that our recruitment is still largely of generalists whose responsibilities have however changed to specialist areas of economics, sociology, technology, sciences. Further our generalist administrators' equipment to meet these new specialized tasks is still the same as that evolved by the British over a century ago. Their systems of information, communication, decision-making, in fact their entire internal dynamics, is based on the hierarchical systems and structures they inherited. Everything is still decided by the file, which embodies a whole culture going back to the Moghul days when, looking exactly as it does today, it was called the *misl,* enclosed in a *basta,* two cardboard sheets wrapped with two cloth flaps and a tape that gave the English language a new word.

The academics, like their counterparts, the administrators and managers, are also highly professional and rank high in world esteem. The best of them are sought abroad in the institutions of highest excellence. We call it a brain drain, when it is really an overflow out of an environment that cannot contain it. It is better to let our springs flow into distant fields than to choke them, as some of the short-sighted among us would have us do.

Excellent in their professionalism and competence, one questions why our academics, administrators and managers have in aggregate achieved so much less than their talent deserves? (The defence, establishment, we shall keep aside. Their professionalism and competence is undoubted and proven, but let them continue to respect the convention of staying aloof). For this we have to look to our fifth sector, the political leadership which, representing the people, is at the apex. Political leaders are expected to interpret the people's aspirations, hopes and needs, and in the process of their fulfilment, coordinate the other sectors in the task of planning and implementation. As leaders, therefore, they need to show deep, and not merely populist, perceptions of the problems the country faces and the solutions, combined with an integrity that inspires confidence in the led. The right political leadership is of great importance in India at the present juncture, when the needs are great but rescues limited: the challenge requires of it a professional excellence, and a set of values like Gandhiji's. How well our leadership fulfils this role is best left an open question.

As this book begins with Punjab, so would I like to end with it. Looking ahead, I can only see a promising scenario, of a Punjab together once again, a Punjab of the Mauryas and Ranjit Singh, not in the political sense but as a community. A few years ago, I was invited to visit Pakistan. In Karachi, Islamabad and Lahore I met a number of groups: public and private enterprise managers, accountants and auditors and administrators. Most among them were Punjabis and they always ended with the same question, at the end of each talk. What do you think, Tandon Sahib, is in our future? Together one day, I said, not politically but as a community, economically and socially together, through agreements and understandings, where small barriers would be progressively shed on travel, customs, movement of goods and people.

For seventy years the French and the German fought three wars, losing millions of their young, twice involving the whole world. Today, forty years after the last war, the very idea of their going to a war again would sound absurd to them, as to the whole world; they are infact the heart of the European Community.

There is a European passport today, total freedom of movement, a European Parliament, a common Agriculture Policy, a Steel Community, soon a common medical degree and other professional curriculae, all this in two generations, during which period we India and Pakistan, have fought three wars, and there is always the threat of the fourth (This was infact a short fourth war, the Kargil event). Where peace treaties, the League of Nations and the United Nations failed, an attempt to bring Europe together through the European economic community has succeeded, leading to the social, economic, fiscal and, one day, according to the latest offer by the German Chancellor, 'Military-Political Cooperation' with a joint Franco-German brigade. Yet the French are as French today as the Germans are German: as the *Economist* captioned the idea: *Jawohl Mon Generale!*

In our own context, we can integrate into a Himalayan Federation with say, 40or 50 states — as the USA is of 49 states that was once threatened by a partition and went through a civil war between the North and the South.

Our united community can have states like East Bengal and West Bengal. East Punjab and West Punjab, Kashmir and Jammu, all as autonomous states but united as a Federation that would be called the Himalayan community. Looking back and looking forward, Punjab, Jammu & Kashmir to me are parts of this togetherness historically, whether under the Hindus and Dogras, Muslims, Sikh or the British. And they will be together again.

European community in the year 2000, EURO currency, NATO, may be the guidelines to our Himalayan country of the new millennium. The Twain Shall Meet!